PEASANTS, POPULISM
AND POSTMODERNISM
The Return of the Agrarian Myth

THE LIBRARY OF PEASANT STUDIES

NEW APPROACHES TO STATE AND PEASANT IN OTTOMAN HISTORY
edited by Halil Berktay and Suraiya Faroqui
(No.10 in the series)

PLANTATIONS, PROLETARIANS AND PEASANTS IN COLONIAL ASIA
edited by E. Valentine Daniel, Henry Bernstein and Tom Brass
(No.11 in the series)

NEW FARMERS' MOVEMENTS IN INDIA
edited by Tom Brass (Preface by T.J. Byres)
(No.12 in the series)

THE AGRARIAN QUESTION IN SOUTH AFRICA
edited by Henry Bernstein
(No.13 in the series)

AGRARIAN QUESTIONS
Essays in Appreciation of T.J. Byres
edited by Henry Bernstein and Tom Brass
(No.14 in the series)

CLASS, STATE AND AGRICULTURAL PRODUCTIVITY IN EGYPT
Study of the Inverse Relationship between Farm Size and Land Productivity
by Graham Dyer (Foreword by Terence J. Byres)
(No.15 in the series)

TOWARDS A COMPARATIVE POLITICAL ECONOMY OF UNFREE LABOUR
Case Studies and Debates
by Tom Brass
(No.16 in the series)

PEASANTS, POPULISM
AND
POSTMODERNISM

The Return of the Agrarian Myth

TOM BRASS

FRANK CASS
LONDON • PORTLAND, OR

First published in 2000 in Great Britain by
FRANK CASS PUBLISHERS
Newbury House, 900 Eastern Avenue
London, IG2 7HH, England

and in the United States of America by
FRANK CASS PUBLISHERS
c/o ISBS,
5804 N.E. Hassalo Street
Portland, Oregon, 97213–3644

Website: www.frankcass.com

British Library Cataloguing-Publication Data

Brass, Tom
　Peasants, populism and postmodernism: the return of the
agrarian myth. – (The library of peasant studies; no. 17)
　1. Land reform – Developing countries　2. Rural development –
Developing countries　3. Peasantry – Public opinion
　4. Political participation – Developing countries
　5. Peasantry – Political activity　6. Peasant uprisings –
History　7. Developing countries – Social conditions
　I. Title
　333.3'1'08863
　ISBN 0-7146-4940-6 (cloth)
　　　0-7146-8000-1 (paper)
　ISSN 1462–219X

Library of Congress Cataloging Publication Data

Brass, Tom, 1946–
　Peasants, populism, and postmodernism: the return of the agrarian myth / Tom Brass.
　　p. cm.
　Includes bibliographical references and index.
　ISBN 0-7146-4940-6 – ISBN 0-7146-8000-1 (pbk.)
　　1. Agricultural laborers – Developing countries – History. 2. Agricultural
laborers – Developing countries – Political activity. 3. Peasantry – Developing
countries – History. 4. Peasantry – Developing countries – Political activity. I. Title.

　HD1542.B73 2000
　305.5'633'091724– –dc21
　　　　　　　　　　　　　　　　　　　　　　　　　　　00-020287

Typeset by Regent Typesetting, London
Printed in Great Britain by
Antony Rowe Ltd, Chippenham, Wilts

For Amanda,
and for
Anna, Ned and Miles

Contents

Acknowledgments — xi

Introduction — 1

1 Peasants, Populism and the Agrarian Myth: The Historical
Background — 9
1.1 The Agrarian Myth and Peasant Essentialism — 11
1.2 The Agrarian Myth, Nationalism and Popular Culture — 12
1.3 Populism as the 'Other' of Marxism — 15
1.4 The Economic Discourse of Neo-populism, or Small
Is Beautiful — 17
1.5 The Politico-ideological Discourse of Populism, or
Penultima Ratio Regum — 19
1.6 Nationalism and the Agrarian Myth in the Nineteenth
Century — 22
1.7 Populism, Nationalism and the Agrarian Myth in the
1920s and 1930s — 25
1.8 Inca 'Communism' and the Agrarian Myth — 27
1.9 Fascism, Populism and the Agrarian Myth in the 1920s
and 1930s — 30
1.10 'Christ, not Lenin' in Eastern Europe — 32
1.11 Conclusion — 35
Notes — 39

PART I – Populist Peasants

2 Trotskyism, Maoism and Populism in the Andes: Latin American
Peasant Movements and the Agrarian Myth — 65
2.1 The Economic Background: La Convención 1900–1958 — 67
2.2 The Structure and Organization of the Peasant Movement
in La Convención — 68
2.3 The Success of the Peasant Movement in La Convención — 70
2.4 The Failure of the Peasant Movement in La Convención — 71
2.5 Trotskyism, Dual Power and 'Dual Power' — 73
2.6 Hugo Blanco, the Agrarian Myth and Capitalism — 74

2.7	Hugo Blanco, Populism and Peasant Essentialism	77
2.8	ANUC and Populism in Colombia	80
2.9	Sendero Luminoso, Maoism and the Agrarian Myth	82
2.10	Conclusion	85
	Notes	88

**3 Socialism, Populism and Nationalism: Tribal and Farmers'
Movements in India** — 98

3.1	Socialism and Peasant Movements in the Pre-Independence Era	99
3.2	Class Struggle from Above, or the Weapons of the Strong	100
3.3	Class Struggle from Below, or the Weakness of the Weapons	102
3.4	Naxalism and Tribal Movements in West Bengal	104
3.5	Maoism, Class Struggle and the Discourse of Tribal 'Otherness'	106
3.6	The 'Newness' of the New Farmers' Movements	108
3.7	The New Farmers' Movements, the Market and the State	109
3.8	The New Farmers' Movements and Urban Bias	111
3.9	The New Farmers' Movements, Gender and Village 'Community'	113
3.10	The New Farmers' Movements and Ecofeminism	114
3.11	The New Farmers' Movements and the Left	116
3.12	The New Farmers' Movements and the Right	117
3.13	Conclusion	120
	Notes	123

PART II – Populist Postmodernism

**4 Postmodernism and the 'New' Populism: The Return of the
Agrarian Myth** — 143

4.1	Global Capitalism and 'Peasant Economy'	145
4.2	The 'New' Populism and the Flight from Socialism	146
4.3	The 'New' Populism, Devictimization and Nationalism	148
4.4	The 'New' Populism and Global Capitalist Expansion	150
4.5	The Privilege of (Academic) Backwardness or the Backwardness of (Academic) Privilege?	152
4.6	The (Post-) Modernization of the Chayanovian Peasant	153
4.7	Postmodernism, Subalterns and New Social Movements	156
4.8	Subalterns, New Social Movements, Class and Consciousness	158
4.9	Revolution, Resistance and 'New' Populist Agency	161

4.10 The 'New' Populism, Bourgeois Democracy, Socialism
and the State 163
4.11 Conclusion 165
Notes 168

**5 Others Who Also Return: The Agrarian Myth, the 'New' Populism
and the 'New' Right** 189
5.1 From Alienated to Empowered 'Otherness' 192
5.2 Marginality and 'New' Populist Agency 194
5.3 'New' Populist Agency and Sorelian Instinctivism 195
5.4 The Agrarian Myth as Link between Postmodernism
and the Right 196
5.5 New 'Right' or 'New' Right? 198
5.6 The 'New' Populism and the 'New' Right: De Te
Fabula Narratur 199
5.7 The 'New' Populism and the 'New' Right: Worlds
of 'Difference' 201
5.8 The 'New' Populism and the 'New' Right: A (Third)
World of (Empowering) 'Difference' 204
5.9 The Agrarian Myth as a Contemporary Mobilizing
Ideology 206
5.10 Conclusion 209
Notes 211

PART III – Populist Culture

**6 Popular Culture, Populist Fiction(s): The Agrarian Utopiates
of A.V. Chayanov, Ignatius Donnelly and Frank Capra** 237
6.1 The Return of Populist 'Community' 238
6.2 Agrarian Utopiates, Populist Fiction(s) 239
6.3 Utopic/Dystopic Discourse 242
6.4 Utopic/Dystopic Nature 243
6.5 Utopic/Dystopic Space 244
6.6 Utopic/Dystopic Time 245
6.7 Dystopic Capitalism, Dystopic Crisis, Dystopic Rulers 246
6.8 Dystopic Workers, Dystopic Struggle, Dystopic Socialism 247
6.9 Agrarian Populist Utopia as Non-technological 'Other' 248
6.10 Agrarian Populist Utopia as Oriental/Pastoral 'Other' 249
6.11 Class Structure in the Agrarian Populist Utopia 251
6.12 Conclusion 253
Notes 254

7 Nymphs, Shepherds and Vampires: The Agrarian Myth on Film   271
   7.1   Film, History and (the Agrarian) Myth   273
   7.2   Plebeian Versions of the Agrarian Myth: The Pastoral   275
   7.3   'I Believe in America . . .'   278
   7.4   Plebeian Versions of the Agrarian Myth: The Darwinian   280
   7.5   Aristocratic Versions of the Agrarian Myth: The Pastoral   282
   7.6   Winning by Appearing to Lose   284
   7.7   Aristocratic Versions of the Agrarian Myth: The Darwinian   285
   7.8   Reel Images of the Land beyond the Forest   286
   7.9   Sex, Death and Emancipation   288
   7.10   From Feudal Vampire to Capitalist Batman   289
   7.11   Conclusion   291
          Notes   292

Conclusion   312

Bibliography   323

Author Index   360

Subject Index   369

Acknowledgements

The arguments in this book possess their origin in the late 1980s, when post-modernism was at its zenith, the height of academic fashion, and carrying all before it. Among its easier conquests were development theory and development studies, a rapid and largely unopposed colonization which took the specific form of a re-essentialization of the peasantry in postmodern analyses of the Third World. At its most cynical, the principle guiding this process seemed to be as follows: if the continued existence of class division under capitalism proves irksome, then just redefine the disadvantageous/(dis-empowering) effects of this economic process as a form of cultural advantage (= picturesque poverty) which, it can then be claimed, corresponds to a unique example of esoteric diversity that confers empowerment.

To challenge or criticize this trend, let alone to point out its epistemological and political affinities with similar ideas in vogue some sixty years earlier (all of which I did while teaching at Cambridge from the late 1980s onwards) was at that time regarded as tantamount to academic heresy, and a confirmation of the intellectual irrelevance of those who continued to be unrepentant Marxists. For this political intransigence, some (myself among them) have paid the price of academic exclusion: despite a public rhetoric about the desirability of political and theoretical plurality, it seemed that exponents of postmodernism in the academy were all following a different practice.

It is a pleasure to acknowledge the following: Lydia Linford of Frank Cass Publishers, who with her usual editorial skill saw this book through production; those members of the Editorial Advisory Board of *The Journal of Peasant Studies* who contacted me in late 1998 to offer support and encouragement; Graham McCann, for encouragement by example; and the Managers of the Smuts Memorial Fund at Cambridge University, for grants which enabled me to present earlier versions of some chapters to conferences and/or workshops in the Netherlands, India and Spain. My thanks are extended to them all.

The cover photograph depicts a mask made to celebrate the Eve of All Saints, when in rural areas the spirits of the dead are said to walk again. It conveys succinctly the themes and concerns outlined in the book. The photograph was taken in England during 1938 by Edwin Smith, and is reproduced here by kind permission of Mrs Olive Smith.

My greatest debt remains, as always, the one I owe to the members of my family: to Amanda, and also to Anna, Ned and Miles. This book is dedicated to them.

Much of Chapter 2 first appeared in 'Trotskyism, Hugo Blanco and the Ideology of a Peruvian Peasant Movement', *The Journal of Peasant Studies*, Vol.16, No.2 (1989), and Chapter 3 draws on materials from 'The Politics of Gender, Nature and Nation in the Discourse of the New Farmers' Movements', *The Journal of Peasant Studies*, Vol.21, Nos.2/4 (1994). Most of Chapter 4 has appeared in 'Moral Economists, Subalterns, New Social Movements, and the (Re-) Emergence of a (Post-) Modernised (Middle) Peasant', *The Journal of Peasant Studies*, Vol.18, No.2 (1991), and Chapter 5 in 'The Agrarian Myth, the "New" Populism and the "New" Right', *The Journal of Peasant Studies*, Vol.24, No.4 (1997). Chapter 6 was first published as 'Popular Culture, Populist Fiction(s): The Agrarian Utopiates of A.V. Chayanov, Ignatius Donnelly, and Frank Capra', *The Journal of Peasant Studies*, Vol.24, Nos.1/2 (1997).

T.B.

September 1999
Richmond, Surrey
(e-mail: tom@tombrass.freeserve.co.uk)

Introduction

' "It is proved," [Dr Pangloss] used to say, "that things cannot be other than they are, for since everything was made for a purpose, it follows that everything is made for the best purpose." ' – An observation by Candide's tutor [*Voltaire*, 1947: 20].

Tracing the way in which the agrarian myth has emerged and re-emerged over the twentieth century in ideology shared by populism, postmodernism and the political right, the argument in this book is that at the centre of this discourse about the cultural identity of 'otherness'/'difference' lies the concept of an innate 'peasant-ness'. In a variety of contextually-specific discursive forms, the 'old' populism of the 1890s and the nationalism and fascism (= the 'old' right) in Europe, North and South America and Asia during the 1920s and 1930s were all informed by the agrarian myth. The postmodern 'new' populism and the 'new' right, both of which emerged after the 1960s and consolidated during the 1990s, are also structured discursively by the agrarian myth, and with it the ideological reaffirmation of peasant essentialism.

Although the economic breakdown of traditional agrarian structures (= depeasantization) in the Third World by post-war capitalist development has been accompanied by a discursive re-essentialization of the peasantry, it is argued that perceptions concerning the kind of political action (resistance-not-revolution) undertaken by peasants have changed. Following the rediscovery of 'popular culture' by postmodern theory, there has been an analogous shift in development debate about agrarian transformation, from 'peasantness'-as-economic-alienation to 'peasantness'-as-cultural-empowerment, leading in turn to an epistemological fusion between 'new' populist and 'new' right discourse.

In considering the combined influence of the agrarian myth plus a resurgent populism and nationalism on theoretical and political debate about agrarian change in the Third World, this book follows a doubly unfashionable path. First, it constitutes an attempt to reassert the value of a Marxist analysis of the peasantry, as set out in the agrarian question. And second, it utilizes a comparative framework that stresses certain similarities between some recent agrarian mobilizations in Latin America and India, when the trend nowadays is in the opposite direction: that is, towards an absolute relativism which stresses the complexity and uniqueness (almost, even, the autonomy) of the individual subject in terms of ideological formation, social composition, and (thus) political interest and disposition. Although the argument fundamentally concerns the agrarian myth and not the agrarian question, therefore, it is the latter which by implication is defended against the former.

Following an initial consideration of nineteenth and early twentieth-century versions of the agrarian myth (Chapter 1), the rest of the book is divided into three parts. The first examines the respective roles of the agrarian myth, populism, socialism and nationalism in a number of grassroots rural mobilizations which occurred in Latin America and India during the latter half of the twentieth century (Chapters 2 and 3), while the second charts the rise of the 'new' populism and the 'new' right over the same period, together with the reasons for this, its implications for development theory in general, and the analysis of agrarian change in particular (Chapters 4 and 5). The way in which the agrarian myth structures specific forms of 'popular' culture (literature, film) is considered in the final section of the book (Chapters 6 and 7).

Chapter 1 outlines the constituent elements of the agrarian myth, its historical background and its political outcomes. The discourse-for of the agrarian myth endorses 'natural'/harmonious rural-based small-scale economic activity (peasant family farming, handicrafts) and culture (religious/ethnic/national/ regional/village/family identities derived from Nature). By contrast, the discourse-against of the agrarian myth expresses opposition to urban-based large-scale economic activity (industrialization, finance capital, the city, manufacturing, collectivization, planning, massification) and hostility towards its accompanying institutional/relational/systemic effects (class formation/ struggle, revolution, socialism, bureaucracy, the state). All the latter are perceived as non-indigenous/inauthentic/'alien' internationalisms imposed on an unwilling and mainly rural population by 'foreigners', and therefore as responsible for the erosion of hitherto authentic local culture, traditions and values.

An 'a-political'/'third-way' discourse that is simultaneously anti-capitalist and anti-socialist, populism is a 'from above' attempt to mobilize the rural grassroots on the basis of the agrarian myth, thereby obtaining support among peasants and farmers opposed to the effects of industrialisation, urbanization and capitalist crisis. In the context of economic depression, therefore, the invocation of anti-semitic/anti-foreigner sentiment or the town/country divide permits landowners and/or rich peasants to deflect, distort or displace class consciousness by emphasizing loyalties not antagonistic to capital (and thus compatible with the continued process of accumulation). Politico-ideologically, the resulting 'peasant-ness' – which populism claims is culturally innate and unchanging – comes to symbolize the 'nation' itself, and depeasantization becomes synonymous with deculturation and the erosion (or loss) of national identity. It was this task which the 'old' populism of the 1890s, the 1920s and 1930s sought to effect by merging the agrarian myth with 'popular' culture.

The rise of agrarian populism during the early twentieth century was an almost universal national response to the capitalist crisis of that period. In the face of what was perceived as a double threat (an 'alien'/international finance capitalism 'from above' and an equally 'alien'/international socialism 'from below'), therefore, the resulting merger between the 'old' populism and the contextually-specific variants of its agrarian myth (*nohonshugi*, 'Merrie England', *strapaese*, *narodnichestvo*, *volksgemeinschaft*, the pioneering frontier spirit, *heimat*, *indigenismo*, etc.) was linked not just to nationalism (as in the United States, Russia, India, and Peru) but also to fascism (as in Germany, Japan, Italy, and some Eastern European contexts). Throughout the 1920s, 1930s and 1940s, moreover, the innate 'peasant-ness' which structured the golden age visions of the agrarian myth also became part of a specifically nationalist anti-colonial discourse.

The first section of the book looks at the effects of the agrarian myth on rural mobilizations in Latin America and India. The role of the agrarian myth in the mobilizing discourse of three Latin American peasant movements is analysed in Chapter 2: FIR in the Peruvian province of La Convención during the 1960s, ANUC in Colombia during the 1970s, and Sendero Luminoso in 1980s Peru. Conjunctural and political differences notwithstanding, all three movements were characterized by a similar combination: a radical ideology – Trotskyism in La Convención, Trotskyism and Maoism in Colombia, and Maoism in the Peru of Sendero – espoused by better-off peasants engaged in the cultivation of cash-crops destined for the international market. In each case, the idioms/programme structuring the mobilizing discourse had more in common with agrarian populism than with socialism.

The main focus is on La Convención in the eastern lowlands of Peru, where one of the most important peasant movements in Latin America took place during the years 1958–62. A central paradox is that although it was led by and reflected the economic interests of an emerging stratum of capitalist peasants, its principal mobilizing ideology in the struggle against the landlord class over this period was Trotskyism. For this reason, the politico-ideological utterances of Hugo Blanco, a Trotskyist who played a leading role in the peasant movement, together with his views about the class structure, the class struggle, and class alliances, are examined in order to ascertain their class-specific acceptability.

In a period during which the price of coffee (the main tenant crop) was high, and faced with the threat of eviction from land on which to cultivate this commodity, rich peasants in La Convención who were estate tenants joined the most radical political group, the Trotskyist FIR (Revolutionary Left Front) led by Hugo Blanco.The latter advocated expropriation of landlord class and the redistribution of property among tenants, and also direct action (strikes, land invasions, non-payment of labour-rent) in furtherance of this.

In the discourse of Hugo Blanco, however, the seemingly radical institutional framework of 'dual power' to be established following the expropriation of the landlord class turns out to be a return to the traditional peasant 'community' – not unlike the earlier Inca 'communism' of Maríategui – and unconnected with the concept as theorized by Trotsky. The resulting idealization of both the struggle and its objective was not merely compatible with but supportive of accumulation project of rich peasants. The latter were able as a result to depict the struggle as that of an homogeneous peasant mass ranged against oppressive landlords, and its objective as the recuperation of a pre-existing and egalitarian rural 'community'.

Challenging received wisdom as to why India is not socialist, the argument presented in Chapter 3 is that in both pre- and post-Independence era this is due mainly to three causes. Two of these derive from the kind of class struggle waged 'from above', by the colonial state, by landlords and by rich peasants: namely, the frequent use of physical violence against poor peasants, tribals and agricultural workers organized by the left, and the resort by the state, landlords and/or rich peasants to the divide-and-rule tactic of communalizing the agrarian struggle with the object of fragmenting the unity of their opponents. The third cause involves the kind of class struggle waged 'from below': as the example of 1970s Naxalism in West Bengal suggests, the mobilizing discourse of Maoism in India has – like its Latin American counterpart – not only invoked a 'from below' communal identity that mimics that projected 'from above' but also endorsed a peasant essentialism associated not with socialism but with populism, and equated socialism itself with a return to the golden age of the agrarian myth.

This same populist discourse structured the 'new' farmers' movements which, together with the environmental and women's movements, emerged in India during the 1980s. Although they are all viewed as part of a new and authentically grassroots form of a-political/anti-state mobilization, it is argued here that the peasant/gender essentialisms invoked in the discourse shared by the 'new' farmers' movement, ecofeminists and some sections of the left, have been those associated historically with the politics of populism/nationalism. In the the Indian context, moreover, such idioms are particularly supportive of the neopopulist/communal/nationalist discourse of the political right. One consequence of this discursive fusion has been the reproduction of a politico-ideological space that was subsequently (re-) occupied by the reactionary Hindu nationalist BJP/VHP/RSS. Another has been the demobilization of class consciousness by diverting/distorting 'from below' struggles into an ethnic/national oppositional discourse.

The reasons for together with wider implications of such developments at the rural grassroots are considered in the second part of the book, which looks at the way in which the post-war re-emergence of the 'new' populism, influenced by postmodern theory in particular, has led not only to a displacement of socialist alternatives with nationalist objectives, and a fusion between the latter and a similarly recuperated agrarian myth, but also resulted in an epistemological overlap with the views expressed by the 'new' right.

Chapter 4 outlines the emergence during the 1980s and consolidation during the 1990s of the 'new' populism influenced by a postmodern cultural analysis – as embodied, for example, in new social movements theory, the 'everyday-forms-of-resistance' framework and the Subaltern Studies project – which not only questions the necessity/possibility of economic development ('post-development') but rejects Marxism, meta-narratives/universals, and 'Eurocentric' Enlightenment discourse ('post-Marxism'). The resulting intellectual retreat, both from the analysis of political economy and from socialist ideas, and their replacement in development theory and historiographical debate with an idealist postmodern relativism possessing epistemological roots in the innate 'peasant-ness' of the agrarian myth, has been justified in academic/intellectual circles by reference to the supposed unfeasability/undesirability/unworkability of socialism itself.

Having abandoned socialist alternatives to a seemingly unstoppable capitalism, exponents of the 'new' populist paradigm have been compelled to seek a non-economic form of empowerment, one that is compatible with the unchanging/unchangeable nature of peasant identity and that can also be realized by non-revolutionary forms of agency undertaken by the rural grassroots. The transformation of the Third World peasantry into an industrial reserve army of labour in the course of post-war capitalist development has been accompanied in development theory by a move away from materialist analysis. Accordingly, the conceptual re-essentialization of an innate 'peasant-ness' has itself undergone a shift, from peasant-as-economic-'other' which characterized neoclassical economic theory about rural development to peasant-as-cultural-'other' which informed the 'new'populist framework influenced by postmodernism.

Also examined in this chapter, therefore, is the way in which peasant movements in both India and Latin America have been reinterpreted by the postmodern and politically revisionist project of the subaltern studies series on India and the new social movements theory on Latin America. Non-class specific categories, such as 'subaltern', which structure both the social composition of 'new social movements' and the grassroots agency of 'everyday-forms-of-resistance', fail to recognize the extent to which this kind of agrarian mobilization/'resistance' reflects the class interests of rich peasants. It is suggested that much of the conceptual analysis embodied in these 'new' populist frameworks is prefigured in the earlier 'moral economy' approach, incorporating the middle peasant thesis of Wolf and Alavi, an epistemological lineage in which the work of J.C. Scott discharges a pivotal role. An additional claim made here is that such frameworks implicitly provide Chayanovian neo-populist economic theory with its missing politico-ideological dimension.

Chapter 5 examines how the postmodern variants of the 'new' populism, such as 'post-colonialism', inherited in turn the political legacy of Fanon and Marcuse, who had themselves combined the anti-colonial/anti-imperial discourse with agrarian myth, in the manner of 1920s/1930s nationalism and socialism. Whereas the earlier views of Marcuse and Fanon expressed fears about alienation involving the estrangement from an 'authentic' peasant self-hood, however, in the Thirdworldist discourse which the more recent and post-modern variants of the 'new' populism share with 'new' right this innate 'peasant-ness' is re-presented ideologically as the recuperation of a cultural 'otherness'/'difference' that can now be celebrated. Alienation thus meta-morphoses into its 'other', 'peasant-ness'-as-empowerment.

Like the 'new' populism, the 'new' right not only emerged after the 1960s and consolidated during the 1990s, but also endorses a similar version of the agrarian myth, and with it the reaffirmation of peasant essentialism. Again like most variants of 'new' populism that are influenced by postmodernism, the 'new' right subscribes to an extreme form of relativism that de-objectifies existence; all knowledge about the latter is thereby deprivileged as necessarily subjective and hence of equal value. Not only does this delegitimize Enlightenment meta-narratives (reason, rationality, science, materialism) but it also relegitimizes a variety of 'othernesses' of Enlightenment discourse: the irrational, the mystical, the nihilistic, and – most importantly – the agrarian myth.

For both the 'new' right and postmodern variants of the 'new' populism, therefore, every political tradition is as valid as any other, and all political traditions are consequently acceptable. Like postmodernism, the 'new' right subscribes to ecological beliefs (since these confirm the sanctity of Nature) and endorses pluralism (religious, national, ethnic) in the name of cultural 'difference'. In this shared discourse rural poverty in the Third World accord-ingly ceases to be a product of capitalism (= economic difference) and – as the presence in such underdeveloped contexts of an unchanging/eternal peasantry confirms – becomes instead evidence for the existence of cultural 'otherness' rooted in Nature. The twofold difficulty faced by this postmodern 'new' populist epistemology, however, is that such relativism not only banishes capitalism as a problem but also licenses precisely those elements (Sorelian instinctivism, the innateness of ethnic identity) which – subsumed under the rhetoric of cultural 'otherness' – are the central ideological emplacements of the 'old' as well as the 'new' right.

The final part of the book examines the different and seemingly contrasting forms taken by the agrarian myth in the domain of popular culture. Whereas the existence of a connection between the agrarian myth and literature is well documented, the presence of a similar connection in the case of film is less well known. The argument here is not just that important elements of the agrarian myth and of populist discourse continue to pervade film, but also that they both inform a number of seemingly unconnected genres (film *noir*, horror film, science fiction).

Given the current resurgence amidst the capitalist crisis of attempts by non-Marxist social theory to construct an 'a-political' concept of 'community', Chapter 6 examines previous attempts – also in the context of capitalist crisis – to construct an 'imaginary' alternative to capitalism and socialism, as projected in the 'community' (= the golden age of the agrarian myth) constructed over a 50-year period by agrarian populism in three literary/filmic texts: *Caesar's Column* (1890) by the North American populist Ignatius Donnelly, *The Journey of My Brother Alexei to the Land of Peasant Utopia* (1920) by the Russian neo-populist A.V. Chayanov, and the 1937 film by Frank Capra of the book *Lost Horizon* by James Hilton (1933).

It is argued that all the latter share a common utopic/dystopic vision based on a series of symptomatic oppositions. The discourse-against of agrarian populism identifies the dystopic (or absence of 'community') as dark, unnatural, and western, where large-scale technified production controlled by finance capital in an urban setting is linked discursively to the threat of socialism and chaos. Its discourse-for, by contrast, identifies utopia (= 'community') as a realm of light that is harmonious, natural and orientalist, in which neither finance capital nor proletariat exists, and which consists instead of small-scale artisan and peasant producers.

The focus of Chapter 7 is on the contrasting representations (plebeian/aristocratic, pastoral/Darwinian) of the agrarian myth on film, and in particular how apparently different themes ('Nature under attack'/'the death of Nature') exhibit the same nostalgia and an accompanying sense of loss for a vanishing landscape, the locus of enduring rural values. The peasant or 'from below' version of the agrarian myth is termed here the plebeian, while the second or 'from above' landlord version is the aristocratic form. Both the plebeian and aristocratic versions subdivide in turn into two further categories.

First, each possesses both a pastoral and a 'red-in-tooth-and-claw' or Darwinian variant. Thus the plebeian pastoral version of the agrarian myth includes films such as *Witness* and *City Slickers*, while *Arachnophobia* is an example of the plebeian Darwinian version. Films like *Nosferatu* and *The Wicker Man* correspond to the arisocratic Darwinian version of the agrarian myth, while the pastoral includes not just *Gone With The Wind* and *The Music Room* but also *The Leopard* and *1900*, as well as the Tamil films of M.G. Ramachandran, in which landlordism is depicted as passive, almost harmless. And second, both have a discourse about 'Nature under attack'/'the death of Nature', in which Nature is depicted as passive (= the object of agency), and also about 'Nature on the attack'/'the revenge of Nature', in which Nature is projected as active, and engaged in struggle to protect itself.

1

Peasants, Populism and the Agrarian Myth: The Historical Background

'Nations are products of Nature: History is merely a progressive continuation of animal development.' – An observation by Alexander Herzen [1956: 178], in 'The Russian People and Socialism: An Open Letter to Jules Michelet', 1851.

'The road to the peasant leads through nature.' – A programmatic observation made during 1936 by Ferencz Szalasi, Hungary's leading National Socialist, in 'The Way and the Aim' [*Weber, 1964: 157*].

'A myth that corresponds to certain interests or traditional customs can always wield a great power in a class society.' – A critical observation at the same conjuncture by Leon Trotsky [1936: 165] about the reasons for the durability of myth.

This chapter considers not just the epistemological and historical overlap between the agrarian myth, populism, neo-populism and nationalism but also the kind of political outcome this generates. The first part analyses the components of the agrarian myth, an historically enduring form of rural organicism/romanticism. Generally speaking, the agrarian myth is a discourse about the desirability/feasibility and 'naturalness'of small-scale economic activity (peasant family farming, artisanry) in the countryside. It is also supportive, therefore, of rural cultural forms/institutions based on this economic activity: namely, the family, village, regional, ethnic and religious identities which are perceived as being derived from Nature.

By contrast, the agrarian myth expresses opposition to all forms of large-scale economic activity (collectivization, massification), particularly those which are urban-based (finance capital, industrialization, planning). It is similarly hostile to their accompanying institutional, relational and systemic effects (class formation/struggle, revolution, socialism, bureaucracy, the state). All the latter are depicted in the discourse of the agrarian myth as non-indigenous, inauthentic and 'alien' (= non-natural) internationalisms imposed on an unwilling and mainly rural population by 'foreigners' and/or their representatives within the context affected, and thus as responsible for the erosion of hitherto authentic local traditions and values.

The second part of the chapter examines the fusion of the agrarian myth and populism, the latter being a mobilizing discourse arising from the former. Like the agrarian myth, populism is an ideology that has a long history, and one which projects itself in terms of a 'a-political'/'third-way' discourse-against that is simultaneously anti-capitalist and anti-socialist. In a variety of guises and forms, populism and neo-populism have emerged and re-emerged periodically as a reaction by (mainly, but not only) peasants and farmers to industrialisation, urbanization and (again, mainly but not only) capitalist crisis: first in the 1890s, and subsequently during the 1920s and 1930s.

The final section of this chapter focusses on the political forms generated by an historical overlap between populism and the agrarian myth. The fact that the rise or resurgence during the 1920s and 1930s of agrarian populism was a characteristic not just of Central Europe but also of such countries as Italy, the United States, Japan, Germany, India and Peru, suggests that it was an almost universal national response to the capitalist crisis of that period. In many of these contexts, therefore, the resurgence in the face of a double threat (an 'alien'/international finance capitalism 'from above' and an equally 'alien'/ international socialism 'from below') of populism and the contextually-specific variants of its agrarian myth (*nohonshugi*, 'Merrie England', *strapaese*, *narodnichestvo*, *volksgemeinschaft*, the pioneering frontier spirit, *heimat*, *indigenismo*, etc.), was in turn linked not just to nationalism (as in the United States, Russia, India, and Peru) but also to fascism (as in Germany, Japan, Italy, and some Eastern European contexts).[1] Equally unsurprising is the fact that significant elements of the agrarian myth structured 'popular culture' in most of these countries.

I

Any consideration of the economic and political discourse of populism must necessarily begin by addressing three interrelated issues. First, the way in which the idealization of peasant society/culture, combined with a suspicious/ condemnatory attitude towards science/urbanism/industrialization, has occupied a crucial historical role in the agrarian myth. Second, the centrality of the agrarian myth itself, and in particular fears about the de-essentialization of the peasantry (= cultural erosion, alienation), to ideas about nationhood. And third, the long-standing debate between populism, neopopulism and Marxism about categorization of the peasantry and consequently the possibility/ desirability of transforming the existing agrarian structure.

1.1 The Agrarian Myth and Peasant Essentialism

A potent form of ruralism with roots in romantic and conservative notions of an organic society, the agrarian myth is an essentialist ideology which in most contexts is defended with reference to a mutually reinforcing set of arguments to do with the innate aspects of 'peasant-ness', national identity and culture. The first of these was about economics, and entailed a discourse ('peasants-as-the-backbone-of-the-nation') in which agriculture was presented as the historical and continuing basis of social organization, peasant farming as the source of national food self-sufficiency, and the peasantry as the source of military personnel – and thus the defence of the nation. The second argument concerned politics, and advanced claims about the peasantry as upholders of the existing hierarchy, and thus as a bulwark against the spread of socialist ideas and the guarantors of political stability. The last and perhaps most powerful component of this discourse was about culture: this entailed a critique of industrialisation, urbanization and modernity based on nostalgia for a vanishing way-of-life, linked in turn to perceptions of an idyllic/harmonious/folkloric village existence as an unchanging/unchangeable 'natural' community and thus the repository of a similarly immutable national identity. Linked to the latter was the view of the countryside generally as the locus of myths/legends, spiritual/sacred attributes, non-commercial values, and traditional virtue.

Many of the diverse, and seemingly distinct, anti-scientific/anti-modern views which inform the agrarian myth possess their origin in the conservative reaction to the spread of Enlightenment ideas. Historically, the politico-ideological object of conservatism has been the legitimization of an existing or rapidly vanishing social order by the attempted ideological naturalization of what are perceived by the ruling class to be its core institutional elements: religion, family, gender, ethnicity, nation, hierarchy, and Nature itself. All the latter have been – and are – perceived/presented by those on the political right as 'naturally-occurring' phenomena, and thus the immutable bases of social existence (= 'being').[2] By elevating 'thinking' above 'being', however, Enlightenment rationalist thought de-essentializes the 'natural'; in the process of challenging what is (or what ought to continue to be), such philosophy has been perceived by a variety of conservative social forces as licensing change, and thus the precursor of revolution.

In so far as 'reason' constitutes the antithesis of the 'natural', which it problematizes and historicizes, therefore, conservatism is necessarily an anti-rational/anti-Enlightenment philosophy. By contrast, since the political right essentializes traditional institutional social forms as 'natural', the latter concept is as a result not only equated with 'being' itself but also (and therefore) constitutes the basis of conservatism generally and the ideology of counter-revolutionary romanticism in particular.[3] It was precisely because they challenged 'natural' institutions that were specific to national culture (individualism exercised in a particularistic form within a 'given' locality), and threatened to supplant them with new (= 'alien'/'foreign') forms imported from (French, Russian) revolutionary contexts, that conservativism generally has been opposed to the notion of universal (= international) socio-economic categories/processes.[4]

To this conservative pantheon of 'natural' categories can be added the concept 'peasant' which lies at the centre of the agrarian myth. Historically, the opposition of the landlord class to science/urbanism, and the aristocratic reaction against industrialization generally, derives in part from the ways in which these combine to break its power over the peasantry. Thus science/machine-based industrial development offers estate tenants not only alternative (and perhaps better-paid) employment in towns but also the possibility of urban residence, both of which challenge the economic and political dominance landlords traditionally exercise over tenants through the control of land, employment and housing in rural areas. Moreover, once it has migrated to town an erstwhile peasantry, hitherto the embodiment of all the 'eternal'/'natural' rural/national/cultural/religious values associated with the agrarian myth, becomes transformed into an urban proletariat (= 'the mob in the streets'), now potentially/actually non-/anti-religious and part of an international working class. In the process it is also reconstituted as a political threat, not only to means of production in the town/city itself but also – and more importantly from the view of the rural landowning class – to property relations in the countryside.

1.2 The Agrarian Myth, Nationalism and Popular Culture

In this connection it is perhaps salutary to recall that 'popular culture' emanating from the agrarian myth is also associated historically with the emergence of nineteenth century European nationalist movements. Hence the importance to the latter of 'reinventing' traditional folkloric concepts linking an ethnically-specific homogeneous 'people' to a particular territory, thereby establishing a politico-ideological claim to its own rightful place/space and simultaneously denying any rival claims to this made by a 'foreign' occupying power. Moreover, in the European context the ideology of ethnic 'primitivism' and 'purism' is essentially 'a label for the assumption that "the people" really means "the peasants". As Herder once put it, "[t]he mob in the streets, which never sings or composes but shrieks and mutilates, is not the people". The peasants were seen as the true People because they lived close to Nature and because they were unspoiled by new or foreign ways'.[5] Popular culture, the agrarian myth, and the discourse of nineteenth and early twentieth-century nationalism are each structured by an idealized/folkloric image/sound of an undifferentiated peasantry, the repository of national culture (embodied in music, language, songs, dress, customs, traditions) and thus emblematic of people/nation/Nature, all of which is counterposed to the proletarian/urban 'other'.[6] Unsurprisingly, the de-essentialization (= alienation) of the peasantry becomes a metaphor for other kinds of loss: the erosion of cultural and national identity.

The concept of alienation discharges a crucial role in the discourse which the agrarian myth shares with populism where, unlike Marxism, for which alienation is a specifically materialist phenomenon linked to the reproduction of labour-power, it refers generally to a process of cultural marginality/estrangement and in particular to the impact of the latter on the peasantry (and through this on national identity). Broadly speaking, alienation corresponds to a process of transformation that constitutes de-essentialization, whereby a particular phenomenon in effect becomes its 'other'. In the specifically materialist analysis of Marxism, alienation is an effect of the development of private property and the division of labour, an historical transformation that leads to the objectification of human labour-power as living labour is embodied in the forces of production and becomes dead labour, to be deployed increasingly against the worker him/herself.[7] In this way, alienation entails the reification/mystification of the social relations of production, whereby commodities manufactured with labour-power are endowed with a false concreteness. The value appropriated by capital from labour in this process generates a multiplicity of contradictions (between private ownership and the social nature of production) that lead in turn to the class struggle from which arises the possibility of a fundamental systemic transition.

The theoretical and political difficulty with alienation-as-estrangement-from-selfhood and concepts of marginality to which it gives rise is that de-objectification and re-subjectification can be either a materialist or an idealist project. Accordingly, the very notion of becoming/being-other-than-oneself is premised on the existence of an innate 'selfhood' that is a-historical and unchanging, a 'natural' identity from which the self has been estranged and hence transformed into something 'alien' (= 'other'). Moreover, this definition of 'selfhood' can extend from the individual through the group to the nation: the result is an all-encompassing concept of 'estrangement' that includes not just the alienation of labour and its reification as commodity but also Rousseauesque/Wordsworthian versions of conservative nationalism, varieties of 'marginal'/'abnormal' identity declared rationally/socially 'other' by

Enlightenment discourse, and an 'authentic' national/ethnic/peasant identity declared culturally/spiritually 'other' by colonialism.

The potentially conservative political linkages between marginality/alienation/estrangement on the one hand and Rousseauesque/Wordsworthian versions of nationalism on the other are not difficult to discern. According to Rousseau, the origin of inequality lies in a debasement of human goodness, an instinctual behaviour from which humanity had become estranged/alienated and which for him was to be found in its 'natural' form in Nature itself. The object, therefore, was to return to this 'natural'/'primitive' state which had been lost, and with it an innately democratic form of existence based on subsistence.[8] Both this belief in and the necessity of recuperating the 'natural' goodness of humanity was not merely shared by the Romantic poet Wordsworth, but formed the basis for his conservative theory of nationalism.[9]

Like Rousseau, Wordsworth maintained that humanity was essentially 'good', but that this 'pure state' had now been lost due to the imposition of an 'artificial' (= 'alien'/alienating/alienated) existence based on hierarchy. To recover this lost state of 'goodness', therefore, it was necessary to re-establish the context in which it thrived, when humanity was closer to Nature. Since the latter was also a context in which an equally pure form of 'general will' (= absence of hierarchy) was exercised, this state of Nature for Wordsworth also constitutes the basis for the presence of an authentic and benign National identity. A consequence of recuperating this 'natural' state, therefore, when a 'naturally good' humanity exercised a political will that was equally 'pure' and (hence) benign, would be to bring into being a 'natural', 'virtuous' and thus 'authentic' national spirit/identity. The importance of this specifically benign source/form of nationalism for conservative theory is that it invites popular consent and thus confers legitimacy on action(s) exercised in its name. The same point about the tradition-invoking ideological role of ethnic and/or peasant marginality/alienation/estrangement can be made with regard to populism and neo-populism.

II

The reaffirmation of peasant essentialism which lies at the heart of the agrarian myth is also central to populism and neo-populism. Combining the ideologically potent 'natural' categories of land and family, populism maintains that an homogeneous peasantry composed of petty commodity producers constitutes a pan-historical socio-economic category the defining characteristic of which is subsistence cultivation. In contrast to Marxism, the economic discourse of neo-populism denies the existence of depeasantization, and maintains instead that the economic reproduction of each individual peasant family farm is governed by its demographic cycle. The political role of populism is to mobilize the grassroots on the basis of non-class forms of consciousness.

1.3 Populism as the 'Other' of Marxism

Combining the economic theory of petty commodity production and the politics/ideology of nationalism, both populism and neopopulism are in many ways the mirror image of Marxism (see Table). Thus the historical subject of the agrarian question is the proletariat, the economic identity of which is linked historically to the development of large-scale industry in the urban sector; its political identity is an international one based on class, and struggle is aimed at systemic transformation (= revolution). By contrast, the historical subject of the agrarian myth is an homogeneous peasantry, the economic identity of which is linked to small-scale family farming in the village community; its non-economic identity is mainly ethnic/cultural/national, and agency (= resistance) is not designed to achieve systemic transformation. As will be seen in the chapters which follow, most variants of populism – 'new' as well as 'old' – subscribe to some or all of these oppositions.

The epistemological divide between on the one hand a materialist/ rationalist emphasis on the objective necessity of internationalism, socio-economic change and industrial development, and on the other an idealist/ irrationalist commitment to the maintenance/reinvention of an 'imagined community', composed of a peasantry wherein reside indigenous national/ cultural/religious values, is itself at the root of the Marxist/neopopulist polemic.[10] All Marxists regard the peasantry as a socio-economic form that fragments into a rural bourgeoisie and a rural proletariat, and for this reason does not itself form a class but is internally divided along class lines.[11] Differentiating the peasantry into rich, middle and poor peasants, Lenin argued that capitalist penetration of agriculture converted the former into a rural bourgeoisie and the latter into rural labour, while the middle peasantry (or petty commodity producers) disintegrates.[12] Whereas a few middle peasants join the rich peasant stratum and become agrarian capitalists, the majority join the poor peasantry and become agricultural workers. This process was accompanied and accentuated by an increase in the utilization of machinery and wage labour, the concentration of landownership, and the displacement of small-scale by large-scale production. Consequently, Lenin concluded, in Russia the village community (mir) was already disintegrating into its opposed class elements, thereby simultaneously providing capitalism with both a proletariat and a home market.

This differentiation of the peasantry licenses not only class formation but also class struggle. According to Lenin and Trotsky, the peasantry discharges

MARXISM		POPULISM
Agrarian Question		**Agrarian Myth**
	Historical Subject	
Proletariat		Peasantry
	Political Identity	
Class		Ethnicity
Economic		Cultural
International		National
	Political Action	
Revolution		Resistance
Struggle		Accommodation
	Sytemic Effect	
Socialism/Communism		Pre-capitalism/ Capitalism
	Economic Discourse	
Conflict		Harmony
Change		Stasis
Progress		Tradition
Political Economy		Nature
Production		Consumption
Manufacture		Handicrafts
Largescale		Smallscale
Surplus		Subsistence
Collective		Individual
Planning		Market
	Politico-Ideological Discourse	
Rationality		Instinct
Science		Religion
History		Myth
Politics		A-Political
State		Village Community
Urban		Rural
Industry		Agriculture
Internationalism		Nationalism

a twofold role in the process of revolutionary transformation.[13] The first stage occurs in the course of the transition to capitalism, and entails a process whereby an economically declining feudal landowning class is challenged and overwhelmed by a peasant movement reflecting the interests of a rising and economically dominant rich peasantry (= rural capitalists). The second stage occurs under capitalism itself, when a rural mobilization led by poor peasants and agricultural workers in turn challenges and overthrows the capitalist peasantry which successfully led the movement against the landlord class. On the agenda at this stage, therefore, is the possibility of a transition to socialism, in that poor peasants and particularly agricultural workers will demand the further socialization of the means of production, and specifically the collectivization of all rural property.

The middle peasantry is not involved in – let alone leads the peasant movement – in either of these two stages, for the simple reason that in Lenin's model this particular stratum is 'depeasantized' in the course of capitalist development. In general terms, classical Marxism has always questioned the revolutionary potential of an undifferentiated peasantry composed of an homogeneous middle peasantry, allocating to it a subordinate political role in a worker/peasant alliance. Some have advocated merely the political neutralization of the peasantry (Lenin, Kautsky), while others regarded it as actively counter-revolutionary, maintaining that once they became proprietors, peasants would resist any further attempts to socialize the means of production (Trotsky, Luxemburg).[14]

Inverting the Leninist framework, populists maintained that an undifferentiated peasantry reproduced itself regardless of the wider economic system; the uniqueness of Russian development was consequently attributed by them to the presence of a subsistence-oriented rural economy which deprived capitalism of a market. Instead of going down the capitalist path, therefore, populists sought to avoid this altogether, in the process conserving the 'natural'/god-given form of petty commodity production, and with it the ancient cultural traditions of what they regarded as the instinctively egalitarian village community.[15] And whereas Marxists insisted that capture of state power was a necessary aspect of the revolutionary process, neo-populists by contrast advocated non-confrontation with the state, a form of indirect political action known as the 'theory of small deeds'.[16]

1.4 The Economic Discourse of Neo-populism, or Small Is Beautiful

Unlike populism, which was grounded in a liberal critique of the dehumanization and inequality associated with nineteenth-century capitalist development, neo-populism is a twentieth century phenomenon opposed not so much to capitalism as to socialism, and in particular to large-scale industrialization and state collectivization of peasant smallholders in the Soviet Union.[17] The most influential exponent of this view was A.V. Chayanov, the prominent theoretician of the Organization and Production School in Russia at the beginning of this century.[18] Just as sociological theory generally can be described as a confrontation with Marx, so the study of agrarian change is similarly a dispute between Chayanov and Lenin. Conducted via their respective frameworks – the agrarian question and the agrarian myth – this dispute involves not just the issue of peasant differentiation *per se* but rather its implications for the role played by rural mobilization in the transition to socialism. The hostility of neo-populism to the latter is embodied in the theoretical opposition between Chayanov and Lenin concerning both the socio-economic differentiation and the politico-ideological disposition of the peasantry.

In contrast to Marxism, therefore, Chayanovian neo-populism views the peasantry as an undifferentiated *sui generis* economic category ('peasant economy', 'peasant mode of production') which both reproduces itself regardless of and simultaneously resists all social systems. According to Chayanov, not only is peasant economy itself a specific mode of production, but the reproduction of the peasant labour farm is determined endogenously, by the consumption needs of the family that works the land. Claiming that in pre-Revolutionary Russia cyclical mobility prevented consolidation of the means of production (land, livestock, horses) by wealthier peasants, and thus the emergence of rich peasant stratum, Chayanov argued that the partition of village lands by the commune prevented the occurrence of economic differentiation, the result being not polarization into classes (capitalist producers, landless workers) but a process of economic levelling.[19] Accordingly, output on the peasant farm was in his view determined not by external factors (such as rent, taxation, or the extraction of surplus labour by those who own/control the means of production) but rather by the motivation of its individual members. Denying that capitalist penetration of agriculture entailed 'depeasantization', he argued instead that the economic reproduction of each individual peasant family farm was governed by its demographic cycle. Landholding size, food output, and work motivation (= 'self-exploitation') by an economically undifferentiated petty commodity producer was for him based on a specific combination of factors: family size, the ratio of working/non-working household members, and the necessity of having to provide all the latter with their subsistence requirements (the drudgery of labour).

Designated the producer/consumer balance, this 'natural' equilibrium constitutes a 'natural' limit to the output of peasant cultivation. From this analysis it follows that substantial capital accumulation and class differentiation cannot occur either in peasant agriculture or in a society organized around the latter. Critiques of Chayanov's theory of peasant economy point out that it conflates rich and poor peasants, it is an historically static entity abstracted from the national and international economy, it embodies a subjective concept of value, it overlooks the operation/effect of land/labour markets and capitalist competition, and ignores class divisions between/within peasant farms together with a differential capacity to utilize technology.[20] In the neo-populist vision of Chayanov, therefore, petty commodity production reproduces itself in the form of the family labour farm, regardless of the presence/absence of feudalism, capitalism or indeed socialism. Unlike Marxist political economy, for which peasant differentiation into small capitalist producers and an agrarian proletariat licenses class-specific revolutionary action designed to capture state power that prefigures a transition to socialism, neo-populism in general and Chayanovian theory in particular reconstitutes the peasantry as an undifferentiated category that resists socio-economic change, a politically conservative position which does not involve a transition to socialism, entails no expropriation/redistribution of existing property, and hence presents no threat to the continued rule of capital.[21]

1.5 The Politico-ideological Discourse of Populism, or Penultima Ratio Regum[22]

Populist discourse has also discharged an important political role as a mobilizing ideology, operating at the level of consciousness where it serves to deflect discourse from class to non-class identity; the imporance of this aspect of populism is evident from the many texts which label it as rhetoric, or a class consciousness displacing discourse-about.[23] Hence the frequent invocation by populism of a necessity for an 'above-politics' or 'a-political' grassroots movement suggests the presence of a class-specific ideology without seeming to be one.[24] The effectiveness of populism as a mobilizing ideology accordingly depends ultimately on its capacity to project class-specific interests as if this were not so; that is, by representing the ideas of a particular class, but in a way that disguises this fact and thus the socio-economic origin of this discourse. That populism frequently eschews the explicitly political, and tends therefore to insist on regarding itself (and being regarded by others) as a 'common-sense' or an 'a-political'/'above-politics' discourse, is precisely because this element of being 'non-political' is central to the very process of appearing not to be class-specific.[25]

This in turn gives rise to a second important political characteristic: because of its epistemological roots in the discourse of the agrarian myth, popular culture and nationalism, populism has also discharged a unique role in mobilizing grassroots support for conservatism. Unlike other texts which categorize variants of populism as compatible with the politics of either the left or the right, therefore, populism is associated here only with the political right.[26] In short, populism is not an autonomous theory/practice that occasionally (and accidentally) overlaps with a largely unconnected conservative theory/practice; much rather it *is* the right, mobilizing or mobilized politically. The reason for eschewing this duality, and classifying populism as a conservative mobilizing discourse is that, although individual socialists/Marxists may on occasion espouse populist views and endorse populist aims, socialism/Marxism as a political programme is in fact not only incompatible with populism but – as the oppositions set out in the Table above confirm – its 'other'. To the degree that it has been – or indeed remains – compatible with populism, therefore, the political theory/practice of what (erroneously) passes for the left cannot be considered socialist/Marxist.[27]

Although it shares with Marxism a discourse-against that attacks big business, political injustice, and the effects of capitalism generally, populism does this not in the name of the common ownership of the means of production (as does Marxism) but rather in the name of individual, small-scale private property. Since it downgrades/denies the existence of class and accordingly essentializes the peasantry, populism also perceives smallholding proprietors as socio-economically undifferentiated and thus casts them all in the role of 'victims', uniformly oppressed by large-scale institutions/monopolies located in the urban sector (the state, big business and 'foreign' capital). As many Marxists have pointed out, the political anxiety that structures the discourse-against of populism is an underlying fear of socialism rather than capitalism. For this reason, the populist discourse-against is directed not so much at capitalism *per se* as at its large-scale monopoly/('foreign') variant which gives rise to the very conditions that lead in turn to socialism.

Like Marxism, populism also combines a pessimism about the present with an optimism about the future. Unlike Marxism, however, populism fails to distinguish between a progressive/modern anti-capitalism which seeks to transcend bourgeois society, and a romantic anti- (or, as will be seen the the chapters which follow, a post-) modern form the roots of which are located in agrarian nostalgia and reactionary visions of an innate Nature. Accordingly, the pessimism which structures the discourse-against of the agrarian myth, populism and neo-populism generates an optimism which is not forwards-looking, or politically progressive, but much rather backwards-looking, and thus corresponds to an attempt to reinvent tradition in a way that has been (and continues to be) supportive of conservative, nationalist and even fascist ideology.

There is no mystery as to why conservatives value the capacity of populism and neo-populism to mobilize grassroots support on the basis of a working-class consciousness-displacing discourse. Despite claims that it is unproblematically associated with 'modernization' *per se*, populism is an ideology which tends to emerge during periods of capitalist crisis, when capitalism is most under threat from a working class mobilizing along specifically class lines.[28] It is precisely at this conjuncture that, from the viewpoint of those interested in its survival, capitalism requires most saving. In such circumstances, any opposition to current forms of accumulation must be prevented from becoming a challenge to the capitalist system itself, a process which requires that opposition to capitalism be permitted but must nevertheless remain under the ideological control of the bourgeoisie.[29] In this way, what is potentially/actually opposition to capitalism can be defused, and transformed into 'opposition'.

As will be seen in the chapters which follow, the advantage for rich peasants in India and Latin America of a populist/neopopulist discourse is that it enables them to operate politically and ideologically on two fronts: against poor peasants and agricultural labourers as well as landlords and/or international capital. The success of this hinges in turn on the displacement of class categories, whereby agrarian subjects who are defined in terms of ownership of or separation from given means of production are redefined in neopopulist terms simply as 'peasants'/'cultivators'/'farmers', or as petty commodity producers in contexts where there is actually great variation in both relations and the scale of production. Such a discursive fusion permits agrarian capitalist producers to claim not only that all rural inhabitants experience a uniform level of suffering in the face of urban and/or 'foreign' exploitation but also that economic growth is located in and confined largely to towns/cities/ industry and/or other nations. By suppressing reference to socio-economic differentiation arising from the process of capitalist development, therefore, rich peasants can challenge landlords and/or imperialism in the name of the peasantry as a whole, which permits them not merely to reinforce and reproduce in discourse shared with poor peasants and agricultural labour the mythic yet politico-ideologically potent image of an homogenous peasantry but also to claim that they represent thereby the voice of 'the people' (= the peasantry), and thus the nation itself.

Two important consequences follow from this nationalist discourse, each of which is supportive of the neo-populist camouflage adopted by rich peasants. First, that self-empowerment is effected at the expense of a foreign and not an indigenous capitalist class; and second, that 'popular culture' becomes identified unproblematically with the 'voice from below', and action based on this is accordingly deemed to constitute an authentic expression of the democratic will.[30] Consequently, anything and everything associated with its grassroots manifestation automatically becomes the embodiment of democratic expression, and can now be invoked/celebrated as the utterance of the hitherto mute and dominated. The difficulty with this is that once the 'popular' is accepted as an *unmediated* construct (or the 'natural' voice of the people), it follows that what is desirable becomes whatever the 'popular' says is so; in short, a procedure that fails to ask precisely how such views are constructed, by whom, and for what political ends. Where precisely a populist grassroots mobilization informed by a discourse combining the agrarian myth and nationalism can lead politically is evident from the historical case studies which now follow.

III

Both the durability of the agrarian myth, and its roots in nationalist discourse, can be illustrated with respect to many different contexts. In the case of English culture, for example, rural nostalgia as embodied in the pastoral has a long, powerful and enduring ideological lineage. Hence the literary invocation of the agrarian myth is the subject of infinite historical regression, stretching back at regular intervals from the 1930s to the 1370s, at each stage of which there is said to exist an image of a (vanishing-to-be-recuperated) 'golden age' constituted by the timeless agricultural rhythms of 'Old England'.[31] Much the same is true of music, where the pastoral style has discharged a crucial role in reaffirming national identity constructed/projected in the course of the English musical renaissance over the latter part of the nineteenth century and the first half of the twentieth.[32] During the capitalist crisis of the 1920s and 1930s the reaffirmation of a connection between national/regional identity and landscape extended from popular fiction to the anti-modern/anti-socialist agrarian populist views of those such as Belloc, Chesterton, and A.R. Orage, all of whom advocated distributism, or a return to a decentralized form of social organization based on the small-scale property of artisan and peasant.[33]

1.6 Nationalism and the Agrarian Myth in the Nineteenth Century

Dismissed by Marxists as *kulak* ideology, the agrarian myth in Russia has a similarly extended genealogy. The polarities which structured the nationalist/ populist ideology informing the Russian version of the agrarian myth were similar to those structuring the *gemeinschaft/gesellschaft* frame-work.[34] Whereas *gesellschaft* entails the adoption of rationalistic/calculating (= scientific) and future-oriented universal values that manifest themselves through public opinion, *gemeinschaft* by contrast is based on religion/ culture/family, its 'natural' will consequently being the expression of ancient faith, custom and folkloric tradition.

The period after 1861 was marked by an attempt on the part of the Russian populists (*narodniki*) to construct within the domain of 'popular culture' an essentialist image of the post-Emancipation peasantry as 'the people' (*narod* = people = peasants).[35] Like *nohonshugi* in Japan, the *narodniki* in Russia blamed the state for permitting capitalism to erode peasant economy/ community. As in the other apparently historically- and contextually-specific examples considered here, therefore, the target of discourse-against of Russian populism was finance capital, and for much the same reason: embodying the doubly 'alien' otherness of 'the urban' and 'the foreign', money was blamed for undermining the economic base of peasant economy, and through this the tradition of the 'eternal peasant' as a pristine cultural subject from which arose an equally 'natural' form of national identity.[36]

Invoking the conservative values and traditions of pre-Petrine Russia against the 'dangerous'/'alien' views of the European Enlightenment, the polarities which structured the nationalist/populist ideology of Russian Slavophiles were stereotypically those of the agrarian myth. Because it threatened on the one hand to expand the urban proletariat and on the other to ruin the small independent peasant producer, the embodiment of traditional religious and nationalist values, Slavophile populists reacted against what was perceived as a foreign (specifically German) capitalist penetration of Russia during the latter half of the nineteenth century.[37] Against the 'artificial', large-scale conflict-ridden system associated with European industrialization/urbanization/bureaucracy that entailed the adoption of rationalistic/calculating (= scientific) and future-oriented universal values, Slavophiles counterposed and invoked the desirability of an a-historical, immanent concept of harmonious/organic small-scale 'community', a predominantly rural and authentically Russian institution composed of 'common people'.[38] Since the latter was based on religion/culture/family, Slavophile populists claimed, its 'natural' will was consequently the expression of ancient faith, custom and folkloric tradition. Backward-looking and opposed to industrialization, Slavophile populism was based on the view that each nation could not but follow its own organic laws of development.[39]

Whereas for Slavophiles peasant identity was basically non-rational and cultural, non-slavophiles such as Semevskii, Engelgardt, Chayanov, and Kondrat'ev all saw the Russian peasant as an economically rational agent.[40] Although the distinction is not absolute, for populism it involved a dual conceptualization of peasant essentialism; on the one hand a social Darwinian peasant, the economic reproduction of which was linked to what Chayanov identified as an infinite capacity for 'self-exploitation' (= survival of the fittest), and on the other a peasant that was culturally pristine. Both identities fused to form an agrarian populist discourse about peasant essentialism, resulting in an economically undifferentiated peasantry the innate culture of which was as a result capable of surviving in any socio-economic formation. For this reason, the Russian peasantry represented for Salvophile and Chayanovian theory alike both a cultural and an economic alternative to capitalism and to socialism.

Superficially, the American and Russian variants of agrarian populism are dissimilar; whereas the latter has its origins in an aristocratic landowning class, the former is rooted in Jeffersonian and Jacksonian democracy.[41] As in Russia, however, the origins of the agrarian myth in the United States lie in a discourse-against emanating from above, and not with some form of 'grassroots resistance' from below.[42] In both cases, therefore, this discourse is anti-intellectual, backward-looking, and nationalist: peasants are presented as the embodiment of national identity, whereby a folkloric peasant/yeoman appears as the bulwark against industrial/urban development, and in both Russia and America this is a discourse about an homogenous rural population of independent smallholders that hides the presence and effects of socio-economic differentiation.[43] Moreover, just as Chayanov supplied Russian agrarian populism with the economic arguments in support of peasant family farming, so Veblen provided its counterpart in America with an economic defence of the yeoman farmer.[44]

Although associated specifically with agrarian mobilizations accompanying the rapid economic change during the 1890s and culminating in the candidacy of William Jennings Bryan in the 1896 presidential election, agrarian populism in America continued throughout the early years of this century to the rise of the People's Party and the Progressive movement.[45] In the context of fears about a declining rural America and the expansion of urban industrial society, populism constituted the reaffirmation of the values (homogeneity, equality of opportunity, civic morality/purity, individualism, rural-based property-owning democracy composed of independent, small-scale and self-sufficient producers) associated with an agrarian tradition based on family farming. Like its Russian counterpart, therefore, American populism in the 1890s was based on the agrarian myth: in the latter case, that of the yeoman farmer, a citizen who embodied the civic and religious values of the nation by virtue of owning the farm on which he worked together with his family.[46]

Ironically, just as antebellum commercialization/mechanization of agricultural production in response to the growth of the national and international market undermined the economic reality on which this myth was based, so the crisis of overproduction during the latter part of the nineteenth century (characterized by a combination of rising costs, falling prices/profits as competition intensified) gave it a new politico-ideological life.[47] As smallholders in the southern and midwestern states of America became less independent economically, therefore, so this agrarian populist discourse became focused increasingly against the corruption of politics, as exemplified in the victimization of the family farm by an urban bureacracy/state and large-scale corporations (= monopoly/finance capital), all of which were identified as being responsible for the land speculation that resulted in the dispossession of the smallholder.[48]

1.7 Populism, Nationalism and the Agrarian Myth in the 1920s and 1930s

This same agrarian populist discourse resurfaced in the United States during the subsequent capitalist crisis, this time connected specifically to perceptions of southern decline. Accordingly, the nostalgic and idealized vision of a rural 'world-we-have-lost' espoused by the Southern Agrarians represented an intellectual reaction against the Great Depression of the 1930s.[49] Opposed to industrialisation, not least because mass production was aesthetically repugnant and undermined good art, the Southern Agrarians not only attempted to recuperate pre-industrial values, among them slavery, but also – and not unlike *nohonshugi* and *volksgemeinschaft* ideology – to construct thereby a common cultural identity on the basis of a shared ethnic/regional background.[50] As in the case of *nohonshugi* ideology, the rejection of progress generally and industrialisation in particular was linked to the fear of socialism and communism, each of which was seen by Southern Agrarians as the inevitable outcome of capitalist development.[51] Like the Russian neo-populists, therefore, the Southern Agrarians regarded small-scale subsistence agriculture based on the individual family farm as a politically desirable, historically traditional and culturally 'natural' organizational form appropriate to the southern economy and society, the 'other' of both finance capital and socialism.[52]

Rejecting the idea that Southern writers 'should adopt somebody else's geography and contrarily write like Northerners – at that, like Northerners made sick by an overdose of their own industrialism', the Southern Agrarians – again like the exponents of *nohonshugi* and *volksgemeinschaft* – invoked instead a specifically agrarian folkloric image of 'popular culture'.[53] Perhaps the best-known and most powerful projection in the realm of 'popular culture' of the antebellum rural society the loss of which was lamented in the agrarian populist discourse of the Southern Agrarians is the film *Gone With The Wind* (1939).[54]

In the case of colonial India, the agrarian myth has a long lineage, and was prefigured in the views expressed not just by Mahatma Gandhi during the 1920s and 1930s but also by Acharya Narendra Deva in the late 1930s and by N.G. Ranga and Rammanohar Lohia during the early 1940s.[55] The impact of pastoral versions of nationalist discourse on the 'popular' culture of colonial India is sufficiently well-known to require much elaboration. Many of the more important actors in the Tamil Cinema of the 1930s actively participated in the nationalist movement itself, and not only was rural life endorsed but this was done with explicit actual/symbolic reference to Gandhi himself: for example, in the form of heroes/heroines returning to the village from the town in order to carry out Gandhian policy.[56]

In many respects, Gandhian theory and practice in India conforms to the classical pattern of nationalist/populist ideology and politics outlined above and below with regard to Japan, Germany, Italy, England, Russia, and the United States.[57] On the one hand, therefore, Gandhi promoted class conciliation, endorsed the notion of an ethnically-specific hierarchy (based on the Hindu caste system), and advocated a return to traditional cultural and religious values as embodied in village India by an undifferentiated peasantry; on the other hand, he denied progress/modernity, was correspondingly suspicious of all things urban (the locus of 'alien' non-Indian western values), and condemned class struggle.[58] Because of the convenient all-embracing character of this populism, in which an externalized oppression/exploitation/ capitalism can be displaced onto an urban/foreign/scientific/Western 'other', the prime movers in the agrarian struggles organized by Gandhi in Bihar and Gujarat during the early part of the century were unsurprisingly the better-off peasants from high castes.[59]

This was the case with regard to the *satyagraha* conducted against European indigo planters in Champaran district, Bihar, where during 1917 Gandhi mobilized tenants against rent increases (*sharabeshi*), illegal levies (*abwabs*), land transfer payments (*salaami*), and the obligation to cultivate the landlord's crops – particularly indigo – on their best land (the *tinkathia* system). The resulting *satyagraha* was led by better-off tenants composed of high caste Brahmins, Rajputs, Bhumihars and Kyasthas, who were caught between rent enhancements coupled with the declining profitability of indigo cultivation on the one hand, and on the other the need to remove existing institutional obstacles to their growing the more profitable foodgrain and sugarcane crops.[60] Much the same was true of the Bardoli *satyagraha* in Surat district, Gujarat, where, because the rental value of land had increased substantially, and the British administration had decided to raise the level of land revenue, rich peasant proprietors belonging to the Patidar caste who cultivated cotton embarked on a 'no-tax' campaign during 1928.[61]

Although Deva, Ranga and Lohia were regarded initially as socialists of some sort, the discourse of each was – like that of Gandhi – basically populist and nationalist.[62] Hence the exploiter is depicted by them as external, the Indian peasant is equated with Nature (= 'pure'/untainted-by-the-city) and is accordingly regarded as an uncorrupted and thus a revolutionary subject. By contrast, the urban worker is 'tainted-by-the-city', corrupted by colonialism, and thus no longer a revolutionary subject. The urban proletariat in metropolitan capitalism is in their perception doubly tainted: simply by virtue of its combined urban/colonial 'otherness', therefore, it can no longer be considered revolutionary. The latter mantle has passed instead to 'colonial toilers' in general and to peasants in particular, who in the view of populists such as Lohia would challenge and destroy capitalism.[63] It is perhaps not without significance that Ranga resigned from the Congress Party in the early 1950s, accusing it of being against farmers, and went on to form first his own peasants' party, the Krishak Lok Dal, and then in 1959 the conservative Swatantra Party, of which he remained leader until the early 1970s.[64]

1.8 Inca 'Communism' and the Agrarian Myth

Turning to Latin America at this same conjuncture, what is striking is the ideological similarity between different political movements and parties on the issue of the agrarian myth. Regarding the latter, therefore, there was – as in the case of India – little to distinguish the views of Peruvian socialists and/or communists such as José Carlos Mariátegui and Hildebrando Castro Pozo from those of Peruvian nationalists and populists such as Víctor Raúl Haya de la Torre.[65] On the basis of a shared epistemology, all of them subscribed to what might be termed a specifically Latin American variant of the agrarian myth: namely, the view that the Spanish Conquest imposed an 'inauthentic' and 'foreign' (= European) feudal tenure structure on what each of them interpreted as being a materially self-sufficient and culturally 'authentic' indigenous Andean peasant community that characterized the pre-Colombian era.[66] More important was the fact that for both Mariátegui and Haya de la Torre, the discourse of the the agrarian myth also possessed a programmatic status: the socialism of the former as well as the nationalism of the latter entailed building on what each perceived as being a still-viable peasant economy, a residue from the golden age of Peru that had survived colonialism.

Politically and theoretically, Mariátegui and Haya de la Torre appear to located at opposite ends of the same spectrum. Widely regarded as the most influential Marxist theorist in Latin America, Mariátegui was not only instrumental in the foundation of the Peruvian Socialist Party (the PSP or *Partido Socialista del Peru*) in 1928 and the Confederation of Peruvian Workers (the CGTP or *Confederación General de Trabajadores del Peru*), but also 'helped to produce a Peruvianized Marxism . . . [and was an intellectual whose] thinking on the agrarian question was without doubt one of his most useful contributions'.[67] By contrast, Haya de la Torre founded APRA (*Alianza Popular Revolucionaria Americana*) during the mid-1920s, a nationalist and populist multi-class front which aimed to represent the 'masses' or 'national majority' composed of workers, peasants, tribals, and elements of the middle class (students, teachers, small agrarian capitalists, etc.) against imperialism and its local representatives (large landlords, merchants), both in Peru itself and also in Central and South America.[68]

Ostensibly structured by anti-imperialism, and strongly influenced by Spenglerian notions of Western decline, therefore, the mobilizing discourse of

APRA combined a powerful nationalism informed by anti-European/anti-American sentiments with an equally powerful idealization of the Indo-American 'working masses', of whom the most significant component was going to be the peasantry. Much the same was true of Mariátegui, his socialism notwithstanding.[69] Smallholders were identified by Mariátegui and Haya de la Torre variously as the source of all production, as embodying an 'authentic' indigenous tradition, and as having been the main victims of 'foreign' (Iberian, North American) domination/exploitation.[70] Unlike the Andean peasant community, which in his view was economically efficient, Mariátegui regarded the large estate as a colonial implantation, a feudal or semi-feudal unit that was economically backward and thus incapable of undergoing a capitalist transformation.[71]

For Mariátegui and Haya de la Torre, the Andean peasant community was for a number of reasons economically and ideologically central to the struggle against a variety of 'othernesses' at the root of economic backwardness (latifundism, feudalism, colonialism, imperialism) as interpreted by the mobilizing ideology of both the PSP and APRA. It was perceived by them as institutionally and organizationally specific to Inca society and Indoamerica (≠ European or 'foreign' implant), the sacred underlying 'other' of an externally imposed profane European feudalism, and as such constituted the embodiment of an 'authentically' indigenous socio-economic form.[72] Furthermore, since it had managed to survive colonization, and thus remained intact, peasant economy was not merely durable but continued to thrive because of its acceptability to existing rural communities: accordingly, it was on this economic survival from what he perceived to be an Incaic golden age of native Peru that Haya de la Torre wished to build his ethnically-specific grassroots 'national sovereignty' (*'La revindicación del indio como hombre y de su sistema como método de producción, son imperativos por razones económicas'*).[73]

Much the same kind of epistemology informed Mariátegui's socialism, according to which the agrarian question in Peru was concerned essentially with two main issues. First, the ending of an externally-imposed feudalism, an historical task which should have been carried out by a democratic bourgeois regime. Since the latter had failed to emerge in Peru, feudal landlords had retained their power.[74] And second, the future role in the national and rural economy of the Andean peasant community: like Haya de la Torre, Mariátegui maintained that feudalism had been built on the ruins of what for him was a pre-existing socialist economy.[75] Among the reasons for his regarding the Inca State as a form of agrarian communism were the presence of institutions such as the *ayllu*, a rural community composed of a clan or kin group claiming descent from a common ancestor, and *mink'a*, a traditional form of co-operative labour.[76] Not only was the pre-Colombian village community in the view of Mariátegui a 'natural' repository of socialist/communist values and practices, but the latter were perceived by him as the basis of its resistance against feudal landlords.[77]

Central to both the nationalist/populist ideology of APRA and the 'socialism' of Mariátegui, therefore, was a specifically Latin American version of the agrarian myth, premissed on the survival of the peasant community together with its accompanying economic institutions (such as *mink'a*, the *allyu*, and the *callpulli*): although Spanish colonization halted the *social* and *political* evolution of ancient/traditional/longstanding grassroots indigenous organizations in Mexico and Peru, it did not in their view succeed in destroying the underlying *economic* system of production and exchange, which had accordingly managed to retain its independence.[78] The programmatic outcome of adherence to this backwards-looking Latin American version of the agrarian myth is not difficult to discern.[79] Having argued variously that the Inca State was a form of 'agrarian communism', that in Peru a domestic bourgeoisie was non-existent, and that consquently power in this context continued to be exercised by a feudal landlord class, the expropriation of the latter and the (re-) construction of a socialist formation necessarily became for Mariátegui the political task of an indigenous peasantry located in the village community.

APRA and Haya de la Torre arrived at the same political destination, but by a slightly different route. Since he equated a proletariat with industrial production and assumed that no landless workers or poor peasants were to be found in agriculture, Haya de la Torre advanced two of the most familiar populist/nationalist arguments heard at this conjuncture: first, that outside Europe and North America no proletariat existed, as a result of which there was correspondingly no constituency in Latin America for the left to mobilize; and second, that ('European'-not-Peruvian) theories arguing for communism and socialism were themselves part of this 'foreign' domination.[80] Reproducing the arguments of Deva, Ranga and Lohia, and likewise anticipating those of Fanon and Marcuse a quarter of a century later, Haya de la Torre maintained further that the industrial working class which already existed in Latin American counties had been bought off (= 'corrupted'/incorporated) by 'foreign' capital, and was thus in a political sense beyond redemption.[81] Given this multiple absence (proletariat = numerically insignificant, confined to urban contexts, and anyway co-opted), he then argued that peasants were the only feasible historical subject at that conjuncture, and consequently *indigenista* ideology would be the mobilizing discourse for any (nationalist) revolutionary action aimed at ending foreign domination.

1.9 Fascism, Populism and the Agrarian Myth in the 1920s and 1930s

In the case of Japan, the nationalist idealization of peasant farming combined with opposition to finance-capital, urbanization/industrialization, socialism and the state are all themes which are present in the ideology of *nohonshugi* (= 'agriculture-as-the-essence-ism') that emerged during the 1890s as a reaction to post-1868 industrialization and modernization. Broadly speaking, the romanticization/glorification of pre-modern rural community in general and in particular the peasant family farm by *nohonshugi* ideology was structured by the belief that external/'non-natural'/'alien' processes (commercialism, socialism) threatened to undermine village life, on which depended in turn the existence of and the sacred authority vested in family, emperor (= God) and nation.

In the work of Gondo Seikyo and Tachibana Kozaburo, the two most prominent exponents of *nohonshugi* who advocated a decentalized form of village autonomy ('self-rule' or *shashkoru*), Japanese agrarian populism merged with nationalism during the 1920s and 1930s. Arguing that the nation-as-people was represented by the emperor and not the state, both equated the latter with the power of the bureaucracy and finance capital (= commercialism) in contrast to the emperor, who for them embodied an authentic national identity and nationalism based on ethnicity, religion and traditional rural hierarchy. This reaffirmation of the centrality of rural community was thus premised on an unmediated link between a 'natural'/ancient process of peasant farming and the peasantry itself on the one hand, and an equally 'natural'/ancient process of imperial rule and the nation itself on the other; in the discourse of *nohonshugi*, moreover, all these sacred and socially fundamental institutional forms were in danger of being undermined by an 'alien' commercialism (= finance capital), the rejection of which correspondingly entailed village self-rule under – and accountable only to – the emperor.[82] In this form of *nohonshugi* ideology, therefore, smallholding agriculture is both synonymous with and mobilizes in defence of 'national essence' (*kokutai*), a discursive fusion whereby family = peasantry = people = warriors = nation.[83]

As elsewhere, in Japan agrarian populist ideas linked to the rise of nationalism were explicitly counterposed to their socialist 'other': thus the independent peasant propietor was presented in *nohonshugi* discourse as a bulwark against the spread of socialist ideas, and the destruction of the former would result in the victory of the latter, which in turn would undermine patriotism and generate class struggle.[84] An important aspect of this process took the form of focusing on the rural/urban divide, with the object of deflecting/diverting the actual/potential development of a consciousness of class among poor peasants and agricultural labourerers in Japan.[85]

Accordingly, the object of the emphasis placed by *nohonshugi* on rural harmony based on a common identity was to abolish or downplay the importance of rural class struggle in the countryside that characterized the 1920s and early 1930s in the form of landlord/tenant conflicts.[86] During this period tenants began to form unions, and while the political objectives of some of these were indeed compatible with populist agrarian nationalism, others were not. For exponents of *nohonshugi* agrarian populism conflict between landlord and tenants in Japan during the 1920s was due not to the unequal ownership of the means of production but rather to the commercialization of agriculture.[87] What is important about the re-emergence at this conjuncture of agrarian populism in Japan, therefore, is that it served amongst other things to deflect some of this agrarian struggle away from class issues into ones linked to national identity and nationalism, in the process off-setting or blocking the spread and influence in the countryside of socialist ideas.[88]

Italy constitutes another instance of the connection between the rise of fascism, class struggle and the agrarian myth, as mediated through popular culture. The centrality of class struggle to this process is clear just from the chronology: in Italy the years 1919–20 were characterized by socialist inspired/led working class mobilization, a potentially revolutionary process that culminated in the factory occupations of September 1920. The subsequent two-year period, 1921–22, was characterized by a reaction to this, in the form of a counter-revolutionary mobilization on the part of employers, landholders and fascists, a process that culminated in Mussolini's march on Rome in October 1922.

The importance of the class struggle in the countryside to the rise of fascism emerges clearly from the examples of Bologna, Tuscany and Apulia.[89] In each of these contexts, therefore, fascism was the 'from-above' resolution to class struggle generated by capitalist development generally and agrarian capitalism in particular. In the case of Tuscany, capitalist competition in the form of American grain imports undermined the *mezzadria* system in Tuscany from the 1880s onwards, as increased tenant expenses (on seeds and fertilizers) led in turn to increased indebtedness and the transformation of tenants into casual labourers. The period after the First World War was accordingly characterized by socialist-led strikes, in the face of which the government capitulated. Landlords, however, bided their time, organized gangs recruited from among the lumpenproletariat, and engaged in counter-revolutionary measures (repression, violence) the culmination of which was fascism.

Much the same is true of Germany, where 'popular culture' was also characterized by an ideological fusion of agrarian populism and nationalism. Like Russian slavophile populism, the agrarian myth in 1930s Germany categorized finance capital as both exogenous and ethnically 'other'. In the discourse of fascism, therefore, finance capital is not merely 'foreign' but also 'Jewish'; the latter identity was equated in turn with usury, and depicted as an external and economically unproductive form of parasitism which preyed upon the endeavours of a productive and ethnically 'pure' indigenous peasantry, the embodiment of all things German. In this way, the nationalist/ culturalist discourse of agrarian populism during a period of capitalist crisis displaced potential/actual criticism of and hostility to capitalism onto finance capital and ethnic relations, each of which was projected as the 'alien'/non-German 'other'.

Central to the anti-modern/anti-urban ideological components of German Fascism (as projected in the writings of Alfred Rosenberg and Richard Walther Darré), therefore, was the concept of immutable laws of nature reasserting themselves to cleanse the nation, the race, and its soil.[90] Like the 'anti-foreigner' Slavophile populism/nationalism of the nineteenth century Russian nobility, this idealization/sanctification of Nature (= the environment = the people = the nation) was also based on the romanticization of a subsistence-oriented smallholding peasantry, projected in politico-ideological terms as the integral embodiment of an ethnically 'pure' German folk culture and the bulwark of a socio-economically atemporal 'natural order' outside history, against which was ranged the town/city, the source of multiple, interrelated and non-Germanic forms of pollution ('Jewish finance capital', socialism, the 'urban mob').[91]

As in the case of Japan and Italy, the rise of agrarian populism in Germany during the 1920s predated yet prefigured the seizure of power by the political right. In rural Lower Saxony, for example, the bourgeoisie mobilized on the basis of an unambiguously *volksgemeinschaft* (= 'people's community'), pronation, above-party and above-class discourse against hyper-inflation, the capitalist crisis and the memory not just of Weimar but also (and more significantly) of the threat posed by the working class in the November 1918 Revolution. Rural artisans sought protection from competition by large-scale capitalist mass production, while farmers in the *landvolk* movement in 1928–29 similarly mobilized against cheaper foreign imports, increasing taxation and the threat of bankruptcy and foreclosure.[92]

1.10 'Christ, not Lenin' in Eastern Europe

A similar set of circumstances linked to capitalist development also gave rise in East European countries during the 1920s and 1930s to the fusion between on the one hand mass peasant mobilizations and on the other a discourse endorsing the agrarian myth, populism and nationalism.[93] Some of these peasant movements, like the Independent Smallholders' Party in Hungary and the Bulgarian Agrarian Union, were simply populist and nationalist, while others, such as the the Christian Slovak People's Party (or Ludaks) in Czechoslovakia, the Croatian Peasant Party, the League of the Archangel Michael and the Iron Guard in Romania, and the Hungarian National Socialist Workers' Party were fascist organizations. As in the United States and Russia, peasant parties in Eastern Europe emerged in the 1890s and consolidated in the 1930s. Although there were obvious differences between them in terms of political programme, all of them adhered to a populist mobilizing discourse, in terms of what they were for and what they were against.

During the 1920s and 1930s, the mobilizing discourse of right-wing agrarian populist organizations in Czechoslovakia, Hungary and Romania not only emphasized the existence of an homogeneous peasantry, consisting of privately-owned smallholdings cultivated by a subsistence-oriented middle peasant, but the presence/desirability of the latter was proclaimed in the party symbols and/or slogans adopted by their leadership.[94] This discourse equated 'the people' with 'the peasantry', and peasant party objectives in most East European contexts aimed both at the maintenance or restoration of a middle peasantry and ultimately at the creation of a peasant State.[95] The latter notwithstanding, East European peasant parties and agrarian populist organizations managed to retain the support of poor peasants, largely because of the non-economic components of their mobilizing discourse. Chief among these was nationalism, which in countries like Romania had informed earlier debates about agrarian reform.[96]

Anti-urban, anti-industrial and anti-semitic ideologies were all pervasive and interrelated aspects of populist discourse in eastern European contexts at this conjuncture.[97] Like their American and German counterparts, therefore, populists in Hungary and Romania categorized commerce in terms not of class but of ethnicity, and thus as an activity conducted not by merchant capitalists but by the Jewish 'other' who as such represented the power of the towns over the countryside and was thereby responsible for the 'foreign' exploitation of an indigenous peasantry, the literal/spiritual embodiment of the nation and hence the 'authentic' bearers of national identity.[98] When combined with anti-urban and anti-industrial sentiments, the discourse of anti-semitism consolidated in particularly potent manner a multiplicity of 'othernesses' linked to the agrarian myth: not only were Jews blamed for the economic dominance of towns in general and finance capital (= usury) in particular, and thus for the ('non-natural') unproductive economic appropriation effected (by 'the urban') from the ('natural') productive economic activity undertaken by smallholders (in 'the rural'), but also for the destruction/deculturation/despoilation of the peasantry and – by inference – the nation itself.

This ideological combination became yet more powerful when linked to the two remaining elements of agrarian populist discourse: on the one hand its hostility towards socialism, communism, Marxism, and – (at this historical conjuncture) especially – Bolshevism, and on the other its endorsement of nationalism. In most East European countries, therefore, agrarian populism was perceived not merely as the discursive 'other' of Marxism but – as in the case of *nohonshugi* in Japan – as the only political force capable of halting the advance in rural areas of Bolshevism.[99] To Marxist calls for internationalism, the necessity for the collectivization of rural property and the argument about the inevitability/desirability of depeasantization, therefore, agrarian populists in Eastern Europe counterposed arguments about the 'naturalness' of national solidarity based on equally 'natural' ethnicities, the necessity for individual private property, the inevitability/desirability of traditional smallholding agri-culture, and the ethnic/national 'otherness' of Bolshevism. The ethnic identity of many East European socialists and Marxists, not to say the Russian Bolsheviks, was accordingly deployed by populists and those on the political right in order to reinforce the claim about the 'otherness' of socialist/ communist theory, and hence to arguments concerning its inapplicability (= 'foreignness') to specific national contexts.[100]

Like the Russian and Peruvian populists in the case of the *mir* and Inca 'communism', Bulgarian and Romanian peasant parties argued for restoration of what they insisted were traditional/ancient – and therefore 'natural' and/or historically 'authentic' – forms of rural organization and/or community.[101] Equally powerful in terms of a mobilizing discourse was the appeal to nationalism, and the emphasis placed by agrarian populists on the peasantry as the 'natural' embodiment of those ancient/traditional religion/languages/ ethnicities/customs/practices which together compose national culture and thus identity.[102] Most peasant parties in Eastern Europe during this period were strongly nationalist, especially those which were or became fascist, and in all cases where it occurred the transformation of nationalism into fascism (Croatia, Czechoslovakia, Romania) was accompanied by an ideological merger between peasant essentialism (an ancient/traditional/eternal 'peasant-ness' = authentic/sacred national identity) that structured the agrarian myth and the discourse-for/discourse-against of populism.[103]

Based on nationalist ideology linked to the agrarian myth, therefore, the mobilizing discourse of agrarian populist organizations throughout Eastern Europe generated much grassroots rural support for right wing (as in Bulgaria) or fascist movements (as in Slovakia, Hungary, Croatia and Romania). In the case of Romania, for example, not only did the membership of the League of the Archangel Michael grow sixfold during the period 1932–37 but four-fifths of this support was composed of the peasantry; at roughly the same conjunc-ture, moreover, the Hungarian National Socialist Workers' Party found strong support among the peasantry in the eastern part of that country.[104] Other elements which took part in this mobilization were members of the lumpen-proletariat.[105] Significantly, and the discourse about the desirability of establishing a middle peasantry notwithstanding, the beneficiaries of populist mobilization by the political right in most parts of Eastern Europe – for example, Romania, Czechoslovakia and Croatia – were not agricultural labourers or poor peasants but rich peasants.[106] In so far as it proclaimed the undesirability of a process of becoming-other-than-oneself that corresponded to peasant (and thus national) deculturation, therefore, early twentieth-century East European 'popular culture' structured by the agrarian myth licensed a now-familiar outcome: the agrarian populist mystification of class and the reification of ethnicity, a combination which – as in the case of Japan, Germany and Italy – either paved the way for or actually became fascist in its political orientation.

1.11 Conclusion

In economic and politico-ideological terms, populism, neo-populism and the agrarian myth all endorse a common ideology which posits or reaffirms an undifferentiated peasantry as the subject of history. The economic discourse to which all three subscribe casts petty commodity producers as smallholders engaged in what is basically subsistence cultivation, where the production/consumption unit corresponds to the peasant family. Politico-ideologically, the resulting 'peasant-ness' which is culturally innate and unchanging symbolizes the 'nation' itself, and protects the latter against a multiplicity of intruding 'othernesses'. These consist of the urban, its proletariat, and thus also its socialism and finance capital, all regarded as 'alien' or 'foreign' impositions that undermine the peasantry, its culture and thus the nation.

Endorsed by a variety of nationalisms (and even some socialists), the agrarian myth is a discourse not just about the existence of a town/country divide but also about the positive/negative characteristics and attributes entailed in such a divide. Since this discourse equates 'the rural' generally with economic and cultural autonomy, villages in the countryside are constituted as socio-economically unchanging 'small-scale' and 'natural' organizational units composed of self-sufficient peasant family farms. Epistemologically, the grassroots historical subject at the centre of this discourse is the 'peasant', the innate 'peasant-ness' of whom becomes thereby a metaphor for a number of conceptually interchangeable identities. Not just for Nature, 'soil', and 'culture', therefore, but through the latter connection also for the timeless, God-given (= sacred), 'natural' and ancient bonds – such as ethnicity (= 'blood' or 'race'), language, religion, customs, dress, songs, traditions – which are said to unite a 'people' on the basis of nationality.

Accordingly, in the discourse of the agrarian myth a 'pure' (or middle) peasantry engaged in smallholding cultivation within the context of an equally 'pure' village community (that is, unsullied by an external capitalism) is presented as embodying all the positive and culturally specific attributes that are constitutive of a 'pure' national identity, which is protected in turn by these same peasants (= warriors-who-defend-the nation). De-essentialization of the peasantry corresponds to alienation from an 'authentic' selfhood and thus estrangement from a 'natural' and ancient identity by a combination of 'foreign' others: capital, socialism and /or colonialism. Since 'peasant-ness' is in this discourse equated not just with smallholding agriculture but also with culture and national identity, depeasantization becomes synonymous with deculturation and the erosion (or loss) of national identity.

In this regard, as in so many others, the agrarian myth is the mirror image of the agrarian question, in which change is the structural dynamic and for which the historical subject is an industrial working class whose political solidarity transcends national boundaries. For the Marxism of the Russian Bolsheviks in general and Lenin and Trotsky in particular, the countryside, the village and the peasantry are all eventually subsumed under capital and accordingly trans-formed by class formation and class struggle. This process licenses in turn the economic development of large-scale manufacture and the revolutionary capture of and rule through the state, first by the bourgeoisie and then by the proletariat. In contrast to both the latter, the peasantry for Marxism does not – and cannot – form a class, and thus cannot discharge the role of historical subject. It does, however, provide the economic foundation for capitalist development.

Unlike the agrarian myth, therefore, the crucial significance for Marxism of the agrarian question concerns the economic role of peasants in the transitions to capitalism and socialism, and more particularly how in a context of under-development the economic resources for accumulation are to be mobilized from within an economically backward agriculture. Central to the economics of the agrarian question was the view that industrialization was the *sine qua non* of economic development, a process structured by a number of inter-related transformations: the emergence of generalised commodity production and exchange, the differentiation of simple commodity producers, the development of the forces of production in agriculture leading to a rise in pro-ductivity, and the consequent generation and release of an economic surplus for reinvestment in industry.

The politics of the agrarian question arise from the resulting dynamic of capital accumulation, the growth of landless labour, and the rising levels of a specifically class consciousness and struggle, all of which generate in turn the necessity for an international working class solidarity. The main obstacle to the latter has been the formation/formulation of an alternative and ideologically plausible discourse: namely, an 'a-political'/'above-politics' one that deflected, distorted or displaced class by non-class (or anti-class) consciousness that emphasized loyalties not antagonistic to capital and thus compatible with the continued process of accumulation. It was this task which populism sought to effect by merging the agrarian myth with 'popular' culture.

Accordingly, the main ideological role of populist discourse has been to mobilize grassroots support in defence of the agrarian myth, while at the same time depoliticizing this process, an objective achieved historically by means of linking 'popular' culture with nationalism and simultaneously delinking both from politics. Not only did popular culture accompany the emergence of nineteenth-century European nationalism, therefore, but in the course of this process the terms 'people' and 'peasants' became epistemologically intertwined. Prefigured in a conservative Rousseauesque/Wordsworthian nationalism based on ideas about a 'natural'/'primitive' goodness rooted in Nature, however, populism is more accurately seen as part of a 'from above' reaction to the Enlightenment critique of 'natural' institutions and social order (which, among other things, supported the power of landlords over peasants).

Hence the importance for this 'from above' ideology of a populist fusion between the agrarian myth and popular culture as a method of emphasizing other (non-class) kinds of 'difference', based on the urban/rural divide. The political advantage of this 'a-political'/'above-politics' stance by populism is that it conceptually erases rural class divisions and thus seemingly confirms the inclusive image of the countryside posited by the agrarian myth, as being a place where landlord, rich peasant and poor peasant all share the same (rural) identity and interests. Depoliticizing discourse is, in short, a way of (re-) ordering the nature of 'otherness', and thereby the meaning of political solidarity and action based on this.

Evidence from a number of different contexts suggests that the 'old' populism of the 1890s, the 1920s and the 1930s enjoyed some success in depoliticizing opposition to the capitalist crises of that period, and channelling this into the discourse-for/discourse-against associated with the agrarian myth. In part, this was due to the fact that neither hierarchy nor accumulation are precluded by the agrarian myth. Unlike unproductive economic activity associated with usury, or undertaken by representatives of 'foreign' monopoly or finance capital invariably located in the urban and operating via the state apparatus, therefore, small-scale enterprise conducted by productive peasant farmers is not excluded from the populist framework. Similarly, opposition to the state does not preclude support for a secular leader (as in Germany or Italy) or a religious one (the Emperor of Japan), since the latter are conceptualized by populism as enjoying a mystical/sacred bond with those at the rural grassroots, who by inference they represent. The same is true of landlord class, members of which in Italy, the American South and India all regarded themselves as among those in the countryside exploited by those in the towns.

While claims about the ancient, immutable and timeless forms of rural organization and community central to the agrarian myth are recognized in references to the existence of a golden age ('Merrie England', Inca 'communism', medieval corporate communities), the 'old' populism not only reaffirmed the importance of the agrarian myth and the desirability of its recuperation in the form of a golden age, but also proclaimed the necesssity of activating the historical agency of the peasantry in countries such as India, Peru, Bulgaria and Romania in order to realize this end. During the capitalist crises of the 1890s, the late 1920s and the early 1930s, therefore, populists in many different contexts reaffirmed the national importance of peasant essentialism and connected this with golden age, legitimizing the resulting identity with reference to the domain of 'popular culture'. By claiming to protect the nation from external 'foreign' influences (colonialism, socialism, finance capital) which sought to undermine its constituent elements, populists endowed nationalism with a democratic veneer.

In the 1920s and 1930s this redemptive nationalism came with a cost. The 'self' of the agrarian myth also required an external 'other', and in the antisemitic discourse of the 'old' populism Jews were constituted as doubly 'alien': not just economically (unproductive exploiters of a productive peasantry) but also culturally (the embodiment of 'foreign-ness'). Populist mobilization accordingly enabled nationalism to construct socio-economic identity in ethnic terms, which in turn informed discourse about agrarian reform in contexts as different as India, Peru and Romania. Just as Gandhi, Haya de la Torre and Mariategui targeted British and American landlordism, not landlordism *per se*, therefore, so Hungarian and Romanian populists targeted Jewish estate managers and not Romanian or Hungarian landlordism.

The historical lessons are clear. Once nationalism is transformed into an 'a-political'/'above-politics' discourse emanating from the grassroots (= 'popular culture'), and is thus seemingly democratic in origin and progressive in orientation, it then becomes possible for its exponents and adherents to argue that nationalism is inclusive and representative, as are actions carried out in its name. By eschewing or discrediting politics in this manner, therefore, populism makes it difficult – if not impossible – to criticize those on the political right on specifically *political* (as distinct from moral) grounds. As the examples of the way in which 1920s and 1930s nationalism, populism and fascism all shared the same epistemology demonstrate, this creates a depoliticized space which the right can then annex, claiming that it too is undertaking an 'a-political' or an 'above-politics' mobilization.

If the 'old' populist claim – that in the absence of capitalism and thus a proletariat and a bourgeoisie, for the purposes of an 'a-political'/'above-politics' mobilization an undifferentiated peasantry constituted the 'authentic' historical subject – was indefensible even in the 1920s and 1930s, how much more is this the case in the period of post-war global capitalist expansion. Yet, as will be shown in the next four chapters, throughout the latter half of the twentieth-century varieties of 'new' populism have continued to make precisely this claim. In the 1960s it was made both by political activists such as Hugo Blanco in Peru and the Naxalites in West Bengal, and also by intellectuals such as Marcuse, Fanon and Foucault. The same claim re-emerged during the 1970s and 1980s, when it extended from the grassroots organizational practice of ANUC in Colombia, Sendero Luminoso in Peru, and the new farmers' movements in India, to intellectuals connected with the latter, such as Sharad Joshi and Vandana Shiva. The 'new' populist version of the agrarian myth was consolidated during the 1990s, in the many theoretical formulations about rural change/agency influenced by postmodernism (ecofeminism, new social movements, 'the subaltern', 'everyday-forms-of-resistance', 'post-colonialism', 'post-Marxism' and 'post-capitalism').

NOTES

1. As is clear from various sources (Rogger and Weber [1965], Cardoza [1982], and Blinkhorn [1990]), many of the characteristics of agrarian populist ideology mobilized by the political right in Germany, Italy and Japan during the 1920s and 1930s were also important in the rise of fascism in other European countries. Thus one sympathetic observer of agrarian populism [*Mitrany*, 1951: 149] concedes that: 'It was significant of the two reactionary mass movements which made their appearance in western Europe that both laid great store upon peasant life and work . . . German National-Socialism especially set the fashion for an almost mystical glorification of the peasant . . . The Spanish Falangists were telling the peasants that "Spain was the countryside". In Germany as in Spain, and later in Vichy France, the peasant family was set up as the hope for national revival . . . France, said Marchal Pétain, "will recover all her strength by contact with the soil". And a Nazi spokesman demanded the "de-urbanization of our whole way of thinking"'. For the link between populism and fascism, see the texts by, among others, Ferkiss [1957; 1961], Holbo [1961], Preston [1990], Sohn-Rethel [1978: 122–3] and Wiles [1969: 176–7]. For the link between populism and anti-Semitism, see below and also Eidelberg [1974], Ionescu [1969: 116–18] and Pavloff [1978: 84ff.].
2. Heidegger's enduring and unrepentant complicity with Nazism [*Ott*, 1993] is one example of this link between an essentialist (to-be-disclosed) concept of 'being'

and the anti-modernist ideology of the political right. On the core elements and epistemological foundation of anti-Enlightenment conservative philosophy, see Mannheim [1953: 74ff.], Epstein [1970: 103ff.], Godechot [1972] and O'Sullivan [1976]. The reactionary character of this discourse is evident from the utterances of those associated with Nazism in Germany and Fascism in Italy during the 1930s (for opposition to the French Revolution and to the Enlightenment on the part of fascism generally, see Nolte [1965]). Hence the anti-Enlightenment proclamation of Italian fascists that '[w]e represent the antithesis . . . of all that world of the "immoral principles" of 1789', while the Nazis stated analogously that 'The year 1789 will be erased from history . . . [w]e wish to destroy the immoral ideology of the French Revolution' (quoted in Guerin [1974: 168]).

3 .'Sociologically speaking,', observes Mannheim [1953: 117], 'most philosophical schools which place "thinking" above "being" have their roots either in bourgeois revolutionary or in bureaucratic mentality, while most schools which place "being" above "thinking" have their origin in the ideological counter-movement of romanticism and especially in the experience of counter-revolution'.

4. In this connection it is important to remember that the basis of conservatism is not merely to oppose but also to roll back the possibility of revolution. On this point, O'Sullivan [1976: 10, 11, 12] notes: 'The principal feature of the two centuries which preceded the Revolution had been an increasing tendency to abandon the traditional pessimism about the human condition reflected in the Christian myth of the Fall and in the idea of original sin. A new optimism gradually replaced the old pessimism. This optimism, which had emerged with the Renaissance and then been bolstered by the growth of scientific knowledge, had two consequences. It produced . . . a belief that the world is an order which is intelligible to human reason without the need for divine revelation, and is responsive to human will, once reason has comprehended its structure. It is, in fact, nothing more than a huge machine . . . which can in principle be dismantled and reassembled . . . The world, in short, now came to be regarded as far more malleable than men had previously considered it to be . . . In order to oppose the ideal of radical change it was necessary for conservative thinkers to show . . . that the world was by no means as intelligible and malleable as men had come to assume.' An integral theoretical component of this anti-scientific/anti-rational political project has been Romanticism, which recuperated and then celebrated as innate precisely those characteristics which conservatives sought to defend. As Porter and Teich [1988: 5, 7] point out, Romantics had a 'passion for the pre-bourgeois past . . . [they] naturally looked within their own nations, seeking to put down new roots in history, in folklore and folksong, in pure, indigenous traditions of language, speech and expression, in bards and ballards. Throughout a Europe recoiling from a French domination which could pretend to advance *universal* progress and rationality, Romantics aimed to uncover national character and even "racial" con-tinuities through which the past, embodied in living memory, could speak to, guide, and nurture the present. [They] offered avenues a-plenty to make sense of or mask the often distasteful realities of oligarchic societies undergoing traumatic capitalist development, industrialization, urbanization, and proletarianization. They conjured up myths of the glories of the past, the drama of the inner self as hero, spiritual voyages into the religious and transcendental, and communion with the mountains . . . [Romanticism] could ally with faith to generate the last great religious "new awakening" of Western Christendom. Frequently the result

was mere escapism. When fleshed out into nationalist and racial fantasies, it might not be so innocent. The Romantics liked to forge solacing ideologies for the developing bourgeois societies they so profoundly despised' (original emphasis). These observations describe much of the discourse not just of Slavophilism but also of the new social movements, the subaltern studies project and ecofeminism, and beyond them all that of the BJP/VHP/RSS and the 'new' right (on which see Chapters 3, 4 and 5).

5. See Burke [1981: 217]. Fear that depeasantization combined with the immigration of Russian and Polish rural labour would undermine German culture was central to the nationalist concerns expressed during the 1890s by Max Weber [Bendix, 1960: 37ff., 55], who blamed this process not on landowning Junkers engaged in workforce restructuring but rather on an ethnically 'other' finance capital.

6. That this image of the proletarian/urban 'other' still permeates the discourse of the farmers' movements in India is clear from the utterances of Sharad Joshi [Omvedt, 1993b: 2709]. At the fifth convention of the Shetkari Sanghatana in October 1993, therefore, Joshi attacked urban workers organized in trade unions for going on strike; he not only urged farmers to withdraw accounts from banks the employees of which were on strike but also advocated that unemployed rural youth be used as strike-breakers in such disputes, replacing unionized public sector employees in the urban sector who had withrawn their labour.

7. It is important to note that for Marxism the concept 'alienation' has always been theoretically problematic, not least because the political right has always laid claim to it [Bell, 1962; Feuer, 1963]. Maintaining that '[s]ince the 1930s Marx's Early Works have been a war-horse for petty-bourgeois intellectuals in their struggle against Marxism', Althusser [1969: 10ff] dissmisses the concept alienation as a pre-Marxist vestige of Hegelian idealism, an existentialist anomaly characteristic of the period before the epistemological break of 1844 that signalled the emergence of the 'mature' Marx. Much the same point is made by Mattick [1978: 160–62].

8. In seeking to explain this loss, Rousseau invokes the element of 'chance', which gives rise to the development that dissipates 'primitive goodness' in the course of generating inequality [Broome, 1963: Ch. III]. He distinguishes between what he categorizes as a benign 'self-interest' (amour de soi), which is compatible with a 'natural' state of 'goodness', and 'selfish interest' (amour-propre), which is not. According to Rousseau the former is a harmless kind of self-centredness (= ego-centricity-relative-to-the-self), whereas the latter by contrast is an altogether less benign egocentricity that is exercised in relation to others, and thus at the root of competitive behaviour and the conflict it generates. This distinction is untenable, however, since the allegedly benign form of self-interested nationalism (= 'pro-self') is in the end no different from the less benign selfish variant (= 'anti-other'): the only difference is that the former is implicitly exclusionary whereas the latter is explicitly so, a point confirmed for example by the 'transformed' utterances of the Ku Klux Klan (see Chapter 5).

9. On this point see Brinton [1926: 58], who observes that 'in 1809 Wordsworth had sketched as completely as Mazzini ever did a theory of nationalism that was to become the political faith of the century'. Significantly, economic nationalism is central to the attempt by a recent populist text [Dolbeare and Hubbell, 1996] to formulate a similar 'political faith' for North America in the twenty-first century,

the realization of which will require 'a drastic middle class Jeffersonian revolution'.

10. Hence the view of Russian Bolshevism [*Trotsky*, 1936: 224] that '[t]he peasantry by virtue of its entire history and the conditions of its existence, is the least international of all classes. What are commonly called national traits have their chief source precisely in the peasantry'.

11. References to the non-coincidence of the terms 'peasant' and 'class' abound in the writings of Lenin and Trotsky. Hence the observation [*Trotsky*, 1934: 331] that: 'The peasantry . . . contains in itself in a rudimentary form all the classes of bourgeois society. Along with the petty-bourgeois of the cities . . . it constitutes that protoplasm out of which new classes have been differentiated in the past, and continue to be differentiated in the present. The peasantry always has two faces, one turned towards the proletariat, the other towards the bourgeoisie.' Although agreeing that a self-sufficient peasantry would be undermined by capitalist production, other Marxists either qualified or emphasized different aspects of this process. For example, Kritsman focused on exploitative relationships within peasant households [*Cox and Littlejohn*, 1984; *Littlejohn*, 1987a], while Kautsky [1988] maintained that although large farms were more efficient than smallholders, they did not necessarily displace them.

12. On the socio-economic differentiation of the peasantry, see Lenin [1964: 70ff., 172–87]. The latter's theory of peasant differentiation was itself based on his view that, where the agrarian sector was composed of latifundia or large landed estates, capitalist penetration of agriculture would follow two distinct paths [*Lenin*, 1962: 238–39; 1963: 139ff.]. One of these, known as the Prussian road, entailed a transformation whereby the landlord expropriated the tenants on his estate, either by depriving them of land altogether or (more usually) reducing considerably their usufruct rights while at the same time increasing the levels of rent. The estate was kept intact as a single unit, and the landlord went on to become a capitalist farmer himself. This he did by preserving the pre-existing relationships with his tenants, such as labour-service. Under the Prussian road, therefore, the power of the landlord class in the state is consolidated, and the majority of the peasantry are pauperized. By contrast, under the American road it was tenants who expropriated the landlord class and subdivided latifundia into individually owned smallholdings, as a result of which some peasants themselves became capitalist producers. The importance of the distinction between the American and Prussian roads to capitalist development, Lenin argued, was that under the Prussian road, where the estate system and with it the economic and political power of the landlord class remained intact, the peasantry would continue having to pay high levels of rent. Consequently, peasants would be unable to afford to improve agricultural production by adopting new techniques, and since they continued to use labour-service, landlords were under no pressure to install new machinery either. The result was a situation inhibiting the development of the productive forces in agriculture, and with it the continued development of capitalism.

13. On this point, see Lenin [1960, 1966] and Trotsky [1962, 1969].

14. The middle peasants that remain must, according to Lenin [1966: 156ff.], be neutralized in the course of the struggle between the proletariat and the bourgeoisie.

15. Malia [1955]. The difference between populists and Marxists is summed up by

Trotsky [1969: 113] in the following way: 'Populists regarded all workers and peasants simply as "toilers" and "exploited ones" who were equally interested in socialism, while to Marxists a peasant was a petty-bourgeois, capable of becoming a socialist only to the extent that he either materially or spiritually ceased being a peasant . . . [a]long that line was fought for two generations the principal battle between the revolutionary tendencies of Russia.'

16. Although the Slavophile interpretation of 'ancient Russian freedom', which structures the discourse of populism, has a negative political view of the state, it is one that is inherently conservative and unconnected with the progressive notion of 'republican liberty'. Whereas the latter was associated with freedom *in* politics, itself premissed on active participation, the former by contrast entailed freedom *from* politics, or the 'right to live according to unwritten laws of faith and tradition, and the right to full self-realization in a moral sphere on which the state would not impinge' [*Walicki,* 1980: 96]. For the 'theory of small deeds' pioneered by Russian populists during the late nineteenth century, see Utechin [1964].

17. For the historical origins and political influence of populism and neopopulism, see Mitrany [1951], Venturi [1960], Ionescu and Gellner [1969], Berlin [1978: 210–37], Walicki [1969; 1980], and Kitching [1982].

18. For details about the work and life of Chayanov [1966; 1991], see among others Kerblay [1966; 1971], Jasny [1972: 200–204], Harrison [1975; 1977], Cox [1979], Durrenberger [1984], Ellis [1988: 102ff.] and Nove [1990]. Texts focusing on agrarian change or populism which unaccountably fail even to mention Chayanov include Long [1977] and Canovan [1981].

19. On these points see the exchanges between Vinogradoff [1975; 1976], Shanin [1976], Moore [1976] and Atkinson [1977]. Claiming that the periodic redistribution of land was an economically rational method of resource allocation which operated to the benefit of (and was thus supported by) all peasant strata in Russia, Vingradoff agrees with Shanin regarding the non-emergence of rich peasantry but disagrees as to the cause. Much the same kind of argument concerning both the existence and effect of indigenous levelling mechanisms is advanced by proponents of Andean peasant economy (see, for example, Alberti and Mayer [1974], Fioravanti-Molinié [1982], Figueroa [1984]), for whom smallholding in the Peruvian highlands is structured around the concept "verticality". The latter refers to exchanges between peasants, rural communities, or land-based kin groups occupying different Andean ecosystems, where survival not surplus is the object of production. It is argued that such culturally-determined reciprocity, as embodied in traditional community institutions (*mink'a, ayni, compadrazgo*), constitutes an indigenous levelling mechanism which not only guarantees the subsistence of the rural population but also prevents capital accumulation and peasant differentiation, and thus accounts for the continued existence of the Andean peasantry. Others, however, have questioned the applicability of this hermetic model, pointing out that "verticality" is theoretically and empirically unsustainable. Peasant smallholders in the Peruvian Andes do market food crops, but find difficulty meeting competition from national and international agribusiness enterprises. Bradby [1982] argues that a specifically ecological "verticality" has been undermined by the emergence on both vertical and horizontal axes of generalized exchange based on money, while Sánchez [1977; 1982] indicates how traditional institutional forms disguise and legitimize unequal

economic exchange inside the rural community itself, and thus facilitate surplus appropriation by rich peasants from poor peasants. Outmigration in search of off-farm employment and income suggests further that community subsistence is not guaranteed. For the prefiguring debate in the work of Mariátegui and Haya de la Torre about Inca 'communism' and the survival of the Andean peasant community, see below.

20. For these points see, among others, Littlejohn [1973a; 1973b; 1977], Shanin [1973], and Patnaik [1979]. Attempts to synthesize the ideas of Lenin and Chayanov include Banaji [1976] and Schulman, Garrett and Newman [1989].

21. As will be argued in Chapter 4, it is now possible to trace a common epistemological and politically conservative lineage from the new social movements and subaltern studies project, both strongly influenced by postmodernism, back through the moral economy argument, the 'middle peasant' thesis, and 'resistance' theory, to the neo-populist concepts which structure Chayanovian theory of peasant economy.

22. Accurately identifying the real nature of political power, the words *Ultima Ratio Regum* (the 'Last Argument of Kings') were supposed to have been inscribed on the muzzles of the cannon belonging to Louis XIV. In so far as it represents the penultimate step before a resort to violence on the part of the ruling class, therefore, populism might be referred to as the 'Last-argument-but-one of Kings', or a variation on the theme of 'if-you-can't-beat-them-join-them' (that is, 'beating-them-by-joining-them').

23. On this point see, for example, Kazin [1995: 1, 2, 3], who defines populism as 'a flexible mode of persuasion, a language whose speakers conceive of ordinary people as a noble assemblage not bound narrowly by class, view their elite opponents as self-serving and undemocratic, and seek to mobilize the former against the latter . . . Populism is thus a grand form of rhetorical optimism'. Much the same point is made by Dolbeare and Dolbeare [1976: 115, 119, 121], who note that in the United States populism 'offered a non-socialist basis for organizing . . . because it assumed the continuity and propriety of the capitalist economic system and social order, it helped to make the labor movement into one of the sustaining forces behind that system. It effectively discouraged consideration of alternatives to capitalism . . . [. . .] The more important distinction to be drawn . . . is that between populism and socialism. The two ideologies are profoundly different. Their thirty to forty year struggle for the soul of the labor movement was won by populism's more moderate elements. By winning, populism . . . prevented socialism from securing the mass base it needed to survive . . . Their differences, and the fact that populism emerged the victor, have shaped the course of American history for the last century. [. . .] . . . populism served to insulate the common people of the United States against socialism, and thereby direct the labor movement into system-supporting forms . . . it seems safe to say that populism's major function . . . was to provide additional defences for the capitalist-liberal system during its period of greatest challenge – roughly 1877 through 1912.' The continuing importance of such populist rhetoric as a working-class-consciousness displacing mobilizing discourse (= 'the discrediting of alternatives' according to Kazin [1995: 271]) for those on the 'new' political right in the United States is clear from the following observation [*Kazin*, 1995: 248,266]: 'Without abandoning their core beliefs, activists and politicians on Right became skilled at courting white Democrats, both North and South, with praise of their

labor, their families, their ethnic identities, and their moral beliefs. Such language did not guide the domestic programs of either the Nixon or Reagan administration – both of which aided the interests of large corporations and did nothing to stem the decline in real wages and good industrial jobs. But it did help frame their policies as correctives to the damage that had supposedly been done by haughty liberals who ignored the desires of the virtuous majority. By capturing the language of populism, conservatives were able, at last, to dominate national politics and to force their long-time adversaries onto the defensive. [. . .] For two decades, from the end of the 1960s to the end of the 1980s, conservative Republicans had posed authentically in populist dress by keeping cultural resentments uppermost in the public mind. Adhering to a disciplined script, GOP politicians ran against a "liberal establishment" composed of federal bureaucrats, the mass media, arrogant academics, and other amoral "special interests". This nexus of power supplanted big business and its political cronies as *the* main threat to the beliefs (and pocketbooks) of the hardworking white majority' (original emphasis).

24. This populist claim to be 'above' politics, or 'a-political', is encapsulated in the following programmatic statement of the 'Village Explorers' – the precursors of the National Peasant Party – in 1930s Hungary [*Jackson*, 1974: 306–7]: 'neither capitalism nor communism, neither Germany nor Russia, neither West nor East, neither political passivity nor direct engagement'.

25. The importance of this consideration is misrecognized by Canovan [1981: 13], who insists on categorizing populism as either agrarian or political, without realizing that agrarian populism is a way of *re*-politicizing the political by appearing to *de*-politicize it. Accordingly, politics is as a consequence an integral part of agrarian populism and not its 'other'.

26. Texts which implicitly/explicitly attribute a politically dual identity to populism include Dolbeare and Dolbeare [1976: Ch. 7], Canovan [1981], Phillips [1982: 33], Lasch [1991], Kazin [1995] and Harrison [1995: 9ff.]. Revisionist critics (such as Goodwyn [1976; 1978; 1986; 1991] and Lasch [1991]) currently attempting to rehabilitate populism as the authentic grassroots version of North American democracy, discount the earlier critique of populism by Hofstadter [1962] because of the 'end of ideology' context in which the latter was made. Hofstadter's argument was that populism would not work because no kind of utopia was possible, and that therefore one should stick with existing (bourgeois) democracy. Unsurprisingly, revisionism opposes Hofstadter's claim that populism is conservative because this is incompatible with the revisionists' own view that it corresponds to a non-bourgeois/non-socialist form of grassroots democracy. Marxists, by contrast, are critical of both the revisionist attempt to rehabilitate populism and of Hofstadter's teleology. Although sharing with Hofstadter the critique of populism as conservative, therefore, a Marxist argument parts company with his over the absolute impossibility of utopia: unlike Hofstadter, therefore, for Marxism a socialist outcome is both desirable and feasible. For the theoretical impact on Hofstadter of the end-of-ideology debate, see Morton [1972: 109ff.].

27. The full significance of this point will emerge in Chapters 2 and 3, where the mobilizing discourse of tribal, peasant and farmers' movements in India and Latin America is analysed. Symptomatic of this problem is the equation of Gandhian ideology with socialism: as is argued below, Gandhism has nothing at

all to do with socialism (towards which it is antagonistic), and represents perhaps the classic manifestation in India of populist ideas.

28. Such crisis can be either economic, when overproduction threatens systemic collapse, or political, when a nascent capitalism is in the ascendant. In either situation, therefore, a potential/actual challenge from the working class represents danger for the continued reproduction of capital. For an example of a text which links populism simply to 'modernization', see Canovan [1981]. She fails to note the existence of capitalist crises, let alone their significance for populism.

29. This is especially important when class struggle becomes particularly acute, as for example in the case of capitalist restructuring that entails the replacement of more value-laden (and hence more expensive) forms of labour-power with less value-laden (and cheaper) equivalents. In such circumstances employers can do one of two different things. They either proceed to replace locals with workers of a different ethnic/migrant identity on the grounds of profitability, or they adopt a populist position and retain local workers on the grounds that these possess the same ethnic/national identity. The latter can then be prevailed upon by employers to accept wage cuts in the name of reciprocity, which in the end achieves the same economic objective.

30. One variant of this position is the cultural ecology of Harris [1966; 1974: 11–32], who argues that because the beef-eating taboo and cow worship are practised by the Hindu population of India, both these cultural phenomena must consequently fulfil (and be an expression of) a 'popular' need. For an example of the extent to which even opposition to 'popular culture' continues to be framed simply in terms 'high/low' culture, rather than politics, see Beik [1993].

31. For the centrality of the pastoral to English culture generally, and the contrast with a demonic image of its urban 'other', see Williams [1973: 8–12; 1985]. After the 1914–18 war, 'a rural England where clocks have stopped' was epito-mized in the pastoral idiom of the Georgian poets [*Timms*, 1985: 113], for whom '[p]overty is quaint because it is rural . . . [t]hese are poets who have closed their minds not merely to social change, but to the transformation of discourse which accompanied it . . . [t]hey are refugees, not merely from the city but from the twentieth century'. It is not necessary to endorse the conclusion presented in the text by Wiener [1981], that in England from the mid-nineteenth century onwards the pastoral myth blocked the development of industrial capitalism, therefore, to accept the validity of his argument regarding the ideological pervasiveness of this myth.

32. On this point, see in particular Stradling and Hughes [1993].

33. Cavaliero [1977] outlines the importance and significance in 'popular culture' of lesser writers such as Eden Phillpotts, for whom the cult of primitivism was pro-jected through a depiction of the innate 'otherness' of isolated rural inhabitants (= different from urban counterparts), as also in the rural fantasy and romance, reaffirming the notion of English-landscape-as-arcadia, which permeated the fiction of Mary Webb, Kenneth Graham, T.F. Powys and H.E. Bates. For examples of Distributist ideas during the same period, see Belloc [1924; 1936].

34. For the *gemeinschaft/gesellschaft* distinction, see Tönnies [1955]; the similarity between the views of the latter and those of Kireevsky, an important organic intellectual of Slavophile nationalism/populism, are outlined by Walicki [1975: 168ff.]. 'German conservatism of the first half of the nineteenth century', Walicki [1975: 174–5] notes, 'was an ideological defence of *Gemeinschaft* against

Gesellschaft . . . Slavophile doctrines as a whole provide a more consistent defence of *Gemeinschaft* than those of the conservative German romantics'. Significantly, Tönnies [1955: 69] regarded peasant society in village India as the embodiment of the *gemeinschaft* category; for the influence of his sociological theory, and its place in the philosophical trajectory that culminated in German fascism, see Lukacs [1980: 591–601]. For an example of the way in which current ecological theory invokes Tönnies' concept of *gemeinschaft* in its critique of industrialization, see Jones [1990].

35. For writers such as Dostoevsky and Tolstoy, as well as Herzen and Chernyshevskii, the peasantry epitomized the spirit of an authentically Russian nationalism. The emergence of 'peasant fiction' as a specific genre during the pre-Emancipation period 1847–61, and the crucial role in this discourse-about of idealized folkloric images of peasant life (the centrality of myth, paganism) threatened/corrupted by the city, is outlined by Woodhouse [1991]. For an account of the artistic, literary and journalistic search in Russia for the peasant 'soul' following Emancipation (from 1861 to 1890) and the importance to this process of Darwinian theory, see Frierson [1993].

36. For Uspenskii, therefore [*Frierson, 1993: 93*]: 'so many of the peasants . . . have been spoiled by corrupting influences from outside the village, most notably by money. The bulk of [his] *From a Village Diary* treats the disintegration of peasants and village culture under the impact of "the accursed silver rouble". The natural, authentic peasant somewhat avoided its touch, while others in the village fell prey to its charms and thereby lost their "peasantness". Uspenskii made this judgement through the [village] stories . . . thus continuing in the tradition of Turgenev of juxtaposing different peasant types to illustrate the moral strength of the pure peasant.'

37. For the link between the espousal by the conservative nobility of Slavophile nationalism and populism, and idealized notions of a subsistence-oriented small-holding peasantry in late nineteenth-century Russia, see Drage [1904: 43ff.], Normano [1949: 69ff.], Utechin [1963: 78ff.,128ff.], Wortman [1967], Walicki [1969; 1975; 1980: 92ff.], Kitching [1982: 145ff.] and Frierson [1993]. Slavophilism, argues Walicki [1975: 177–8], 'was the ideology of the hereditary Russian nobility who were reluctant to stand up on their own behalf as a privileged group defending its own selfish interests, and therefore attempted to sublimate and universalize traditional values and to create an ideological platform that would unite all classes and social strata representing "ancient Russia" '. That an important reason why Slavophiles adhered to the agrarian myth was a fear of the consequences of the emergence of a proletariat is clear from the following [*Drage* 1904: 44]: 'The peasant with his strength of passive endurance, his non-resistance to oppression, his few wants and absolute content with any circumstances short of starvation, is the ideal which [Slavophiles] are trying to preserve. Western culture and freedom of thought would destroy it, and thereore the Slavophiles opposed all intellectual progress, being in this supported by the Orthodox Church. "The social order of the West rests upon a false foundation", wrote Aksakoff; "Aetheism, Anarchism, and Materialism, and the growth of the proletariat are its natural consequences . . . It is a blessing for Russia that she detests all Western culture and has preserved her Orthodox faith. Our Church remains pure, and the State has its foundations in the absolute will of the Tsar." According to this view, . . . the hope of the nation lay in the people – that is, in the

peasant.' Significantly, both the fear of the urban proletariat as 'the mob in the streets' and the countervailing desirability of the rural artisan in the village commune was echoed in symptomatically pathological utterances by nineteenth century Slavophiles such as von Tengoborski, 'who argued that the development of handicraft helped Russia escape from the "*sore* of the proletariat"' (original emphasis), and Baron August von Haxthausen, who declared that '[t]he commune distinguished Russia from Western Europe . . . in that it preserved Russian society from "the cancer of a proletariat"' [*Normano*, 1949: 75; *Petrovitch*, 1968: 208].

38. According to Walicki [1969: 53], the views of Mikhailovskii on the undesirability of progress 'expressed the very essence of the backward-looking populist utopia, a utopia which idealized the primitive peasant economy by setting a high value on its autarchy, on its independence of the capitalist market. Mikhailovskii constantly repeated that the interests of individuality coincided with the interests of "undivided", non-specialized labour, i.e. with the interests of the Russian peasantry. The Russian peasant, like primitive man, lives a life which is poor but full; being economically self-sufficient he is, therefore, an independent, "all-round", and "total" man. He satisfies all his needs by his own work, making use of all his capacities – he is a tiller and an artisan, a shepherd and an artist in one person. The peasant community is egalitarian, homogeneous, but its members have differentiated, many-sided individualities. The lack or weak development of complex co-operation enables them to preserve their independence and simple co-operation unites them in mutual sympathy and understanding. This moral unity underlies the common ownership of land and the self-government of the Russian "mir".'

39. As confirmed by a recent exchange between Patnaik [1995] and Brass [1995b], what are in fact nationalist/populist views about the uniqueness of national paths of development continue to masquerade as Marxist political economy.

40. For Kondrat'ev, see Jasny [1972: 158ff.]; for Semevskii, see Petrovich [1963]. In addition to his work on the long cycle and the inter-sectoral terms of trade, Kondrat'ev also contributed to the formulation of the NEP. Since in economic terms he favoured agriculture over industrialization, Kondrat'ev also advocated the adoption of measures and policies to encourage the growth of a rural bourgeoisie: the latter were in his view the most productive elements of the agrarian economy. An early social historian of the Russian peasantry, Semevskii also regarded the peasantry as potentially the most productive elements in Russian society. His essentialist concept of the peasantry is evident from the fact that the workforce employed in the Siberian gold-mining industry towards the close of the nineteenth century was for Semevskii simply a case of 'peasants in overalls'. Unsurprisingly, therefore, Semevskii – like Mikhailovskii – was opposed to 'progress' involving the destruction of peasant economy.

41. Because for Herzen both Russia and America were examples of non-European classless societies, however, the precursor of Russian populist ideology perceived a potentially similar trajectory in terms of future development: 'Classless democratic America and peasant Russia, which is moving towards classlessness,' he noted during the mid-1860s, 'remain for me, as before, the countries of the the immediate future' (cited in Kucherov [1963: 35]).

42. In America the agrarian myth 'was not a popular but a literary idea, a preoccupation of the upper classes, of those who enjoyed a classical education, read pastoral

poetry, experimented with breeding stock, and owned plantations or country estates' [*Hofstadter*, 1962: 25].

43. Notwithstanding these similarities, Canovan [1981: 14] maintains wrongly that 'American and Russian populism were very different indeed: the fact that they share the same name is, in fact, accidental'.

44. On the relationship between Veblen and populist ideology in America, see Riesman [1953: 142–8], who observes that: 'We might even suggest that Veblen's theory of economic crisis, with its populist preoccupation with the role of finance, is traceable to his farmer origins . . . It is a theory in which capital, credit, interest, and price – the most significant influences on farm production – play the principle roles, while the category of wages, which plays so large a part in Marx's crisis theory, play almost no part in Veblen's . . .'

45. Headed by Robert M. La Follette, the Senator from Wisconsin, the Progressive movement represented a continuity of rural protest by Grangers and Populists against monopolies and big business [*Hicks*, 1963: 79ff.]; La Follete, its Presidential candidate, received nearly five million votes in the 1924 elections. Dismissing third party initiatives generally as the 'conciliationist illusions of the petty bourgeoisie, primarily the farmers', Trotsky [1945: 12ff., 323–4] criticized the American Communist Party during the early 1920s for collaborating with the Progressive movement. Trotsky himself [1945: 12–14] compared this third party mobilization in America to that of the populist *narodniks* in pre-revolutionary Russia, and outlined the political dangers of this kind of class collaboration in the following uncompromising manner: 'It is quite self evident that the path which certain American comrades are ready to follow has nothing in common with Bolshevism. For a young and weak Communist Party, lacking in revolutionary temper, to play the role of solicitor and gatherer of "progressive voters" for the Republican Senator LaFollette is to head toward the political dissolution of the party in the petty bourgeoisie. After all, opportunism expresses itself not only in moods of gradualism but also in political impatience: it frequently seeks to reap where it has not sown, to realize successes which do not correspond to its influence. . . . the inspirers of this monsterous opportunism, who are thoroughly imbued with skepticism concerning the American proletariat, are impatiently seeking to transfer the party's center of gravity into a farmer milieu – a milieu that is being shaken by the agrarian crisis. By underwriting, even with reservations, the worst illusions of the petty bourgeoisie, it is not at all difficult to create for oneself the illusion of wielding influence over the petty bourgeoisie. To think that Bolshevism consists of this is to understand nothing about Bolshevism.' Certainly those on the political right (e.g., *Filler*, [1976]) have no difficulty in claiming the Progressive movement as part of what they perceive as an 'authentic' American tradition.

46. For the importance of the agrarian myth in American history, see Hofstadter [1962: 23ff.]. The agrarian myth overlapped with and was itself structured by the frontier myth (on which see Hofstadter and Lipset [1968]), in that the latter enabled an infinite expansion of the smallholding economy idealised by the former.

47. See Hofstadter [1969: 12–14], who points out that American grain farmers faced competition from Argentina, Canada and Australia, and those cultivating cotton from India and Egypt.

48. Observing that in the 1880s and 1890s the anti-finance/anti-foreign capital, anti-

state discourse of the Populists was nevertheless aimed at the reform of American capitalism, not its overthrow, Vann Woodward [1960: 159] points out that 'they denied the commercial character of the agricultural enterprise and sometimes dreamed of a Golden Age. In their economic thought they overemphasized the importance of money and oversimplified the nature of their problems by claiming a harmony of interest between farmer and labor, by dividing the world into "producers" and "non-producers", . . . and by thinking that too many ills and too many remedies of the world were purely legislative'.

49. On this point, see Vann Woodward [1989: 203ff.]. Part of the Southern literary renaissance, the Southern Agrarians included among its ranks writers and poets, many of whom were found among the contributors to the programmatic and seminal text *I'll Take My Stand* [*Twelve Southerners*, 1951]. The importance and influence of the latter on the political discourse of/about the South in particular and of/about American conservatism in general is considered by, among others, Kirk [1978: 414–15], Lora [1971: 107–23], Nash [1976: 36ff., 57ff., 70, 199ff.], Conkin [1988] and Genovese [1994]. For the current reaffirmation by conservatives of the views of the Southern Agrarians, see Fifteen Southerners [1981] and Bradford [1985: Part Three, and especially 83ff.].

50. The defence of plantation slavery in the American South, not just by the Southern Agrarians [*Twelve Southerners*, 1951: 14, 76ff.] but also by earlier apologists for slavery such as Fitzhugh [1960], was based on an objection to modernity and capitalism. Arguing that slaves were provided with a guaranteed subsistence, shared in any benefits which accrued to their master (= 'trickle down' theory), and were generally happy with the paternalistic regime on the plantation, Fitzhugh defended the Southern conservative agrarian tradition against Northern industrial capitalism on the grounds that the latter would generate a socially and economically disruptive process of class struggle leading to the eventual destruction of the 'natural' social order which its supporters believed the system of plantation slavery to be.

51. That industrialisation was rejected by the Southern Agrarians largely because capitalism would lead to socialism and communism is clear not only from their own observations on this linkage (e.g., Twelve Southerners [1951: 49–50], Conkin [1988: 74–7, 174]), from the perception of marxism as their 'other' [*Conkin* 1988: 98–9, 110, 112, 150, 160] but also from the fact that *I'll Take my Stand* was originally entitled 'Tracts Against Communism' [*Conkin*, 1988: 71].

52. For programmatic statements by the Southern agrarians regarding the desirability of a back-to-the-land movement based on subsistence agriculture carried out on individual smallholdings, see Conkin [1988: 106, 110–13, 125]. For the theoretical and ideological affinities between the Southern Agrarians and the Distributionist movement of Belloc, and the links between them, see Lora [1971: 120–21] and Conkin [1988: 111–14].

53. For this point, see Twelve Southerners [1951: 55, 59], where the components and configuration of 'popular culture' are clearly delineated in the following manner: 'The South has been rich in the folk-arts, and is still rich in them – in ballards, country songs and dances, in hymns and spirituals, in folk tales, in the folk crafts of weaving, quilting, furniture-making . . . If the Southern [artistic] tradition were an industrial tradition, it would deserve to be cast out rather than cherished. It happens, however, to be an agrarian tradition'.

54. For the political significance of the film *Gone With The Wind*, see Chapter 7.

55. Acharya Narendra Deva (1889–1956) founded the Congress Socialist Party in 1934, the main political plank of which was its anti-imperialist programme, led the 'Quit India' movement in 1942, and played an important role in organizing the peasantry during the pre-Independence era. Like Deva, Rammanohar Lohia (1910–67) was also an important member of the Congress Socialist Party, and in the mid-1950s he left the Praja Socialist Party and formed the Lohia Socialist Party. Similarly influential in the peasant movements of the 1920s and the founding of the All-India Kisan Sabha, N.G. Ranga (1900–1995) resigned from the Congress Party and went on to form the conservative Swatantra (= 'Freedom First') Party, described by him [*Ranga,* 1968: 541] as 'the party of agriculturalists *par excellence'.*

56. For these points, see Baskaran [1981: 102–3, 109, 116–18].

57. For example, R.G. Fox [1990] equates Gandhian philosophy with socialism and then argues that it amounts to an expression of popular cultural autonomy or resistance to the kinds of colonial domination encoded in Orientalism. Significantly, some of those who write in the Subaltern Studies framework (see Chapter 4) also find in Gandhi the true expression of Indian grassroots tradition, a similar embodiment of the authentic 'voice-from-below' (see, for example, Amin [1984] and Chatterjee [1984; 1986]).

58. Hence the endorsement by Gandhi of the Hindu caste/varna hierarchy as an immutable (and therefore 'natural') social order stemmed from a corresponding rejection of class struggle as a necessary effect of industrial modernization. In his view, therefore, the advantage of the caste/varna system was that in India its 'object..is to prevent competition and class struggle and class war . . . because it fixes the duties and occupations of persons' (cited in Ambedkar [1946: 287–9]). In much the same vein, Bharatan Kumarappa, the Assistant Secretary of the Village Industries Association and a Gandhian who advocated a village based rural revival, observed [1935: 1–2]: 'One of the great differences between our Civilization and that of the West is that our Civilization takes its root from rural life while that of the West centres round cities . . . The centre of life in our country has always been the village . . . Towns and cities were mainly distributing agents of village products, the village being the real producing centre . . . Our culture is best understood only when the agricultural background out of which it has arisen is taken into account. That being so, no mere imitation of the West which has developed on lines fundamentally different from our own, can at all fit in with our national heritage.' This fear of the town/city and of the 'urban mob' accords well with the view expressed by the Bombay Pradesh Committee during the late 1920s, whose objective when confronted with increasing militancy on the part of striking mill workers was to '[s]pare no money and no efforts to draw workers away from the communists. They [the workers] ought to be made to understand that the more important struggle [is] between the British government and the people, rather than between capital and labour' (cited in Lieten [1988: 75]).

59. That the agrarian struggles organized/led by Gandhi in Bihar and Gujarat were basically rich peasant movements is clear from, among others, Dhanagare [1975; 1983: 88ff.] and Pouchepadass [1980].

60. On these points, see Brown [1972: 52ff.], Dhanagare [1975: 22–30], Sen [1982: 29ff.] and Das [1983b: 57ff.]. Significantly, the indigenous Indian component of the landlord class was not included among the targets of the Champaran

mobilization, and its objectives included neither a redistribution of land to poor peasants nor wage increases for landless workers. One of the main reasons why Gandhi subsequently chose the salt monopoly rather than the land tax as the object of his non-cooperation campaign against the colonial power was precisely his fear that peasants might extend non-payment of rents from British to Indian landlords [*Brown*, 1972: 76–7; *Dhanagare*, 1975: 28–9; and *Tidmarsh*, 1960: 100].

61. Hardiman [1981], Charlesworth [1985]. It is again significant that, as in the case of the Champaran *satyagraha* a decade earlier, no attempt was made to address indigenous employer/employee relationships: 'Gandhi did not attack the economic basis of the *hali* system nor did he disapprove of the then prevailing serf-master relationship. He simply expected his Patidar followers to be more compassionate towards Dublas and liberalize their conditions of work because . . . such compassion would bring more prosperity to Patidar landowners' [*Dhanagare*, 1975: 92].

62. Although he warned against communalism and populism (= 'peasantism'), Deva nevertheless incorporated much of the latter into his own political pronouncements. In his 1939 Presidential Address to the annual conference of the All-India Kisan Sabha, on 'The Peasant in Indian Revolution', Deva [1946: 33ff.] maintained that as the objective of the Indian peasantry was freedom, the agrarian programme of Congress should abolish all feudal and colonial exploitation and seek to protect the peasantry from the effects of the 1929 Depression; peasants should be against landlords/moneylenders/imperialism but not anti-Congress. Influenced by the anarchism of Kropotkin, Deva [1946: 42, 44] equated 'peasant' with 'class', and inferred that the main conflict would be between the latter on the one hand and landlords and colonialism on the other; in short, foreign but not national capital would be the target. The unambiguously populist nature of this discourse is confirmed by his programmatic exclusion of agricultural labour and its political interests. According to Deva, therefore, social justice for agricultural labour was not – and should not be – on the agenda; Deva recognized the deserving case of agricultural labour, but insisted that it was more important for the nationalist mobilization against imperialism to obtain the support of peasant proprietors and 'landowners with small incomes', a multi-class alliance not dissimilar to the Subaltern category associated with the work of Ranajit Guha (see Chapter 4). Agricultural labourers could not expect either to lead or to benefit from the agrarian movement, he maintained, nor should they advocate policies that were not also in the interests of peasants. Otherwise, argued Deva, the peasantry would be lost to the anti-imperialist/anti-colonial struggle. He went further, and asserted that it was landlords who put workers' issues on the political agenda, with the object of dividing the rural support Congress might hope to obtain. Like Ranga, therefore, Deva subordinated class to national identity/struggle, and like Sharad Joshi and the new farmers' movements of the 1980s (see Chapter 3) he insisted that only a rise in crop prices would enable peasant farmers to pay their workers higher wages.

63. 'The worst sufferers under capitalism', observed Lohia [1963: 29–30] in 1943, 'are the colonial masses. Presuming the validity of the communist law of class struggle, there is obvious need to change its basis. Not the working class in capitalist countries, but the colonial masses are the principal grave-diggers of capitalism. Imperial labour can at best be an ally of colonial toilers in the destruc-

tion of capitalism. The class of colonial toilers pours its life-blood into the capitalist system from its birth, carries it along through its various phases, and is itself steadily impoverished until it reaches a stage when its own extinction spells the decay of capitalism, while its purposeful rise into manhood ushers in a new world . . . the future of capitalism depends not so much on the behaviour of labour in capitalist countries as on the behaviour of colonial masses. The student of the capitalist future will have his eyes pre-eminently on the political action of colonial toilers.' In a footnote [*Lohia*, 1963: 30] to this same observation, he concludes that: 'Whatever Marxists may say about the impossibility of regarding the colonial toilers as a single class, even under Marx's tests of community, political consciousness, and national organization, the colonial toilers as a whole are more justifiably a class than is the working class of capitalist countries.'

64. On this point see Erdman [1967] and Ranga [1968]. In many ways, the views of Ranga not merely embody all the elements of populist discourse (peasant = nation = nature) but were in this respect remarkably consistent over time. He was an exponent of 'urban bias' *avant la lettre*, maintaining among other things that the 'greatest social problem in the world is the exploitation of the vast masses of agricultural peoples by the industrial peoples and countries through the unequal exchanges imposed upon the former by the latter through their control over world markets and finance . . .' [*Ranga*, 1946: vi]. Adopting the anti-socialist/anti-capitalist position of populism, Ranga [1946: 87–8] maintained that adequate 'community' control – as exercised through the traditional hierarchy based on tribal chieftainship – already existed at the grassroots, the inference being that this was the model 'democracy' which would replace British imperial rule. Unsurprisingly, he [*Ranga*, 1946: 51, 84] also insisted that national identity overrode class; accordingly, he saw no benefit to be gained from opposition against capitalists attempting to segment the labour market in the form of unity between local workers in Malaysia and indentured immigrants, arguing much rather that the latter should be excluded on the grounds of ethnic 'otherness'. Not only did he make no distinction between European workers and capitalists, regarding both as exploiters of the colonized [*Ranga*, 1946: 38, 50–51, 77], but he also idealized traditional subsistence agriculture undertaken by an undifferentiated peasantry [*Ranga*, 1946: 45, 53, 68]. The extent of the discursive overlap between his nationalism and agrarian populism is evident from the observation [*Ranga*, 1946: 90–91] that 'The Western Socialists are hankering after industrial democracy, as an escape from and an alternative to the prevailing capitalist dictatorship. If the coloured peoples have saved themselves, even partially, from the claws of world capitalism, it is because they have remained loyal to their cottage industries, collective ownership and cultivation of land, and the self-sufficiency economy of their villages and tribes. They enjoy quite a good bit of economic freedom and democracy.' Such positions were consolidated after independence, when Ranga continued to uphold all the traditional populist shibboleths: these included not just opposition to Marxism, socialism and secularism as non-Hindu forms of 'otherness' inappropriate to the Indian context, but also to Nehruvian attempts at modernization/planning because they threatened individual proprietorship and peasant family farming [*Ranga*, 1968: 123, 418, 445, 529, 532, 537, 538, 542].

65. For these versions of the agrarian myth, see Mariátegui [1968], Haya de la Torre [1936a; 1936b], and Castro Pozo [1924; 1936]. With the exception of the last one by Castro Pozo, all these texts were written and published in the late 1920s.

66. This very point is in fact conceded by Mariátegui [1968: 40, 69, note 18], who not only admits to the existence of a close connection in Peru between *indigenista* ideas and socialism but also accepts that his own views about the Andean peasant community are the same as those of Haya de la Torre (*'[e]scrito este trabajo, encuentro en el libro de Haya de la Torre . . . conceptos que coinciden absolutamente con los míos sobre la cuestión agraria en general y sobre la comunidad indígena en particular. Partimos de los mismos puntos de vista, de manera que es forzoso que nuestras conclusiones sean también las mismas'*). For literary and filmic representations of Chayanovian and populist concepts of peasant 'community', see Chapter 6.

67. On this last point, see Chavarría [1979: 169, 171].

68. See Haya de la Torre [1936b: 35, 40, 65]. It is clear, however, that when he referred to 'Indoamerica', Haya de la Torre [1936b: 177] meant the Andean Republics with large peasant populations (Venezuela, Colombia, Ecuador, Peru and Bolivia). The similarity between on the one hand the components of the 'old' populist multi-class front of APRA during the 1920s and 1930s, and on the other the elements constitutive of the 1990s 'new' populism, such as the Subaltern Studies project (see Chapter 4), is striking. Equally significant is the fact that the combination of internal/external enemies (feudal landholders + imperialism) targeted by APRA was subsequently also that of the CPI in India (see Chapter 3).

69. For an example of his anti-imperialism, see Mariátegui [1968: 78ff.]. The specifically Marxist nature of Mariátegui's theory continues to be the subject of debate. During the 1930s, his views were criticized by Miroshevsky [1942], who pointed to the similarity beween Mariátegui's socialism and *indigenista* romanticism, and to the dissimilarity between his interpretation of the agrarian question and that of Lenin. Subsequent defences of Mariátegui have shifted the terms of the debate: for example, in an otherwise useful analysis Chavarría [1979] insists that Mariátegui's views should be interpreted as belonging to a Latin American and not a European Marxism. More recently, Löwy [1998] has attempted to rescue Mariátegui from the critique of Miroshevsky by claiming that he was not a romantic – clearly Mariátegui was – but that such romanticism was and is compatible with Marxism. Such a defence entails a certain amount of historical revision: having claimed that Marxist ideas were no different from those of the Russian populists, Löwy then dismisses critiques of the latter as a 'Menshevik dogma', an assertion which overlooks the anti-populist arguments of Bolsheviks such as Lenin and Trotsky.

70. Preferring the specifically ethnic designation 'Indoamerica' to the term 'Latin America', Spanish and Portuguese colonialism and American imperialism were all described by Haya de la Torre [1936a: 29] as an 'ethnic occupation' (*invasión étnica*). On the economic importance of smallholding production (*'[n]uestros países feudales, al emanciparse, tienen que dar preeminencia a la clase campesina, a la clase productora de la tierra . . .'*), see Haya de la Torre [1936b: 149]. The latter point is also made by Mariátegui [1968: 69].

71. See in particular Mariátegui [1968: 83].

72. As expressed by Haya de la Torre [1936b: 178], the inference is that European feudalism was an appropriation not just of land but of Nature itself (*'[e]l feudalismo es la profanación de la tierra, hasta entonces libre, su apoderamiento'*), a view which was to be reproduced subsequently in the populist/ nationalist discourse of the BJP/VHP/RSS in India (see Chapter 3). The same

kind of argument was made by Mariátegui [1968: 71–2], who identified the peasant community in Peru as the first line of defence of traditional indigenous beliefs/forms against attacks on these by feudal landlords (*'Disolviendo o relajando la "comunidad", el régimen del latifundio feudal, no sólo ha atacado una institución económica sino también, y sobre todo, una institución social que defiende la tradición indígena, [y] que conserva la función de la familia campesina . . .'*).

73. See Haya de la Torre [1936b: 181]. The epistemological overlap between the 'socialism' of Mariátegui and the populism/nationalism of Haya de la Torre is underlined by the extent to which each subscribes to the following set of oppositions:

Peruvian 'Self'	Non-Peruvian 'Other'
Rural community	Latifundio
Peasantry	Landlord
Indigenous	Foreign
Inca	Spanish
Ancient	New
Efficient	Inefficient
Egalitarian	Hierarchical
Communist	Feudal

74. See Mariátegui [1968: 42ff.].

75. See Mariátegui [1968: 14, 24]. It it equally clear that Haya de la Torre [1936b: 170–71, 177] also regarded the Inca empire as a socialist system (*'Desde el sur de Columbia hasta el norte argentino queda la huella étnico-social del Imperio Incaico. Aquella vasta zona occidental de Sudamérica, característicamente agraria, ha conservado los restos del primitivo socialismo del antiguo imperio peruano. La comunidad o ayllu incaico, no puede incluirse en ninguna de las clasificaciones sociales planteadas por la ciencia europea'*).

76. See Mariátegui [1968: 45, 52, 64–7 note 15]. Not the least of the many difficulties with such a theorization is its vulnerability to a counter-attack from those opposed to Marxism. In the case of claims about the socialist nature of the ancient Incas, therefore, just such an attack was mounted in a 1928 book by Baudin (reissued some thirty years later with an endorsing Foreword by Ludwig von Mises [*Baudin*, 1961]), where he concurred with the view that it was indeed the case that 'both agrarian collectivism and state socialism existed in Peru', and then went on to argue that as such it was characterized by all the negative attributes he associated with 'totalitarianism': namely, the compulsory relocation of entire populations, forced labour, and economic stagnation. His conclusion is instructive [*Baudin*, 1961: 231]: 'it seemed as if in the twentieth century the Incas would scarcely be mentioned any longer . . . [b]ut today we see them once more emerging from the shadows. The reason for this is to be found in the predominant interest presently [i.e. *circa* 1928] taken in economic questions. The conflicts between the advocates of different systems are becoming very sharp. Specialists, statesmen, and demagogues are in search of arguments and examples. Now the doctrine opposed to liberalism that ruled the world in the nineteenth century is socialism, and pre-Columbian Peru provides the only available example of the application of this doctrine to a great empire. The problems we have just been examining are those we face today. We are witnessing in Europe the advance of

etatism or of general syndicalism, the establishment of a controlled economy, and the destruction of individuality and hence of the elite. The America of the pre-Columbian era provides us with valuable lessons in this respect. Let us hope that we can hold fast to them and put them to good use. There is no such thing as historical inevitability. It is incumbent upon us to take action if we do not wish to become the subjects of a new Inca empire.'

77. See Mariátegui [1968: 68] for these claims, where it is clear that he mistakes grassroots organization *per se* as evidence for the presence of socialism (*'Demuestran . . . la vitalidad del comunismo indígena que impulsa invariablemente a los aborigenes a variadas formas de cooperación y asociación . . . El comunismo . . . ha seguido siendo para el indio su única defensa . . . en las aldeas indígenas donde se agrupan familias entre las cuales . . . subsisten aún, robustos y tenaces, hábitos de cooperación y solidaridad que son la expresión empírica de un espíritu comunista. La "communidad" corresponde a este espíritu. Es su órgano. Cuando la expropiación y el reparto parecen liquidar la "comunidad", el socialismo indígena encuentra siempre el medio de rehacerla, mantenerla o subrogarla'*). As will be seen in Chapter 2, Hugo Blanco in the eastern Peruvian province of La Convención during the early 1960s made a similar mistake, believing that 'dual power' corresponded simply to the traditional institutional structure of peasant economy that existed prior to the implantation of the landlord estate.

78. For the details of this argument (*'[p]ero en ninguno de los grandes centros poblados de Indoamérica – Mexico y los varios países de hoy que comprendía el viejo imperio peruano, por ejemplo – el importado sistema feudal, de trescientos años de colonaje . . . pudo erigir una organización propia, realista y firme. Una lucha . . . entre las masas de población indígena, contra sus opresores feudales . . . representa la profunda oposición de las formas primitivas y tradicionales de reparto y propiedad de la tierra, contra el feudalismo europeo importado por los españoles . . . España vence, pues, militarmente a los imperios indígenas, pero su victoria, capaz de construir el mecanismo político de los pueblos que conquista, no logra derribar totalmente sus estructuras económicas. La conquista trae un nuevo sistema, pero no puede acabar con el sistema anterior'*), see Haya de la Torre [1936b: 170–72].

79. The political problems raised by rural mobilization on the basis of a backwards-looking agrarian myth can be illustrated with reference both to peasant movements in Peru and India (see Chapters 2 and 3), and also to the Cristero movement in Mexico, perhaps the most characteristically populist agrarian mobilization in Latin America at this conjuncture. A patriotic and religious mobilization which might be described as a specifically Mexican equivalent of the Vendée, the *Cristiada* uprising of the late 1920s was a reaction to the anti-clericalism of the Mexican State on the part of a rural petty-bourgeoisie: not only did the mobilizing discourse of the latter reproduce the central emplacement of populism (rural = pure, urban = bad), therefore, but for the peasantry involved '[t]o extirpate Catholicism . . . was to impose a process of deculturation' [*Meyer, 1976: 183,189*]. Even Meyer [1976], who presents the *Cristiada* in a sympathetic light, cannot disguise the reactionary and backwards-looking nature of the movement. 'The religion of the Cristeros', he observes [*Meyer, 1976: 195*], 'was . . . the traditional Roman Catholic religion, strongly rooted in the Hispanic Middle Ages'.

80. On the absence of a proletariat and its political consequences, together with his dismissal of (European/Russian) communism as a 'foreign' philosophy which was inapplicable to Peru, see Haya de la Torre [1936b: 46ff., 54–5, 148].

81. See Haya de la Torre [1936b: 64–5]. For Fanon and Marcuse, see Chapter 5.

82. On this, see Havens [1974: 194ff.]. In many ways, this reaffirmation by *nohonshugi* ideology of the spiritual/sacred/ethnic/national unity between leader (= emperor) and the led (= the peasantry) parallels the similar *volksgemeinschaft* discourse in Germany about the nature of the link between an indigenous peasantry and the *führer* as well as that in Slavophile discourse in pre-Revolutionary Russia concerning the bond between peasant and tsar.

83. Thus one influential exponent (cited in Havens [1974: 155, 160]) of *nohonshugi* views observed that: 'If any one of them [family/peasant/nation] perishes, the others will perish too . . . [a]griculture in our country has the family system as its base and is a system of agriculture which is well articulated with the family system . . . [f]amily-managed farming, i.e. the small-farm system, promotes and nutures the broad spirit of protecting the *kokutai* [= "national essence"]. I believe that this is the true meaning of "agriculture is the foundation of the country" [= *nohonshugi*]'.

84. On this point, see Havens [1974: 126–7, 128]. It is important to note that not all the beliefs advanced by those who regarded themselves as on the political left were in fact incompatible with agrarian populism. For example, in the 1930s the powerful anarchist movement in Japan advocated a decentralized village society of self-sufficient peasants and artisans [*Crump*, 1993], a programme that was in a large measure indistinguishable from that of *nohonshugi* exponents such as Gondo Seikyo.

85. In Japan during the early part of the twentieth century [*Totten*, 1960: 199], therefore, for 'the villagers, urbanism represented the complex and unknown, the source of ideas subversive of true rustic samurai virtues . . . The suspicion and fear of urbanism could be built upon by conservative elements in the agricultural villages to combat "divisive" and "class" ideas. The landlords emphasized village "solidarity" *vis-à-vis* the cities and fanned urban-rural tensions . . . with the rise of nationalism in Japan *nohonshugi* gained strength. It came to be thought of as unpatriotic sectionalism for labor and tenant farmers to be organized within narrow class interests.'

86. For the spread and extent of class struggle in the Japanese countryside during the 1920s and the early 1930s, see Wakukawa [1976] and Dore [1959: 54–85, especially Table 2].

87. Havens [1974: 156]. In the discourse of *nohonshugi*, both landlords and tenants were presented as being equally exploited by finance capital.

88. For the demobilization of the labour movement in Japan during this period, see Large [1981: 128ff.]. 'There is no doubt', observes another source [*Dore*, 1959: 105], 'that the events of the years 1930–37 – the suppression of left-wing activity, the depression, the rise of peasant anti-urban feeling, the resurgence of *nohonshugi* ideas, the rise of patriotic sentiment as Japan began her great gamble in Asia, the appearance of the Army as the champion of the peasant, ...wrought a great change in the political atmosphere of the villages. The stirrings of revolt which had begun to seem dangerous in the mid-1920s were no longer to be seen. There was no longer any question of the peasant being alienated from the goals and symbols of the nation, or of tenant resentment against the landlord turning into

resentment against authority as a whole. The old virtues of resignation and sub-
mission had been restored. Peasants, and in particular tenants, were still poor and
debt-ridden. They occasionally muttered. But spiritually they were integrated
parts of a nation which was moving into an age of glory.'

89. In Bologna [*Cardoza*, 1982], Tuscany [*Snowden*, 1979] and Apulia [*Snowden*,
1986], fascism emerged directly from opposition by landlords, commercial
farmers and/or rich peasants to rural working class mobilization.

90. On these points, see Bramwell [1985] and Pois [1986]. The words of Darré himself (cited in Mosse [1966: 148–50]) are unambiguous about the nature of the
nation/race/soil/peasant interrelationship: 'First there was the German peasantry
in Germany before what is today served up as German history. Neither princes,
nor the Church, nor the cities have created the German man. Rather the German
man emerged from the German peasantry. Everywhere one will find primordial
peasant customs that reach far back into the past. Everywhere there is evidence
that the German peasantry, with an unparalleled tenacity, knew how to preserve
its unique character and its customs against every attempt to wipe them out . . .
One can say that the blood of a people digs its roots deep into the homeland earth
through its peasant landholdings, from which it continuously receives that life-
endowing strength which constitutes its special character.'

91. This concern with ethnic 'pureness' extended to clothing [*Jacobeit*, 1991]: males
and females were encouraged in an authentically populist manner to forsake
international (= 'Jewish') high fashion in favour of an indigenous folkloric
'German style' in general and rustic design (= peasant costume) in particular.

92. Fritzsche [1990: 114–18] suggests that during the late 1920s the peasant movement in Lower Saxony mobilized on the basis of a classic populist discourse that
was not only anti-systemic, anti-big business, anti-semitic, anti-socialist, but also
anti-public spending and anti-bureaucracy (both of which were identified by
peasants themselves as the source of high taxation). The role of petty commodity
producers in the rise of German fascism is confirmed for the rural areas of
Schleswig-Holstein and Hanover where, in contrast to poor peasants and agricultural labourers who supported the Socialists and Communists, the majority
of the support for Nazis in the 1932 election was provided by peasant family
farmers [*Loomis and Beegle*, 1946].

93. For Romania, see Weber [1964: 96ff.; 1965; 1966], for Hungary see Weber
[1964: 88ff.] and Deák [1965], for Bulgaria see Bell [1977], and for Eastern
Europe generally see Mitrany [1951], Ionescu [1969], and Jackson [1974]. As
Warriner [1950: ix] notes: 'In 1938, the outstanding fact about eastern Europe as
a whole, with the exception of Czechoslovakia, was that it was Fascist-ruled. The
regimes headed by Horthy, Boris, Beck, Stojadinovic and Antonescu were not the
creation of Nazism: on the contrary, they had come to power long before Hitler
appeared on the European scene, as a result of the victory of internal reaction in
the nineteen-twenties.'

94. Thus, for example, Švehla, leader of the Czech Agrarian Party, coined the slogan
'All the countryside is one family' (i.e., peasant = kinship = 'natural' category),
while Böszörmény, the leader of Hungarian National Socialist Workers' Party,
chose as the emblem of the latter a pair of crossed scythes, and Codreanu, leader
of the Iron Guard in Romania, dressed in traditional peasant costume [*Jackson*,
1974: 303; *Deák*, 1965: 384–5; *Ionescu*, 1969: 121]. Typical perhaps of the
idealization at this conjuncture of the peasantry is the text by Viski [1932], in

which the Hungarian smallholder is depicted not only as undifferentiated (= all-cultivators-are-the-same) but also as a timeless and innately cultural being whose entire custom-bound (= 'traditional'/unchanging) existence was governed by Nature.

95. Ante Radic, who formulated the ideology of the Croatian Peasant Party, equated 'the peasantry' with 'the people', as did Stambolisky, who wanted to make Bulgaria 'a land of prosperous middle peasants', and the Romanian populist leader Constantin Stere, for whom the peasantry were 'a coherent [= undifferentiated] social group' embodying the 'national genius' of the Romanian people; both the Bulgarian Agrarian Union and the Croatian Peasant Party aimed to create a peasant 'homeland' (*domovina*) or state [*Jackson*, 1974: 286, 290–91, 293, 295; *Bell*, 1977: 168].

96. The ethnicization of debate about agrarian reform was effected in Romania at the beginning of the twentieth century by Protopopescu, 'a leading exponent of the rising wave of agrarian nationalism' who in 1903 not only announced that the target of legislation should not be landlords but rather their estate managers (*arendasi*) – who were responsible for administering landlord property, subletting portions of this to peasants and collecting labour-rent, and many of whom were of Jewish ethnic origin – but also described them as 'foreigners [who] constitute not only a social and economic, but also a national, menace' [*Eidelberg*, 1974: 120–21]. At one stroke, therefore, he shifted the debate from one about class to one about race and national 'belonging'/'otherness', in the process winning over much support in rural areas.

97. Like the Slavophile populists in Russia, the populist Constantin Stere wished to prevent the introduction into Romania of what he considered to be the avoidable 'evils' of industrialization, a position echoed by Hungarian populists during the 1930s, while Stambolisky, leader of the Bulgarian Agrarian Union and prime minister of Bulgaria in the period 1919–23, expressed his hostility towards 'the urban' in uncompromising terms ('The city people live by deceit, by idleness, by parasitism, by perversion'), and – like Ante Radic of the Croatian Peasant Party – maintained that 'the urban' and 'the rural' were in fact culturally distinct entities [*Jackson* 1974: 289, 292,295,307]. Hence the ideological efficacy of the following oppositions:

	Bulgaria, Croatia
'Other'	'Self'
City	Countryside
Western or Graeco-Roman	Slavic/rural/superior

98. In the case of Romania, for example, '[t]o the peasants the Jews represented the farm-stewards or farming trusts exploiting their labour, the innkeepers and shop-keepers lending them money at usurious rates . . .' [*Weber*, 1966: 115]. For the equation in late nineteenth-century Romania of Jews with the power towns exercised over the countryside, see Eidelberg [1974: 64]. Although not linked specifically to one ethnic group, village moneylending in other Eastern European countries was similarly the target of peasant hostility: in late nineteenth-century Bulgaria, for example, it was referred to as 'Godless usury' (i.e. moneylending = the profane 'other' of productive cultivation by smallholders), and took the form of forward-buying of peasant crops, which merchants then profitably sold back to these same cultivators in times of scarcity [*Bell*, 1977: 14–15]. For instances of

anti-semitism generated by late nineteenth-century American populism, see Chapter 6.

99. See Jackson [1974: 286]. On the anti-Marxism of the Legion in Romania, see Weber [1966: 105]. That the role of agrarian fascist discourse was in many instances simply one of preventing/pre-empting the development of a consciousness specifically of class is evident from an observation (cited in Deák [1965: 385]) by one of the Hungarian 'village explorers' that, when he encountered impoverished seasonal workers on a large estate in 1934, all of whom were members of the Scythe Cross movement, they informed him that ' "We fight for the Idea" . . . but were unable to tell [him] what the "Idea" was about. They hated the Communists and the Gentlemen'. When over a hundred peasants who were members of the Scythe Cross were arrested and tried subsequently, they '[a]ll declared themselves ready to die for the "Idea", but were unable to provide the judge with further elucidation. [Most] owned neither house nor land . . . [t]hey wore torn trousers, miserable short overcoats or old sheepskin vests; none of them wore a shirt . . . [t]he judge permitted most of the defendants to return to their poverty' [Deák, 1965: 386].

100. Thus the reactionary Hungarian populist Gömbös dismissed Socialism and Marxism as 'a destructive heresy foisted on simple workers by self-seeking international Jews', and more generally [Weber, 1964: 89, 90, 97] Hungarian nationalists and fascists 'were anti-semitic because they equated the Jews with exploitation and the money power [and also because] many . . . of the Commissars of Bela Kun's red republic of 1919 were alleged to have been Jews . . . To young Romanian nationalists, most of whom were poor students or intellectuals, often just up from the land, the economic claims of peasants and of workers were just; they were however confused with Communism . . . it appeared that a majority of Communist leaders were Jews, a national group which in Eastern Europe far more than in the west appeared as a separate community, set apart by custom, language and, frequently, by dress. The equation between Jews and Communism [and thus] Jews and the foreign threat, suggested itself at once to the adolescents whom Codreanu gathered around him . . .'. Hence the emphasis placed on ethnicity in the following oppositions involving the leadership of Romanian socialists and populists [Ionescu 1969: 101]:

C. Dobrogeanu Gherea	Constantin Stere
socialist	agrarian populist
Russian Jewish origin	*Romanian yeoman origin*
internationalist	nationalist
revolutionary	constitutionalist

101. Codreanu, the leader of the fascist Legion in Romania, 'was interested in the particular historical survival of the Razasi – free villages whose inhabitants traced their descent from a common free (noble) ancestor and claimed a customary freedom to run their own affairs through a council of village elders', while Stambolisky maintained that the Bulgarian Agrarian Union was based on the idea of *suslovie*, 'an estate in the medieval sense of the word', and the ideal of the fascist Ludaks in Czechoslovakia was similarly based on the restoration of a medieval corporate society [Weber, 1966: 111; Jackson, 1974: 289, 305]. Significantly, the Romanian Legion received strong support from areas where these 'free villages' predominated

102. 'It was in this guise', notes Jackson [1974: 294–5], 'as a party respresenting the desire of a national minority for greater self-government . . . that the Croatian Peasant Party retained its popular support . . . [i]n this sense the Croatian Peasant Party, by educating the Croatian people to see the national question as the key to all problems, paved the way for the creation of the Croat fascist State of Ante Pavelic during World War II, a State in which many Croatian Peasant Party leaders participated'.

103. The mobilizing slogan of the Romanian Iron Guard, for example, was 'All for the Fatherland' [*Weber*, 1966: 102]. About the dynamics and prevalence of the nationalist/populist/fascist combination, Jackson [1974: 304–5] notes: 'the Christian Slovak People's Party, or the Ludaks, . . . along with the Croatian Ustaše movement and the Iron Guard in Romania, serve as an excellent example of the ease with which agrarianism, virulent nationalism and fascism could be blended in Eastern Europe . . . [the Ludaks] drew significant support from the village and paid much attention to it . . . they resembled the Croatian Peasant Party in their focus on the myth of a people's or peasant State (People's Slovakia), and their notion that national virtue was best represented in the slovak peasant . . . [t]hey strongly supported the rights of property, opposed communism and socialism and called for social peace ('Christ, not Lenin') . . . the Ludaks tried and succeeded in creating a genuine fascist state.'

104. On these points, see Weber [1966: 107,117].

105. For the importance of lumpenproletarian elements in the support of the Legion in Romania, see Weber [1966: 105].

106. On this point, see Jackson [1974: 293, 296, 304]. Ante Radic, for example, is referred to by Trotsky [1936: 227] as 'the banker-leader of the Croatian rich peasants'.

PART I
Populist Peasants

Trotskyism, Maoism and Populism in the Andes: Latin American Peasant Movements and the Agrarian Myth

'There is no deceiving the kulak. He does not judge by words but by deeds, by taxes, by prices, and net profit.' – An observation by Leon Trotsky [1936: 139].

' "Should the situation in fact arise," said the prince, "we may hopefully expect the conducting of the affairs of our country for the sole benefit of its people." The word people had become fashionable since the war. It was used by persons of every shade of political opinion, and took on a different meaning in different mouths. When the prince said "people" he meant himself and the members of his immediate family.' – The description by Norman Lewis [1953: 47] of the benefits of nationalizing foreign agribusiness enterprises as perceived by a fictional Siamese prince during the early 1950s.

In rejecting economistic approaches to the analysis of the peasantry and peasant movements, the focus of a number of important studies undertaken over the past 20 years has been not just on politics and ideology but more crucially on the language of protest and opposition. While in a general sense this is a welcome and much needed development, the danger of such an approach is the tendency to view all grassroots (or 'from below') resistance as inherently radical, thereby losing sight of not only the *class*-specific basis of opposition to the existing social order but also how different – and apparently 'innocent' – components of discourse can in these circumstances form a potent expression of *bourgeois* (or 'from above') class consciousness.

While 'subaltern', 'oppressed' or 'supressed' socio-economic categories associated with such analyses of peasant resistance/protest recognize the existence of conflict, therefore, they are unable to identify the class-specific nature of the struggle involved, and thus the kind of political outcome it prefigures. The three case studies from Latin America presented below all illustrate the way in which a seemingly radical politico-ideological discourse of opposition and protest actually reflects and promotes the class interests of a rich peasant leadership.[1]

The first of these case studies concerns the peasant movement which took place in the eastern lowlands of Peru over the period 1958–62, on the large rural estates in the province of La Convención. It was one of the most important agrarian mobilizations to have occurred in Latin America during the latter part of the twentieth century.[2] Two distinctive characteristics of this movement were that it was led by rich peasant tenants, who had most to lose from eviction and most to gain from high coffee prices, and that at the hight of the struggle many of these better-off elements abandoned unions affiliated to the Peruvian Communist Party (PCP) and the APRA in order to join the Trotskyist Revolutionary Left Front (FIR) led by Hugo Blanco.

The conventional explanation of this political shift is that, on the fundamental issue of landownership, both the PCP and APRA were conservative whereas the FIR was more radical, and thus offered a strategy based on direct action which suited the immediate objectives of rich peasants. Such an explanation, focusing as it does on the element of political opportunism, is undoubtedly true in part; however, it fails to transcend two basic contradictions. The first is Trotsky's own negative views regarding the political role of the peasantry in the revolutionary process.[3] And the second is the fact that a programme based on Trotskyism possessed inherent dangers for rich tenants, in that it might be turn against them subsequently by poor peasants and landless labourers.

Unlike the Maoism of Sendero, for example, Trotskyism does not immediately suggest itself as a suitable politico-ideological vehicle for the mobilization of a peasant movement, let alone one led by and reflecting the socio-economic interests of capitalist rich peasants. In contrast to most critiques of Hugo Blanco, therefore, this chapter will make three points.[4] First, that on questions such as the (revolutionary) role of peasants in the struggle against both the landowning and capitalist class, their superordinate/subordinate relationship to the working class in this conflict, and their role in the transition to socialism, his politico-ideological position constitutes a fundamental break with Trotskyism (its alleged mentor).[5] Second, the idealist manner in which these processes are depicted in Blanco's discourse is in fact ultimately compatible with the non-socialist character and objectives of the dominant elements in the peasant movement. And third, that the discourse of Blanco and the rich peasantry is much rather that of populism, the mobilizing ideology of a capitalist rich peasantry.

The second and third case studies examine peasant movements which occurred in Latin America in each of the next two decades: the first is ANUC, a Colombian peasant movement in the 1970s, while the second is the better known Sendero Luminoso, a 1980s movement with an important rural component. Although these case studies are presented in less detail than the first, each is very similar to the earlier peasant movement led by Hugo Blanco, and in many ways both follow the pattern of what happened in La Convención: namely, mobilizations which reflected the class interests of rich peasants, the discourse of which nevertheless invoked a radical politics (Maoism in the case of Sendero) and idealized images of an economically uniform peasantry seeking to re-establish subsistence cultivation in the face of oppression/exploitation by a domestic 'feudal' landowning class and/or urban/'foreign' outsiders.

I

The extent, nature, and political effects of the break between Blanco and Trotskyism can be illustrated with reference to the way in which the concepts 'dual power', 'permanent revolution', and 'peasantry' appear in the discourse of both Trotsky and Hugo Blanco, and in particular how the latter elaborates them with regard to the events which unfolded in La Convención during 1961–62.

2.1 The Economic Background: La Convención 1900–1958

La Convención, the largest and northernmost province in the Department of Cusco, is situated on the semi-tropical eastern slope of the Andes, and constitutes an ideal location for the cultivation of cash-crops such as sugar, cocoa, tea, coca and coffee. Although its geographical inaccessibility prevented extensive colonization and settlement of this frontier region until the early twentieth century, the area has since the mid-sixteenth century formed part of the rural estate system (*hacienda*) imposed at the Spanish Conquest. During the early part of the twentieth century, owners of these *latifundia* leased uncultivated plots (on the non-demesne sector of the estate) to peasant migrants from the southern highlands, who thereby became tenants (*arrendires*) contributing a contractually-stipulated number of days labour-service on the landlord enterprise (or demesne sector of the estate) as rental.

Before the 1940s, labour-rent payments by tenants to landlords were low but, following the rise during the next two decades in the global demand for primary commodities grown in the province (tea, cocoa, and especially coffee), landlords increased the amount of labour-rent payable by tenants. The latter in turn leased a portion of their holding to one or more sub-tenants (*allegados*), who henceforth discharged all the labour-service obligations owed by the tenant to the landlord.[6] With the rise in coffee prices, a small but economically powerful stratum of rich peasants began to accumulate capital by growing this cash-crop for the export market with credit obtained from local merchants. Tenant obligations to the landlord now became an economic obstacle to further accumulation, as the decline in the real level of the remuneration paid by the landlord to substitute workers fulfilling labour-service requirements coincided with a rise in the amount of labour-rent per leased hectare.

Accordingly, these capitalist tenants increasingly came into conflict with the landlord class in the province over the control of labour-power and means of production on the estate system. The response of landlords to this exercise of economic and political power by the estate peasantry was non-renewal of non-demesne leases coupled with eviction of tenants from their holdings.[7] The latter maneouvre became more common during the late 1950s with the expansion in volume and profitability of coffee production on tenant hold-ings.[8] In addition to its specifically economic purpose, however, eviction also possessed an explicit and symbolic *political* object: the expulsion (and neutralization) of unionized tenants in general, and union leaders in particular. Faced with the threat of eviction, therefore, tenants were compelled either to adopt a more radical political position in their struggle against the landlord class, and to bring into question the property relation itself, or accept dis-possession of their non-demesne holdings. It was precisely the continuation of legalistic forms of struggle by both APRA and the PCP which contributed to the shift by tenants from the latter to support FIR's extra-legal challenge to the power of the landlord class.[9]

2.2 *The Structure and Organization of the Peasant Movement in La Convención*

The dissolution of landlord power in La Convención during the late 1950s and the early 1960s was coterminous with (and largely determined by) the emergence of politico-ideological power exercised by estate tenants (and to a lesser extent sub-tenants), the specific characteristics of which were the organization from 1947 onwards of peasant unions and the formation in 1958 of the Provincial Federation of Peasant Unions (*Federación Provincial de Campesinos de La Convención y Lares*). From its inception, peasant unioniza-tion was based on active rank-and-file membership at the level of each indi-vidual estate in the province. Each union branch was allowed to send two elected delegates to federation meetings, the combined delegate strength forming the Federation membership. This organizational structure based on affiliated union branches permitted rank-and-file peasants in individual estates not only to receive mass support from one another but also to participate in the struggles against the landlord class as a whole. In 1958 the 15 peasant union branches in different estates throughout the province had a membership of only 1,500 tenants and sub-tenants; by 1959, this figure had increased to 40 union branches with 5,500 members, and during the 1961–62 period of acute struggle with landlords these numbers rose to 122 branches and 12,500 members.[10]

With regard to the social composition of the union leadership, this consisted of the most literate and longest settled peasants in the province, many of whom joined either the PCP or the FIR. Most union leaders were Roman Catholics, despite the assertion by some texts that a 'surprisingly large minority' belonged to protestant fundamentalist sects.[11] Although corresponding to only 17 per cent of peasants on the estates, tenants accounted for 80 per cent of the union leadership in 1961. By contrast, sub-tenants who amounted to 44 per cent of the estate peasantry accounted for only 18 per cent of the leadership, while agricultural labourers who constituted 39 per cent provided only two per cent of the leadership.[12]

Although unionization developed from the grassroots, it was nevertheless linked to three politico-ideological tendencies.[13] These were the Peruvian Communist Party (*Partido Comunista Peruano* or PCP), the influence of which was mediated through the Cusco Workers Federation (*Federación de Trabajadores de Cusco* or FTC), the American Popular Revolutionary Alliance (*Alianza Popular Revolucionaria Americana* or APRA), and the Revolutionary Left Front (*Frente de la Izquierza Revolucionaria* or FIR).[14] The PCP and APRA were both reformist, and operated within a legalistic context defined by the existing property relation. Their activity was therefore limited to the implementation of existing legislation, which confined the level of landlord rent to 20 per cent of tenant produce and permitted a possessing subject to buy his holding at the free market price.

The line adopted by the FIR was more radical: it not only allocated primacy to direct union action (mass mobilizations, land invasions, strikes) over legalistic activity, but also advocated a break with the existing property relation (the conversion of non-demesne usufruct rights into ownership rights, the expropriation and redistribution of demesne land belonging to repressive landlords). Evidence suggests that, in the course of the class struggle occurring in the province during 1958–62, not only did the FIR receive support principally from among rich peasant tenants while middle and poor peasant tenants and sub-tenants supported the PCP, but further that a significant proportion of this rich peasant tenant support which was originally received by APRA subsequently moved to the FIR.

An examination of the average area of peasant holdings in estates located in each individual district of La Convención reveals that rich peasant tenants constituted the predominant stratum in the districts of Santa Teresa, Ocobamba and Echarate, while middle peasants predominated in the district of Lares. By contrast, Santa Ana, Huayopata, Vilcabamba and Maranura are poor peasant tenant and sub-tenant districts.[15] If this information is linked to shifts in support for particular politico-ideological tendencies in the province over the period in question, then an additionally significant pattern emerges. Thus rich peasant tenants in APRA strongholds (the districts of Santa Teresa and Echarate) transferred their allegiance to the FIR and (to a lesser extent) to the PCP, the latter retaining its control over those districts where poor peasant tenants and sub-tenants were the principal stratum.

2.3 The Success of the Peasant Movement in La Convención

The years 1961–62 marked the zenith of the peasant movement in La Convención, a period characterized by rising levels of oppression exercised by the landlord class in conjunction with the repressive apparatus of the state (police, military, judiciary). Thus attempts by estate tenants either to resist or prevent the landlord from evicting them from their non-demesne holdings escalated increasingly into physical confrontation.[16] The peasant response took the initial form of a general strike throughout the province, action which subsequently developed into land invasions, and finally the emergence of what Blanco termed a 'dual power' structure and the guerrilla movement.

Within the context of the estate system in La Convención, strikes involved not so much the withdrawal of tenant-provided labour-power (= labour-rent) from the landlord demesne as its redeployment from this sector onto the peasant enterprise. When landlords rejected a series of peasant union demands made by the FIR and presented through the Federation, the latter called for an indefinite general strike throughout the province. Although this mass withdrawal of tenant-provided labour-power lasted for only two months, the politicization and militancy of the peasant movement resulted in continuous strikes, action that involved the withdrawal of labour from 70 estates at the hight of the class struggle in 1962.[17] This form of peasant action ceased in April that year when the legislative abolition of all forms of labour-rent by state decree confirmed its success. Organized by union militants from the FIR under the slogan 'Land or Death' (*tierra o muerte*), land invasions commenced in 1961, a process in which 120 union branches occupied some 250,000 hectares on 100 estates throughout La Convención.[18] This involved both the re-occupation of holdings from which tenants had been evicted and encroachments onto the uncultivated portions of the landlord enterprise itself.

From the viewpoint of Hugo Blanco and the FIR, these land seizures, together with the cessation of labour-rent, plus the simultaneous emergence of an alternative structure organized and administered by peasant unions, signalled the advent in the province of dual power (*un semi-gobierno campesino*).[19] Managed through peasant unions, it included not only peasant-controlled judicial tribunals, schools, health centres and militias, but also infrastructural improvements (construction/extension of roads, irrigation canals, bridges, demesne housing) and the peasants' own agrarian reform decree.[20] The latter was issued by Hugo Blanco himself from the occupied estate of Chaupimayo during the early months of 1962, and argued for the conversion of usufruct rights on the non-demesne sector of the estate system into ownership, the right of 'just'/'good' landlords to retain ownership of the demesne, the distribution of uncultivated demesne land to poor peasants, and the exclusion of 'authorities in the service of the landlord' (= state agencies) from any part in this process.[21] In response to the view that the defeat of the landlord class would merely signal a new struggle against rich and middle peasants, Blanco maintained that once dual power was established the existing tenure patterns would again be transformed but this time on a collective basis, thereby incorporating the hitherto excluded landless agricultural labour.[22]

2.4 The Failure of the Peasant Movement in La Convención

The existence in La Convención of what Hugo Blanco called a dual power structure gave rise to conflict within the peasant movement itself, a situation which in turn led to military intervention by the state and armed resistance by the peasantry in the form of guerrilla activity. The divergence between the reformist line advocated by the PCP and the radical line of the FIR culminated in a split between these two principal politico-ideological tendencies within the Peasant Federation. Following the election of Hugo Blanco, the FIR candidate, to the important post of Secretary-General, the losing reformist minority not only rejected the victory of the radical majority but also withdrew from the Federation and requested the intervention of the state in order to expel Blanco and his supporters from La Convención for 'politicizing' the struggle of the peasant unions.[23] Accordingly, by the end of 1962 not only was the province under military occupation but peasant union support for the radical policies and methods of the FIR had ceased, resistance to the occupation being confined to the peasant militias in the estate of Chaupimayo and taking the form of clandestine guerrilla operations.[24] No longer permitted to function as Secretary-General to the Federation and increasingly isolated, Blanco was captured by the police in May 1963.[25]

The two land reforms carried out by the Peruvian state over 1963–64 were an important factor in the decline of the peasant movement. In the first of these reforms, promulgated in March 1963, only tenants received ownership rights to their non-demesne holdings, and this itself was conditional on payment by the beneficiaries of an agrarian debt. The latter was rejected by the Federation, which pointed out that tenants had already purchased their holdings many times over by providing the landlord with labour-rent over a period of years, and the state soon abandoned attempts to extract payment for tenant holdings.[26] Under the provisions of the second reform law, promulgated in 1964, peasants excluded from the reform of the previous year were given land titles.

By the mid-1960s, therefore, former tenants and sub-tenants were both established as peasant proprietors on the non-demesne sector of the estate system in La Convención. However, this cannot account for peasant demobilization or the political marginalization of Hugo Blanco and the FIR. Given the fact that both reforms which converted usufruct rights into private property did no more than consolidate the unequal land distribution embodied in the pre-reform tenure structure, the widespread acceptance by the peasantry of a mobilizing ideology based on Trotskyism would have signalled just the *beginning* – not the end – of this acute stage of class struggle in the province. It is accordingly necessary to examine Hugo Blanco's Trotskyism in more detail.

II

For Trotsky, dual power is merely one phase of a continuous two-stage revolutionary transformation, a process in which the initial stage corresponds to a struggle between a feudal landowning class and the bourgeoisie (the latter challenging and displacing the former) while the subsequent stage consists of a struggle between the 'newly crowned' bourgeoisie and the 'third power' or the proletariat (the latter similarly challenging and displacing the former).[27] The principal contradiction in this struggle is located by Trotsky at the level of class relationships (feudal landowners against the bourgeoisie, the latter against the proletariat), the social category of 'peasants' being as a result assigned a politically subordinate position. This lack of an independent political role for the peasantry is in turn determined by its heterogeneous socio-economic composition; in the course of class struggle, therefore, different peasant strata are to be found in the camp of either the bourgeoisie or the proletariat, depending on the extent and form of capitalist penetration of agriculture, the development of the productive forces, and the forms taken by the social relations of production.

The significance for the working class of this political duality exhibited by an internally differentiated peasantry is that it is the peasantry which determines not only the balance of class forces at the critical moment of revolutionary conflict but also what is – and what is not – possible as the outcome of struggle. For this reason, Trotsky advocated an immediate transition to the dictatorship of the proletariat, rather than risk the possibility of peasant counter-revolution in the intervening bourgeois democratic stage. As he observes, the working class 'is inevitably and very quickly confronted with tasks the fulfilment of which is bound up with deep inroads into the rights of bourgeois property. The democratic revolution grows over directly into the socialist revolution and thereby becomes a *permanent* revolution.'[28] It is precisely this convergence between dual power and permanent revolution, together with the economic and ideological reasons for this, which is missing from the politics of Hugo Blanco and the FIR.

2.5 Trotskyism, Dual Power and 'Dual Power'

Superficially, the concept 'dual power' elaborated by Hugo Blanco and the FIR (and 'applied' in La Convención during 1962) occupies a similar theoretical and political terrain to that of Trotsky. This occupation, however, is one of name only. A number of observations are necessary, therefore, in order to identify the extent of and the reasons for this divergence between Blanco and Trotsky. These will accordingly focus on four specific aspects of 'dual power' as elaborated by Hugo Blanco: the spatial element (the locus of 'dual power') and the temporal element (the political conjuncture in the Peruvian social formation), each of which relate to the national context, while at the local level both the form of 'dual power' (the peasant-controlled institutional framework) and its content (the class-specific configuration and acceptability of the 'alternative' structure) will be considered.

The first discrepancy between the 'dual power' of Hugo Blanco and the dual power of Trotsky concerns locus. Whereas for the latter the concept has meaning only at the level of the social formation, for the former by contrast it materialises not at the national but at the local context.[29] Significantly, the examples of dual power cited by Trotsky are *England* in 1640, *France* during 1790–91, *Germany* in 1848, and *Russia* in 1917, while for Blanco dual power in 1962 occurs not in Peru but in *La Convención*, one of its provinces.

The second discrepancy, which follows from and relates directly to the first, concerns the acuteness of the class struggle at the level of the social formation. Thus for Trotsky dual power is not only coupled with the generalised dissolution of the state apparatus but is also synonymous with the existence of a civil war waged by opposed class forces throughout the nation.[30] Hence the examples of dual power cited by him refer to England in *1640*, France during *1790–91*, Germany in *1848*, and Russia in *1917*, each of which corresponds to a widespread and generalised crisis of the state absent from Peru in 1962.

The third discrepancy concerns the form taken by the dual power structure itself. On this point Trotsky notes: 'Either the bourgeoisie will actually dominate the old state apparatus, altering it a little for its own purposes, in which case the soviets will come to nothing; or the soviets will form the foundation of a new state, liquidating not only the old governmental apparatus, but also the dominion of those classes which it served.'[31] Thus the alternative institutional structure (based on the soviet) which emerges during and characterizes dual power is antagonistic to and fundamentally incompatible with not only the decayed pre-existing institutional structure (the autocratic state embodying the interests of a landowning class) but also the subsequently modified institutional structure (the democratic state apparatus controlled by and operating on behalf of the bourgeoisie).

The existence of on the one hand a convergence between the old and 'new' state apparatus (the bourgeoisie 'altering it a little for its own purposes'), and on the other a divergence between this old/'new' state apparatus and the specifically working class institutions which develop in the course of dual power, suggests that close attention must be paid to precisely what kind of class interests are served by any institutions which emerge during this process or are retained subsequently.

2.6 Hugo Blanco, the Agrarian Myth and Capitalism

Regarding the origins and form of the institutional framework which emerged in La Convención during 1962, Blanco has written: 'Communal decision-making is reborn or strengthened in all respects: local justice, public works, education, health, commerce. Mutual aid in agriculture is also strengthened . . . In reality, the peasants of the hacienda form a community . . .; that community has moved from being governed almost absolutely by the landlord to being governed collectively – that is, to peasant democracy.'[32]

This quote indicates the true nature of the politico-ideological terrain occupied by Blanco. Following the expropriation of (or in some cases simply the negation of power exercised by) the landlord class in La Convención, the dual power structure of Blanco revealed the presence on the non-demesne sector of the estate system of an already-constituted peasant 'community', the existence of which corresponds merely to the absence of the landlord class. That is, 'dual power' for Blanco involves the *same* (non-demesne) structure, but controlled by a different subject. The discursive function of the term 'community' as employed here by Blanco is, in short, to refer its (socio-economically heterogeneous) subjects to a 'surviving' and 'historically immutable' existence which simultaneously deflects or supresses mention of internal differentiation (and the antagonism deriving from this), the politico-ideological effect of which is acceptance of the present (the social order 'reborn' in the course of dual power) premissed on the reaffirmation of its 'normal' or *eternal* form.

What we have here, in other words, is the invocation by Blanco not of dual power as understood by Trotsky but rather of the agrarian myth as propagated by populism. The contradiction between on the one hand the identification and idealization by Blanco of peasant 'community' as a prefigurative socialist form within the dual power structure of La Convención, and on the other its mobilizing role in bourgeois ideology, possesses a distinct political and theoretical history. As has been outlined in Chapter 1, populists believed that the most effective bulwark against the spread of capitalism in pre-revolutionary Russia was the village community composed of petty commodity producers whose economy was located outside capitalism, a view shared in 1920s/1930s Peru not just by nationalists such as Haya de la Torre but also by socialists like Mariátegui. By contrast, Russian Marxists in general and Lenin in particular argued that capitalist relations had already penetrated the village community, which was as a result disintegrating into its opposed class components; traditional rural institutions could not be regarded, therefore, as prefigurative socialist forms *per se*.[33]

The reasons for the ideological acceptability of the agrarian myth to rural capitalist producers in La Convención during the early 1960s is not difficult to discern. It is no accident, therefore, that the framework of Blanco's (already-present-only-to-be-revealed) 'dual power' includes not only 'local justice', 'public works', 'education' and 'health' but also 'mutual aid' and 'commerce', since at this conjuncture the latter correspond to institutional forms that prefigure not so much socialism as capitalism. Furthermore, the institutional forms in the 'dual power' structure were not merely compatible with capitalist production but actually supportive of the accumulation process in La Convención.[34] Thus the provision of local medical and educational facilities contributed both to the reproduction of labour-power and to the increasing social and technical division of labour; on the one hand by improving the health of the labouring subject, and on the other through the displacement of rich peasant kin from the labour process (training them as administrators and technical functionaries). Non-capitalist producers did not benefit from these resources to the same extent; since children became unavailable for agricultural work during school hours, local educational facilities frequently deprived poor peasants of significant portions of their workforce, while private health was for these same subjects economically inaccessible.

In so far as they contributed to the output and marketing of cash crops, moreover, improvements to the demesne infrastructure carried out as a result of peasant-controlled self-help projects (for example, construction of roads and irrigation canals) initiated during the period of 'dual power' in La Convención were also compatible with rich peasant accumulation. That such 'alternative' institutional forms posed no threat to the bourgeois state is demonstrated by the subsequent continuation of many of these self-help projects by state agencies during the mid-1960s. The traditional work arrangements endorsed by Hugo Blanco under the rubric of 'mutual aid' were similarly compatible with the accumulation process on the non-demesne. Thus the institution of fictive kinship (*compadrazgo*), usually presented in terms of reciprocal – and therefore non-explotative – exchanges between smallholders, was used by rich peasants in La Convención to discipline and maintain control over the labour-power of poor peasant co-parents (*compadres*) and/or god-children (*ahijados*).[35] Forms of exchange labour (*ayni, mink'a*) were also used in much the same way by rich peasants, who exchanged not personal labour with one another but rather the labour-power of poor peasants and agricultural workers under their control.[36]

In assessing the 'dual power' framework as perceived by Hugo Blanco, it is also necessary to consider those institutional forms which either did not cease to function during this period, or which were not implemented. The most notable is the continuation (and in some instances the extension) of private property in land on the peasant enterprise. Although labour-service payments by tenants to the landlord on the demesne sector of the estate system ceased, those made by poor peasant sub-tenants and their kinsfolk to rich peasant ex-tenants on the non-demesne sector continued, as did debt bondage relations in this context. Similarly, neither an increase in wages paid to hired labour nor a reduction in the working day to eight hours was implemented on the non-demesne sector.

What is common to each institutional form of 'dual power' is that in economic terms its presence or absence was determined not by some (unspecific) popular demand but rather by a compatibility with capital accumulation effected on the non-demesne at this conjuncture by rich tenants.[37] Moreover, this 'alternative' institutional structure also meets the equally pressing requirement for a favourable politico-ideological projection of this development on the part of its dominant class elements – tenants from the rich peasant stratum – simultaneously engaged in a twofold struggle: on the one hand against the landlord class, and on the other against tenants and sub-tenants from the middle and poor peasant strata.

The already considerable theoretical and political distance between Hugo Blanco and Trotsky manifests itself most clearly with regard to the fourth and final discrepancy, the concept 'class' underpinning the political and economic objectives incribed in the programmatic statements by Blanco and the FIR. As regards the social forces constitutive of 'dual power' in La Convención, Blanco observes: 'It is certain that in Peru the duality of power on a national scale will not occur between bourgeois power and the peasantry, but between bourgeois power and the proletariat . . . [b]ut this does not contradict the local development of incipient dual power between the bourgeois government and sectors of the population other than the proletariat, which is practically non-existent in many zones'.[38]

Whereas for Trotsky dual power arises from an initial antagonism between the landlord class and the bourgeoisie, which then develops into a struggle between the latter and the proletariat, for Blanco by contrast the conflict that results in the emergence of 'dual power' is not only limited just to the initial phase, but the antagonism involves 'feudal' landowners and *peasants*, the latter inserted by Blanco into the space which for Trotsky is occupied in turn by the bourgeoisie and the proletariat. This substitution of peasant for both bourgeoisie and proletariat constitutes nothing other than a displacement of *class* categories (subjects defined in terms of ownership of or separation from given means of production) by an indeterminate social category (subjects engaged in small-scale agriculture where production relations take various forms). It also underlines the affinity between Blanco's discourse and that of populism.[39]

2.7 Hugo Blanco, Populism and Peasant Essentialism

Within the realm of Trotskyist theory, this economic displacement licenses an equally specific political effect. While both bourgeoisie and proletariat in their separate class capacity are capable of executing an *independent* revolutionary role in the class struggle (the bourgeoisie in relation to the landowning class, and the proletariat in relation to the bourgeoisie), the 'intermediate layer' of peasants is denied precisely this political coherence which class confers, and as such is incapable of playing an independent role in revolutionary transitions.[40] Not only does the non-involvement in Blanco's 'dual power' of a large landless workforce present in La Convención on a seasonal and/or permanent basis make problematic its application in this context, but the opacity of the term 'peasant' subsequently assigned the central emplacement in this 'dual power' structure ensures that the nature of the *class* forces opposed to landlordism is never posed.

Symptomatic of this is the fact that for Blanco exploitation occurs only at the level of the landlord/tenant relation, and that consequently the absence of a landlord (following his expropriation) indicates a simultaneous end to exploitative rlationships on the estate system of La Convención.[41] The fiction of an homogeneous peasantry makes it unnecessary for him to identify exploitation within the peasantry, and to link this to the process of capital accumulation taking place on the non-demesne, which in turn would indicate the presence there of heterogeneous class subjects (migrants and those poor peasant sub-tenants whose principal source of income derived from working for others).[42]

A corollary of the failure to locate class differentiation and exploitation on the non-demesne sector of the estate system in the province is that it now becomes possible for Blanco to proclaim the existence in this context of a *material* basis for a political 'united front' incorporating all the peasantry.[43] Proof of this consists of his assertion that a decline in the amount of labour-rent tenants owed the landlord necessarily entailed a corresponding reduction in the workload of sub-tenants. Such a view overlooks the fact that, because of its labour-intensive nature, capitalist expansion on the non-demense sector of the estate system of La Convención depended on increasing the input of labour-power, the conflict between landlord and tenants having been as much over the control of this resource as about land.[44]

Accordingly, the principal beneficiary of the anti-landlord struggle where this concerned a reduction in the rent for tenant leases (and a corresponding diminution in or cancellation of labour-rent payable on the demesne) was the rich peasant, a gain not passed onto the poor peasant sub-tenant either as a reduced workload or a decrease in the length of the working day. In fact, much rather the opposite, since labour-power saved in this manner was – in the context of labour scarce yet labour-intensive non-demense production – redeployed onto the non-demesne holdings of the tenant.[45]

The conceptually coherent idealization by Blanco of the peasantry as an undifferentiated socio-economic category was undermined by subsequent events. Unlike tenants, sub-tenants received no titles to their non-demesne holdings in the agrarian reform of March 1963; accordingly, the 1963–4 period was characterized by acute struggle within the peasantry of La Convención as capitalist ex-tenants sought to repossess the land they had previously leased to sub-tenants.[46] The observations by Blanco on these and succeeding developments are instructive. He notes:

> The bourgeoisification of the better-off tenants has come about as a consequence of their abandoning the unions . . . [s]ome people have allowed themselves to be deceived, especially wealthy ex-tenant farmers. The scheme of the exploiters is to ally with them to crush poor peasants and the agricultural labourers, and they think that after crushing us it will be easy to show the door to the wealthy ex-tenant farmers, whom they have deluded. Those comrades must understand that if they help smash the peasants and their federation, the government's sweet reasonableness toward them will not last very long, for the exploiters will seize their land and there will be no one to defend them. Perhaps we do not remember that there has never been justice for peasants?[47]

He continues:

> There are many comrade tenants who fought against exploitation and who now wish to become exploiters. They even use the same words as the landlords used to use against them. These comrades do not understand reality, they believe that La Convención is an island, that it has nothing to do with the rest of the world, that things are not going to change there, that they are always going to remain in their present state . . . [t]here is no middle way [for rich ex-tenants], there are only two roads. Either they join the side of the workers, all the workers including agricultural labourers; or they join the side of the exploiters with the knowledge that afterwards the latter will crush them when they are no longer needed.[48]

These quotes reflect clearly the viewpoint of Blanco at a later conjuncture (July 1970), when the events of the intervening period had established concretely that the 'dual power' structure which developed in La Convención during 1962 signalled a transition not to socialism but to capitalism, and as such afforded him the opportunity of recognizing the reality of this process: the non-socialist direction of the peasant movement in general, and in particular the role in this of rich peasants. As the following four points confirm, however, Blanco's original perspective has not changed, and the principal component of his politico-ideological framework – peasant essentialism – remains intact.

First is the view that better-off tenants have been transformed into capitalist peasants as a result of abandoning peasant unions, a causal inversion whereby the economic is displaced by politico-ideological determination. Much rather it was because they were already part of a new rural bourgeoisie that rich peasants abandoned unions, and not the other way round. Second, one notes the proposition that wealthy ex-tenants who 'do not understand reality' have been deceived by 'exploiters' who, after having destroyed poor peasants and wage labourers with the aid of the former, will then turn on these same wealthy ex-tenants and 'seize their land'. Again, this posits a peasant essentialism from which capitalist ex-tenants are held to have deviated as a result of 'deception' practised by non-peasant exploiters, a position which fails to recognize not only that rich peasants are themselves exploiters of poor peasants and/or migrant workers but also that these agrarian capitalists are in fact part of the same exploiting class which Blanco places in opposition to his concept of peasant essentialism.

Third is the notion that although rich peasant 'comrades' are now considering whether or not to join the camp of the 'exploiters', they have not in the past belonged to and indeed do not yet form part of this camp. This is a position which similarly locates capitalist ex-tenants within an homogeneous peasant mass opposed to and distinct from the exploiters who are not themselves peasants. Fourth and last is the idea that in the process of struggle it is necessary for rich ex-tenants to choose between the 'side of the workers' and 'the side of the exploiters'. This combines peasant essentialism with a non-materialist voluntarism, in which the political position of its subjects is determined not by class interest but by personal preference.

Despite recognizing the extent of the divergence which existed between on the one hand the peasant movement as he viewed it in the 1958–62 period, and on the other the fact that its dominant stratum was by the 1970s following a separate path, Blanco nevertheless continued to misrecognize the cause. This was due in turn to the populist nature of his framework, structured as it was by the agrarian myth and peasant essentialism.[49] The 'false' direction followed by rich peasants was therefore attributed by Blanco to an *absence of 'peasant' consciousness* rather than its actual determinant: *a manifestation of class consciousness* on the part of this new rural bourgeoisie.

III

It might be objected that the example of La Convención during the early 1960s is unique, and that other peasant movements in Latin America have not embraced populism or the agrarian myth as a mobilizing ideology. As two instances from the subsequent decades – ANUC in Colombia and Sendero Luminoso in Peru – demonstrate, the deployment by rich peasants of a populist discourse beneath the veneer of Marxism is far from uncommon. Where Maoism is concerned, however, its deployment in this manner presents fewer surprises than the Trotskyism of Hugo Blanco.

In contrast to Trotskyism, therefore, Maoism not only allocates an important revolutionary role to the peasantry, in the form of a peasant/worker alliance as distinct from a worker/peasant alliance, but also locates the principal socio-economic contradiction between on the one hand (external) monopoly capital and (internally) a semi-feudal landlord class, and on the other a united front composed of the progressive national bourgeoisie plus a non-capitalist peasantry.[50] However, the Maoism of Sendero Luminoso – just like the Trotskyism of Hugo Blanco – turns out to be nothing other than a variant of populism structured by the discourse of the agrarian myth.

2.8 ANUC and Populism in Colombia

The rise and fall of the peasant movement in Colombia over a period of two decades, a process which began with the formation of the National Peasant

Association (*Asociación Nacional de Usuarios Campesinos* or ANUC) in 1967, reached a peak with the land invasions of 1971, and ended in the late 1970s when the struggle for land ceased. Because it did not result in a substantial 'repeasantization', this movement is regarded by Zamosc – its principal chronicler – as a failure.[51] Although in the course of this struggle and the subsequent agrarian reform some 66,000 families had obtained land by the end of the 1970s, a greater number had in fact become landless during the two previous decades.[52] The mobilizing ideology of ANUC was influenced by both Trotskyism (in the form of the Socialist Bloc) and Maoism (the Marxist-Leninist Communist Party or PCML); the political strategy of the more influential PCML was aimed at securing a 'popular democratic revolution on the road to socialism', an objective to be realized by the peasantry.[53]

Like that of Hugo Blanco in the case of La Convención, Zamosc's analysis of ANUC is structured by an idealized view of the peasantry, which in turn leads to a misrecognition of the reasons for the agrarian struggles he describes. Apart from a few token footnote references, no attempt is made to address the existing literature on and debate about capitalist development, rural socio-economic differentiation, and the peasant economy.[54] Instead of differentiating the peasantry in terms of class, Zamosc follows Shanin – whose enthusiastic endorsement precedes the main text – and adopts a neo-populist framework in which not only is the peasantry itself recast in terms of 'class' but the self-sufficient peasant family farm is regarded as a non-capitalist alternative form of development.[55] That such a theoretical framework is impossible to sustain rapidly becomes apparent, since Zamosc's view of peasants as a class soon begins to co-exist uneasily with references to the presence of rich, middle, and poor peasants.[56] Subsequently he admits that the existence of a socio-economically differentiated peasantry undermined the peasant movement, and concludes by noting that the demise of ANUC was due largely to this factor.[57]

Although his argument is based on the Chayanovian concept of the independent peasant family farm, Zamosc actually tells us little about its internal socio-economic structure, organization, and dynamic. For example, he omits to provide data on crucial points such as changing household composition, the kinds and amounts of labour employed (personal, family, hired), cropping patterns and per hectare yields, and whether or not such units generated production surpluses. Instead, the defining criterion is land, a methodological procedure which, when coupled with the unproblematic adoption of census land-holding categories, involves Zamosc following 'the accepted convention that ... considers units smaller than twenty hectares to be peasant units'.[58] That the economic interests of those at the top of this category might not be the same as those at the bottom is a question Zamosc never poses. According to the 1960 agricultural census, cultivators owning under twenty hectares accounted for 61 per cent of total output and, more significantly, for half the output of coffee, the principal cash-crop exported by Colombia.[59] This undifferentiated land-holding category would therefore have included not only poor peasants, whose main income derived from the sale of their labour-power, but also small agrarian capitalists producing coffee for the international market.[60]

The theoretical contradictions inherent in Zamosc's neo-populist teleology reproduce those of Hugo Blanco (see above), and are perhaps nowhere more evident than in his assessment of the agrarian reform that followed the peasant movement. Trapped by his essentialist concept of a peasant 'class' composed of family farmers whose main objective and defining characteristic is landownership for subsistence cultivation, it is necessary for Zamosc to depict the peasant movement in Colombia during the 1970s as an attempt to realize this goal by establishing a 'peasant economy'.[61] Thus the failure of the co-operative institutional structure (*empresas comunitarias*) set up by the Colombian agrarian reform agency INCORA after the land struggles is attributed principally to the external agency of 'adverse state policy', despite acknowledgement that 'an individual economy of small entrepreneurs and affluent peasants' operated inside the co-operatives.[62] However, Zamosc – like Hugo Blanco – regards the existence of the latter subjects not as evidence of capitalist development in Colombian agriculture but much rather as an indication of 'distorting repeasantization' and 'a failure of the peasant economy'.[63] Symptomatically, he blames such deviations from the path of peasant essentialism on the decline of a (non-existent) peasant 'class solidarity'.[64]

Like many of the new social movements theorists who write about the peasantry (see Chapter 4), Zamosc also makes explicit the political practice consequent on his analysis. Notwithstanding the inescapable weight of evidence against his essentialist view of the peasantry, therefore, Zamosc continues to argue against the 'indiscriminate use of such notions as "emergent peasant bourgeoisie"', and insists on reaffirming his neo-populist vision that 'the first task of a sensible opposition [in Colombian politics] is to restore the spirit of autonomy among the peasants'.[65]

2.9 Sendero Luminoso, Maoism and the Agrarian Myth

Much the same kinds of difficulty confront the attempt by McClintock to theorize the support received by the Sendero Luminoso guerrillas in rural Peru throughout the 1980s in terms of a combined 'moral economy', 'middle peasant', and new social movements framework.[66] Invoking both Scott and Wolf to sustain her argument, McClintock claims that economic decline, population growth, and ecological crisis in locationally remote Ayacucho have all resulted in a threat to the subsistence of 'smallholders . . . relatively unintegrated into the capitalist market' from among whom Sendero consequently draws its support.[67] Although not categorized as such, these smallholding proprietors are clearly regarded as middle peasants, a point which McClintock confirms in another text.[68] Since peasant proprietors remain socio-economically undifferentiated, are all regarded as uniformly impoverished and downtrodden, and undertake action merely to defend the *status quo*, little or no attempt is made to account for the changing socio-economic composition of Senderista support in rural areas and to link this in turn to the *class*-specific acceptability of Sendero's ideology.[69]

The problematic nature of McClintock's populist analytical framework emerges clearly when she attempts to explain the changed socio-economic composition of Senderista backing in the Peruvian countryside. With the exception of one particular location, the Upper Huallaga valley in the department of Huánuco, rural support for Sendero in the Andean region declined over the 1983–86 period. McClintock is clearly baffled by this development, and observes that – unlike the impoverished Ayacucho area – there was no reason why the Senderistas should either seek or hope to find support among the better-off peasants cultivating coca in the Upper Huallaga Valley.[70]

Since most of the texts dealing with the cocaine economy tend to focus only on the large amounts of money generated in the course of and as the rewards linked to the high-risk marketing/distribution from Colombia of the already processed drug, little reference is made to the profitability of the first stage in its production, the cultivation in Peru (and elsewhere) of the coca crop itself. From the viewpoint of cocaine production in the Andean region, the highest-yielding coca leaves are to be found in the Upper Huallaga Valley, where during the mid-1980s a peasant producer might expect to gross on average an astonishing US$12,600 per hectare of coca cultivated.[71] In contrast to McClintock's 'moral economy' and new social movements argument, therefore, it is clear that in the Upper Huallaga valley rural support for Sendero no longer corresponded to a stuggle by uniformly impoverished middle peasants belonging to the same ethnic group in defence of a threatened subsistence base but much rather involved rich peasant colonists who grew and benefited substantially from the coca crop.[72]

This shift in the socio-economic composition of Senderista backing raises the additional issue of precisely why the same politico-ideological position is apparently acceptable to such different agrarian class subjects. In short, the question concerns the seeming incompatibility between the Maoism of Sendero and the class interests of coca-growing rich peasants in the Upper Huallaga valley. Two opposed views exist regarding the political and ideological position of Sendero. One maintains that what is important about Sendero's rural appeal is not so much its Maoism as Andean messianism, the latter invoking a mythical Incaic past where the traditional Pre-Conquest cultural values of the Quechua population will once again dominate.[73] The other, which includes new social movements theorists such as McClintock and Gianotten *et al.*, rejects the claim that Sendero is attempting to recreate an archaic cultural tradition. In support of this view, McClintock points out that '[w]ords such as "feudalism", "bourgeoisie", "imperialism" are common, whereas references to the Incan past, indigenous customs, and popular anecdotes are non-existent'.[74] Similarly, Gianotten *et al.* argue that: first, because the Andean peasantry in now integrated into the market, Sendero is faced with the impossibility of reconstituting the self-sufficient rural community; and second, Sendero has anyway attempted to break the existing political and economic structures of the Andean peasant community by replacing communal authorities with its own militants.[75]

In so far as they are mutually-exclusive, however, neither of these positions is wholly correct; much rather, the ideology of Sendero ought to be perceived as a *synthesis* of Maoism and Andean messianism. Thus, the objection made by Gianotten *et al.* regarding the impossibility of reconstituting the eroded material base of peasant economy together with the Andean rural community overlooks the extent to which it is possible for Sendero to obtain support as a result of an *ideology* based on the desire to recuperate this materially impossible objective. Furthermore, it is significant that Sendero does not challenge the concept and structure of 'community' *per se*, but – like the 'dual power' of Hugo Blanco in La Convención two decades earlier – merely replaces its personnel.

Neither view considers the degree to which and the reasons why Sendero Luminoso's Maoism is compatible with the more important politico-ideological components of Andean traditional beliefs, either by reproducing the latter directly or merely by not challenging them. Thus the anti-urbanism, anti-imperialism, ethnic chauvinism and peasant essentialism (*campesinismo*) of Sendero not only possess strong affinities with the politico-ideological form and content of indigenous Andean beliefs such as the town/country opposition, nationalism and ethnic chauvinism, but also reproduces the central tenet of neo-populism, 'urban bias'.[76] In short, it contributes to and reinforces the mythical existence of a middle peasantry while at the same time permitting a rich peasant stratum to operate.[77]

One important consequence of classifying the Peruvian social formation as 'semi-feudal', therefore, is that the principal contradiction is located not between capital and labour but between on the one hand an external imperialism coupled with its internal ally, the 'feudal' landlord class, and on the other an anti-imperialist alliance composed of peasants, workers, and a 'progressive' bourgeoisie, in which the peasantry constitute the dominant element. Not only are Maoism, populism and nationalism interchangeable in this discourse, but its specifically Maoist component also allocates the main role in the defence of the nation against 'outsiders' to an undifferentiated peasantry. Thus in politico-ideological terms 'the nation' (= 'the people', 'the popular masses') is equated largely with the peasantry as a whole, while 'outsiders' – or non-peasants – of whatever kind (= urban dwellers, technocrats, bureaucrats, foreigners) are unproblematically associated with 'imperialism' (peasants: outsiders :: nation: imperialism).

From the viewpoint of prosperous coca growing peasants in the Upper Huallaga valley, therefore, the politico-ideological acceptability of Senderista Maoism/messianism lies precisely in the fact that, when combined with the historical image of coca as a 'traditional' crop associated with subsistence/ survival and the Incaic past, an outside enemy permits rich peasants to exter-nalize capitalist exploitation, and thus to deflect/supress any reference to the occurrence of socio-economic differentiation and surplus appropriation within the peasantry itself. Accordingly, when linked with anti-urbanism, ethnic chauvinism and peasant essentialism in this manner, the anti-imperialism of Sendero Luminoso reinforces not politically progressive internationalist/ socialist concerns but a more narrow and reactionary set of nationalist/ conservative beliefs that is compatible with and indeed reflects the *class* position of rich peasants.

Like other texts on Sendero, that by McClintock emphasizes the discon-tinuity between the rural guerrilla movements of the 1960s, and those of the 1980s, pointing to the absolute failure of the former when compared with the relative success of the latter.[78] By contrast, it is argued here that, in at least one important respect, significant continuities do exist between these two periods: as has been argued above with regard to Hugo Blanco in La Convención, there are instances of peasant movements during the 1960s that were a success for rich peasant subjects, and similarly not despite but much rather because of a seemingly radical ideology. It is tempting to speculate in passing that, just as the Latin American guerrilla movements of the 1960s were linked to the profitability of the coffee crop, so those of the 1980s in Peru and Colombia may be linked similarly to the profitability of the coca grown for cocaine pro-duction.[79]

2.10 Conclusion

Although there are obvious differences between the three peasant movements considered here, on a number of crucial issues the similarities are striking. Thus the FIR in La Convención during the early 1960s, ANUC in Colombia during the 1970s, and Sendero in Peru during the 1980s all possess a number

of shared economic and political characteristics. Common to each mobilization was a strongly differentiated peasantry, the better-off elements of which
were engaged in cash-crop production for the international market (coffee,
coca). These rich peasants not only led their respective movements but – in the
case of La Convención and Colombia – also became the beneficiaries of the
subsequent agrarian reform programmes. In terms of the mobilizing discourse,
the similarities are equally striking. Despite an ostensibly Marxist orientation
and politics (Trotskyism in the case of FIR, Trotskyism and Maoism in the
case of ANUC, and Maoism in the case of Sendero), therefore, the mobilizing
discourse of all three Latin American peasant movements exhibited a strong
affinity with populism and the agrarian myth.

Combining anti-imperialism and an hostility to urban values with a non-
class specific notion of the grassroots ('nation', 'people', 'masses'), the FIR,
Sendero and ANUC not only subscribed to an idealized view of village 'community' based on enduring rural traditions/values/practices but also sought to
recuperate idealized visions of an Andean peasant economy. Where better-off
elements are in the forefront of rural mobilization, therefore, apparently radical socialist idioms may in fact be compatible with (and serve to disguise) the
more conservative meanings inherent in peasant essentialism and the agrarian
myth, which either support or do not challenge the politico-ideological objectives and economic interests of rich peasants. The contextually specific
reasons for this emerged most clearly in the case of FIR, and the apparently
paradoxical acceptability of Hugo Blanco's 'Trotskyism' to the rich peasantry
of La Convención during the early 1960s.

Class struggle in La Convención at that conjuncture was characterized by a
challenge from rich peasant tenants to the power of the landlord, a process
which involved both the formation of peasant unions and a simultaneous
conflict over the politico-ideological meanings of those basic institutional
forms on the estate system that were supportive of landlord power (labour-
service, the fiesta system, non-demesne property rights). Over the same
period, however, differentiation within the peasantry resulted in the development of a similar politico-ideological struggle between its opposed class
elements: the capitalist ex-tenants owning non-demesne means of production,
and poor peasant sub-tenants possessing non-demense means of production.
Until the peasant movement, the landlord projected and sought to obtain
acceptability for his own class-specific version of intra-estate 'community', a
view which supressed or defused any reference to the unequal exchanges
occurring within his property. In the course of the struggle that culminated in
'dual power', it was similarly necessary for rich tenants not only to challenge
and reject the politico-ideological acceptability of the landlords' version of
'community' but also to construct their own class-specific replacement. It

was in these circumstances that the 'Trotskyism' of Hugo Blanco assumes significance.

Although certain components of a common discourse which until the early 1960s signalled and permitted the politico-ideological dominance exercised by the landlord class were challenged and superceded by opposed meanings, these same discursive elements nevertheless subsequently reappeared in the same form but with a different content.Thus the supercession of politico-ideological components at one axis of the struggle (between landlord and tenant on the demesne, where the meanings of the former were displaced by those of the latter, emphasizing the coercive/extractive nature of institutions such as labour-rent and fiesta sponsorship, the meanings of which change in the course of conflict while the content remains the same) did not prevent the continuation of some of these same components at the other axis of struggle (between capitalist peasants and subordinate petty commodity producing and/or landless labouring elements on the non-demesne, where the meanings of the former emphasize a supra-class notion of equality in an attempt to defuse the coercive/extractive/exploitative nature of labour-service and/or debt bondage relations linking non-demesne subjects, a process whereby the politico-ideological forms remained the same while the economic content changed).

Hence the existence of an interlocking and mutually supportive series of political representations framing discourse on the demesne ('community', 'mutual aid') were vacated in an ideological sense by the landlord class, only to be annexed in turn by the victorious rich tenants, and fused with an analogous discourse about the non-demesne (absence of capitalism, 'homogeneous peasantry', 'united front', 'peasant democracy'). The presence of contradictory meanings at either end of this axis of struggle notwithstanding, the exceptional nature of the conjuncture ('dual power') momentarily conferred legitimacy on *both* discourses (anti-landlordism, peasant essentialism). In this process of producing class-specific knowledge, therefore, Hugo Blanco (at this conjuncture the ideological representative of the new rural bourgeoisie) discharged a pivotal role: the insecurity implicit in these contradictory meanings (which threatened the acceptance by poor peasants of the class-specific discourse of the new rural bourgeoisie) was countered by the radical 'Trotskyism' of Blanco himself, through which the form and object of the struggle was recast and closed off.

Against those who maintain not only that the peasant movement in La Convención failed but also that failure was in some way linked to Hugo Blanco's Trotskyism, it is argued here that largely because his ideology was *not* Trotskyist the movement was for its rich peasant leadership a success. In short, Blanco's Trotskyism enabled capitalist peasants simultaneously engaged in a twofold class struggle (against middle and poor peasant tenants and sub-tenants, as well as landlords) to operate successfully on two fronts. By supressing reference to the non-demesne socio-economic differentiation arising from capitalist development, it permitted them to challenge the landlord class from within an (heterogeneous) anti-landlord front; and by expropriating the landlord class in the course of establishing 'dual power', it simultaneously enabled them to reinforce and (temporarily) reproduce potent images of egalitarianism in a discourse shared with the subordinate elements of the anti-landlord front. As will be seen in the following chapter, many of these points also apply in the case of peasant and farmer movements occurring in India throughout the twentieth century.

NOTES

1. As will be seen in Chapter 3, the Latin American case studies presented here have similar parallels elsewhere.
2. This is the view of Hobsbawm [1969a: 31]. For other accounts of the peasant movement in La Convención, see Quijano [1967], Craig [1967; 1969: 274–96], Hobsbawm [1967], Villanueva [1967], Pumaruna [1968], Neira [1968], Huizer [1970a: 142–55; 1973: 73–83], Gott [1970: 237–47], Béjar [1970], Blanco [1972], Fioravanti [1974], Alfaro and Ore [n.d.], and Aranda and Escalante [1978: 63ff.].
3. The reasons for this are outlined in Chapter 1. Referring to the conditions which permit an alliance between the proletariat and the peasantry, Trotsky [1936: 139] warned: 'The ally [= the peasantry] must first be educated. This can be achieved, on the one hand, by paying great attention to all its progressive and historical needs, and, on the other hand, by displaying an organized distrust towards the ally, and fighting tirelessly and relentlessly against its every anti-proletarian tendency and custom.' Not only would the position of the peasantry in such an alliance always be secondary to that of the workers, therefore, but the alliance itself was premissed on a willingness of the former to adopt a politically progressive outlook and abandon those customs/traditions which were incompatible with the development of a working class consciousness. In short, a worker/peasant alliance was possible only where/when the peasantry discarded the agrarian myth as a mobilizing ideology.
4. Born in Paruro in the Department of Cusco in 1935 to a bourgeois family, Hugo Blanco Galdós received a secondary education at the College of Sciences in Cusco, and in 1956 joined the Revolutionary Workers' Party attached to the Peruvian section of the Fourth International. Blanco was arrested in 1958 for taking part in a workers' strike. While in jail, he encountered peasant leaders from La Convención who had been committed to prison by Alfredo Romainville, landlord of Chaupimayo, for having organized a union branch there. On his release, Blanco travelled to the province and became a sub-tenant in Chaupimayo, where he devoted himself to the tasks of politicization, and organizing peasant unions in other estates. During the 1958–63 period, Blanco's name became synonymous with anti-landlord agitation, both within La Convención itself and throughout the southern sierra of Peru [*Fioravanti*, 1974: 192–5]. In emphasizing the importance

of Hugo Blanco, this chapter adheres to the notion that the role of leadership in a peasant movement is not so much to *impose* a political viewpoint as to *express* it. It is for this reason that the ideas of Hugo Blanco merit attention, and the focus here will be on the class-specific acceptability of his politico-ideological utterances. By contrast, other texts concerned with the peasant movement in La Convención during 1958–63 tend to overemphasize the significance of his *person*, the charismatic nature of which is regarded as either the sole or the all-important determinant of the class struggle that took place in this period [for example, *Craig*, 1967, 1969; *Neira*, 1968; *Huizer*, 1970b: 398; 1973: 120ff.]. Blanco himself is rightly critical of the voluntaristic element in this approach, and observes [*Blanco*, 1972: 88]: 'The bourgeoisie, like the exploiting classes of the past, fosters a belief in redeemers. Basically this belief is similar to religious alienation; it is another opiate of the people . . . [the] bourgeoisie will even exalt authentic revolutionaries, even though it may be through insults and slanders. They are eager to extol the individual at the expense of the masses. As long as the masses believe in a redeemer, no matter how revolutionary he may be, the bourgeoisie feels relatively secure. This redeemer can be bought off, jailed or killed; they cannot do this to the masses.'

5. Unlike Debray [1967: 36ff.; 1973: 137–40], who in the course of a critique of Blanco dismisses Trotskyism (Blanco = Trotskyist), it will be argued below that the politico-ideological position elaborated by Blanco with regard to the class struggle has nothing in common with the views of Trotsky on the same question (Blanco ≠ Trotskyist). Given the extent and nature of the divergence between Blanco and Trotsky, it is surprising that texts addressed specifically to the peasant movement in La Convención either accept (uncritically) Blanco's claim to Trotsky as a theoretico-political precursor [e.g., *Craig*, 1967: 42; *Huizer*, 1970a: 183; *Aranda and Escalante*, 1978: 82–3, 115–19] or else, recognizing this divergence, nevertheless fail to pursue its political implications with regard to the form and direction of the class struggle in the province [e.g., *Villanueva*, 1967: 103; *Béjar*, 1970: 48].

6. For labour-rent in La Convención, see Cuadros [1949], Tupayachi [1959], CIDA [1966: 206ff.], Craig [1967], and Hobsbawm [1969a].

7. For the duration of non-demesne leases, see Cuadros [1949: 80ff., 90–91] and Fioravanti [1974: 81ff., 150ff.].

8. Coffee was ecologically more adaptable to cultivation on tenant holdings than on the landlord demesne. During the period 1945–54 the price index for this crop increased from 100 to 1,221 [*Craig*, 1969: 283], and over the years 1940–50 the index for coffee output in the province went from 100 to 187 [*Fioravanti*, 1974: 94, Table 18].

9. Legislation abolishing the right of a landlord to evict tenants from non-demesne holdings on his estate in La Convención was promulgated by the Prado government in April 1962.

10. For these data, see Fioravanti [1974: 181]. The subsequent decline in peasant unions in La Convención is demonstrated by the fact that the number of active union branches decreased from the 1962 peak of around 120 to only 25 a decade later. The percentage increase in the number of inactive peasant union branches over the 1969–74 period is shown in the following table:

Year	Inactive Union Branches
	%
1969	58
1970–72	50
1973–74	79

Note: The term 'inactive' refers to affiliated union branches whose delegates fail to attend Federation meetings.

Source: Compiled from data in Alfaro and Ore [n.d.: 59, 92].

11. Craig [1967: 38–9] and perhaps more surprisingly Hobsbawm [1969a: 45] and Béjar [1970: 37] report the existence of a strong evangelical influence among the peasant union leaders in La Convención. The former observes that 'interviews with several of these men revealed that each of them had seen in the labor movement an opportunity of bringing about the objectives of "social justice" which they claimed to have derived from the Scriptures. As one leader succinctly put it: "The Bible says that the meek shall inherit the earth, and we are the meek".' This claim is rejected by Fioravanti [1974: 180–81, Table 22] who, on the basis of interviews conducted with leaders of eleven peasant union branches in the province, found that 92 per cent were Roman Catholics and only six per cent followers of evangelical sects.

12. Fioravanti [1974: 91, 180]. As the latter points out [1974: 178, note 72], the fact that – with the single exception of Hugo Blanco, who arrived in the valley at the end of 1958 – all the union leadership consisted of tenants and sub-tenants resident in the province since the 1940s contradicts the assertion by Quijano [1965] and Singelmann [1981: 144, 176] that peasant unions were organized by 'outsiders'.

13. The concept 'politico-ideological tendency' is used here instead of the term 'political party' since the former refers more accurately to the presence of a combination of a specific political programme (content) and tactics (methods) where formal party status and/or apparatus may either be minimal or non-existent. Thus, although both the APRA and the PCP recruited and operated in La Convención on the basis of national and local party organizations, this was not the case with the FIR. Indeed, in the latter case Hugo Blanco (incorrectly) attributes subsequent failure as regards peasant mobilization to the absence of a strong and formally constituted party apparatus [*Blanco*, 1972: 36ff.; *Fioravanti*, 1974: 199–200].

14. For the role of the PCP in the implantation of peasant unions in La Convención, see Neira [1968: 73], Craig [1969: 286–7], Blanco [1972: 20–21, 50, 85–6], Fioravanti [1974: 146–9], Alfaro and Ore [n.d.: 6], and Aranda and Escalante [1978: 67ff.]. For the areas of Firista influence, see Blanco [1972: 37–8], Fioravanti [1974: 205] and Alfaro and Ore [n.d.: 14]. For information on Aprista peasant unions in the province, see Fioravanti [1974: 156ff.] and Aranda and Escalante [1978: 78ff.,109]. The extent to which political discourse in La Convención continued to be rooted in the events of 1958–62 long after these had passed is illustrated by the utterance of an ex-tenant, now a rich peasant, who in 1974 identified his own political affiliation as 'a communist of Nikita Khrushchev's type' (*soy comunista tipo Nikita Kruschev*). The peasant movement in La Convención took place when Khrushchev was First Secretary of the CPSU and Premier of the USSR, and his name would have been invoked by the PCP in the course of politicization/unionization carried out among estate tenants in the province.

15. Tenants and sub-tenants are categorized as belonging to the rich, middle or poor peasant stratum on the basis of the quantity of non-demesne land possessed. The latter was a significant element in differentiating the peasantry because of its crucial role in the production of coffee, the most profitable cash-crop grown in the province. Although coffee was best suited to cultivation on the fertile, well-drained soils of the peasant holdings situated on the hillsides of the estates, the topography of such areas prevented mechanization. Increases in coffee output were therefore obtained by expanding the area under cultivation (and hiring in more workers). Accordingly, the area of non-demesne holdings available for current and future coffee production became an important factor in the non-demesne accumulation process and levels of profitability on the peasant enterprise. Rich peasants operated in excess of ten non-demesne hectares, and constituted the economically dominant element among the tenants; they not only possessed the most extensive holdings but also disposed of the largest quantity of uncultivated land on which to expand coffee production. Middle peasants held between five and ten hectares of non-demesne land, and although possessing less extensive holdings than rich peasants they were nevertheless capable of sustained and substantial accumulation in good harvest years. Poor peasants had less than five hectares of land, and virtually no reserves for future expansion. In one particular estate, for example, the average rich peasant landholding amounted to 15 hectares, that for middle peasants to seven hectares, and that of poor peasants to just over two hectares. There were no sub-tenants among the ranks of the rich peasants, while the middle peasantry consisted of sixty per cent tenants and 17 per cent sub-tenants. By contrast, only a quarter of poor peasants were tenants, and nearly seventy per cent of them sub-tenants; the economically inadequate nature of their landholdings was recognized in the official designation of those ex-sub-tenants with access to insufficient means of production as *deficitarios*.

16. Examples of deaths resulting from police action in La Convención during 1962 include 43 peasants massacred at Chaullay, two killed in the estate of Echarate and one in the estate of Pujiura [*Espinosa and Malpica*, 1970: 230–3; *Villanueva*, 1967: 63–5, 149].

17. See Neira [1968: 92] and Blanco [1972: 50–52]. During the early stages of the strike action, this form of anti-landlord struggle was opposed by both the PCP and APRA on the grounds that it constituted a provocation which would result in further repression by the state.

18. Sources for the land invasions in La Convención include Villanueva [1967: 125–7], Neira [1968: 101ff.], Blanco [1972: 61, 71], Fioravanti [1974: 166–7, 201–2, 205–6], Alfaro and Ore [n.d.: 12, 15], and Aranda and Escalante [1978: 83, 85ff.]. The slogan 'Land or Death' originated with the peasant movement of La Convención, and was subsequently taken up by other peasant unions engaged in land seizures throughout southern Peru. Its antecedents were two other slogans with similarly revolutionary associations: hence 'Land or Death' combined 'Land and Freedom' (*tierra y libertad*) used by Zapata during the 1911 Mexican revolution and 'Fatherland or Death' (*patria o muerte*) employed by Castro during the 1959 Cuban revolution.

19. For information on the nature of the 'dual power' structure in La Convención during 1962, see Villanueva [1967: 135–9], Neira [1968: 94], Blanco [1972: 53–6], Fioravanti [1974: 195–8, 216], Alfaro and Ore [n.d.: 12ff.], and Aranda and Escalante [1978: 82ff., 118–20].

20. For infrastructural improvements/extension during the period of dual power, see Blanco [1972: 59], Fioravanti [1974: 213], and Alfaro and Ore [n.d.: 11].
21. For the peasants' agrarian reform decree, see Villanueva [1967: 127–9], Blanco [1972: 58–9], and Fioravanti [1974: 208–11].
22. Rich tenants were regarded by Blanco as the most progressive component of the peasant movement, since subjects from this stratum were most active in the struggle against the landlord class [*Alfaro and Ore*, n.d.: 17–18]. Indeed, he points out with evident approval that 'a number of such farmers were members of the guerrilla band' [*Blanco*, 1972: 73]; that is, the most steadfast political support for Blanco and the FIR derived from rich peasants. This support continued into the post-reform era: during the mid-1970s, rich ex-tenants on one agrarian co-operative in the province continued to project strongly the view of Blanco-as-revolutionary, in a number of significant ways. These instances, all of which circulated at the grassroots level, and thus operated within the domain of 'popular culture', included stories recounted about him, songs composed/sung about him, and photographs of him displayed prominently in non-demesne dwellings. The iconic symbolism of this discourse is not difficult to discern. The object was to deflect criticism of and thus secure acceptance for the existing tenure structure (which left intact the holdings of rich peasants), not just by reference to its radical inception ('this is what we all fought for against the landlords') but also by emphasizing simultaneously the fact that revolution was now in the *past*. That is, accomplished and thus precluding the necessity for further land reform.
23. For the conflict inside the Federation during 1961–62, see Craig [1967: 42–4], Blanco [1972: 22, 65ff.], and Fioravanti [1974: 206–8].
24. One long-term legacy of the peasant movement and the guerrilla operations of the 1960s has been that La Convención continued to be regarded by the Peruvian state as a politically-sensitive area: a large police contingent was permanently based in the provincial capital, Quillabamba. In the course of carrying out fieldwork there during 1974–75, I was arrested for talking to peasant union leaders, imprisoned, tried in front of a military tribunal, and subsequently expelled from Peru (about which see Brass [1982]).
25. After a confrontation with the police, in which one of the latter was killed, Blanco together with 28 of his comrades was put on trial in Tacna and sentenced to 25 years' imprisonment. Released in the amnesty of 1970, he was exiled to Mexico the following year. Blanco returned to Peru in July 1978 for the Constituent Assembly elections, and secured a large personal vote in Lima where he stood as a candidate for the left-coalition Worker, Peasant, Student Popular Front (*Frente Obrero, Campesino, Estudiantil y Popular* or FOCEP). During the late 1980s he became a member of PUM (*Partido Unificado Mariateguista*), the largest Marxist party in Peru, and switched the focus of his political activity to the southern province of Puno [*Taylor*, 1983: 20–21].
26. For details about the government land reform decrees of the early 1960s, see CIDA [1966: 216, 398–9], Craig [1967: 45], Neira [1968: 95], Fioravanti [1974: 214], and Alfaro and Ore [n.d.: 74ff.]. Even the notoriously anti-socialist Peruvian military, in the form of high-ranking army personnel sent to supress the peasant movement in La Convención, argued for an agrarian reform programme [*Stepan*, 1978: 137ff.], understanding perhaps better than Hugo Blanco that once the better-off tenants already engaged in capitalist accumulation became individual proprietors they would not merely cease to support the FIR but actually oppose any further

attempts to socialize the means of production through the redistribution of private land.

27. See Trotsky [1934: 223–32] for the theorization of 'dual power'.

28. See Trotsky [1962: 154, original emphasis]. On the the link between the necessity for the proletariat to effect 'deep inroads into the rights of bourgeois property' and permanent revolution, Trotsky [1962: 235] notes: 'The programme of the equal distribution of the land thus presupposes the expropriation of all land, not only privately-owned land in general, or privately-owned peasant land, but even communal land. If we bear in mind that this expropriation would have to be one of the first acts of the new regime, while commodity–capitalist relations were still completely dominant, then we shall see that the first "victims" of this expropriation would be (or rather, would feel themselves to be) the peasantry. If we bear in mind that the peasant, during several decades, has paid the redemption money which should have converted the allotted land into his own private property: if we bear in mind that some of the more well-to-do of the peasants have acquired – undoubtedly by making considerable sacrifices, borne by a still-existing generation – large tracts of land as private property, then it will be easily imagined what a tremendous resistance would be aroused by the attempt to convert communal and small-scale privately-owned lands into state property. If it acted in such a fashion the new regime would begin by arousing a tremendous opposition against itself among the peasantry.' This warning against the counter-revolutionary potential of a rich peasantry, and consequently the need for permanent revolution, might have been written with La Convención in mind. For a useful discussion of the importance and political significance of the concept 'permanent revolution' in the theory of Trotsky, see Deutscher [1954: 145ff.].

29. On these points, compare Trotsky [1934: 231] with Blanco [1972: 57].

30. See Trotsky [1934: 225, 228, 231].

31. Trotsky [1934: 230].

32. Blanco [1972: 57–8].

33. As will be seen below, the idealised notion of an undifferentiated peasant 'community' was still being used in Peru during the 1980s, but now by the Maoist Sendero Luminoso movement.

34. Because tenants and sub-tenants were themselves originally immigrants from smallholding communities in the Peruvian highlands, many institutional forms from the latter context (such as the fiesta system, ritual co-parenthood, and exchange labour) were also found on the estate system of La Convención. However, institutions which performed a non-capitalist function in the highlands possessed a specifically capitalist role in La Convención, the similarity in form notwithstanding.

35. Of particular importance to the accumulation process is the fact that although fictive kinship is capable of projecting an ensemble of positive meanings that serve to defuse or deflect antagonism between godparents and co-parents occupying different class positions, it simultaneously enables a rich peasant godfather to exercise a unique and powerful form of social control (based on patriarchal and/or co-parental authority exerted through actual/fictive kin networks) over poor peasants and agricultural workers who are also his co-parents or godchildren. For an analysis of the *compadrazgo* relationship in La Convención, see Brass [1999: Ch. 2].

36. In La Convención *ayni* corresponds to a dyadic relationship involving just two smallholders who agree to work on each other's land over a given period, while

mink'a refers to a large work party called for a particular day during which many smallholders repay a day's labour owed to the peasant on whose land the *mink'a* takes place. Both these forms of institutionalized exchange labour are accompanied by festive drinking and eating, and are therefore frequently theorized [e.g., *Alberti and Mayer*, 1974; *Guillet*, 1980; *Skar*, 1982] as non-monetary but materially reciprocal transactions which characterize the traditional (= non-capitalist) Andean peasant economy. In La Convención, however, such exchanges are called by capitalist peasants producing cash-crops for the national and international market, and are structured not only by the employment of substitute workers to whom monetary payments are made but also by the social division of labour. For example, middle or poor peasants exchange their own personal labour-power on such occasions, whereas two rich peasants linked by an *ayni* relation exchange not their own personal labour-power but that of their workers. Similarly, middle or poor peasants contribute their personal labour to a working group, thereby repaying days of labour owed to its organizer. By contrast, repayment of working days owed by a rich peasant takes the double form of his own personal labour plus that of his worker. Labourers who participate in such exchanges, and accompany and/or discharge the work obligations of their employer, not only receive payment from the latter for this participation but also undertake the more difficult agricultural tasks allocated by the peasant organizing the *mink'a*. For a useful account of how these 'traditional' socio-economic forms are used by rich peasants in the Peruvian highlands, see Sánchez [1982].

37. Significantly, those traditional institutions which did constitute an obstacle to rich peasant accumulation, such as obligatory fiesta sponsorship (see Brass [1986]), were discontinued during this period. Along with labour-rent and usufruct rights to non-demesne land, fiesta sponsorship was structured by a discourse which contributed to the notion of an intra-estate 'community' as perceived by (and reflecting the interests of) the landlord class.

38. See Blanco [1972: 57]. In claiming that no proletariat existed in La Convención, Blanco overlooks the presence of a sizeable pool of landless workers in the province, composed for the most part of kinsfolk of peasant proprietors and migrants from the highlands of Cusco, many of whom had no access to land.

39. For the substitution by populism in general of 'peasant' for 'class', in particular by the nationalism/populism of Haya de la Torre and APRA, together with the opposition of Marxists to such a procedure, see Chapter 1.

40. On the 'independent' revolutionary role of the peasantry, Trotsky [1962: 153, 154] writes: '[N]o matter how great the revolutionary role of the peasantry may be, it nevertheless cannot be an independent role and even less a leading one. The peasant follows either the workers or the bourgeois. This means that the "democratic dictatorship of the proletariat and the peasantry" is only conceivable as a *dictatorship of the proletariat that leads the peasant masses behind it . . .* an insurmountable obstacle on the road to the creation of a peasants' party is the petty-bourgeoisie's lack of economic and political independence and its deep internal differentiation' (original emphasis).

41. See Blanco [1972: 32].

42. Class conflict frequently took the form of disputes between kinsfolk. For example, speaking of that time, one ex-tenant boasted in the mid-1970s of the long and acrimonious struggle to evict a sub-tenant from his own larger holding; the sub-tenant concerned was also his brother, and the dispute over property rights was couched

in the discourse of kinship (trust, obligation).

43. See Blanco [1972: 32]. Both Craig [1967: 112] and Fioravanti [1974: 148] adopt a similar line on the question of the unproblematic existence at this conjuncture of a peasant 'united front' on the non-demesne sector of La Convención.

44. For details about this, see Brass [1999].

45. Sub-tenants were required not only to discharge the labour-rent obligations owed by rich tenants to the estate landlord but also to work on the non-demesne holdings of these subjects. In the course of an interview during 1974, an agricultural labourer who was himself the son of an ex-tenant characterized pre-reform tenants as small landlords who leased tiny plots of land to sub-tenants in order to secure labour-power, both for their own non-demesne holdings and also to carry out their labour-service obligations to the owner of the estate (*cuando tu eres arrendire, asi es que vas a partir el arriendo a fin de que te ayude en tú chacra y en la hacienda al mismo tiempo. Así es que ya eres como segundo hacendado, es como mini hacendado, asi es que al allegado tú lo obligas*) This view was confirmed by a poor peasant ex-tenant who, describing the tenant as a landlord in his own right, explained that in the pre-reform era it was necessary to work six days per month on his tenant's land, and then to undertake a further six day's work on the latter's behalf in order to meet the labour-rent payable on the demesne (*al arrendire lo hacía condiciones de seis días al mes, y a la hacienda otro seis días por cuenta de eso otro tambíen. Gamonal era, pues, el arrendire*). The use of the term *gamonal* in this manner is significant, in that a perjorative word generally applied by peasants only to landlords in order to signify the parasitic socio-economic role of the latter is here extended to include the tenant, who is thereby identified by the sub-tenant as the same kind of exploiter/oppressor.

46. The acute conflict within the peasantry during 1963–64 underlines the precarious nature of access to land by poor peasants at this conjuncture. In general terms, the support given to the peasant movement by tenants and sub-tenants from the middle and poor peasant strata derived from two related causes. First, and most importantly, a desire to become proprietors of non-demesne land leased directly from the landlord or indirectly through the tenant. In this respect, the position of sub-tenants – the vast majority of whom were poor peasants – was particularly vulnerable: not only was their tenure status prior to 1964 legally non-existent, but future property rights could only be obtained at the expense of those tenants in whose holdings the sub-tenancies were located. And second, the existence of debt bondage relationships linking tenants and sub-tenants. This doubly-structured power exercised by rich peasants over poor peasants may have contributed to a lack of politico-ideological independence among the latter during the initial stages of the anti-landlord struggle, and the resulting ability of rich peasants to push through – rather than having to obtain acceptance for – their own economic objectives.

47. See Blanco [1972: 35, 157].

48. Cited in Alfaro and Ore [n.d.: 120–21, 122, Appendix 10]. This *ex post facto* rationalization by Hugo Blanco is open to the same kind of criticism as that made by Trotsky [1936: 176] of the opportunistic support extended by the Comintern to the Chinese Kuomintang during the mid-1920s: 'If yesterday the Chinese bourgeoisie was enrolled in the united revolutionary front, then today it is proclaimed [by Stalin and Bukharin] to have "definitely gone over to the counter-revolutionary camp". It is not difficult to expose how unfounded are these transfers

and enrollments which have been effected in a purely administrative manner without any serious Marxian analysis whatsoever. It is absolutely self-evident that the bourgeoisie in joining the camp of the revolution does so not accidentally, not because it is light-minded, but under pressure of its own class interests.'

49. Both the role and the discourse of Hugo Blanco are in some important respects similar to those of Sharad Joshi in India during the 1980s (see Chapter 3). Like Blanco, therefore, Joshi also held populist views (anti-landlordism, peasant essentialism, individual peasant proprietorship); unlike Blanco, however, Joshi did not claim to be a Trotskyist.

50. For an example of Peruvian Maoism, see Paredes [1974]. Although of the two mobilizations considered below Sendero is most clearly the one influenced by Maoism, ANUC in Colombia also possessed linkages to Maoist organizations [*Zamosc* 1986: 4]. For the politico-ideological potency of Maoism as a mobilizer of the Indian peasantry during the Naxalite movement of the late 1960s and early 1970s, see Chapter 3.

51. In addition to being an account of the peasant movement itself, the text by Zamosc [1986] contains much important information on the political economy of Colombia, and also about the opposing politico-ideological positions in debates concerning rural transformation.

52. See Zamosc [1986: 149, 203].

53. There is no mystery as to why Trotskyism in Colombia was less successful than Maoism as a mobilizing discourse for the peasantry. According to Zamosc [1986: 115], the reason was that 'there were doctrinal differences that made the ML's message more suitable for the peasants. The Trotskyites insisted on the proletariat as the main force of the revolution, downgrading the peasant struggle. Their motto, "land without masters", confused the peasants, many of whom perceived a contradiction between its proletarian content and their own aspiration for an economy based on individual landownership. The Maoist slogan "land for those who till it" avoided this problem, because . . . the slogan was sufficiently ambiguous . . . Since the ML concept also placed the peasantry at the centre of the revolution, Maoist ideology proved to be far more appealing [to peasants] than that of Trotskyites.'

54. Zamosc [1986: 215–16]. Where he does address the issue of the agrarian question, Zamosc [1989: 103, 108–9] poses it in terms of a two-paths development process characterized by 'peasant agriculture' on the one hand and by 'entrepreneurial landlords on the other, thereby banishing peasants from the ranks of capitalist producers – in much the same way as Hugo Blanco (see above).

55. See Zamosc [1986: : xi–xiv, 2, 7, 27, 37, 39, 46, 50ff., 215–16 footnotes 1–2].

56. See, for example, Zamosc [1986: 41, 124–5, 140, 231 footnote 81, 224 footnote 83].

57. On these points, see Zamosc [1986: 170–71, 204–5].

58. See Zamosc [1986: 23].

59. These data are cited in Zamosc [1986: 25].

60. The extent of economic differentiation among Colombian peasants owning/operating less than 20 hectares of land emerges most clearly from a study [*Reinhardt*, 1988] of the 1970s agricultural modernization in and its effects on a rural community in the southwest of the country. One result of the Green revolution programme applied in the latter context was that the average value of per farm marketed output of those with more than 12 hectares of land was twice that of peasants owning 3–12 hectares, eight times that of peasants owning 1½–3½

hectares, and 21 times larger than peasants with less than 1½ hectares of land (calculated from data presented in Reinhardt [1988: 166, Table 6.1]).

61. See Zamosc [1986: 130, 146, 149ff., 163, 165, 202].

62. See Zamosc [1986: 160ff.].

63. See Zamosc [1986: 146, 165].

64. See Zamosc [1986: 163].

65. See Zamosc [1986: 212, 213].

66. The significance of this combined 'moral economy', 'middle peasant', and new social movements framework will become clearer in Chapter 4.

67. For these claims, see McClintock [1984: 49, 58ff., 63, 74, 76–7, 82; 1989a: 67–70, 95].

68. See McClintock [1989b: 358].

69. The element of class is similarly ignored in the presentation of Senderista/state relations by Bourque and Warren [1989], which is itself based on the postmodern 'culture of terror' thesis of Taussig [1987]. Bourque and Warren [1989: 13ff.] accordingly emphasize the regional and ethnic dimensions of this conflict.

70. Hence the observation by McClintock [1989a: 87–8] that: 'Many analysts were surprised at the appearance of Sendero in this zone. In contrast to the Southern highlands, this valley is prosperous. The people living on these lower Andean slopes are less likely to be descendants of the Incas than the people in the Southern highlands. Sendero apparently chose to recruit in the Huallaga Valley to take advantage of the popular opposition to the coca-eradication programs sponsored by the US and Peruvian governments. Sendero did mobilize and support coca-growers, and became the dominant authority at several sites.'

71. See Morales [1989: 55–6] for these figures. According to another and more con-servative estimate, by growing coca for cocaine production a peasant was able during the 1980s to earn seven and a half times the amount per hectare that could be made from the cultivation of profitable cash-crops such as coffee or cocoa ('Peru: State of Fear', *Internationalist*, No.197, July 1989, p.17).

72. Much the same was true of Colombia, where even in the early 1970s some peasant proprietors cultivating marihuana for illegal export to the United States were able to realize six times the profit of other commercial crops [*Zamosc*, 1986: 137].

73. An example of this view is Taylor [1983: 20–21]. For the prefiguring discourse about a mythical Incaic past, see chapter 1.

74. See McClintock [1989a: 83].

75. See Gianotten et al. [1985: 192ff.].

76. For an account of the way in which categories such as 'nationalism', 'regionalism' and 'ethnicity' displace 'class' in Senderista ideology, see Montoya [1986].For the connection between 'urban bias' and neo-populist discourse, see Chapters 1 and 3.

77. Even this middle peasant disguise has been disgarded by Maoism elsewhere. During the 1980s, therefore, the Chinese Communist Party no longer saw a contra-diction between the re-emergence of rich peasant capitalists and building socialism [*Chossudovsky*, 1986: 59].

78. On this point, see McClintock [1984: 49, 77ff.; 1989a: 76ff.].

79. For the link between the profitability of coffee production during the 1960s and the peasant movements in Latin America during that decade, see Gott [1970: 15].

3

Socialism, Nationalism, and Populism: Tribal and Farmers' Movements in India

'It was not flexibility that served (nor should it serve today) as the basic trait of Bolshevism but rather *granite hardness*. It was precisely of this quality, for which its enemies and opponents reproached it, that Bolshevism was always justly proud.' – Leon Trotsky [1936: 141, original emphasis].

'It is said that the industrial worker is much better off than the bulk of the rural population and that there is, therefore, much less need for the State to do anything for him than for the rural population. I have noticed that this plea most often proceeds from people who want the State to do nothing either for the one or the other.' – An observation made by D.R. Gadgil [1945: 101] in the Banaili Readership Lectures given at Patna University during March–April 1940.

Given the view that socialism has been and is possible in India, this chapter considers the reasons for its absence. Accordingly, it will be argued here that the absence of socialism is due in part to three causes. First, ruling class violence and communalization of agrarian struggle. Second, that on the issue of the social forces and idioms utilized in the process of agrarian mobilization, the parties of the Indian left have – like their counterparts in Latin America – espoused not merely non-socialist but anti-socialist theory and practice, adopting instead of socialism the politics of populism/neo-populism (in the discourse of which nation = people = peasants = Nature). And third, that the outcome of such non-socialist theory/practice on the part of the left has been to create a politico-ideological space now occupied by the parties and movements of the political right.

This process will be examined with reference to agrarian mobilization in both pre- and post-Independence India, and especially the way in which political parties of the left have supported any/all grassroots rural agitation in ways which frequently have been indistinguishable from parties opposed to socialism. Crucially, this has usually entailed the ideological reproduction of those very ideas about an innate and historically eternal 'peasant-ness' which inform populism and the agrarian myth. Not only have socialist objectives been replaced on such occasions by popular frontism (the target of which is not agrarian capitalism but an exernal imperialism + internal feudalism), but an additional result has been that the restitution of pre-existing (and non-socialist) tribal/peasant socio-economic structures has then been presented as the realization of socialism.

As in the case of Peru, the main grassroots exponents of this populist discourse have been rich peasants. Claiming to break with the socialist/nationalist politics/practice of the past, the new farmers' movements which emerged in India during the 1980s mobilized against a 'looting', unecological, economically uniform urban industrialization (urban India, or *India*), and in in support of village community (rural India, or *Bharat*), women as 'natural' protectors of the environment, and an undifferentiated peasantry. Much of this discourse was subsequently appropriated by the BJP/VHP/RSS, which attribute environmental degradation and the decline of the caste system to foreign industrialization and non-Hindu ideas, and maintain that the sacred Indian earth is best conserved by caste Hindu village women. Central to this chapter, therefore, is the role of populism as a mobilizing ideology, not least because it points to similarities with long-standing forms of agrarian discourse and action.[1]

I

As has been argued in earlier chapters, the real importance of populist ideology lies in its impact on political practice: it forbids socialism, and encourages bourgeois democracy and nationalism. It is necessary to ask, therefore: in the case of colonial and post-colonial India, to what extent has this denial by populist discourse to those below (rural workers, poor peasants) of the existence/possibility/desirability of a *class* voice, as evidenced by a general refusal of politics and more particularly by a withdrawal of commitment to socialist politics, been offset by arguments/struggles for socialism on the part of the Indian left operating at the grassroots?

3.1 Socialism and Peasant Movements in the Pre-Independence Era

The central question remains, therefore, why has the attempt of the left in India to organize/mobilize rural support for socialist objectives not met with greater success? Just under three quarters of all labour is still employed in agriculture, and landless workers amount to a significant component of the rural population. If one adds to this poor peasants, sharecroppers, and tenants, whose income derives mainly from the sale of labour-power and not the product of labour, there can be little doubt about the presence, size and importance of a potential/actual socialist constituency. In short, elements which would benefit not from an economic and political emphasis on individual peasant smallholding but rather from a programme of common ownership of the means of production, distribution and exchange. This in turn would entail not just opposition to the state – as in the case of the farmers' movements (see below) – but rather control of the state, which would permit a socialist government to expropriate private property and implement a system of collective agriculture, to integrate the latter into a national plan reflecting socialist (and not capitalist) objectives, to invest in raising the level of the productive forces in agriculture, and finally to protect this programme from a hostile national/international capitalist class.

Linked to this is the failure of the numerous and extensive rural mobilizations to lead to a socialist transformation. Why, therefore, have poor peasants and agricultural labourers not moved more resolutely and successfully towards socialism? Against the characterization by Barrington Moore of rural India as politically passive, there is actually a long history of agrarian struggle.[2] It could be argued, for example, that the 1940s was a particularly fruitful time in which to put socialist ideas on the political agenda of rural India. To begin with, it was a period marked by the imminence of Independence, when the shape of the future was itself the object of discussion, conflict and decision. More importantly, the capitalist crisis of the 1930s, the 1943 Bengal famine and war-time devaluation had all combined to undermine petty commodity production in economic terms, and with it any residual 'loyalty'/ legitimacy hitherto accorded to the landlord class.[3] And finally, the period was characterized by two significant and potentially revolutionary agrarian mobilizations: the *Tebhaga* or sharecroppers movement in Bengal, and the Telengana movement in Hyderabad state (now Andhra Pradesh).[4]

3.2 Class Struggle from Above, or the Weapons of the Strong

Much of the argument about the failure of socialism in India tends to focus on problems specifically to do with socialism itself.[5] For example, the alleged incompatability between the socialist idea on the one hand, and on the other the hard realities of everyday economic facts, as demonstrated by the impossibility of central planning, plus the inherent individualism of human nature. Socialists themselves have not only invoked these as reasons either for not advocating radical changes or for abandoning socialism altogether, but have also contributed to this political introspection (problem = socialism) by theorizing class struggle as a process waged largely – albeit unsuccessfully – from below. Implicit in such a view is the mirror image of the struggle-from-below, or the notion that those from whom land, property, wealth, and title have been taken will meekly accept this situation and simply go away. Against such a view of ruling class passivity, there is abundant evidence that the ruling class in India has not merely struggled to great effect in order to retain/ reproduce its power, but has done this relying on two weapons in particular: physical violence and dividing the opposition.

In both the colonial and post-colonial era violence and communalisation have frequently been used by the ruling class in India in the struggle to protect their interests. What is frequently underestimated, not least by socialists themselves, is the capacity of and necessity for the ruling class not merely to demobilize but also to destroy potential/actual opposition. In the case of India, therefore, violence (both actual and threatened) plays an important role in maintaining existing property relations, the major part of this violence being directed against the non-parliamentary left and its grass-roots support. Over the 1982–86 period in Bihar, for example, there were around 16,000 recorded killings of labourers and poor peasants by large landholders, their private armed gangs, and the para-military agents of the state.[6] In this connection it is as well to remember two things: first, that these are officially recognized levels of agrarian violence, the actual figure being much higher; and second, that – like the 'disappeared' of Latin America – India has with the term 'encounter' similarly contributed to the international vocabulary of political torture and violent death.[7]

The second important weapon utilized by the ruling class in India has been the capacity to divide and rule potential/actual opponents by communalizing the agrarian struggle.[8] For example, when the power they exercised over their Tamil coolies was marginally curtailed by legislation enacted during the 1920s, and recognizing that labour was becoming more independent and assertive as a result, tea planters in Ceylon turned explicitly to caste distinctions. Paying particular attention to religious observances and social custom, therefore, was a method of continuing control over labour by means of reinforcing and encouraging caste identity among their workers. For planters, the main attraction of caste was not its element of hierarchy, but rather the primacy and innateness of intra-workforce 'cultural' division; in short, a system in which everyone knew his/her place as ordained (and thus rendered immutable) by 'nature'. The role of the caste system in such a context was accordingly the reproduction of an inherent (or 'natural') sense of otherness *within* the ranks of the workforce that maintained a sense of unity (and thus work discipline) while simultaneously hindering any attempts to combine effectively against the planter class.[9]

This attempt to divide and rule by communalizing the agrarian struggle was not confined to the British colonial ruling class. Like its British counterpart, therefore, in the course of the Tebhaga movement in Bengal and the Telengana movement in Andhra Pradesh during the 1940s, both Hindu and Muslim components of the landlord class in India invoked and emphasized communal identities in an attempt to counter the class identity constructed/exhibited by their tenants. Within the muslim community, where religious leaders discharged an important role in the transmission/reproduction of the authority and power exercised against muslim peasants by muslim landlords, religious identity was used in order to discourage muslim sharecroppers from participating in the process of agrarian mobilization. Muslim landowners in Andhra Pradesh and Bengal emphasized that communist-led peasant unions in both contexts were first and foremost Hindu organizations. In Bengal they also repeated the Muslim League argument that the economic demands advanced by muslim sharecroppers would be met in an independent Pakistan, thereby subordinating the class question to the national question.[10]

3.3 Class Struggle from Below, or the Weakness of the Weapons

It might be objected that the success of any or all these attempts to impose a particular kind of political consciousness from above is of necessity limited by the emergence from below of countervailing and antithetical forms of political consciousness. It is necessary to ask, therefore, about the extent to which just such a countervailing political consciousness has in fact developed at the rural grassroots: specifically, one that is either actually socialist or at least prefigurative of socialism. The dangers inherent in equating 'the popular' with the existing can be illustrated in the case of pre-Independence India by reference to three interrelated issues. First, by the problematic espousal on the part of left political parties of nationalist and/or populist politics. Second, by the kinds of socio-economic forces (an undifferentiated peasantry) mobilized by the left as a result of this nationalist/populist political practice. And third, by the kind of ideology (communalism) it is necessary (or expedient) to invoke in this process.

The first point, about contradictory theory and practice, may be illustrated by the ambivalent manner in which the Indian left have viewed and continue to view both nationalism and Mahatma Gandhi as embodiments and expressions of 'the popular'.[11] To begin with, in the perception of the Soviet Union, Indian socialists and communists, the political role of Gandhi changed from a reactionary one during the 1920s to a progressive one in the anti-imperialist national movement during the anti-Fascist Popular Front of the 1930s.[12] More importantly, although critical of Gandhian politics, many on the Indian left nevertheless separate this from and simultaneously acknowledge his charisma and widespread personal following. To illustrate the view that leaders do not mould followers but are moulded by them, the influential CPI theoretician S.A. Dange has argued that: 'Gandhi learnt from the masses and led them. The individual became the instrument of history, made by the masses in action, who wrote with their blood the glorious pages of our freedom movement'.[13] By endorsing in this manner the view that a political leader like Gandhi unproblematically embodies 'the popular', the left necessarily becomes doubly entrapped: not only by having to support all those he claims to represent (the socio-economically undifferentiated 'masses') but also in the specific ways designated by him (nationalist/populist discourse and practice).

Having identified 'feudalism' and not capitalism as the principal enemy and focus of struggle in the countryside of pre-Independence India, therefore, the CPI have used this as a means for postponing revolutionary action in furtherance of socialism, and advocated instead political alliance with the 'progressive' national bourgeoisie against an external monopoly capitalism (plus its internal ally, feudalism). But even in cases where revolutionary action has been undertaken by the Indian left, its connection with socialism remains problematic. Ignoring the fact that for Marxism the peasantry does not itself form a class but is internally divided along class lines, and for this reason has no independent historical role, the CPI, CPI(M) and CP(ML) have – like the populist and neopopulist opponents of Marxism – insisted on the political unity of the peasantry. Consequently, sections of the left have not only avoided confronting the economic issues which divided peasants along class lines but – in the name of a spurious national and/or peasant unity – have also on occasion actively suppressed an emerging class consciousness among poor peasants and agricultural labourers.

For example, in the late 1930s the CPI refused to continue in alliance with untouchable or Dalit organizations because the latter wished to make all landlords and industrialists the object of struggle; that is, those in the Congress party as well as the British. By contrast, the CPI maintained that as Congress had to lead the 'joint national struggle against imperialism', it could not itself be the object of struggle.[14] Similarly, in the course of the sharecroppers' movement which took place in Bengal during the late 1940s, when tensions arose between peasants who employed sharecroppers and sharecroppers themselves, CPI activists in the peasant union attempted to encourage compromise, and argued that the focus of the peasant movement should be on anti-landlord policies, or the abolition of the *zemindari* system, on which no difference existed between rich and poor peasants.[15]

Significantly, evidence from both Northeastern and Southern India suggests that tribals and poor peasants *are* willing to be organized along class lines and, where the left has formed a separate union for agricultural workers, a specifically class consciousness has indeed emerged.[16] Instead of encouraging the development of class consciousness, however, there is in pre-Independence India a long history of communist support for communal groups. In other words, just like parties of the right, those on the left have actively promoted and encouraged communalization, in the form of ethnic, caste or tribal consciousness. For example, in order to gain the support of the local tribal population in Tripura during the 1930s, the CPI advocated the disenfranchisement of royal ministers and bureaucrats not on the grounds of class but because they were immigrant Bengalis.[17] In Kerala during the 1940s the CPI not only recruited a mass base by means of caste mobilization through caste associations but also – like other political parties – chose parliamentary candidates from among the regionally dominant religious/ethnic community (Hindu, Christian, or Muslim) in order to attract the maximum support in that area.[18]

It could be argued that, given the necessity of securing Independence, the struggles conducted by the left during the colonial era necessarily focussed not on the agrarian but the national question. Once Independence had been achieved, therefore, the national question (and its accompanying discourse stressing non-class identities) would for those on the Indian left cease to be a political issue; socialism would then move to the centre of the political agenda. The case of Naxalism in West Bengal, however, suggests otherwise.

II

Among the more serious reasons offered for the absence of a socialist India since Independence are regional/linguistic disparities, economic backwardness, the absence of a rural proletariat, and the Sino/Soviet split of 1964, with its resultant fragmentation and disunity among political parties/groups on the Indian left.[19] While all these may indeed be important contributory factors to the absence of socialism, here it is intended to focus on different causes connected with the form and content of the agrarian class struggle itself. The latter contention may be illustrated with respect to Naxalism as a Maoist mobilizing discourse used by tribals in West Bengal during the late 1960s and early 1970s.

3.4 Naxalism and Tribal Movements in West Bengal

Neither isolated culturally from the rest of the population nor economically undifferentiated, tribals in northeast India have participated historically in agrarian struggles not just as producers in their own traditional areas but also as agricultural workers (for higher wages, better working conditions, etc.) in the Assamese tea plantations and in the coal mines of Bihar.[20] The extent to which class differentiation operates within the tribal population emerges clearly from a study by Bose in 1980 of five districts of West Bengal (Birbhum, Bankura, Burdwan, Midnapore and Purulia).[21] Not only were the beneficiaries of government reservation schemes in this context rich peasant tribals, who composed only one per cent of all households yet owned 16 per cent of the land, 44 per cent of which was irrigated, but they also engaged in moneylending, owned more livestock, and used more chemical fertilizer than any other peasant strata.[22] Middle peasants, who constituted seven per cent of households, owned 23 per cent of the land, 22 per cent of which was irrigated, while poor peasants who amounted to 68 per cent of all households, owned 60 per cent of the land only 20 per cent of which was irrigated.[23]

A quarter of middle peasants and three quarters of poor peasants in these West Bengal villages purchased no labour-power, whereas all rich peasants employed outside labour; by contrast, no rich peasant, a few middle peasant, most poor peasant and all agricultural labour households sold labour-power.[24] Tribal peasants who hired tribal wage-labourers treated them no better, and in some cases worse, than non-tribal peasants hiring tribals as agricultural labour.[25] Rich peasant tribals also employed young labourers (*bagels*) to herd their cattle, either without paying them wages or merely on the promise of meeting their marriage expenses when they came of age.[26] In politico-ideological terms, variations in tribal kinship patterns were determined by class, as was intra-kin conflict; there was little evidence of intra-tribal unity, rich tribals being regarded by their poorer counterparts as possessing not just different but antagonistic interests.[27]

Significantly, these same West Bengal districts of Midnapore, Birbhum, and Bankura were also areas of Naxalite guerrilla activity over the 1967–71 period.[28] Formed in 1969 after a split with the pro-Moscow CPI(M), the Maoist CPI(M-L) initiated the Naxalite guerrilla movement in this region, and drew its main support from the tribal population. Just as in the case of Sendero Luminoso in Peru, Naxalite Maoism in West Bengal exhibited millenarian characteristics that were ultimately not only compatible with but supportive of the existing tribal structure, regardless of the extent to which it might be differentiated socio-economically.[29] Claiming that India was a semi-colonial/semi-feudal social formation, therefore, rural Naxalites externalized capitalist exploitation on the one hand, and on the other emphasized tribal cultural particularism together with the element of continuity between the politico-ideological objectives of the present struggle and those of the past.[30] Claims by Duyker to the contrary notwithstanding, such an approach leads inevitably to the displacement of class struggle (which licenses intra-ethnic conflict) by ethnic struggle (which licenses intra-class conflict) as the primary focus of Naxalism.[31]

3.5 Maoism, Class Struggle and the Discourse of Tribal 'Otherness'

In contrast to the claim by subaltern studies texts regarding the irreducible nature of ethnic categories (see Chapter 4), the Naxalite movement in West Bengal provides evidence that at the bottom end of the social structure proletarian class solidarity does indeed transcend tribal/caste distinctions. Following the introduction of the Green Revolution package in this region during the mid-1960s, there was an increase in the incidence of *de facto* proletarianization as landholders not only no longer leased out land to new tenants and rotated existing ones in order to prevent them claiming ownership rights, but also increased product rents and decreased wage levels.[32] On the basis of a common experience as sharecroppers and agricultural labourers, therefore, Santals united with other tribals (Munda, Mals, Rajbansi, Oraons) and lower caste Hindus (Bagdi, Bauri, Doms).[33]

While such evidence confirms the existence of and the reasons for the transcendence of ethnic divisions by class solidarity at the lower end of the social structure, the same study only hints at the occurrence of a similar differentiating process at its top end. Duyker notes the emergence of a rich peasantry following the Green Revolution, but omits to indicate whether or not this stratum extended to include Santals.[34] However, nearly half the killings carried out by Naxalites in Birbhum were of peasants with less than 25 acres, while those who owned more than this amount accounted for only 22 per cent of annihilations, a point underlined by one CPI(M-L) leader who observed that 'the fundamental contradiction was not between (big) landlords and their sharecroppers, tenants and labourers, but between *jotedar*-kulaks and share-croppers, labourers and tenants'.[35] The significance of this lies in the fact that, as the study by Bose demonstrates, a numerically small but economically important stratum of precisely this kind of peasant was to be found *within* the tribal population itself.

The existence of actual/potential Naxalite targets among the Santals themselves raises in turn the crucial issue of the reasons for an absence of intratribal class struggle. Why, if a *de facto* Santal proletariat was able to unite with other tribals and/or non-tribals along class lines, was it not also capable of directing subsequent action against those of a different class inside the same ethnic group? As with Sendero Luminoso, the answer to this question must necessarily address the complicity between the politico-ideological position of the CPI(M-L) itself and that of the 'traditional' tribal authorities, the corresponding failure to challenge – let alone break – the strong ties of authority inside the village community, and the resulting deflection of class struggle by ethnic conflict.

Duyker suggests that in both Midnapore and Birbhum districts the

CPI(M-L) micro-level organization 'owed more to indigenous cultural factors than to its April 1969 resolution on political organization.' Accordingly, 'Naxalite cells and action squads had hierarchies, lines of communication and logistic support which were rooted in the local kinship system . . . as whole familes of Santals joined the movement, kinship organization began to parallel guerrilla organization . . . the natural authority of the elders, i.e. fathers, uncles and husbands, appears to have become a political and military authority over sons, nephews and wives who also joined the movement'.[36]

In other words, guerrilla activity mobilized through the kinship system was actually structured by – and thus could not but reflect the interests of – the *existing* socio-economic order, as embodied in the authority of tribal elders.[37] The difficulty with this is that even in a tribal context (as Bose, Pathy and others show), such authority can also correspond to that exercised by rich peasants over agricultural labourers and sharecroppers (all of whom happen to be tribal kinsfolk), and would therefore not only not be 'natural' but in *class* terms could not be neutral. In the (unlikely) event of their own socio-economic position being challenged/threatened, therefore, rich peasant tribals would be able to counter any attempt on the part of the CPI(M-L) to mobilize Santals as class subjects (landless labourers, poor peasants, sharecroppers) by proclaiming a politico-ideological unity based on ethnicity.

In the light of all this, it is necessary to ask how is it possible to advocate socialism and construct a specifically socialist politics, when no account is taken of the fact that tribals and peasants are not just internally differentiated along class lines, but are willing to mobilize on this basis; when it is implied that the future for which socialists are fighting is no different from an idealized tribal past; and when no attempt is made to create prefigurative socialist forms (choosing instead to lock on to existing ones, and operate through these). When, in short, what is promoted or engaged in is not merely non-socialist but actually *anti*-socialist political practice. The significance of this can be demonstrated with regard to the discourse of the new farmers' movements, perhaps the most important mobilization of agrarian capitalists in India since Independence.

III

Emerging from the late 1970s onwards, the farmers' movements operated under different names in specific contexts throughout India. The most important of them were: *Shetkari Sanghatana* in Maharashtra, led by Sharad Joshi; the *Bharatiya Kisan Union* (BKU), led by M.S.Tikait in Uttar Pradesh, and by Ajmer Singh Lakhowal, Balbir Singh Rajwal and Bhupinder Singh Marn in Punjab; the *Bharatiya Kisan Sangh* in Gujarat; the Tamil Nadu Agriculturalists' Association (*Tamilaga Vyavasavavigal Sangham* or TVS) in Tamil Nadu; and the Karnataka State Farmers' Association (*Karnataka Rajya Ryota Sangha* or KRRS) in Karnataka, led by M.D.Nanjundaswamy. It is impossible to ignore or underestimate the powerful effect the farmers' movements have had on local, regional and national politics in India during the 1980s. Their impact extends from demonstrations, blocking the food transportation system, denying officials access to villages, refusing to pay outstanding loans (tax arrears, electricity dues, bank loans), and withholding crops from local markets (which resulted in price rises), to an important role in the overthrow of Rajiv Gandhi's Congress government in the 1989 elections.[38]

3.6 The 'Newness' of the New Farmers' Movements

The novelty of the farmers' movements which emerged in the Green Revolution areas of India during the late 1970s and early 1980s has generally been attributed to a number of characteristics which they are said to have in common. Unlike past anti-landlord movements, led by and reflecting the class interests of rich peasants, the farmers' agitation of the 1980s is regarded as a non-political form of mobilization, aimed specifically against the state by all peasants who are no longer divided along class lines but now united as commodity producers, and consequently demanding not land but remunerative prices.[39]

A result of the overall commercialization of production combined with a slowdown in economic growth experienced in these areas of capitalist agriculture at this conjuncture, it is argued, is that surplus generating peasants blamed the state – as the effective institutional regulator of input/output prices, and through this the economic reproduction of the peasantry as a whole – for adverse terms of trade between industry and agriculture. Hence the opposition to the state on the part of all peasants, and the demand by the latter for 'remunerative prices', or lower costs for inputs (energy, irrigation and credit) and higher returns for output (crops, livestock). Such an interpretation of the new farmers' movements is faced with a number of difficulties.

First, as confirmed by earlier instances in rural India of mobilization aimed against government on questions of remunerative prices for agricultural commodities and lower taxes, opposition to the state on these issues was not new.[40] Second, land continued to be on the agenda of the new farmers' movements, albeit not in the usual form of an egalitarian redistribution; much rather the opposite, since the demand was for the abolition of land ceilings, or the opportunity for the better-off to extend/consolidate rural property.[41] Third, the balance of the resource flows from the agrarian sector implied in the concept 'urban bias' ignored the existence of substantial direct/indirect subsidies to agriculture by the state.[42] And fourth, the support of not only agricultural labourers but also poor peasants for the new farmers' movements, and with it the multi-class nature of such mobilization, was questionable; again, much rather the opposite appeared to be the case, since peasant proprietors confronting the state over 'remunerative prices' were simultaneously engaged in conflict with their workforce over wage levels and the restructuring of the labour process.[43]

Hence the antagonism of the new farmers' movements towards the state was itself partial and class specific: while state intervention on the issue of remunerative prices was perceived as desirable and thus actively sought, there was simultaneously an equally strong opposition by the new farmers' movements to the (actual or potential) implementation by the state of legislation enforcing land ceilings and minimum wages.[44] In short, in these regions of capitalist agriculture rich peasants who supported the new farmers' movements wanted political power exercised through the state not only commensurate with their economic position but supportive of this: that is, the deregulation of state control over land, labour and the price of agricultural produce.

Both the free market philosophy structuring the discourse of the new farmers' movements and the contradictions to which this gave rise emerged most clearly with regard to debate over the propositions formulated by Arthur Dunkel, the GATT Director General in the period 1980–93, as outlined in the *Draft Final Act Embodying the Results of the Uruguay Round of Multilateral Trade Negotiations*. The latter was endorsed by Sharad Joshi and the farmers' movement in Maharashtra, both because it challenged price-distorting 'urban bias' and state intervention, and because in his view the liberalization of international trade and the accompanying elimination of agricultural subventions on a global scale would benefit ('heavily taxed') Indian peasants at the expense of ('heavily subsidized') farmers in the US, the EEC and Japan.[45] By contrast, the farmers' movements in Uttar Pradesh and Karnataka (led by Tikait and Nanjundaswamy) were both opposed to the suggestions contained in the Dunkel draft, on the grounds that free trade would permit foreign capital to undermine national economic sovereignty and depress the domestic prices of agricultural produce.[46]

3.7 The New Farmers' Movements, the Market and the State

This debate about the effect of Dunkel and GATT liberalization policies on the farmers' movements in India highlighted the partial and contradictory position of Sharad Joshi on the interrelated connections between free trade, market competition and the role of the state. To compensate for the low prices determined by 'urban bias', he argued, required that farmers be permitted to export agricultural produce, irrespective of local and/or national food shortages (a result of which would be to increase existing prices for domestic produce); however, this committment to free trade was in turn dependent upon state intervention, in the form of tariff protection against foreign competition, to prevent import penetration and a consequent decline in existing prices for domestic produce.[47]

The partial nature of this free market philosophy was similarly contradicted by Joshi's equivocal attitude towards government subsidies. The latter were to be retained not only for export promotion but also to guarantee the reproduction of existing property relations (for smallholdings which 'are, by their very size and character, uneconomic') and also to raise the level of the productive forces (land consolidation, installation of irrigation, purchase of seeds, hire of machinery).[48] Accordingly, the free market philosophy of Joshi entailed a central paradox: the demand for the freedom of farmers to commodify production in response to price advantages on national/international markets depended in turn not only on state provision to these same farmers of export subsidies but also – like Tikait and Nanjundaswamy – on denying foreign capital a similar capacity to engage in free trade (and thus in effect negating GATT).

The political differences over GATT between the *Shetkari Sanghatana* on the one hand and the BKU and KRRS on the other should not obscure their agreement about the fundamental issues: all the farmers' leaders blamed the Indian government for implementing foreigner-favouring/anti-farmer policies, and all wanted some form of tariff protection to ensure higher domestic prices. And although seemingly divergent in terms of policy towards Dunkel and GATT, the position of all the farmers' movements nevertheless made reference to and thus invoked the same populist/nationalist discourse.

Accordingly, Sharad Joshi maintained that even the 'middle-layer farmer' in India could outcompete the 'foreigner' once the latter was deprived of subsidies, while both Tikait and Nanjundaswamy sought protection for this same smallholding peasant from this same 'foreigner'.[49] The policy of agricultural liberalization announced by the Namasimha Rao government at the end of March 1993 to coincide with yet another farmers' rally in New Delhi not only constituted an attempt by the ruling Congress (I) party to gain the support of the new farmers' movements by conceding one of Joshi's principal demands (for export-oriented free trade) but also licensed thereby a more acute process of class differentiation within the new farmers' movements themselves, between the rich peasant beneficiaries of such a policy and those mainly poor peasants for whom it would mean proletarianization.[50]

These considerations notwithstanding, leaders of and activists in the new farmers' movements denied the importance/existence of class and stressed instead the a-political nature of mobilization on the part of a rural population (peasants/tribals/women) uniformly exploited by and thus in conflict with an 'urban' state. For example, Sharad Joshi – like Gandhi – rejected class struggle within the peasantry, and thus socialism as the outcome, and argued instead not only that all peasants were united as producers and consumers of commodities the prices of which were controlled by the state, but also that higher prices received by farmers for their output would enable them to pay their workers higher wages.[51] Echoing both the Chayanovian concept of a family farm, and also the 'urban bias' thesis of Michael Lipton and Charan Singh, Joshi maintained that the principal contradiction was no longer found within the agrarian sector (between rich, middle, and poor peasants) but was now located between a powerless, uniformly poor rural population (= *Bharat*) on the one hand, and on the other a powerful, uniformly rich urban population (= India) and its state apparatus.[52]

3.8 The New Farmers' Movements and Urban Bias

At the centre of the farmers' discourse, and a crucial aspect of their mobilization, therefore, was the claim about the existence/effect of 'urban bias', as encapsulated in Sharad Joshi's politico-ideologically powerful slogan 'Bharat versus India'. Some recent analyses of the new farmers' movements in India question the viability of this distinction, and provide evidence that theoretically and empirically it is unsustainable, while others maintain that in terms of resource transfers, terms of trade, pricing policies, etc., urban bias possesses a material as well as an ideological reality. [53] In a review of the debate about 'urban bias', Varshney has argued that farmer empowerment in India is attributable to the fact that democracy preceded industrialization, a situation which confers on the rural sector the capacity to exercise an electoral veto on unfavourable (= anti-rural) policy.[54] He makes two points regarding the extent of this rural empowerment: first, the absence of an external obstacle to its consolidation, in the form of the inability of the Indian state to tax agriculture; and second the presence of an internal obstacle to consolidation, in the form of non-economic fissures (caste, ethnicity, religion).[55]

Noting that since the mid-1970s taxation in India has amounted to 15–17 per cent of GDP, that agriculture is untaxed, and that further revenue from this source could only take the form of direct taxation, Varshney nevertheless dismisses the feasibility of taxing agriculture, for three reasons in particular: that such a policy option would result in yet more tax evasion, that for the Indian state to concede farmers' demands for higher prices and then to claw back such gains by means of taxes would further alienate the rural sector, and that anyway administrative problems connected with its implementation together with the opposition of politicians would render such a policy unviable.[56] About this view three points can be made. First, the argument that the actual/potential incidence of tax evasion is a sufficient reason for not imposing *additional* taxation could also be used as justification for not having *any* taxation, and is therefore unacceptable. Second, to observe that farmers and their political representatives would be alienated by taxation is tautological: to cite this as a reason for not taxing is to accept the farmers' case (about unequal terms of trade, price differentials, relative supply, and cost escalation), which Varshney clearly does not. *Of course* farmers would object to such a policy, but this would be equally true of landlords, industrialists and millionaires generally, all of whom could similarly be expected to block/avoid/evade this.[57] Not surprisingly, owners of means of production are (and historically have been) opposed to any kind of measure (expropriation, nationalization, land reform, income redistribution) that directly or indirectly threatens their property rights.

Much the same kind of difficulty faces the attempt by Varshney to explain the failure of the farmers' movements to realize their economic objectives by reference to the fragmenting effect of non-economic identity.[58] In his view, therefore, a combination of religious/caste/ethnic issues have overridden the unifying economic identity of the 'rural sector' in India, in the process placing limits on the politics of farmer empowerment. What Varshney fails to understand, however, is that – as the examples of ANUC in Columbia, FIR and Sendero in Peru, and Naxalism in West Bengal all demonstrate – capitalist farmers and/or rich peasants are unable to cohere around economic issues because in order to mobilize effectively, it is necessary for them to obtain the support of those categories (poor peasants, agricultural labourers) whose *class* position is not just different from but in economic terms antagonistic to their own. Precisely for this reason, therefore, a necessary condition for such agrarian mobilization to occur is that its discourse-against focuses on issues and identities unconnected with class divisions. Accordingly, contradictions at the level of the economic require that farmers' discourse project 'otherness' in populist terms, or the 'innate'/'natural' identities of caste, religion, nationality and sector (urban/rural divide). Having recognized the theoretically unsustainable nature of the concept 'urban bias', Varshney is nevertheless unable to explain why this is so. In other words, the fact that both taxation and communalization are fundamentally political questions to do with *class* and contradictory effects of capitalist accumulation, an issue which Varshney does not confront.[59]

3.9 The New Farmers' Movements, Gender and Village 'Community'

Given the political importance of 'urban bias' as a mobilizing ideology, however, it is unsurprising to find that the peasantry, peasant women and 'womens
power' were all identified by Joshi as the major liberating forces in rural India,
and the main form of oppression was violence, or 'looting', which he regarded
as primary and unrelated to property.[60] As was clear from the objectives of the
village-level *Laxmi Mukti* ('liberation of housewives') project of inter-gender
property transfer developed by the Shetkari Sanghtana in Maharashtra, however, the form taken by womens' self-empowerment was in class terms very
specific: not only were landless rural women excluded from the programme,
but land operated by the peasant household and 'gifted' by men to women was
to be cultivated by the latter in a traditional (non-technical/natural/organic)
manner solely for the purpose of family subsistence provision.[61] In this way
the discourse and practice of the new farmers' movements reinforced the
potent mythical image of an ageless/unchanging (= 'natural') subsistence agriculture carried out largely by women, with the object of preserving traditional
peasant household production (peasant = woman = Nature = *Bharat Mata* =
nation).

At first glance, many of the economic demands made by agrarian capitalist
producers of the new farmers' movements would appear to have little in
common with the rustic traditionalism of Gandhian philosophy.[62] However,
this is to overlook the main role of the latter as a mobilizing ideology,
designed – like the 'Trotskyism' of Hugo Blanco and the Maoism of Sendero
Luminoso (see Chapter 2) – to deflect attention from the process/effects of
peasant differentation and thus obtain widespread support in rural areas (the
' "us"ness-of-we' as against the ' "them"ness-of-they') for what was in fact
a class-specific agrarian programme/policy. For precisely this reason,
opposition by rich peasants to what they identified as Nehruvian 'socialism' in
post-Independence India has generally been framed in Gandhian neopopulist
terms: for example, the replacement of Nehruvian 'socialism' by a Gandhian
alternative was central to the neopopulist agrarian policy of Charan Singh,
political representative and organic intellectual of India's rich peasantry.[63]
Claims to the contrary notwithstanding, therefore, the idioms which structured
the mobilizing ideology of the new farmers' movements which emerged
during the 1980s did not in fact break with this prefiguring discourse.[64] Not
only were H.S.Rudrappa, the founder president of the KRRS, and M.D.
Nanjundaswamy, its leader, both staunch Gandhians, but the farmers' movement in Maharashtra resorted to Gandhian methods of protest, and the anti-
intellectual 'rustic' ideology projected by M.S Tikait was a thinly-disguised
version of Gandhian/Liptonian 'urban bias'.[65]

In a similar vein, Sharad Joshi not only rejected Nehruvian 'socialism' and advocated a return to the Gandhian model of development but – like Gandhi himself – located the reasons for this in a specifically nationalist discourse: accordingly, the existence in India of 'urban bias' was attributed by him to the dual inheritance of the colonial regime, a process of post-Independence industrial growth predicated on the imitation of a 'foreign' lifestyle made possible only by the continued exploitation of the farmer.[66] And like not only Mahatma Gandhi and Charan Singh in India but also the populists in Russia, and Hugo Blanco and Sendero in Latin America, the main objective of Sharad Joshi was to reconstitute the village community: economically, by retaining within it the surplus otherwise appropriated through 'urban bias'; socially, by providing an employment-generating self-sufficient village economy based artisan production; and politically, by devolving power from the state to the traditional village *panchayat*.[67]

3.10   The New Farmers' Movements and Ecofeminism

Although the economic relationship between ecological concerns and the new farmers' movements were complex and potentially contradictory, at the level of discourse a significant measure of agreement existed. For example, Sharad Joshi blamed industrial pollution, industrialization, and 'urban bias' for declining soil fertility and environmental degradation in India generally and the centuries-old process of appropriation from the farmer. In his view, an ecologically sustainable use of 'appropriate' (= small-scale) agricultural technology would lower production costs and make farmers less dependent on state control over input prices.[68] Much the same kinds of arguments have been deployed by the influential ecofeminist Vandana Shiva, who not only acted as an advisor to M.S.Tikait but also addressed the 1993 farmers' rally organized jointly by the BKU and the KRRS in New Delhi.[69] When combined with the the views of Sharad Joshi regarding the way in which not only peasants but the environment and women are 'looted' by a 'foreign'/urban/industrial development pattern, therefore, a politico-ideological affinity emerges between the discourse of the new farmers' movement and that of ecofeminism.

Like Sharad Joshi, Vandana Shiva attributes environmental degradation to a specifically urban and western industrial science and technology, and advocates instead the mobilization of women as 'natural' protectors of Nature in the context of the traditional Hindu village community.[70] Again like Sharad Joshi, she links women to subsistence production, and like Gandhi, she rejects not only capitalist accumulation but also economic growth generally as 'alien' (= western) impositions on India. Equating the universalizing tendencies of science and development with modern western patriarchy, Shiva maintains that all these forces combine to exercise violence not only against Nature itself (a manifestation of which is the Punjab conflict) but also against tribals, peasants and rural Indian women ('still embedded in nature'), thereby replicating both process ('violence'/'looting') and target (women/peasants) identified in the discourse of Sharad Joshi; instead, she argues for a reversion to subsistence agriculture that would simultaneously reinstate *prakriti* (= Nature/female = source of life), enhance the position of women, tribals and peasants, and (yet again like Sharad Joshi) thereby restore social peace and ecological harmony to rural India.[71]

The compatibility between the analytical approach of Shiva and that of new social movements theory influenced by postmodernism (see Chapter 4) is evident from her positive/negative characterizations: on the one hand, therefore, she advocates a politics of human rights and 'democratic resistance' in pursuit of 'new civic spaces', and celebrates endogeneity/difference/ diversity/decentralization as ends in themselves; on the other hand, she is opposed to the (non-class-specific) state, and rejects development/progress/ class/modernity as unacceptable universal categories associated exclusively with a western 'colonial' Enlightenment project.[72]

Similarly, her affinity with nationalism and populism is clear from the way in which she classifies ethnicity and romanticizes the agrarian social structure that preceded the Green revolution. Accordingly, not only is the oppressed Nature/female couple equated with ethnicity but for Shiva economic growth *per se* is identified as a form of 'new colonialism' and the Green Revolution is the result of a specifically 'foreign' science, 'foreign' politics, and 'foreign' knowledge produced by 'foreign' experts.[73] Against the externally imposed, urban oriented, surplus extracting, large-scale/hightech, non-natural, agribusiness of the Green Revolution from which women, tribals and peasants derive no benefit, Shiva counterposes an unambiguously Gandhian vision of small-scale, subsistence-oriented, needs-meeting, survival guaranteeing natural agrarian structure composed of an undifferentiated peasantry.[74] Indeed, one of her main objections to the Green Revolution is that it disrupted the stability of pre-existing traditional society by eroding tribal and/or peasant 'cultural norms and practices', 'co-operation' and 'mutual obligations'.[75]

Since the romanticized concept of a pristine 'tribal' (itself a colonial invention) is central to this critique, it is necessary to ask: to what historical stage of its development does Shiva wish to restore the 'tribal', and why? Tribal populations throughout India have experienced a continuous process of socio-economic change; by the late 1970s many were already differentiated along class lines, the unequal pattern of intra-tribal landholding and income distribution being similar to that for the non-tribal population as a whole.[76] As has been noted above, better-off tribals in West Bengal have benefitted disproportionately from welfare provision (thereby intensifying the very differentiation process such measures are designed to prevent), have converted tribal land to private property, utilize high yield variety seeds, invest in means of production, and exploit the labour-power of less-well-off tribals.[77]

3.11 The New Farmers' Movements and the Left

Significantly, despite being distrusted by the farmers' movements, sections of the left in India also regard it as anti-monopoly capital and thus politically progressive.[78] The way in which the CPI perceives the issue of remunerative prices, and consequently policy towards the new farmers' movements, demonstrates clearly the extent to which its agrarian policy is – like that of Hugo Blanco – still anti-feudal/pro-kulak/pro-democracy rather than anti-capitalist/pro-labour/pro-socialist, and thus deeply complicit with the bourgeois nationalism of the Indian National Congress some 40 years after Independence.

Rejecting the argument from those to its left that remunerative prices enrich and strengthen kulaks, the CPI instead invokes a resolution passed by Congress at Lahore in 1929 to the effect that it was the inalienable right of the Indian people 'to be free' and 'to enjoy the fruits of their labour'. Reasserting that it is not rich peasants but a combination of landlords/usurers/merchants who were the exploiters and thus the enemies of democracy, the CPI maintained during the early 1980s that remunerative prices would enable farmers to pay minimum wages to agricultural labourers and, further, that the drain of investible resources from rural areas must be reversed since unremunerative prices would eventually ruin marginal, small and middle peasants, and lead to their proletarianization.[79] Although it scarcely seems necessary to draw attention to the theoretically and politically problematic nature of the way in which the new farmers' movements are inscribed in such an analysis, the following three points will serve to underline the distance between the CPI and socialism.

First, as has been seen in previous chapters, concepts of an undifferentiated peasantry have more in common with populism and neo-populism than with Marxism. Second, on the wages question the CPI adopted the discredited 'trickle-down' thesis which overlooks the role of class struggle in determining/maintaining the pay levels and working conditions secured by agricultural labour. And third, the ruination of small/middle peasants – which the CPI wished to halt – is precisely the effect of agrarian differentiation; that is, again like populists and neo-populists, the CPI adopted a thinly disguised 'urban bias' argument in order to advocate the retention/preservation of an undifferentiated peasant economy which could successfully resist proletarianization by reproducing itself as an homogenous stratum of petty commodity producers.[80] Ironically, and notwithstanding claims that the new farmers' movements were different from the left, both politico-ideological agendas did indeed have much in common; not, however, because the ideas/positions on agrarian change propounded/advocated by the left were connected with socialism, but much rather because they were not.

3.12 The New Farmers' Movements and the Right

When combined within a single framework, all the views considered above give rise to the set of politico-ideological oppositions illustrated in the following Table.

		New Social Movements, New Farmers' Movements, Ecofeminism, CPI, BJP/VHP/RSS
('Other')	('loots')	('Self')
West	⇒	East
Foreigners	⇒	Hindus
India	⇒	Bharat
Urban	⇒	Rural
Industry	⇒	Agriculture
Science	⇒	Culture
Development	⇒	Environment
State	⇒	Peasants
Class	⇒	Community
Men	⇒	Women
(Profane)	⇒	(Sacred)

These politico-ideological oppositions structure the discourse not just of/about the new farmers' movements, ecofeminism, and the analysis by the left of agrarian change, but also – as will be seen in Chapters 4 and 5 – that of the postmodern 'new' populism (new social movements, 'popular culture', subaltern studies, 'everyday forms of resistance', etc.). Most significantly, these same politico-ideological oppositions are not merely shared with the Hindu chauvinist BJP (*Bharatiya Janata Party*), the VHP (*Vishwa Hindu Parishad*, or World Council of Hindus), and the RSS (*Rashtriya Swayamsewak Sangh*, or National Volunteer Corps), but are in fact more effectively mobilized (and indeed in this form find their authentic expression) from within the specifically anti-socialist, populist, nationalist, and communal discourse of the political right.[81] Along with the scheduled castes and scheduled tribes, it is unsurprising both that women became an electoral target of BJP activity, and that in Maharashra, Gujarat and Karnataka the BJP gained political/electoral support at the expense of the farmers' movement.[82]

This actual/potential electoral shift must in turn be linked to the way in which changes can and do occur in the possession/control exercised over the circulation of specific discursive forms that are shared by competing political groups/parties. Although it is true that no discourse is ever wholly 'owned' by a specific politics, a result of the strong historical link between the political right and religious/nationalist/communal issues is that where such components are currently part of another discourse (remunerative prices + free trade in agricultural produce + female/tribal/peasant/farmer self-empowerment + nationalism + environmentalism + populism + anticapitalism) it becomes possible not just to reappropriate the main individual components themselves (nationalism + populism) but through them to dispossess the current 'owners' – such as the new farmers' movements and the new social movements generally – of the remaining components linked to these views, and thus to gain control over the whole discourse.

When narratives which emanate from distinct – even formally opposed – political positions, and by virtue of making empowering reference to the same elements are both initially and in their continuation linked discursively, it is the wider socio-economic context together with immediate form taken by the class struggle which confers politico-ideological acceptability. In the case of India, therefore, such a relay-in-statement is made possible not only by the complicity of the political left with nationalism/ neopopulism (and hence the absence of a recognizably distinctive alternative, a discourse-against), by the a-political/anti-political nature of contemporary forms of 'popular culture' and accompanying modes of self-empowerment/ resistance (by women, tribals, peasants, as well as the new farmers' movements), but also by an overdetermined and unambiguously chauvinist nationalism (in the discourse of which circulate narratives about Ayodhya in general and the events of 6th December 1992 in particular, about communalism and the desirability of a non-secular state, supported by the filmic/ televisual resurgence of Hindu epics and the media prominence given to action undertaken by the BJP). Accordingly, where political power entails (paradoxically) a transformation not in the political content of discourse itself but rather in the political control exercised over this, it is not necessary for a group/party of the political right to espouse/project all components of a discourse in order to be able to exercise actual/potential control over the whole discourse itself.[83]

The extent of and similarity between the negative/positive components which structure the politico-ideological discourse of the new farmers' movements and that of RSS is indeed striking, and suggests that a more general reappropriation by the political right would not be difficult.[84] Like new social movements generally and the new farmers' movements in particular, the RSS is opposed to – and claims to stand above – politics, arguing that it belongs neither to the right nor to the left of the political spectrum but takes a '"common man's [sic] approach to economic problems"'.[85] And just as the repoduction of 'urban bias' is linked by Sharad Joshi to the imitation of 'foreign'/'western' patterns of industrial economic growth, so the RSS blames disintegration of national values/culture on a '[w]esternized elite who propose capitalism, socialism, or communism as solutions for Indian development'.[86] Like Gandhi, the RSS condemns 'foreign' philosophies because the material development linked to them generates class antagonism that disrupts social harmony.[87] Instead, the RSS endorses an unambiguously populist/nationalist approach to agrarian change, and – again like Gandhi, Charan Singh and Sharad Joshi – not only supports the cause of 'the small entrepreneur and the yeoman farmer', advocates the abolition of landlordism, but also promotes the concept of village-based artisan production ('cottage industry').[88] The RSS also subscribes to a variant of 'urban bias', in that it opposes co-operative agriculture on the grounds that this presents bureaucrats and politicians with more opportunities to exploit farmers.[89]

It is now possible for the BJP/VHP/RSS to operationalize a potent relay-in-statement, composed of the following politico-ideological matrix.[90] In so far as the Hindu caste system regulated the occupations in which its subject could engage, it can be claimed that it created an 'ecological space' whereby Hindu society was (and could be again) in harmony with Nature.[91] Since the environment of India is god-given and hence sacred, ecological destruction offends against Hindu religion, and its perpetrators are thus profaning the sacred.[92] Many of these politico-ideological themes crystallized around the dispute in the early 1990s between Hindus and Muslims over the issue of the temple on the Ram-Janmabhoomi/Babri-Masjid site at Ayodya in Uttar Pradesh.[93] Significantly, in celebrating the sacrifices undertaken to further the construction of a Hindu temple at Ayodya, the discourse of the BJP/VHP/RSS commemorated not only 'martyrs' killed in communal riots but also their mothers and wives.

Within this discursive framework, moreover, the current environmental degradation in India can be blamed on the implantation/operation over a 700-year period of 'foreign' non-Hindu ideas (Christianity, Islam, Secularism) that do not value – and therefore do not conserve – Nature.[94] The depletion of natural resources belonging to and emblematic of the nation can then be (re-)presented not only as the result of commercial exploitation by 'foreign' domination and industrialization, but also (and thereby) as being a threat to and thus against the interests of an authentically indigenous village-based sustainable agriculture structured by the organizing principle of caste. Similarly, the actual/potential impoverishment of middle and poor peasant proprietors can be blamed on soil erosion, which is in turn attributable to the environmental degradation that is itself the fault of 'foreigners'.

The role of gender in this chain of signification is especially important. Not only do women themselves have direct experience of oppression (physical assault, dowry deaths), but in the discourse of the political right they discharge both an active and a passive function: they are equated with the role of motherhood-as-racial-preservation and also the last line of resistance against the corrupting values of 'western'/(urban) modernization.[95] Hence the potency of the combined image of gender-specific/ethnic-specific assault frequently invoked by the VHP, particularly since a Hindu woman raped by a Muslim is also a metaphor for a similarly violent attack by 'foreigners' on a constellation of sacred symbols: the cow (= Mother-Cow/*Gau-mata*), the Hindu mother (-land), her/(its) traditional values, and Nature itself.[96] Such a view is simultaneously supportive of Hindu nationalism, of a politically conservative form of female self-empowerment, of the ecofeminist argument that environmental conservation is best left to women in the traditional Indian village community, and of the specifically populist concept 'urban bias'.

Finally, in associating exploitation with the 'foreigner', the BJP also reproduces and reinforces the image of capitalism as an unproblematically external phenomenon, a view which annexes the concept of an economically undifferentiated rural population promoted by the new farmers' movements, ecofeminism, populists and the left. In the context of economic liberalization then being applied in India, which licensed even more ruthless competition from international capitalism, with an attendant withdrawal of government subsidies, declining prices and shrinking markets, the farmers' movements experienced a twofold pressure: from external (= 'foreign') capital on the one hand, and from the domestic working class on the other.[97] Accordingly, the resulting hostility of the farmers' movements towards international capital reinforced the politico-ideological acceptability of nationalist concepts of 'foreigner' (= 'other'), the same being true of antagonism expressed against workers in analogously communal idioms.[98]

3.13 Conclusion

Because class struggle is generally regarded as a process waged largely – albeit unsuccessfully – from below, there has been a tendency to underestimate both the capacity and willingness of the colonial and post-colonial ruling classes in rural India to protect their interests by waging class struggle from above. Traditionally, the latter has taken two forms. First, violence by landlords, their private gangs, and the state, directed against the left in general and in particular its grassroots support among poor peasants and agricultural labourers. And second, the attempt from above to divide potential/actual political opponents by communalizing the agrarian struggle.

Instead of opposing attempts to undermine class struggle by challenging communal identities invoked 'from above', however, sections of the Indian left have themselves invoked communal identity 'from below'. By not only suppressing class issues in the name of a non-existent peasant unity but also directly or indirectly communalizing the agrarian struggle, the CPI/CPM/ CP(ML) have – like their political opponents – also contributed to the under-mining of a socialist project. Ironically, therefore, the parties on the Indian left have long adhered to precisely that mobilizing discourse (operating through existing ideology/identity) which many of those critical of socialism now wish them to adopt.

Like their Maoist counterparts in Latin America (Sendero in Peru and ANUC in Colombia), Naxalites from the CPI(ML) in West Bengal over the 1967–71 period not only mobilized tribal support on the basis of cultural particularism, claiming that no difference existed between present struggles and those of the 1855 tribal insurrection, but also organized guerrilla activity on the basis of existing tribal and kin group authority at the village level. Unsurprisingly, therefore, by the late 1980s, the CPI(ML) was engaged not in class but in caste struggle, mobilizing backward caste Yadavs against high caste Rajputs. Although Rajputs have traditionally consisted of substantial proprietors, a few of the latter are now also to be found among the ranks of the Yadavs, so in this situation caste does not correspond to class.

This displacement of class by caste reached its apogee in the populist dis-course of the new farmers' movements which emerged in India during the 1980s. Claiming to break with the socialist/nationalist politics/practice of the past, farmers have mobilized in support of village community (rural India, or *Bharat*), women as 'natural' protectors of the environment, and an undifferen-tiated peasantry, against a 'looting', unecological, economically uniform urban industrialism (urban India, or *India*) and its state. However, important components of this discourse, and in particular its structuring principle of an urban/rural divide, are prefigured in and symptomatic of the politics and ideo-logy of neopopulism/nationalism: in Europe from nineteenth-century nationalist movements to twentieth-century fascism, and in India from the freedom movement of Gandhi, through the post-Independence mobilizations of Charan Singh to the communalism of the BJP/VHP/RSS.

In this neopopulist/nationalist discourse, the city is the locus of negative/(profane) attributes: a large-scale, science-based, polluting industry, protected by a wasteful bureaucracy in the taxation/surplus-extracting state, the revenues of which are used solely for the benefit of an externally-oriented/ ('treacherous') westernized/('decadent') elite and its potentially/

actually politically menacing proletariat ('the mob in the streets'). Behind all the latter, moreover, are to be found the economic and political interests of 'the foreigner'. In short, precisely a combination of agents/institutions/processes which are perceived to undermine petty commodity production, and through this the nation itself.

By contrast, 'the rural' is inscribed by this same discourse with stereo-typically positive/(sacred) attributes: the locus of an harmonious/traditional/(atemporal) ethnic/gender/religious/('natural') purity embodied in a small-scale, ecologically sustainable village-level agriculture and artisan production. The latter, however, are condemned to poverty/inefficiency precisely by virtue of the violence/profligacy/('looting') engaged in by their 'other': 'the urban' and its 'foreign' backers. It is these neopopulist/nationalist politico-ideological oppositions that the discourse of the new farmers' move-ments, ecofeminism, and elements of the left either endorses or does not challenge.

At the core of this neopopulist/nationalist conceptual matrix, in which a number of innate identities are symbolically interchangeable (rural = Nature = woman = nation) and on which 'popular culture' is based, lies an equally symptomatic – yet politico-ideologically potent – view of 'peasant' as the embodiment of traditional and enduring cultural/religious values. Hence the displacement of a class-differentiated by undifferentiated concept of 'peasant' in the discourse of new farmers' movements, ecofeminism and sections of the left, enables – indeed encourages – the recasting of the now-homogeneous peasantry as a (non-economic) cultural category, and therefore as a bearer of natural/ahistorical characteristics which can in turn form the basis of an eternal/ever-present (folkloric) national identity and thus nationhood.

The metamorphosis of 'popular culture' from a passive to an active historical role is linked in part to its being the source of self-empowerment on which grassroots 'resistance' is based. Whereas in India the process of agrarian mobilization (of nation against colonialism, of peasant against land-lord) for neopopulists such as Gandhi and Charan Singh was largely defensive, a segment of the new farmers' movements has gone onto the offensive, and now regards global free trade as advantageous to the (rich) peasantry. At the level of discourse, this metamorphosis has been matched by an analogous shift in the realm of nationalist/communal ideology on the part of the BJP/VHP/RSS, resulting in a confluence not merely of discourses but more importantly of political action (= self-empowerment) linked to them.

This in turn can lead to the demobilization of agrarian *class* struggles by transforming/deflecting consciousness of class into (false) ethnic/national con-sciousness and conflict. Accordingly, organization/conflict undertaken by agricultural workers and poor peasants against class opponents becomes converted/diverted into a struggle on behalf of nation, against the external and/or internal 'foreigner' (who is to be resisted, and then expelled or killed). By virtue of being resistance in a context where all politically unspecific resistance is regarded as positive (action/discourse-against), however, it remains possible for some to continue to interpret even this kind of mobilization as progressive.

In these ways, and for these reasons, therefore, not only is the radical new agenda claimed by/for new social movements neither radical nor new, but the complicity of the new farmers' movements, ecofeminism, and sections of the left with what is an historically longstanding neopopulist/nationalist/(communal) discourse about the interrelationship between people/peasants/gender/ Nature/nation has contributed towards the reproduction of an ideological space which permits right-wing political organizations to reappropiate the Indian past (to undertake 'resistance' in defence of 'popular culture', in other words) with the object of creating an ethnically specific Indian state. The next two chapters will accordingly examine the wider significance of this process, in terms of the co-terminous rise of the 'new' populism influenced by postmodern theory, and also the political implications of such a development.

NOTES

1. Words that could apply to the Indian farmers' movements of the 1980s, to the effect that they were mobilizations by 'a class of cash-conscious commercial farmers, producing staples both for the world market and linked to the bustling, competitive petty capitalist life of the expanding small towns of the . . . interior' which 'aimed, above all, to restore agrarian profits and to scale down agrarian debts . . . [and] assumed that general prosperity could be restored without a thoroughgoing reconstruction of the economic or constitutional order..', are in fact those used by Hofstadter [1969: 9, 26] to describe the rural supporters of American populism one hundred years earlier.

2. See Moore [1967: 202], and for the many instances of peasant mobilization spanning the Moghul and the post-Independence era, see Gough [1979: 85–126]. Texts on agrarian movements in India include Desai [1979, 1986], Dhanagare [1983], Gupta [1986], Karna [1989], Nadkarni [1987], Pavier [1981], Pouchepadass [1980], Sen [1982] and Wood [1987].

3. For the link between on the one hand the capitalist crisis of the 1930s, the wartime devaluation, the development of what Patnaik identifies as a 'pre-famine conjuncture', and the 1943 Bengal famine, and on the other the politico-ideological delegitimization of the landlord class in Bengal and the subsequent participation by their sharecroppers and tenants in the *Tebhaga* movement, see Patnaik [1991], Greenhough [1982], and Cooper [1988: 247–8].

4. Given the importance of both these peasant movements, the literature on them is large. For background, together with debates by participants and others (about social composition, political alliances, possible outcomes, etc.), see Sen [1972], Sundarayya [1972], Rao [1972], Pavier [1981], and Cooper [1988].

5. For example, Yadav [1993b] not only unproblematically blames socialism for its own political difficulties but also proposes a 'rethought' variant of the same that no longer resembles the original. Accordingly, his 'socialism' is unconnected with metanarratives (= 'European models'), requires the abandonment of the concept 'false consciousness' and a corresponding political acceptance (= 'understanding') of the 'existing moral traditions' (caste, religion, 'popular culture', 'rural society') that amounts to no more than a diluted variant of the nationalism/populism of the subaltern studies project (see Chapter 4).

6. Official statistics published in the *Indian Express*, 14 April 1987. Gough [1979: 118] reports that some ten thousand peasants linked to the communists in India were killed during the 1967–70 period of the Naxalite movement. For the continuing incidence and impact of landowning class violence in Bihar, see Prasad [1989: 75–94].

7. On this point see Amnesty International [1983: 61–8].

8. It is important to note in this connection that the communalization of struggle from above frequently triggers a corresponding communalization as a response from below, resulting in a mutually constructed discourse that leads to the displacement of class. For example, arguing that it would have been possible for Gandhi to have advanced an anti-untouchability campaign if he had been serious about it, Ambedkar [1946: 257] observes that: 'He [Gandhi] could have proposed that if a Hindu wishes to enroll himself as a member of Congress he should prove that he does not observe untouchability and that the employment of an Untouchable in his household should be advanced in support of his claim in this behalf . . .' The practicality of such a test, Ambedkar continues, lay in the fact that 'almost every Hindu, certainly every high caste Hindu, keeps more than one servant in his household'. In other words, Ambedkar was challenging untouchability while simultaneously accepting the class structure of which it was a part. That Hinduism was for Ambedkar the enemy is a point conceded by Omvedt and Patankar [1992: 386]; that is, the framing (or acceptance) of conflict in ethnic terms cannot but elicit an opposite reaction in similarly ethnic terms (on this point, see also Engineer [1992]). Unsurprisingly, therefore, not only were the 1993 Assembly elections in the states of northern India characterized by a process of ethnic/caste/communal consolidation (from below as well as from above), but opposition to the existing structure on the part of the *Dalit Voice* spoke from the perspective of a petty-bourgeois dalit cultural nationalism against a 'Brahmanical Social Order' [*Omvedt,* 1993a: 2403–4].

9. A manual by Green [1925] advising planters on the importance of caste ritual/practice makes explicit the political object of reinforcing caste distinctions among the plantation workforce.

10. Much the same kind of argument ('we appeal to peasants not to launch direct action this year . . . [t]he new government of independent India . . . must be given an opportunity for fulfilling its promises through legal channels') was used by the CPI similarly to defuse agrarian class struggle in Bengal during this period [*Pouchepadass,* 1980: 151].

11. Generally speaking, the potentially reactionary nature and mobilizing role of non-politically-specific (= 'a-political') concepts of 'the popular' can be illustrated by reference to the epistemological overlap between Gandhian philosophy and anarchism, and between variants of the latter and much current right-wing libertarian theory (Barry [1986: 161–91], Block and Rothwell [1988], Dupré [1985],

Pirie [1988], Nash [1976: 313–19], Nozick [1974], Rothbard [1978: 191–207]).

12. For Soviet perceptions of Gandhi, see Kautsky [1956] and Tidmarsh [1960: 86–115]. Throughout the 1920s and 1930s, Gandhi was regarded by the CPSU in a somewhat contradictory light: as a reactionary, but nevertheless necessary, component of the nationalist struggle for independence from British colonialism. Although located politically on the right-wing of the Indian nationalist movement by Soviet theoreticians, therefore, his reformism was in many ways an accurate reflection of the primacy accorded to national revolution by Comintern strategy during the 1935–43 period. From 1949 onwards, the Soviet Union turned to the Peoples Republic of China as an ally against western imperialism, and correspondingly downgraded the importance of struggle in India. Accordingly, Gandhi was henceforth described as a 'progressive' who fulfilled a 'major and positive role ... in the history of the struggle of the Indian people'; his non-violence was now reinterpreted in positive terms, as was his emphasis on tribal self-determination and more generally the mobilization of the masses in support of the independence movement. Most significantly, the reactionary elements of Gandhian philosophy were now recast. Not only were the negative aspects of his anti-industrial views dismissed as insignificant, but his opposition to western technology was reinterpreted as being politically acceptable: as evidence of an authentic Indian rejection of Western European colonial tradition, and thus the only way in which the peasantry could be persuaded to oppose/overthrow colonialism. This rehabilitation of Gandhi at the very moment when the Indian bourgeoisie assumed power sanctified not merely the continuation of an anti-imperialist (= nationalist) rather than an anti-capitalist (= socialist) programme but also a reactionary version of this, and thus could not but legitimize the politics of class collaboration subsequently pursued by the CPI.

13. See Dange [1969: 10]. Much the same point has been made by R. Palme Dutt and E.M.S. Namboodiripad (see Ghose [1971: 121, 133], Namboodiripad [1959: 111ff.; 1966: 46]).

14. See Omvedt [1990c: 12–22].

15. Much the same occurred in Kerala during the 1960s, where a class of agrarian capitalists emerged from among the ranks of tenants who had themselves been active in the anti-landlord struggles led by the CPI(M), and who were also the beneficiaries of the land reform carried out during that decade [*Krishnaji*, 1986: 384–402]. Contradictions subsequently arose within this anti-landlord front, when on the wages question agricultural labourers encountered fierce opposition from their rich and middle peasant employers, activists who had been in the vanguard of the earlier struggles against the landlord class. The same was true of Andhra Pradesh during the 1980s, where in order to maintain 'peasant unity' the CPI(M) refused to act against rich and middle peasants who employed bonded labour [*Balagopal*, 1986: 1401–5].

16. As the work of Alexander [1981], George [1984: 47–51], Gough [1989: 473–7, 478ff.] and Kannan [1988: 248ff.] shows, in parts of Kerala and Tamil Nadu, where the left has organized on the basis of class and excluded small farmers and tenants from unions of agricultural labourers, not only have the latter succeeded in obtaining higher wages and better working conditions but higher and backward caste workers have become members of the same union.

17. On this, see Bhattacharya [1990: 2209–14]. The similarity between the 'anti-foreigner' position adopted by the CPI with respect to Tripura in the 1930s and that

of new social movements in Assam during 1979–80 is noted below.

18. On this point, see Hardgrave [1973: 134]. By contrast, an ethnically-specific ideology is an appropriate mobilizing discourse for agrarian capitalists, as the case of the new farmers' movements demonstrates (see below).

19. Banaji [1980: 233], for example, attributes the political dominance of the Indian bourgeoisie to the 'exceptional backwardness of the Indian Communist Party in its early phases of attempted formation'. Das, Rojas and Waterman [1984], by contrast, regard the Indian left as too vanguardist, and like the left generally in peripheral capitalist societies of the so-called Third World, too focussed on the mobilization of organized workers in the urban sector. Instead, Das et al. advocate the adoption of an Autonomist position, whereby all 'labouring people' and not just the proletariat are mobilized outside formal party structures in a common struggle for autonomy from capital and the state. The problem with this view is that – like populism – it fails to distinguish between the two different forms of anti-capitalism, and thus conflates petty-bourgeois elements, such as artisans and petty commodity producers which are opposed not to capitalism but only to specific variants of this (finance capital, large-scale industry, foreign/international capital), with urban/rural proletarians opposed to capitalism per se. As has been noted above, whereas the latter have an interest in socialism, the former do not, and are in some instances strongly anti-socialist in political outlook.

20. On tribal migration in northeast India see, for example, Rao [1986], Bhowmik [1981], and Vidyarthi [1970]. Until the development in the 1940s of pan-tribal movements, Santal and Bhumij culture had for a long time been incorporating Hindu beliefs and behaviour, while Munda ceremonial and religion had similarly been influenced by both Hinduism and Christianity [Bose, 1985: 22ff.].

21. See Bose [1985]. Similar observations concerning the socio-economic differentiation of tribal peasants in other parts of India at this conjuncture are made by, inter alia, Datta [1989], Mishra [1987], Pathy [1976] and Pathy [1987].

22. Pathy [1984: 25,185ff.] makes much the same observation about the fact that welfare measures aimed at tribals invariably benefit the better-off elements, and thus paradoxically intensify and hasten the very differentiation process they are designed to prevent.

23. See Bose [1985: 75, 80, 84, Tables 3.10, 3.14, 3.16].

24. See Bose [1985: 51, 86–7, 88–9].

25. See Bose [1985: 94–5].

26. Tribals who are rich peasants engage in productive moneylending to secure labour-power cheaply, and 71 per cent of tribal agricultural labour households are in debt to such landholders. The economic object of this activity is described by Bose [1985: 95, 101–2] in the following terms: '. . . all the rich peasants advance money to tribal labourers so that during the peak season, when the demand for labour is high, they get them at comparatively cheaper rates . . . [t]he loans are mainly consumption loans, which labourers take during the lean period . . . [these have] to be repaid [in the form of] labour during the peak agricultural season'.

27. See Bose [1985: 112–13, 118–19, 121–2].

28. See Duyker [1987].

29. See Duyker [1987: 110, 124]. Despite maintaining that Santals expected a classless society to emerge from the Naxalite movement, Duyker [1987: 123] furnishes no evidence to support this assertion.

30. See Duyker [1987: 101–2, 117]. One CPI(M-L) leader noted that: 'When we went

to the Santals we used to emphasize their [1855 Insurrectionary] heroes . . . We told them that Sidhu and Kanhu were our predecessors and that "New Democracy was no different from what they had fought for" ' [*Duyker*, 1987: 118].

31. Duyker [1987: 118]. The Maoist Communist Centre, which Duyker [1987: 152] notes as consolidating its position in West Bengal from the 1970s onwards, was by 1987 engaged not in class but caste struggle in neighbouring Bihar, a communalization that culminated in the killings of Rajputs by Naxalite-led Yadavs in Aurangabad district. As one commentator observed, 'Over the years, the new, better-off class among the backward castes transformed itself into the kulak lobby. Today, the same people who were once in the forefront of the Kisan Sabha movement are the oppressors. 'Another source makes much the same point, commenting that 'Yadavs occupy a peculiar position on the socio-economic scale in this part of Bihar. They are both exploiters and exploited. Many of them own land and are said to maltreat Harijan agricultural workers.' See Kanchan Gupta, 'Communism through caste in Bihar', *The Statesman*, 16 June, 1987; Chandan Mitra, 'Caste-Class War In Bihar To Go On', *The Times of India*, 3 June 1987.

32. See Duyker [1987: 50ff.].

33. See Duyker [1987: 133ff.].

34. See Duyker [1987: 60ff.].

35. See Duyker [1987: 62–3].

36. See Duyker [1987: 89, 103–4].

37. In the case of Uttar Pradesh, for example, the organizational success of the BKU has been attributed to caste and clan solidarity among the Jats, clan heads having acquired leadership of BKU units, and the support for the new farmers' movement in Karnataka is strongly rooted among the Lingayat and Okkaliga castes (Dhanagare [1988: 30; 1994], Nadkarni [1987]; see also Hasan [1994] and Gill [1994]).

38. It was the National Front government of V.P. Singh which replaced Congress that convened the Standing Advisory Committee on Agriculture (see Government of India [1991]), chaired by the leader of Shetkari Sanghatana, Sharad Joshi.

39. Among those who hold this view are Rudolph and Rudolph [1984, 1987: 333–92], Lenneberg [1988], Gupta [1988], Weiner [1989: 129ff.], Lindberg [1990], and Athreya, Djurfeldt and Lindberg [1990: 314–15]. For the similarity between the new farmers' movements view of the state, and those of the Russian populists, see Chapter 1.

40. Thus the 1928 Bardoli 'no-tax' campaign is one example of mobilization by rich peasants against the attempt by the colonial state to increase revenue in line with land values. Similarly, rich and middle peasant mobilization in Andhra Pradesh during the 1950s centred not only on landholding but also on tax reduction, better provision of agricultural inputs (irrigation, electricity), and the fixing by the state of remunerative prices for their agricultural produce [*National Labour Institute Report*, 1986]. As is clear from an interview he gave in 1947 to Colin Clark, an economist advising the Indian Planning Commission about development strategy, Gandhi also espoused an earlier version of 'remunerative prices' for peasant farmers. Clark [1984: 63] reported that: 'Gandhi . . . proved to be a convinced free-market economist, strongly critical of . . . price controls, rationing, and compulsory purchase of farm crops . . . The right solution, [Gandhi] said was to raise the price of food, then everyone would have to work harder. The source of India's troubles [he thought] was that the people were thoroughly idle.' The issue of remunerative

prices for peasant farmers was also central to Charan Singh's neopopulist programme of the 1960s and 1970s [*Singh*, 1978: 35ff.].

41. For the claim both that in the Green Revolution areas of India land is no longer a political issue, and that this is one of the distinctively new aspects of the farmers' movements of the 1980s, see Lindberg [1990] and also Athreya, Djurfeldt, and Lindberg [1990: 314]. For the continued importance of the land question in India, see Das [1988: 17]. Adopting a somewhat contradictory position, Rudolph and Rudolph [1984: 284] argue that land redistribution remains an objective of the farmers' mobilization, but only in so far as it does not threaten existing property relations. For the importance of land as well as marketing and prices as an issue defining the new agrarian movements in Mexico, see Harvey [1990: 41].

42. Between 1981/82 and 1985/86 direct subsidies for items such as food, fertilizers, etc., paid by the Union government to agriculture doubled (from Rs 19,460 million to Rs 41,880 million), an increase which takes no account of the infrastructural expenditure (or indirect subsidies to agriculture) on roads and transportation over the same period [*Mehta*, 1992: 224–5, Table 3]. More generally, from Independence onwards the terms of trade have moved in favour of agriculture [*Chattopadhyay, Sharma and Ray*, 1987: 158–60]. The economic unsustainability of the concept 'urban bias' is echoed in politico-ideological terms by scheduled caste agricultural labourers from Karnataka, who reject it on the grounds that for them the main contradiction remains one between 'private property owners and the non-propertied' in all sectors, and not one between workers in rural and urban contexts [*Nadkarni*, 1987: 150–51].

43. In Karnataka, for example, the farmers' demand for an increase in the price of paddy is strongly opposed by their Dalit workforce, both because it would result in a corresponding rise in the purchase price of rice consumed by poor peasants and agricultural labourers, and because – contrary to the claims made by the farmers themselves – wages would not be increased to meet such price rises. Much rather the opposite: when Dalits challenge farmers to pay them rates stipulated in existing legislation, employers respond by replacing them with externally recruited migrants [*Nadkarni*, 1987: 152]. That is, restructuring the agrarian labour process by recomposing its workforce. For an analogous instance of class struggle leading to workforce restructuring by farmers in Haryana during the late 1980s, see Brass [1999: Ch. 3]. For the views of Sharad Joshi on the issue of 'remunerative prices', see Government of India [1991: 14–15, 33–4, paragraphs 37, 84–8]. Joshi himself provides evidence that any link between the receipt by farmers of higher crop prices ('remunerative prices') and the payment by them of higher wages ('trickle down' argument) is problematic when he claims high wage costs as a reason for higher prices: if wage costs are already too high, then any increases in product prices would merely serve to offset these high wages, and consequently would not – as Joshi maintains – be passed on to agricultural workers in the form of wage increases. For Joshi's contradictory utterances on this issue, see Dhanagare [1990: 362, 363].

44. In contrast to the new farmers' movements, by whom the state is perceived as largely negative (denial of remunerative prices, potential/actual implementation of land ceilings and minimum wages legislation), agricultural workers from the scheduled castes in Karnataka regard the state in more positive terms, as provider both of protective legislation and of alternative non-rural employment oppor-

tunities. As one of its adherents admitted, the new farmers' movements hostility towards the state is due in part to the fact that 'if the labourers get monetary or material benefits or loans from the government, . . . they would develop their own activities (like livestock rearing) and would not come for agricultural coolie work..[a]griculture would then suffer without coolies' [*Nadkarni*, 1987: 152–3].

45. Joshi [1993: 3,4,6] extols and evaluates the advantages to the farmers' movements of the Dunkel proposals in the following manner: 'it emphasises the importance of rural-urban balance as a structural precondition to a free trade system . . . [t]his anti-statism and free marketism has its practical side too. The Indian primary produce is generally in a position of comparative advantage in the international market despite fragmentation of land, low capital formation and sustained State repression. The advantage is sizeable in fruit, cotton, some foodgrains and health-foods . . . The middle-layer farmer is quietly confident of being able to compete in the international markets if only the Government kept its cotton-picking hands off . . . [t]he new epoch of destatisation, liberalisation and globalisation comes like a fresh breeze.'

46. The unambiguously nationalist discourse structuring this opposition to the free trade proposals of GATT is evident from the following comments made by peasants attending the farmers' rally in New Delhi: 'What they [the Indian govern-ment] are trying to do to the farming community is selling them to the *foreigners* . . . Our leaders have said that the *foreign* paper [Dunkel draft] is an evil design to sell Mother India to *foreigners*. For a kisan, the life support are his land, seed and plough. If the Rao government sells these to the *foreigners* what will happen to the national pride . . . we are against the Government policies which are not only destroying the farmers's economy in a phased plan but also corroding the country's industry and culture . . . We are now self-sufficient in crop production: so why this sell-out to MNCs?' (emphasis added). Other proposals made by the farmers' movement and framed in a similarly nationalistic discourse included banning multinational corporations from having access to agricultural land. See 'Farmers against Dunkel Draft', *The Hindustan Times*, 4 March 1993.

47. On these points, Joshi [*Government of India*, 1991: 36, 42–3, paragraphs 88, 105, 106–7] observes: '[A] certain minimum export should be permitted, in the case of commodities which have an international market, irrespective of the supply situa-tion in the domestic market. In cases where the domestic supplies are insufficient, shortfall should be made up by compensatory imports rather than by restriction on exports . . . All zonal restrictions on the movement of produce should be scrapped . . . .the industrial lobbies are for ever active to minimize any exports of agri-cultural produce with the objective of keeping the domestic prices low.'

48. Government of India [1991: 17, 23, 24, 26, 29, 30, 42–3, 49 paragraphs 40, 55, 60, 64, 73, 78, 106–7, 126]. It should be noted that the issue of ownership of crop species and seed varieties is at the centre of the opposition by Tikait, Nanjundaswamy and Shiva to the position adopted by GATT on intellectual property rights. Unsurprisingly, resistance by the new farmers' movements to the threat by transnational agribusiness corporations to patent indigenous seed varieties, and thus establish legal title to an important component of the agrarian productive forces in India, is projected by Shiva [1993a: 555, 557, 560] in nationalist terms: that is, as a challenge by the 'foreigner' both to 'national sovereign rights to biodiversity and patterns of its utilization' (= 'colonization'), and to the 'inalienable cultural rights' of 'traditional' farmers in 'traditional'

societies, emphasizing thereby the extent to which for Shiva 'nation' = Nature. Moreover, the mobilizing slogan 'Seed *Satyagraha*' (see Shiva [1993a: 555]) encountered at the farmers' rally of 3 March 1993 asserts this right to control such productive forces in unambiguously Gandhian terms.

49. For the hostility of the farmers' movement in Karnataka towards the GATT proposals, and the perceived threat to the farming sector in India of pressure from the IMF and the World Bank for the adoption of economic liberalization policies, see Kripa [1992: 1183], Omvedt [1993b] and Assadi [1994].

50. As demanded by Joshi, Indian peasants were henceforth permitted to export staple foodgrains, regardless of the domestic situation. Furthermore, agrarian capitalists were able not only to import equipment and raw materials duty free, a concession hitherto enjoyed only by export processing zones, but also to sell half the output produced on the domestic market. In keeping with the prognosis of Sharad Joshi, one report characterized the effects of this change in agricultural policy as 'the most significant liberalisation of the country's farm trade . . . since independence', and forecast that Indian farmers 'could well become internationally competitive exporters'. See 'Farmers Reap Benefit of Indian Reform', *Financial Times* (London), 1 April, 1993.

51. For the views of Sharad Joshi on the issue of agricultural wages and the related question of the fairprice Public Distribution System, see Government of India [1991: 37–9, paragraphs 89–98]. Significantly, by demanding wage increases for hired labour and payment for peasant family labour employed in agriculture, Joshi not only presented himself in a positive manner politically but also (and perhaps more importantly) strengthened his case for remunerative prices linked to higher production costs. As has been noted above, there is no evidence that such wage payments/increases would be passed on to those who actually supply the labour-power; and even if they were, such benefits would be cancelled out by the contraction of the Public Distribution System, another of Joshi's policy recommendations. Unsurprisingly, given his support for the free market and higher crop prices, Joshi was opposed to a Public Distribution System based on state procurement of fixed-price food. At the level of discourse, however, he was able to circumvent this contradiction by maintaining that the main beneficiary of fairprice shops is the urban population, and consequently the Public Distribution System constituted yet more evidence of 'urban bias'.

52. Hence the observation by Sharad Joshi that '[i]t is a conspiracy on the part of the Indian elite to try to divide Bharat in terms of big, medium and small farmers. There is no line of contradiction between the big and small with regard to prices' (quoted in Nadkarni [1987: 142]). The mobilizing slogan adopted by the followers of Charan Singh in 1979 ('Today, India's villages are the colony of the city') not only contains echoes of 'urban bias' but is similar in this respect to the one ('Bharat versus India') subsequently popularized by Sharad Joshi. The latter's observation [Government of India, 1991: 18, paragraph 42] that '[t]he size of the holding of any family is more directly related to the familial situation than to the economic one' suggests a Chayanovian concept of the peasant family farm, the reproduction of which is determined not by exogenous ('economic') categories such as rent and wages but by the endogenous ('familial') category of the producer/consumer balance (see Chapter 1). Significantly, the Bharat/India opposition projects not just an urban/rural divide but also the implication that behind the process of urban exploitation of the rural producer lies the 'foreign'/'other' (see,

for example, Government of India [1991: 6, paragraph 14]), which in turn licenses the symbolic fusion of Bharat = nation and thus a correspondingly nationalist appropriation of the Bharat/India opposition itself. It became possible, therefore, for the Hindu chauvinist BJP to argue that, as all rural inhabitants were the authentic components of *Bharat*, they were consequently the embodiment of nationalism and thus the true inheritors of post-colonial state power. For Joshi's views on the pervasive concept 'urban bias', see Government of India [1991: 3, 6, 45, paragraphs 9, 10, 18, 113].

53. Among those writing about the new farmers' movements, Dhanagare [1994] and Assadi [1994] question the presence of 'urban bias' while Hasan [1994], Lindberg [1994], Gill [1994], and Omvedt [1994b] all subscribe to its existence.

54. See Varshney [1993a; 1993b]. It is somewhat curious, to put it no more strongly, that in a collection of essays dealing with the issue of 'urban bias' [*Varshney, 1993c*] no mention is made of Marxist views (for example, Mitra [1977], Chattopadhyay, Sharma and Ray, [1987]) about this concept. Perhaps the most plausible explanation for such an omission is a straightforwardly political one: a Marxist approach is not merely incompatible with but undermines much of the argument contained in the contributions to the collection, all of which comes from a neo-classical economic position (for example, Lipton [1993], Bates [1993]). In the case of Varshney, this involves issues of 'choice-making' subjects and institutional constraints [*Varshney, 1993b: 202, 207*]. Significantly, he shares with Sharad Joshi the perception of the fiscal burden as a 'problem' of unnecessary administrative expenditure [*Varshney, 1993b: 202*].

55. Given his view that the existence of democratic political structures enables (= empowers) peasants and farmers to exercise pressure for higher prices, it is unsurprising that Varshney [1993b: 210] holds the converse to be true: that is, 'that *there is no systematic ruralising tendency in authoritarian polities*' (original emphasis). This is a surprising claim, and shows an unfamiliarity not just with the agrarian myth but also with debate about the agrarian question, and in particular Lenin's concept of a Prussian road (see Chapter 1).

56. See Varshney [1993b: 179, 200].

57. Symptomatically, in considering the potential/actual role of taxation in India, Varshney makes no mention of the seminal contribution to this debate by Kalecki [1976], who argued that the political unwillingness of the state to directly tax agriculture – a consequence of the class nature of Indian society and the state – would lead to deficit financing and precisely the economic problems that Varshney attempts to address.

58. See Varshney [1993b: 202, 205, 208, 210].

59. The fact that the notion of *contradiction* must be inserted into questions about empowerment (of one category/class at the expense of another category/class) seems to escape Varshney. Although acknowledging the importance of including agricultural labour in any consideration of 'urban bias', therefore, he excludes them from his conceptualization of 'rural sector' (= peasants, farmers) and then proceeds to argue for a situation of general 'rural well-being' that fails to take into account the antithetical interests of rural workers [*Varshney* 1993b: 210, 211, footnote 1].

60. For the position of Shetkari Sanghatana on the desirability of a political alliance beween the farmers' movement and the womens' movement, together with Sharad Joshi's reasons for this, see Government of India [1991: 6, paragraph 17] and

Omvedt [1986: 2085–6]. It is clear from the latter text, and also from Omvedt [1990a: 238, 246], that the *Sanghatana Mahila Aghadi* activists were predominantly women from middle caste and rich or middle peasant family backrounds who wanted a better deal under existing propery rights, not to change property rights themselves.

61. Guru [1992: 1463–65] and Government of India [1991: 22, paragraph 54]. The acceptability of this intra-household system of property transfer was not unconnected with the ability of rich peasant supporters of the new farmers' movements to use the *Laxmi Mukti* programme as another form of *benami*; that is, to undermine existing agrarian reform laws by evading land ceiling legislation. In a similar vein, Joshi himself justified opposition to land ceiling legislation not in terms of a capacity on the part of better-off peasants to retain/consolidate property but in the spuriously progressive framework of gender equality; accordingly, and somewhat perversely, his argument emphasized that land reform would prevent rural women from becoming proprietors [*Government of India*, 1991: 22, paragraphs 52–3].

62. As noted by one observer [*Baxter*, 1971: 314; see also Graham, 1990: 189–90] about an earlier period, much the same kind of dilemma confronted the parties of the political right: 'The Jana Sangh would like to import western technology and use western capital while barring the entry of western secularism and liberalism. It is doubtful that such a policy can succeed'.

63. This Gandhian populism is outlined in Singh [1978: 90ff.; 1981: 269ff., 393ff.]. For details about the post-Independence growth in the political influence of the kulak lobby, together with the participation and role of rich peasants in the movements of the 1980s, see among others Nadkarni [1987], Chattopadhyay, Sharma and Ray [1987: 173ff.], Hasan [1989a; 1989b], Prasad [1991], and Dhanagare [1994].

64. For this reason, it is necessary to disagree strongly with the attempt by Rudolph and Rudolph [1984: 330–31; 1987: 357–8] to differentiate the 'old agrarianism' of Gandhi, which they rightly describe as conservative and anti-statist, from what they wrongly regard as the more progressive 'new agrarianism' of the new farmers' movements. For similar attempts to differentiate the 'robust realism' of the new farmers' movements from the backward looking peasant movements of earlier periods, see Dhanagare [1990: 360] and Gupta [1992]. And although they all disagree substantially on the political character of the new farmers' movements, Balagopal [1987a: 1546] and Omvedt and Galla [1987: 1926] deny the presence/importance of Gandhian themes.

65. On these points, see Nadkarni [1987: 142, 226–7], Kripa [1992: 1182–3], Guru [1992: 1464], and Gupta [1992].

66. Hence the complaint by Joshi [*Government of India*, 1991: 3, 7, paragraphs 9, 19] that 'The economic tenets of the Mahatma . . . were quickly abandoned. Industrialisation became synonymous with development. Development came to mean native replication of western industrial model . . . The nation is reaping the harvest of the anti-Mahatma economics it sowed.' For the differences between Gandhian and Nehruvian approaches to questions of development and the environment, see Roy and Tisdell [1992].

67. The structure of the Gandhian model of village development envisaged by Joshi [*Government of India*, 1991: 8, 9, 25, 47–9, paragraphs 21, 24–5, 62, 123–30] can be glimpsed from the following programmatic statements: 'This logic of develop-

mental model makes a major deviation from the model utilised since Independence guided by the "Mahatma's Talisman". It bases itself on a flourishing agrarian economic and village autonomy. The Gandhian model does not look upon under-development as either a vicious cycle or a natural state of affairs. It holds that growth is a natural process and can be in fact an enobling and happy experience . . . [t]he long-term solution to the problem of rural unemployment can come only from self-employment generated from the surplus that the farmers are allowed to retain . . . [t]he control from the state or the centre should be minimized and maximum powers vested in the community . . . [d]ecentralization of power and resuscitation of village panchayat is an important instrument of the present agricul-tural policy . . . .[t]he long-standing tradition has it that the village elders hold a position of respect . . .'. This position is very similar to that outlined in the mid-1930s by Kumarappa [1935: 10, 15], who claimed that: '[O]ur solution should be one which has room in it both for the profit-motive and for social control. And we believe that such a remedy is to be found in decentralising production and in practising the ideal of Swadeshi. Decentralising means refusing to dictate from the centre how things are to be produced and what kind they are to be, but leaving that always to the good sense and initiative of the producer . . . our ancient village organization sought to curb the profit-motive, to provide a subsistence to all, so that there are no great inequalities of income, to make villages self-contained and to give first place to personality or things of the spirit. All these objects are . . . best served by decentralising production.' Like Joshi and Kumarappa, Charan Singh also wanted to shift investment from heavy industry to employment-oriented artisan production in the village context [*Franda*, 1979: 83]. For an example of the attempt to recuperate a concept of village-based peasant economy for development theory generally, see Bideleux [1985].

68. For the endorsement by Shetkari Sanghatana of natural/organic farming, see Omvedt [1991b]. On the relationship between 'urban bias', environmental degra-dation, social unrest, and the necessity of 'appropriate' technology, Joshi [*Govern-ment of India*, 1991: 11–12, 15, 28, paragraphs 30–1, 37, 72] commented: 'In an old community where for centuries agricultural surplus has been expropriated for medieval luxuries . . . and industrial capital accumulation . . . land is fragmented and degenerated to low levels of fertility . . . the ecology [is] devastated . . . .[t]he short-sighted rush for industrialization has left the country . . . with a seriously damaged life support system – land, water, vegetation. Even before starting to resolve the ecological problems of the bullock-cart era, the nation is facing the problems of industrial pollution. The unbalanced economic policies are threaten-ing to tear the social fabric . . . [a]n alternative technology will need to be resorted to . . . initiating a real green revolution that would be less dependent on the rapidly depleting petroleum resources . . . [i]n order to improve the efficiency of small farms, . . . it will be necessary to introduce small agricultural implements and machinery along with appropriate technology.' More recently, Joshi [1993: 6] has invoked the ecosystem as a countervailing 'natural' advantage enjoyed by Indian peasants competing in global markets ('third world countries have a natural advan-tage in natural biodiversity'), to be offset against the highly technified/mechanized productive capacity of farmers in metropolitan capitalist countries.

69. A report in *The Hindustan Times* of 4 March, 1993, about the farmers' rally in New Delhi noted that Vandana Shiva 'who seemed to have earned the respect of senior farmer leaders, said . . . "[w]e are here [at the rally] to make the movement

sharper. Our goal is to give the farmers' revolution a proper shape and create a political direction and impact".'

70. For these views, see Shiva [1988; 1990; 1991a; 1991b; 1992a; 1992b; 1993b; 1998]. For the political importance and influence of her ideas, see among others Omvedt [1990b: 27ff.], Merchant [1992: 200ff.] and Jackson [1993]. It is important to situate the work of Shiva in the political shift experienced globally by feminist theory over the period from 1970 to the mid-1980s. In its first phase, feminist theory developed a specifically materialist critique of gender difference as a social/historical construct; maintaining that gender subordination/oppression was largely economic, the political solution it advocated was the elimination of masculinity/femininity difference [*Eisenstein*, 1984]. By contrast, the second phase was characterized by a reactionary form of gender essentialism that not only emphasized gender difference but equated biological female identity with self-empowerment/liberation. Like ecofeminism generally, which in Third World contexts is opposed to the devaluation of women and Nature by Western culture and accordingly seeks to protect traditional ways of life, the work of Shiva is a product of this second phase. The extent to which her work is structured by this wider project of innateness based on gender essentialism is clear from the following observation by Merchant [1992: 185, 190–92]: 'Many cultural feminists celebrate an era in prehistory when nature was symbolized by pregnant female figures . . . which were held in high esteem as bringers-forth of life. An emerging patriarchal culture, however, dethroned the mother-godesses and replaced them with male gods to whom the female deities became subservient. The scientific revolution of the seventeenth century further degraded nature by replacing Renaissance organicism and a nurturing earth with the metaphor of the machine to be controlled and repaired from the outside. The ontology and epistemology of mechanism are viewed by cultural feminists as deeply masculinist and exploitative of a nature historically depicted in the female gender. The earth is dominated by male-developed and male-controlled technology, science, and industry. Often stemming from an anti-science, anti-technology standpoint, cultural ecofeminism celebrates the relationship between women and nature through the revival of ancient rituals . . . For cultural ecofeminists, human nature is grounded in human biology . . . Sex/gender relations give men and women different power bases . . . The perceived connection between women and biological reproduction turned upside down becomes the source of women's empowerment and ecological activism. Women's biology and Nature are celebrated as sources of female power . . . .' For the individualist basis of feminist theory, and hence an inherent epistemological compatibility with the neo-classical economic framework structuring the neo-populism of Chayanov, see Fox-Genovese [1991: 113ff.].

71. Shiva [1988: xiv, xvi, xvii, xviii, 6, 7; 1991a: 11–12]. Her target is encapsulated in the concept 'patriarchal mode of economic development in industrial capitalism' [1988: xvii]. Although considered politically to the left of Shiva (whose work she has influenced: see Mies and Shiva [1993]), Mies [1986: 217ff.] nevertheless ends up invoking as a specifically feminist and alternative perspective of a new society a similarly idealized image of a subsistence-oriented, autarchic peasant society. Interestingly, the World Bank [1992] has also endorsed the concept of women as 'natural' protector of the environment.

72. Shiva [1988: ix, xi–xii, xiv, xv, xviii, xx, 5, 219; 1991a: 11, 15, 233].

73. Shiva [1988: 2, 11; 1991a: 14, 29ff.]. For a similar claim that the principal contra-

diction is no longer between capital and labour, but between on the one hand 'colonized' indigenous peasant women in peripheral Third World contexts, and on the other an exploitative combination of white/male workers and capitalists at the industrialized core, see Mies, Bennholdt-Thomsen and von Werlhof [1988]. For an early invocation by essentialist feminism of woman-as-colonized-subject, see Morgan [1992: 74–7].

74. Shiva [1988: xiv, xix, xvii, 2, 4, 9, 10, 11, 55ff.; 1991a: 47, 49, 94–5]. For her endorsement of 'urban bias', see Shiva [1991a: 178]. This view of rural women in India generally as victims of 'urban bias', together with women's movement as a response to this, is also advanced by Omvedt [1990a: 231]. For the invocation by Shiva of Gandhian views concerning the non-applicability in Indian conditions of western industrial development, the spinning wheel as reassertion of traditional culture, and a self-sufficient peasantry, see Shiva [1988: xviii, 6; 1991a: 16, 27–8, 236, 238–40, 257, 263]. For the pervasiveness of Gandhian philosophy among gender-specific new social movements in India generally, see Sen [1990: 7]. That the wider object of the *charkha* revival was not only to displace machine-made imports from England with indigenous handspun textiles but also to preserve thereby small-scale artisan-based village production and with it the peasant economy by preventing further outmigration from rural areas (and hence the formation of an urban proletariat, or the feared 'mob in the streets') is clear from Puntambekar and Varadachari [1926: 120ff., 218ff.], a text introduced by Gandhi himself and endorsed by Congress.

75. Shiva [1991a: 171, 173, 175, 185, 191]. Significantly, in support of her views about the traditional and subsistence-oriented nature of peasant society she [1988: 4, 12] invokes both the 'limited good' concept of Foster [1962] and the Chayanovian exegesis of Sahlins [1972]. There are numerous instances from other contexts of a similar ideological convergence between populism and ecology. In the case of Africa, for example, ecological knowledge is equated with traditional knowledge [*Richards,* 1983; 1985; 1986; 1990], a position which in turn licenses a return to the past and thus a reaffirmation of Nature. Much the same is true of current attempts to recuperate a romanticized image of the North American Indian as the 'original ecologist', a golden age when the latter subject lived in timeless harmony with Nature.

76. About the unsustainability of the tribal/non-tribal distinction, Kosambi [1956: 25] has commented that '[t]he entire course of Indian history shows tribal elements being fused into a general society'.

77. A similar process of socio-economic differentiation is reported for tribals in the Northeastern Indian states of Assam and Arunachal Pradesh [*Goswami,* 1983: 266–75].

78. For the contributions to the debate about the characterization and the politically progressive/non-progressive nature of farmers'/social movements in India, see among others Rudolph and Rudolph [1984: 328ff.], Nadkarni [1987: 136ff.], Balagopal [1987a, 1987b], Omvedt and Galla [1987], Ray and Jha [1987], Das [1988], Lindberg [1990: 15ff.], Hasan [1989b], Dhanagare [1990], Banaji [1990], Omvedt [1991a] and Mehta [1992: 223ff.]. As an activist involved with the All-Women's Front (*Samagra Mahila Aghadi*) associated with Sharad Joshi's *Shetkari Sanghatana* in Maharashtra, the contributions to this debate by Omvedt are of particular interest (in addition to the above mentioned texts by her, see also Omvedt [1988; 1989; 1990a; 1991b]). As Ray and Jha [1987: 2229] rightly dis-

cern, a consequence of support she initially extended to Sharad Joshi because of his pronouncements on gender oppression is that Omvedt has shifted politically from a Marxist to a populist position (that is, a politico-ideological relay-in-statement).

79. All these issues are presented in Sinha [1982: 7, 8, 9, 10, 11, 12–13]. For resolutions of support from the CPI dominated All India Kisan Council, both for the new farmers' movements and their demands for lower taxes and remunerative prices, see All India Kisan Sabha [1981: 34–9, 49–50].

80. In this connection, it is perhaps worth recalling the warning of Karl Kautsky during the 1880s and 1890s against the trend towards electoral opportunism within German Social Democracy [*Salvadori*, 1979: 48ff., *Husain and Tribe*, 1984]. Against those like von Vollmar, who wished to build an electoral base among the peasantry, and who – as in the case of the new farmers' movements in India a century later – advocated an agrarian programme of price supports and debt write-offs in order to secure a following among the crisis-ridden small and middle peasantry, Kautsky argued that as ultimately the small peasant farm was an historically doomed institution, no attempt should be made to revitalize it.

81. For the politico-ideological fusion of RSS discourse with that of the BJP and VHP, together with the RSS background of the BJP leadership after 1986, see Anderson and Damle [1987: 228, 230, 235, 236–7] and Basu *et al.* [1993]. Significantly, prior to the emergence there of the Shetkari Sanghatana during the 1980s, M.G. Bokare, now a spokesperson for the RSS-dominated *Swadeshi Jagran Manch*, was an organizer/theorist of the cotton producers movement in Maharashtra [*Omvedt*, 1993a: 2402].

82. Sarkar [1991: 2057], Nadkarni [1987: 111], Lenneberg [1988: 447], Shah [1991]. To counter the influence of Sharad Joshi and draw support away from the farmers' movement, the BJP in Gujarat has supported the attempt by the BKS (*Bharatiya Kisan Sangh*) to mobilize the peasantry from 1986 onwards. 'In order to mobilise peasants', one observer [*Shah*, 1991: 2923] notes, 'the party took the support of spiritual leaders of different sects, invoked religious symbols and aroused Gujarati sentiments'. Similarly, in Karantaka, where the KRRS participated in the elections for the first time in 1991, it lost the votes of farmers' movement supporters to the BJP over the temple issue (Kripa [1992: 1182], Manor [1992], Gill [1994] and Hasan [1994]). For the inroads made by the BJP into the tribal constituencies of Congress in the 1993 Assembly Elections, see Yadav [1993a].

83. In this connection, it is necessary to emphasize two points. First, that just as the BJP can reappropriate nationalist/populist discourse from the new farmers' movements, ecofeminism, new social movements and the left, so this same discourse can in turn be appropriated – or in the case of Congress (I), reappropriated – from the BJP. And second, the populist/communal discourse under consideration here is supportive of nationalism *per se*, and not just the Hindu chauvinist variant espoused by the BJP/VHP/RSS: that is, of non-Hindu (or anti-Hindu) regionally-specific nationalism(s) in other parts of India (Punjab, Assam, Tamil Nadu).

84. The increasing rural support for the RSS has been noted by Anderson and Damle [1987: 248–9], who comment: 'Since its formation in 1925 the RSS has attracted support almost exclusively in urban areas, and largely from the salaried lower middle class and small-scale shopkeepers. These are groups whose social and economic aspirations are undermined by inflation, by scarcity of job opportunities, and by their relative inability to influence the political process. The RSS has had

little success among the peasantry . . . However, as change comes to affect increasingly large numbers of Indians, the revivalist appeals offered by the RSS (and by other groups as well) are likely to become more popular, and there are now signs that the RSS is making some headway in certain rural areas.'

85. Anderson and Damle [1987: 81, 103 footnote 50].

86. Anderson and Damle [1987: 72]. For the threat to India of an alien 'consumerism' generated by 'western industrialization' and more generally by ('foreign') economic imperialism, as conceptualized in the discourse of the RSS-influenced *Swadeshi Jagran Manch*, see Omvedt [1993a].

87. Anderson and Damle [1987: 73–4, 81]. Significantly, in the discourse of the BJP, Muslims are not merely externalized as a passive 'other' ('not-us') but are actively identified with the 'West' ('with-them'): hence the view that 'Muslims always do the opposite of what Hindus do. If the east is sacred to the Hindu, then the Muslim will worship the West' [*Basu et al.*, 1993: 77].

88. Anderson and Damle [1987: 81, 103 footnote 50]. Like the RSS, Sharad Joshi and Kumarappa, the Vice-President of the BJP, Sunder Singh Bhandari, has observed that the BJP similarly endorses the process of economic and political decentralization to village *panchayats* [*Basu et al.*, 1993: 49].

89. Anderson and Damle [1987: 194].

90. On this issue see in particular Sarkar [1991: 2059], who observes: 'The RSS occasionally plugs into a whole range of otherwise radical issues – ecology, world peace, interrelated critiques of western materialistic and monolithic notions of truth that lead to imperialist suppression of non-western identities.'

91. For an exposition of this view, see Dwivedi [1990]. An important prefiguring text in this regard is that by Kumarappa, who in the early 1930s observed [1935: 3] that: '[one of] the basic ideas which underlie our village life and organization [is] to avoid competition and the uncurbed play of the profit-motive, and conversely to promote cooperation. The caste-system distributed the work of society among its various members [and thus avoided] upsetting the whole social equilibrium, as happens today . . . The caste system also promoted group loyalty and cooperation, the absence of which is now so evident in us who are city-bred.'

92. For the RSS conceptualization of the 'sacred geography' of India, see Anderson and Damle [1987: 77]. For a Gandhian view equating peasant farming with 'the sacred', see Kumarappa [1935: 2].

93. Symptomatically, the CPI [*Rao and Faizee*, 1989: 3, 4ff.] condemned the communalism generated by the temple issue not because it diverted attention from socialist politics but because it endangered bourgeois democracy.

94. On this point, Sarkar [1991: 2059] comments: 'The discourse starts with the unique philosophical concept of tolerance within Hinduism . . . This very pluralism and tolerance, however, characterize a single national ethos which is essentially Hindu and to which all immigrant religions have adapted themselves. The notion of an essentially Hindu national ethos came under attack when "fanatic" Muslim rulers ruled the land and tried to destroy it with "brute strength". The British, however, "planned to subvert the Hindu mind itself". This was achieved through a seemingly successful mode of western knowledge which . . . substituted alien categories of thought for self-knowledge. The perception of a single national ethos was broken up and Indian history was restructured to prove that the nation means simply a geographical space . . . [According to the discourse of the BJP/VHP/RSS this] false and alien notion of secularism destroyed the single shared culture

and fractured the sense of wholeness, led to communalism and violence, and eventually culminated in partition.' For RSS claims that the Christian and Muslim influences undermine/denationalize India, and further that the disintegration of Hindu society dates from the period of Islamic invasions around the first millenium, see Anderson and Damle [1987: 72].

95. For the racially-specific reproductive role of 'motherhood' in the discourse of the political right, and for the gender-specific appeal of the latter generally, see Macciocchi [1979], Koonz [1987] and Bree [1991]. The potency of this combination of passive/active female roles in the recent communal mobilization, whereby women take part in the liberation of a male Hindu deity, is noted by Basu *et al.* [1993: 81–2], who comment: 'The reversal of roles equips the communal woman with a new and empowering self-image. She has stepped out of a purely iconic status to take up an active position as a militant'.

96. On the interrelatedness and sacred nature of this Hindu symbolism, see Sarkar [1991: 2057–58, 2061] and Pandey [1991: 2998, 3003–4]. On the same point, Anderson and Damle [1987: 77] note that for the RSS '[t]he metaphor of the Divine Mother is used to describe both the nation and the "sacred" geography where the nation resides . . . [t]he metaphor offers RSS publicists emotionally-packed imagery to convey their message. The Mother image informs feelings for the homeland, that piece of earth which has nourished and sustained the people through history and is the true setting for the life of the people today; RSS literature is filled with references to the historical desacration of this land. *The division of the subcontinent in 1947 is described as "rape". Those who threaten the nation of the "sacred" geography are portrayed as lustful masculine figures.* In the 1980s, the RSS and its affiliates used the symbol of the Mother-Godess in mass campaigns to inspire loyalty to the country' (emphasis added). Another example of a politically reactionary womens' self-empowerment in contemporary India is the anti-foreigner movement which took place in Assam during 1979–80. This mobilization by indigenous Assamese was aimed principally at Muslims coming from Bangladesh after its secession from Pakistan (the 'post-1971 foreigners'), and also against immigrant Nepalis; as well as the disenfranchisement/deportation of the non-Assamese ethnic population, its political demands included the closing of the border between India and Bangladesh. Not only did women play an important role in the movement, but the politically reactionary direction of this gender-specific mobilization passes without comment – either by the authors [*Barthakur and Goswami*, 1990] or by the editor [*Sen*, 1990] – in a collection of texts celebrating female self-empowerment. Not the least of the difficulties accompanying the (active) process of female self-empowerment under the aegis of the political right is that the way in which gender is inscribed in – and takes its ideological structure from – the concept Nature means that women in general and rural women in particular are trapped in a discourse that emphasizes female passivity, which in turn places obstacles to the kind of active roles women themselves are permitted to discharge. Like the earth itself, therefore, woman is in ideological terms cast as the passive recepient of (male) seed ('ploughed'), the produce of which she raises and nourishes at considerable cost to herself (= self-denial, sacrifice). In this chain of signification, therefore, female is equated with Nature/'seed'/field', all of which are controlled/owned/(fertilized) by males. On this point, see Dube [1986: 41].

97. Much is made of the fact that the main victims of this economic crisis were not peasant cultivators but the 'trading classes' which profited from the consumer

demand generated by the Green Revolution (see, for example, Datta [1991: 2522]). However, such a view overlooks the point that many 'traders' were actually peasant farmers who diversified out of agriculture, yet continued to own rural property [*Banaji*, 1994]. For the role in Punjab of fundamentalist Sikh gangs in the attempted suppression by Sikh farmers of struggles by Hindu agricultural workers for higher wages, see A Correspondent [1987]. For instances of the communalization of conflict in Karnataka by caste Hindu farmers, see Nadkarni [1987: 149–150, 153–5].

98. It should be noted that nationalist sentiment was fuelled by the different responses of the farmers' movements to economic liberalization: for Joshi, therefore, it was an effect of Indian farmers' capacity to compete with international counterparts on equal terms, while for Tikait it was an effect of their fears about an inability to do so. Not surprisingly, the BJP capitalized electorally on nationalist anti-foreigner sentiment generated by this neo-liberal economic climate. As one observer noted, '. . . in the recent meeting of its national executive the [BJP] toyed with the idea of launching an agitation against the Dunkel proposals and the signing of the GATT treaty as a stepping-stone to a widespread "national economic campaign" which could later be developed into a "swadeshi" [= 'freedom'] campaign . . . [a]ccording to the thinking of a large section in the party, [it] may be able to influence sections of farmer and business interests with its rhetoric of anti-Dunkel "Swadeshi"' ('BJP: Conflicting Pulls', *Economic and Political Weekly*, Vol.29, Nos.1–2, 1–8 Jan. 1994).

PART II
Populist Postmodernism

4

Postmodernism and the 'New' Populism: The Return of the Agrarian Myth

'To bring back yesterday is now the sole prescription of the democratic reformers of capitalism: to bring back more "freedom" to small and middle-sized industrialists and businessmen, to change the money and credit system in their favour, to free the market from being bossed by the trusts, to eliminate professional speculators from the stock exchange, to restore freedom of international trade, and so forth *ad infinitum*. The reformers even dream of limiting the use of machines and placing a proscription on technique, which disturbs the social balance and causes a lot of worry.' – An observation by Leon Trotsky [1940: 29] some sixty years ago.

'Those freed from the past are chained to reason; those who do not enslave reason are the slaves of the past' – Georges Bataille [1985: 193].

'I'll be back' – Arnold Schwarzenegger as a T-100 cyborg in the film *The Terminator* (1984).

Claims about the persistence of petty commodity production notwithstanding, it is clear that throughout the period after the second world war, the economic base of 'peasant economy' in the so-called Third World has been subject to constant erosion by capitalism, and that consequently the majority of peasants are now no more than part-time/full-time providers of labour-power for a world-wide industrial reserve army of labour. Ironically – but unsurprisingly – this trend towards economic globalization, or the attempt by capital to impose the law of value on an international scale, has been (and continues to be) accompanied both by the rejection on the part of peasants, farmers' movements and intellectual/academic circles alike of the universal categories associated historically with a socialist future, and by a corresponding retreat into the national/regional/local/ethnic particularisms/identities which characterize what is termed here the postmodern 'new' populism.

Although the latter appears progressive in political terms, it is argued here that many currently-fashionable forms of intellectual/academic/activist opposition to modern/international capitalism derive their epistemological and political roots not from a forward-looking, progressive/modern anti-capitalism which seeks to transcend bourgeois society, but much rather its opposite: a backward-looking, romantic anti- (or post-) modern form of 'discourse-against', located in nostalgic and reactionary visions of an innate Nature that possess their roots in the agrarian myth and are thus supportive of conservatism and nationalism. These culturally-essentialist postmodern variants of the 'new' populism all combine to fill the ideological space implied in Chayanovian theory of peasant economy, and signal the return of the agrarian myth.

Accordingly, this chapter will argue that the more important epistemological components – together with their political implications – of a populist lineage can now be traced directly from the 'old' populism of Chayanov through the 'middle peasant thesis' and the 'moral economy' argument of Wolf, Alavi, and Scott, to the current studies of agrarian mobilization that use a postmodern subaltern studies and new social movements framework. These 'new' populist frameworks, it is further argued, also provide Chayanovian theory about peasant economy with its missing politico-ideological dimension: in so far as the subaltern studies and new social movements approach is structured by the increasingly fashionable methodology of discourse analysis and resistance theory, therefore, its conceptualization of ideology and action is decoupled from class and revolution, becomes pluri-vocal, and hence diffuse in its origins, causation, effect, and ultimately in its political direction.

I

The term 'new' populism encompasses three interrelated discourses, two of which have been influenced strongly by postmodernism. The latter consist of on the one hand a number of seemingly disparate analytical approaches to the issue of economic development in the Third World, and on the other grass-roots movements affected by this process. Both tend to stress the importance of 'peasant-ness'-as-empowerment. By contrast, the emphasis of the third, and earlier, component of the 'new' populism – as embodied in the work of Fanon, Marcuse and Foucault – is on 'peasant-ness'-as-alienation, a prefiguring discourse which is examined in Chapter 5. Since details about peasant and/or farmers' movements in India and Latin America have already been presented in Chapters 2 and 3, the focus here and in the following chapter will be on situating this 'new' populist discourse in its wider global and institutional context, by delineating the nature of the formative influences and indicating how and why such theoretical influences resuscitated the peasant essentialism central to the agrarian myth for new social movements to use as a mobilizing ideology.

4.1 Global Capitalism and 'Peasant Economy'

The seemingly unstoppable expansion of capitalism, and the continuous reno-
vation of the new international division of labour itself, in the form of reloca-
tion/restructuring and workforce recomposition (in terms of national/ethnic/
regional/gender identity), raises an important theoretical question about the
way we analyse capitalism, both in terms of its past and its future. This in turn
leads us back to the unjustly neglected work of Rosa Luxemburg regarding the
limits to capitalism, and in particular her views about the way in which non-
capitalist formations are vital to the existence and further reproduction of
capital.[1] The significance of her views about the relation between the non-
terminal nature of capitalist crises (in the short term) due to the ability of
capital to reproduce itself through access to hitherto untapped sources in
non-capitalist contexts of cheap labour-power, and current theory about the
globalization of the industrial reserve army concern two developments. First,
the contribution of peasants driven off the land in so-called Third World
contexts to the expansion of the global industrial reserve army of labour. And
second, the role in this process of ex-socialist and actually existing socialist
countries which are now being incorporated into the new international division
of labour, and the resulting crisis of overproduction.

Since the global pattern of agrarian transformation suggests that the major
portion of Third World peasantries have no future simply as subsistence cultivators, what then are the implications for development theory of their
economic role as part-time/full-time providers of cheap labour-power in what
has been described as the new international division of labour?[2] According to
the latter view, post-war economic development has been characterized by a
shift in production from the metropolitan capitalist countries, initially to the
newly industrializing countries (Hong Kong, Korea, Singapore, Taiwan) and
subsequently to yet other national contexts (China, Vietnam, Thailand,
Malaysia). This continuing process of restructuring/recomposition/relocation
– and with it the globalization of the industrial reserve army of labour – has
been made possible by the breakdown in 'traditional' agrarian structures, the
development of transportation and communication technology, the fragmentation of the labour process, and the deskilling of the workforce.[3] Significantly,
many of the workers employed in the world market factories and export processing zones that characterize the new international division of labour come
from rural backgrounds, expelled from the land as 'peasant economy' ceases
to be viable.[4]

As the examples of what are now *de facto* or *de jure* ex-socialist social
formations (Russia, Eastern Europe, China, Vietnam) demonstrate, the new
international division of labour applies not only to the relations between

metropolitan capitalist countries and newly industrializing countries but – and perhaps more importantly – to the relations between the latter and other less developed countries. These are now engaged in what amounts to a Dutch auction, whereby governments attempt to undercut one another in terms of the cheapness and compliant nature of the workforce they are able to deliver to international capital. Accordingly, it can be argued that the labour-power of peasants in actually existing and ex-socialist countries is now being mobilized to give new life to – and prolong the existence of – the world capitalist system. The extent of this paradox may be illustrated by the fact that both actually-existing and ex-socialist countries will be at the centre of the two main regional political economies now in the process of formation. One of these corresponds to the Pacific rim, and will involve the access by US and Japanese capital to the labour reserves of China. The other will be located in Europe, and will entail a similar access by European and other capitals to the labour reserves of Russia and Eastern European nations.

The resulting development of an authentically global capitalist economy, in which all countries adopt export-oriented production and simultaneously depress the living standards of their own workers in order to become more competitive, raises once again Luxemburg's thesis about the systemic limits to the realization of surplus-value and the collapse of capitalism. Sooner or later, a situation is reached in which everyone is producing for export to populations who have had their own consuming power cut back in order to achieve the same end (that is, the realization of a classic overproduction crisis). It is significant, therefore, that – although not identified as such – not only is over-production at root of farmers' grievances worldwide, in that the political slogan 'remunerative prices' is nothing other than a demand for prices higher than those which the free market 'awards', but more generally the trend towards globalization has been accompanied by the resurgence in many contexts of nationalism. Not only has the political right made gains throughout Europe, India, Russia and North America, therefore, but even in those cases where its electoral support has not increased it has nevertheless extended its influence in terms of defining the agenda of other ('moderate'/'democratic') political parties.[5]

4.2 The 'New' Populism and the Flight from Socialism

The list of left scholars worldwide who have abandoned socialism (either directly, or indirectly by discarding its basic tenets) because of the seeming unstoppability of capitalism and/or the perceived difficulties with socialism itself is now very long. It extends from those in the UK who were associated with the journal *Marxism Today* – whose 'designer socialism' emphasized revolutionary form (style, consumerism) at the expense of revolutionary content, and who have not only made their peace with neo-liberal capitalism but now regard the latter ('new times') as a victory for the workers – via the urban sociologist Manuel Castells, the main theoretician of the new social movements (who between the 1970s and 1980s moved from Marxism to a self-avowed populism), to the genuinely confused.[6] There are also other reasons for such changes of political position, which have more to do with the prevailing intellectual fashion within academic contexts.

Recent events in Eastern Europe and the Balkans have been widely interpreted as the atavistic resurgence of long-suppressed national/ethnic identities, or the reaffirmation of a 'natural' social order (Nature reasserting itself). Consequently, the absence/demise of socialism is attributed by many of these ex-socialists, as well as non- or anti-socialists, to its unfeasibility, unworkability, undesirability, or to a combination of all these.[7] It is necessary, therefore, to ask the following three questions: why has this move away from socialist views taken place, why in so many instances have socialist views been replaced with populist ones, and what is the role of intellectuals in this transformation?[8]

Since the 'old' populism was both the conduit of the agrarian myth and also the 'other' of Marxism, it is in a sense unsurprising that 'new' variants of the same discourse should position themselves politically in an analogous manner, and this is indeed what has happened. Varieties of currently fashionable environmentalism, postmodernism, feminism and conservatism have thus all combined to form the 'new' populism, with the same twofold object as the 'old' populism: first to identify, and then to celebrate, the innateness of peasant cultural identity in the ('post-colonial') Third World.[9] Together with ex-Marxists who have joined the ranks of the *pentiti* ('the repentent ones'), those who fuel this kind of reaction now devote much of their time to the formulation of warnings about the impossibility of progress, the end of development in general and large-scale industrialization in particular, and hence the inevitable demise of Marxist political economy.

Accordingly, the 1980s and 1990s have witnessed a confluence between on the one hand academic discourse – as embodied in the the highly influential subaltern studies series, edited by Ranajit Guha, in the 'moral economy' framework connected with the historiographical work of E.P. Thompson, and in the 'everyday forms of resistance' approach of James Scott – and on the other the political practice in India, Latin America and elsewhere of what are termed new social movements.[10] The latter consist not only of regionally-specific mobilizations by farmers and/or peasants but also of environmental movements (composed of tribals and forest-dwellers) and more generally the women's movement, which – as was shown in Chapter 3 – has played a prominent role in both the ecological and the new farmers' movements. This process has been accompanied by an analogous theoretical trend in the field of development studies, extending from Manuel Castells' analysis of urban social movements to the 'post-development'/'post-Marxist' conceptual framework associated with the 'impasse' position and the views of Serge Latouche.[11]

Although the subject of much debate, the 'new' populism which re-emerged during the 1960s and became entrenched during the 1990s encompasses – like its 1890s/1920s/1930s counterpart – a number of recognizable characteristics. Generally speaking, therefore, it expresses antagonism towards the large scale, and more especially towards politics, class, capitalism, socialism and the state; by contrast, it endorses the 'peasant-ness' of the agrarian myth, the small scale, and especially the idea of non-class-specific common interests ('the masses', 'the people') operating on the basis of grassroots/local initiatives.[12] Antagonistic to Eurocentric metanarratives premissed on Enlightenment rationality, and to Marxist theory/practice in particular, the romantic anti-capitalism of the 'new' populism influenced by postmodern theory endorses instead a process of 'resistance'/'empowerment' based on non-class identities that celebrate 'diversity', 'difference' and 'choice'.

Like its 'old' counterpart, the idealized or romantic anti-capitalism of 'new' populist theory is opposed not to capitalism *per se* but only to big business and/or foreign capital; for this reason, therefore, much of the 'new' populism is not just compatible with an indigenous/(small-scale) capitalism but is also nationalist in its (political) orientation. The latter notwithstanding, the 'new' populism operates with an anti-party-political framework ('above politics'/ 'non-political') which amounts to a 'refusal of politics'. Accordingly, it constitutes an attempt to de-politicize opposition to the state apparatus by capitalizing on and the mobilizing of 'resistance' without at the same time adressing the question of the class/classes which rule through this institution. Significantly, this 'refusal of politics' characterizes not only the 'old' populism but also much postmodern theory as well as the approaches of the 'impasse' and the new social movements.[13]

4.3 The 'New' Populism, Devictimization and Nationalism

The widespread endorsement of 'resistance' and 'popular culture' in the 'new' populist discourse by/about these new social movements is due in part to the way in which such concepts challenge the notion of passivity, by recognizing the voice and action of those historical categories (women, agricultural labourers, tribals, peasants) usually perceived as mute and/or dominated. On the face of it, such a process can be viewed as politically progressive. It is

frequently argued, therefore, both in academic discourse about these movements, and by the spokespersons of the latter, that what is on offer here is
nothing other than a radical new agenda, or a complete break with a socialist/
nationalist/male past and thus the shape of an entirely new future.[14]

The implication of such an approach is that opposition to the existing social
order derives not from class formation, class struggle, and the politics of class,
but from a hitherto undiscovered authentic grassroots voice (= 'popular
culture') re-presented in subaltern/movement/ecofeminist/'post-development'/'post-Marxist' texts as a *de*politicized discourse untainted by discredited overarching metanarratives. Like the 'moral economy' position,
primacy is allocated to customs, traditions, culture, and practices as these
already exist within the peasantry and the working class, a view which
contrasts with that of Marxists who – as outlined in Chapter 1 – have emphasized the backward-looking, politically reactionary and historically trans-
cendent role of much of what passes for resistance based on an already
existing 'popular culture' (racism, nationalism, religion).

Unfortunately, it is now usually forgotten that, historically, political opposition to and the rejection of capitalism as an economic system has taken – and,
as the 'old' populism generally and Latin American peasant mobilizations and
farmers' movements in India in particular demonstrate, still can take – two
opposing forms.[15] On the one hand, therefore, anti-capitalism may involve the
progressive 'going-beyond' of Marxism, which argues for both the desirability
and possibility of socialism (the expropriation of property, its control by the
working class through and by means of state power, and the harnessing of the
means of production/distribution/exchange for social rather than private ends).
On the other hand, anti-capitalism can also take a reactionary form, or the
regressive 'going-back' to a pre-/non-capitalist 'golden age'.[16] The latter form
of anti-capitalism, based as it is on the agrarian myth, entails a process of
empowerment/resistance based on non-class identities (nationalism, ultra-
conservatism, fascism), and is based on two distinct visions of Nature: the first
(and merely conservative) operates with a concept of Nature which is harmonious, while the second (and more openly fascistic) operates with a
concept of a violent Nature, or Nature as 'red-in-tooth-and-claw'.[17]

In terms of constituency, because the postmodern 'new' populism is anti-
Marxist, and thus denies the existence/importance of class and class struggle,
it claims as a consequence to be able to speak pluri-vocally, in the name of all
socio-economic classes and interests within a given national context.[18] In this
way, and for this reason, the postmodern 'new' populism not only focuses on
an external enemy (foreign/international capital) but in the process discovers
(and ideologically sanctifies) a spurious unity amongst a plurality of socio-
economically differentiated components of 'the nation', and thus gives a

(false) concreteness to 'nationhood'/'nationality'. Missing from this endorsement of 'plurality' is the element of contradiction, or the incompatibility between what are opposing political views which arise on the basis of irreconcilable economic positions.

The difficulty with this endorsement by the postmodern 'new' populism of diversity/difference is that, once the premiss of plurality is conceded, it then becomes possible to apply it to spheres beyond the 'cultural'; in short, it can now be argued that the uneven distribution of means of production, of wealth and power, is nothing more than a recognition of this principle at work.[19] It should be recalled also that the apartheid system in South Africa was consecrated ideologically precisely by the principle of ('separate') development based on ethnic/racial/tribal 'diversity' and 'difference'. This same principle structures not just claims to territorial sovereignty advanced by the contending parties to the conflict in ex-Yugoslavia but – as was argued in Chapter 3 – the political programme of the Hindu chauvinist BJP in India.

4.4 The 'New' Populism and Global Capitalist Expansion

The link between the the resurgence of populism and the current territorial expansion of capitalism is not difficult to identify. In a context of a globally rampant neo-liberal capitalism, therefore, what is a universalizing (economic) process necessarily licenses as its (politico-ideological) antithesis the invocation of the particularistic. Accordingly, throughout the so-called Third World (but by no means confined to it), this process of economic change is experienced ideologically as a cultural de-naturing, or a threat to religion, kinship, family, community, region, and nation. Consequently, in order to preserve all the latter against capitalist development, a rejection of capitalism defines itself against not only the economic aspects of this universalizing tendency but also against its accompanying epistemology (the pervasiveness of a western/modern/Enlightenment 'other').

Unsurprisingly, therefore, the specific form of anti-capitalism associated with the current spread of international capitalism manifests itself as a defence of the particular, or that which-is-specific-to-us (the ' "us-ness"-of-"we" ', the capitalist other's 'other'). Accordingly, in the absence of a specifically socialist project (see Chapters 2 and 3), or in cases where such a project is under attack or in retreat, the internationalization of capitalism licenses mobilization/resistance which is based not on class but on national/ethnic identity – or precisely that ' "us-ness"-of-"we" ' which, by denying class, creates a space for the romantic anti-capitalist 'above-politics' agency of the 'new' populism which is nevertheless compatible with continued accumulation by indigenous/national capital.[20]

Equally problematic in this regard is the claim by many exponents of the postmodern 'new' populism that, if nothing else, it has at least an effective programme of action. Designed to achieve empowerment at the grassroots, therefore, populist agency in so-called Third World contexts is undertaken not by political parties but rather by non-party/'a-political' non-government organizations (NGOs).[21] Guided by the latter, such action takes the form of de-politicized mobilization ('popular participation') or resistance by the 'people' or 'masses', and its object is merely to restore the status quo ante ('redemocratization').[22] Such organizational initiatives, however, are not just contradictory but also irredeemably reformist, doing no more than work within the limits imposed by (an international) capitalism to which populism is in theory opposed.[23] In terms of politics, this kind of micro-level activity is at best of limited value: hence NGOs create the impression not only that problems are being solved but further that they can be solved locally, thereby diluting antagonism towards the existing class structure and diverting mobilization away from other, large-scale and thus more effective forms of action.

The difficulty here is that in order to claim the accomplishment of grassroots empowerment based on resistance, it is necessary to deny what is interpreted as the passivity of 'victimhood'. Those who merely contrast the (positive) activity of resistance with (negative) passivity, and unproblematically endorse every/all variants of the former simply because they negate the latter, fail to notice that in its undifferentiated form ('action-against'), the process of resistance/empowerment subsumes radically different political solutions. [24] Hence the denial-of-victimhood requires in turn not merely the dissolution of analytical categories based on or leading to conflict (class, struggle) but much rather their inversion: accordingly, those social relationships hitherto regarded as forms of opression/exploitation can now be celebrated as evidence of empowerment/resistance.[25]

The process of historiographical revision which results from this inversion has entailed, amongst other things, the relativization of slavery and fascism.[26] Despite claims to 'newness', such theory is in fact both traditional and politically conservative. The appropriateness of the latter designation stems from epistemology: it invites us to change our perceptions (negative $\Rightarrow$ positive) of – and hence to accept – the system in question (slavery, colonialism, capitalism, fascism). Furthermore, in so far as the existing is represented as the desirable, not only is there no need to change it but such situations are now actively to be sought. Not the least important issue raised by this kind of ontological transformation is the role played by the academy and its intellectuals in the current process of 'rethinking' politics generally, and in particular the spread of postmodernist views regarding the (im-)possibility/(un-) desirability of development.

4.5 The Privilege of (Academic) Backwardness or the Backwardness of (Academic) Privilege?

There are a number of reasons for the shift in the current intellectual climate and the form this has taken. To begin with, for specifically material reasons the academy itself is extremely sensitive to changes in political power.[27] Linked to this is the theoretical/political effect of the contraction in academic employment: the postmodern method of deconstruction is politically expedient in a conservative or reactionary climate, since it renders valid anything and everything intellectuals have to say about a text – any text – and thus makes it possible for one thousand interpretations to bloom where only ten operated previously. Furthermore, postmodernism means that academics no longer have to be oppositional, nor do they have to represent views other than their own.[28] In other words, it legitimizes not just a much wider range of theory but also the politically 'safe' views that are supportive of its practitioners' employment prospects within the academy. To some degree, therefore, the depoliticization/(repoliticization) of debate in the public arena has occurred not in spite of but much rather because of a similar process at work in academic discourse.[29]

In the field of development studies, for example, much current non-/anti-Marxist theorizing about the subject of agrarian change is divided between economists who mathematize it and non-economists who deny its possibility. Into the latter category fall postmodernists, for whom Marxism is the main target, and who instead identify/endorse a process of 'resistance'/'empowerment' based on plural identities that celebrate 'diversity', 'difference', and 'choice'.[30] As Petras suggests, therefore, the change in political climate generally has produced a corresponding change in the views which prevail inside the academy.[31] Accordingly, if conservative ideas are once again academically in vogue, then it is not because the ideas themselves are intrinsically right (= theoretically acceptable) but rather because the times are right (= politically acceptable), in both senses of the term.[32]

Despite eschewing metanarratives, it is evident from a number of examples that postmodern theory can be – and in the case of its application to so-called Third World contexts is – a discourse not just of nationalism but also, and ultimately, even of fascism. Two opposed views exist concerning the origins of this discourse, and the reasons for its impact on development theory. According to Petras postmodernism ('indeterminacy') is a Trojan horse that has entered development discourse from western capitalism.[33] He attributes the decline of the organic intellectual and the coterminous ascendancy of the institutional intellectual to the funding of the latter by overseas agencies and research organizations, in the course of which neo-liberal, conservative and even fascist agendas emanating from the political right in metropolitan capitalist countries have been transferred to so-called Third World contexts, amounting to an ideological process justifying the accompanying economic recolonization.[34]

By contrast, Ahmad has suggested that the postmodernization of the intellectual is due to the opposite cause: the transfer of what is actually a traditional form of cultural nationalism from Third World colonial/ex-colonial contexts to metropolitan capitalism through a process of privileging the migrant intellectual ('the figure of exile'), a point which applies with particular force to many of those who have contributed to the Subaltern Studies project.[35] The philosophy of Rorty is yet another example of the epistemological link between postmodern theory and what has been termed the 'new' nationalism.[36] For Rorty, therefore, a 'commonsense' ethnocentrism is both inevitable and at the centre of his own postmodern discourse. Since what he defends/endorses/celebrates is a socially non-specific notion of 'democracy', the locus of which is (an equally unspecific) 'society', because in his discourse the latter concept is theoretically interchangeable with 'nation', Rorty's philosophy is a defence of 'nationhood'/'nationalisms'.[37] There is, however, a third trajectory, and one in which the Chayanovian concept of 'peasant' plays a crucial role.

II

Perhaps because of the intrinsic tensions in the neo-classical paradigm, the debate about development in general and its applicability to the Third World peasantry has shifted, away from economics and once again towards culture. The resulting conceptual re-essentialization of the peasantry, mainly by postmodern variants of the 'new' populism (the 'moral economy' approach, the middle peasant thesis, new social movements' theory, and the subaltern studies project) has been characterized by the emergence within development studies of a discourse about 'peasant-ness'-as-empowerment.

4.6 The (Post-) Modernization of the Chayanovian Peasant

Ironically, development theory was influenced intitially not by culturalist but by economic variants of the 'new' populism. This was at a time when, at the end of the 'development decade' of the 1960s, the long dominant peasant-as-cultural-'other' approach of anthropology had been joined by the peasant-as-economic-'other' approach associated with the work of Chayanov.[38] Following the availability in English translation of texts by the latter, their version of neo-populism began to influence the debate about the centrality to development strategy of peasant economy.[39] Like other interventions in debates about the peasantry during the 'development decade', it was its politics as much as anything that made Chayanovian analysis so acceptable once again in the 1970s and 1980s, particularly amongst economists and sociologists working for international food and development agencies.[40] Based on the peasant family farm and small-scale technology, Chayanovian theory presented the possibility of agricultural production without having substantially to reform the existing agrarian structure. In other words, it entailed neither rural property redistribution nor collectivization, and as such was not merely compatible with capitalism but would also not lead to socialism.[41]

However, while Chayanovian theory outlines the *economic* logic of the peasant family farm, it tells us nothing about the nature of the *political* action which corresponds to and follows from this economic role. And it is this very gap that the 'new' populist theory advanced not only by Scott, Alavi and Wolf but also by the subaltern studies and new social movements framework together with the 'impasse debate' concerning the nature and object of individual or collective action undertaken by the peasantry fills so neatly. In other words, it is Chayanov's peasant family farm which, as the 'eternal' middle peasant, either engages in revolutionary action against capitalism, or simply resists it on a day-to-day basis, the object in both instances being to restore the *status quo ante.*

Unlike the Leninist concept of 'depeasantization' and Trotskyist denial of an 'independent' political role to the peasantry, therefore, the 'middle peasant thesis' propounded by Wolf and Alavi allocates a revolutionary role to its subject, and thus opens up a *politico-ideological* space for the economic theory of Chayanov. Superficially, the seminal texts by Wolf and Alavi covering twentieth-century peasant movements in Mexico, Russia, China, India, Vietnam, Algeria, and Cuba appear to be compatible with a Marxist framework.[42] Thus agrarian mobilizations are regarded as a response to the impact of capitalist development, and the peasantry itself is differentiated on the basis of rich, middle and poor components. Wolf's analysis of peasant movements has been endorsed by no less a person than A.R. Desai, who not only maintains that he uses 'some of the major elements of a Marxist approach [and] adopts an approach which comes closest to a Marxist [framework]' but goes so far as to commend the resulting break with ahistorical anthropology in which peasants 'are treated as passive, unchanging, . . . traditional and . . . major obstacles to the modernization of the Third World'.[43] However, both Alavi and Wolf share the (un-Leninist) belief that the middle peasant is not located between the rich and poor peasantry but much rather corresponds to a different sector of the rural economy, composed of independent smallholders who own their land which they cultivate with family labour.[44] Both also share the (un-Leninist) view that poor peasants are the least militant elements of the peasantry as a whole because of patron-client ties which bind them to their masters, and similarly that the the most militant elements are the middle peasantry.[45]

The mutually reinforcing theoretical overlap between the 'middle peasant thesis' and the 'moral economy' framework provides Chayanov with two additional forms of superstructural material. First, it constitutes a break with the Leninist concept of revolutionary action and the role of different peasant strata in this process (the political significance of which will become clear below). Instead of revolutionary or insurrectionary activity involving peasants as a mass, rural mobilization in the 'moral economy' framework has been recast by Scott as 'everyday forms of peasant resistance'.[46] The latter refers to small-scale and apparently innocuous activity undertaken by peasants on an individual basis, corresponding to 'generalized non-compliance by thousands of peasants', and consists of actions such as foot dragging (or go-slows) dissimulation, desertion, false compliance, feigned ignorance, slander, arson, and sabotage.[47] The importance of such actions, Scott argues, lies in the fact that they require little or no coordination or planning (= spontaneous), they make use of implicit understandings and networks, they often represent a form of individual self-help, and they typically avoid any direct confrontation with authority. He concludes that in many ways 'everyday forms of peasant resistance' is a more effective form of action, in that through this peasants are more likely to achieve the goals they fail to obtain in the course of the more dramatic large-scale rural mass mobilizations.

And second, just as the Chayanovian subject is reconstituted theoretically in the 'middle peasant' thesis, so the 'moral economy' framework emphasizes its ahistorical character (or 'naturalness') in protecting the subsistence ethic against an external capitalism.[48] A theoretical position which this time Wolf shares with Scott, 'moral economy' maintains that peasants are moved to protest when capitalist penetration of the countryside leads to the loss of subsistence as a result of the breakdown in patron–client relations linking them to elites.[49] The 'moral economy' element consists of the fact that pre-capitalist relationships and institutions protect the peasantry against hardship and starvation, and it is this pre-existing form of insurance or subsistence guarantee which is destroyed by capitalism. Therefore, Scott and Wolf claim, the object of peasant resistance against capitalism is to protect or restore this traditional source of provision. Unlike Lenin, for whom capitalist development not only benefits rich and poor peasants in different ways but also prefigures socialism, for 'moral economists' it merely provokes a return to a pre-capitalist socio-economic structure (= golden age), and thus cannot prefigure anything.[50]

4.7 Postmodernism, Subalterns and New Social Movements

At first sight, both the subaltern studies project and new social movements theory seem to have little in common in terms of time and space. Thus the subaltern studies project is basically a critique of the historiography of colonial India, and focuses on issues connected largely with rural transformation; by contrast, the emphasis of the original new social movements texts is on urban social mobilization in contemporary Latin America, which is regarded as a response to new forms of social subordination (commodification, bureaucratization, and massification).[51] More recently, however, the scrutiny of new social movements theory has not only shifted from urban to rural mobilizations but has also begun to combine with the 'middle peasant thesis', the 'moral economy' framework and 'everyday forms of resistance' theory, where it finally (and logically) joins forces with the subaltern studies project.[52]

It is impossible to situate the theoretical concerns and political direction of subaltern studies and new social movements without reference to the way in which their discourse is structured by postmodernism. As will be seen in Chapter 5, postmodern theory has transformed the disillusion of 1968 into a Nietzschean pessimism which licenses and in politico-ideological terms epitomizes the conservatism of the 1980s and 1990s.[53] In rejecting totalizing/ Eurocentric meta-narratives, postmodernism also denies thereby the possibility of a universal process of socio-economic development embodied in the notion of history-as-progress (regardless of whether or not this is actually realized).[54] Such a view necessarily signals the abolition of the Enlightenment project, or emancipation as the object and attainable end of historical transformation, and along with it socialism and communism.[55]

The epistemological link between on the one hand the 'middle peasant thesis' and the 'moral economy' framework of Wolf, Alavi, and Scott, and on the other the postmodern underpinnings of the subaltern studies project and new social movements theory, is evident from the positive/negative thematic classification that structures their discourse. In general terms, therefore, Eurocentrism, universalism, together with the emancipatory object of history-as-progress all constitute methods/processes/concepts the efficacy of which is denied. The collective is replaced by the autonomous/fragmented individual subject, and the latter is defined not by production but by consumption. The realm of 'the economic' gives way to 'the cultural', while Lenin and Marx are similarly pushed aside by Gramsci and Foucault.[56] Action is guided not by class structure/formation/struggle but by subaltern/elite identities and/or those based on ethnicity/gender/religion/region; a change in the very nature of action itself entails that revolution be replaced by resistance, and in terms of the desirable/(possible) outcome of such action socialism is displaced by bourgeois democracy (or worse).

This nihilistic anti-systemic/anti-progessive position derives in part from the epistemological underpinnings of postmodern theory itself. In methodological terms, postmodernism is the mirror image of historical materialism: its unit of analysis is the individual, and its sphere of intervention/determination 'the ideological'.[57] As with language itself, each and every discursively constituted subject in postmodern theory is in ideological terms fragmented and hence autonomous: instead of people speaking univocally (as a class), the individual speaks plurivocally (as a gender/ethnically/regionally specific subject).[58] In contrast to the Marxist analysis of, for example, Volosinov, for whom language is a materially determined arena of class struggle, whereby rival significations are reproduced or transcended and meanings constructed inter-subjectively, for postmodernism the subject is unproblematically constituted by and through language, outside of which there is no existence and therefore no meaning.[59]

In common with two of its theoretical precursors Gramsci and Foucault, the analytical focus of postmodernism is on 'the ideological': unlike historical materialism, however, an important socio-*economic* concept such as 'power' is theorized by Foucault as an ideological phenomenon, as an end in itself (an innate human characteristic), and thus not as a means to an end (ownership/control of the means of production).[60] Accordingly, the determining role of 'the economic' is either denied or downgraded: ethnic- or gender-specific sociological categories are decontextualized economically, only to be reconstituted in postmodern discourse as cultural subjects.[61] In the case of subaltern studies, this methodological procedure results in the depeasantization of tribals (or the tribalization of peasants), which in turn licenses the dei-/rei-fication of the 'other'.[62] With regard to rural mobilizations during the colonial era, therefore, Ranajit Guha downgrades the concept 'class' on the grounds that it was overdetermined by religious or ethnic solidarities; however, one important theoretical effect of this position is the conceptual reproduction of the 'tribal', paradoxically a central emplacement of colonial discourse (the demystification of which is Guha's objective).[63] As O'Hanlon rightly hints, behind the deconstructed subject of the subaltern studies project necessarily lurks another (or 'an other') subject, potentially or actually reconstituted.[64] The latter, it is argued here, is none other than the 'other' which the totalizing discourse of historical materialism had apparently dis-mantled earlier.

Hence the *ideological* difference embodied in (and recognized by Marxism as) 'ethnicity' not only reappears in subaltern studies discourse but can now be recuperated as a *material* difference, occupying the terrain previously held conceptually by 'class'. Accordingly, in rejecting/displacing historical materialism, with its universal/totalizing *economic* analytical categories, and then contrasting the 'degenerate'/'corrupt'/(sinful) Eurocentrism of the latter with the immanent 'goodness'/'naturalness' of the *ideological* categories that constitute 'indigenous' discourse, the subaltern studies framework creates a theoretical space for the rescue of the 'tribal' from the dustbin of (colonial) history, and thus breathes new life into the Rousseauesque myth of the 'noble savage' who, together with its contemporary variant, the middle peasant, is everywhere to be found engaged in 'everyday forms of resistance' to remain the same.[65]

In rejecting history-as-progress, postmodernism is nevertheless required to identify a less alienating version of the present, and (its ahistoricism notwith-standing) unsurprisingly retrieves from the past an idealized version of a world-we-have-lost. Accordingly, the postmodernist philosopher Lyotard expresses nostalgia for a pre-modern (traditional) society, which rests on non-scientific knowledge such as myth, magic, folk wisdom, while the 'New Philosopher' Nemo makes a similarly unfavourable constrast between the dehumanized anonymity of commodity relationships under capitalism and the (more desirable) personal bond between master and servant under feudalism.[66] This advocacy by postmodernism of a return-to-Nature both merges neatly with and simultaneously reinforces not only the 'moral economy' argument and the 'middle peasant' thesis but also the neo-populist vision of Chayanov that lies behind them. In denying either the possibility or even the desirability of emancipation, therefore, postmodern theory supports the view of an 'eternal' peasant economy as a 'natural' category outside and against history, and thus confers politico-ideological acceptability on the struggle of its con-stituent subjects to remain the same.[67] Postmodernism also reproduces and reinforces the theoretical emphasis placed by Chayanovian theory on the role of consumption (as distinct from production) in defining the subject.

4.8 Subalterns, New Social Movements, Class and Consciousness

In typically postmodern 'new' populist fashion ('a plague on all your houses'), the critiques undertaken by subaltern studies, new social movements, and Scott, all object to a similar combination of overarching theoretical frame-works. Thus the trinity composed of 'conservative paternalism, . . . [and] the technicist understanding of history by Latin American Marxists' against which new social movements theory argues is analagous to the tripartite model of colonial/nationalist/Marxist interpretations challenged by subaltern studies.[68] In much the same vein, Scott rejects both 'conservative officialdom and revo-lutionary vanguard'.[69]

In subaltern studies and new social movements texts, as well as in the work of Alavi, Wolf and Scott, the concept 'class' is either used incorrectly, questioned, downgraded or rejected. Although he uses the terms rich, middle and poor peasants, therefore, Alavi nevertheless questions the utility of such concepts.[70] In a similar vein, Wolf claims that peasant interests override class alignments, as demonstrated by the fact that rich and poor peasants unite as kinsfolk (kinship = affective relation) rather than divide as economic subjects.[71] For Scott, the concept of 'class' is synonymous with the category 'peasant', and seemingly radical notions such as 'ordinary means of class struggle' together with 'everyday forms of class resistance' thus refer mainly to conflict between the peasantry as a whole and the state (see below).[72] Significantly, because of this conflation ('class' = 'peasant'), Scott is then able to claim that, as a 'class', peasants are able to discharge an *independent* historical role, the antithesis of Marxist views on this subject.[73]

The irrelevance of class differentiation in relation to the peasantry emerges most clearly in a collection celebrating Scott's concept of 'everyday forms of resistance', where the editor unambiguously asserts that:

> For the sake of convenience the rural poor are described as peasants. Numerous discussions about what constitutes a peasant remain inconclusive. At times it is important to acknowledge the heterogeneity of the rural poor. Not so here. Thus the definition adopted is broad, with only two easily satisfied characteristics: (1) the peasant works in agriculture, and (2) he or she has a subordinate position in a hierarchical economic and political order.[74]

Much the same is true of the approaches which adhere to the new social movements and subaltern studies framework. Because it is tainted with universalism and Eurocentrism, and hence deemed to be inapplicable to the Third World, both deprivilege class as an analytical category.[75]

Instead of class difference, the opposition is rather between the 'elite' and its 'state' on the one hand, and on the other the 'masses'/'popular masses'.[76] Thus Guha's category of the 'subaltern' encompasses all forms of 'subordinate' who do not belong to the 'elite'; that is, all those 'of inferior rank ... whether this is expressed in terms of class, caste, age, gender and office or in any other way'.[77] It is these same 'subalterns' who correspond approximately to Scott's 'weaker party' or 'relatively powerless groups' that engage in 'everyday forms of resistance' against the state.[78] The politically and sociologically problematic nature of the 'subaltern' is evident from its all-embracing social composition: among its ranks, therefore, are to be found 'the lesser rural gentry, impoverished landlords, rich peasants and upper middle peasants'. The fact that it includes those whose *class* position and interest correspond to those of an agrarian petty-bourgeoisie, and as such are opposed to those of a rural proletariat, rightly identifies the 'subaltern' as an all-encompassing ('new') *populist* category.[79]

The political and analytical depriviledging/demise of class that characterizes the theoretical approaches under consideration stems from a particular epistemological chain of causation. Because classical Marxism – with the exception of Lukacs – failed to develop an adequate theory of class-determined ideological forms and practice, this terrain has been annexed by non-Marxist postmodernists who now use it to throw doubt on the current and historical existence of class itself.[80] Thus subaltern studies and new social movements theory argue that, as agrarian mobilization and resistance to colonialism/capitalism has more to do with the experience and ideology of gender, ethnicity, region, ecology, or religion, these kinds of 'difference' cannot be understood by (and are therefore not reducible to) the class position of the subject. This incompatibility between ethnic/gender/religious/regional identity and experience on the one hand, and class-specific ideological forms on the other, leads in turn and inevitably to the non-emergence of class consciousness, which is then taken as evidence for the non-existence of class itself. Within such an unambiguously idealist framework there is no need to probe the surface appearance of non-class idioms/language/identity/ experience, and hence no contradiction is perceived to occur between the latter and the socio-economic position of the subject(s) concerned. Accordingly, the question of precisely what ideological forms constitute consciousness of class, together with the reasons for their absence, is never (and indeed cannot be) posed.[81]

In the case of Latin America, therefore, the argument is that as peasants are unable to make the transition from a 'class-in-itself' to a 'class-for-itself', any attempt to analyse rural mobilizations in terms of 'class' is consequently inappropriate.[82] At no point do such texts consider what ideological forms such a transformation (class-in-itself $\Rightarrow$ class-for-itself) would entail, let alone the possibility that for the leading strata such movements are actually a success. As has been shown in Chapters 2 and 3, the operationalization of apparently politically 'innocent' pre-/non-capitalist ideological forms serve to disguise and simultaneously to advance the *class*-specific objectives of rich peasants, since only in this way can relationships which in economic terms are unequal be represented ideologically as equal. Similarly, in the case of India politico-ideological inversions in which 'Brahmans . . . would behave like Sudras and Sudras like Brahmans' that seem to reverse (and hence subvert) the existing hierarchy, may in certain situations also serve to obscure the presence of economically opposed subjects within the category of the subaltern/subordinate itself.[83] A consequence of accepting the surface appearance of these relationships is to endow them with a false concreteness, a reification which not only results in the (mis-) recognition of middle peasants as the sole agents and benefactors of agrarian mobilization but also sustains thereby a rejection of history-as-progress.

This acceptance of surface appearance of relations of production, which derives from the epistemological impossibility of admitting the presence of false consciousness, also structures the subaltern studies critique of the non-fulfilment of the liberal bourgeois project on the part of the British Raj. That the latter did not displace pre-capitalist social forms in its colony, as embodied in the contrast between the introduction of Liberalism/Democracy/Liberty/Rule-of-Law, etc., leading to the elimination of unfreedom in the metropolitan context yet the absence of the very same combined with the persistence of unfreedom in the Indian subcontinent, is regarded as evidence for the failure of the totalizing capitalist project and implicitly confirms the impossibility of history-as-progress.[84] Because the issue is theorized largely at the level of the superstructure, however, even a perceptive subaltern studies contributor like Ranajit Guha fails to distinguish between the spread of capitalism as an *economic* project, and Liberalism/Democracy/Liberty/Rule-of-Law, etc., as contingent *politico-ideological* aspects of this process, any or all of which may be absent without necessarily hindering the reproduction of the capital relation itself.

Accordingly, capitalism does not everywhere need – and indeed sometimes cannot operate with – the superstructural forms that constitute the liberal bourgeois project: much rather, in specific contexts and at particular moments, the accumulation process actually depends on their absence. Unfree (or 'feudal') relations of production constitute a good example of this paradox, since both historically and currently the development of a specifically *proletarian* class consciousness linked to the existence of the free wage relation not only threatens the profitability of capitalism in the short term but confronts this soci-economic system with the possibility of its own demise in the long term.[85] In such circumstances, therefore, the continuation of pre-capitalist socio-economic forms in non-metropolitan contexts is in fact a *realization* and not a negation of the universalist project of capitalism.

4.9 Revolution, Resistance and 'New' Populist Agency

As has already been noted, Marxism denies middle peasants an independent historical role in any revolutionary process. As small capitalist producers, rich peasants are in the vanguard of the struggle against the landlord class in the course of a capitalist transition, only to be displaced in turn by the proletariat and poor peasantry in the course of a transition to socialism. Because of its continuous 'depeasantization', the middle peasantry does not – and indeed *cannot* – discharge a similar historical role, and for this reason is not considered by Marxism to constitute an independent revolutionary force. Having recuperated this very same subject for the historical process, Wolf and Alavi nevertheless experience difficulty in reconciling the innate dissonance between on the one hand its revolutionary political action and on the other its conservative socio-economic disposition.[86] The work of Scott offers a plausible solution to this contradiction, in so far as it shifts the locus of peasant action from revolution to 'everyday forms of resistance', thereby banishing or downgrading revolution from the historical agenda and simultaneously restoring to the middle peasant an independent historical role embodied in this kind of all-pervasive and continuous political activity.

Scott is in many ways a pivotal figure in the whole discourse under consideration here. His methodology based on 'everyday forms of resistance', together with its theoretical effects, forms a crucial (and continuing) link between earlier texts by Wolf and Alavi, and the later texts belonging to the subaltern studies and new social movements framework. Thus the micro-level responses embodied in Scott's ubiquitous concept, deployed by Wolf to describe peasant reaction to capitalist penetration, reappear in the work of Laclau as the 'new forms of struggle and resistance' undertaken by new social movements, which in turn lead to 'new socio-cultural patterns of everyday sociability . . . the embryos of a popular counter-foundation' as perceived by Evers.[87] As an organizational form, the concept of 'everyday forms of resistance' also structures the actions undertaken by subalterns: in contrast to the elite, whose activity is legalistic/constitutional, cautious and controlled, and consists of vertical mobilization, therefore, subalterns engage spontaneous/ violent (= 'natural') action that entails the operationalization of traditional horizontal linkages based on kinship and territoriality.[88]

Most importantly, the element of hegemony, implied in the work of Wolf and Alavi, is challenged and displaced by Scott. The latter thereby transforms peasants from passive accepters of existing ideology into its active challengers. Hence middle peasants are not just occasionally engaged in overt conflict, such as going to war, rioting, rebelling, or undertaking revolutionary activity to stay middle peasants but are now depicted by Scott as being actively and continuously engaged in covert struggle to remain middle peasants. In short, the periodic and defensive action attributed by Wolf and Alavi to middle peasants in order to preserve their status as such is in the work of Scott transformed into incessant and offensive action. As significant is the fact that in the course of this epistemological break, the central focus of peasant resistance has shifted from withstanding capitalism (as in the work of Wolf and Alavi) to opposing socialism (in the work of Scott, subaltern studies and new social movements), thus not only reinforcing the Chayanovian concept of the peasantry as a socio-economic form which reproduces itself independently regardless of the mode of production but also licensing opposition by rich peasants to attempts at the further socialization of means of production.

The shift from revolution to resistance as the main type of peasant action licenses a break not just with the revolutionary form itself but also with its political content. A consequence of downgrading the act of revolution in this manner is a corresponding denial of history-as-progress linked to and dependent on the revolutionary process itself; in short, a procedure which banishes emancipation generally, and in particular abolishes not merely the inevitability but even the possibility of socialism as the outcome.

4.10 The 'New' Populism, Bourgeois Democracy, Socialism and the State

As the focus of new social movements is the individual subject, the target of whose activity is the state apparatus, it is unsurprising that its postmodern discourse is – like that of populism and the agrarian myth – unequivocally anti-state. Thus new social movements, for whom the 'question of a reappropriation of society from the state has become thinkable' are characterized as generally 'anti-authoritarian, anti-institutional'.[89] Wolf, Scott and Redclift all identify the state as the object of action undertaken by peasants.[90] Since without knowing the class composition of a movement against the state it is impossible to say what kind of socio-economic contradictions permeate its political programmes and objectives, the decoupling of state and class immediately raises a number of politically important issues.

At a general level, this decoupling generates a certain amount of conceptual confusion; for example, the claim by Redclift that in Latin America during the 1970s and 1980s the state has replaced the landlord as the source of repression in the agrarian sector allocates to the state (an adminstrative apparatus where – as is the case here – the class interests are unspecified) the role previously filled by the landlord *class*.[91] It also obscures the *class* origin and object of action against the state. Hence a simplistic peasant/state opposition reproduces and reinforces the all-powerful-state/all-subordinate-peasantry dichotomy, which in turn conceals the extent to which it is *rich* peasants who successfully resist the attempts by a capitalist state to impose controls on the direction of their own accumulation project.[92] Similarly, 'everyday forms of resistance' can be undertaken by any and all socio-economic agents against the state, a point conceded by Scott.[93]

He attempts to rescue his characterization of this kind of action as resistance-from-below by claiming that it usually involves a 'weaker' party struggling against an 'institutional' opponent that controls the state apparatus, and that all those engaged in such action operate with a concept of injustice-which-needs-rectifying.[94] The problem with this is that landlords and capitalists are not only capable of undertaking 'everyday forms of resistance' but – like poor peasants and workers – also do this on the basis of 'injustice' (for example, state expropriation of privately-owned factories or latifundia). A further problem is that, although new social movements are directed against the state, both their mode (resistance-not-revolution) and form (the aestheticization of revolt, or cultural opposition) of mobilization effectively preclude a realistic challenge to the power and existence of the state itself. This point is recognized by Evers, who observes that new social movements are basically about 'everyday social [and socio-cultural] relations' and *not* about the capture of political power.[95]

That the state apparatus remains intact in this manner – for the bourgeoisie to (re-) occupy – is unsurprising, since the political objective of new social movements and subaltern studies framework is an understanding of the difficulties associated with the realization not of socialism but bourgeois democracy.[96] Hence the project of subaltern studies has been defined by Guha as 'a "new democracy" – *it is the study of this failure which constitutes the central problematic of the historiography of colonial India*' (original emphasis), while that of the new social movements similarly addresses issues relating to the (re-) construction of a hegemonic democracy encompassing the 'popular sectors'.[97] However, the rejection by Scott of 'hegemony' indicates the difficulty of reconciling 'everyday forms of resistance' with any social structure, since the element of politico-ideological acceptance implicit in the concept is by its very nature incompatible with this kind of (almost nihilistic) peasant activity.[98]

The long-term political direction of a theoretical framework with a socially non-specific state at its core, and thus as the focus of peasant action, finally emerges when it becomes clear that it licenses resistance not only to the capitalist state but also to a socialist state and behind this socialism itself.[99] Hence the observation by Slater that 'we must not assume that there exists a linear relationship between new social movements and a progressive political orientation, because obviously it cannot be assumed *a priori* that every new struggle or demand will somehow automatically express a socialist content'.[100] This point is reiterated elsewhere by Slater and also by Evers, who comments that 'some observers have pointed to the puzzling fact that some of the new impulses coming out of these base level groupings have similarities with the ultra-liberal ideology of [Milton] Friedman'.[101] Significantly, in rejecting revolution as a means of securing change, Scott argues that socialist revolutions are more exploitative than capitalism and, like Laclau and Mouffe, makes no distinction between Leninism and Stalinism.[102] For Scott, therefore, the focus of peasant opposition has now become the socialist state, and his examples of 'everyday forms of resistance' embodying state/peasant conflict are all drawn from non-capitalist contexts: the Soviet Union in the 1920s and 1930s, Hungary during the 1940s and 1950s, and China 1949–78.[103]

Although this particular development in the work of Scott constitutes an fundamental break with Wolf, for whom the focus of peasant opposition is the capitalist state, it nevertheless licenses an equally important continuation with the earlier views of Chayanov. Thus the type of peasant he defends in general terms against the socialist state is precisely that which Chayanov was accused of protecting in the Soviet Union, and for much the same reasons. At first sight, therefore, the self-sufficient family farmer, whose 'autonomy' is threatened by the socialist state, whose life-sustaining link between production and consumption is broken by collectivization, and who because of this engages in 'everyday forms of resistance' exhibits all the socio-economic characteristics associated with – and indeed appears to be nothing other than – the middle peasant.[104]

However, just as Chayanov conflated middle peasants and kulaks, thereby providing the latter with a politico-ideological defence that permitted them to resist further socialization of the means of production under the guise of petty commodity producers rather than rich peasants, so Scott tacitly acknowledges that in socialist Hungary 'everyday forms of resistance' was a defensive strategy adopted by kulaks to block state procurements.[105] Despite being aware of the petty bourgeois disposition and element among the peasantry in such contexts, therefore, Scott refuses to make a political distinction between action undertaken by incipient/actual agrarian capitalists against a socio-economic system attempting to prevent them from becoming once more or continuing as small capitalists, and that undertaken by workers and poor peasants against capitalism. Whereas both activities share the same form, the political content of the former is reactionary, and must be differentiated from resistance against capitalism which seeks to go beyond it and establish socialism.

4.11 Conclusion

Any attempt to analyse the rise of new social movements worldwide, and to link this to the return of the agrarian myth, must begin by locating this process in the context of post-war capitalist development. The latter has been characterized by a shift in production from metropolitan countries to newly industrializing and less developed countries, a relocation made possible (amongst other things) by the globalization of the industrial reserve army of labour, leading to the loss of landholdings, livelihood and employment on the part of many peasants and workers in the so-called Third World. It is only as a response to this process of the internationalization of capitalism, therefore, that the resurgence in many parts of the globe of both the 'new' populism and of 'new' populist movements, all of which proclaim resistance/empowerment on the basis of a romantic anti-capitalism, can be understood.

In this conservative political climate, the role of the academy in general and intellectuals in particular has been to provide not so much explanations for this shift as justifying ideologically that which happens to exist. Many non-/ anti-Marxist intellectuals who have abandoned socialist politics for the 'new' populism now espouse a form of *laissez-faire* ideology (choice-making individuals selecting an identity through which to achieve empowerment by means of resistance) to match the *laissez-faire* economics of neo-liberal capitalism (the exercise of subjective preference in the free market by choice-making individuals). Consequently, in much contemporary analysis of the micro-level agrarian mobilization occurring in the so-called Third World (the grassroots response to this globalization and market liberalization), the prevailing orthodoxy within the academy is that political empowerment/ resistance structured by a postmodern rejection of metanarratives/universals always and everywhere constitutes an unproblematically desirable end, a view arrived at without asking by whom and for what such a process is conducted.

One influential example of this 'new' populist approach is to be found in the way in which peasant action and peasant movements have been theorized in the period following the development decade. The latter saw a shift from peasant-as-economic-'other' associated with the 'old' populism of Chayanov to peasant-as-cultural-'other', initially in the work of Alavi and Wolf, and then in the the work of Scott, and most recently in the approach which characterizes texts on the new social movements and subaltern studies. When combined, all these 'new' populist approaches focussing on the peasant-as-cultural-'other' provide the economic theory about the Chayanovian peasant family farm with its missing politico-ideological dimension. To a large degree, this process is structured by the de-/re-constructions effected as a result of postmodern epistemology, an importance consequence of which has been the conceptual re-essentialization of 'peasant-ness' that is central to the agrarian myth.

Mediated through the subaltern studies and new social movements framework, the postmodern project is in a number of important ways particularly supportive of the 'middle peasant thesis' and 'moral economy' argument advanced by Wolf, Alavi, and Scott, and behind them the neo-populism of Chayanov himself. On the one hand, therefore, postmodernism attacks the teleological roots belonging to the traditional political opponents of neo-populist visions of a self-sufficient peasantry: the overarching meta-narratives of Marx and Lenin on the universality of class and class struggle, collectiviza-

tion and socialism as outcomes of the latter, the necessity/desirability/possi-
bility of emancipation which structures the notion of history-as-progress,
and the state as the object of revolution. On the other hand, it attempts to
recuperate conceptually a politico-ideological project which sustains that
very same 'new' populist vision: the ideological pluralism of the subject, the
autonomy of the individual, the political importance and acceptability of (self-
defined) relativism as embodied in 'the cultural' ('the tribal', 'the peasant'),
the wholesale legitimacy of any/all 'everyday forms of resistance', and bourgeois democracy.

In keeping with their postmodern antecedents, therefore, analyses based
on a new social movements or subaltern studies framework claim that the
object of peasant activity – whether 'everyday forms of resistance' or large-
scale mobilizations – is unconnected with socialism because the latter is
unrealizable/undesirable. While it is true that peasant activity may not necessarily lead to socialism, this is *not* for the reasons indicated by the subaltern
studies and new social movements framework. These imply that all smallholders are middle peasants interested only in remaining as such, and as a
result adhere to non-class based ideologies which stress regionalism, ethnicity,
or gender. It is one thing to maintain that class struggle has not developed as
predicted, it is quite another to argue that class is of little or no relevance to the
understanding of the formation/reproduction of politico-ideological consciousness and the (equally class-specific) kinds of conflict this permits subsequently. Thus the transcendence of ethnic solidarity by class solidarity
among poor peasants and agricultural workers, and the subsequent displacement either of class consciousness by ethnic identity or free wage labour by
'semi-feudal' relations of production, is itself an integral part of the class
struggle, and constitutes evidence only of the resort by rich peasants to
'traditional' institutional forms supportive of their economic power when/
where necessary, and not of the undesirability of socialism or the impossibility
of historical progress *per se.*

The political dangers inherent in unproblematically equating the 'popular'
with the existing, or an unmediated (and hence 'authentic') voice-from-below,
is evident both from the socio-economic forces that have (and continue to be)
mobilized in rural areas by the left and from the ideology it uses for this
purpose. As previous chapters have suggested, agrarian mobilizations such as
ANUC in Colombia, FIR and Sendero Luminoso in Peru, Naxalism in West
Bengal and more generally the new farmers' movements in India all underline
the extent to which it is rich and not middle peasants who are in the forefront
of rural protest/revolt, and further that apparently radical political discourse
may in particular contexts reflect the politico-ideological interests and objectives of rich peasants.

In order to maintain what is in effect a spurious peasant unity, moreover, grassroots leftist organizations such as the CPI, the CPI(M) and the CPI(ML) in India, the FIR and Sendero in Peru, and ANUC in Colombia have not merely avoided confronting issues which divide the peasantry along class lines but on occasion actively suppressed an emerging class consciousness among poor peasants and agricultural labourers. Rather than class as a mobilizing ideology, the left has – like its political opponents – frequently ethnicized/ communalized the agrarian struggle, either by promoting/encouraging or by not challenging ethnic, caste and/or tribal consciousness, thereby legitimizing and creating a politico-ideological space for anti-socialist discourse and practice.

The importance of this lies in its impact on the political response to capitalism. Like the 1920s and 1930s, therefore, the capitalist crises of the 1980s and 1990s have licensed a nationalist resurgence; unlike the 1920s and 1930s, however, a strong countervailing socialist politics, with its emphasis on class and internationalism, is largely absent. In part, this absence is due to the attempt by intellectuals generally and some socialists in particular to replace socialism with the 'new' populism, an idealist form of anti-capitalist theory. Contrary to received wisdom, therefore, the argument advanced here is that – in the case of India and Latin America – socialism has failed to prosper not because the ground has been unfertile, nor because socialist ideas are unacceptable to workers, but much rather because the proponents of socialism have not been socialist enough, and consequently a socialist agenda has not actually been offered to workers. The significance of the latter is, as Rosa Luxemburg reminds us, that political choice is and can only be one between socialism and barbarism; the implications of this point are pursued in the following chapter.

NOTES

1. See Luxemburg [1951], who argued that the basic contradiction facing capitalist accumulation was the inability of consumption to keep pace with production. In other words, the necessity on the part of capital to keep down the living standards of the working class necessarily placed a limit on the demand for its own commodities. However, in the short term a countervailing mechanism exists in the form of the ability of capital to unload part of its production onto populations outside the closed capitalist system; that is, capitalists can still find market outlets in non-capitalist contexts. But, she argued, the very process of capitalist expansion eventually destroys this safety valve, as increasingly acute competition for markets means that even non-capitalist contexts are ultimately incorporated into (and thus become a part of) capitalism. In the long term, therefore, this initial tendency toward crisis cannot be avoided.

2. There is now a vast literature on the new international division of labour, a theory associated with Fröbel *et al.* [1980]. For more recent texts on this subject, covering a variety of production processes in different contexts, see (among others) Boyd, Cohen and Gutkind [1989], Bustamante *et al.* [1992], Castles and Miller [1993], Chapkis and Enloe [1983], Chossudovsky [1986; 1988], Cohen [1987], Deyo [1989], Henderson and Castells [1987], Hoogvelt [1987], Kaplinsky [1993], Levidow [1991], Mitter [1986], Munck [1988], Ong [1987], Portes *et al.* [1989], Safa [1995], Sanderson [1985], Sassen [1988], Sawers and Tabb [1984], Sklair [1990], Southall [1988], Stichter and Parpart [1990], Watts [1992], and Yonghong [1989]. It is important to note that, in contexts where there is a history of successful working class movements and/or organization, the neo-liberal economic policies associated with the new international division of labour require an un-/anti-democratic government and repressive politics (a strong state or military regime), in order either to pre-empt or to roll back gains obtained by local/migrant workers. In the case of Chile, for example, on the advice of the neo-liberal economists belonging to the Chicago school the Pinochet dictatorship restored expropriated land to previous owners, banned political activity, cut wages, ended food price controls for the urban working class and subsidies to smallholders. With the resulting collapse of domestic purchasing power, and the reversal of the internally-oriented development strategy advocated by the Economic Commission for Latin America (ECLA), agrarian capitalists in Chile now export traditional staple foods which the locals can no longer afford to inter-national markets (Hojman [1990; 1993], Korovkin [1992], Silva [1990]).

3. This particular development, linking the continuation of capitalist accumulation worldwide to an expansion in the global industrial reserve army of labour, would have come as no surprise to those Marxists belonging to earlier generations (such as Maurice Dobb) who both knew their Marx and remained Marxists. Writing in 1950, amidst the bout of end-of-ideology triumphalism which accompanied claims that a Keynesian solution had banished recurring capitalist crises, Dobb [1955: 215–25] warned against the illusion that capitalism was compatible with a stable condition of full employment ('a situation where the sack had lost a good deal of its sting as a disciplinary weapon, with the virtual disappearance of the industrial reserve army'), and pointed out that sooner or later capitalist profita-bility would require the restoration of unemployment.

4. It is important to note that the continuing disintegration of 'peasant economy' is due as much to economic stagnation as to growth. Although Green Revolution programmes have been effected in both India and China, therefore, export pro-cessing zones draw their labour-power from those who have been expelled from the land both as a result of more efficient productive technique and because of a lack of investment in agriculture. Hence the example of India, and in particular the pattern of migration from Bihar to Calcutta, suggests that as important as the displacement of rural labour due to economic development is the displacement of rural labour due to economic stagnation. And as the example of India [*Kumar*, 1989] also confirms, export processing zones are not merely a method whereby international capital circumvents domestic legislation regarding minimum wages, welfare provisions, employment of women and legal minors, trade union membership and the right to strike. Local capital producing for export also utilizes export processing zones to get around regulations protecting its own workforce. In this respect, workforce restructuring effected by international

capital is in fact no different from the workforce restructuring by national (as well as international) capital effected through the informal sector economy.

5. This issue will be examined in more detail in Chapter 5. For the resurgence of the political right in India, see Chapter 3.

6. Initially perceiving urban contexts as places where class struggle was undertaken by industrial workers interested in socialist objectives, Castells [1977, 1983] subsequently changed his mind, and maintained that no urban social movements were – or could be – class-based mobilizations opposed to capitalism; rather, they were – and always had been – sociologically heterogeneous organizations defending their place in the existing system. This shift away from Marxism, Castells [1983: xv–xvi] agreed, meant that '. . . most existing research on community organizations and social movements (including those of this author) combine romantic descriptions with populist ideology'. Among the genuinely confused are to be found ex-socialists such as Ernesto Laclau, Chantal Mouffe, André Gortz, Julia Kristeva, David Selbourne, Paul Hirst, and Marvin Harris. For recantations, together with reasons, see *inter alia*, Gortz [1982], Hall and Jacques [1989], Harris [1992], Laclau [1990: 97ff.], Selbourne [1985: 181–210; 1987]. For critiques of this kind of political shift, see (among others) the texts by Callinicos [1989], Miliband [1985], Norris [1993: 1–28], Palmer [1990] and Sivanandan [1990: 19–59]. Significantly, one ex-socialist now claims that 'a society of yeomen . . . could well return, if we work at it' [*Hirst*, 1998: 1197]; equally significantly in the light of the connection between the 'new' populism and ecology, a number of ex-socialists have changed their political colour from red to green (Bahro [1982], Gortz [1980], Lipietz [1992]).

7. Socialism is dismissed in this way by, among others, ecofeminism, new social movements, the 'impasse' and subaltern studies theory (see below and also Chapter 3). In this regard it is perhaps salutary to recall comments made by Trotsky about a similar period of socialist disarray during the first world war, when nationalist divisions among socialists resulted in the collapse of the Second International. 'At first glance', he observed [*Trotzky*, 1918: 34–6], 'it may appear that the social revolutionary prospects of the future are wholly deceptive. The insolvency of the old Socialist parties has become catastrophically apparent. Why should we have faith in the future of the Socialist movement? Such skepticism, though natural, nevertheless leads to quite an erroneous conclusion. It leaves out of account the good will of history, just as we have often been prone to ignore its ill will . . . It is not Socialism that has gone down, but its temporary historical external form. The revolutionary idea begins its life anew as it casts off its old rigid shell. This shell is made up of . . . an entire generation of Socialists that has become fossilized in self-abnegating work of agitation and organization through a period of political reaction, and has fallen in the the habits and views of national opportunism or possibilism.'

8. Historically associated with the formulation of rules, the objectification of knowledge (= science), and the legitimation/exercise of power [*Chomsky*, 1982; *O'Brien and Vanech*, 1969; *Said*, 1994], intellectuals generally have been distrusted by populist movements. Such anti-intellectualism notwithstanding, as the example of not only Sharad Joshi himself but also Vandana Shiva and Gail Omvedt demonstrate (see Chapter 3), intellectuals do in fact discharge important agenda-setting roles in the farmers' movements in India. In short, the political views of intellectuals *are* important, and *do* matter.

9. The list of texts which, under the influence of currently fashionable postmodern theory, in one way or another end up denying the possibility/desirability of socio-economic development is now very long, and would include Guha [1982–89], Laclau [1985; 1993], Spretnak [1986; 1990], Shiva [1988; 1991a], Scott [1990], Pieterse [1992], Escobar and Alvarez [1992], Prakash [1992], Latouche [1993, 1996], Omvedt [1994a], and Booth [1994].

10. The subaltern studies project is presented in – but by no means confined to – the collection of texts edited by Guha [1982–89]. The latter series as a way forward is endorsed by Chakrabarty [1992: 83–4], who observes that: 'serious and undogmatic discussions on Gandhi (and Gandhian politics) in the pages of *Subaltern Studies* have now opened up, in India, an intellectual space for dialogue between Marxists critical of Eurocentrism and non-Marxist, liberal Indian thinkers . . . who have developed criticisms of Eurocentric ideas of modernity'. For the influence of the subaltern studies project, both within and outside India, see Sathyamurthy [1990]. For 'moral economy', see Thompson [1991: 184ff.]. For discussions from different perspectives of new social movements as global phenomena, see Slater [1985], Fuentes and Frank [1989], Eckstein [1989], Foweraker and Craig [1990], J. Fox [1990], Escobar and Alvarez [1992], Calman [1992], Wignaraja [1992] and Eder [1993]. Although Fuentes and Frank [1989: 184, 187–9] are correct to observe that 'new' social movements are neither new nor comprehensible without reference to class composition, they mistakenly believe that '[i]n the Third World social movements are predominantly popular/working class' and thus overestimate the socialist content and potential of such mobilization. For a discussion of the divergence between Marxism and the ego-centric resource mobilization theory of collective action that structures much new social movements analysis, see Melucci [1989: 184–92].

11. See Castells [1983] for an important early formulation of the theory about urban social movements, and Rahnema and Bawtree [1997] for an elaboration of the concept 'post-development', a term extended to cover the views of 'old' populists like M.K. Gandhi and 'new' populists such as Scott, Shanin, Sahlins, Escobar, Illich, Latouche and Shiva. As formulated by Booth [1985; 1993; 1994], Corbridge [1990], and Schuurman [1993], the 'impasse' position takes the double form of on the one hand a currently fashionable disenchantment with Marxism and on the other a resulting espousal of a populist/postmodern framework, a combination that negates not just much of the conceptual analysis that makes the study of development possible but also and thereby the very concept development itself. The 'new' agenda for development theory proposed by Booth turns out to be nothing more than yet another thinly-disguised postmodern endorsement of 'resistance/empowerment' inside the capitalist system, a process based on plural identities celebrating 'diversity', 'difference' and 'choice' (for a critical discussion of the 'impasse' position, see Brass [1995a]). This denial of the possibility/(desirability) of progress is also central to the work of Latouche [1993], which in many respects not only anticipates much of the current 'impasse' argument but also pushes the 'impasse' position itself to its logical conclusion. He categorizes the 'have-nots' in the so-called third World as 'castaways shipwrecked by modernity', and – like Shiva (see Chapter 3) – identifies development itself as the problem, not the solution. Maintaining that industrialization is an inappropriate Western imposition on 'non-Western' contexts, Latouche concludes that under-development stems from a specifically *cultural* incompatibility between so-called

Third World countries and western capitalism. Since in his view the price of development is the destruction of traditional solidarities and economic security, he unsurprisingly ends by celebrating/privileging the cultural plurality/diversity (= polysemic history) of the so-called Third World as an alternative to economic development itself. For Latouche, in short, 'post-development' not only means *cultural* empowerment via the existing, but has also and thereby become code for no more economic development.

12. Examples of the quasi-mystical belief by 'new' populist texts in the efficacy of any/all discourse/action-from-below include not just Canovan [1981: 257] and Sinha, Greenberg and Gururani [1997], but also – and more importantly – Scott and many of the contributors to the Subaltern Studies project (see below). The discursive overlap between the 'new' populism, postmodernism and ecofeminism is perhaps nowhere more evident than in an observation by an exponent of the latter [*Spretnak*, 1986: 157] that to head the 'new' populism in North America she 'nominate[s] the postliberal, postsocialist, post-finance-capitalist body of ideas for our era called Green politics. It combines global responsibility and the values of decentralist, Jeffersonian democracy with the ecological wisdom of a sustainable, steady-state economy, one based on maximum private ownership by the maximum number of citizens . . . [the 'new' populism] is an ecological, holistic, and feminist movement that transcends the old political framework of left versus right. It emphasizes . . . .the embeddedness of individuals and societies in the processes of nature.'

13. An example of the postmodern 'refusal of politics' is Foucault [1991: 173]. There are many variants of this 'refusal of politics'. One is to announce, as many anthropologists have done [*Clifford and Marcus*, 1986; *Geertz,* 1988], that after all their form of practice is too subjective, and thus a way of knowing about the 'self' rather than the 'other'. In part, this reconstituting of participant/observation research methodology as a variety of literary practice (anthropology = fiction) is a conjuncturally symptomatic way of abolishing/denying the politically unpalatable reality (the effects of capitalist development, the non-existence of the 'noble savage' and the agrarian myth) that much contemporary fieldwork discloses (for evidence of which see Geertz [1988: 99–101], although he himself does not make this point). Another variant of this 'refusal of politics', also in the realm of development discourse, is the concept of 'rent-seeking' associated with neo-classical/neo-liberal 'new political economy', a theory whereby the political right challenges what it perceives as the illegitimate operation of government monopoly in the capitalist market. As Bagchi [1993: 1729] correctly observes, 'there is nothing particularly novel about the idea of earning rent as an obstacle to progress. What is novel is a deliberate restriction and in some cases an arbitrary redefinition of the concept of rent-seeking and its application to denigrate all government intervention and virtually abolish the domain of politics in LDCs'. It scarcely needs pointing out that the postmodern 'refusal of politics' from below coincides rather too neatly with the argument from above about the desirability of a similar 'refusal of politics'; unsurprisingly, the reason why the political right advocates that the state should not be an object of class struggle is precisely because its capture by the proletariat is the one (revolutionary) act that ruling classes everywhere fear most.

14. The claim that it is necessary to break with not only a male/socialist/nationalist past but also industrial economic growth which structures this, and to construct

instead a future based on the ecological/social/women's movements is made by, among others, Mies, Bennholdt-Thomsen and von Werlhof [1988].

15. That conservatives lay claim to this anti-capitalist tradition is clear from many sources (see Chapter 5), not least those written by conservatives themselves. As one of them [*Nisbet*, 1966: 26] has observed, 'the indictment of capitalism that comes from the conservatives in the nineteenth century is often more severe than that of socialists. Whereas the latter accepted capitalism at least to the point of regarding it as a necessary step from past to future, the traditionalists tended to reject it outright, seeing any development of its mass industrial nature – either within capitalism or a future socialism – as but a continued falling away from the superior values of Christian-feudal society. It was what the socialists *accepted* in capitalism – its technology, modes of organization, and urbanism – that the conservatives most despised. They saw in these forces cause of the disintegration of what Burke called the "inns and resting places" of the human spirit, Bonald, "les liens sociales," and Southey, "the bond of attachment" ' (original emphasis). For a similar defence of tradition by a conservative, see Shils [1981]. The fact, the history and the strength of this claim by the political right on the discourse of anti-capitalism is forgotten by socialists at their peril: by endorsing politically non-specific/undifferentiated forms of anti-capitalist discourse and action, they put the weapons (incorporation, dilution) of the class struggle into the hands of the enemies of socialism.

16. The redemptive myth of a 'golden age', which structures the many and recurring proclamations in the midst of capitalism by populists/populism announcing the 'end-of-history' and the 'end-of-ideology', is also present in the symbols, rites, and religious customs/ceremonies of most non-capitalist social formations [*Eliade*, 1954], where it involves the ideological attempt to replace the mortality of profane time (= history) with the immortality of sacred time (= the eternal present in the Garden of Eden). Far from disappearing, it is argued by Bausinger [1990] that such traditonal beliefs expand/extend to accompany the spread of capitalism, a process structured by the commodification/reinvention of folklore. A similar point is made by Shils [1981: 206–8].

17. A synthesis of these apparently antithetical views about Nature is contained in the work of Hardin (see below), for whom the 'natural' violence of famine, floods, drought, infanticide, etc., in so-called Third World countries is nothing other than Nature systematically restoring the 'natural' carrying capacity (= 'harmony') of given national populations in these contexts (Hardin [1977: 63–4, 68, 93–5, 113–14; 1993: 175], Hardin and Baden [1977: 113–25]). Unlike Hardin, for whom the violence of Nature is rational, for Foucault it represents the desirable 'otherness' of irrationality: the Dionysian rejection of reason on the part of Foucault, therefore, is an attempt to recuperate a concept of 'the pre-rational/primitive' (see Chapter 5), a process whereby the act of death/self-obliteration itself becomes a surrender to the ultimately unconquerable and innate power of Nature.

18. There are numerous examples of 'new' populist hostility to Marxism. According to Castells [1983: xvi–xvii, xx], therefore, '. . . we want to work out a theory of urban social movements . . . this theoretical purpose is informed by a methodological perspective that is distrustful of former experiences involving the useless construction of abstract grand theories . . . [w]hat we need now are not trans-historical theories of society [= Marxism]'. The same is true of the 'impasse' position. As is clear from the mutually admiring exchanges between Booth [1985;

1994] and Corbridge [1990; 1994: 93], what they both regard as the 'impasse' – or the 'post-Marxism' that the 'impasse' has now become – refers to Marxist and Marxist-influenced development theory generally and to Marxist political economy in particular (characterized variously as 'Warrenism', dependency, and debates about the mode of production and the real/formal subsumption of labour under capital). It is equally clear from his observation that '[t]he range and substance of what we might now dare call "post-impasse" research on . . . development is a cause for celebration' that Booth [1992: 3] feels that the 'impasse' debate has now succeeded in exorcising the Marxist spectre at the development feast. Booth objects to Marxism because in his view it ignores 'complex heterogeneity' (= 'difference'), is reductionist, it cannot explain change and is thus for him 'conceptually redundant'; by contrast, he approves of the 'diversity' of development based on 'choice', the latter to be guided by 'responsible actors in LDCs' [*sic*], new social movements and 'empowering' NGOs [*Booth*, 1992: 3, 4, 6, 7, 8, 34, 141–2]). Notwithstanding the admission that the 'impasse' possesses no theory of development, for Booth [1992: 15, 17] the 'rediscovery of diversity' means in theoretical terms 'an increased sensitivity to systemic variation, that is to say diversity about which it is possible to *generalise* at a certain level' (original emphasis). The difficulty with this argument is that generalizing (or, to use his own words [*Booth*, 1992: 5], ' "reading off" from [the] universal') is precisely what Booth objects to in Marxism, since it leads to what he dismisses as 'class reductionism'. More examples of an almost visceral antagonism to Marxist theory on the part of the 'new' populism will be presented below, and also encountered in Chapter 5.

19. For more on this point and the ones which follow, see Chapter 5.
20. This is particularly true of urban social movements which, according to Castells [1983: xviii], mobilize in defence of 'cultural identity associated with . . . a specific territory'. Indeed, the same souce indicates with evident approval that '[t]he role of territoriality in the definition of cultural identity and symbolic meaning . . . [is among the main] forces at work in the redefinition of the relationship between the state and civil society by people's demands for self-management and local autonomy'.
21. Like new social movements, much NGO activity is frequently built around a single issue (gender, region, religion, ethnicity, or ecology), is non-class-specific, is anti-state, and seeks to improve – but not transcend – bourgeois democracy. In part, therefore, the current acceptability of voluntary organization activity in many so-called Third World countries can – again like new social movements – be attributed to the attempt to foster development without politics in general, and without the politics of class in particular.
22. See Castells [1983: xviii] for the view that 'redemocratization' is the object of agency undertaken by new social movements.
23. That NGOs are not merely conservative but in some instances profoundly reactionary is clear from the following two examples. The first concerns base Christian communities in Brazil, which have been described in a text [*Lehmann*, 1990] that is a paean to the virtues of NGOs as politically progressive organizations which enable an 'authentic' process of 'from below' empowerment (*basismo*) to take place. That such a claim is nonsense emerges clearly from research conducted by Burdick [1993] and Hewitt [1998], both of whom show how conservative base Christian communities are, and how these kind of

organizations have in effect depoliticized grassroots agency in Brazil. The second example concerns the case of what proudly claims to be 'the oldest human rights organization in the world', the Anti-Slavery Society. During the mid-1980s, one of the members of its governing body published a text [*Sawyer*, 1986] defending the apartheid system in South Africa, a book which carried an endorsing foreword by the joint President of the Society. That complicity of this kind has a long history where this particular NGO is concerned is evident from the experiences of Sol Plaatje, the first secretary of the African National Congress, who described the Anti-Slavery Society as 'the South African government's most sturdy defender' [*Willan*, 1984: 201].

24. Much of this kind of theorization is associated with the arguments of those who adhere to the currently fashionable 'everyday forms of resistance' framework derived from the analytical approach of Scott (see below). What such theorizations overlook is that, in a period of capitalist crisis when an authentically socialist alternative is absent (in other words, where parties of the left are reformist, on the retreat, and trade unions are under attack), empowerment/ resistance arising from working class opposition to and protest about capitalism can easily be channelled into the romantic/reactionary form of anti-capitalism of the political right. This is especially true of situations where a lack of trade union and class solidarity/experience is combined with a capitalist restructuring of its workforce that results in competition for jobs among workers of different ethnic/national/gender identities. In such circumstances, the result is that anti-capitalist antagonism/conflict is projected in the (racist/nationalist/communal/ sexist) idiom of ethnicity/nationality/gender.

25. It can now be argued that, because women are (obviously) neither passive nor ignorant, whatever they do is what they choose to do. In the case of gendered economic activity such as informal sector participation in so-called Third World contexts, therefore, it follows that women 'choose' and benefit from low-paid forms of self-emploment such as street vending. With this kind of essentialist assertion, it is possible to not merely to justify but actually to characterize as empowerment any and all forms of economic exploitation.

26. As the case of the German *historikerstreit* suggests, historiographical revisionism of all kinds begins by relativizing horror/terror/(exploitation/unfreedom) and ends up by rehabilitating it. Like the attempt to 'normalize' fascism, revisionist historiography about unfree labour during the nineteenth century attempts to combat negative portrayals of black slaves on the cotton plantations of the ante-bellum American South, of bonded labour in the Indian state of Bihar, and of Pacific island labour employed on the sugar plantations of Queensland by empha-sizing what is claimed to be the 'positive' aspects of economic and/or politico-ideological autonomy. For adherents of this viewpoint, the driving force in this tension-free economic model is not the coercion associated with class struggle and surplus extraction but rather the non-conflictive process of individual choice-making workers exercising autonomy ('subjective preference') by responding to 'pecuniary rewards' in an harmonious free market. Accordingly, slave labour on the cotton plantation of the American South, bonded labour in Bihar, and inden-tured Pacific islanders in Queensland are consequently depicted by revisionist historiography as uncritical collaborators in their own exploitation by the planter, moneylender or farmer. For critiques of revisionist arguments about unfree labour in Latin America, Asia, and elsewhere, see Brass [1999].

27. There is an overwhelming sense of *deja vu* regarding the current rush within the academy to distance itself from Marxism. In their reviews of the history of the 'post-Marxist' retreat of intellectuals, both Callinicos [1989: 162ff.] and Petras [1990: 2145] show how exactly the same kind of arguments claiming to have superceded Marxism were deployed in the 1930s, the 1950s and the 1960s. As suggested by the case of the media publicity accorded in the mid-1970s to the 'new philosophers' [*Jenkins*, 1977: 116–24], a group of vehemently (ex-)/anti-Marxists proclaiming 'end-of-ideology'/'a-political' views such as 'in the end, there is no world, only discourse', 'reason is totalitarianism', and celebrating the 'new resistants' (feminists, ecologists, minority groups), it cannot be accidental that the increasing access of intellectuals to a mass audience via the electronic media [*Debray*, 1979] is accompanied by a self-imposed or – more usually – a willingly espoused conservatism/conformity.

28. Significantly, one important political effect of the challenge by postmodernism to the notion of representation is that – in the name of 'self-empowerment' – it henceforth frees intellectuals from the need to base their arguments on the views of an 'other' (about which, see Foucault [1991: 159–60]), and in particular of a working class 'other'. They can now espouse bourgeois ideology without guilt.

29. This goes against received wisdom, as embodied in the periodical lamentation by those in the academy (for example, Ignatieff [1998], Geras [1998], Rowbotham [1999]) bemoaning their exclusion from the political decision-making process from the 1980s onwards, and insisting how much better political practice would be now if only those in power during this period had listened to tenured intellec-tuals. As always, the truth is almost the exact opposite: conservatives in power throughout the 1980s and the 1990s were indeed listening, and heard in academi-cally fashionable ideologies like postmodernism not merely a justification but actually a celebration of their own reactionary views. This issue is examined in more detail in Chapter 5.

30. For attempts to apply a postmodern/(post-structuralist) framework to develop-ment theory, see the texts collected in Pieterse [1992] and Hobart [1993]. Although rightly seeking to locate labour studies in a global context, and simi-larly aware of the threat that postmodernism constitutes for such a project, Bergquist [1993] nevertheless insists on the value of a postmodern approach in the process of 'constructing a viable democratic politics in the world today'.

31. As with all fields of academic study, development theory has at the margins its share of unserious practitioners (= 'intellectuals') who, not having anything of significance to say, nevertheless feel sufficiently emboldened to proclaim old/new political allegiances in keeping with these neo-liberal times. Some have now emerged from the political closet: unsurprisingly, therefore, the 'search' by one such (Hawthorn [1991; 1993a; 1993b]) for a 'new' text about Third World politics leads back to Hume and Constant (for the latter's endorsement of views about the sacredness of individual property and the market, the central emplace-ments of 1990s neo-liberalism, see Fontana [1988]; for Constant's position in the pantheon of conservatism, and evidence of his now-fashionable pessimism struc-tured both by a nostalgia for 'ancient liberties' and by a distinctly postmodern aporia, see Hayek [1967: 160], O'Sullivan [1976: 44–52] and Eatwell [1992: 66–7]).

32. As Petras [1990: 2146] comments wryly: 'Under conditions of maximum capitalist power . . . the cost to the intellectuals of retaining their Marxist commit-

ments goes up and the benefits go down, increasing the incentives to rationally choose to operate within the framework of neo-liberal political economics.' That even Social Darwinist discourse has penetrated the agenda of development strategy is evident from the transformation that has taken place in the discussions of the political right concerning famine. This is best illustrated by comparing two symptomatic texts, both by important members of the (Atlantic) ruling class, but with the crucial difference that one was made in the development decade of the 1960s and the other during a subsequent and less optimistic (postmodern/neo-liberal) conjuncture, when the hitherto unutterable was once again back on the political agenda of capitalism. In the opening address to the Conference on *Subsistence and Peasant Economics* in 1965, John D. Rockefeller announced that the main issue confronting humanity was to increase food supply to meet the rising population levels (see Wharton [1970: 3–5]). His proposed solution was to expand the output of the subsistence producer, an objective of the subsequent Green Revolution programme. Nearly a quarter of a century later, the position had been reversed. In another keynote intervention, the Duke of Edinburgh [1989], who married into a large landowning family, argued in the 1989 Richard Dimbleby Lecture that humanity was now in a situation where the 'natural' balance had been upset. According to this view, ecological disaster threatened because demographic growth was due to the fact that more efficient food pro-duction permitted more people to survive. In other words, whereas for Rockefeller in 1965 the main problem was that population increase had to be met with a corresponding increase in food production (that is, the objective is to buy off potential opponents), for the Duke of Edinburgh in 1989 the main problem had now become one where an increase in food output itself enabled more people to survive, which in turn threatened humanity with ecological disaster. From this discourse it follows that, to maintain the existing ecological balance requires less food, the desired object of which is to enable less people to survive (that is, the policy has now become to kill off potential opponents). The sub-text of this argument is nothing other than a 'green' variant of Social Darwinism which synthesizes ruling class fears about population growth as a threat to its power with popular concerns about food overproduction and ecological destruction. The price humanity is being asked to pay to avoid the latter and maintain Nature itself in a 'natural' balance is once more to accept the inevitability (or 'naturalness') of famine as a solution to population growth in the so-called Third World. That Social Darwinism continues to flourish within the academy itself is evident, for example, from the 'lifeboat ethics' associated with the work of Garrett Hardin [1960, 1977, 1993; see also Hardin and Baden 1977], a 'deep ecologist' whose views about the demographic impact on the environment of the removal of Malthusian 'checks' are perhaps the most sinister confronting development strategy. Like the Duke of Edinburgh, Hardin posits a 'natural scarcity' in which resources are finite, and is accordingly opposed to technical progress and development generally because these overload global 'carrying capacity' and threaten existing (= capitalist) property relations. Hardin's view is that global resource transfers from rich to poor nations either discourage self-sufficiency (economic aid = 'permanent parasitism', a view echoed by Kirk [1968]) or deplete common resources (= non-individual property); consequently, he main-tains that inequality is functional for survival, he defends private property as a 'natural' arrangement, and to protect the latter he advocates the adoption of immigration controls by rich nations (Hardin [1977: 46ff, 80–81, 92–3, 125–6; 1993: 23–5, 278ff., 300, 309], Hardin and Baden [1977: 16ff., 27, 67]). For Hardin [1960: 53, 55, Figures 3–4 and 3–5], therefore, for whom the laws of Nature must be obeyed, the equilibrium of neo-classical economic theory represents within society exactly the same kind of 'natural' balance as the Darwinian scheme favouring the 'survival of the fittest' in Nature itself. His reactionary views combine the sociobiology of Wilson, Ardrey and Dawkins with (among other things) the politics of Edmund Burke and the economics of Soddy, a 'money-reformer' with fascist connections [*Hardin*, 1977: 98, 112–13, 137, 145; 1993: 76]. For the epistemological link between on the one hand sociobiology, and on the other racism, conservative ideology and Hume's philosophy of nature, see Barker [1981]; for the influence of Hardin's views on debates about ecology, population and the environment in so-called Third World contexts, see Basu and Mishra [1993], Bradford [1989], Bramwell [1989: 217–18], Davis and Bernstein [1991: 315ff., 323ff.], Ferkiss [1993: 176–7], Jodha [1990], McCormick [1992: 69ff.], Mellor [1989: 32–3], Merchant [1992: 66–8] and Thompson [1992: 14–15, 129–31, 162, 164–5, 172–5].

33. Petras [1990].

34. In seeking to understand the link between intellectuals, nationalism, peasants and populism, it is necessary to recognize just how deeply entrenched conservatism is in many of the academic institutions of metropolitan capitalist countries. Thus the emergence in North American and Australian academic circles of a revisionist historiographical approach to the issue of chattel slavery in the antebellum American South and Pacific island indentured labour in Queensland has (amongst other reasons) been due to the need to create a 'usable history', or a requirement on the part of the inheritors to present the process of plantation slavery and colonization in a more favourable light. In the UK the process has been somewhat different, since behind the rhetoric of plurality and democracy the ancient academic institutions continue to be under the sclerotic political control of the same kind of madrigal singers and recorder players so accurately depicted many years ago by Kingsley Amis [1961]. Like the Welches, therefore, those who subscribe to a culturally-determined concept of 'Merrie England' nearer home unsurprisingly extend this same analytical framework into the cultural domain of the 'other' in so-called Third World contexts. Celebrating culture on their own account, they are quick to identify in the cultural *specifica diferentia* of the 'other' a similar form of empowerment within the existing socio-economic system, contributing thereby to the now increasingly familiar refrain of 'Merrie Everywhere Else'.

35. Ahmad [1992]. Concerning the contradiction which derives from the privileging of the migrant-in-exile without taking into account the class origin of this subject, and the way in which this structures the political content of his/her discourse, Ahmad [1992: 12–13] observes that 'the ideological ambiguity in these rhetorics of migrancy resides in the key fact that the migrant in question comes from a *nation* which is subordinated in the imperialist system of intra-state relationships but, simultaneously, from the *class*, more often than not, which is the dominant class within that nation [which] makes it possible for that migrant to arrive in the metropolitan country to join not the working classes but the professional middle strata, hence to forge a kind of rhetoric which submerges the class question . . .' (original emphasis).

36. For the theorization of the 'new' nationalism(s), see Billig [1993]. Significantly, the concept of 'new nationalism(s)' finds an exact echo in Hardin [1993: 295], for whom the 'formula for survival and progress is . . . [u]nity within each sovereignty: diversity among sovereignties'. Equating nationalism with a 'natural' tendency towards 'tribalism' and 'tribal competitiveness/warfare' (tribe = nation = Nature), Hardin [1977: 132] accepts that such a position amounts to a naturalization of the existing socio-economic system (= bourgeois nationalism), and hence a justification of its inequalities. Although he notes that a system based on 'many antagonistic but coexisting tribes . . . sounds very much like the world we now live in', and is thus profoundly conservative, Hardin [1977: 133] nevertheless concludes that 'it is essential that we see that it would be unwise to try to escape this condition'.

37. Hence the observation [*Billig*, 1993: 78] that: '. . . the phase "the institutions of democracy" (which Rorty often uses) omits something crucial. In the modern age, democratic institutions developed within the nation-state, and, therefore, nationhood can be seen as one of the institutions of democracy. If so, then Rorty's argument has an unstated theme: to protect democracies and their institutions, one ("we") must protect the "societies" in which they are situated. Unless otherwise stated, this means protecting the institutions of nationhood ("our" nationhood). To protect a nation is to protect a national identity, which, as Rorty recognizes, distinguishes that community from other communities. In the context of nations, this means preserving the nationalist myths by which nations depict themselves as unique "imagined communities" – as "our country". In this way, Rorty's argument contains within itself an implicit defence of the world of nations, and thus a world of nationalisms.'

38. For examples of the peasant-as-cultural-'other' approach of anthropology, see among many others the classic texts by Redfield [1956] and Wolf [1966]. Historically, such culturalist images of peasant society have been particularly dominant in the case of Puerto Rico and Mexico, where the peasantry were depicted by anthropologists as belonging to (and constitutive of) a self-contained and hermetically sealed socio-economic system. For example, Foster's [1962, 1965] concept of 'limited good' and Redfield's [1930, 1941] concept of 'folk culture' were both applied to rural communities in Mexico between the 1920s and the 1940s. Such 'folk peoples', according to Redfield [1930: 2], 'enjoy a common stock of tradition; they are the carriers of a culture [which] preserves its continuity from generation to generation . . . such a culture is local'. Similarly, the concept 'culture of poverty' – associated with the work of Oscar Lewis [1962, 1966, 1967a] – attributed rural poverty to psychologically innate negative cultural traits, while for Malinowski the participation in or withdrawal from market activity by Mexican peasants was governed by cultural factors, and not competition or declining prices/profits [*Malinowski and de la Fuente* 1982: 177–9]. In responding to Stavenhagen [1967: 490], who accused him of saying 'being poor is terrible, but having a culture of poverty is not so bad', Lewis [1967b: 499] not only seems almost to agree but also to anticipate the postmodern celebration of culture-as-empowerment when he states: 'I am also suggesting that the poor in a pre-capitalistic caste-ridden society like India had some advantages over modern slum-dwellers because the people were organized in castes and *panchayats* . . . [p]erhaps Ghandi [*sic*] had the urban slums in mind when he wrote that the caste system was one of the greatest inventions of mankind.'

39. For examples of the peasant-as-economic-'other' approach, see texts by Wharton [1970], Lipton [1974], and Richards [1985]. Among the many studies of the peasantry which have either utilized a Chayanovian analysis, or been influenced by this, are Wolf [1966: 14–15], Sahlins [1972], Cutler [1975], Kofi [1978], Hunt [1979], Shanin [1981], Durrenberger [1984], Scott [1985a], Maclachlan [1987], Cancian [1989], and Durrenburger and Tannenbaum [1992]. For critiques of Chayanov, see Littlejohn [1977, 1987b], Archetti and Aass [1978: 114–19], Kitching [1982: 46–55], and Jonsson, Köll and Pettersson [1991: 68–9]. Chayanovian theory has been dismissed as inapplicable to Java [Aass, 1980], to Ireland [Curtin, 1987], to India [Krishnaji, 1995], and to Pakistan [Akram-Lodhi, 1995]. It should be noted that the theoretical provenance of Chayanovian arguments concerning the peasant family labour farm is neo-classical economics. Hence the categorization by the latter of the wage received by the industrial worker as a 'reward' for the disutility of labour finds a direct parallel in Chayanov's drudgery-averse peasant, whereby a 'natural' producer/consumer equilibrium results from a subjective evaluation by the peasant family of the balance between the drudgery of labour and the satisfaction of wants. The political significance of this is as follows: whereas classical economics stressed the role of socio-economic conflict between classes over an exogenous concept of value generated in the sphere of production, neo-classical economics which emerged during the 1870s was by contrast an explicitly anti-Marxist response to the development of the labour movement, and thus emphasized social harmony premised on the existence of an equilibrium in which a psychologistic (and therefore relative) notion of value is conceptualized internally by each individual subject and located at the level of exchange. In his critique of the latter position, Bukharin [1927: 32] observed that the 'methodological difference between Karl Marx and [the Austrian marginalists] may be summarized . . . as follows: objectivism – subjectivism, an historical standpoint – an unhistorical standpoint, the point of view of production – the point of view of consumption'. Not only was adherence to the Austrian marginalist school one of the charges levelled against Chayanov by his Marxist critics (see Chayanov [1966: lxix, 84–5, 220]), but the terms used by Bukharin to describe the way which neo-classical economics diverges from Marxism could be used verbatim to differentiate the latter from postmodernism.

40. In what came to be known as the 'development decade' of the 1960s, there was a widespread concern among non-Marxist intellectuals generally and economists in particular about the implications for 'political stability' of an economically backward agriculture in the Third World, not least because of fears that food scarcities occasioned by population growth would fuel revolution (an apprehension seemingly confirmed by the events in Cuba during 1959). This concern led to a consideration of the ways in which Third World peasant agriculture might be modernized so as to generate food surpluses, which resulted in among other things the installation of the Green revolution. It is not without significance, therefore, that the 1965 Conference on Subsistence and Peasant Economics [Wharton, 1970] concerned the ways in which peasant farming might be modernized so as to increased food output, which would in turn enhance consumption among the rural poor, thereby preventing famine/starvation in the rural Third World and hence the possibility of revolution by the rural poor. Non-Marxists have long had a similar interest in the potential impact of peasant mobilization.

For example, in his 1940 Presidential Address (on the theme of 'The Peasant and Politics') to the Conference of the Indian Society of Agricultural Economics, Malcom Darling [1940: 7, 8, 9] noted: 'Man, said Aristotle, is a political animal. This may be true of urban man, perhaps even of western man, but it is certainly not true of the Indian peasant. On the contrary he is essentially a non-political animal. He has always "let the legions thunder past" and plunged in work again, in the work of wrestling for daily bread with a despotic and capricious nature. But great changes are taking place . . . The [1914–18] war released forces which are spreading all over India, and their effect upon the peasant has been to set him thinking about his rights instead of his obligations. Three years ago, too, he was given the vote. This may prove to be a momentuous change in his political history. [. . .] How dangerous a situation . . . can be when the peasant asserts his rights and the landlord relies for the defence of his interests upon hereditary right rather than upon service to his tenants and the community is shown by what happened in Europe after the [1914–18] war. In Roumania the landlord was deprived of nearly 12 million acres in return for an almost nominal compensation. In Poland he also lost much of his land and was only partially compensated, and in Russia he lost everything. In all three countries this was done by the party in power to gain the political allegiance of the peasant, in the first two to avoid revolution, in the last to confirm it. In India the rapid increase in population is already putting the tenant at a disadvantage, and if we are to avoid serious disturbance, of which there are already ominous signs, he will have to be increasingly protected. But it is not easy to say how this can best be done and the problem is essentially one for politician and economist to consider together.'

41. Moreover, since even a rise in output from smallholding agriculture was never going to be large enough to feed domestic populations, let alone export food to other markets, this kind of policy was also extremely favourable to food-exporting metropolitan capitalist countries.

42. See Wolf [1971] and Alavi [1979].

43. See Desai [1979: 760ff.]. As will become clear below, Wolf adheres closely to the anthropological framework that is supposed to have been transcended, and in fact reproduces those very concepts which Desai claims are absent.

44. See Alavi [1979: 673f.] and Wolf [1971: 291f.].

45. Wolf and Alavi both acknowledge a mutual influence, and each claim that his own hypothesis concerning the peasantry is supported by the work of the other (compare Wolf [1971: 291] and Alavi [1979: 716, footnote 2]).

46. See Scott [1976, 1985a, 1985b, 1989, 1990]. Exponents of the 'impasse' position concerning Third world development who find merit in 'everyday forms of resistance' and/or 'moral economy' include Booth [1992: 9–10], Corbridge [1994: 114] and Harriss [1994: 181ff., 188, 192]. As the collections edited by Scott and Kerkvliet [1986], Colburn [1989], Haynes and Prakash [1991], and Joseph and Nugent [1994] all testify, the 'everyday forms of resistance' framework has generated a large following among those who study development in the so-called Third World.

47. See Scott [1985b: xvi, 11]. It cannot be without significance that Scott's theory about the alternative nature and 'from below' operational efficacy of 'everyday forms of resistance' in challenging the existing power exercised 'from above' by capital is in many ways no different from the efficaciousness of 'dual power' in La Convención as perceived by Hugo Blanco (see Chapter 2). Each overestimates

the extent to which 'everyday forms of resistance' or 'dual power' constitutes a break with capitalism, notwithstanding the array in both cases of a specifically oppositional discourse.

48. The generally opaque link between the 'moral economy' argument and the micro-economic theory that structures the Chayanovian concept of a subsistence-oriented, risk-avoiding, choice-making, utility-maximizing peasantry can be seen most clearly in the work of Scott [1976: 13–15].

49. For a useful critique of the 'moral economy' theory, see Popkin [1979]. Although strictly speaking Alavi cannot be categorized as an adherent of the 'moral economy' position, some of its more important concepts are nevertheless present in his work: for example, the view that peasant response is triggered by the violation of traditional norms [1973: 35], together with the crucial role of patron–clientage in peasant–master relations [1979: 714].

50. From the Marxist viewpoint, one of the main objections to the 'moral economy' argument is that it denies the *active* striving of the different components of the rural population as *class* subjects; that is, either by rich peasants to become small agrarian capitalists or by poor peasants and agricultural labourers to improve their position as workers (by organizing in pursuit of higher wages, better working conditions, a shorter working day, etc.). Without this capitalist struggle, together with the equally specific kinds of socio-economic contradictions to which it gives rise, there can be no transition to socialism.

51. Although the Subaltern Studies project is about the peasantry in the colonial era, some contributions cross the boundary into the post-colonial period (for example, Chandra [1983], Das [1983a], Chakrabarty [1984]), while others claim that its methodological and/or theoretical approach transcends the colonial/post-colonial divide (for example, Chatterjee [1983: 77]). Implicitly or explicitly, therefore, the Subaltern Studies framework can also serve as a model for analysing contemporary peasant movements.

52. For examples of this shift, see Eckstein [1989] and Redclift [1988]. The publication in both *Subaltern Studies IV* and the volume edited by Colburn [1989] of the same text by Ramachandra Guha [1989] underlines this trend towards theoretical (and political) cross-fertilization and compatibility. More recently, the Subaltern Studies project has ceased to be confined to the historiography of India, and now extends to Africa and Latin America [*Latin American Subaltern Studies Group*, 1993; *Prakash*, 1994; *Mallon*, 1994; *Cooper*, 1994]. Interestingly, the rejection by Scott of 'hegemony' (see below) on the grounds that, while peasants may accept the inevitability of their overall subordination, this does not imply that they regard it as just, finds a strong echo in a recent text by Ranajit Guha. The latter [*Guha*, 1989: 266ff.] similarly displaces 'hegemony' with a variant of the 'moral economy' argument, whereby 'dharmic protest' or 'rightful dissent' by peasants derives from a pre-colonial Indian tradition that legitimizes 'the morality of struggle against . . . [the ruler's] failure in his protective function [towards the ruled]'. The antithesis between 'hegemony' and 'resistance' is another reason why Guha [1989: 299], like Scott, questions its existence.

53. On this point, see, *inter alia*, Sarup [1988] and Callinicos [1989].

54. For the rejection of universalism and/or Eurocentrism by Subaltern Studies, see Guha [1983: 6; 1989: 272ff.]. The latter, however, then goes on to base his concept of 'negative class consciousness' on Hilton's study of *European* peasant movements [*Guha*, 1983: 20].

55. New social movements texts that question emancipation include Evers [1985: 61] and Redclift [1988: 254].

56. In a similar vein, Castells [1983: 138] privileges the 'cultural' by maintaining that 'the emergence of a social movement and its transformation into a political force [takes place] through the spatial organization of a self-defined cultural community'.

57. For the link between Subaltern Studies and 'the ideological', see Guha [1983: 13].

58. Thus Laclau [1985: 28] observes that 'the social agent's positions become autonomous – it is this new autonomy which is at the root of the specificity of the new social movements'. Similar views regarding the autonomy of the subject are expressed by Slater [1985: 5] and Evers [1985: 59]. The fragmentation of the subject's consciousness is identified by Evers [1985: 45, 61] as the main characteristic of postmodern discourse, while the effects of the 'individualizing techniques of power' on peasant resistance are noted by Redclift [1988: 251–2]. For the importance of ethnic/gender/regional identity/inequality in the discourse of the Subaltern Studies and new social movements framework, see Guha [1982a: vii], Slater [1985: 3], Gianotten et al. [1985: 185] and Redclift [1988: 252]. Significantly, Wolf attributes a similarly important role to the element of regionalism in the 'middle peasant thesis'. Accordingly, the location of a middle peasantry in geographically peripheral areas is regarded as one of the main reasons why such 'tactically mobile' peasants are able to successfully engage in revolutionary action [*Wolf*, 1971: 291].

59. This difference is encapsulated in the comment by Volosinov [1973: 13] that: 'Individual consciousness is not the architect of the ideological superstructure, but only a tenant lodging in the social edifice of ideological signs'.

60. Among those who endorse/invoke/apply Foucault's theory with regard to peasants are Redclift [1988: 252–3] and Scott [1989: 8], while those who do the same with regard to Gramsci include Guha [1983: 10,19ff.] and Chatterjee [1989]. The political significance of both a Gramscian and a Foucauldian framework is considered in more detail in the next chapter.

61. This emphasis on culture permeates all the texts under consideration here: for Wolf [1971: 279], the transformation of non-capitalist contexts as a result of capitalist penetration entails a corresponding change from a cultural system to an economic system, while the 'everyday forms of resistance' undertaken by new social movements are similarly presented as manifestations of popular culture, 'an alternative moral universe in embryo – a dissident subculture', or the defence of cultural identity (Evers [1985: 43,49,50], Gianotten et al. [1985: 183], Scott [1976: 240; 1989: 24]).

62. For instances of the tribalization of peasant movements, see Chapter 4. For a useful critique of the tribalization (and hence abolition) of peasant movements, see Sengupta [1982, 1989]. For an example of the tribalization of peasants in Latin America, see Burger [1987].

63. See Guha [1983: 166ff.].

64. See O'Hanlon [1988: 196].

65. For a similar view to that of Guha, see Sen [1987: 204]. Although Guha [1983: 15, 26] hints at the existence of intra-tribal socio-economic differentiation, he fails to explore this in terms of ethnic identity as false politico-ideological consciousness generated in the process of agrarian class struggle. The colonial ori-

gins of the concept 'tribe', together with the way in which it was used by the British to divide and rule, are discussed by, *inter alia*, Pathy [1984: 2] and Singh [1985: 104ff.].

66. On these points, see Sarup [1988: 132] and Dews [1980: 10].

67. In part, the penetration of peasant studies by postmodern discourse has been effected via anthropology in general and the ahistorical structuralism of French 'Marxist' anthropology in particular. From the latter emerged both Clastres [1977], who in true postmodern fashion counterposed an idealized image of the (non-Western) acephalous primitive society to the (Western) state, and the high priest of postmodernism Baudrillard [1975], for whom a dematerialized political economy of production has symbolic meaning only. In many ways it is unsurprising that postmodernism has been embraced so enthusiastically by anthropology, since the latter regards the project of the former as a vindication of its own specific theoretical/methodological practice, elements of which include both superstructural autonomy and the reification of the peasant and/or tribal as an ever-present 'other'. Of particular significance in this respect is the trajectory followed by Sahlins [1972: 102ff.], whose initial attempt to recuperate Chayanovian theory in the form of the 'domestic mode of production' has now culminated symptomatically in postmodern cultural determinism [*Sahlins*, 1985]. In terms of methodological and theoretical emphasis, the differences between anthropology and historical materialism on the one hand and the similarities between postmodernism and anthropology on the other may be illustrated by the following set of oppositions:

Anthropology (Postmodernism)	*Marxism* (Historical Materialism)
micro-level	macro-level
relativism	universalism
culture	economy
community	state
individual	class
stasis	change

Postmodernism might be described as the revenge wreaked by anthropology on development theory for the theft by the latter of the object belonging to the former.

68. See Evers [1985: 45], Slater [1985: 4, 5] and Guha [1983: 4]. In keeping with the new social movements theoretical approach, Redclift [1988: 249] dismisses the applicability to Latin American peasant movements of the 1960s of both the modernization paradigm as exemplified by Landsberger and Hewitt [1970] and the Marxist framework of Quijano [1967]. This point is echoed by Guha [1989: 270], who observes that '[the popularity of] a dynamic modernity . . . has declined with the end of the development illusions generated by post-war capitalism to "modernize" an archaic Third World'.

69. See Scott [1989: 4].

70. See Alavi [1979: 672–3].

71. See Wolf [1971: 289].

72. See Scott [1985b: xvi–xvii; 1989: 5, 7]; see also Guha [1983: 92–3]. The reference by Scott [1989: 23] to class as 'social stratification' rather than relations

of production confirms his non-Marxist use of this term. In his introduction to a collection of texts on Peru, Miller [1987: 14] also rejects class as a determinant of peasant struggles during the colonial period in preference to the 'moral economy' approach.

73. In what he accepts is 'a celebration of the *petite bourgeoisie*', Scott [1985a: 185, 186] places the agency of the peasantry at the centre of his ubiquitous 'everyday-forms-of-resistance' theory, and similarly invokes 'a libertarian reason' for believing that 'the petty bourgeoisie represents a precious zone of autonomy and freedom in state systems increasingly dominated by huge bureaucratic institutions'. The extent of theoretical/political confusion this generates is evident from the fact that for Scott [1985a: 196–7] the petty bourgeoisie (= the peasantry) are the 'natural' bearers of socialism, a view which he derives in turn from the mistaken belief that 'the popular ownership of the means of production' is the same as common ownership. Unsurprisingly, therefore, socialism is for Scott simply the result of non-class-specific 'from-below' grassroots mobilization by 'the popular', a view which ignores the fact that peasant smallholding entails (individual/private) property relations which are incompatible with common ownership of the means of production. The denial that the framework of Scott is in any way Chayanovian (by, for example, Harriss [1994: 182]) could only be made by someone unacquainted with this particular text of his.

74. See Colburn [1989: ix]. That Scott himself does not subscribe to a concept of an internally differentiated peasantry is evident from his resort to inverted commas when using the word ' "kulak" ' [1989: 17, 32 footnote 28]. Zamosc [1989: 122] also puts inverted commas round the term ' "rich peasant" '.

75. See, for example, Guha [1983: 166ff.], Evers [1985: 62], Laclau [1985: 29, 30], and Slater [1985: 5, 15].

76. For a similar view of struggle as involving the people (= 'the whole structure of social classes') versus the state, see Castells [1983: 176–7]. The latter goes on to observe [1983: 178] that '. . . the possibility of these ['popular'] sectors becoming a bank for an alternative political scheme, makes them at once dangerous . . . [t]hus our hypothesis is that the nation-states tend to be the mediators between the multinational corporations dominating uneven economic growth and the local communities trying to rebuild a new urban world on their own from the debris of their disrupted rural past and from the memory of their cherished traditions'. It is clear, therefore, that Castells regards the rebuilding of a 'new urban world' by the 'popular sectors' (= the lumpenproletariat) based on a 'disrupted rural past' and the 'memory of . . . cherished traditions' as an acceptable 'alternative political scheme', despite the fact that such an 'alternative' corresponds to the reactionary variant of anti-capitalism associated not just with populism but also with the agrarian myth. He attempts to rescue his position by arguing [*Castells, 1983:* 180ff.] that empirical data from Santiago de Chile in 1966 and Caracas in 1978 indicate that those on the urban margins 'were not the unemployed street vendors of Third World mythology, but mainly industrial and construction manual workers [= proletariat] of the small companies'. However, Castells then proceeds to indicate that these urban margins were 'the home of people with a broad range of occupations and social positions', a situation pointing to socio-economic heterogeneity. The latter notwithstanding, Castells [1983: 183–4] insists that marginal settlement dwellers did not possess a rural identity, and that they were mainly an urban working class, despite the presence among them of petty traders

and artisans (categorized by him as a 'subproletariat'), as well as beggars and prostitutes, whom he accepts constitute a lumpenproletariat. The romanticization of the latter as core agents of the new social movements which pose a challenge to the existing social order in the Third World is in many respects no different from the prefiguring argument of Fanon, who at an earlier conjuncture similarly identified the lumpenproletariat as actual/potential revolutionary subjects (see Chapter 5).

77. See Guha [1982a: vii–viii], and also Sen [1987: 203].

78. See Scott [1989: 5].

79. Significantly, the 'subaltern' category shares this characteristic not only with the Maoism of Sendero Luminoso and the Naxalites but also with the 'Trotskyism' of Hugo Blanco and the FIR (see Chapters 2 and 3); that is, the heterogeneous nature of the class elements subsumed under its rubric. For the analogous usage of a dichotomy composed of 'elite' and 'rural poor'/'popular masses' in the case of Latin America, see J. Fox [1990] and Zamosc [1990].

80. The theoretically pre-eminent Marxist analysis of class consciousness remains that by Lukacs [1971].

81. Part of the difficulty here is that such a procedure is epistemologically impermissible, since consciousness of class is an Eurocentric concept that involves an 'outsider' imputing a politically appropriate, logically consistent and historically necessary set of universalistic beliefs to particular socio-economic agents.

82. For examples of this kind of argument, see Wolf [1971: 289] and Redclift [1988: 250].

83. See Guha [1983: 30ff.]. Although Guha agrees that in so far as they 'empty rebellion of its content and reduce it to a routine of gestures in order to reinforce authority by feigning defiance . . . ritual inversion stands for continuity turned into sacred tradition' [1983: 31,36], such reversals may in fact be supportive of the status quo by *deflecting* rebellion, he nevertheless fails to consider the extent to which *successful* uprisings do not similarly incorporate symbolic inversions that also reinforce the existing social order, thereby subverting the act of rebellion/opposition itself.

84. For this view, see Guha [1989: 235–7, 273–4, 277], who poses the central question thus: 'Why did the universalist drive of the world's most advanced capitalist culture, a phenomenon that corresponded to the universalizing tendency of the most dynamic capital of the time, fail, in the Indian instance, to match the strength and fulness of its political dominion over a subject people by assimilating, if not abolishing, the pre-capitalist culture of the latter?' [*Guha, 1989: 272–3*].

85. In the course of actute class struggle between agrarian capital and its workers, therefore, the former introduces/reintroduces unfree relations in an attempt to maintain control over the cost/availability of the latter by pre-empting/undermining/reducing their bargaining power [*Brass, 1999*]. That poor peasants do in fact struggle to become or remain a proletariat in the face of landlord and/or rich peasant attempts to prevent this, refutes the 'moral economy'/'middle peasant' position of Alavi and Wolf (see above) which maintains that subjects from this particular rural stratum are too downtrodden and oppressed to do this.

86. This dilemma is signalled in the observation by Wolf [1971: 292] that 'it is the very attempt of the middle and free peasant to remain traditional which makes him revolutionary'. This same view – that it is middle peasants reacting to

external change rather than rich or poor peasants challenging the existing social order – is implied in the wish of Redclift to reconstruct the 1960s peasant mobilizations in the image of new social movements theory. Hence the comment [*Redclift*, 1988: 251] that '[i]t is easier today to see the [Latin American] peasant movements of the 1960s as a symptom of transformation than the *agency* of transformation . . .' (original emphasis)

87. See Wolf [1971: 282], Laclau [1985: 27], and Evers [1985: 63]. Significantly, the concept 'alienation' as estrangement-from-an-essentialist-peasantness is central both to the 'moral economy' argument of Wolf and the Chayanovian exegesis of Netting. In each case, therefore, capitalist development is perceived as a process of (mainly cultural) dislocation that not only 'threatened the stability of peasant equilibrium' but also prevented the middle peasant from realizing what is posited as the 'authentic selfhood' of petty commodity production. For the essentialist concept of a peasantry-that-is-alienated-from-peasantness, see Netting [1993: 328ff.], who observes that 'the smallholder represents a bastion of resistance to the alienation of employment in capitalist industry'. Much the same is true of Wolf [1971: 280], for whom capitalist development involved the 'liberation from accustomed social ties and the separation which it entailed constituted the historical experience . . . of "alienation". The alienation of men from the process of production which previously guaranteed their existence; their alienation from the product of their work which disappeared into the market only to return to them in the form of money; their alienation from themselves to the extent to which they now had to look upon their own capabilities as marketable commodities; their alienation from their fellow men who had become actual or potential competitors in the market: these are not only philosophical concepts; they depict real tendencies in the growth and development of capitalism'. For an earlier version of the same argument, see Röpke [1950].

88. See Guha [1982b: 4–5].

89. See Evers [1985: 61] and Slater [1985: 3].

90. See Wolf [1971: 294–5], Scott [1989: 23] and Redclift [1988: 251].

91. See Redclift [1988: 250].

92. This is illustrated by the case of Peru, where the state has been unable to stop rich peasants either from privatizating co-operative land and assets (see Gonzales and Torre [1985]) or from growing coca for and profiting from cocaine production (see Chapter 2).

93. See Scott [1989: 23].

94. See Scott [1989: 24].

95. See Evers [1985: 43].

96. That the control of the state is not the object of anti-colonial conflict is the theme of one of Guha's lengthiest contributions to the Subaltern Studies project, where he argues [1989: 213–14] that 'the indigenous bourgeoisie . . . abjured and indeed resolutely opposed all forms of armed struggle against the raj, and settled for pressure politics as their main tactical means in bargaining for power'.

97. See, for example, Guha [1982b: 7], Slater [1985: 5, 9, 16, 18], Evers [1985: 46, 58, 63], Redclift [1988: 251]). By contrast, both Miller [1987: 11] and McClintock [1989a: 73] talk of 'landlord hegemony' [*sic*]. That democracy (= 'citizenship') and not socialism is to be regarded as the main object of mobilization by the 'rural poor' in Latin America emerges clearly from a collection edited by J. Fox [1990]. In his contribution to the latter, Zamosc [1990: 45] observes

symptomatically that 'democracy can still provide a substantial part of the remedy for Colombia's ills'.

98. See Scott [1985b: 314ff.]. Although Guha [1989] also rejects the concept 'hegemony', he does so for a different reason: it applies to the failure of British colonial rule in India to displace pre-capitalism with the liberal bourgeois project (Liberty/Democracy/Rule-of-Law, etc.) of capitalism itself.

99. Hence the observation by Evers [1985: 63] that: 'States themselves have fallen into discredit'.

100. See Slater [1985: 7].

101. See Slater [1985: 14] and Evers [1985: 63]. The same kind of unintended admission regarding an affinity between neo-liberal economics and populism, in this case involving the 'old' variant in the United States, has been made before by Salutos [1968: 115], when noting that: '. . . the monetary views of Milton Friedman . . . whose name was linked with Senator Barry Goldwater's during the presidential campaign of 1964, sound very similar to those of the [1890s American] Populists'.

102. See Scott [1989: 3–4, 18] and Laclau and Mouffe [1985]. The trajectory of Ernesto Laclau, an adherent of new social movements theory and one of the main exponents of the 'new' populism who is currently to be found in the vanguard of the politico-ideological counter-revolution within the academy, offers a salutary lesson. Initially, and by implication, Laclau [1977: 15–50] sided with those who argued against immediate revolution, on the grounds that capitalist relations of production had yet to develop in Third World contexts, and it was therefore necessary for advocates of socialism to wait until they had. For him, like for so many others, the revolution is now not merely postponed but cancelled, along with class and class struggle. Instead, Laclau [1985; 1990] – like exponents of the 'impasse' – advocates a populist/postmodern form of mobilization based on new social movements, or a plural-identity/non-class form of emowerment within (and thus compatible with the continued existence of) capitalism.

103. See Scott [1989: 15ff.]. Symptomatically, one enthusiastic exponent of 'everyday-forms-of resistance' [Colburn, 1994] now dismisses revolution as an Eurocentric intellectual fashion that is inappropriate for Third World countries generally.

104. See Scott [1989: 15].

105. See Chayanov [1966: lxx, 43ff.] and Scott [1989: 17]. Decollectivization and the introduction of the family responsibility system in post-Maoist China is described symptomatically by Scott [1989: 16] as an effect of peasant resistance, the object of which was 'subsistence and survival'. Another text [Chossudovsky, 1986: 75], however, attributes this same process to a very different cause. Since the People's Commune 'failed to eliminate the rich peasantry as a class, decollectivization emerged from *within* the structure of collective agriculture, leading initially to the collapse of the collective work process and to the restoration of private production under the household responsibility system' (original emphasis).

5

Others Who Also Return: The Agrarian Myth, the 'New' Populism and the 'New' Right

'Fascism has opened up the depths of society for politics. Today, not only in peasant homes but also in city skyscrapers, there lives alongside of the twentieth century the tenth or the thirteenth. A hundred million people use electricity and still believe in the magic power of signs and exorcisms.' – An observation by Leon Trotsky in 'What is National Socialism?', written in November 1933 [*Trotsky*, 1971: 413].

'What does this [non-socialist, non-capitalist "Third Way"] mean, in practical terms? . . . it means first and foremost that we should again become conscious of the economic, social and communal foundation of the primary organic process, i.e. agriculture. Of course, not agriculture *per se*, but a form of agriculture with a very special economic and sociological structure, one carried on by a free peasantry. It is not so much the production of food and organic raw materials as such which interests us here, as that particular form of production which we call peasant production, for it alone possesses the inestimable sociological importance which we have made the basis of our argument and we have it alone in mind when we speak of agriculture as the last mighty refuge in the face of the collectivization, mechanization and urbanization of our time and lament its decline as the "flight from the land". [Plantations and collective farms] appear to us from this point of view not only as uninteresting, not only as the mere transfer of the pattern of large-scale industrial enterprises to basic organic production, but as something far worse: the annihilation of the peasantry which is the very corner stone of every healthy social structure, and as a refusal to oppose spiritual collectivization even when such strong and natural forces [= peasants] would aid us . . . Not agriculture *per se* is the backbone of a healthy nation but peasant agriculture alone . . .' – The justification/defence in the early 1940s by Wilhelm Röpke [1950: 201–2] of peasant economy as a non-capitalist/non-socialist 'Third Way'.

'Nor must we lose sight of the fact that the South African Negro is not only a man of an utterly different race but, at the same time, stems from a completely different type and level of civilization . . . Apartheid means, therefore, that certain appropriate possibilities for development will be given the two ethnic groups in South Africa, black as well as white, through the establishment of "Bantustans" . . . Justice demands refutation of the idea that South Africa's Negroes, as a whole are [under apartheid] a persecuted and unhappy mass of people . . . I, personally, have the liveliest and most pleasant memories of the happily-waving children in the native villages; the humorous farmer from North Transvaal, who earned sufficient money to buy a cow by working in our hotel for several months as an elevator boy, and the magnificent dances put on by the individual tribes represented among the seasonal workers in the gold mines. These were their great Sunday entertainments at which they merely tolerated the presence of their white employers, whom they caricatured drastically in a refreshingly disrespectful way.' – The justification/defence of the South African apartheid system by Wilhelm Röpke [1964: 8, 9, 10, 11] during the mid-1960s.

'Though they call themselves *New* Conservatives, no one shows a higher regard for things that are old – old families, old houses, old manners, and especially the old structure of classes.' – An observation by Edward McNall Burns [1963: 304, original emphasis].

This chapter addresses two crucial issues that arise from the previous one: from what immediate epistemological precursors did the postmodern 'new' populism of the 1980s and 1990s obtain its reputation for being a politically progressive discourse, and in what political direction does it actually go. Just as the culturalist discourse of the postmodern 'new' populism provided the prefiguring economic discourse of Chayanov with its missing ideological dimension, therefore, so it in turn draws its own radical political credentials from the earlier anti-colonial/anti-imperial arguments of Fanon and Marcuse, and more generally from its connection with the events of 1968. The latter conjuncture, however, also provided a point of departure for others of a politically less progressive outlook. As has been argued in earlier chapters, problems arise when this anti-colonial/anti-imperial legacy merges with the conceptual re-essentialization of an innate 'peasant-ness' (anti-imperialism + the agrarian myth = nationalism).[1]

The focus of this chapter is accordingly on the way in which the 1980s/1990s version of the agrarian myth is part of a much broader and politically less progressive discourse, and how this in turn possesses implications for all its exponents. It cannot be accidental, therefore, that the anti-Marxism, the peasant essentialism structuring claims about the cultural 'otherness'/ 'difference' of the so-called Third World, and the emphasis on 'choice' in many 'new' populist texts are also all central to the ideology of 1980s/1990s neo-liberalism and conservativism.[2] In a development which ought to generate more concern and attention than it does, this discourse is one which the more recent and postmodern variants of the 'new' populism (ecofeminism, new social movements, 'the subaltern', 'everyday-forms-of-resistance', 'post-colonialism', 'post-Marxism' and 'post-capitalism') share not just with the 'new' right but also in many instances with its counterpart from the 1920s and 1930s.[3]

The more recent versions of the 'new' populist agrarian myth are characterized by two important transformations: on the one hand revolutionary agency passes from the proletariat to the peasantry, and then ceases even for the latter; and on the other, 'peasant-ness'-as-alienation metamorphoses into its 'other', 'peasant-ness'-as-empowerment. Accordingly, the discourse-against of Marcuse and Fanon is characterized by the domination of non-materialist concepts of 'alienation' which, unlike the specifically materialist concept of alienation that structures Marxism, are also shared by those on the 'new' political right. Whereas the prefiguring discourse of both the 'old' right and 'new' populists such as Fanon and Marcuse identifies the 'estrangement' of the peasantry by capitalism as a problem, so that of its more recent post-modern/post-colonial/post-capitalist/'new' right inheritors declares this estrangement to be at an end, a problem that has in effect been solved. Sorelian myth as a mobilizing discourse has in process become a reality.

Unsurprisingly, the 'old'/'new' populism and the 'old'/'new' right also share an additional set of epistemological assumptions. Unlike Marxism, each subscribes to the presence of essentialist identities said both to predate and be alienated/marginalized/estranged by the discourse of rationalism. Again unlike Marxism, each endorses the continued existence of many 'traditional' institutional forms linked to a supposed ability to meet basic grassroots needs. Most significantly, the 'old'/'new' populism and the 'old'/'new' right share what is for Marxists a *dis*empowering belief in the undesirability of change that substantially transforms existing (= 'traditional') property relations. In so far as it advocates micro-level empowerment of non-class (national/ethnic) identities on the basis of romantic anti-capitalist ideology realized by means of ('everyday forms of') resistance to the state acting in the interests of large/ foreign/finance capitals, therefore, the 'new' populism – no less than the 'old' variant – not only creates a space for but in some instances actually licenses nationalism, conservatism, and perhaps even fascism.[4]

The presentation which follows is divided into three sections. The first outlines the way in which postmodern variants of the 'new' populism (the 'post-colonial' approach in particular) theoretically recuperated and re-empowered the peasant 'other' identified by Fanon, Marcuse, and Foucault as marginalized/alienated, while the second second investigates the extent to which the epistemological fusion between the 'new' populism and the 'new' right can be traced to a common emphasis on cultural 'difference' and a shared endorsement of agrarian myth. The final section examines the implications of the latter both for a similarly overlapping Thirdworldism and also for political mobilization in metropolitan capitalist contexts.

I

Towards the end of the 1960s, important elements of the agrarian myth re-emerged to combine with the radical politics of struggle against imperialism and colonialism in the work of those who might be termed the immediate precursors of the 'new' populism: Fanon, Marcuse and Foucault. As is clear from Chapter 1, many of the central ideological components which informed Fanonist, Marcusian and Foucauldian variants of the 'new' populism have a long lineage in Third World contexts. In India, for example, they were prefigured in the views expressed not just by Mahatma Gandhi but also by Deva in the late 1930s and by Ranga and Lohia during the early 1940s, while in Latin America they permeated the views of Maríategui and Haya de la Torre during the late 1920s and 1930s. It was specifically from this earlier tradition of anti-colonialism/anti-imperialism that the 'new' populism inherited its reputation for progressive/radical politics, a legacy enjoyed first in the 1960s by Fanon, Marcuse, and Foucault, and then in the 1980s/1990s by the postmodern variants.

5.1 From Alienated to Empowered 'Otherness'

Such a project, combining non-class identities ('diversity'/'difference') and interests with the agrarian myth, could be said to structure much recent social theory about the so-called Third World.[5] Accordingly, the 'new' populism is evident in the concept of an alienated/marginal 'otherness' that informs the theory of Marcuse, Fanon and Foucault. It also present, albeit with a radically different meaning, in the tribal/peasant/gender/ethnic/national 'communities' implied in or disclosed by the many variants of postmodern theory: the discourse of ecofeminism, new social movements, 'the subaltern', 'everyday-forms-of-resistance', 'post-colonialism', 'post-Marxism' and 'post-capitalism'. As has been shown in Chapter 4, most of the latter contextualize empowerment within the domain of 'popular culture', a procedure which challenges the notion of passivity by recognizing the voice and action of oppressed historical categories (= 'those below') usually perceived as mute and/or dominated. Recuperating a Rousseauesque notion of a 'general will' in a state of Nature, 'popular culture' becomes identified with the voice-from-below and anything/everything associated with it can now be celebrated by postmodern 'new' populism as the embodiment of an authentically democratic expression.[6]

One teleological effect of postmodern nominalism, whereby the meaning of language has no purchase on any existence outside of itself, is the naturalisation of 'culture', a concept which consequently not only no longer needs to be problematized politically but also (and thereby) becomes a substitute for economic development.[7] Implicitly conceding the arguments made by those on the political right, that there is now no longer a coherent alternative to capitalism, that the latter is consequently here to stay, and that further opposition to capital is accordingly pointless, much postmodern 'new' populist discourse now seeks to present the the *status quo* in the best possible light.[8] In order to put the best face on the existing situation, therefore, it is necessary for postmodern 'new' populists to redefine it: cultural identity becomes a substitute for economic identity, as a result of which a 'from below' empowerment can be said to have already been accomplished. In so far as all 'those below' categories (lumpenproletarians, tribals, peasants, women of any/every ethnic/national identity) previously alienated/marginalized/estranged have suceeded in realizing 'selfhood' within the domain of 'popular culture', no further struggle is necessary.

In the discourse of anti-/post-colonialism, alienation is linked conceptually to the experience of blackness, the definition of which when contructed by (colonial) whites is not – cannot be – represented as an 'authentic' experience. For Fanon, therefore, alienation corresponds to the experience of estrangement whereby the colonized is an 'alien' in his/her own national environment.[9] By regaining national autonomy in the act of violently displacing/expelling the 'alien' colonizer, the post-colonial subject realizes a liberating selfhood: the act of decolonization effected by a national liberation movement entails amongst other things the recuperation by the self of the respect which preceded and was negated by the basic 'otherness' of alienation.[10]

Much the same applies to the categories of marginalized/estranged/ 'alienated' subjectivity recuperated by postmodernism. Like Fanon and Marcuse, Foucault not only demonizes the Eurocentric metanarratives of Enlightenment discourse but also romanticizes marginality simply because of its 'otherness'. To the varieties of 'selfhood' established by Enlightenment discourse (reason/rationality/science/knowledge = 'the normal', 'the social'), its related practices (gaze/speech = rule/power) and sanctifying institutional effects (sanity/legality/heterosexuality/life), therefore, Foucault counterposes de-centred 'other' forms of marginal 'selfhood' (madness/criminality/homosexuality/death) which find their expression not merely in a multiplicity of 'othernesses'/'marginality' but 'othernesses'/'marginality' which are also taboo (= 'ab-normal').[11] The latter are thus alienated by virtue of being discursively stigmatized as 'a-social' (= socially marginal) and accordingly politically/institutionally excluded from the realm of scientifically sanctioned (= 'rational') forms of social existence (= the 'normal').

Because he blames Enlightenment rationalism for inventing 'normality' and thus 'abnormality', Foucault attacks the former in the name of the latter. The invention of an 'abnormality' simultaneously licenses the creation of 'marginality' and 'alienation', since the 'non-normal' is not merely consigned to the margins of 'the social' (and becomes thereby the 'a-social') but stigmatized as the 'other' that requires social regulation. In this process of carnivalesque inversion, therefore, not only is the 'normal'/'abnormal' distinction dissolved (itself an uncontentious procedure) but – more controversially – Marxism is itself inculpated as part of 'scientistic' and tainted Enlightenment discourse that contructed the opposition between 'normality' and 'abnormality' in the first place.[12] Moreover, since it is considered by Enlightenment discourse as 'irrational' and thus its 'other', traditional folkloric memory – the embodiment of a 'from-below' discourse and the central emplacement of popular culture – is for Foucault part of this same category of 'otherness', and therefore belongs in the pantheon of stigmatized-to-be-recuperated voices.[13]

5.2 Marginality and 'New' Populist Agency

This process of marginality/alienation was central not just to the link between 1920s/1930s populism and the 'new' variants but also to the return of the agrarian myth. In contrast to Marxism, which allocates society-transforming revolutionary agency to the working class, this same role in the 'new' populism of Fanon, Marcuse and Foucault is discharged not by the proletariat but rather by marginal socio-economic elements that are similarly alienated from capitalism. For both Fanon and Marcuse, capitalism has succeeded in buying off its workers. The latter are therefore dismissed as privileged, and hence no longer revolutionary. According to Fanon, it is in the colonies 'where a real struggle for freedom has taken place', the inference being that class struggles in the metropolitan capitalist countries have either been non-existent or 'unreal'.[14] Noting that support for political parties is urban, and composed not just of teachers, artisans and shopkeepers but also workers, all of whom 'have begun to profit . . . from the colonial set-up', Fanon concludes that workers in particular want no more than wage increases and are thus prepared to compromise with colonialism.[15]

This view about the privileged and hence non-revolutionary nature of the urban industrial proletariat in metropolitan capitalist contexts is in an important sense endorsed by Marcuse.[16] For the latter, as for Fanon, the western industrial proletariat has been co-opted by capitalism to the degree that it is no longer capable – and perhaps no longer even willing – of realizing its historical task of self-emancipation by overthrowing the system in a revolutionary act.[17] This process of working class incorporation ('introjection of the subject by its master') is for Marcuse a 'repressive tolerance' determined in part by the capacity of capital to generate artificial (= 'alienating') needs; the resulting working class consumerism is linked by Marcuse in turn to the technification of domination (a procedure not dissimilar to Foucault's discourse/techniques/practice of power).[18] Indeed, in so far as the alienation that stems from the cultural estrangement of the worker (= spiritual disenchantment with the existing) is not eradicable, it now becomes a permanent obstacle to emancipation. Like Foucault's 'power', therefore, Marcuse's 'alienation' appears to be innate and systemically non-transcendable.[19]

In terms of social composition, the element of 'marginality' covers a heterogeneous ensemble of 'othernesses', extending from the alienated deskilled (students, intellectuals) in metropolitan capitalist contexts, through variants of the 'abnormal'/'a-social' (criminals, prisoners, homosexuals, the insane) in both metropolitan and peripheral capitalism, to the peasantry and lumpenproletariat in the so-called Third World. Although Fanon accepts that peasants and a lumpenproletariat composed of landless peasants are reactionary, anti-modern, anti-urban in outlook, and counter-revolutionary in terms of action, for him the revolutionary potential of these alienated elements stems from the fact of their marginality.[20] Unlike the urban proletariat, neither the peasantry not the lumproletariat have been 'corrupted' by colonialism; moreover, each retains its spontaneous revolutionary tendencies that derive from its as-yet undiscarded background (= 'peasant tradition').[21] The 'marginality' of Marcuse is a similarly all-embracing category composed of 'the underprivileged'. Accepting that the latter cuts across class boundaries, he nevertheless identifies it as revolutionary simply by virtue of it being 'the mass basis of the national liberation struggle against neo-colonialism in the third world'.[22]

5.3 'New' Populist Agency and Sorelian Instinctivism

In terms of agency, the alienated/estranged/marginal is perceived by much 'new' populist discourse to be the 'natural' locus of an equally 'natural' innate/spontaneous 'resistance' to capitalism. Hence the peasantry is for Fanon 'the only spontaneously revolutionary force', while for Marcuse it is included among the 'underprivileged' sections in the Third World that are the repository of a radical 'pre-revolutionary' political consciousness.[23] As with Fanon, therefore, the recognition by Marcuse of the non- or indeed the counter-revolutionary potential of déclassé petit bourgeois elements or lumpenproletariat does not prevent him from claiming that – simply on account of an 'oppressed' status – such elements possess an innate interest in challenging the capitalist system.[24] Again like Fanon, the potentially revolutionary character of this oppositional disposition is attributed by Marcuse to the fact that the lumpenproletariat is imperfectly incorporated into capitalism. Moreover, both attribute an elemental/(non-rational) character to the agency of the alienated/marginal in the Third World. For Fanon the violence of the masses (= peasants + lumpenproletariat) is 'innate', almost 'natural', thereby reproducing the stereotype of 'native' = 'savage', while Marcuse similarly notes the 'instinctual' nature of revolt.[25] At the centre of the 'new' populist discourse of Fanon and Marcuse, therefore, is to be found a concept of pristine 'peasant-ness' not dissimilar to that which informs the earlier versions of the agrarian myth associated with the ideology of *nohonshugi*, 'Merrie England' and *volksgemeinschaft*.

Much the same is true of the 'from below' mobilization which structures the postmodern 'new' populist framework of Foucault and others, for whom the concept of agency amounts to a politically non-specific form of individual resistance, 'a certain decisive will not to be governed'.[26] And just as Foucault claims an 'authentic' system of values is essentially religious, non-materialist and pre-capitalist in origin, so he identifies an equally 'authentic' form of resistance not in Marx but rather in religious dissent during the pre-capitalist era. In many respects, the precursor of Foucault and others who adhere to a postmodern concept of agency is Sorel, for whom the cleansing violence of the revolutionary act was more important than its socio-economic cause and political outcome.[27] Like Foucault, Sorel not only questioned the possibility/ desirability of progress but linked mobilization to a Bergsonian intuitiveness based on myth.[28]

The importance of myth for Sorel is its specifically anti-intellectual quality: since it is based not on analysis (= 'facts'/'thinking') but on instinct (= 'intuition'/'feeling'), myth – like religion – is unamenable to rational critique and hence refutation.[29] A significant result of this de-objectification of knowledge is that action linked to it becomes contextually de-linked, correspondingly voluntaristic and thus 'spontaneous'/'elemental' in character.[30] To the extent that the 'new' populism generally argues for the mobilization of all/every category of 'marginal' supposedly alienated from capitalism, therefore, it endorses the realization of Sorelian myth. The difficulty with this is that, as in the case of 1920s/1930s populism (see Chapter 1), such mobilization is supportive not of the political left but much rather of conservatism, and even of the political right.

5.4 The Agrarian Myth as Link between Postmodernism and the Right

As the recently-disclosed fascist sympathies/links of a number of prominent intellectuals (Heidegger, Blanchot, de Man, McLuhan) who either prefigure or are associated with the postmodern project suggest, the latter is compatible not just with nationalism *per se* but also with its most reactionary form.[31] Although postmodernism's complicity with fascism is deemed 'uninteresting' by one commentator, it is impossible to dismiss the political and theoretical significance of this connection quite so easily.[32] In the case of Heidegger and McLuhan, for example, such complicity derives from the same cause: not only do both share a common anatagonism towards technology, but each espouses much the same kind of populist belief in a mythical/folkloric concept of 'primitive'/'natural'/(unspoiled) man, a central emplacement of the agrarian myth.[33] In the case of McLuhan, the politically reactionary provenance of this anti-modernism/anti-capitalism is clear from his nostalgia for the lost tradition of the aristocratic/agrarian American South, which he contrasts favourably with the commercial/industrial utilitarian capitalism of New England.[34] In so far as he endorsed a policy of national self-sufficiency based on agriculture and small-scale industry, such views possessed for McLuhan a programmatic status.[35]

At first sight, the inclusion of the academically unfashionable work of Marshall McLuhan in the postmodern pantheon may be surprising.[36] Although not identified as such, however, many of the extremely fashionable views currently associated with the high priests of postmodernism such Lyotard and Baudrillard are in fact prefigured in texts by McLuhan. For example, an opposition to metanarratives in general and Marxism in particular, and also the view about the impossibility/undesirability of representing the 'other'.[37] Of equal significance in this connection is the fact that, for McLuhan, the form of the electronic media is more important than its content in determining meaning, a theory which directly anticipates the view about 'hyperreality' now held by Baudrillard.[38]

Moreover, in keeping with postmodern theory, McLuhan operated with a concept of ideological indeterminacy, he deprivileged 'high' culture by erasing the boundary between it and the 'popular', and more generally focussed on culture/consumption/ideology at the expense of the economic and production.[39] Similarly, his affinity with the populism of the new social movements is evident from the way in which he condemned the corruption of the modern, eschewed politics for specifically 'non-political' ecological concerns, and his views about the desirability of decentralization to the small-scale.[40] For Heidegger, a universally objectifying (= 'inauthentic') technology similarly represents a negation not only of the subjectivity (= 'authenticity') of 'being' but also and with it of Nature and ecology.

Of particular significance in this regard is the fact that the object of McLuhan's interest in technology in general and specifically the electronic media was to understand their dynamics in order to prevent them from bringing about the kind of social order he feared.[41] Unsurprisingly, therefore, McLuhan's concept of 're-tribalization' by means of the electronic contraction of time/space, was itself premised on the recuperation of an idealized version of a small-scale pre-literate society ('tribal culture') in which oral communication between individuals would be possible once again.[42] In a similar vein, Heidegger laments the appearance of television antennae on peasants' dwellings, a view which suggests that – as with McLuhan – against modern technology (= 'artificial'/industrial/urban) is counterposed an a-historical, romanticized concept of immanent (= 'natural'/rural) 'being'.[43]

II

Inculpating liberalism for giving rise to an egalitarianism that prefigures socialism and culminates in communism (= 'totalitarianism'), the 'new' right – like its 'old' counterpart – identifies as the target of its discourse-against the combined and interrelated processes of large-scale urbanization, industrialization, capitalism, socialism, modernity, and technology.[44] Among its more significant pre-figuring and/or organic intellectuals are Alain de Benoist, Marco Tarchi, Julien Freund, Gianfranco Miglio, Henning Eichberg, Friedrich Hayek, Milton Friedman, Roger Scruton and John Gray.[45] Also important in this regard is the political theory of Julius Evola (1898–1974) and Carl Schmitt (1888–1985), each of whom not only rejected rationalism as the progenitor of an humanistic liberalism/(socialism/communism) but also constitutes a link between the 'old' and 'new' right.[46] Central to much contemporary debate about political theory, both on and within the 'new' right, is the extent to which the latter now exercises a politically unchallengeable hegemony (= transcendence of the left/right polarity), a result both of distancing itself from its past (= decline of the 'old' right) and of the demise of the 'old' left.

5.5 New 'Right' or 'New' Right?

Perhaps the most frequently repeated of contemporary myths – propagated mostly by those on the 'new' right itself – is that the left/right political divide has ceased to possess any meaning, since the 'new' right has broken with its undemocratic past and now shares many of the positions endorsed by the 'new' left while the 'old' left remains mired in irrelevancy, and increasingly endorses what are widely regarded as anti-democratic positions.[47] The 'new' right, it is claimed, has adopted an 'a-political'/'above-politics' stance. Not only is the European right now opposed to the state, to the 'Americanization' of the globe, to Christianity, and even to specific forms of capitalism, therefore, but (so the argument goes) its pro-Thirdworldism, its espousal of feminism and sexual choice, environmentalism, the right to cultural 'difference', together with its advocacy of economic and political decentralization (= 'small-is-beautiful') and local self-determination, all constitute evidence of its progressive politics, its pluralism, its non-authoritarian character and hence the veracity of its self-proclaimed democratic credentials.[48] It is, its supporters/apologists maintain, not the political right of old but much rather an authentically new right.[49]

By contrast, the continued adherence by those on the left to Eurocentric universals (class, science, progress, development, etc.) and their internationalism, their advocacy of an environmentally unsustainable large-scale industrialization and defence of the state is again widely seen by those on the 'new' right not only as outmoded and correspondingly unprogressive, but also (and therefore) as anti-democratic and ultimately incompatible with a variety of sought-after de-alienated 'selfhoods'. The sub-text of this argument is unmistakable: since the 'new' right possesses fresh ideas that both engage with and offer solutions to socio-economic issues which neither the 'old' left nor the 'old' right have been able to address or to solve, its views should be taken seriously and henceforth incorporated into the domain of 'acceptable' political discourse.[50] Linked to this are claims about the fragmented nature of right-wing discourse itself, the sub-text here being that a consequence of this non-monolithic politics is a correspondingly non-threatening disposition.

Claims to the contrary notwithstanding, there are good reasons for supposing not just that the 'new' populism is in a number of important respects indistinguishable from the 'new' right but also that a crucial element in this shared epistemology is the common endorsement of the agrarian myth.[51] First, some on the 'new' right define themselves as part of the 'new' populism.[52] A second point of overlap is chronology. Like that of the 'new' right, much of the 'new' populist thinking emerged during the 1960s generally, and in relation to the events of 1968 in particular.[53] The combination of an anti-American/anti-capitalist/anti-progress/technophobic discourse-against and an environmentalist/Thirdworldist discourse-for that characterized the events of 1968 and the emergence of new social movements linked to these issues influenced the political thinking of those on the 'new' right as much as those who were linked to the 'new' populism. Third, and more importantly, both emphasize cultural not economic struggle, whereby 'selfhood' is realized within the domain of 'popular culture'.

5.6 The 'New' Populism and the 'New' Right: De Te Fabula Narratur

In terms of practice, both the fact and the extent of the overlap between the 'new' right and contemporary variants of populism is not difficult to discern. For both the 'new' right and the 'new' populism, struggle is not so much economic or political as cultural. Central to this process of imbrication is the appropriation by the former from the latter of Gramscian theory/practice of cultural hegemony; like contemporary populism, the 'new' right now allocates primacy to conducting its struggle within the domain not of politics but of culture.[54] Each endorses existing forms of 'from-below' discourse simply because it is 'from-below', a position which avoids problematizing how and why current ideology circulates among the grassroots and who or what is responsible for its reproduction. The important difference is that, whereas the 'new' populism has attempted to *de*politicize its analysis of cultural struggle, the 'new' right has by contrast *re*politicized this process. While the high/low cultural divide remains intact, therefore, low (= 'popular') culture is now celebrated rather than denigrated. For the 'new' right, as for the 'new' populism, the sole criterion for the acceptability of any/every view is that it currently circulates among (and by implication enjoys the support of) the grassroots.[55]

A similarity of emphasis on cultural practice notwithstanding, it might still be objected that hardly any similarity exists between the 'new' populism and the 'new' right in terms of the political content of such struggle. The evidence, however, suggests the opposite is true. In certain important respects, therefore, little separates the discourse-for/discourse-against of the 'new' populism and that of the 'new' right, particularly with regard to on the one hand a common anti-Americanism and a shared distrust concerning the possibility/desirability of socio-economic progress, and on the other an espousal of 'difference' generally and in particular as this encompasses multiple forms of 'otherness' in the so-called Third World.

To begin with, the discourse-against of both the 'new' populism and the 'new' right is characterized by a nationalistic anti-Americanism. In a way that was subsequently to be appropriated almost wholesale by those on the 'new' right, therefore, the anti-capitalism of Marcuse is expressed in terms of antagonism towards generating and replicating a specifically North American pattern of consumption.[56] In terms of discourse, it is but a small step from a critique of capitalism-as-American-consumerism to a critique of the latter as a threat to the cultural specificity of the 'other'. This nationalist sub-text emerges clearly in the anti-Americanism of the 'new' European right.[57] Far from being evidence of a politically progressive transformation, the anti-Americanism of the European 'new' right in general and of de Benoist in particular is actually in keeping with that of the traditional right on this issue.[58] Not only is this anti-Americanism grounded in an attempt to protect what is presented as an innate cultural identity – which requires the prevention of a universalizing 'American' (= capitalist) influence from undermining non-American cultures – but it is also rooted in the economic competition between nationally-specific capitals.

Another characteristic which the 'new' populism shares not just with the European 'new' right but also with its 'old' counterpart is a pessimistic view about historical progress, and thus about the possibility, the effectiveness and even the desirability of social change. Like the 'new' right, the analytical approach of the 'new' populism to socio-economic transformation associated with Enlightenment notions of 'progress' is at best equivocal. Fanon not only rejects 'western values' as Eurocentric but appears to associate economic development with a specifically European experience, the implication being that it has nothing to offer those in the so-called Third World.[59] Because large-scale industrialization undermines not just traditional culture, religion and national identity, but also (and thereby) human nature and Nature itself, most postmodern variants of the 'new' populism – like the 'new' right – are similarly technophobic and/or opposed to progress.[60]

This questioning of progress (= the denial of modernity) is itself linked historically to the rejection by conservative intellectuals of a linear conception of time, and its replacement by cyclical notions of time based on the annual cycle of birth/death in Nature.[61] In contrast to the political left, for which progress involves a unilinear process of technical/mechanical/relational change, therefore, for those on the political right Nature/time (= particularistic knowledge/wisdom/culture) is suspended in an 'eternal present', which is divinely and/or 'naturally' ordained and ordered, and its hierarchy/'difference' (= heterogeneity, diversity) is therefore sacred and/or 'natural'.[62] For de Benoist and Evola, therefore, there is no time but the present, into which both past and future are incorporated: all the central and interrelated elements of social existence (= farming/tradition/culture/ethnicity) accordingly exist outside time/(history), unchanging and unchangeable in an 'eternal present'.[63]

5.7 The 'New' Populism and the 'New' Right: Worlds of 'Difference'

Certainly the most significant epistemological – and perhaps the most important political – component in the theoretical framework shared by the 'new' populism and the 'new' right is the concept 'difference'/'otherness' on which cultural empowerment is based.[64] In contrast to the political left, for which empowering universals override disempowering alterity (= 'otherness'/'difference'), this anti-universalistic espousal of the irreducibility of cultural 'otherness' is a characteristic of 'new' populism in general, and of its postmodern variants in particular. Not only does Fanon himself refer to the colonized 'original inhabitants' of 'native society' as 'the others', therefore, but it is precisely this emphasis on and endorsement of 'otherness' that exponents of postcolonial theory find useful in his approach.[65] Similarly, in much of the 'new' populist discourse cultural 'difference' is presented as being at the root of underdevelopment in the so-called Third World: not merely is industrialization perceived as an inappropriate Western imposition, but its absence

(= underdevelopment) is itself vindicated/celebrated as a the accomplishment of a form of cultural empowerment specific to the Third World 'other'.[66]

Along with many on the 'new' right, de Benoist argues for 'the right to difference', a principle which is to operate across all areas of human activity and existence: culture, religion, sexuality, ethnicity, politics and economics.[67] The significance of this is that, unlike the left, for which a specifically international identity/experience/(consciousness) of class undermines national/ethnic/cultural particularism, for the 'new' populism and the 'new' right by contrast it is precisely this national/cultural/(ethnic) identity which over-rides/displaces what is perceived by them as an 'alien'/unfeasible/(undesirable) internationalism.[68]

The focus of this 'difference', it is claimed both by those on the political right and by their defenders, is no longer race but culture, and distinctive ethnic/national identities/practices are now perceived not as racially superior/inferior but merely as culturally 'other'.[69] Such a position is not only compatible with but actually supportive of the invocation and/or exercise by the 'other' of an analogous form of particularism: the acceptability of the latter practice to those on the political right derives from the fact that it adheres to the same defining principle of 'otherness', and is thus to be encouraged so long as it does not undermine or threaten the distinctiveness of those – like a ruling aristocracy – whose culture is built on (and indeed symbolizes) economic power. It is for this reason that – historically and currently – those on the political right oppose the 'sameness' implied in the advocacy by the political left of universals.

A number of problems confront those such as Taguieff who claim to identify a political break in the views of de Benoist and the right generally, between an explicitly racist/nationalist/anti-communist position of the 1960s and a seemingly more enlightened phase during the 1970s when biologistic determinism has been replaced with an advocacy of cultural 'otherness'. To begin with, in a general sense biologistic determinism is not the ideological *sine qua non* of the 'old' European right.[70] Not the least of the many difficulties facing those who deny the continuing complicity with fascism of non-biologistic views about 'racial otherness' (as does Taguieff in the case of de Benoist), is a failure to consider the extent to which views unconnected with race are also a product of fascism, and thus not merely compatible with but actually symptomatic of a politico-ideological *project* of right-wing reaction. Only by focussing on the single issue of race, and maintaining (falsely as it turns out) that the 'new' right has purged itself of discredited notions of 'otherness', is it possible for those such as Taguieff to claim that because a particular politics is no longer tainted with racism it is *ipso facto* no longer fascist and thus acceptable.

More importantly, the 1960s and 1970s were decades when throughout Europe and North America those belonging to the 'old' right were re-inventing the definition of innateness central to their political beliefs and in the process themselves.[71] And as with many other of its components, this particular element of 'new' right ideology has a long genealogy in the discourse of the traditional right. Thus it is clear that for some of those on the political right during the 1930s the undesirability of the historical trend towards mass society was the eradication not just of cultural 'otherness' itself but – and perhaps more significantly – the capacity to reproduce this: namely, the material base which gives rise to this *specifica diferentia* in the first place.[72]

Behind the defence by the political right of a specifically *cultural* 'difference', therefore, is to be found a more important sub-text: the defence of the capacity to retain the *economic* power on which this cultural difference is based, and indeed, which makes it possible to be 'different'.[73] In short, it is a defence not so much of cultural 'otherness' as of the economic basis of class power: the ownership of or control over the means of production which enables the owning/controlling subject to command both cultural resources (art, music, architecture) and – by withdrawing from productive labour – the time to indulge in them.[74] Accordingly, the advocacy of the desirability of cultural 'otherness' by those who continue to regard themselves as politically progressive ignores the fact that it is to the advantage of a global capitalism which reproduces an economically uniform class position to endorse precisely this kind of *specifica diferentia* by emphasizing cultural heterogeneity as the basis of national/ethnic 'difference', in order to disguise not merely this element of relational 'sameness' worldwide but also – and more importantly – to prevent political mobilization on the basis of this economic uniformity.[75]

III

Both the existence of and the reasons for the Thirdworldist views of the 'new' populism and the 'new' right derive in each case from the rejection of what are perceived as culturally-eroding universals (such as economic development/progress and its concommittant process of large-scale urban industrialization), and a corresponding endorsement of what is perceived as a 'natural' culturally-based form of pre-capitalist existence (= the 'golden age' of agrarian myth) which entails the reproduction of those traditional institutional forms and a peasant economy threatened by these universals. In short, the underdeveloped/less-developed countries in general and their rural population in particular epitomize the 'otherness'/'difference' which is central to the 'new'-right/'new'-populist Thirdworldist discourse-for.

5.8 The 'New' Populism and the 'New' Right: A (Third) World of (Empowering) 'Difference'

Like the discourse-for of the 'old' populism and the 'old' right, most variants of the 'new' populism subscribe to the agrarian myth and thus undertake a backwards looking recuperation of (and in the process idealize) non-/pre-capitalist rural society in the so-called Third World. Although he accepts that colonialism 'tribalizes' its opponents (with the object of dividing and conquering), that it 'encourages chieftancies' (because traditional institutions are complicit with colonial rule), and further that 'town workers and intellectuals' who support political parties have no repect for and indeed struggle against traditional institutions (= 'customary chiefs'), therefore, Fanon nevertheless insists that in the course of the anti-colonial struggle the authority of chiefs should be supported.[76] The reasons for this are twofold: because the authority of tribal chiefs is recognized (= legitimated) by the peasantry, and also because it is a source of an authentically pre-colonial national identity. Marcuse also comes close to idealizing non-capitalist society in terms of already existing 'natural needs' which do not involve having to go down the capitalist path.[77]

Much the same is true of the more recent variants of the 'new' populism influenced by postmodern theory. Like the Rousseauesque/Wordsworthian combination of a 'natural' state of human 'goodness' exercised as a 'general will' in Nature itself, the Subaltern Studies/Post-colonial framework seeks to recuperate a similarly pristine pre-colonial subject who – once the distorting/occluding encrustations of an 'alien' colonialism have been erased – is, it seems, 'naturally' good and therefore by implication also possesses a politics that amounts to an equally 'authentic' exercise of the 'general will'. This attempt to identify the presence at the grassroots in many rural Third World contexts of what is presented as an alternative, anti-capitalist and anti-socialist, and hence new and politically progressive discourse, is less than persuasive, for two reasons in particular. First, the very flimsy evidence on which the case for this 'alternative' discourse rests. And second, because important components of what are identified as an 'alternative' discourse are in fact nothing other than variants of the agrarian myth espoused by the 'old' populism.

A similarly idealized notion of pre-capitalist society informs the work of Foucault. His argument both that prior to the sixteenth century those who were mad were tolerated and not incarcerated, and that before the modern 'invention' of sexuality what modernity subsequently reclassified as 'unnatural' was accepted as 'natural', suggests that Foucault does indeed adhere to a Rousseauesque vision of primitive goodness.[78] Moreover, not only is pre-Christian antiquity for Foucault a source of a new politics, but it also represents a return to a pre-/anti-Enlightenment system of values corresponding to what he refers to as a 'political spirituality'.[79] In a similar vein, the backwards-looking 'new' populism of those associated with the 'everyday-forms-of-resistance' framework, the Subaltern Studies project and the new social movements theory as well as texts by those such as Latouche, Shiva, Mies and Omvedt reproduce the romanticization of pre-capitalist society that structures the agrarian myth. All maintain that economic growth *per se* is an inappropriate and hence a disempowering 'Western' imposition on less developed countries: in order to protect/enhance the position of – and thus empower – a variety of Third World 'others' (women, tribals and peasants), therefore, such texts advocate instead a reversion to a subsistence agriculture.[80]

Attempts by 'new' populist discourse to present an idealized notion of pre-capitalist society as an empowering, new and alternative form of non-capitalist/non-socialist social existence invariably overlooks its historical genealogy. As the Thirdworldism of the 'new' right suggests, this kind of 'alternative' is not only not new, nor simply compatible with a reactionary (= tradition-invoking) form of 'golden age' anti-capitalism of the agrarian myth, but actually supportive of the latter. Unsurprisingly, therefore, the 'new' right evinces a similar approval of a traditional Thirdworldist 'otherness'/ 'difference' that is the basis of a distinctive national identity and – for this reason alone – is perceived by it as empowering.

Like nineteenth-century Romanticism and twentieth century fascism, the European 'new' right invokes as its 'golden age' an idealized vision of an ancient Indo-European/'Aryan' civilization, when subsistence-oriented and economically self-sufficient tribal cultivators lived 'naturally' in harmony with Nature.[81] In the case of Evola, this Thirdworldist discourse is linked to his Orientalist engagement with the Eastern cultural 'other'. Turning away from the 'decadent' materialism of 'the West', the 'new' right romanticizes what it takes to be an organic and thus culturally pure 'otherness' of the East that is the the source of its own primordial Indo-European past. This redemptive myth of a 'golden age', which structures the the ideology of *nohonshugi*, *strapaese*, 'Merrie England', *heimat* and *volksgemeinschaft*, is also present in most pre-capitalist social formations, where the immortality of sacred time (= the eternal present in the Garden of Eden) replaces the mortality of profane time (= history).[82] In the discourse of the 'new' right, therefore, underdeveloped (= 'primitive'/peasant) societies represent a lost innocence, a desirable purity and an harmonious existence (= 'primitive goodness') that it perceives as empowering and thus wishes to recuperate. For those such as de Benoist, such a process of recovering a lost past entails an alliance between the European 'new' right and the mainly rural populations of the Third World (where this 'primitive goodness' still survives in the form of peasant economy) against the undesirable universalizing/de-naturing processes emanating from the United States.[83]

Also supportive of this Thirdworldist discourse-for is the religious pluralism of the European 'new' right, which derives from the perception of Christianity as part of the Judeao-Christian 'other'; as in the case of Foucault, therefore, Christian beliefs are deprivileged and displaced in the discourse-for the European 'new' right by an earlier – and what for it is thus a more 'authentic' form of religious belief – paganism.[84] Not only is this consistent with 'new'-populist/'new'-right views regarding the rural grassroots practice of an empowering form of 'popular culture', but the endorsement of any/all religious belief also constitutes a negation of Enlightenment rationality. Just as the 'new' right subscribes to a form of ancient religious faith that predates a universalizing Christianity, therefore, so it accepts that the same can be true of 'different' pre-Christian mythical belief systems which are culturally specific to the Third World 'other'.

Neither is there any mystery about the fact that the ecological beliefs now espoused by the 'new' right and the 'new' populism alike similarly uphold their Thirdworldist views.[85] To begin with, ecological theory and its practice, environmental preservation, constitutes a potent discourse-for about the same kind of Nature-based 'naturalness' that structures the gender/peasant/national identity that is at the root of Third World 'otherness'/'difference'. Environ-mentalist discourse is also supportive of (and licensed by) the powerfully combined   anti-state/anti-industrial/anti-modern/anti-progress/technophobic discourse-against shared by the 'new' populism and the 'new' right. Accord-ingly, 'new'-populist/'new'-right discourse maintains that in so far as identity/ 'difference' is determined by space/place, change that undermines ecology also threatens the traditional institutions/organizations/'community' of the Third World 'other'.[86] For this reason, therefore, environmentalism-as-preservation-of-Nature confirms the 'new'-populist/'new'-right view that economic growth is not a desirable objective for Third World countries.[87]

5.9 The Agrarian Myth as a Contemporary Mobilizing Ideology

To the ostensibly plausible objection that, while it may still persist in Third World contexts, the historical link between the agrarian myth, the 'new' populism and nationalism could not possibly have any ideological resonance or relevance at the end of the twentieth century in a country with a modernized agriculture, a brief but immediate reply would point to the fact and significance of the actual/potential role of just such a link in two apparently unconnected processes/episodes, both of which occurred in late 1990s England. First, the mass support for and the discourse surrounding the two

Countryside Marches in London in 1997 and 1998; and second, the structure and popular impact of the oration by Earl Spencer at the funeral of his sister, Princess Diana in 1997. Each of these examples is informed by the same discourse, or an ensemble of meanings ordered (or re-ordered) by a common epistemology, not least that of Sorelian instinctivism.

Seemingly a multi-class/single-issue coalition (= new social movement) opposed to anti-hunting legislation, the Countryside Alliance organized two well-attended rallies in London, of some 100,000 in 1997 and an estimated quarter of a million protesters in 1998, which in the name of 'liberty' brought together agricultural workers, environmentalists, rural employers as well as field sports enthusiasts to defend a rural 'way of life', its 'traditions and communities against the town and its state'.[88] Notwithstanding claims about the 'classless' nature of this mobilization, and the voluntary participation of rural employees, it is clear not only that the main organizers were big landowners and businessmen but also that many tenants and agricultural labourers were ordered by their rural employers to attend the 1998 Countryside March (a process referred to by one landowning aristocrat as 'marshalling the peasantry').[89]

The link between on the one hand the agrarian myth, nationalism, and a 'new' populist defence of existing property relations, and on the other the mobilizing discourse invoked by those attending and/or organizing the Countryside March is similarly clear. Uppermost in the minds of big landowners, therefore, were the implications for rural property rights of potential right-to-roam legislation, a class specific political concern that it would have been difficult to justify in the absence of a more general defence of the countryside: that is, a populist mobilization rooted in 'popular culture' uttering an 'a-political'/'above-politics' warning against tampering with Nature, its innate 'difference', 'natural' traditions and hierarchies (Nature = natural = countryside ≠ the town).[90] Claiming that he, too, was a 'country person' at heart, the New Labour prime minister unsurprisingly backtracked on the right-to-roam issue.[91] Equally unsurprising is the fact that the far right equated the attack on rural tradition as an attack on national identity, thereby setting in train the ideologically powerful link between the agrarian myth and nationalism (countryside = rural tradition = Nature = 'natural' = 'natural' identity = national identity).[92]

A form of class struggle waged largely 'from above' that nevertheless needs to masquarade as a 'from below' defence of rural 'popular culture' (= countryside-as-a-way-of-life), the Countryside Alliance is the epitome of the contemporary manifestation of the mobilizing power and 'new' populist character of the agrarian myth. Its anti-state, 'a-political'/'above politics' discourse in defence of rural tradition and community is, in short, aimed at suppressing the class divide in rural areas by appealing to a common identity as 'country people' and simultaneously invoking the opposed images of a 'naturally' Darwinist (= violent) and pastoral (= peaceful) Nature.[93] As is evident from the preceding chapters, this discourse and its related themes are all ones which reoccur throughout history. Much the same is true of the second example. Thus the continuing power and forwards march of the agrarian myth, the 'new' populism and nationalism can also be illustrated with reference to an earlier phenomenon that characterized the 1990s: the life and death of Diana, Princess of Wales, and the way in which these episodes permitted the construction of a pseudo-radical oppositional discourse (about deprivation, about the monarchy, and about the nation itself) that was in effect politically conservative.

During her life in the public domain it was frequently observed in the press that Diana embodied the 'caring face' of royalty (= 'the people's princess'). In this respect, she fulfilled a classic populist role: namely, evincing public concern about issues such as social deprivation, poverty and inequality, without however questioning the system which produced them, let alone suggesting that the only feasible method of eradicating these phenomena necessitated its overthrow.[94] Similarly, at her funeral, widely thought to represent the public nadir of royalty, when the monarch was called upon by the press to display public contrition and remorse, the most explicit and dramatic challenge to its institutional role came not in the form of a republican critique, couched in politically progressive terms, but rather from her brother, himself a member of the landowning aristocracy, whose invocation of 'blood family' ties could quite easily have come from a medieval text or a Shakespearean play about conflict over dynastic rule and succession.[95]

By placing themselves at the head of grass-roots protest and/or mobilization, or being placed there by others whose class interests they embody or represent, therefore, an English princess, a landowning aristocrat, or a class of landowners generally can in the 1990s – no less than a leader of a 1960s Peruvian peasant movement or a 1980s Indian farmers' mobilization – formulate and/or give voice to a combined discourse-for/discourse-against in a climate where existing anger and dissatisfaction remain politically unfocussed, and thereby shape the structure taken by opposition to the existing socio-economic order. Rather than an attack against tradition, as claimed by the press, the object of this discourse is to preserve the existing institutional and/or property structure, either by threatening the state with consequences of doing so, or conversely by warning about the failure of not adapting ideologically to present circumstances. [96] In other words, it was a defence, both by the Countryside Alliance landowners generally and by Earl Spencer in particular, of a traditional and ancient power system (founded on the control of land) of which both they and he were an integral part, and in the case of Earl Spencer the main position in which he confidently expected his nephew at some point to inherit.

The advantages of mobilizing the grass-roots sentiment generated by the death of Diana were not lost on the then recently elected Prime Minister, Tony Blair, perhaps the most populist of English politicians.[97] Just as the discourse about Diana proclaimed the rebirth of a 'new' compassion/caring/feeling/ hugging society to replace the previous one based on debate/strife/class, so Blair put a similar emphasis on the importance not of an equal but of 'a compassionate society'.[98] He also took the next logical step, and equated the 'new' compassion represented by the princess with a 'new' nation and a 'new' Labour Party (Princess Diana = 'New' Britain = 'New' Labour), thereby annexing nationalist discourse in the familiar 'a-political'/'above-politics' manner which is specific to populism. There is no mystery about political object of this discourse. Like the pseudo-radical 'opposition' of the Princess of Wales to deprivation, and the 'anti-royalist' sentiments of her brother Earl Spencer, the New Labour discourse about 'New' Britain is a deeply conservative ('new') populism which serves ideologically to unite a nation divided along class lines. In short, it enables the rich to retain their wealth by not overtly antagonizing the poor: that is, by telling the latter how much they (the rich) *care* about the plight of the poor, which however continues as before (or worsens).[99]

5.10 Conclusion

The discourse of both the 'old' populism and the 'old' right spanning the period from the 1890s to the 1930s, and also the 'new' populism of Marcuse and Fanon during the 1960s, together with the postmodern varieties of the 1980s and 1990s, as well as the 'new' right, all in their different ways subscribe to the agrarian myth, which amounts to a reaffirmation of peasant essentialism. In the discourse of the 'old' populism, the 'old' right and the 'new' populism of Marcuse and Fanon, this takes a negative form of a fear about alienation, which expresses anxieties about the undesirability of depeasantization, a process whereby peasants are deprived of (= estranged from) their 'authentic' selfhood and reconstituted as other-than-peasants. Lamenting the loss of this innate 'peasant-ness' and with it national cultural identity, each of which is undermined by the 'alien' forces of finance capital and/or colonialism, the object of the agrarian myth in this negative form (*nohonshugi*, 'Merrie England', *volksgemeinschaft, narodnichestvo*) is to signal the desirability of reversing this process, and preventing this threatened self-hood from vanishing.

Much the same is true of the postmodern variants informing the more recent 'new' populism ('popular culture', ecofeminism, new social movements, 'the subaltern', 'everyday-forms-of-resistance', 'post-colonialism', 'post Marxism' and 'post-capitalism'), where the inescapable (= essentialist) 'naturalness' of 'peasant-ness' is similarly confirmed, albeit in a discursively distinctive form. Instead of lamenting the loss of peasant identity as a manifestation of alienation, these postmodern variants of the 'new' populism proclaim that the recuperation signalled by the agrarian myth has in fact been realized. The same essential identity of 'peasant-ness' is now projected in a positive discursive mode, and celebrated as having survived due to its culturally indissoluble 'natural' character. Declared by postmodern variants of the 'new' populism to be no longer under threat of alienation, this innate 'peasant-ness' is (re-) presented as an empowered form of cultural 'otherness'/'difference' firmly rooted in Nature. On the basic elements structuring the agrarian myth, therefore, there is in the end no epistemological break in the discourse of both the 'old' populism and the 'old' right on the one hand, and that of the 'new' populism and the 'new' right on the other.

This overlapping discourse about the agrarian myth is itself structured by a similarly shared Thirdworldism. Instead of a racial hierarchy in which the rural populations of the so-called Third World are dismissed as inferior, they are merely recategorized in a discourse which the 'new' right shares with the 'new' populism as 'other'/'different'. In keeping with its espousal of inter-national pluralism and an acceptance of polytheism, therefore, this replacement by the 'new' right of racial hierarchy with a concept of cultural 'difference' is not merely not anomalous but in keeping with the specific form taken by Thirdworldism in the discourse of the political right generally, not least because for it Orientalism is a reaffirmation of that mysterious 'otherness' (= the unknown, the unknowable) which is in fact historically central to conservative philosophy.

Together with the 'old' populism and the 'old' right, therefore, both the 'new' populism and the 'new' right could be said to share a number of inter-related epistemological procedures. A consequence of an antagonism to Marxist theory (class, class struggle) is that the 'old'/'new' populism and the 'old'/'new' right all reject Marxist categories of action/agency (revolution, proletariat) which are replaced in their discourse with the agency or non-agency of the non/anti-Marxist alienated/marginal/estranged 'other', premissed on a non-class identity of 'difference'. The existence of class is either denied or downgraded and instead a community of interests is declared to exist between and unite those 'above' and 'below'. As the case of the Countryside Alliance demonstrates, this kind of populist mobilizing discourse based on the agrarian myth is not confined to the Third World.

The fundamentally disempowering effect of this discourse generally, and in particular the discursive shift to a culturally empowered 'peasant-ness' is unmistakable. By reclaiming culture but not the economy or politics, the 'new' populism not merely mimics the struggles of the 'old' and 'new' right but fails to recognize what the latter and the left long ago understood; that without a supportive economic infrastructure and politics, any/all culturally specific formations – and especially those of a ruling class – would not be reproduced and thus could not survive. For the 'old' and 'new' right, therefore, arguments for the retention of particular cultural forms were and are a way of making oblique statements about the continuation of the relations of production on which its own survival was/is predicated. In short, the defence of culture was and is – as always – a defence of the economic power of which this culture was an expression.

Like 'old'/'new' right views about alienation and modernity, the 'new' populism posits the existence of an 'authentic' non-class cultural identity through which the hitherto alienated subject is now able to realize him/herself. Since no cultural identity is any longer an 'estrangement', none can be regarded as alienating. By declaring that henceforth any/all forms of cultural alterity are non-alienated, the 'new' populism has consequently not merely banished the problem of alienation but effected an abolition that simultaneously makes the transcendence of capitalism unnecessary.

From the viewpoint of metropolitan capitalism, the advantages of such a 'new'-populist/'new'-right ideology is that it severs the economic link between itself and un-/underdeveloped areas of the so-called Third World. This it does by conferring on the latter a specifically cultural identity that sanctifies poverty and economic backwardness as 'quaint', chosen by its subject, and eternal, all of which remove underdevelopment from the realm of the transformable. Enlightenment metanarratives in general and Marxism in particular are demonized for daring to attempt such transformation, a suggestion dismissed in 'new'-populist/'new'-right discourse where the desirability/possibility of change are presented as 'alien' impositions of Eurocentric discourse. The so-called Third World is thereby excluded from the possibility of economic growth, and the advantages it confers, which discursively (and by default) become the preserve of metropolitan capitalism.

NOTES

1. Not the least of the problems generated by this merger is the substitution of a crude anti-Americanism for anti-imperialism, a displacement which licenses a corresponding switch from a socialist to a nationalist politics.
2. For an existentialist like Sartre (who endorsed Fanon's argument), therefore, it was possible to choose a revolutionary agent. Because the urban industrial proletariat, both in metropolitan capitalist and colonial contexts, can no longer be considered a

revolutionary subject committed to self-emancipation and the emancipation of the 'other', it becomes possible simply to select (= choose) a replacement. Accordingly, for Fanon and Marcuse, the lumpenproletariat and the peasantry are chosen as revolutionary agents, interested in and capable of accomplishing the revolutionary tasks which the urban working class is no longer willing or able to carry out. Unsurprisingly in view both of its rejection of any/all forms of government and/or regulation and its emphasis on individual choice-making, Foucault was also sympathetic to liberalism generally and to that of of von Mises and Hayek in particular. For the attractiveness to Foucault of liberalism, not least because it licensed choice in the domain of sexuality as much as in other areas, see Miller [1993: 310–11, 327]. The latter concludes that '[a]s much as any figure of his generation, [Foucault] helped inspire a resurgent neo-liberalism in France in the 1980s' [*Miller*, 1993: 315].

3. Given the received wisdom that postmodernism and right-wing theory/politics are not merely unconnected but antinomic, pointing to the existence of a connection – let alone an epistemological affinity – is a controversial undertaking. Although it is obviously not the case that current exponents of postmodernism are fascistically inclined, the same cannot be said about a number of important precursors: the fascist sympathies/complicity of those such as Heidegger, Blanchot, de Man and McLuhan are a matter of record (see Farias [1989], Ferry and Renaut [1990], Kermode [1991: 102–18], Lehman [1991], Marchand [1989], Mehlman [1983], Hamacher, Hertz and Keenan [1989], Norris [1990: 222ff.], Ott [1993], and Sluga [1993]). The following kind of 'new' populist/postmodern argument (for example, Chakrabarty [1995]) is typical of much recent writing about the rise of nationalism and its political implications for so-called Third World contexts. Since fascism is a European phenomenon and an historical one at that, and as it emanates conceptually from Eurocentric discourse generally and that of liberalism in particular, for these reasons alone, the postmodern 'new' populists declare, it is impossible to speak of its actual/potential presence in non-European contexts. Nationalist dicourses linked to traditions and cultural forms which are authentically indigenous to the Third World, it is further claimed, are not merely not inherently or potentially reactionary but actually a bulwark against the rise/spread in such contexts of fascism. The prevailing discursive dominance of an emancipatory postmodernism (advocating diversity/plurality, upholding the rights of 'the marginal', and opposed to power in general and that of the state in particular), together with the vigilance of scholars influenced by this, it is inferred, is itself a guarantee against the political legitimization of fascist ideology. Among the many objections to this kind of complacency is the fact that, while it is true that with liberalism comes capitalism, and with capitalism fascism, it is nevertheless incorrect to conclude from this that hankering after a traditional/indigenous/(non-socialist) alternative to capitalism precludes fascism. Much rather the opposite, since it is precisely on this same kind of mythic/folkloric/('blood-and-soil') nostalgia that fascism draws in order to construct its own discourse-for. Another text, by Vanaik [1994], that is not postmodern but nevertheless similarly dismissive of the fascist label, arrives at a somewhat contradictory conclusion that in India a non-fascistic 'Hindutva [constitutes] a reactionary right-wing and dangerously authoritarian form of populism'. In the view of this writer the latter definition is in fact perfectly compatible with (not to say an excellent description of) fascism.

4. Attributing an 'alien'/'cosmopolitan' communism to an equally 'alien'/'cosmo-

politan' capitalism, therefore, the politically reactionary Zhirinovsky has described his agenda for Russia as follows: 'Today we are in the bath-house. We are washing off this muck, this filth, plastered on us by the twentieth century. Sometimes this calls forth blood. It's bad, but apparently necessary for us and our bitter country, so that we can finally wash away the satanic dirt [= Bolshevism] which came to us at the beginning of the century, let loose on us by the West to poison this country and destroy us from within . . . via cosmopolitanism, via the influence of alien religions, alien ideas and an alien way of life. We will get rid of it all.' ('Bear with a Sore Head', *The Guardian*, London, 7 Jan. 1994).

5. This social theory, heavily influenced by postmodernism, has as its neo-liberal economic counterpart the similarly designated 'new political economy', the equally class-specific political object of which is to theoretically justify – and thus contribute to the ideological legitimation of – the economic redistribution of resources from the poor to the rich [*Bagchi*, 1993; *Leys*, 1996; *Vieux and Petras*, 1996].

6. The current dangers in endorsing what is in effect a depoliticized 'popular culture' are clear from many examples, of which the following are typical. Right-wing Christian groups in North America are mobilizing politically on the basis of popular culture, the object being to achieve 'crossover into the mainstream market' in videos, pop music, television, films and books, all forms borrowed from their secular counterparts but given an explicitly non-secular and politically reactionary content. Much the same is true of a depoliticized notion of 'empowerment', a concept which similarly can be applied to any and every kind of activity. It becomes possible, therefore, for Rodriguez [1994] to celebrate religious faith in Our Lady of Guadaloupe, a traditional icon of conservative Catholicism in Mexico, as evidence of gender empowerment. Similarly, in the case of Italy the 'post-fascist' Gianfranco Fini was invited by the PDS (the ex-Communist Party) to its annual conference in July 1995, where he was received with rapture and applause: both the invitation and the reception were justified by the PDS leadership in terms of the fact that Gini represents a grassroots movement. This too is a familiar argument, loved by and symptomatic of the postmodern 'new' populism. Because a view comes 'from below' or has grassroots support, therefore, this it is claimed is enough to make it acceptable. Such a position, which postmodernism shares with the 'old' populism and the 'new' right, fails to ask what the *politics* of these grassroots views are. On this 'logic', it would be possible to endorse not only fascism but also genocide and racism.

7. Not only does the colonial/postcolonial duality signals its nationalist epistemological underpinnings, but it is clear from texts by its exponents [*Bhabha*, 1991; *Prakash*, 1995] that postcolonialism addresses mainly – and in most cases only – questions of ideology; that is, of the way in which the colonized 'other' is (mis-) represented in the discourse of the colonizer. Because it depicts the colonized 'other' as passive (= victim), postcolonial theory eschews the domain of 'the economic' (= 'sociology of underdevelopment'/'dependency') as this encompasses the specifically economic dimension of the colonizer/colonized relationship. For a particularly effective critique of postcolonialism, which points out the way in which it has been inflated in temporal/spatial terms, see Ahmad [1995].

8. Like all the postmodern variants of the 'new' populism, those which maintain that societies are now 'post-capitalist' and can only be understood in terms of a 'post-Marxist' theory adhere to an analytical framework from which class, class formation and class struggle have all been banished, and in which ethnic/'tribal'/

national identities are regarded as innate. Proponents of 'post-capitalism' [*Dahrendorf*, 1959: 241ff.; *Bell*, 1971; *Drucker*, 1993] maintain that, as production has now been displaced by knowledge as a source of value in the global economy, the resulting knowledge-intensive society is no longer premissed on the opposition between capital and labour. The anti-Marxist nature of this particular agenda was accurately delineated many years ago by Macpherson [1972: 18], who observed that: 'there is a good deal of loose writing these days [1964] about something called "post-capitalism". The same publicists and theorists who use this term are apt to talk also about post-Marxism. The idea in both cases is the same: to suggest that the thing now hyphenated has in fact disappeared and has been replaced by something really quite different. If one cannot deny, in either case, that something superficially similar to the old thing is still around, one can perhaps exorcize its spirit by calling it "post-". Thus, as capitalism, old-style, has become increasingly difficult to justify in terms of any acceptable social ethic, it becomes highly advantageous to find that it has given way to something else. And as Marxism, old-style, continues to give trouble, it can perhaps more easily be dealt with by announcing its demise and replacement.'

9. On this point, see Fanon [1968].

10. A parallel could be made here, not only with medieval corporate society of eastern Europe and the Inca 'communism' of Mariátegui during the 1920s/1930s (see Chapter 1), but also with the postmodern theory of Prakash [1992: 18], for whom underneath the externally-imposed colonial encrustation there lies an 'authentic' Indian-ness, a pristine identity of 'self-hood' which colonialism neither affected nor disturbed. Marcuse [1970: 104–5] also implies that the negation of the established order will take place on the basis of an appeal to Rousseauesque/Burkean 'natural rights' (= ancient principle).

11. Unlike Foucault, for Marcuse [1970: 81] there is such a thing as rational authority, but like Foucault he endorses 'a new dimension of protest, which consists in the unity of moral-sexual and political rebellion' [*Marcuse*, 1970: 92]. In the light of his sadomasochism, his thanatological disposition and his somatic reductionism (on which see Miller [1993]), the detailed description by Foucault [1977: 1–6] of all the distressing minutiae of the execution in 1757 of the regicide Damiens appears worryingly to be more a celebration than a critique of this event. For Foucault, it seems, death is not just the ultimate but perhaps even the only form of empowerment – a very religious sentiment indeed. Alternatively, the fact that his description can be read either as critique or as celebration is perhaps no more than a measure of the extent of Foucault's postmodern aporia.

12. For the theorization by Foucault of Enlightenment rationalism as the 'other' of freedom, and his dismissal of Marxism as a variant of Enlightenment 'scientism', see Foucault [1991: 118] and Rabinow [1984: 52–3]. The specifically anti-Marxist epistemology of Foucault was recognized by Sartre in 1966 [*Eribon*, 1992: 164]; more generally, Foucault's vehement anti-communism is well-known, and a matter of extensive record (on which see Eribon [1992: 136]). In the case of Marcuse, there can be no doubt about his Marxist committment. The case of Fanon is more problematic: although characterized by Caute [1970: 52] as a socialist, it is evident from what Fanon [1963: 78] himself writes that he was as much anti-socialist as anti-capitalist.

13. On the displacement of rationalism by the 'from-below' discourse of traditional folkloric memory, Foucault is unambiguous: 'Unreason would be the long

memory of peoples,' he observes, 'their greatest fidelity to the past' (cited in Eribon [1992: 118]). Unsurprisingly, much the same kind of reification of spontaneity/elementalism as a 'natural' (and thus non-transformable) aspect of human existence has long been the stock-in-trade of the political right. Like Foucault, therefore, Ortega y Gasset [1961] invokes the authority of Nietzsche for his view that rationalism is necessarily and always displaced by an innate irrationalism.

14. Fanon [1963: 37].
15. On these points, see Fanon [1963: 47]. 'It cannot be too strongly stressed', he observes [1963: 88], 'that in the colonial territories the proletariat is the nucleus of the colonised population which has been most pampered by the colonial regime. The embryonic proletariat of the towns is in a comparatively privileged position. [It] has everything to lose . . . .' According to Fanon [1963: 48], the result is the emergence of an urban proletariat the members of which 'fight under an abstract watchword: "Government by the workers", and . . . forget that in their country it should be *nationalist* watchwords which are the first in the field' (original emphasis).
16. Marcuse's denials notwithstanding [1976: 71], that he no longer perceived the urban industrial working class in metropolitan capitalist contexts as a revolutionary agent is clear from many of his texts [*Marcuse*, 1969: 14–15; 1970: 70, 99–100].
17. On this point, see Marcuse [1976: 66]. Ironically, this kind of thinking also lies behind the postmodern celebration of what used to be regarded as alienation: not only is social fragmentation (= alienation) inverted and re-presented by postmodernism as the empowerment of identity politics, but the generation by capitalism of artificial (= alien) demands amounting to consumerism-as-the-negation-of-selfhood is similarly reborn in its 'other' postmodern form of consumerism-as-the-realization-of-selfhood (= 'shop-till-you-drop').
18. On the significance for accumulation of this capacity to generate seemingly endless demand, and its connection with the political integration of the proletariat into metropolitan capitalism, see Marcuse [1976: 66–7]. For this reason, moreover, social transformation must be preceded by a change in the definition of needs [*Marcuse*, 1969: 4, 18–19; 1970: 80].
19. Since for Foucault power is everpresent, for this reason alone there can be no process of emancipation. For different reasons, the concept 'represssive tolerance' is faced with similar problems. Hence the pessimism of Marcuse [1970: 100–101; 1976: 66] about the implications for working class emancipation of this process of incorporation stemmed in part from the conjunctural perception – also shared by the end-of-ideology theory – that capitalism had in the short term solved the problem of crisis (= overproduction). Consequently, for those on both the political right and left, the urban proletariat in metropolitan capitalist countries was regarded as no longer having a reason to oppose the the capitalist system. The responses from both ends of the political spectrum, however, were different: those on the political right proclaimed the end-of-ideology (= a foreclosure on class and class struggle), while some of those on the left searched for an alternative revolutionary subject.
20. For his views on the peasantry and the lumpenproletariat, see Fanon [1963: 90–91, 93, 95–6, 103–5, 109]. As is evident from Chapter 1, this kind of anti-colonial discourse associated with the 'new' populism, involving the search for an alterna-

tive revolutionary subject that is neither urban, working class nor tainted by capitalism, is not in fact new.

21. Hence the view [*Fanon*, 1963: 103] that: '. . . the rebellion, which began in the country districts, will filter into the towns through that fraction of the peasant population which is blocked on the outer fringe of the urban centres, that fraction which has not yet succeeded in finding a bone to gnaw in the colonial system. The men whom the growing population of the country districts and colonial expropriation have brought to desert their family holdings circle tirelessly around the different towns, hoping that one day or another they will be allowed inside. It is within this mass of humanity, this people of the shanty towns, at the core of the lumpenproletariat that the rebellion will find its urban spearhead. For the lumpenproletariat, that horde of starving men uprooted from their tribe and from their clan, constitutes one of the most spontaneous and the most radically revolutionary forces of a colonised people.' Not only does this romanticization of the urban lumpenproletariat as potentially revolutionary continue to pervade analyses of the contemporary urban informal sector economy in the so-called Third World (for example, Scott [1994]), but – like the 'peasant-ness' of the agrarian myth as perceived by postmodern 'new' populism – this kind of alienated/marginal existence is also represented as a locus where the poorly-remunerated and highly exploited self-employed realize 'empowerment' (for example, Scott [1985a: 191ff.], Nuñez [1993], Sherman [1992: 73–4,179], and Latouche [1993: 127ff.; 1996: 108ff.]).

22. Marcuse [1970: 85]. 'These masses', he continues, 'can perhaps now be considered the new proletariat and as such they are today a real danger for the world system of capitalism'. For similar claims, see also Marcuse [1970: 93, 94–5, 100–1; 1976: 72], where he recognizes not just that such opposition might be mobilized as easily by the political right as by the left but also that a successful overthrow of the capitalist system can only be achieved by the combined opposition in metropolitan and Third World contexts.

23. On these points, see Fanon [1963: 99] and Marcuse [1969: 56–7]. About the revolutionary role of a peasantry ignored or disdained by political parties, Fanon [1963: 48] notes: 'it is clear that in the colonial countries the peasants alone are revolutionary, for they have nothing to lose and everything to gain. The starving peasant, outside the class system, is the first among the exploited to discover that only violence pays'.

24. For the denial of the lumpenproletariat as a revolutionary force, see Marcuse [1969: 51; 1970: 73]. Accepting that it may '[regress] to bourgeois or, even worse, aristocratic ideologies', Marcuse [1969: 52] nevertheless persists in identifying the lumpenproletariat as the bearer of 'a new, spontaneous solidarity'. As has been noted in Chapter 1, there is much historical evidence to the effect that not only is the lumpenproletariat not revolutionary but that it is much rather counter-revolutionary. In the case of Johannesburg in the early twentieth century [*van Onselen*, 1977], for example, the criminal activity (= 'resistance') of urban gangs whose members were a depeasantized lumpenproletariat resisting proletarianization and seeking instead a process of repeasantization, was directed against black migrant workers (from whom they stole and by whom they were feared).

25. On these points, see Fanon [1963: 56–7] and Marcuse [1969: 9]. Among those who have recognized in Fanon an echo of their own populism is Reinaga [1969: 67–71, 77, 155], a prominent Bolivian *indigenista*, who invoked Fanon's claims about the instinctual revolt of the Third World 'other' in support of his own arguments con-

cerning the innateness of indigenous ethnic identity in rural Latin America.

26. For the epistemology of this 'resistance' based on what Foucault similarly categorizes as a politically non-specific process of individual 'critique', see Miller [1993: 301–5].

27. The same is true of Bataille [1985, 1991, 1994], another postmodern precursor who not only lamented the loss of myth entailed in progress/modernity but also celebrated the cleansing effect of 'primitive' violence as a 'natural' reaffirmation of myth in pre-capitalist social formations akin to the elemental/destructive force of Nature itself (see note 32).

28. For his critique of progress, see Sorel [1969]. For the link between Sorel's theory and the French political right, see Wilde [1985]. The description of Sorel [*Wilde*, 1985: 16] as 'neither a political or social theorist but merely a critic . . . his views regarding the distribution of political and economic power are limited to abhorrence of the *status quo* . . . he remains firmly on the side of intuition when dealing with the potential forces for liberation from the stranglehold of democratic society' might apply just as accurately to many postmodern 'new' populist texts.

29. For the importance of myth, see Sorel [1916: 22ff.]. The extent to which myth is perceived by him not merely to lie beyond the realm of 'the rational' but to derive advantage from precisely this element of 'unknowability' is clear from the observation [*Sorel*, 1916: 32–3] that 'myths are not descriptions of things, but expressions of a determination to act. A Utopia is, on the contrary, an intellectual product; it is the work of theorists who, after observing and discussing the known facts, seek to establish a model to which they can compare existing society in order to estimate the amount of good and evil it contains. . . . A myth cannot be refuted, since it is, at bottom, identical with the convictions of a group, being the expression of these convictions in the language of movement; and it is, in consequence, unanalysable into parts which could be placed on the plane of historical descriptions.' For the centrality of the invocation of mythical/traditional/religious/sacred themes to the process of fascist mobilization, see Mosse [1978].

30. Not only does this 'spontaneous'/'elemental' characterization apply also to the way postmodernism and 'resistance' theory interpret agency but, the claims to accurately represent an authentically 'from below' discourse about mobilization notwithstanding, both the former share what is actually a patronizing attitude towards 'those below' (= talking-down-to-the-'other'), a position that is not just politically disempowering but also wrong. Much the same point about talking-down-to-the-'other' has been made by Larsen [1993: 282, 285], who observes: 'Those super-exploited and oppressed at the periphery . . . become pegged with a sort of sub-political consciousness, as if they couldn't or needn't see beyond the sheer fact of survival . . . [postmodernism] rests on an intellectual distrust of the masses, a view of the mass as beyond the reach of reason and hence to be guided by myth. The Latin American masses have a long history of being stigmatized in this way by both imperial and creole elites . . . . [I]n the era of "postmodernity" we are being urged, in exchange for a cult of alterity, to relinquish this conception of the masses as the rational agents of social and historical change, as the bearers of progress. Given the increasing prevalence of such aristocratism, however it may devise radical credentials for itself, it becomes possible . . . to be seduced by the false Nietzschean regard for the masses as capable only of an unconscious, instinctual political agency.' Significantly, this observation about 'instinctual political agency' applies with particular force not just to Foucault, Scott and Latouche, or

indeed to Fanon and Marcuse, but also to the Sorelian concept of myth and its mobilizing role.

31. As worrying as the postmodernism/fascism link – or, indeed, perhaps more so – is the refusal of those such as Derrida either to accept the fact of this complicity or to acknowledge its importance (about which, see Ferry and Renaut [1990: 52–3], Lehman [1991: 234ff.]).

32. See Harvey [1989: 357]. Even in the case of Bataille, an (perhaps 'the') important precursor of the postmodern problematic [*Pefanis*, 1991], there exists an uneasy relationship between his anti-fascism on the one hand and his Nietzschean philosophy on the other, a contradiction unsatisfactorily explained in terms of the absence of a clear-cut distinction between the politics of left and right during the 1930s. Of significance, therefore, is the fact that during the mid-1930s not only was Bataille accused by Breton of being *sur-fasciste*, and he himself admitted to a 'paradoxical fascist tendency', but the 'endorsement' Bataille extended to the Popular Front in France was on account of its force/violence rather than its politics [*Bataille*, 1985: xi, xviii, 161–8]. Like Foucault, who identifies both Blanchot and Bataille as seminal influences [*Foucault*, 1991; *Foucault and Blanchot*, 1990] and whose own work is described in turn by Blanchot [*Foucault and Blanchot*, 1990: 95–8] as being about a 'society of blood', there is in the case of Bataille an obsession with and an emphasis on death, destruction, execution and torture, amounting at times to a Nietzschean celebration of the nihilistic/irrational. Interestingly, for Foucault [1975: 24–9] the eroticization of power/(death) embodied in the aethetics of Nazism leads almost to 'normalization' of fascism in the name of 'popular culture'. According to Bataille [1991: 367, 399–400, 457], who rather weakly disavows the existence of a link between fascism and Nietzsche, the latter recognized that the effect of an 'anything-goes' philosophy, or 'the sovereignty of a "free spirit"', would be moral relativism, or precisely the licence that postmodern theory extends to fascism (= 'horror'). The attempt to exculpate Nietzschean *volkische* beliefs is equally unconvincing: having proclaimed his own concept of 'sovereignty' innocent of a desire to recuperate an idealized agrarian past, Bataille somewhat arrogantly accuses Nietzsche of not being aware of the difference between a 'nostalgia for the feudal' (= traditional sovereignty) and Bataille's own sovereignty of the 'free spirit'. That the latter is in fact itself similarly structured by romantic/folkloric concepts of the 'primitive', however, is clear not only from his celebration of the elemental/(destructive) forces of Nature, his explanation of capitalism largely in terms of pre-capitalist socio-economic forms (the sacred, sacrifice-as-expenditure) but also from his wish 'to stimulate a rebirth of the kind of social values [he] espoused . . . the rebirth of myth and the touching off in society of an explosion of the primitive communal devices leading to sacrifice' [*Bataille*, 1985: xix–xx, 200–201; 1992]. The suspicion remains that the combination of destruction/sacrifice/Nature which so fascinates Bataille and structures his 'transgression'/(otherness) is in the end no different from the ideology/(worship-of-the-sacredness) of violence/blood/soil which characterizes fascism. (It is precisely this dimension, reactionary anti-capitalism, that Habermas [1987: 211ff.] overlooks in the course of identifying Bataille's heterology simply as a 'discourse-against'; at some point, therefore, the seeking out of 'otherness' merely in order to transgress cannot but posit the notion of 'fascinating fascism'.)

33. This complicity with fascism, in the name of 'popular culture' suggests the continued relevance of the observation [*Walicki*, 1969: 3] about Russian populism that

'. . . in the [eighteen] eighties and nineties, the view that the ideas of the intelligentsia should give way to the [unmediated] opinions of the people was upheld, and came close to reactionary obscurantism'.

34. It should be remembered that the defence of plantation slavery in the antebellum American South, initially by apologists such as Fitzhugh and subsequently by the Southern Agrarians (see Chapter 1) was based on a similar objection to modernity and capitalism. In the case of India, Gandhi objected to western capitalism for exactly the same reason: that the price of industrialization was the accompanying growth of an urban proletariat which was both politically disruptive and a bearer of 'alien' beliefs/values.

35. For the influence on McLuhan of agrarian populism, see Marchand [1989: 27], Miller [1971: 22ff.] and Kermode [1991: 82–92]. Of particular interest in this regard is the link between on the one hand a decentred postmodernism, where all views are deprivileged, and on the other the McLuhanite concept of the 'acoustic', together with its chain of signification. For McLuhan [*McLuhan and Fiore*, 1967: 111], therefore, not only is the more desirable 'acoustic' itself decentred ('the ear favors no particular "point of view"'), but discursively it is linked to other key concepts (acoustic = the South = 'the desirable' = tradition = rural = primitive = intuitive = 'the natural') in his framework (see Marchand [1989: 67, 95, 260]). By contrast, for McLuhan the visual is equated with the undesirable, which in turn is linked discursively with the North, the logical, industrialization, urbanization, and (unsurprisingly) technology. This framework gives rise to the following politico-ideological oppositions:

desirable	undesirable
acoustic	visual
intuition	logic
primitive	modern
South	North
rural	urban
tradition	industry
Nature	technology

36. The intellectually unfashionable status of McLuhan during the recent past can be gauged from a patronizing reference to him by Debray [1979: 139] as 'a curious gentleman'. Interestingly, in acknowledging the influence of Mumford and Giedion on the one hand, and on the other the New Criticism of the 1930s, McLuhan anticipates postmodernism by constructing a theory about the social based originally on ideas about architecture and literature. The latter's role in this genealogy is particularly significant, since both McLuhan and postmodernism have roots in the romantic nostalgia of the Southern Agrarians in the United States, who not only attempted to recuperate pre-industrial values, but also via the work of Robert Penn Warren, John Crowe Ransom and the *Kenyon Review* influenced the revival of an a-historical, desocialized, innate aestheticism associated with the New Criticism (for which see Eagleton [1983: 47–53]).

37. For McLuhan's views on these issues, see Marchand [1989: 144, 196, 222]. In addition to his nostalgic and idealized vision of a rural 'world-we-have-lost', the anti-modern/anti-Marxist views of McLuhan were also structured by his Roman Catholicism, his views about the sanctity of the family and the importance of individual liberty, a general admiration for the traditions of a Christian Europe – which

he counterposed to socialism, and the strong influence of G.K. Chesterton [*Marchand*, 1989: 23–4, 27]. In part, McLuhan's antagonism towards Marxism derived from what he regarded as its technological bias, and by implication its role in hastening the kind of future he was trying to avoid (see, for example, McLuhan [1951: 34]).

38. For a genuflection in the direction of McLuhan by the high priest of post-modernism, see Baudrillard [1981: 164ff; 1983: 35]. That the work of the latter is prefigured in that of the former is also recognized by Rose [1991: 25–8], who – unlike the position taken here – nevertheless links their views on the electronic media to the project of modernity rather than to post-modernism.

39. On these points, see McLuhan [1951], and also Marchand [1989: 107, 121, 144]. Like McLuhan, Bataille [1988, 1991] also based his theory of general economy on the primacy of consumption (expenditure of wealth) rather than production.

40. On these points, see Marchand [1989: 186, 207]. About politics, McLuhan is on record [*Marchand*, 1989: 186, 216] as observing not just that political parties were a thing of the past but also that: 'Instead of having a line or party to follow, the political candidate must become an image capable of including all the hopes and wishes of the electorate.' These utterances reveal a symptomatic political combi-nation of populism ('above-politics', or the absence of class) + new social move-ments theory ('no more parties', or non-political mobilization) + postmodernism ('politics-as-image').

41. For his critique of modernity/media/industrialization, see McLuhan [1951]. '[T]he process of renewal', observes McLuhan [1949: 15], 'can't come from above. It can only take the form of reawakened critical faculties. The untrancing of individuals by millions of individual acts of the will. Psychological decentralization. A merely provisional image of how it might (not how it should) occur could be formed by supposing every mechanical agency of communication in the world to be suspended for six months. No press. No radio. No movies. Just people finding out who lived near them. Forming small communities within big cities . . . If something like this doesn't happen it is quite plain what will happen . . . The machine is power. And practical politics mean quite simply that the machine must assume increasingly its most powerful form. The shape and rational form of man is now irrelevant.'

42. For McLuhan's endorsement/advocacy of the 'preliterate', see Marchand [1989: 131]. That for McLuhan the 'global village' was a return to the 'normality' of a *tribal* village, or the *ruralization* of decentralization, is clear from the visual material he presents in support of his argument [*McLuhan and Fiore, 1967: 66–7*]. '"Time" has ceased, "space" has vanished,' he observes [*McLuhan and Fiore, 1967: 83*], 'we now live in a *global* village . . . we are back in acoustic space. We have begun again to structure the primordial feeling, the tribal emotions from which a few centuries of literacy divorced us.' In this regard, McLuhan himself was influenced by the views of Mumford [1934], who, in order similarly to counter the expansion of large-scale factory production and its accompanying process of urbanization, advocated a decentralization to and restoration of rural, community-based artisan production ('small-is-beautiful').

43. See Heidegger [1969: 50]. For the connections between Heideggerian philosophy, German fascism and the theory of 'deep ecology', see among others Lukacs [1980: 489–522], Bramwell [1989], Taylor [1992] and Ferkiss [1993: 164–7].

44. The resurgence of the European political right extends from the Italian 'Alliance for Freedom' (composed of the Northern League of Umberto Bossi, Forza Italia of

Silvio Berlusconi, and the neo-fascist National Alliance or MSI of Gianfranco Fini), the Republicaner Party in Germany, the Freedom Party in Austria, the National Front of Le Pen in France, to attempts in Spain to rehabilitate Franco (Betz [1994], Cheles, Ferguson and Vaughan [1991], Ford [1992], Gunn [1989]). In North America, the resurgence of the political right has taken the form of populist politics advocated by Ross Perot in the USA and Preston Manning in Canada, and in Russia the populist politics of Yeltsin have created a space now occupied by the 'ultra-nationalist'/(fascist) Zhirinovsky. Texts about/by the 'new' right generally include Cohen *et al.* [1986], Phillips [1982: 46ff.], Levitas [1986b], Gottfried and Fleming [1988], Gamble [1988], Habermas [1989], Gunn [1989], Sunic [1990], Cheles *et al.* [1991], Hoeveler [1991], Ford [1992], Eatwell and O'Sullivan [1992], Basu *et al.* [1993], Gray [1993], Hayes [1994], Diggins [1994], Gingrich [1995], Sarkar and Butalia [1995], Mazumdar [1995] and Eatwell [1995].

45. For the theoretical importance and political influence of de Benoist, see Sheehan [1980; 1981], O'Sullivan [1992: 174ff.], Sunic [1990], and Taguieff [1994a]; for Tarchi, see Sacchi [1994]; for Freund, see Sunic [1990: 158] and Ulmen [1995]; for Miglio, see Campi [1994] and Gottfried [1994]; for Eichberg, see Bodemann [1986] and Biehl [1995]; for Hayek and Friedman, see Bosanquet [1986], Gamble [1988] and Shackleton and Locksley [1981: 53ff.,87ff.]; for Scruton and Gray, see Ryan [1986], Gamble [1988: 161–2], O'Sullivan [1992: 175ff.] and Hayes [1994]. In terms of the practice linked to this theory, the North American right has exercised influence not only through periodicals such as *The Public Interest, Commentary,* and *The New Criterion,* but also via foundations/institutes (Heritage Foundation, American Enterprise Institute); de Benoist was instrumental in the foundation of the umbrella group for the European political right, GRECE (*Groupement de Recherche et d'Études pour la Civilisation Européenne*), while Scruton (and others) exercised agenda-setting influence on Thatcherite discourse in Britain via rightwing 'think-tanks' (on which see Cockett [1995]).

46. For the influence on the 'new' right of Evola and Schmitt, together with their general theoretical/political importance, see Sheehan [1981], Sunic [1990: 43ff.], Bendersky [1983], Gress [1986], Gottfried [1990b], Ward [1992: Ch. 8], Sacchi [1994: 72ff.], Eatwell [1995: 202ff.], and Neocleous [1996]. According to Schmitt, the impossibility of liberal (and other/all forms of) democracy stems from the fact that it requires a correspondingly unrealizeable social homogeneity, the absence of which in effect precludes its existence. Like de Benoist and others on the 'new' right, Schmitt denies the presence of humanistic universals, the formulation of which he blames on a spurious rationalism which in turn gave rise not just to an alien politics (liberalism = socialism = communism) but also and thereby to equally artificial forms of calculation (science/technology/economics).

47. For an examples of this kind of argument, see among many others Phillips [1982], Gottfried and Fleming [1988: vii–viii], Sunic [1990: 6–7], Piccone [1994: 7, 9–10, 11–12, 20], Sacchi [1994: 71], Latouche [*Sacchi,* 1994: 76; *de Benoist,* 1995: 79], Benvenuto [1994], de Benoist [1995: 73ff.], and Tarchi [1995: 181ff.]. Significantly, the claim that the left/right divide no longer informs political theory/ practice emanates invariably from texts which subscribe to a 'new'-populist/ 'new'-right position. Equally unsurprising is the fact that in place of the left/right opposition such texts offer the 'a-political'/'above-politics'/('common-sense') interpretation based on (in economic terms a tension-free) 'community' where 'otherness' takes the form of cultural 'difference'.

48. The most sustained claim for the existence of a political/epistemological break between 'new' and 'old' right discourse relates to the question of gender/sexual identity, issues over which the traditional right has exercised an authoritarian hold. Although adhering to what is ostensibly an enlightened view on issues of gender and sexual identity, the the European 'new' right nevertheless incorporates this within the framework of the historical right. Accordingly, the European 'new' right attributes female oppression and homophobia specifically to Christianity, and claims that paganism would result in a 'natural' process of gender/sexual empowerment [*Wegierski*, 1994: 59–60].

49. Accepting the presence of continuities in the discourse of the 'old' and 'new' right, apologists for the latter hasten to utter strident disclaimers which nevertheless fail to persuade. Hence the assertion by Piccone [1994: 22] that: '[F]ar from constituting any kind of public danger . . . the French New Right, notwithstanding its obsessive opposition to any kind of administratively imposed equality (which may be its only remaining link with the Old Right) has made a significant contribution [to current political debate] at a time when original ideas are hard to come by. As such, it deserves to be taken seriously . . .'. Adler [1994: 26] similarly maintains that the 'new' right 'has nothing whatsoever to do with "fascism" as such', as do Wegierski [1994: 69] and Gottfried [1990a: x], while Taguieff [1994a: 34–5, 39] insists on the presence of a divergence between the early/fascism and late/'antifascism' of de Benoist, claiming that the current emphasis of the latter on 'otherness'-as-culture represents not just an epistemological but also a political break with his previous view of 'otherness'-as-biology. The views of de Benoist have received endorsement not only from Jean-Marie Le Pen, leader of the French National Front, but also from Raymond Aron, the cold warrior of old, who has defended the right of de Benoist 'to be heard' [*Taguieff*, 1994a: 49–50; *Marcus*, 1995: 22–4]. Unsurprisingly, Gianfranco Fini, leader of the far-right MSI/AN (*Movimento Sociale Italiano/Alleanza Nazionale*), has proclaimed himself a 'postfascist', and Marco Tarchi, another Italian 'new' right leader, has argued that it is necessary to stress the term 'new' and not the term 'right' [*Wegierski*, 1994: 55].

50. Somewhat ingenuously, Wegierski [1994: 65] protests that the European 'new' right 'cannot be held responsible for the adoption of some of its ideas by groups such as Le Pen's National Front, or the Anglo-American or German far right'. Just why traditionally right-wing political parties would incorporate the 'fresh' ideas of 'new' right intellectuals if these were in any way fundamentally opposed to or incompatible with the *project* of the historical (= 'old') right is a question that is rarely asked. Since the combined discourse-for/discourse-against of the right is above all a *mobilizing* ideology (see Chapter 1), what seems to have actually occurred is that the politically-unacceptable views of the 'old' right have been not so much discarded as hidden. This is borne out by a number of sources, not least the observation that during the mid-1970s the Italian 'new' right continued to endorse 'an organicist concept of the world founded on a rank order among identities that differ because of their origins, development and functions' [*Sacchi*, 1994: 74].

51. Because the discourse of the 'new' populism is cloaked in the ideology of 'commonsense' (= a 'naturalness' that denies the efficacy/existence of political alternatives), the occurrence and extent of its rightwards shift frequently goes unrecognized by many 'new' populists themselves. The response of the latter to anyone who points out the affinity between the 'new' populism and the 'new' right is thus one of incredulity, or worse. Shortly after my review [*Brass*, 1995a] of the

'impasse' appeared, I was left in no doubt as to what 'worse' might entail. In an academic equivalent of road rage, one of the exponents of the 'impasse' criticized on precisely these grounds personally confronted me in my faculty room in Cambridge and, having burst unannounced/uninvited through my door uttering abuse and threats (his aggressive body language suggesting that physical assault was imminent), proceeded to expostulate at length about the review. Although he claimed that it had gone beyond the accepted boundaries, when asked what these were, who defines them and how, he was unable to provide any answers. Agreeing that, as had been pointed out in the review, he had failed to mention the importance for political change of property relations, and that he should have in fact done so, he finally departed in a rather more subdued manner.

52. For the equation by those on the 'new' right of their own views with populism, see for example, Gottfried and Fleming [1988; 21–2, 77ff., 92ff], Glendening [1994], Taguieff [1995], and Dolbeare and Hubbell [1996: 19, 43]. This self-identification is also true of some postmodern texts, where a 'new' populist influence is tacitly acknowledged. For example, Isaacman [1993: 264], who edits and contributes an essay on rural social protest in Africa to a collection [*Cooper, Mallon, Stern, Isaacman, Roseberry*, 1993] advocating the replacement of Marxist theory about development by postmodernism, acknowledges the influence of Boyte [*Boyte, Booth and Max*, 1986], a prominent commentator on and exponent of the 'new' populism (for details of which see Reed [1992: 167–8, 197–8]). This is recipro- cated by Boyte himself [*Boyte, Booth and Max*, 1986: ix], in an acknowledgement of Isaacman's influence on his own views.

53. The link between the events of 1968, which signalled the global emergence of new social movements, and the 'new' populism is a matter of record (see, for example, Kazin [1995: Ch. 8] and Latouche [1996: viii–ix]). On the importance of 1968 for Foucault, and of Foucault for 1968, see among others Rabinow [1984: 58], Foucault [1991: 135–6], and Eribon [1992: 122, 124, 135–6]; for the 1968/Fanon connection, see Katsiaficas [1987: 74] and Fraser [1988: 70]; on the 1968/Marcuse connection, see Marcuse [1969: ix,22], Katsiaficas [1987: 22, 126, 223, 229–30], and Fraser [1988: 49, 106–7, 124–5, 141, 143, 144]. It must be emphasized that, unlike criticism of the political legacy of the events of 1968 which identifies it as too leftwing, the position taken here is that by contrast it was not leftwing enough. For the emergence of the 'new' right during the 1960s and early 1970s, see Phillips [1982: 46], Gottfried and Fleming [1988; 37ff., 59ff., 77ff.], Wegierski [1994: 56], and Kazin [1995: 222ff.]. The conjuncturally-specific origin of this 'new' right/'new' populist convergence is also noted by Sacchi [1994: 72–3], who observes that: 'Evola's philosophy became an important point of reference . . . for a younger generation of political activists who grew up in the middle of the economic boom of the late 1950s and 1960s. For these people (including most of the future leaders of the Italian New Right) who chose the wrong side, Evola pro- vided an organic and and coherent *weltanschauung* to oppose their peers in the mainstream culture in the 1960s. Of course, the fascination with Evola's work in esoteric Eastern cultures also had to do with the spirit of the times – a period when there was a quest among the young for alternatives to Western materialism and bourgeois lifestyles.' Although the received wisdom is that the 'new' right in North America emerged as a reaction against the events of 1968, such a view over- looks the extent to which the former was able to incorporate the latter. In so far as it entailed opposition to the expansion of large-scale factory production and its

accompanying process of urbanization on the one hand, and on the other advocated a decentralization to and restoration of rural, community-based artisan production ('small-is-beautiful'), therefore, right-wing libertarians (for example, Rothbard [1970: 291]) had no difficulty in identifying with much of the ideology which characterized the events of 1968. What is frequently overlooked is that anarchist views about the desirability of political decentralization and individual freedom/ self-empowerment coincide with the view of the libertarian right concerning the importance of the competitive 'choice-making' individual in the context of the 'minimal' state. For the extent of 'anarcho-capitalist' beliefs among those on the political right, see Evans [1996].

54. On the primacy of cultural struggle generally and the 'Gramsciism of the Right' in particular, see Levitas [1986a], Sunic [1990: 29ff.], Wegierski [1994: 63], Sacchi [1994: 71] and Kazin [1995: 246,248]. Wegierski makes it clear that it is not the Marxist but the populist content of Gramscian theory which has been appropriated, while Sunic [1990: 4, 35ff.] displays evident confusion about this process by implying that such an appropriation constitutes evidence of the extent to which the 'new' right is politically progressive in outlook (= 'European Leftist Conservatives'). For a not dissimilar view, see Gress [1986].

55. The potentially reactionary political implications of this 'new' populist approach are nowhere better illustrated than in the admission by Piccone [1994: 20–22 note 19] that the unproblematic endorsement of any/every 'from-below' discourse may indeed involve the acceptance/advocacy of slavery and/or racism. In a similar vein, Latouche [1996: 123–4] implies that practices such as infibulation, the stoning of adulterers and cutting the hands off thieves are all unchallengeable – not to say acceptable – forms of cultural 'otherness'.

56. See, for example, Marcuse [1969: vii]. The opposition by many postmodern 'new' populists to the current spread into the so-called Third World of North American or Eurocentric *cultural* universals overlooks the fact that the latter are themselves the product of a universal *economic* process, capitalism.

57. For the anti-Americanism of de Benoist and the European 'new' right, see Taguieff [1994a: 48] and Wegierski [1994: 68]. Significantly, an analogous form of anti-Americanism is to be found historically within the United States itself, propounded during the 1930s by Southern Conservatism. Because they identified themselves as part of a cultural tradition linked to a feudal European past, therefore, the Southern Agrarians objected to what they too categorized as a culturally-eroding process of 'Americanization' associated with the expansion of industrial capitalism in the North [*Karanikas*, 1966: 29–30].

58. For example, during the 1930s Oswald Mosley [1932: 62–6], leader of the British Union of Fascists (BUF), not only espoused anti-Americanism but did so for precisely the same reasons as the European 'new' right does now. Just as the anti-Americanism of the BUF was linked to increased competition from US capital in markets traditionally dominated by Britain, therefore, that of the European 'new' right is similarly linked to current inter-capitalist rivalry in international markets.

59. On these points, see Fanon [1963: 75ff.; 1967: 125]. Much the same kind of argument structures the 'new' populism of Latouche, for whom the current de-culturation/(de-naturing) of the indigenous Third World 'other' is a result of mimetic industrialization (= 'Westernization'). At the centre of this discourse, however, lies a theoretically untenable contrast: between on the one hand the economic rationality/calculation of modernity, in which culture-as-distinction

characterizes the passive consumption of 'alien' cultural forms/practices, and on the other the more positive/desirable situation of culture-as-meaning that operates in pre-modern societies, where an active (= 'natural') process of cultural formation is not only all-pervasive but also based on the indissoluble proximity of production and consumption [*Latouche*, 1996: 39–41]. 'By alienating Third-World peoples from their own culture,' he asserts [*Latouche*, 1996: 41], 'Westernization makes them . . . uncultured, turning them into passive consumers'. Significantly, perhaps, the ideas of Latouche regarding the desirability of terminating the economic development of the so-called Third World, and its replacement with an indigenous 'cultural empowerment', have attracted 'considerable attention' among and the interest of the 'new' right in France and Italy (on which see Sacchi [1994: 77, note 4] and Taguieff [1994b: 164]).

60. See the previous chapter for texts by 'new' populists which for these reasons either explicitly or implicitly question/dismiss the possibility/desirability of progress. Unsurprisingly, a recent text by Scott [1995] exhibits a symptomatic 'new' populist binary opposition between a discourse-for at the centre of which is a positive invocation of Nature, and a discourse-against aimed at all those elements associated conceptually with the notion of progress (science, technology, the state, the large-scale, and modernity itself). For the technophobia and antagonism towards progress on the part of the 'new' right, see Wegierski [1994: 56].

61. See Bailey [1958] for the significance of the rejection by Nietzsche, Spengler, Pareto, Ortega y Gasset and Le Bon of a linear conception of history and their views regarding the non-achievability of progress as characterized by the rise of 'mass society' and a civilization in decline.

62. Unlike the political left, both the 'new' populism and the 'new' right maintain that since the grassroots are 'naturally' conservative, there is consequently little point in attempting to radically change the existing structure. The very possibility of 'progress' is thereby deemed not merely undesirable but unrealizable. While the political left also accepts that the grassroots may currently be conservative, it parts company with both the 'new' populism and the 'new' right in that it contextualizes/historicizes this situation, with a view to changing it. In short, unlike either the 'new' populism or the 'new' right, Marxists see nothing 'natural' or enduring about this grassroots conservatism.

63. For the rejection of historical linearity by Evola and de Benoist, see Sacchi [1994: 72], Wegierski [1994: 59] and Eatwell [1995: 202]. This concept of an unchanging/unchangeable 'eternal present' structures the view of an innate 'peasant-ness' that is at the centre of the non-capitalist/non-socialist "Third Way" propounded by Wilhelm Röpke (1899–1966), a contemporary of Evola and like him a member of the political right, whose ideas influenced European and American conservatism (on which see Lora [1971: 197], O'Sullivan [1976: 139, 144, 147], Nash [1976: 27, 33, 34, 142, 148, 175, 179–82, 357, 392], Kirk [1978: 408], and Berger [1987: 226]). The significance of Röpke is that his views constitute an epistemological fusion of the agrarian myth, populism, neo-liberal economics and the 'traditional' conservatism of the political right. Hence the centrality to his argument of an economically viable smallholding agriculture premissed on the recuperation of an idealized peasant proprietorship [Röpke, 1950: 201ff.; see also Röpke 1948: Ch. IX, 'The Peasant Core of Society – Danger of Agrarian Collectivism'] is itself linked to the wider political project of the right, incorporating ideological support for small-scale rural production/exchange (artisan, petty trading) and opposition to

the large-scale (the state, monopolies). For Röpke, therefore, the importance of peasant family farming is that, since it is immutable and basically individualistic/ conservative, it operates as an ever-present economic/political/cultural bulwark against the political dangers represented by economic progress, urbanization, mechanization, class struggle, proletarianization, socialist planning and collectivization. In support of his argument for the conservation of the peasant family farm, Röpke invokes not just the same texts as Chayanov (e.g., by Ernst Lauer, the Secretary of the Union of Swiss Peasants [cf. *Röpke, 1950*: 207; *Chayanov, 1966*: xxxi–xxxii, 89]) but also the same kinds of economic argument (for example, '. . . the peasant freeholder tends to stick to his holding and his calling in spite of the most adverse conditions and if necessary accepts the hardest possible working conditions which, materially speaking, push him far below the existence level of an industrial laborer . . .' [*Röpke, 1950*: 203]). Claiming that smallholding agriculture based on private property 'brings men and nature together' in a way that 'counterbalances the industrial and urban aspects of our civilization with tradition and conservatism, economic independence and self-sufficiency [that derive in turn from a] proximity to nature, . . . a natural and full existence near the sources of life . . .', Röpke [1950: 202–3] warns that 'the peasant world together with other small sectors of society, represents today [the early 1940s] a last great island that has not yet been reached by the flood of collectivization, the last great sphere of human life and work which possesses inner stability and value in a vital sense. It is a priceless blessing wherever this reserve still exists . . .'. Where such a discourse about an a-temporal/a-historical peasantry leads when applied to the Third World 'other' is not difficult to discern. In the case of South Africa, therefore, apartheid entails separate development which, according to Röpke [1964: 10], also involves 'appropriate development' for those segregated along ethnic lines. In other words, 'appropriate development' for whites is deemed inappropriate for blacks, and *vice-versa*. Precisely what Röpke envisages as 'appropriate development' for those categorized as 'different' in this way emerges subsequently: in his opinion, therefore, the black population of South Africa is – and will remain – a 'natural'/ a-temporal peasantry ('One of the major aims of this policy [of establishing Bantustans] is . . . to teach them modern agricultural methods'). Consequently, within this discourse not only do South African blacks experience an innate 'peasant-ness' as a specifically cultural form of empowerment (= 'appropriate development' for the tribal/ethnic/peasant 'other'), but they are also ideologically forbidden the 'un-natural' transformation of becoming a potentially threatening and thus politically dangerous proletariat in the towns (= 'the-mob-in-the-streets').

64. That an apparently progressive endorsement of diversity/difference is not merely compatible with but actually supportive of the political right is evident from the following observation [*Epstein, 1970*: 115]: 'Conservatives not only emphasize variety, they also love it. The spontaneous development of human society has led to a colorful richness which conservatives find emotionally and aesthetically satisfying. They do not bother to rationalize this preference in terms of any metaphysical system, for they consider it to be simply "natural", that is in accordance with the "real" needs of "uncorrupted" human nature. Conservatives usually accuse radicals of wishing to destroy existing variety – expressing what is old and familiar – by implementing the precepts of an abstract and uniform rationalism . . . The conservative view of the world affirms in theory (not always in practice) the existence of a plurality of competing values.' (That diversity/difference has an

important place in the conservative canon is also confirmed in the influential text by Kirk [1978].) The reactionary programmatic application of diversity/difference is evident not just from the obvious example of 'separate development' which structured the Apartheid system in South Africa (see previous note), but also from the pronouncements of Gianfranco Miglio, an organic intellectual of the Northern League in Italy, whose secessionist proposal to re-establish 'Etruria' is based on claims of ethnic difference/diversity between the productive inhabitants of the Northern region and the unproductive/parasitical Mediterranean 'mentality' of southern Italy ('Prophet of Italy's Loss', *The Guardian*, London, 1 Dec. 1993). Like the de-internationalized/anti-universalist ultra-nationalism/(fascism) of Zhirinovsky in Russia, it is only by a process of 'ethnic cleansing' that the nationalism of the Northern League can be recuperated and restored to a pristine authenticity within Italy as a whole, so as to be able then to co-exist and/or compete with other such (internally 'cleansed' but externally 'polluting') nationalisms

65. On this point, compare Fanon [1963: 33] and Bhabha [1987]. The irreducibility of cultural 'otherness'/'difference' was of course a principle which those on the 'old' right extended to colonial subjects. Asked whether he would impose a culturally 'other' education on colonized India, for example, Mosley [1936: 86] replied: 'We [the BUF] will certainly attempt the education of the Indian masses, *but not on Western lines*. The mistake has been the imposition of western culture on oriental life . . . Under Fascism, Indian leaders will arise to carry forward their own traditions and cultures within the framework of Empire . . .' (emphasis added). The same principle informed the policy of 'separate development' that structured the apartheid system in white South Africa.

66. See Chapter 4 for 'new' populist texts which attribute underdevelopment in the so-called Third World to a non-transcendental 'difference' which is then equated with cultural empowerment. The intellectual history of the 'new' populism is already being rewritten, and a number of surprising candidates are being allocated (or are allocating themselves) a starring role in its political unmasking. Among the more bizarre claims advanced in this connection is the one made by Vanaik and also by Sarkar [1997: 82ff.], a one-time contributor to the 'new' populist Subaltern Studies, that the initial and most powerful critique of the Subaltern Studies project was the internal one mounted by Sarkar himself. Vanaik [1997: 224, note 106; 1998] has adopted the role of cheerleader in making unsustainable claims on Sarkar's behalf: namely, that it was the latter who first identified the complicity between on the one hand anti-Enlightenment epistemology, the postmodern discourse of the Subaltern Studies, and an emphasis on cultural 'difference', and on the other the rightwing/conservative Third World nationalism of the BJP/VHP/RSS. Not only did non-dissenting contributions by Sarkar continue to appear in Subaltern Studies III and VI [*Guha* 1984, 1989], when the political trends to which he now objects were already well-established (why no opposition at that point?), but his critique emerged for the first time only in 1994, some while after the same objections had already been raised by a number of scholars outside the Subaltern Studies project. Of the many ironies structuring this claim, two are worth mentioning. First, the kind of Marxism Sarkar now defends, the 'from-below' historiography of E. P. Thompson, is in many important respects no different from the postmodern 'new' populism informing the Subaltern Studies project. And second, Vanaik [1994] himself has earlier decried a connection between European fascism and the Indian political right (BJP ≠ fascist), when some of those external critiques

of the Subaltern Studies project were making precisely this point (BJP = fascist).

67. For the views of de Benoist and the French National Front concerning 'difference', see Piccone [1994: 10] and Adler [1994: 26ff.]; for the centrality to contemporary conservatism of 'difference', see Gottfried and Fleming [1988: ix–x]. In fact, it is difficult to think of a right-wing discourse – either 'old' or 'new' – which does not imply the existence of 'difference'; it is clear, for example, that the 'perspectivism' (= 'point of view' = plurality of perception) of Ortega y Gasset [1961: 86ff.] is an earlier invocation of 'difference'. That the seemingly neutral concept of 'citizenship' which is ideologically central to the new social movements framework is similarly compatible with appeals to 'difference' in the mobilizing discourse of the 'new' right is clear from Kazin [1995: 227, 246], who shows how the populism of the American 'new' right has been informed (among other things) by a notion of *white* citizenship.

68. According to Wegierski [1994: 61], therefore, 'The ultimate goal [of the "new" right] is *the Europe of a Hundred Flags* – a patchwork quilt of colourful, traditional principalities' (original emphasis). His claim that such emphasis on small-scale as distinct from large 'homogenizing' territorial units constitutes a departure from the ideology of the 'old' right is wrong, since what is central to the discourse-for of the political right is that any organizational unit – whether large or small – is based on a 'natural' kinship/ethnic/national identity. In the end a small-scale regionalism/localism is no different from a large-scale nationalism: not only is the claim of each to existence/legitimacy founded on the same kinds of identity (culture, ethnicity), therefore, but the object of regional/local autonomy is invariably the political creation of yet another national unit, in the process realizing what its advocates claim is an underlying and thus more 'authentic' identity.

69. 'Thus', Adler [1994: 26] notes, 'the "native French had a right to preserve the integrity of their culture against the "invasion" of Third World immigrants, the primary source of all France's ills. This was a new and highly effective way of rendering racism (illegitimate in its biological-hierarchical form) acceptable; it became the basis of the [French] National Front's program.' In part, the sub-text to this emphasis on cultural specificity is a fear of becoming like the Third World 'other' in economic terms, an anxiety which structures the discourse of both the political right and contemporary populism in North America, the latter sharing with the former the view that immigration should be limited [*Dolbeare and Hubbell*, 1996: 59ff., 98]. In other words, the Third World 'other' is acceptable only in so far as it continues to occupy its own 'natural' place/space. For the claim that, with the exception of 'extreme fringe elements', American conservatism is no longer racist, see Gottfried and Fleming [1988: xii].

70. On this point one commentator [*Soucy, 1995: 152*] observes: '[I]t would be unhistorical to make racism a litmus test for all fascism . . . The major bonds between German, Italian and French fascism before 1940 were anti-Marxism and anti-liberalism, not racism and anti-semitism'. It is anyway necessary to note that 'scientific' racism associated with the 'old' right has not only not disappeared but is now in the process of making a comeback (on which see Kohn [1995]).

71. In two important texts about the epistemology of what he termed the new racism, Barker [1979, 1981] attributes its (re-) formulation in British politics to the last of three speeches made by Enoch Powell in 1968, in which the latter stated that 'difference' was 'a matter of culture and assimilation, not race' [1981: 39–40]. Interviewed on British television in 1969, Powell denied that he was in fact a

racist, since: '[I]f by racist you mean a man who despises a human being because he belongs to another race, or a man who believes that one race is inherently superior to another in civilization, then the answer is emphatically no'. In the United States during the mid-1970s, the ideology of the Ku Klux Klan was undergoing a similar kind of metamorphosis: 'The Klan believes in England for Englishman, France for Frenchmen, Italy for Italians, and America for Americans: Is there anything objectionable about this? The Klan is not anti-Catholic, anti-Jew, anti-Negro, anti-foreign, the Klan is pro-Protestant, and pro-American' (cited in Sargent [1995: 142]).

72. Writing in the 1930s, Ortega y Gasset [1950: 12–13] gives classic expression to this fear of 'mass man' and the loss of cultural 'difference'/'otherness'. *The characteristic of the hour'*, he observes [1950: 12–13], *'is that the commonplace mind, knowing itself to be commonplace, has the assurance to proclaim the rights of the commonplace and to impose them wherever it will . . .* The mass crushes beneath it everything that is different, everything that is excellent, individual, qualified and select. Anybody who is not like everybody, who does not think like everybody, runs the risk of being eliminated. And it is clear, of course, that this "everybody" is not "everybody". "Everybody" was normally the complex unity of the mass and the divergent, specialized minorities. Nowadays, "everybody" is the mass alone. Here we have the formidable fact of out times, described without any concealment of the brutality of its features' (original emphasis).

73. Both the ease and the significance of extending the principle of 'difference' from the domain of 'the cultural' to that of 'the economic' should not be underestimated. Just as the relativism of 'popular culture' in the realm of ideology licenses postmodern aporia, so relativism in the realm of economics confers acceptability on and thus licenses the *laissez-faire* doctrine of neo-classical economic theory (i.e. unto each his/her own – or no 'meddling' by the state).

74. This view is implicit in much conservative writing. In the case of Ortega y Gasset [1950: 13–14], for example, the perception of a threat posed by (and hence opposition to) the emergence of 'mass man' is clearly linked to (and indeed, a reaction by) his own 'radically aristocratic interpretation of history'. As long as it remains within the domain of culture, however, such 'from above' aristocratism is not incompatible with 'from below' agency. That the political right is not just comfortable with but actually approves of those specifically cultural forms of grassroots agency identified by 'new' populists as empowering displays of 'resistance' is evident from the second of the two epigraphic quotes by Röpke at the head of this chapter.

75. It comes as no surprise that 'new' populist arguments about cultural 'otherness' are now being deployed by those on the political right to defend the employment of unfree labour in the so-called Third World (on which see Brass [1999]).

76. On these points, see Fanon [1963: 73, 88–9, 109]. 'The traditional chiefs are ignored', he complains [1963: 91], 'the old men, surrounded by respect in all traditional societies and usually invested with unquestionable moral authority, are publicly held up to ridicule'.

77. Marcuse [1970: 75].

78. On this point, see Foucault [1971; 1978].

79. Miller [1993: 324]. Symptomatically, in expressing support for mass mobilization against the Shah in Iran during 1978, Foucault endorsed the subsequent exercise of theocratic rule as a form of 'political spirituality' [*Miller*, 1993: 306ff.]. What was

important for Foucault, therefore, was the fact that Iranians were attempting 'to change not only the form of government but the shape of their everyday lives, casting off "the weight of the order of the entire world". Inspired by a "religion of combat and sacrifice", they had forged an authentically "collective will" . . .' [*Miller*, 1993: 309]. Not only did this constitute an idealist as distinct from a materialist interpretation of the Iranian revolution, but what Foucault appears to have found most desirable in this 'resistance' was precisely its most reactionary element (= death/sacrifice/religion/mysticism). In so far as it involves for Foucault the rejection by those 'from below' of modernity in the name of a pre-modern ideology, this suggests that – like Rousseau – Foucault subscribes to a notion of a pre-capitalist 'general will' that was both good and rooted in an instinctive/ elemental force of Nature.

80. For more details on these points, see the previous chapter. For a similar advocacy of family farming by American 'new' populists, and its importance to support they receive from an agrarian petty bourgeoisie (smallholders, small businesses), see Boyte, Booth and Max [1986: 132ff.] and Reissman [1986: 62]. The American far right also mobilized in support of small farmers resisting dispossession/repossession during the farm crisis of the 1980s. Not only was the latter attributed to a global conspiracy between the US State and international (= 'Jewish') bankers, but vigilante groups such as the Posse Comitatus received considerable support from small farmers in rural areas where the agrarian economy was in depression [*Ridgeway*, 1990: 24, 27, 50, 100, 109ff., 113, 132].

81. For a similarly orientalist invocation of the 'Asiatic soul' as instinctively 'different', the tradition-embedded 'other' of rationalism, see Ortega y Gasset [1961: 49, 64–5, 68, 74, 79]. 'This romanticized past is important,' observes Wegierski [1994: 58], 'because many of the [European 'new' right] referents, such as paganism, naturalism, particularism, a sort of feminism, and ecology, are predicated on it'. That the origins of much contemporary academic conservative Thirdworldism are still to be found in the agrarian myth is clear from many sources, not least those written by conservatives themselves. A prominent exponent of conservative Thirdworldist views [*Berger*, 1979: 168–9] observes: 'One funny thing that happened to me in the Third World was that I developed a strong sympathy with tribalism . . . I gained an enormous respect for the positive values of such intact premodern communities as still exist in the Third World – communities of kinship, tribe, locality, and region – and the frequently moving efforts to preserve these communities under the violent pressure of modernization.'

82. For the elements composing the discourse about a pre-capitalist 'golden age', see Chapter 1. For an admission that his own vision of an 'International New Order' is essentially the recuperation of a medieval 'golden age', see Röpke [1950: 236, 238–9]. Just as the 'golden age' of Rousseau posits a vanished-to-be-recovered form of primitive goodness, when humanity was closer to Nature (and thus more 'natural'), so 'new' populist ecofeminists [*Shiva*, 1988; 1991a; 1991b, *Spretnak*, 1986; 1990] identify this same lost state with a pre-existing 'natural' form of female empowerment in the context of traditional communities. Accordingly, ecofeminism equates masculinity with patriarchy, and both with a secular/profane dominance over – and hence a denial of – a religious/sacred Nature/(nature) that is female. Whereas males are destructive, and their power takes a negative form (conflict, economic growth, industrialization, mechanization, science), that of females by contrast takes the positive form of conservation: the latter is therefore

associated by 'new' populist ecofeminism with peasant/tribal subsistence, ecological balance, social harmony and cyclical regeneration.

83. On the link between the anti-Americanism and pro-Thirdworldism of the European
'new' right, see Taguieff [1994a], Wegierski [1994: 63–4], and Sacchi [1994: 72].
It should be noted that the American 'new' right also espouses what it regards as
pro-Thirdworldist views [Gottfried and Fleming, 1988: 68]. That pastoral
visions/versions of the 'rural' continue to be important in the discourse of those on
the English 'new' right is clear from many sources. For example, it emerged in a
television programme ('Think of England: A Green and Pleasant Land', BBC2, 22
Oct. 1991) in which Roger Scruton presented an exegesis of stability/continuity
as embodied in the innateness of the English countryside (the persistence of
seigneurial attitudes, the importance for humans and animals of breeding, since
this is the way in which 'natural' hierarchy – royalty, aristocracy, prize livestock –
is reproduced). The same kinds of argument also inform a recent collection about
the urban/rural divide in the UK [Barnett and Scruton, 1998]. Symptomatically,
the perpetuation of the agrarian myth in many parts of rural England is currently
undertaken not by local agricultural workers but rather by members of the bourgeoisie; the latter, having acquired land in rural areas for residential purposes
(= 'gentrification'), then oppose economic development in such contexts on the
grounds that it destroys the aesthetic (and thus the financial) value of their
property.

84. On this point, see Wegierski [1994: 57–8] and Taguieff [1994a: 48]. Not only does
Lyotard equate postmodernism with paganism but he also appears to identify the
latter as the basis for an instinctual/innate form of political/ethical/aesthetic judgement [Lyotard and Thébaud, 1985: 15–16]. It is clear that some elements on the
'old' right (for example, Mosley [1936: 10]) also espoused a form of polytheism. It
is not without significance that polytheism is also compatible with an existentialist
concept of 'choice' that is not dissimilar to the self-empowering choice-making
subject at the centre of neo-classical economic theory.

85. For the pro-ecological/environmental-preservationist views of individuals/institu-
tions on the European 'new' right – such as Evola, de Benoist, GRECE, and
Henning Eichberg – see Bodemann [1986], Taguieff [1994a: 35 note 7] and
Wegierski [1994: 56, 62–3]. In keeping with the 'common-sense'/'above-politics'
approach of the 'new' populism, the editor of The Ecologist defended his decision
to address the annual meeting of GRECE in November 1994 in terms of the
a-political nature of environmental issues (cf. 'Leading Ecologist to Address Far
Right', and 'Ecologists and Their Right to be Independent', The Guardian, 25
Nov. and 5 Dec. 1994). It cannot be accidental, moreover, that the rightward
political trajectory of the prominent new social movements theorist Rudolph
Bahro, a process culminating in his espousal of Fascism (on which see Biehl
[1995: 48–58]), was accompanied by an endorsement of ecological and spiritual
beliefs at the centre of which were essentialist concepts of Nature and 'natural'
ethnic/national identity.

86. The 'new nationalists' of the 'new' right, such as Eichberg, oppose 'state centralist
industrial [= socialist] societies [since] highly technological industrial systems
colonize the peoples in the world [and] deprive them of their national and cultural
identity' (cited in Bodemann [1986: 151]).

87. Linked to this is the fact that, since ecological theory/practice in its current form is
largely incompatible with development, it posits 'natural' limits to economic

growth and therby hands the control of resources to specific ethnic/cultural groups, also deemed 'natural'. For an earlier version in the discourse of the political right of the argument that, as the peasant family farm is a 'natural' form of agriculture, it is therefore appropriate for the Third World (underdevelopment = 'natural'), and also the equation of environmental conservation with the recuperation of peasant economy, see Röpke [1950: 244, 246 note 4].

88. A typical comment reported in the press was by a Conservative councillor, who said '[t]he countryside is under attack. The town is out to get us and a way of life is being threatened . . .' ('Flames of Rural Anger Stoked', *The Guardian*, London, 27 Feb. 1998).

89. That the claim about 'classlessness' was bogus is evident from the fact that the Duke of Roxburghe admitted to a reporter that the rally was 'a good way of linking social classes' ('Faithful Gather in Countryside Blood Feud', *The Guardian*, London, 11 July 1997). The same contradiction is unintentionally revealed in the following comment from the right-wing press: 'Clubland had done a roaring breakfast trade and there were few rooms to be had in St James's but, overall, there was a deliberately classless atmosphere. The last thing the organizers wanted was a parade of toffs' ('The Country Comes to the Town', *The Daily Telegraph*, London, 11 July 1997). Not only was Prince Charles subsequently revealed as being one of a number of wealthy and aristocratic 'anonymous backers', therefore, but a list of the latter indicates that 'far from being a broad-based rural protest group, the Alliance is actually the creature of prominent Tory landowners and the British aristocracy' ('Charles's Dangerous Alliance', *The Observer*, 26 Sept. 1999). It was equally clear, moreover, that some of the rural workers and tenants who participated did not do so voluntarily. Hence rural estates instructed employees to attend in terms that conveyed undisguised menace (for example, '[the owners of the estate] have indicated that they would wish all members of staff to attend . . . together with their wives/husbands and families,' indicated one estate manager, concluding ominously, '[p]lease let my secretary know if you are unable to attend, together with the reasons'), the most vulnerable to this kind of threat being those agricultural workers who were in tied houses or dependent on a local source of rural employment ('Yeomen Get Marching Orders', *The Guardian*, London, 21 Feb. 1998).

90. Hence the view expressed by one participant that: 'The British countryside is a wild, cruel place, of checks and balances. We change its structure at our peril' ('Faithful Gather in Countryside Blood Feud', *The Guardian*, London, 11 July 1997).

91. Hence the claim made by Tony Blair in *Country Life* that 'I wouldn't live in a big city if I could help it. I would live in the country. I was brought up there, really' ('Blair Woos Country Folk', *The Guardian*, London, 25 Feb. 1998). For the climb down on a statutory right-to-roam, see 'Blair Puts Brake on Legal Right to Ramble', *The Guardian*, London, 26 Feb. 1998.

92. According to the British National Party and the National Front, those who attended the countryside rally were 'under attack by an urban majority ignorant of rural values, traditions and beliefs . . . [t]here are a lot of people in England who are angry about these continual assaults on the English way of life' ('Extremists Join Country Lobby', *The Guardian*, London, 30 Oct. 1997).

93. The significance of these seemingly distinct representations of Nature is examined in Chapter 7.

94. In his funeral oration at Westminster Abbey, Earl Spencer described his sister as 'the very essence of compassion, of duty . . . [a]ll over the world she was a symbol of selfless humanity . . . a standard bearer for the rights of the truly downtrodden [someone] who was classless' (*The Guardian*, London, 8 Sept. 1997)

95. A random selection of newspaper headlines (for example, 'The crown tarnished before our eyes', 'Earl Captures Nation's Mood', *The Observer*, 7 Sept. 1997) conveys the impact of the funeral oration. One of the more restrained press accounts ('Brother's Rapier Thrust that left the Windsors Wounded', *The Guardian*, London, 8 Sept. 1997) described the effect of these words in the following manner: 'Five minutes that shook the royal world. They will be returned to again and again. That oration at that funeral. The words that caused the winds of applause already swirling around the crowds outside to overwhelm the congregation.'

96. That the funeral oration by Earl Spencer was interpreted as an endorsement of modernity is evident from some of the press headlines (for example, 'The Nation Unites Against Tradition', *The Observer*, 7 Sept. 1997) and also from commentaries by celebrity intellectuals. Examples of the latter include Martin Jacques and 'six commentators [gathered] to chart the way ahead for what now really is a new Britain', one of whom insisted '[Diana] was seen as the modern against the traditional . . . the country is moving into a modern phase', Elaine Showalter, who opined that '[i]t is daily becoming more apparent that Diana's death has become a political occasion, a moment of subdued, but very British, revolutionary sentiment . . . a mass demonstration of anger towards the monarchy', and the playwright David Edgar, who hoped that '[a] new, post-market, post-individualist may be stirring' ('We've Changed . . . but What Will We Become?', *The Observer*, London, 12 Sept. 1997; 'Storming the Wintery Palace' *The Guardian*, London, 6 Sept. 1997; 'The Floral Revolution', *The Guardian*, London, 10 Sept. 1997). Even an initial reading of the actual text of the funeral oration reveals, however, that it was not an attack on but rather *a defence of the monarchy as an institution* ('On behalf of your mother and sisters, I pledge that we, your [i.e. Diana's] blood family, will do all we can to continue the imaginative and loving way in which you were steering [her sons] . . . .We fully respect the heritage into which they have been born, and will always respect and encourage them in their royal role'.)

97. Unsurprisingly, when the monarchy was being criticized in the British press for not showing a more 'caring' response to the death of the princess, it was Blair who came to its rescue ('How Blair Gave the Monarchy a Millbank Makeover', *The Observer*, 7 Sept. 1997).

98. For this, see the text of Blair's speech to the 1997 Labour Party Conference ('Blair Calls for the Age of Giving', *The Guardian*, London, 1 Oct. 1997).

99. Subsequent analysis confirms that the mass hysteria generated by the death of the Princess of Wales was in a large degree media constructed, a process described by some who did not subscribe to it as the 'touchy-feely fascism' ('don't think, just get in touch with your feelings; we all care, we are all the same', etc.) which characterizes populist rhetoric and Sorelian instinctivism. One of those interviewed observed: 'We kept being told that the country was united, which it was in the sense that we were all watching the same television programme. But in another sense – that divisions of class and race were being healed, for example – well, it's crap' (see Ian Jack, 'Those Who Felt Differently', *The Guardian Weekend*, London, 27 Dec. 1997).

PART III
Populist Culture

Popular Culture, Populist Fiction(s): The Agrarian Utopiates of A.V. Chayanov, Ignatius Donnelly and Frank Capra

'The populist tradition offers no panacea for all the ills that afflict the modern world' – An observation by Christopher Lasch [1991: 532].

'We were created to live in Paradise, and Paradise was designed to serve us. Our purpose has changed; that this has also happened with the purpose of Paradise is nowhere stated' – Aphorism 84 in Franz Kafka [1973: 97].

'You don't win a hat like that playing mumbly pegs' – An aside by Bob Hope to Bing Crosby, about the size of the hat worn by the High Lama, in the film *Road to Hong Kong* (1962).[1]

In a world characterized on the one hand by dystopic images of widespread poverty, unemployment, famine, 'ethnic cleansing', refugee flight, depeasantization, ecological disaster and war, all generated by a seemingly unstoppable capitalism, and on the other by a triumphalist and widely announced 'death' of Marxism together with its vision of progress rooted in the possibility/ desirability of planning, technology, industry and urbanization, one of the most urgent and frequently-asked questions has become: are there any alternative visions of the future, and if so of what do they consist? In short, if Marxism is no longer to be permitted a role in the design of Paradise/Utopia (= community), what sort of place will the latter be, and who/what will decide this?

One alternative vision of the future that has a long history is that advocated by agrarian populism. Accordingly, in this chapter it is intended to examine the depiction in the domain of 'popular culture' by the 'old' populism (see Chapter 1) of what purports to be its non-capitalist/non-socialist alternative: in short, the socio-economic and political structure of its 'imaginary' as this involves a symptomatic opposition between the utopic and dystopic (or the combination within populist ideology of a discourse-for and a discourse-against about utopia and its 'other'). This dystopic/utopic opposition structures each of the three populist texts considered here: the American novel

Caesar's Column (1890) by Ignatius Donnelly [1960]; the Russian text *The Journey of My Brother Alexei to the Land of Peasant Utopia* (1920) by A.V. Chayanov [*Kremnev*, 1977]; and *Lost Horizon* in both its literary and cinematic forms, the English novel by James Hilton [1933a] and the film produced in America during 1937 and directed by Frank Capra.

These three literary/filmic texts share a common negative/positive vision that is typical of the agrarian myth, in which a dystopic/('evil') urban is contrasted with an utopic/('good') rural. To the 'natural'/god-given social order of the populist utopic, therefore, is counterposed the dystopic chaos of a dark/dangerous/closed world inhabited by the variants of non-natural *untermensch* ('mob', 'lower classes', 'underclass'). Accordingly, it is argued here that what is significant about the fictional portrayals of utopia by Donnelly, Hilton and Capra – all of which had a powerful impact in the domain of 'popular culture' – is not just that each text was a reaction in the midst of a capitalist crisis to capitalism itself, nor that each was nationalist, orientalist and even racist in outlook, but also (and perhaps most importantly) that all were an expression of fear that such a situation would lead to socialism. This latter anxiety also informs the fictional utopia of Chayanov, except that in his case the danger is now in the past.

I

6.1 The Return of Populist 'Community'

The received wisdom that utopias have been and are basically the 'imaginaries' of the political left overlooks the long history of similar attempts by those on the centre/right of the political spectrum to construct an alternative 'imaginary'. It is not without significance, therefore, that following the demise of the Soviet Union much (non-Marxist) social theory is currently engaged in an attempt to recuperate a specifically non-socialist variety of community. This project extends from the still fashionable 'communitarianism' of MacIntyre, Etzioni and Lasch, with its fear of the loss of and an advocacy of a return to traditional family and community values, to a community of autonomous individuals that structures the contractarianism of Rawls and the postmodernism of Rorty.[2] Such a project could be said also to include the tribal/peasant/gender/ethnic/national 'communities' implied or disclosed in much recent social theory about the so-called Third World that is produced from within on the one hand the 'cultural-not-racial-difference' discourse of the allegedly 'post-fascist' European 'new' right, and on the other the postmodern approach of the new social movements and Subaltern Studies framework.[3] Despite some obvious theoretical differences, all the latter share a common characteristic: the attempt either to identify or to construct an ethically based 'moral' community, without having regard to class differences or having to transform substantially existing property relations.[4] In short, this search for a depoliticized form of 'community' signals the return not just of populism but in some instances also of the agrarian myth.

As argued in previous chapters, the way in which populism has been propagated historically, in terms of form and content, demonstrates the problematic nature of claims that it corresponds to an authentically grassroots discourse-against. Hence in a significant number of historical cases from the 1890s to the 1940s the agrarian myth has not only been disseminated in the domain of 'popular culture' in a form that is either aristocratic or plebeian but its politico-ideological content has similarly been an historically and/or contextually specific response from above to an actual/potential threat from below, posed in the case of an aristocracy by the bourgeoisie and in the case of the latter by the proletariat.[5] Accordingly, antagonism to international capital and condemnation of economic 'greed' serve to exculpate (and thus to protect) capitalism by endowing populism with an oppositional voice that is both nationalist and plebeian in tone (for example, 'peasants-as-warriors').[6]

6.2 Agrarian Utopiates, Populist Fiction(s)

Two of the three texts considered here were produced in the context of a capitalist crisis, and all three idealize the small-scale, rural life, the lone individual, and are against the large-scale, finance capital, against the city, and against the state. Set in New York a century into the future, the first of the three agrarian populist utopias, Caesar's Column (1890) by Ignatius Donnelly, consists of a series of letters written to his brother by Gabriel Weltstein, a sheep farmer from the new African state of Uganda.[7] Like all the rest of modern capitalist civilization, Donnelly's New York of 1988 is polarized between on the one hand a small aristocratic ruling class of wealthy finance capitalists (= the Plutocracy), and on the other a large urban industrial proletariat (= the 'great, dark, writhing masses' which inhabit the 'underworld'). Organized into the Brotherhood of Destruction and led by an ex-farmer called Caesar, the American working class overthrows the ruling aristocracy of financial capitalists, in the course of which modern urban industrial civilization worldwide is itself extinguished. While Caesar celebrates the victory of the proletariat amidst the ruins of New York by building a column out of the bodies of the slain, Weltstein and a few others succeed in escaping to an idyllic rural 'garden in the mountains' located in Africa.[8]

Using the pseudonym of Ivan Kremnev, the Russian neo-populist theoretician A.V. Chayanov wrote the utopian fiction The Journey of My Brother

Alexei to the Land of Peasant Utopia (1920).[9] The central character in this narrative is Alexei Kremnev, a socialist living in the drab Soviet Russia of 1921, who is suddenly transported forward in time by sixty years to Moscow in 1984, where he is mistaken for an American visitor.[10] Half a century on, he finds that socialism has collapsed, towns have been abolished, and Moscow is now a rural arcadia without either heavy industry or proletariat.[11] Established as a result of peasant opposition to socialism, the labour-intensive agrarian economy of what has now become the Russian Peasant Republic is in the fiction of Chayanov based on the restoration of private property in the form of the peasant family farm, and the corresponding absence of planning and state intervention. Discovering that half a century earlier he himself was responsible for the suppression of the peasant movement in Soviet Russia, and by implication the idyllic pastoral (= agrarian utopia) that Russia would have become had this not been done, Kremnev repents and rejects his socialism in favour of populism.

For a number of reasons, perhaps the most interesting of the three examples of agrarian populist utopia considered here is that projected in the book *Lost Horizon* by James Hilton, and in the film of the same name, directed by Frank Capra.[12] Both film and book versions of *Lost Horizon* follow roughly the same plot.[13] Escaping from a revolutionary crowd in China, European passengers on the last plane out are kidnapped and transported to a mysterious, idyllic Tibetan 'garden in the mountains' (the valley of the Blue Moon or Shangri-La) high in the Himalayas.[14] In the film version those kidnapped consist of the British Foreign Secretary elect, Robert Conway, and his brother George, together with a paleontologist (Alexander P. Lovett), an incurable invalid (Gloria Stone), and a speculator (Chalmers Bryant, whose alias is Henry Barnard) who swindled small investors during the Wall Street crash. 'Discovered' on the unexplored Tibetan plateau by a Capuchin priest at the beginning of the eighteenth century, Shangri-La remains mountain-locked and unaffected by the economic depression, the impending world war, or indeed time itself.[15] In short, it embodies the Garden of Eden of legend, in which no one grows old or lacks for anything. However, shortly after the death of the two-hundred years old High Lama, the original 'discoverer' of Shangri-La, the main protagonist Robert Conway and his brother attempt to return to external 'civilization'. In the course of this journey, one of the accompanying inhabitants of Shangri-La ages rapidly and dies, while Conway's brother falls off the mountain to his death. Conway himself reaches the plains below, but then changes his mind about staying and decides to return once more to Shangri-La, which he succeeds in doing as the film ends.

The context – and the background to the successful appeal – of both novel and film versions of *Lost Horizon* is the capitalist crisis of the 1930s, which has in turn given rise to the criticism that the narrative corresponds simply to an unfocussed form of escapism, a discourse-against that lacks an 'other'.[16] This critique, which is reinforced textually by the flight from (and the juxtaposition of) a context governed by chaos/war to one structured by order/peace, is true only in a superficial sense.[17] *Lost Horizon* is not simply an expression of pessimism devoid of an accompanying optimism, but is rather the combination of a pessimism/optimism couple in which the optimism possesses (and thus projects) a particular socio-economic configuration. Although pessimism generated by economic crisis in metropolitan capitalism is not confronted internally, in that no solution is sought within (and arising from) the structure of modern industrial capitalism itself, it does contain an external 'other'. An alternative is present, therefore, in that the optimistic 'other' is to be found not in the form of a transformation of existing society but rather outside industrial capitalism altogether, in an idyllic arcadia located deep within the Himalayas. Accordingly, this is a case not of (an 'otherless') escapism *per se*, as many of the critics maintain, but rather its opposite: the *reaffirmation* of a traditional and – as is argued here – a conservative form of 'otherness' which, as well as being anti-industrial (anti-modern/anti-urban/anti-technological) in outlook, is not only (and therefore) specifically rural but also populist and orientalist.[18]

Much of the 'old' populist discourse which structures the agrarian myth is present in other films directed by Frank Capra and other novels written by James Hilton. Capra directed not just *Lost Horizon* (see below) but also *Mr Deeds Goes to Town* (1936), *Mr Smith Goes to Washington* (1939) and *It's a Wonderful Life* (1946).[19] All these films celebrated the populist values associated with the rural conservatism of an idealised small-town America, as epitomised by an individual saviour in the form of 'the little man' from a small-scale rural background (= purity, innocence) who takes on and triumphs over city bankers and financial interests in the corrupt and large-scale urban setting. Thus *Mr Deeds Goes to Town* celebrates a seemingly irrational/insane use of inherited wealth to resettle farmers dispossessed by the capitalist crisis, and culminates in a courtroom reaffirmation of small community anti-intellectualism (= 'natural, rural common-sense') against the false sophistication of the city. Similarly, in *It's a Wonderful Life* Capra contrasts the small/'good' capitalist from an unchanging/small-scale rural community background with the large/'bad' financial capitalist and a nightmarish large-scale/mechanised urban future.[20]

Much the same is true of the other novels written by James Hilton. In *Goodbye Mr Chips*, for example, the kind of values to be taught in an English public school, Brookfield, are the subject of struggle between the two main protagonists. One is the hero, Mr Chips, a classics teacher who is 'old-fashioned' and respresents 'tradition'; the other is the new headmaster,

Ralston, who teaches science, is 'up-to-date' and modern in outlook, and represents 'efficiency'.[21] The victor in this struggle, Mr Chips, is given to making anti-semitic jokes, and stands for and defends tradition, conservatism and a specifically rural English national identity, the decline of which he abhors.[22] He gives voice to all the familiar components of populism, both its discourse-for and also its discourse-against: not only does Mr Chips invoke the declining values of 'old gentlemanly traditions' (= custom) and the landed aristocracy (= 'broad acres'), therefore, but he also inveighs against an ascendant finance capital and technology.[23] His vision of the future, a democracy of 'duke and dustman', is a populist one based on the reproduction of an old (= 'traditional') hierarchy in which everyone enjoys mutual repect (= no *cultural* snobbery) but nevertheless knows his/her place (= 'natural' socioeconomic order).

II

6.3 Utopic/Dystopic Discourse

The three agrarian populist texts considered here – *Caesar's Column, The Journey of My Brother*, and *Lost Horizon* – all combine and simultaneously juxtapose what might be termed the symptomatic discourse about the 'dystopic' and 'utopic', an opposition which delineates a form of political, economic and social existence that is either desirable (small-scale production, yeoman farmer, rural arcadia) or undesirable (technology, large-scale industry, urbanization, socialism, finance capital and the proletariat).[24] In short, for agrarian populism utopia corresponds to its 'community' while dystopia constitutes the absence of the latter. More generally, the discourse about utopia/dystopia extends from (and epistemologically unites) the 'high culture' of the ancient world and traditional Christian beliefs on the one hand to the literary/filmic depiction of 'future worlds' in modern science fiction (time-travel and/or space-travel) on the other.[25] In so far as it addresses the desirability/undesirability of the structure/content of future worlds, therefore, it is a genre that not only transcends the 'high'/'low' cultural divide but also and thereby licenses the political construction/reproduction of a 'popular culture' that is specifically populist.

An important distinction between the texts considered here is that whereas for Chayanov the dystopic is disclosed and warned against by a shift in time, for Hilton and Capra the same objective is achieved by a shift in space. The text by Donnelly combines a shift in both time and space. Accordingly, the utopic vision of Chayanov entails traversing time but not space; the protagonists in his narrative are projected forward into a future within the same demarcated space. By contrast, in the the utopic vision of Hilton and Capra it is space which is traversed and not time; both utopic and dystopic exist in the same moment but occupy a different terrain. Central to the discourse about 'the utopic' and/or 'the dystopic', therefore, is a sub-text concerning the sacredness (or profanation) of Nature, space and time.

6.4 Utopic/Dystopic Nature

An important element of the discourse about utopia/dystopia is the concept of a violent/harmonious Nature, whereby dystopia is equated with all that is 'unnatural' and utopia with 'natural' forms of social organization and existence. Seemingly antithetical, violent/harmonious concepts of Nature are actually different sides of the same ideological coin, and constitute a discourse in which humanity (instead of shaping) is shaped by Nature. Accordingly, the harmony which exists in the pastoral version is in fact underwritten by the violence of the 'red-in-tooth-and-claw' variant, in that a 'natural' order is not merely incribed in Nature but the latter periodically exercises its physical power in order to restore/maintain this.[26] This discourse structured by the view that change of all kinds is organic, and beyond the capacity of human agency to alter, licenses in turn a pessimistic view about humanity and historical progress, and thus about the possibility, the effectiveness and even the desirability of social change: where/when it takes place, the latter is regarded as a 'natural' process, as part of a project of innateness.

Fears about the destruction of Nature – and with it a 'natural' peasantry – invariably structure the utopic/dystopic portrayals that arise historically as a response to the depeasantization that accompanies economic crisis. This kind of anxiety manifests itself in the implicit/explicit identification of a combined threat: (financial) capitalism and its even more nightmarish 'other', socialism. Thus the economic depression of the 1880s in England generated a whole literary genre projecting contrasting dystopic/utopic images of society, at the centre of which is a discourse about Nature.[27] In the utopias of William Morris and Richard Jefferies, for example, not only is Nature central to the narrative but in each instance it represents two different sides of the same coin; the former depicts a pastoral and the latter a Social Darwinist image of nature.[28] For the agrarian populist utopic, therefore, the objective is not, as with Marxism, one which entails that humanity be in control of Nature, but much rather its opposite: that (an active) Nature be in control of (a passive) humanity.

6.5 Utopic/Dystopic Space

The ideological and metaphorical significance of symbolic spacing in the utopic/dystopic project derives in part from Christian tradition, in which a salvation that is non-material but spiritual is always to be found in heaven – located above (literally and metaphorically) the earth – where the innocence/purity/light of the Garden of Eden (= pastoral) is to be recuperated. Thus high physical space (= mountaintop) signals not only salvation but also the recovery of innocence and its accompanying primitive essence which is also rural (heaven = purity = redemption = peace = Nature = utopia = 'the above'). By contrast, in the same religious tradition the earth (= purgatory, limbo) is the physically intermediate domain of 'the material' and the 'sinful-but-redeemable', a context that is both 'pure' (= rural) and 'impure' (= urban) where the (class) struggle (between capital and labour) for salvation which takes place results in either redemption or damnation.

Beneath them all, however, lies the underworld (= hell = violence = dystopia = 'the below'), the domain of 'the unredeemable-sinful' and thus metaphorically and literally the 'other' of Eden/heaven: the dark realm of death and the damned (= the urban proletariat, the 'underclass' or the 'mob-in-the-streets').[29] Unsurprisingly, the dystopic character of this symbolically potent physical 'otherness' is a pervasive theme in many of the literary/cinematic depictions in 'popular culture': examples from the science fiction genre include *The Underground Man* by Gabriel Tarde [1905], the film *Metropolis* (1926) directed by Fritz Lang, and – most notably – *The Time Machine* by H.G. Wells [1895], in which 'those below' were the violent/(productive) Morlocks, the workers underground who provided for and then consumed the gentle/(parasitical) Eloi, 'those above' who led an idyllic rural existence in the 'Upper World'.

The importance of symbolic spacing in *Lost Horizon* is twofold. First, like the 'mountain' film genre in Germany during the same period, the physical location of Shangri-La within the highest/(undiscovered) peaks of the Himalayas similarly projects an aura of sacredness/spirituality linked to it being the abode of the gods, a perception reinforced by its mythical/legendary status.[30] And second, the physical occupation by the lamasery of the middle foreground raised mightily over the valley floor (a spatial distinction that is very evident in the film), accurately conveys the relative importance in the class structure of its respective inhabitants: its mainly European rulers are situated 'up above', while the indigenous peasantry (= 'natives') that is the object of this rule occupies the space 'down below'.

The same kind of symbolism is if anything even more pronounced in the physical ordering of space in *Caesar's Column*: in the underworld, below everyone, is the 'under-class' or proletariat, while immmediately above them occupying the middle ground is the aristocracy of finance capital; above them all, 'amidst the high mountain valleys of Africa', is the colony of 'the saved'.[31] As significant is the fact that, as Donnelly observes, those below (= the urban proletariat) cannot by travelling 'that narrow, gloomy, highwalled pathway, out of which they could never climb' escape from their dystopic situation up the mountain to utopia.[32] Like the case of Shangri-La in *Lost Horizon*, therefore, the working class inhabitants of the 'Under-World' in *Caesar's Column* will not be permitted to reach Eden, there to find redemption.

6.6 Utopic/Dystopic Time

As important and symbolic as space in the 'utopic' project is the element of time. Accordingly, in the sacred context of utopia the passage of time is itself suspended, and with it history, the object being to halt – if not to reverse – the economic development in an 'eternal present', which is divinely and/or 'naturally' ordained and ordered, and its hierarchy/'difference' (= heterogeneity, diversity) is therefore sacred and/or 'natural'. The suspension of time in utopic discourse also contributes to the reproduction of a number of mutually reinforcing stereotypes: the myth of an a-historical, ever present, self-sufficient/subsistence-oriented peasant farmer, the eternal 'lazy native' whose alleged indolence stems from the 'unchanging timelessness' (= the essential sameness) of Nature itself, a conceptualization which in turn lies behind most of the orientalist nations about the 'primitive'/'otherness' of Africa and the East.

Perhaps the most potent ideological manifestation of this view is the redemptive myth of a 'golden age', which not only structures the many and recurring proclamations in the midst of capitalism by populists/populism announcing the 'end-of-history' and the 'end-of-ideology', but is also present in the symbols, rites, and religious customs/ceremonies of most non-capitalist social formations, where it involves the ideological attempt to replace the mortality of profane time (= history) with the immortality of sacred time. Hence the timelessness of Shangri-La in *Lost Horizon* represents the attainment of sacred time, the eternal present of the Garden of Eden: no one who does not leave Shangri-La grows old.[33]

III

Before considering the positive elements of the populist utopic as presented in these texts by Donnelly, Chayanov, Hilton and Capra, it is important to establish the negative structure (together with its determinants) of their dystopic 'other': that is, the mirror image of the utopic.

6.7 Dystopic Capitalism, Dystopic Crisis, Dystopic Rulers

Unlike *Journey of My Brother*, in which the dystopic is socialist, both *Caesar's Column* and *Lost Horizon* are characterized by a capitalist dystopia. In both the latter texts, however, the anti-capitalist discourse is of a specific type: in each case the responsibility for – and hence the target of their political attack – is not capitalism *per se* but finance capital (= usury). Not only does Donnelly portray finance capital as all-powerful (a force that 'has the whole world in its grasp') and responsible for the plight of the indebted yeoman farmer and thus the undermining of the agrarian myth, but he also – and most significantly – inculpates financial capital with creating the urban proletariat which destroys the whole of existing civilization.[34]

As depicted in *Caesar's Column*, therefore, the ruling class responsible for the dystopic condition of New York in 1988 is not only composed of aristocratic representatives of finance capital, but the latter is also closely associated in Donnelly's narrative with an ethnically 'foreign'/'alien' Jewish 'other'.[35] This opposition between an idealized and ethnically 'pure' American republicanism and its 'impure' aristocratic ruling class 'other' is underlined in the narrative by the fact that one of the two principal female characters, who is a lineal descendent of the first president, is sold as a concubine to Prince Cabano, the ruling financier.[36] Hence the purchase by 'Jewish finance capital' of that most sacred of American symbols permits a relay-in-statement of negative identities (urban = foreigner = Jewish = finance capital = non-American 'otherness'). By contrast, the two principal female characters (Christina, Estrella) not only come from (and thus symbolically represent) rural backgrounds, but also (and thereby) embody moral virtue and racial 'purity', licensing a series of symbolically interchangeable positive identities (woman = virtue = purity = rural = Nature = Aryan = civilization = authentically American).[37]

Much the same is true of *Lost Horizon*, in which the economic crisis of the 1930s is presented not as a systemic effect of capitalism itself but rather as the fault of financiers and intellectuals, thereby combining populist anti-capitalism and anti-intellectualism.[38] Significantly, the representative of (unproductive) finance capital, the speculator Barnard/Bryant, not only finds redemption in Shangri-La, where he reverts to a productive role, but is exonerated by Conway who, as the representative of the state, also inculpates himself for the existing capitalist crisis.[39] The sub-text in this particular case is that the capitalist system would function adequately if financiers, intellectuals and the state were all prevented from interfering with it.

6.8 Dystopic Workers, Dystopic Struggle, Dystopic Socialism

Perhaps no other component of agrarian populist discourse-against is allocated quite such a negative role in precipiating a dystopic armageddon, and thus depicted in quite the same pathological manner, as the urban working class. Symptomatically, therefore, for Donnelly the existence of the urban industrial proletariat in the New York of 1988 is the mirror image of his rural paradise: in contrast to the yeoman farmer of the agrarian myth, the 'haggard', 'hopeless' workers inhabit an urban anti-utopia which corresponds to a literal and metaphorical 'underworld' that is 'death in life', 'the resurrection of the dead' and 'hell'.[40] Like its 'other' and creator, finance capital, the American proletariat of *Caesar's Column* is similarly 'impure', being composed of ethnically diverse migrants (= 'invading Mongolian hordes').[41] Indeed, the less 'controllable' and the more revolutionary the working class becomes, the more the narrative of *Caesar's Column* focuses on its ethnic composition, a discourse in which the latter is equated with the 'alien'/'darkness' both of urban 'otherness' and of the destructive 'otherness' of 'barbarism'/'chaos'.[42]

Of greater concern to Donnelly than the oppression and exploitation of the industrial workforce, however, is the fact that a century hence it has become organized, and formed the Brotherhood of Destruction.[43] Not only does the latter have a global membership of one hundred million, but workers are now routinely familiar with Marxist theory and have acquired a consciousness of class, as a consequence of which it is no longer possible to control them.[44] Most significantly, for Donnelly this is a transformation that is not only unnecessary but one that must be reversed, a view which contrasts with that of Marxism which *celebrates* such a transition. His fear is that by de-naturing the peasantry of the agrarian myth, and turning the yeoman farmer into a landless labourer in the city, finance capital creates not just its 'other' but an 'other' in its own brutal image.[45]

Once a peasantry is transformed into a proletariat, Donnelly warns, it loses not only its land but also its passivity and thus its political inhibitions: accordingly, he implies, the yeoman farmer of the American agrarian myth should be retained not so much for economic reasons (= the viability of self-sufficient cultivation) as for political reasons.[46] In short, to prevent an historically 'eternal' category of petty commodity producers from being separated by (finance) capital from its traditional means of production, in the process becoming what all fractions of the bourgeoisie fear most: a class conscious urban proletariat no longer under their collective control, or the 'mob-in-the-streets' that pervades the dystopia of agrarian populism.[47]

Since much of the anti-modern and anti-technological discourse of agrarian populism is founded on the fear of the 'mob-in-the-streets', it is unsurprising to encounter in *Caesar's Column*, in *Journey of My Brother* and in *Lost Horizon* a pervasive anti-socialist politics. In the case of *Lost Horizon*, therefore, the film version by Capra commences with a literal and symbolic flight by Conway (and the others) to escape from a Chinese revolutionary 'mob-in-the-streets'. Hence the journey which ends in Shangri-La/utopia commences by leaving behind the 'twin evils' that structure the dystopia of agrarian populism: finance capital and its 'other', the revolutionary working class.[48] For Donnelly the impossibility/undesirability of socialism is similarly evident from his apocalyptic vision of New York once the proletarian revolution is realized: not only is the latter process depicted as nihilistic, a pointless act of destruction by the 'mob-in-the-streets', but for him the overturning of the existing division of labour appears 'unnatural'.[49] Furthermore, the revolutionaries are presented as in the end being no different from the financiers who ruled them, and thus incapable of constructing an alternative to the whole oppressive/exploitative system which they have overthrown.[50]

Chayanov regards a socialist alternative to capitalism in similarly negative terms, although in his case it is an alternative that has already been tried and found wanting. In the course of his time-travel to the Moscow of 1984, therefore, Kremnev learns that the socialist system of the 1920s was of short duration, and collapsed into its national components amidst a more general process of war and European fragmentation, since when 'the system had been slowly evolving towards an increasingly peasant regime'.[51] Significantly, it was the collapse of socialism that led to the re-emergence of its 'other': the system of peasant family farming. Dismissing the Bolsheviks as 'ideologists of the working class', Chayanov concludes by claiming that they were 'enlightened absolutists' who had been responsible for reducing Russia to 'a condition of anarchic reaction'.[52]

IV

Turning to the physiognomy of the agrarian populist utopia, not only are finance capitalism, technology, the urban proletariat and socialism – the dystopic effects of time and historical progress – absent, but in terms of class position and ethnic origin political power is exercised by a different subject.

6.9 Agrarian Populist Utopia as Non-technological 'Other'

Since at the centre of most literary/filmic representations of anti-modern dystopias lies the nightmare vision of a planned (= rational) future, unsurprisingly an important aspect of existence in the utopic 'other' is its non-/anti-technological socio-economic structure.[53] The historical appeal of the latter to agrarian populism is unsurprising, since technology has been the visible manifestation of the large-scale economic power of capital, and the method whereby smallholders were not only separated from their means of production (= physically displaced-from/replaced-on the land) but also lost control over both their land and their own labour-power, each of which were ideologically deeply rooted in a discourse about Nature.[54]

In *Caesar's Column*, *Journey of My Brother* and *Lost Horizon*, therefore, a large-scale technology/industrialisation (and, by implication, modernity itself) is represented in negative terms.[55] Hence the government of the utopian 'garden in the mountains' located in the Uganda of 1988 discourages the invention of labour-displacing techniques, since in this context the desired objective is 'not cheap goods or cheap men, but happy families'.[56] Similarly, the Moscow of 1984 has reverted to a non-technified labour-intensive peasant agriculture, while in Shangri-La technology – like modernity generally – is presented as an unwelcome 'contamination' from the 'outside' below, the process of 'machine-power multiplying' being equated with the familiar dystopic theme of technology-beyond-the-control-of-humanity.[57]

6.10 Agrarian Populist Utopia as Oriental/Pastoral 'Other'

Given the negative/dystopic elements (capitalism, socialism, urbanisation, technology) which structure the discourse-against of agrarian populism, it is equally unsurprising that its positive/utopic reproduces and reaffirms the importance of two distinct forms of 'otherness': it is both orientalist and rural. A return to this rural/'primitive'/Eastern 'otherness', therefore, is celebrated in a specifically orientalist mode: imperial colonization. Hence the utopia of *Caesar's Column* is not only located in the new state of Uganda in the African confederation, where English is the universal language, but has been colonized by the family of the main character for a period of seventy years.[58] Furthermore, Africa is depicted as the exotic/mysterious/unknowable 'other' of imperial discourse, the mirror image of urban New York in 1988; it is accordingly described by Donnelly both as 'primitive' and as 'that strange, wild, ancient, lofty land'.[59]

Much the same is true of *Lost Horizon*. Just like the Southern Agrarians in the United States, whose response to the capitalist crisis of the 1930s was to advocate a return to the non-capitalist 'natural' values embodied in the cultural 'otherness' of the antebellum American south, so Frank Capra in the midst of the same capitalist crisis similarly attempted to recuperate a seemingly 'authentic' non-capitalist, agrarian and culturally-specific form of 'otherness' physically removed from the present, but this time located in the 'orient'. For Capra and Hilton, therefore, the utopia of Shangri-La in *Lost Horizon* is orientalist, located in the domain of the Eastern 'other' in Tibet.[60] Indeed, the utopias in *Caesar's Column* and *Lost Horizon* both share the same geography, and thus symbolic spacing: rural arcadias in exotic colonial settings, situated within – and protected from the outside by – high mountain ranges. Hence the description by Donnelly of the physical location of his utopia-in-Uganda in the inaccessible high mountain valleys of Africa could just as easily apply to Shangri-La in *Lost Horizon*.[61]

In literary practice the pastoral tradition is structured by the opposition between on the one hand a simple/happy/('natural') life in the tranquillity of the countryside that is light and open, and on the other the corruption/depravity/pollution of 'unnatural' existence in the city, which is dark, narrow and dangerous. The utopic of agrarian populism, therefore, is essentially the attempt to recuperate the traditional values associated with a 'natural' but vanishing rural social order threatened by the violent expansion of industrial/financial capitalism and its accompanying 'other', socialism. This is especially true of the utopia in *Caesar's Column*, which constitutes the epitome of the American agrarian myth based on nostalgia for a 'golden age': that is, a 'little world [that] is a garden of peace and beauty', or a combination of 'the primitive, simple shepherd-life' and homestead farming, a situation characterized by an 'equal distribution of wealth' in which no individual landholding would exceed one hundred acres.[62] Similarly, the Valley of the Blue Moon in *Lost Horizon* is described by Hilton as 'nothing less than an enclosed paradise of amazing fertility . . . crops of unusual diversity grew in profusion and contiguity, with not an inch of ground untended.' The idyllic nature of this rural arcadia emerges most clearly in the pastoral imagery which structures the film version, the visual impact of which led Graham Greene to describe Shangri-La as a place of 'flirtatious pursuits through grape arbours, splashings and divings in blossomy pools under improbable waterfalls and rich and enormous meals'.[63]

The same is true of *Journey of My Brother*. The Russia of 1984, in which towns no longer existed, was now a land of abundance, an agrarian society dominated economically by the peasant family farm, which emerged and consolidated following the implosion of socialism during the 1920s and peasant revolution of the 1930s.[64] As in *Caesar's Column* and *Lost Horizon*, the resulting social order of utopia based on peasant farming is depicted by Chayanov as a return to an ancient and natural condition which neither capitalism nor socialism had been able to suppress for long.[65] Accordingly, the Russia of the mid–1980s is characterized by an absence of 'large fortunes', an economic situation referred to by Chayanov as 'the democratisation of national income'.[66] In short, a context in which no socio-economic differentiation of the peasantry occurs, and consequently an economy in which all petty commodity producers remain the same.

6.11 Class Structure in the Agrarian Populist Utopia

Claims about peasant economy notwithstanding, it is important to note that the agrarian populist utopia does not exclude the possibility of small-scale capital accumulation, and hence the persistence and/or development of class relations. Thus it is only finance capital and not capitalism *per se* that is to be banished from the agrarian populist utopia of *Caesar's Column*. Criticizing usury which 'kills off the enterprising members of a community by bankrupting them', therefore, Donnelly not only presents small-scale manufacturing in a positive light but also accepts in principle the process of accumulation and the unequal distribution and inheritance of wealth, maintaining that 'only in their excess [do] they become destructive'.[67] The same appears to be true of Russia in 1984 where, as Chayanov makes very clear, the continued existence of the peasant family farm is not itself incompatible with the survival of the market, a 'residual capitalism' described by him as 'tame' and non-exploitative.[68]

As with the dystopia of agrarian populism, the nature and ethnic origin of the ruling class in its utopia is equally specific. Accordingly, in *Caesar's Column* those who flee from the New York in 1988 to the safety of 'the garden in the mountains' in Uganda are in the main of 'Aryan' ancestry, while in the case of *Lost Horizon* the traditional political ruling hierarchy in Shangri-La is a theocracy at the apex of which are similarly to be found representatives of the 'Nordic' races, a ruling class that is periodically replenished mainly by Europeans who arrive from the outside.[69] Although neither the Ugandan colony in 1988 nor the Moscow of 1984 is a theocracy, Christian religion discharges an important role in the former while in the latter context political power is exercised by a monastic order (the Brotherhood of Saints).[70]

The structure of class rule in utopia is evident from the similarity in the nature of political power and role of the state in all three texts considered here. As Donnelly makes clear, although nominally democratic, power in his agrarian populist utopia is actually exercised by a ruling class, albeit of a different kind from that which ruled its dystopic urban 'other'.[71] In Chayanov's Moscow of 1984, the state operates a *laissez-faire* principle whereby the ruling peasant regime 'for the most part relied on social methods of solving problems, not measures of state coercion'. Based on peasant councils, the state has neither role nor substantial power, having been stripped of 'virtually all social and economic functions' and replaced by what appear indistinguishable from grassroots non-government organizations.[72] Symptomatically, the benign role of the state attributed by Chayanov to the peasant regime is contrasted with the coercive, surplus-extracting state apparatus under socialism: in the latter context, it is argued, the state exploited the workers in order to maintain a wasteful bureaucracy, thereby reproducing once again a central ideological premiss not just of agrarian populism but also of the political right.[73] Exactly the same *laissez-faire* principle structures politics in Shangri-La, where the 'prevalent belief' of its ruling class is in 'moderation'.[74]

Notwithstanding the tranquillity implied in the idyllic character of ruling class existence in the utopias of *Caesar's Column, Journey of My Brother* and *Lost Horizon*, each is nevertheless structured by a sub-text that is aggressively nationalist and/or exclusionary.[75] Thus 'the saved' who manage to escape from a dystopic New York of 1988 not only take with them examples of ruling class culture but also as the inhabitants of 'the garden in the mountains' in Uganda then erect a wall to prevent those still on the outside from entering utopia.[76] In the case of Moscow during 1984, the Russian Peasant Republic conscripts Nature itself (a cyclone) in order to protect itself from and to vanquish Germany, characterized by Chayanov as 'the defeated hordes', a conflict which itself mimics the nationalist defence of a subsistence-oriented smallholding peasantry mounted by Slavophile populism against German (= 'foreign') capitalist penetration of Russia during the late nineteenth century.[77] Much the same kind of discourse is evident in *Lost Horizon*, where – as in the case of *Caesar's Column* – the fear is that the capitalist crisis 'outside' will result in the destruction not so much of society but of ruling class culture; accordingly, the object of the 'utopic' is in this case to protect/ preserve the latter against a rapacious modernity and its machine.[78]

Most importantly, in none of the utopias depicted in these three agrarian populist texts is there a sizeable urban working class. Thus a potentially threatening proletariat is largely absent from Donnelly's Uganda in 1988, and wholly absent from the Shangri-La of Hilton and Capra in the 1930s: in both these contexts, the main producers are self-sufficient cultivators.[79] Neither is there an urban proletariat in the Moscow of 1984 as depicted by Chayanov. The reason for this is significant: towns had been abolished because of the threat posed by the proletariat which resided and worked in them. In short, for Chayanov the fear of industrialisation and urbanization that would lead to socialism – via the kind of apocalypse predicted in the texts by Donnelly, Hilton and Capra – had resulted in the pre-emptive and counter-revolutionary destruction by the Russian peasantry of urban habitation and the decentralization of production.[80]

For all these reasons, it is necessary to disagree with Marin, for whom utopia represents an equilibrium, a neutral space between rival powers in which neither prevails.[81] Although corresponding to many other aspects of 'the utopic', therefore, Shangri-La during the 1930s, Moscow in 1984 and Uganda in 1988 are not so much 'neutral'/'in-between' (= liminal) spaces, in which power is negated, but much rather a locus of its *expression*.

6.12 Conclusion

The resurgence of a 'communitarian' political agenda which seeks to construct a concept of 'community' (= utopia) that does not entail a radical transformation in property relations indicates yet again the historical pervasiveness amidst recurring capitalist crises of populist ideology. To a significant degree, the agrarian populist discourse-for and discourse-against in *Caesar's Column*, in *Journey of My Brother* and in *Lost Horizon,* overlaps with and is thus supportive of the oppositions which in turn structure utopic/dystopic discourse (high/low space, time/timelessness, and most importantly the rejection/ recuperation of Nature), albeit with some variations and additional elements.

Hence the dystopic 'other' of these 'old' populist texts spanning the half century from 1890 to 1937 is characterized by the absence of 'community', or a situation in which a modern financial capitalism generates an urban environment, a technology and a workforce none of which can be controlled: that is, an urban industrial proletariat which threatens armageddon/(damnation) by becoming both revolutionary and socialist. The latter possibility is the subject of warnings contained in all three texts; Chayanov, however, issues his from within the context of a socialist dystopia which already exists and which can thus be avoided if an alternative path based on peasant economy is not suppressed, whereas Donnelly, Hilton and Capra do so in reverse, by charting the dystopic role of finance capitalism which occurs precisely because such an agrarian populist course was not followed.

Furthermore, both finance capital and the proletariat are united in their 'otherness' for agrarian populism by virtue of being not merely the harbingers of the dystopic but also because each is the 'inauthentic' ethnic/national 'other'. Accordingly, it is Jewish finance capital that is blamed for creating its 'other', an urban proletariat containing a large black component, a discourse which mimics that of the political right (for which Jewish finance capital creates its 'other', Jewish Bolshevism). All the dystopic elements (finance capital, the proletariat, urbanization, industrialization) in *Lost Horizon* and *Caesar's Column* not only have a specific ethnic identity but have their origins in and/or are associated with 'western civilization'. By contrast, all the utopic elements (small-scale accumulation, the rural, the peasantry) tend to be located in the domain of the Eastern 'other', thereby implicitly conceding the fear by agrarian populism of large-scale industrialisation/urbanization associated with both capitalist and socialist development as in nationalist terms a specifically 'alien' and Western 'other'.

The desired utopia (= 'community') in all three texts is therefore not only orientalist and rural, but is also characterized by the suspension of time, and with it history, the object being to halt economic development, if not to reverse it. An effect of this a-historical timelessness is that it permits in turn the celebration/(salvation) of the traditional small-scale producer (artisan, farmer, peasant) in the context of the Edenic pastoral. Although in each case the discourse is against capitalism, the latter – like socialism – encompasses only large-scale industrial manufacturing: specific forms of small-scale accumulation, such as handicraft/artisan/peasant production, are thus acceptable within the context of the agrarian populist utopia.

The refusal to admit large numbers of those on the 'outside' who might wish to enter both the Ugandan colony and Shangri-La as a result of the capitalist crisis suggests further that access to these particular utopias is constrained in two specific ways: not only is it restricted in terms of ethnic and class composition, but it is also limited to those who appreciate/know/respect the upper-class cultural values that such utopias desire to conserve/preserve. These agrarian populist utopias constitute, in short, the 'utopic' as ordained by a (mainly) white European ruling class, in which hierarchy is ordained by God, is 'natural', is based on Nature, and is presented either as acceptable to (and thus not challenged by) those below, or as beyond the capacity of the latter to challenge.

NOTES

1. Although less serious than the utterances of Robert Conway about Shangri-La in the film *Lost Horizon*, this aside by Bob Hope a quarter of a century later nevertheless makes an oblique reference to the same kinds of 'otherness' (the 'East' in general, the Tibetan lamasery in particular, and the kind of the power exercised in the latter context).
2. See MacIntyre [1981], Etzioni [1990, 1993], Lasch [1991, 1995], Rawls [1993], and Rorty [1989]. For much the same reason – attempting to identify 'community' where none exists – the 'communitarianism' of Etzioni has come under attack from those on the neo-liberal political right as well as those on the political left. Accordingly, those on the left criticize 'communitarianism' from the viewpoint of a socialist alternative, based on the control by the state of market forces. Similarly accepting that markets destroy communities, neo-liberals on the political right (for an example of which see John Gray, 'Hollowing out the core', *The Guardian*, London, 8 March, 1995) maintain by contrast that the impossibility of 'communitarianism' derives from the unviability/undesirability of state control over the market. For the heterogeneity of political and economic views subsumed under the concept 'community', see Kamenka [1982].
3. On these points, see Chapters 4 and 5.
4. Hence the current appeal of a 'communitarian' ideology to a wide spectrum of centre/right political opinion (for example, Democrats in America; Liberal

Democrats, New Labour and Conservatives in Britain) is precisely because it does not to any great degree question existing property relations. It is in short an attempt to construct a concept of 'community' that is compatible with the continued reproduction of capitalism. As Etzioni himself observes: 'But what about socioeconomic rights? What is the communitarian economic agenda? The short answer is, there is none. . . . Our agenda, so far, has largely been "cultural" . . . Cultural factors need attending to and are, indeed, at the core of the communitarian mission.' ('Common Values', *New Statesman and Society*, 12 May 1995). Moreover, the work of MacIntyre [1981] suggests that communitarian ethics are traditional and thus backward-looking, to be retrieved from an idealised 'golden age' of Medieval Christianity and Ancient Greece. Unlike the concept of 'community' which structures the liberal social theory of Etzioni, Rawls and Rorty, the same concept as used by socialists can have an existence only where all means of production are also subject to common ownership. Significantly, the attempt by current 'communitarian' ideology to establish 'community' without transforming property relations is itself prefigured in the views of agrarian populists in America. Thus for Lasch [1995] – as for Donnelly – the threat to democracy comes from 'new elites' which control not just information (= intellectuals) but also globally-mobile money (= international finance capital); again like Donnelly, the suspicion remains that what communitarians such as Lasch really fear is that 'the revolt of the elites' in the form of a refusal by the rich to recognize the existence of social obligations to, a shared humanity and common bonds with the poor and less-well-off will lead to 'the revolt of the masses'. Noting that communitarianism and populism both attach importance to small-scale property, family values and tradition, and each is anti-state and rejects the untrammelled freedom of the market (because this undermines small property), Lasch [1995: 92–114] accepts that both ideologies are essentially the same. In contrast to Marxism, which seeks to abolish both private property and class by means of revolutionary action, therefore, communitarians such as Lasch and agrarian populists like Donnelly [1960: 5, 66] want merely to reform the existing system and establish a 'brotherhood between classes' while leaving property relations largely intact. Evidence of this earlier communitarianism in *Caesar's Column* takes the form of, for example, appeals by Gabriel Weltstein to the ruling class to spare humanity, his defence of a clergyman preaching reconciliation between capital and labour, and the conversion of political conservatives to utopian ideals [*Donnelly*, 1960: 137–9, 167–71, 310]. There are also constant references in the film version of *Lost Horizon* to Shangri-La as a 'community'.

5. See Chapter 7 for the distinction between the aristocratic and plebeian versions of the agrarian myth as depicted on film.

6. This characterization by populism of capitalist crisis as the effect not of accumulation but rather of 'human greed' emerges most clearly in two of the texts considered below, in which the dystopic is a specifically capitalist phenomenon. In *Lost Horizon*, therefore, Hilton [1933a: 148–9] observes that the Great Depression of the 1930s which resulted from speculation on the financial markets was itself the consequence of people 'want[ing] something for nothing'. Similarly, in the case of *Caesar's Column*, the apocalyptic destruction of modern civilization is blamed by Donnelly [1960: 71–2] on 'human greed, – blind, insatiable, human greed – . . . selfish instincts, these have done this work!'. Such a theorization, in which the solution to the crisis entails not systemic but individual transformation,

is of course compatible with the continued existence of capitalism, albeit on a small scale. The theme of peasant-as-warrior, together with the negative consequences for the nation of this ceasing to be the case, is particularly marked in the agrarian populist discourse of *Caesar's Column*. Noting that in America towards the end of the nineteenth century the numerous uprisings by the working class were suppressed by 'sons of farmers', one of the characters [*Donnelly*, 1960: 96] laments that as the number of farmers had declined this source of defence can no longer be relied upon. The resulting situation is clearly outlined by Donnelly [1960: 97]: 'Hence the materials for armies have disappeared. Human greed has eaten away the very foundations on which it stood . . . when the Great Day [of the revolution] comes, and the nation sends forth its call for volunteers, as in the past, that cry will echo in desolate places . . . [there will be no] desire or capacity [among those farmers which remain] to make soldiers and defend their oppressors.' Of especial significance, therefore, is the fact that by proletarianizing yeoman farmers, and transforming them into their 'other' (= the 'mob-in-the-streets') finance capital has destroyed not only the peasantry (= warriors) which protected its own class power by defending the latter against the proletariat but also and thereby the nation itself.

7. Ignatius Donnelly, who was born in Pennsylvania in 1831 and died in 1901, was perhaps the most influential agrarian populist in the United States during the latter part of the nineteenth century. Like Chayanov, he was engaged in a wide range of activity; in addition to *Caesar's Column* Donnelly not only wrote books on a wide variety of subjects, but also founded a Populist newspaper, drafted the programme of the People's Party, played an important role in the Farmers' Alliance, led the Granger movement against railroads, and was a senator for Minnesota and a vice-presidential candidate [*Ridge,* 1962]. Together with his political activity and speeches, the fiction/non-fiction of Donnelly contributed to the construction/consolidation of anti-finance/anti-foreign capital, anti-state discourse that constituted the mobilizing ideology of farmers' protest movements (the Grangers, the Greenbackers, the Farmers' Alliance) in the mid-western and southern states of America over the last three decades of the nineteenth century, a mobilization that culminated in the formation of the People's Party in 1892. The mass appeal and hence political impact of *Caesar's Column* in the domain of 'popular culture' is beyond question; a decade after publication some 230,000 copies of the book had already been sold in the United States and 450,000 in Europe [*Ridge,* 1962: 267], and as Vann Woodward [1938: 139] has noted: 'Thumbed copies of Donnelly's *Caesar's Column* . . . were circulated from hand to hand. Those [farmers] who did not read them heard them quoted by those who had.'

8. Contrary to the assertion by Kumar [1987: 128] that 'the insurrection [of the Brotherhood of Destruction] is brutally crushed', it in fact succeeds, which for Donnelly (and populism generally) is the crux of the problem. However, the victory of the proletariat in *Caesar's Column* is short lived, and – with the single exception of 'the saved' in the mountain valley of Uganda – the world quickly reverts to a state of social darwinian Nature (starvation, famine, plague), in which three quarters of all humanity perish [*Donnelly*, 1960: 310]. The dystopic symbolism of both the building of and the form taken by Caesar's column itself is unmistakable: a pyramid of dead bodies covered with cement, it carries an inscription – composed by Gabriel Weltstein – commemorating 'The Death and Burial of Modern Civilization' [*Donnelly*, 1960: 274, 282]. What is being celebrated, there-

fore, is the destruction of a multiplicity of 'othernesses' which are the targets of agrarian populist discourse-against: the end of the proletariat and finance capital, the bodies of which constitute the column, of modern industrial society, and the death of the city itself. All are interred beneath a structure of concrete (= the building material of the urban) in the shape of a pyramid (= tomb of past civilizations, never to rise again).

9. Like that of Ignatius Donnelly, the written work of Alexander Vasilevich Chayanov is wide-ranging, and includes not just literature but extends also to cover rural sociology, economics, art and history (see the bibliography in Chayanov [1966: 279ff.]). Best known and most influential as an agronomist, Chayanov was a prominent neo-populist theoretician who took an important part in the debates about the nature and future development of the peasantry in the Soviet Union during the 1920s (see Chapter 1). Born in 1888, he was Director of the Moscow Institute of Agricultural Economy until the 1930s, and 'disappeared' in Stalin's purges at the end of that decade. The views expressed by him in the *Journey of My Brother* constitute an attempt to represent in fictional form the systemic effect of his economic theory: in short, it is an account of what a future society composed of and ruled by an economically viable peasantry might look like in practice.

10. The date 1984 immediately invites a comparison with the dystopic novel by Orwell [1949], and raises the issue of a possible connection between the latter and Chayanov, via the dystopic novel by Zamyatin [1977], not least because (as Deutscher [1955: 35–50] has shown) the plot of Orwell's *1984* is based on Zamyatin's *We*. The possibility of a Chayanov-Zamyatin-Orwell link arises from the fact that – as Smith [1977: 9–10] suggests – Zamyatin, who knew Chayanov, himself spent time in England, in this way disseminating via literary circles the utopic significance of 1984 that was subsequently incorporated by Orwell into his own text.

11. In this fictional portrayal of Moscow as it would be in the mid-1980s, Chayanov [*Kremnev*, 1977: 90] reproduces one of the central arguments made by agrarian populists in Russia during the 1920s, namely that: 'Thanks to its fundamentally healthy nature, agriculture had avoided the bitter cup of capitalism and [the ruling peasant regime of 1984] had no need to direct [its] developmental process into that channel.' Such a view contrasts with that of the Bolsheviks in general and in particular Lenin, who argued that the Russian village community was not a bulwark against capitalism (as populists maintained) but much rather had already been penetrated by this economic form, as a result of which the peasantry was disintegrating along class lines (see Chapter 1).

12. First published in September, 1933, the book had already gone through sixteen printings by August 1936 (the edition owned by this writer). Over the 40-year period from its publication until the mid-1970s, the combined hardbound and paperback sales of the book *Lost Horizon* amounted to some 3.7 million copies [*Hackett and Burke*, 1977]. Adapted by Robert Riskin from the novel by Hilton, the screenplay for the film has only recently been published [*McGilligan*, 1997: 469–575]. The 1937 film of *Lost Horizon* was produced by Columbia Studios and cost US$2 million (= US$30–40 million at current prices) to make; similarly popular, the film was nominated for four Academy Awards and eventually became a box-office success. For the background to the making of the film, and the quarrels between director and producer over budget and editing, see McBride [1992: 351–66]. Interestingly, a 1973 remake of the film *Lost Horizon* – but this time as a

musical – was a critical failure and incurred a financial loss; made just after the development decade, the message of the film seemed at that particular conjuncture to be irrelevant.

13. Although as Hilton himself has observed [*McGilligan*, 1997: xlvi] '[i]t was really amazing to see how [the screenplay by] Robert Riskin has kept the feeling [and] the spirit of the book', there are a number of differences between the book and film versions of *Lost Horizon*. For example, in the film Father Perrault is Belgian, whereas in the book he is of Luxembourgeois nationality; Hugh Conway, the main character in the book, becomes Robert Conway in the film; Captain Charles Mallinson, one of the two colonial officials in the book, is in the film transformed into George Conway, brother of Robert; and the character Roberta Brinklow, a missionary in the book, is in the film version changed into Gloria Stone, an incurable invalid. The film also contains an additional character: Alexander P. Lovett, a paleontologist (played by Edward Everett Horton). Significantly, perhaps, the only character who retains his identity and name in both book and film versions is the speculator, Chalmers Bryant alias Henry Barnard. In the book Robert Conway is merely a minor colonial administrative official (HM Consul) who flees a revolutionary uprising in Baskul (= Kabul?) on the north-west frontier of India; the kidnap flight to Tibet and Shangri-La is eastwards, across the Karakorum mountains. In the film version, however, both Baskul and the revolutionary uprising are located in China, Conway is now the British Foreign Secretary elect travelling to Shanghai, and the kidnap flight towards Tibet and Shangri-La goes westwards (but remains within the domain of 'the East'). There are also differences between book and film in terms of chronology: whereas the book is set in 1931, the film locates the same episode in 1935. The significance of the latter date is that it coincided with the Long March of 1934–35, a period that signalled the re-emergence of the Chinese Communists, and thus underlined the element of a socialist 'threat'. The year in which film itself was made is also crucial in reinforcing its warnings: the Marco Polo Bridge incident, which took place in 1937, marked the start of Sino-Japanese conflict and – along with the Civil War in Spain – the beginnings of the Second World War.

14. Since a horizon is by definition a place which is never reached, and thus like Utopia itself is a non-existent place, plus the fact that the name of the valley makes an oblique reference to a time ('once in a blue moon') that is similarly rare, the 'lost' element has a twofold meaning. It refers both to a double unattainability (that-which-cannot-be-reached either in physical or temporal terms), reinforcing thereby its element of mystical 'otherness', and also to a literal and symbolic opacity in relation to the surrounding world (= chaos).

15. For references by Conway and others to the economic depression 'outside' Shangri-La, see Hilton [1933a: 133–4, 148–52]. The metaphorical opposition between the 'outside' and Shangri-La itself is highlighted early on in the film when, following their rescue from the plane crash, Conway and the other passengers enter Shangri-La for the first time: outside the entrance a storm continues to rage, whereas inside it is calm and peaceful. This contrast is underlined visually by the astonished reaction of Conway himself, who first looks down into the valley and then once again glances behind him at the tempest on the other side of the entrance. The assumption about the pivotal role of Robert Conway, and hence the politico-ideological importance of his utterances, is based on the fact that Capra himself strongly identified with the character [*McBride*, 1992: 356].

16. McBride [1992: 355–6] misses the underlying element of continuity that structures Capra's populist discourse when he complains that, unlike the director's previous films in which positive solutions (a vindication of and a return to the 'common-sense' traditional values of the countryside) are counterposed to and overcome the negative elements (the corrosive effect of technology, corruption, and finance capital in the big city), *Lost Horizon* lacks a coherent alternative to the chaotic world Conway leaves behind, and is thus merely an exercise in escapism. Much the same point is made by Graham Greene, who claims similarly that Capra's discourse-against is merely unfocussed escapism. Hence the observation [*Parkinson*, 1993: 270] that: 'The director [Capra] emerges as a rather muddled and senti-mental idealist who feels – vaguely – that something is wrong with the social system. . . . it is useless trying to analyse the idea behind the Capra films; there *is* no idea that you'd notice, only a sense of dissatisfaction, an urge to escape . . .'

17. The box-office failure of the Korda film, *Things to Come*, based on H.G. Wells's *Shape of Things to Come* and the success of *Lost Horizon* is attributed by Brosnan [1978: 63–4] specifically to a negative audience reaction to the issue of techno-logical progress; in other words, a popular rejection of Wells's celebration of technology/modernity and a corresponding endorsement of the anti-technological/anti-modern themes projected by Hilton/Capra. Such a view is supported by the adverse audience reaction to the Orson Welles radio dramatization in the United States of H.G. Wells's *The War of the Worlds* in October 1938 [*Cantril*, 1982], when panic was generated not only by insecurity linked to the capitalist crisis but also the impending European war and the technological/mechanical means by which this would be waged.

18. It is clear from research conducted by Mass Observation [*Richards and Sheridan*, 1987: 96, 122, 127, 131, 132, 200ff.] into audience reaction to films screened during a period extending from the late 1930s to the early 1940s not only that the film *Lost Horizon* had a strong appeal to cinema audiences generally but also that the latter perceived an optimistic programmatic element ('uplifting moral vision') in the message both of the film itself and in its ending. This perception by cinema audiences of a programmatic aspect is evident, for example, from responses such as: 'the discussion in town after *that* picture's [i.e. *Lost Horizon*] visit shows that spiritual uplift is beginning to attract in pictures' (original emphasis); and '*Lost Horizon* [had] a certain amount of moral behind it'. Similar kinds of positive reaction were elicited by its ending (= the final cinematic 'fade out' in which Conway struggles back over the mountains to Shangri-La). In dismissing *Lost Horizon* as 'the typical middlebrow novel', therefore, Graham Greene [*Parkinson*, 1993: 426] unwittingly identifies one of the main reasons for its successful appeal to film audiences. On this point he asks rhetorically: 'What common ideas can be assumed between the middle-western farmer and the Cockney clerk, between the New York stockbroker and the unemployed man in a Welsh village? Few, I'm afraid, less vague and sentimental than the ideas of *Lost Horizon*.' (For a similarly dismissive view, see Morton [1952: 205–6]) Significantly, in his consideration of the way in which populist ideas were disseminated in America, Hofstadter [1962: 6] allocates an important role precisely to 'middlebrow writers'.

19. For the connection between Capra's films and populist ideology, see Richards [1970], Rohdie [1970], Levy [1991], and McBride [1992: 253–4, 259]. Capra, who himself invested substantially in land and became a millionaire by the end of the 1930s, can aptly be described [*McBride, 1992: 329, 382]* as someone whose film

oeuvre 'balances . . . Republican economic principles with a democratic fantasy of nonconformity . . . by and large, a safe nonconformity, without risk of adverse economic or social consequences and therefore a meaningless form of pseudo-revolt'.

20. In the version of *It's a Wonderful Life* scripted by Dalton Trumbo, one of the Hollywood Ten who was blacklisted by the McCarthyite House Committee on Un-American Activities (HUAC), no distinction is made between 'good' and 'bad' capitalist. As McBride [1992: 521–2] notes: 'Trumbo's George [Bailey] is a politician who rises from an idealistic state assemblyman to a cynical congressman contemptuous of the people he represents . . . [in Trumbo's script] there is no [Henry S.] Potter to serve as George's nemesis, for George, in effect, serves as his own Potter – a ruthless modern businessman who carelessly spoils the town for his own profit. The harsh, explicit social criticisms of Trumbo's script cut too close to the bone for Capra [who] retreats from the Marxist implications of Trumbo's view of capitalism, carefully balancing its unfavourable (and unbelievable) portrait of an evil businessman (Potter) with a favourable portrait of a good businessman (George) . . . *It's a Wonderful Life* paints the Bailey-Potter conflict in the Manichaean rhetorical terms of the Populist Party in the 1890s, showing the extent to which Capra had become locked into an anachronistic, and by then reactionary, thought pattern.'

21. See Hilton [1934: 70ff.]. Significantly, the downfall of the new headmaster Ralston is caused by his 'monkeying on the Stock Exchange' [*Hilton*, 1934: 80]; that is, entering into a symbolic alliance with ('Jewish') finance capital.

22. Someone for whom 'the world viewed from the haven of Brookfield [the public school at which he taught] seemed to him full of distasteful innovations', Mr Chips 'once . . . had got into trouble because of some joke he had made about the name and ancestry of a boy named Issacstein'; he is described not only as 'a conservative in politics' who 'did not hold with all this modern newness and freedom' but also as a person who 'whatever happened and however the avenues of politics twisted and curved . . . had faith in England, in English flesh and blood' [*Hilton*, 1934: 28–30, 41, 67–8, 77]. Mr Chips, Hilton [1934: 68] concludes, 'had been left a vision that grew clearer with each year – of an England for whom days of ease were nearly over'.

23. The new headmaster Ralston, observes Mr Chips [*Hilton*, 1934: 76,77], 'was trying to run Brookfield like a factory – a factory for turning out a snob-culture based on money and machines. The old gentlemanly traditions of family and broad acres were changing, as doubtless they were bound to; but instead of widening them to form a genuinely inclusive democracy of duke and dustman, Ralston was narrowing them upon the single issue of a fat banking account . . . Financiers . . . vulgar ostentations . . . all the hectic rotten-ripeness of the age.'

24. Despite conforming to a classical dystopian/utopian framework, neither *Journey of My Brother* nor *Lost Horizon* is mentioned in two influential texts on utopia/utopianism (Kumar [1987], Bann and Kumar [1993]), and *Caesar's Column* is referred to only in passing – and then incorrectly (see note 8 above).

25. For the political heterogeneity and the long historical lineage of discourse about the utopic/dystopic, see among others Manuel [1967; 1972: 69ff.], Passmore [1972], Finley [1975: 178–92], Manuel and Manuel [1979], and Kumar [1987].

26. For more about the pastoral and 'red-in-tooth-and-claw' versions of the agrarian myth, see Chapter 7.

27. The political trajectory covered by such arguments may be illustrated by reference to the ideological fusion of the ideas advanced by W.H. Hudson, H.J. Massingham and Rolf Gardiner (about which see Griffiths [1983: 142–6] and Abelson [1988]). The pro-agrarian/anti-industrialization views propounded by Hudson were instrumental in persuading Massingham to question and then strongly reject the desirability/possibility of modernism, progress, industrialization and urbanization. The importance of Massingham, a widely-read writer about the English countryside, is twofold. First, by arguing for the centrality to notions of 'Englishness' and 'belonging' of Nature, the aesthetics of landscape and the countryside generally, it was he more than any other writer who (re-) constructed the agrarian myth in English 'popular culture' during the inter-war period, thereby reproducing/ reinforcing the view that national identity was essentially rural. And second, this combination of a lament for the cultural decline of England, the nostalgia for and romanticization of a vanishing rural arcadia, and his anti-socialist/anti-industrial/ anti-urban views, led Massingham in turn to endorse the attempt by Gardiner – a prominent Nazi sympathiser and enthusiast of 'Nordic solidarity' – to re-invent what was belived to be an authentic 'Merrie England' through the restoration of the 'traditional village community' composed of cultivators and artisans.

28. Examples include Morris [1885/1970], Jefferies [1885/1939], Hudson [1887], and Forster [1909/1947]. The view taken here is different from that advanced by Fortunati [1993: 84ff.], who maintains that the structuring principle of these texts is the Biblical myth of the Apocalypse. Here it is argued that as important as the millenarian element is the fear about the way in which capitalism was transforming rural society; indeed, given the sacred ideological status of Nature itself in this discourse, and further the ideological interchangeability of Nature/'nation'/'sacred', this difference is merely one of emphasis, since both are variants of the same discourse. (For the extent to which current Hollywood films are structured by religious themes of Armageddon (= the end of time), see Ostwalt [1995].)

29. The same opposition between above/good and below/bad structures the dystopia of E.M. Forster [1947: 115–58], where an anomic, unnatural, undesirable existence – controlled by 'the Machine' – in the city underneath the surface of the Earth is contrasted with the long lost and now forbidden 'natural'/rural/desirable existence on the surface of the Earth. Although in the 1936 film *Things to Come* directed by Korda, the utopia of H.G. Wells is located underground – thereby transgressing this most fundamental symbolic spacing – this contradiction is resolved ideologically by locating salvation above ground, in the form of an escape by means of a 'space gun' to the Moon.

30. It could be argued that the physical location of Shangri-La actually *within* the mountain peak itself (a visual image that is very clear in the film version) signifies protection by the gods. For the significance in Germany during the 1930s and early 1940s of the 'mountain' film genre, see Chapter 7. The symbolic spacing informing *Lost Horizon* also structures a subsequent film, *Foreign Correspondent* (1940) directed by Alfred Hitchcock, for which James Hilton wrote the script. Escaping by plane to a neutral USA, the heroine tells her father, the treacherous head of the Peace Party, that she wishes they could both live forever in the clouds, thereby avoiding the war and chaos breaking out beneath them; that is, in the physical equivalent of a Shangri-La, high above the conflict taking place below.

31. Donnelly [1960: 7]. As with *Caesar's Column*, the above/good and below/bad metaphor in *Lost Horizon* also extends to include the opposition between dark

(= bad) and light (= good). In contrast to the dark and ominous atmosphere of scene in which Conway and the others escape from the revolutionary 'mob-in-the-streets' at the beginning of the film, the arrival in Shangri-La is by contrast bathed in light.

32. Donnelly [1960: 38].

33. That the utopic element of timelessness/agelessness was for Hilton a central aspect in the reproduction of an innate purity that dystopic time/age corrupts is reinforced by the fact that Mr Chips [*Hilton*, 1934: 86] informs his schoolboys that '[i]n my mind you never grow up at all. Never'. This in turn underlines what for Hilton was the multiple symbolic interchangeability of agelessness/ timelessness: Garden of Eden = Shangri-La = Brookfield. '[L]ike some baulked monster, waiting outside the valley to pounce', time in Shangri-La is represented by Hilton [1933a: 101, 185–6, 201] as an 'external contamination', a specifically Western and dystopic characteristic, whereas timelessness is presented as a characteristic of the utopic Eastern 'other'. A similar theme structures the Powell and Pressburger film *Black Narcissus* (1947), in which the spirituality of an innate and timeless Oriental 'otherness' overcomes Christian nuns who attempt to establish a convent in the Himalayas.

34. For these points, see Donnelly [1960: 26, 43, 95]. Significantly, the 'unnatural'/ Machine-controlled urban industrial civilization of the dystopic underground city in 'The Machine Stops' by E.M. Forster [1947] is also destroyed.

35. For the epistemological connection between a discourse about an ethnically 'foreign'/'alien' Jewish 'other' and the agrarian myth, see Chapter 1. Anti-semitic utterances occur throughout *Caesar's Column*. For example, 'the aristocracy of the world is now almost altogether of Hebrew origin', Jews 'are the great money-get-ters of the world', 'the real government is now a coterie of bankers, mostly Israelites . . .', 'Europe is a banking association conducted extensively for the benefit of bankers . . . The world today is semitized' [*Donnelly*, 1960: 31–32, 97–8]. This anti-semitism – a pervasive element of American populism (see *Vann Woodward* [1938: 431ff.]) – is not confined to observations about members of the Plutocracy: hence the vice-president of the Brotherhood, himself of Jewish ethnic origin, ultimately absconds with the funds belonging to the proletariat [*Donnelly*, 1960: 283]: 'He took several of his trusted followers, of his own nation, with him. It is rumoured that he has gone to Judea; that he proposes to make himself King in Jerusalem, and, with his vast wealth, re-establish the glories of Solomon, and revive the ancient splendours of the Jewish race, in the midst of the ruins of the world.'

36. On this point, see Donnelly [1960: 48–9].

37. The importance of 'Aryan ancestry', which is in turn equated with 'civilization', is made clear by Donnelly [1960: 242].

38. 'High finance . . . is mostly a lot of bunk . . . A feller does what he's being doing for years, and what lots of other fellers have being doing, and suddenly the market goes against him. He can't help it, but he braces up and waits for the turn. But somehow the turn doesn't come as it always used to, and when he's lost ten million dollars or so he reads in some paper that a Swede professor thinks it's the end of the world. Now I ask you, does that sort of thing help markets,' Barnard/Bryant observes, and when challenged by Mallinson that the money he lost belonged to other people, replies: 'There isn't safety anywhere, and those who thought there was were like a lot of saps trying to hide under an umbrella in a typhoon . . . the

whole game's going to pieces . . . there isn't a soul in the world who knows what the rules [of the game] are' [*Hilton* 1933a: 148–9, 150].

39. 'As for Bryant, whom [Conway] decided he would still think of and address as Barnard, the question of his exploits and identity faded instantly into the background, save for a single phrase of his – "the whole game's going to pieces". Conway found himself remembering and echoing it with a wider significance than the American had probably intended: he felt it to be true of more than American banking and trust company management. It fitted Baskul and Delhi and London, war making and empire building, consulates and trade concessions and dinner parties at Government House; there was a reek of dissolution over all that recollected world, and Barnards's cropper had only, perhaps, been better dramatised than his own. The whole game *was* doubtless going to pieces, but fortunately the players were not as a rule put on trial for the pieces they failed to save. In that respect financiers were unlucky' [*Hilton,* 1933a: 151–2, original emphasis]. Ironically, a recent financial scandal reproduces much of the symbolic structure of *Lost Horizon*: in February 1995, therefore, a 'rogue trader' Nick Leeson (= speculator Barnard/Bryant), accused of being responsible for losses of some £700+ million and the collapse of Barings Bank, fled eastwards from Singapore to Malaysia, where he travelled to Kota Kinabalu and took refuge in an hotel named the 'Shangri-La'. Unlike the Barnard/Bryant character in *Lost Horizon*, however, Leeson found no redemption in his particular Shangri-La.

40. Donnelly [1960: 36, 38].

41. Donnelly [1960: 37–8]. Much the same theme – blaming an ethnically specific (Jewish) finance capital for importing ethnically specific (black/hispanic) cheap labour with which to undermine an ethnically specific but indigenous (white or 'authentic American') workforce – is central to the discourse of American fascism [*Sargent*, 1995: 126].

42. Thus Donnelly [1960: 71, 123–4] compares the approaching 'universal conflict, savagery, barbarism, chaos' of working class revolution in New York of 1888 to the 1791 slave revolt in Santo Domingo, and notes that all the black workers in the American South are members of the Brotherhood of Destruction because: 'Their former masters have kept them in a state of savagery, instead of civilizing and elevating them; and the result is that they are as barbarous and bloodthirsty as their ancestors were when brought from Africa, and fit subjects for such a terrible organization [= the revolutionary proletariat].' Later the working class leader, Caesar, is described by Donnelly [1960: 149] in the following terms: 'his [Caesar's] skin was quite dark, almost negroid'. And when Caesar captures the palace belonging to – and in effect becomes – his 'other', Prince Cabano, Donnelly [1960: 272] comments: 'He [Caesar] was so black with dust and blood that he looked like a negro . . . his eyes were wild and rolling.' For Donnelly, therefore, the proletariat = revolution = black = blood/bloodthirsty = dirt = savage/wild = uncontrollable. That agrarian populism in America has a long history of complicity with racism in general and southern racism in particular is clear from many sources (see, among others, Van Woodward [1938] and Conkin [1988]). Significantly, the way in which black Americans from the inner cities are currently perceived by the white middle class as a 'problem' of an 'uncontollable underclass' (as theorized by Murray [1990, 1994]) reproduces much of the discourse which structured this century-old agrarian populist fear of the 'mob-in-the-streets'.

43. It should be emphasized that Donnelly is not unaware of the dynamics of capitalist

exploitation and oppression. For example, he observes [*Donnelly*, 1960: 39] that '[i]t was the same story everywhere. Here we saw exemplified, in its full perfection, that "iron law of wages" which the old economists spoke of; that is to say, the reduction, by competition, of the wages of the worker to the least sum that will maintain life and muscular strength enough to do the work required.'

44. On these points, see Donnelly [1960: 67, 161], who notes that workers 'are wonderfully intelligent . . . there have arisen, from among the very labourers, splendid orators, capable organizers, profound students of politics and political economy . . .'. The inability of employers to control a class conscious (= 'intelligent') proletariat is attributed by Donnelly to the benefits of state education, the implication being that the revolutionary overthrow of capitalism has in an important sense been made possible by public expenditure ('our taxes'). Interestingly, the latter point anticipates the argument currently advanced by many of those on the neo-liberal political right in metropolitan capitalist countries for cutting public expenditure.

45. As Donnelly [1960: 149, 280] makes clear, a proletarianized/brutalized peasantry is 'not natural' (depeasantized peasant ≠ warrior ≠ nation ≠ Nature). 'Brutality above had produced brutality below'; he observes, 'cunning there was answered by cunning here; cruelty in the aristocrat was mirrored by cruelty in the workman . . . [. . .] Crowds of farmers from the surrounding country kept pouring into the city. They were no longer the honest yeomanry who had filled, in the old time, the armies of Washington, and Jackson, and Grant, and Sherman, with brave Patriotic soldiers; but their brutalized descendents . . . They [de-natured peasants] were murderers not warriors.'

46. See Donnelly [1960: 92, 96], whose view about the political necessity of reproducing what may in fact be an economically unviable peasant economy contrasts with that of Chayanov, for whom the survival of the peasantry was determined by its economic viability (see Chapter 1).

47. An example of the dangers inherent in such a transformation effected by finance capital is the case of Caesar himself, the commander of the Brotherhood of Destruction. Originally a peasant farmer and a 'good' man, Caesar is transformed by cumulative, high-interest debt into his 'other', a 'bad' man at the head of the 'mob-in-the-streets': consequently, he 'who was once a peaceful farmer' becomes a 'brute' responsible for 'universal conflict, savagery, barbarism, chaos' [*Donnelly*, 1960: 71, 126-7, 190]. The moral of this particular fable is clear: the dangers inherent in tampering with Nature (= a 'natural' peasantry, which is 'naturally' passive) – which is precisely what finance capital stands accused of in agrarian populist discourse-against.

48. This hostility to socialism on the part of the author of *Lost Horizon* emerges clearly both in another novel published in the same year [*Hilton*, 1933b] and also in the 1937 film based on this, *Knight Without Armour*, directed by Jacques Feyder, which incorporates the similar theme of a successful flight from the Bolshevik revolution by a Russian countess.

49. Not only does he dismiss the efficacy of revolutionary transformation, therefore, but Donnelly [1960: 60–1, 65–6, 70–1, 256, 257] also describes the revolutionary proletarian 'mob-in-the-streets' as 'the molten mass of horror . . . sweeping away all this splendour into never-ending blackness and ruin. [. . .] A foul and brutal and ravenous multitude . . . dark with dust and sweat, armed with the weapons of civilization, but possessing only the instincts of wild beasts . . . Civilization is

gone, and all the devils are loose! . . . That which it took the world ten thousand years to create has gone in an hour'. In his view [*Donnelly*, 1960: 227-8], moreover, the building of Caesar's column 'was Anarchy personified: – the men of intellect [merchants, lawyers, clergymen] were doing the [manual] work; the men of muscle were giving the orders'.

50. For Donnelly [1960: 190, 258], therefore, the proletarian revolutionaries who constitute the 'mob-in-the-streets' 'have decided to keep all these fine residences for themselves! They will be rich. They will do no more work. [. . .] The difference is, they [the financiers] are brutes who are in possession of the good things of this world; and Caesar is a brute who wants to get into possession of them'.

51. Kremnev [1977: 86–7]. The fact that the earlier dystopia of E.M. Forster [1909/1947] is ruled by a Central Committee suggests that it, too, might be socialist.

52. For evidence of Chayanov's anti-Bolshevik/anti-communist discourse, see Kremnev [1977: 89, 90–91, 92]. In attributing the collapse of Bolshevism during the 1920s to a combination of socialist 'anarchy', the impossibility of planning, and an innate nationalism, and maintaining that communism 'removed all incentive [to] work' and merely reproduced the inherent 'servitude' of the proletariat, Chayanov not only omits to mention external factors (for example, the invasion of Soviet Russia during 1918–19 by Polish, British, American, French, Czech and Turkish forces in an international anti-Bolshevik crusade) but also reproduces the arguments about the impossibility/collapse of socialism advanced by those on the political right.

53. Thus it is mathematical rationality to which Zamyatin [1977] objects in his dystopic novel *We*. Much the same is true of the underground, urban dystopia in 'The Machine Stops', about which Forster [1947: 148] observes: '. . . Humanity, in its desire for comfort, had over-reached itself. It had exploited the riches of nature too far. Quietly and complacently, it was sinking into decadence, and progress had come to mean the progress of the Machine.' On the historical pervasiveness of anti-science ideology, see Passmore [1978]. As always, it is important to distinguish between two distinct forms of anti-scientific/technological discourse. On the one hand, a Marxist critique of science/technology as value-free technique, which points out that under capitalism it constitutes the productive forces whereby capital extracts more surplus-value from labour-power, but which under socialism could be used for social rather than private ends (for the benefit of rather than against workers). And on the other, an idealist all-embracing rejection of science and technology *per se*, as presented for example in the work of Shiva (see Chapter 3).

54. Symbolically, therefore, the (capitalist) machine becomes the method whereby capital consumes both land/(Nature) and ('natural') time spent working on this. That anti-technological discourse necessarily categorizes American populism as a form of conservatism is denied by Lasch [1991: 226], who observes that: 'Populists condemned innovation because it undermined proprietary independence and gave rise to "wage slavery", not because it tore apart the delicate fabric of custom. They had little use for custom as such, nor did they cultivate a reverence for the past.' Because it ignores the discursive imbrication between national identity, custom, tradition and 'proprietory independence' on the one hand, and on the other mistakenly regards non-specific opposition to wage slavery as politically progressive (rather than as motivated by fear of a potentially/actually revolutionary 'mob-in-the-streets'), this attempt by Lasch to de-link populism and conservatism fails to persuade.

55. Observing that the physical isolation of Shangri-La would prevent it from being 'contaminated' by the outside world, Conway points out that the word 'contaminated' encompasses most aspects of modernity ('dance bands, cinemas, electric signs, and so on'). 'Your plumbing', he explains [Hilton, 1933a: 88], 'is quite rightly as modern as you can get it, the only certain boon, to my mind, that the East can take from the West. I often think that the Romans were fortunate; their civilization reached as far as hot baths without touching the fatal knowledge of machinery.'

56. Donnelly [1960: 309].

57. Thus Kremnev [1977: 84] asks: 'Why the devil do you [Russians] expend so much human labour on the fields? Surely your technology, which easily controls the weather, is capable of mechanising agricultural labour to free work hands for more skilled occupations?' To which the reply is: 'Agriculture has never been as manual as now. And at our population densities, this is no fad, but sheer necessity'. Chayanov goes on to describe large-scale manufacturing industry as 'a pathological, monsterous condition' [Kremnev, 1977: 90]. For the anti-technological views (= 'machine-power multiplying') of those who rule Shangri-La, see Hilton [1933a: 190–91].

58. For these points, see Donnelly [1960: 13, 26].

59. See Donnelly [1960: 7, 141]. A recent text by Pieterse [1992] that examines the way in which images of Africa structured Western 'popular culture' unfortunately fails to make any mention of the way these pictorial/visual stereotypes were themselves reinforced by the references to Africa contained in Caesar's Column.

60. Thus the central character in Lost Horizon, Conway, is not only described at the beginning of the film version as 'a man of the East' but is said in the book to 'get on with' the Chinese, and to be reminded of China by the valley of the Blue Moon [Hilton, 1933a: 130]; for rather less idyllic versions of the socio-economic conditions 'enjoyed' by the peasantry in China at this time, see Buck [1930] and Tawney [1932, 1938]. Notwithstanding its literary/filmic impact on the domain of 'popular culture', and the resulting popularisation/reinforcement within pre-war metropolitan capitalism of the stereotypically timeless/mystic/Eastern 'other', Lost Horizon is not mentioned by Said [1978, 1994] in his consideration of the historical instances and dissemination of orientalist ideology.

61. For descriptions of utopia as 'the garden in the mountains' that is 'shut out from attacks by ice-topped mountains', see Donnelly [1960: 245, 299].

62. On these points, see Donnelly [1960: 7, 45, 105, 313]. Denying the grassroots efficacy of the agrarian myth, some revisionist texts now engagaged in the attempt at the political rehabilitation of the American populist tradition maintain, among other things, that it was not based on nostalgia but was 'broadly egalitarian and humanistic [on] issues of race and gender as well as economics' [Goodwyn, 1991: 42–3]. In a similarly sympathetic account of populism, Donnelly's utopia is wrongly described by Canovan [1981: 57] as involving 'a fairly socialistic program'.

63. For these descriptions of Shangri-La, see Hilton [1933a: 129] and Greene [1972: 148]. Much the same is true of the description in 1920 by Chayanov [Kremnev, 1977: 94–5] of Moscow as it would be 50 years in the future, where 'The passing centuries had changed nothing in rustic delights, and only a careful observer would have noticed the considerable quantities of preserved pineapple, the bunches of bananas and the extraordinary abundance of good chocolate. As in the good old

days, little boys whistled on gilded clay cockerels, just as they had done in the days of Tsar Ivan Vasilevich and in Novgorod the Great. A double accordion played a fast polka. In a word, everything was fine.' The recuperation/rejection of the 'primitive'/'natural' element in the film version of *Lost Horizon* is mediated through the four main relationships: between Robert Conway and Sondra, Lovett and Barnard, and the latter and Gloria, all of whom either remain in or return to Shangri-La and whose relationships symbolize the realization of an 'authentic' selfhood, and between George Conway and Maria, who deny this 'authentic' self-hood and each of whom dies whilst attempting to escape from Shangri-La. In the case of Lovett, for example, this self-realization is depicted filmically by a rejection of his own facial image reflected in a mirror on the lid of a Chinese lacquer box, which he shuts (= denying selfhood): having accepted Shangri-La, and decided to stay, he then opens the same Chinese lacquer box in order now to enjoy his own reflection (= discovery of selfhood in Shangri-La/'Eastern' artefact). The key relationship in the film is that between Robert Conway and Sondra: she is the one who suggests that Conway be brought to Shangri-La, and thus represents its desirable 'otherness'. Their relationship blossoms amidst the idealized rural imagery depicting the Valley of the Blue Moon: indeed, his initial pursuit of her through its arcadian scenery (waterfalls, lake) mimics the hunt in the classic pastoral, and his subsequent meeting with her takes place among similar bucolic images, after Robert Conway encounters further evidence of harmonious unchanging/unchangeable Nature in the form of 'natives' herding livestock and 'native' artisans at work. On this occasion he takes over from her the conducting of 'native' children who are singing, a metaphor for his inheritance of power over the 'natives' in the rural Eden of Shangri-La itself. Lovett and Bryant/Barnard also experience conversion and redemption in a similarly arcadian context: the latter abandons plans to mine gold in favour of an engineering project to improve the water supply in Shangri-La while the former undertakes to teach 'native' school-children (informing Chang of his discovery that the 'native' artisans seem very happy), again metaphors for transcendance of two forms of 'otherness' unacceptable to agrarian populism (finance capital, intellectuals). Much the same happens to the invalid Gloria Stone, who simultaneously recovers her health and discards her makeup, thereby signalling her rejection of the 'evil'/'outside' (= 'unnatural'/'corrupting modernity) by regaining her 'natural' physical/(spiritual) purity. By contrast, Robert's brother George not only persists in his desire to leave Shangri-La, an attitude signalled by his retention of 'western' clothing long after the others have 'gone native', but he also takes with him an inhabitant of Russian origin, Maria, who symbolizes the expulsion of the socialist 'other' from the Eden of agrarian populism.

64. For the civil war of the 1920s, the peasant revolution of the 1930s and the re-emergence of both abundance and the Russian peasantry, see Kremnev [1977: 75, 86–7, 88, 90]. Consequently, Kremnev [1977: 82] is informed, the situation is now one in which 'the whole area for hundreds of miles around Moscow is a continuous agricultural settlement, intersected by rectangles of common forest, strips of co-operative pastures and huge climatic parks. In areas of farmstead settlement, where the family allotment is no more than 8–10 acres, you will find peasant houses almost side by side for dozens of miles'.

65. In reply to his question about the origins of the new organizational form based on peasant agriculture, Kremnev [1977: 88] is told: 'You want to know about those

new principles . . . which peasant power introduced into out social and economic life. In fact, we had no need of any *new* principles; our task was to consolidate the *old*, centuries-old, principles on which from time immemorial the peasant economy had been based . . . Our economic system, like that of the ancient Rus', is founded on the individual peasant farm. We considered it, and still do so, the ideal model of economic activity. In it, man confronts nature . . . This is man's natural condition, from which he was exiled by the demon of capitalism' (original emphasis).

66. Kremnev [1977: 96].

67. Donnelly [1960: 26, 101–4].

68. For the existence of residual capitalist production in the fictional Russia of the mid-1980s, see Kremnev [1977: 91, 92]. The peasant regime which replaced socialism, argues Chayanov [*Kremnev*, 1977: 92], 'took over the management of the economy [and] immediately put in motion all the mechanisms which stimulate private economic activity – piece rates, bonuses for managers and premium prices for those products of peasant farming which it was essential to develop . . .'.

69. For the rural, ethnic and national origins of 'the saved' in the case of *Caesar's Column*, see Donnelly [1960: 225–6, 236, 242]. On the nature of theocratic rule in Shangri-La, together with the ethnic composition/recomposition of its ruling class, see Hilton [1933a: 123, 174–5]. 'Our best subjects,' observes Perrault [*Hilton, 1933a: 181*], 'undoubtedly, are the Nordic and Latin races of Europe; perhaps the Americans would be equally acceptable . . .'. Given that in *Journey of My Brother* Kremnev is himself mistaken for a visitor from America, the ethnic composition in all three agrarian populist utopias is roughly the same: European and/or North American whites.

70. On this point, see Donnelly [1960: 3, 292–3, 297, 302, 309, 313] and Kremnev [1977: 83].

71. The governing body of the utopia in Uganda is known as 'The People', and is composed of three branches: producers (peasants, workers), employers (merchants, manufacturers), and intellectuals, who hold the balance of power: 'For good purposes and honest instincts we may trust the multitude,' observes Donnelly [1960: 301–2], 'but for long-sighted thoughts of philanthropy, of statesmanship and statescraft, we must look to a few superior intellects'.

72. On these points, see Kremnev [1977: 89, 98–9, 100]. Should any organization defy or exceed the wishes of grassroots opinion, Chayanov suggests, it will be subject to the power of 'moral authority' exercised by these same grassroots. However, no mention is made of what happens in the event of a confrontation between competing but mutually irreconcilable interests.

73. For evidence of Chayanov's anti-state discourse, and in particular the equation by him of the state with the bureaucracy, see Kremnev [1977: 89, 91, 97–9]. On the question of exploitation of the worker by the bureaucracy, Chayanov [*Kremnev*, 1977: 91] claims that '[the] labour laws protect the worker from exploitation even better than the laws of the dictatorship of the proletariat under which a colossal share of surplus value was absorbed by the herds of officials in the Chief Administrations and the Administrative Centres'. For the centrality of this kind of claim (state = wasteful, unnecessary bureaucracy) to the discourse of agrarian populism in general, and in particular the new farmers' movements that emerged in India during the 1980s, see Chapter 3.

74. The *laissez-faire* principle structuring political power in Shangri-La is clear from

the observations by Chang [*Hilton,* 1933a: 90–91, 137, 139], that '. . . I should say that our prevalent belief is in moderation . . . [i]n the valley . . . there are several thousand inhabitants living under the control of our order . . . we rule with moderate strictness, we are satisfied with moderate obedience . . . we believe that to govern perfectly it is necessary to avoid governing too much'.

75. In response to an observation by Conway that 'there are many people in the world nowadays who would be glad enough to be here', Perrault replies [*Hilton,* 1933a: 234]: '*Too* many . . . [w]e are a single lifeboat riding the seas in a gale; we can take a few chance survivors, but if all the shipwrecked were to reach us and clamber on board we should go down ourselves' (original emphasis).

76. On these points, see Donnelly [1960: 245, 300], who notes that those fleeing to 'the garden in the mountains' in Uganda take with them 'a great library of books . . . literature, science, art, encyclopedias, histories, philosophies. . .', and then build a wall 'that would completely cut off communication with the external world', adding that it 'was a melancholy reflection that [the 'saved'] were thus compelled to exclude [their] fellow men'. This twofold course of action is also followed by the inhabitants of Shangri-La in *Lost Horizon.*

77. Kremnev [1977: 106]. See Chapter 1 for the late nineteenth-century connection between Slavophile populism, Russian nationalism and the defence of the peasantry against 'foreign'/German capitalism.

78. Hence the reply given to Conway by Perrault [*Hilton,* 1933a: 191], to the effect that '[w]e may expect no mercy [from the chaos outside], but we may faintly hope for neglect. Here we shall stay with our books and our music and our meditations, *conserving the frail elegancies of a dying age . . .*' (emphasis added). Asked by the High Lama whether or not he considered Shangri-La to be unique, Conway answered no, because [*Hilton,* 1933a: 210] '. . . it reminds me very slightly of Oxford [University], where I used to lecture. The scenery there is not so good, but the subjects of study are just as impractical . . .' Indeed, the parallel is exact, since in both contexts the object of existence is precisely to conserve 'the frail elegancies of a dying age'. This sense of the impending loss of traditional values which must themselves be preserved is reinforced by what Hilton writes elsewhere; describing the menaced tranquility of his public school in Cambridge (Brookfield = the Leys) during the First World War, he observes [*Hilton,* 1938: 44]: 'Behind the murmur of genitive plurals in dusty classrooms and the plick-plock of cricket balls in the summer sunshine, there was always the rumble of guns that were destroying the world that Brookfield had made and that had made Brookfield'. '[I]t seems to me,' concludes Hilton [1938: 49], implicitly contrasting an internal and idyllic pastoral/ (cultural) setting (public school/ancient university/Shangri-La) threatened by an external chaos, 'that Brookfield in wartime was . . . less barbarian than the world outside it'. This protective attitude towards traditional culture is also encountered in *Journey of My Brother*: the futurist painting that symbolised revolutionary socialism in Russia during the 1920s has been replaced in the Russian Peasant Republic of 1984 by a return to the artistic styles of the pre-revolutionary ruling classes [*Kremnev,* 1977: 77].

79. For the abundance of food grown by inhabitants in their own smallholdings in 'the garden in the mountains' in Uganda, and the presence of self-sufficient cultivators in Shangri-La, see Donnelly [1960: 310] and Hilton [1933a: 139].

80. Noting that the 'rising of 1937 was the last manifestation of the political role of the towns before they dissolved in the sea of the peasantry', Chayanov [*Kremnev,*

1977: 80, 87] observes that: 'In 1934, when power was firmly in the hands of the peasant parties, the . . . government, persuaded by many years' experience of the danger to a democratic regime from huge conglomerations of urban population, decided on a revolutionary measure. At the Congress of Soviets they carried through a decree . . . on the abolition of towns with more than 20,000 inhabitants . . . The factories were gradually evacuated to new railway junctions throughout Russia.'

81. See Marin [1993: 9–10].

7

Nymphs, Shepherds, and Vampires: The Agrarian Myth on Film

'It is, I think, a fact that any efficient director, when he gets down to making a film about the soil and the people of the soil, loses much of his triteness and mannerism, and produces something that is related to the simplicity of the earth itself. The nearer a film draws to the fields and the hills and the prairies, the better, as a rule, it is.' – An observation by the conservative film critic C.A. Lejeune [1931: 232].

'Noble Savage Syndrome: Thrown into the company of a native tribe of any description, the protagonist discovers the true meaning of life and sees through the sham of modern civilization . . . Such movies seem well intentioned at first glance, but replace one stereotype for another; the natives seem noble, but never real. They may be starving, but if they're noble and have a few good songs, why worry?' – A cinematic cliché noted by Ebert [1995: 78].

'In the end, he who screens the history, makes the history'. – An observation by Gore Vidal [1992: 81].

When in the mid-1990s the last Conservative Prime Minister, John Major, extolled the virtues of 'long shadows on country cricket grounds', 'warm beer' and 'old maids bicycling to Holy Communion through the morning mist' in support of his back-to-basics campaign, he was derided for adhering to outdated images of national identitity as rural. Popular culture, critics pointed out, had long since moved on, and now either celebrated or reflected different and more accurate kinds of non-traditional, non-rural identity. Perhaps without knowing it, John Major had invoked one of the central emplacements of conservative ideology: the pastoral variant of the agrarian myth, or a benign, a-political or politically neutral arcadian image associated in Britain with Ealing film comedies of the 1940s. His critics, however, failed to understand two things. First, that such images are historically far more common, far more durable and far less benign politically than usually thought. And second, that plebeian and aristocratic versions of the agrarian myth continue to structure popular culture in general and its most powerful medium, the cinema, in particular, where they have been far more dominant than is generally realized. It is on this second aspect that this chapter will focus.

In the case of England, this seemingly benign 1940s image of 'Merrie England', or Englishness-as-rural-arcadia, was projected in the films produced not just by Ealing Studios but also by Powell and Pressburger.[1] The output of all the latter endorsed most powerfully and effectively a populist vision of England and English culture as essentially agrarian and historically unchanging/unchangeable, an image fused with and supported by concepts of an innate and mutually-reinforcing Nature and ethnic (= tribal) 'otherness'.[2] Equally symptomatic, this pastoral image of Englishness-as-landscape/village/country-church is in the films produced both by Ealing Studios and by Powell and Pressburger counterposed to what was then emerging as an alternative politics of socialism.[3] In short, what was being reproduced in the domain of 'popular culture' was on the one hand antagonistic towards the implied socio-economic 'sameness'/'uniformity' associated with socialist politics, large-scale industry, and modern planning, and on the other a celebration of what was being projected as an alternative to this: its 'a-political' populist 'other', where the emphasis was by contrast on an 'eternal present' as embodied in an immutable cultural diversity mediated through the traditional (= anti-modern) rural community where difference was 'natural', enriching and acceptable.

Such nymphs-and-shepherds depictions of the English pastoral should warn against the appearance in the domain of 'popular culture' of oversimplified versions of the agrarian myth. Accordingly, film representations of the latter can be categorized in two distinct ways. As has been argued in earlier chapters, the agrarian myth is supportive of rural-based small-scale uniform/harmonious/'natural' economic activity (artisanry, peasant family farming) and culture (religious/ethnic/national/regional/village/family identities derived from Nature). However, it can be equally supportive of landlordism as part of the same ancient – and thus 'natural' – rural hierarchy to which a peasantry also belong. The first category of film, the peasant or 'from below' version of the agrarian myth is termed here the plebeian, while the second or 'from above' landlord version is the aristocratic form.

Both the plebeian and aristocratic versions subdivide in turn into two further categories. First, each possesses both a pastoral and a 'red-in-tooth-and-claw' variant. And second, both have a discourse about 'Nature under attack'/'the death of Nature', in which Nature is depicted as passive (= the object of agency), and also about 'Nature on the attack'/'the revenge of Nature', in which Nature is projected as active, and engaged in struggle to protect itself. These polarities are of course not mutually exclusive: not only can 'the death of Nature' itself be a form of struggle, which in the end combines with and becomes 'the revenge of Nature', but 'Nature on the attack' can be transformed into 'Nature under attack'.

I

Frequently encountered claims that film is the most advanced of twentieth-century art forms, in terms of both technological prowess and representational verisimiltude, and the most extensive form of popular culture in terms of audience, convey the impression of a medium with an innate bias towards modernity and political progressiveness. Such a view conflates the modernity of form with that of content, and consequently fails to comprehend the extent to which film, by its very nature, is able to enhance the claims to reality of a content which in material terms is non-existent/unreal. It is for this reason that cinema might be described as the medium not just of popular culture but of populism in general and of the agrarian myth in particular.[4] That is, a capacity to combine a technologically modern form with a politically reactionary content, and thus to project as real – and to persuade as to its authenticity – a set of images about that-which-is-unreal.

7.1 Film, History and (the Agrarian) Myth

Although socialists have always been aware of the role of the media in the class struggle, they have nevertheless tended to underestimate both the importance and the extent of its negative impact in constructing/reproducing/reinforcing/deflecting particular forms of political consciousness.[5] Hence the enthusiasm manifested among those on the left in Russia, Europe and the United States during the 1920s and 1930s for cinema as a form of popular culture that would contribute substantially to the political advancement/emancipation of the working class was in many ways similar to the current postmodern obsession with popular culture as a medium for 'from-below' empowerment.[6] Only later did politically progressive film criticism come to recognize that in a capitalist context the agenda of what constituted the 'popular' was set largely from above and not below.[7]

As many have argued, the powerful ideological role of film derives in a large part from a seemingly antithetical combination of on the one hand its capacity to fictionalize discourse, by ordering (or reordering) time, space and plot, and on the other the realism of the medium itself.[8] Where the agrarian myth is concerned, for example, it may entail depicting as 'natural' or immutable either the rural/urban divide or a given set of social relationships (peasants, landlords) found within agriculture. The control over the composition of sequence/narrative/characterization, in terms of projecting as acceptable (= real, 'natural') the kind of plots/resolutions that are in fact implausible, and *vice versa*, in turn confers on film the power to construct and either reproduce, challenge or constitute political meaning. This may vary, from the capacity to give a new meaning to an old event/issue/subject, to the ability to re-emphasize an old meaning already associated with the latter, or alternatively to introduce an entirely new event/issue/subject while at the same time defining its meaning.[9] When the reproduction of bourgeois social relations (and thus society) requires it, therefore, the object of populist discourse as projected through film is to remind, reinsinuate in and/or reinterpret for the popular memory a particular event/issue/subject.

As important is the agenda-setting role, or the capacity to foreclose plot resolution once problems have been identified, and it is in this respect that film discharges an important function in the formulation/acceptability of populist discourse. When it is no longer possible to avoid confronting an event/issue/subject, therefore, the ideological role of cinema shifts from denial to the projection of specific kinds of solution, a process that in effect downplays or precludes an alternative political outcome.[10] The result is to offer as plausible a solution that reconciles opposed interests, and thereby seemingly embodies the interests of 'those-below' (= 'the masses', 'the people'), which for Marxism amounts to the sanctification of false consciousness. Accordingly, the requirement on the part of film to 'smuggle in a [politically] respectable way of thinking', or a plot resolution/outcome that does not fundamentally challenge the existing socio-economic order, is nothing other than the classic function of populism as mobilizing discourse. That is to say, one that points in particular directions (compatible with the existing) and away from others (incompatible with the existing), or the construction/reaffirmation of what in class terms is a false (re)solution.[11]

This power to constitute/reproduce/recuperate political meaning – without appearing to do so – derives in turn from the capacity of film narrative to define salvation (= naturalize outcomes) in terms of values, unit and agency.[12] An important ideological aspect of film is thus to establish in terms of positive/negative attributes the kind of values (for example, honesty, principle, heroism, betrayal) associated with the event/issue/subject that is recalled, reinsinuated or reinterpreted.[13] This is particularly important where the agrarian myth is concerned, since the multiple object here is to underline the enduring quality not just of the values but also of the politico-ideological project (the 'naturalness' of tradition, family, kinship, community, the countryside, peasant farming, landlordism, etc.) linked to them.[14]

Because historically film plots have focussed on the agency of individuals, occasionally through whom the wider events/issues are ideologically re-configured, this has given rise to a reductive tendency akin to methodological individualism. Although the element of individual agency may operate in two very different ways, therefore, the focus remains on individual as distinct from mass agency.[15] A consequence is that plot resolutions are projected in terms not just of a particular subject but also formulated in discourse appropriate to this unit. Accordingly, the nature of the-problem-to-be-addressed also shifts, from wider structural/societal to individual attributes.[16] The result is a double decoupling of 'problems'/'solutions' from society and class: first, because 'problems'/'solutions' posed at the level of the individual are not necessarily those of society or even the class to which a given individual belongs; and second, because invariably cinema tends to represent individual 'problems'/ 'solutions' psychologistically, as innately 'human' ones that apply equally to everyone regardless of class.[17]

In this connection it is important not to underestimate two things. First, the extent to which film characters do in fact represent specific class interests, and hence the degree to which their actions are correspondingly those of individuals engaged in class struggle. And second, the way in which even those values projected by threatening/doomed/dangerous (= 'villainous') characters can in certain situations be made to appear desirable/attractive.[18] As the example of *Nosferatu* considered below confirms, the repulsion/attraction integral to the anti-hero is one way in which film discourse about the agrarian myth creates an ideological space for the construction/reproduction within the domain of 'popular culture' of political meaning in a manner that is supportive not just of populism but also of nationalism and fascism.

II

The plebeian or 'from below' version of the agrarian myth takes two forms: the peasant pastoral, and the peasant 'red-in-tooth-and-claw'. The peasant pastoral characterizes the three most powerful cinematic genres in the popular culture of western capitalism: not just the Hollywood western, with its emphasis on the frontier/pioneer achievement (= resistance) of the small farmer defending a stereotypically idyllic rural existence (against big landowners, railway interests, bankers and businessmen), but also – and more surprisingly – *film noir* and the gangster film.[19] This version of the agrarian myth also includes the 1960s films of Pasolini, and also films from the 1980s and 1990s, such as *Heimat*, *City Slickers*, and *Witness*. By contrast, it can be argued that post-war horror and science-fiction films as well as more recent ones, such as *Arachnophobia*, all contain a plebeian/peasant 'red-in-tooth-and-claw' theme.

7.2 Plebeian Versions of the Agrarian Myth: The Pastoral

Symptomatic of the way in which the peasant pastoral version of the agrarian myth operates in the domain of popular culture are the films of Pier Paolo

Pasolini. Although a sometime member of the Italian Communist Party (PCI), his work embodies both the contradictions and the discourse-for/discourse-against not just of populism but of its agrarian variant.[20] At the centre of his films, therefore, is a mythical/folkloric concept of 'primitive'/'natural'/ (unspoiled) man. Like Fanon and Marcuse in the 1960s, Pasolini romanticized both the peasantry and the lumpenproletariat, and condemned capitalism for undermining the purity of smallholding cultivation.[21] Again like Fanon and Marcuse, he also regarded the industrial working class as corrupted by consumerism, and argued that as a consequence the PCI should become a party of 'the poor'.[22] Much like Foucault, moreover, the attraction for Pasolini of the agrarian myth is linked to the issue of sexuality: just as the peasantry are part of Nature, a 'natural' form of existence under threat from capitalism, so a non-repressed sexuality in general (and homosexuality in particular) is also part of a pre-capitalist pagan existence, in tune with Nature and thus by inference 'natural'.[23]

Even the New German Cinema, which emerged in the Federal Republic during the late 1960s, and is widely perceived as one of the most politically progressive film movements, was not immune from elements of the agrarian myth.[24] From the early to the mid-1970s, the 'worker film' (*arbeiterfilm*) genre constituted an attempt on the part of directors such as Fassbinder and Ziewer to recuperate/re-present contemporary forms of a specifically working class experience by means of a realistic depiction of 'everyday' workplace relations and struggles as recounted by the subjects concerned.[25] Although the New German Cinema began with an ostensibly radical project of rediscovering the voice-from-below, therefore, by the mid-1970s a number of directors (Herzog, Reitz) associated with this project were producing films (*The Enigma of Kaspar Hauser, Aguirre Wrath of God, Nosferatu, Fitzcarraldo,* and *Heimat*) depicting not just a rural/historical version of grassroots discourse, and thus recycling ideological components emanating from the backward-looking agrarian myth, but in some instances also the reactionary forms of nationalism linked to this.

In the case of Edgar Reitz's film *Heimat* (1984), for example, it is the peasant/pastoral version of the agrarian myth that is recuperated. Like its Italian counterpart *strapaese* (see below), the German term *heimat* refers to films (and literature) incorporating elements of the agrarian myth.[26] Perhaps the most influential recent example of this genre is the mid-1980s version directed by Reitz who, like Hertzog, was an influential exponent of New German Cinema. An eleven-part film series shown on West German television, *Heimat* chronicled the life of three families over four generations in a rural Rhineland area, and was a critical and popular success.

Reitz's *Heimat* depicted everyday village life in this context between 1919 and 1982 in an unambiguously nostalgic manner, a rural idyll where a largely self-sufficient 'natural' peasant community lived in day-to-day harmony with Nature. Unsurprisingly, an effect of this (depoliticized) 'history-from-below' embodied in the film is the familiar one of naturalizing popular culture, and through this effecting a politico-ideological redemption of the grassroots as it exists at a given historical conjuncture. By focusing on and emphasizing the 'ordinariness' of peasants engaged in everyday activity, therefore, Reitz's positive film images of village life during the Nazi era have contributed to the wider process of normalizing fascism.[27]

Accordingly, in the case of Germany during the period 1933–45, this 'everyday-ification' of rural life under fascism corresponds to a double form of normalization (= 'every-deification' of the existing): explicitly in the case of village life/inhabitants, and – more insidiously – implicitly of the Nazi regime.[28] During the later episodes of *Heimat*, dealing with the post-war economic miracle in the Federal Republic, the modernity/technology associated with the latter is inculpated for the symbolic/physical erosion of the village ethos/landscape depicted in an idealized form during the earlier episodes. This sense of loss is reinforced metaphorically by a pervasive anti-Americanism; in the film those who migrate to and return from America are represented negatively, embodying all the unacceptable 'othernesses' of *heimat* (cosmopolitanism, industrialization, urbanization, the large-scale).[29]

Reitz's 1980s depiction of the Nazi era is thus no different from the plebeian version of the agrarian myth in German films of that period. The framing discourse of the latter, the audience for which increased dramatically between 1933 and and the early 1940s, was Nature, and in particular the way in which forests and mountains symbolize both Nature and nation.[30] The cinematic representation of such 'blood and soil' themes extended from extolling traditional/folkloric values and peasant customs as the basis of national identity, commending rural inhabitants for their closeness to Nature and the extent of their sacrifice (as depicted in the struggles conducted by villagers against representatives of finance capital) to the idealization of a specifically rural and timeless *volksgemeinschaft*.[31] This denial of historical time was an important component of other forms of 'popular culture' in Germany during the 1930s and early 1940s, when artistic genres such as painting and photography were dominated by anachronistic representations of farming without either machinery or agricultural labourers, reproducing thereby the 'traditional'/folkloric images of a self-sufficient peasantry.[32]

7.3 'I Believe in America . . .'

The peasant pastoral version of the agrarian myth, as embodied in the anti-thesis between rural/(= good) and urban/(= bad), also informs an unexpected genre of cinematic popular culture: *film noir*, with its fear of the loss of order and the shadowy menace of unseen forces (= 'the mob in the streets') in the American city. Although it possesses a variety of sub-texts, not least the fear of the independent female on the part of demobilized males, and can thus be read in a variety of ways, *film noir* underlines the 'otherness' and at the same time the desirability of the pristine rural, and thus simultaneously endorses dis-course supportive of the agrarian myth.[33] Because it constituted an expression of urban alienation, therefore, *film noir* also exhibited important elements of populist discourse-against about the threats posed to small-scale (petty-) bourgeois individualism by the large-scale (capital, the state, the bureau-cracy).[34] In this respect, *film noir* forms a continuity with, and in a political sense prefigures, what might be termed American 'red scare' movies, or the version of the agrarian myth in which the peasantry is depicted as 'red-in-tooth-and-claw'.

The thematic role of *film noir* as the 'other' of the agrarian myth extended to include the gangster film. Hence the negative portrayal of the urban under-world as a dark place where corruption, alienation, betrayal, and despair were the norm, to be contrasted as such with its 'other' the rural, depicted positively as the locus of redemption/light/hope, informs *The Asphalt Jungle* (1950), directed by John Houston. The main protagonist of this film, a petty criminal, not only exhibits many of the same characteristics (honour, decency) as the private investigator of *film noir*, therefore, but he also dreams about using his portion of the robbery to purchase the small farm where he was born. Betrayed, wounded and pursued, he escapes from the city and returns to die on the farm, thereby symbolically equating the latter with a process of spiritual redemption.

Elements of the same discourse structure what is unquestionably the most influential example of this genre, the *Godfather* trilogy (1972–90) directed by Francis Ford Coppola.[35] Like *film noir*, this version of the gangster genre is similarly informed by populist ideology: despite amassing/controlling sub-stantial power and wealth, therefore, its main characters are depicted sympa-thetically as no more than upholders of what are the simple/basic (= rural) social institutions and traditions (kinship, honour) of peasant life.[36] Although usually interpreted as a defence of the family and the romanticization of organized crime, therefore, each part of this trilogy is also structured by a variant of the agrarian myth. However, the latter is in this instance to be found not within the United States itself, where the narrative focus is on urban New

York and Las Vegas, but rather in rural Sicily.[37] This theme emerges most powerfully in the final part of the trilogy, where the redemptive desire of Michael Corleone to effect a transition from illegality to legality with regard to his economic operations coincides with the return to and an idealization of his rural Sicilian family roots.[38]

The film *Witness* (1985), directed by Peter Weir, is a recent example of the peasant pastoral version of the agrarian myth, in which an idyllic rural setting in the United States – in this case the purity/harmony of the Amish – is invaded by hostile forces from the urban, in the form of violent/corrupt/drug-dealing detectives from the big city. Significantly, the sole 'good' representative of 'the impure urban' – the good policemen, as in *The Wicker Man* (see below) – finds only temporary redemption in its 'other', the 'pure'/ harmonious/rural existence of the Amish, and finally returns to and becomes part of 'the urban', thereby underlining both the 'otherness' of the rural and simultaneously its incompatibility with the urban.

The film *City Slickers* (1991), directed by Ron Underwood, is a comedy about three members of the urban middle class who search for and find redemption in the traditional (= 'authentic') values of the 'old west' associated with rural America, and subsequently take these back to the city. Symbolically, the narrative is about how a jaded urban bourgeoisie finds its salvation by recuperating – and thereby reaffirming – the 'pure'/traditional values of rural America associated with the agrarian myth. This is in fact a variant of the familiar theme contrasting the impurity of the urban to the purity of the rural, and suggests that waning/depleted urban values can and should be reinforced by their still-relevant rural counterparts.

Although ostensibly about masculinity, male bonding, and the response of American men to a mid-life crisis in the form of an attempt at rejuvenation by undertaking an adventurous *rite de passage* normally associated with youth, therefore, the film *City Slickers* is also about the importance of the agrarian myth and its role in sustaining life and values in the American city itself. The story focuses on Mitch, a jaded middle-aged media executive in urban America who receives as a birthday present from his two best friends a holiday on a 'real working ranch' of the 'old west', and the opportunity to participate with them in a cattle drive. In short, a chance to 'come out city slickers, go home cowboys', and thereby regain his self-esteem.[39] And just as in horror genre the agrarian-based power of Dracula becomes transformed into that exercised in urban contexts by Batman (see below), so in plebeian pastoral film comedies such as *City Slickers* the urban bourgeois feeds off and in the process is itself rejuvenated by the agrarian myth.

7.4 Plebeian Versions of the Agrarian Myth: The Darwinian

Turning to the second, and darker form, of the plebeian or 'from below' variant of the agrarian myth, here too one encounters significant areas of popular culture colonized by film discourse about peasants 'red-in-tooth-and-claw'. Ostensibly, the theme associated with Dracula (and thus the aristocratic version of the agrarian myth), that of 'taking over' ordinary people close to oneself and turning them into 'other' than themselves, also permeated many of the science fiction films during the post-war period, where the concept of 'alien' operated as a metaphor for a threat from a specifically terrestial as distinct from extra-terrestial form of 'otherness'. It is a commonplace, therefore, that 1950s films such as *The Thing* (1951), *Them!* (1954), *The Quatermass Experiment* (1954), *Quatermass II* (1956) and *Invasion of the Body Snatchers* (1956), in which the prevailing theme was invasion linked to the appropriation of the human body, all had as their sub-text the fear of a 'communist takeover', or a situation in which the 'other' side is winning the class struggle.[40] As in the Dracula myth, moreover, this political conquest is effected by means of an (illicit) adoption of the form belonging to erstwhile friends, neighbours and relatives, or the very people deemed to be immune to its power.[41]

Significantly, however, in these films both the initial struggle against invading 'alien' forms and subsequently the seat of grassroots resistance to them are located in rural contexts that correspond to small-town America. This suggests a continuity not so much with the landlord as with the plebeian version of the agrarian myth: namely, the transformation of the peasant pastoral into its 'other' Social Darwinist variant, the peasant 'red-in-tooth-and-claw'. Of equal significance in this regard is the fact that such discourse about 'alien' invaders of the American countryside was extended subsequently in horror films to include invasion of 'the rural' by urban inhabitants generally and city-dwellers in particular.[42]

The same theme, that of a plebeian (or peasant) variant of the 'red-in-tooth-and-claw' version of the agrarian myth, resurfaced in the domain of horror genre from the 1970s onwards. The significance of the latter is that horror not only constitutes a form of popular culture that reaches a large cinema audience (= possesses a mass following) but also licenses a form of presentation which emphasizes dramatic impact and thus projects more effectively content (the immanence/sacredness of Nature, the 'revenge of Nature' and warnings about its destruction) linked to this. Accordingly, such films – horror and non-horror alike – depict situations in which a double threat emanates from Nature itself, one active, the other passive.

The first form corresponds to 'Nature on the attack'/('the revenge of Nature'), and includes those films which show how various components of

Nature (animals, the environment) actively strike back at human society.[43] With the horror film *Arachnophobia* (1990), produced by Steven Spielberg, about how the inhabitants of a small town in the United States fall prey to lethal spiders that are accidentally imported from Amazonia in the coffin of a victim, the 'revenge of Nature' theme combines with and becomes the-revenge-of-Third-World-Nature. Significantly, the house in which the deadly Venezuelan spiders make their nest, and from which they launch attacks against the inhabitants of the surrounding countryside, is that of the doctor, an outsider who has recently arrived from urban America. There is accordingly a twofold assault conducted by Nature: from its base in the Third World against the ('invading') United States, and by rural America against (an 'invasion' from) urban America.

In the second form, by contrast, films portray 'Nature under attack' or the 'death of Nature', in which the ecological system is radically transformed, to the detriment of a large section of humanity or indeed human society as a whole. Examples include most of the films directed by Werner Herzog, an important and fluential exponent of the New German Cinema.[44] These either warn against tampering with Nature or portray the effects of this on those rash enough to subjugate Nature/'the natural' both in European and in Third World contexts (Africa, Latin America). Unsurprisingly, his films are informed by an explicitly social Darwinist version of the agrarian myth, in which an all-powerful Nature struggles against and in some instances successfully resists attempts at conquest.[45]

Accordingly, films by Herzog are structured mainly by the related and variant theme of 'Nature on the attack', or 'the revenge of Nature'. Thus *Aguirre, Wrath of God* (1972), is about the way in which the Third World indigenous 'other' successfully resists European/(Spanish) colonization; Nature itself, in the form of the Peruvian jungle and the Andean mountains, contributes towards this defeat of the *conquistadores*.[46] Like the main pro-tagonist in *Aguirre*, *Fitzcarraldo* (1982) is also about the successful resistance on the part of the combined forces of the Third World 'other' and an 'untamed'/'untamable' Nature to attempts at European cultural colonization. As in the case of *Aguirre*, the Amazonian forest frustrates and finally over-whelms the attempt by Fitzcarraldo to build an opera house (= urban/European values) in its midst.

III

Aristocratic versions of the agrarian myth, or film images of landlordism as seen 'from above', can be politically supportive of the latter in a number of different and seemingly contradictory ways. One is the pastoral, in which the landlord is depicted as benign, and the countryside or peasant communities over which he rules as tension-free, content and harmonious. The inference here is either that there is no need for struggle between rural classes, or that landlords as a class are weak, and thus unwilling and certainly incapable of defending their economic position; consequently, they are unable to prevent/pre-empt their expropriation, should this occur. A variant of the pastoral is the conversion of powerful landlords into weak equivalents. As in the case of plebian or 'from below' versions, there is also a darker, 'red-in-tooth-and-claw' aristocratic variant of the agrarian myth, in which landlords are depicted as villainous/powerful/aggressive, and capable of undertaking (and willing to engage in) combat in order to defend their interests.

The first category, that of landlord pastoral, is exemplified by films such as *Gone With The Wind* or *The Music Room*, while in films such as *The Leopard* and *1900*, landlordism is shown as passive, almost harmless, and in an important sense 'not worth bothering about'. The theme of social redemption, whereby a member of an hitherto powerful and/or aggressive/combative/villainous landlord class willingly elects to reform him/herself and adapt to changed circumstances, not only becoming thereby a benign character but also (and significantly) retaining his/her property rights, is represented by the Tamil films starring M.G. Ramachandran. Into the second category, the 'red-in-tooth-and-claw' aristocratic variant of the agrarian myth, come films such as *The Birth of a Nation*, *Nosferatu*, *Dracula*, and *The Wicker Man*, all of which depict members of the landlord class as villainous, active and on the offensive in order to defend their class interests/position,

7.5 Aristocratic Versions of the Agrarian Myth: The Pastoral

The common theme structuring the aristocratic pastoral version of the agrarian myth is evident from a comparison of two films which in many other respects could not be more dissimilar. One is perhaps the best-known Hollywood film portrayal of the agrarian myth in the realm of popular culture: *Gone With The Wind* (1939), directed by Victor Fleming, a cinematic epic in which an idealized/romanticized antebellum plantation society is celebrated as a 'land of Cavaliers and Cotton Fields', a doomed civilization the passing of which generates nostalgia and regret.[47] The other is an Indian film, *The Music Room* or *Jalsaghar* (1958), directed by Satyajit Ray, which evokes a similar nostalgia for and laments the passing of a bygone age and culture associated with Bengali landlordism.[48] The plot concerns the futile attempt of an financially bankrupt landlord to outcompete a rising businessman in terms of cultural display, in the process losing his own life as well as that of his wife and son.[49]

The contemporary historical context is crucial to an understanding of the anxieties expressed by both films.[50] Although *Gone With The Wind* is set in the period of Reconstruction, it accurately conveys the forebodings connected with the capitalist crisis of the 1930s. It was, in short, part of the much broader and conservative intellectual reaction against the Great Depression, which among other things gave rise to the nostalgic and idealized vision of a rural 'world-we-have-lost' espoused by the Southern Agrarians; it is the views of the latter which permeate *Gone With The Wind*.[51] Much the same is true of *The Music Room*: although set in the 1920s, it is perhaps a more accurate expression of the concerns felt by Indian landlords during the late 1950s, when the historical position of this class was under increasing threat from land reform legislation.

The political effects of an overlap between the aristocratic pastoral version of the agrarian myth and populism is evident from the case of Italy. Notwithstanding the acuteness of agrarian class struggle in Italy during the 1920s and 1930s, films tended to underplay or deny this and depict the Italian countryside as a locus of class collaboration. This is particularly true of *strapaese* films, which depicted rural existence in terms of the agarian myth.[52] Hence the rural 'community' was idealized as the locus of indigenous virtue and a source of national identity, an ideological fusion that also informed the discourse of Italian fascism during the 1920s and 1930s, a relay in statement which in turn permitted the identification of anti-Fascism as anti-Italian.[53]

During this period many of the films associated with the *strapaese* ideology, and particularly those directed by Blasetti, projected within the domain of 'popular culture' the themes structuring agrarian populism, combining its discourse-for and discourse-against.[54] On the one hand, therefore, rural life in Italy is depicted in positive terms, a tension-free and virtuous domain where a spiritually-fulfilled and culturally empowered peasantry coexists harmoniously with landlords, while on the other the city – synonymous with alienation/'greed'/materialism – is presented as a context in which rural inhabitants who go there are betrayed and/or misled.[55] Such is the case with the film *Terra Madre* (1931), where the subsequent return home (in the countryside) by the aristocratic hero signals not only a disillusion with and a rejection of the urban and its 'alien' values, but also the reaffirmation/celebration of all those 'authentic' rural values (religion, family, hierachy, 'community', harmony) informing what is presented as an immutable cultural identity on which in turn the nation and nationalism depends.

Ironically, in the case of post-war Italian film, not only is the landlord class depicted as benign/paternalistic and unconnected with the rise of fascism, but this is a cinematic discourse the ideological construction of which has been the work of directors with Marxist sympathies (Visconti, Bertolucci, Pasolini). In contrast to the *Dracula* films, where a declining landlord class is engaged in struggle with elements of the urban bourgeoisie, in *The Leopard* (1963) Visconti portrays the landlord class as surviving-by-adapting, in the form of a fusion with a rising urban bourgeoisie, which then symbolically combine both to unite Italy (= nationalism) and defeat and execute the (mainly working class) rebels.[56] Much the same is true of the film *1900* (1976), directed by Bertolucci, in which the active complicity of the landlord class with the rise of fascism is not merely downplayed but effectively denied. Indifferent to the anti-working class activity of fascists such as Attila, and shocked by the murders the latter commits, the landlord Alfredo is portrayed as a politically weak and an essentially benign/humane character, whose socio-economic position/interests are unconnected with (perhaps even opposed to) right-wing reaction, and indeed someone for whom its manifestations (= 'excesses') are abhorrent.[57]

7.6 Winning by Appearing to Lose

The degree to which landlord pastoral versions of the agrarian myth are supportive of populist politics is also evident from the case of the south Indian actor-turned-politician M.G. Ramachandran (MGR), and the way in which the electoral success of his political party (*All India Anna Dravida Munnetra Kazhagam*, or AIADMK) and government in the state of Tamil Nadu was linked to a political persona constituted by his screen roles.[58] Despite the fact that the policies of his government were designed to redistribute income from the poor to the rich, M.G. Ramachandran retained the support of agricultural labourers and poor peasants with the result that the AIADMK was elected for three successive terms (1977–87). This contradiction can only be explained by reference to the film roles of M.G. Ramachandran himself, and their/his impact on the formation of political consciousness. From the 1960s onwards, his screen image increasingly invoked and celebrated traditional Tamil Nadu popular culture, in which immortal (= eternal) low caste heroes protect low caste property (land, females) against high caste villains.[59] By depicting himself as characters (agricultural labourers, poor peasants) engaged in an empowering 'from below' struggle against the oppression of landlords and moneylenders, these films enabled M.G. Ramachandran successfully to portray himself as 'one of us' in the eyes of his potential/actual political constituency.[60]

In political terms, however, this process is far from progressive or empowering. To begin with, the films of M.G. Ramachandran are not about the collective struggle of agricultural workers and poor peasants: in keeping with their mythic derivation, at the centre of these portrayals is the individual-as-hero with superhuman attributes/qualities, whose death consequently represents a closure not just of the character but also (and politically more importantly) of the struggle itself. Linked to this is the ambiguousness of the manner in which the 'from above' struggle is resolved. Accordingly, landlords as a class remain undefeated and – again, more importantly – unexpropriated: thus 'bad' landlords experience personal conversion, in the process not only becoming 'good' landlords who redeem themselves by seeing the error of their ways but also (and thereby) retaining their property rights. Most significant, however, is the fact that, because conflict is framed by ancient myths of traditional popular culture and folk theatre in Tamil Nadu (a discourse familiar to the audience), the struggle of the oppressed is not a forward-looking one but rather an attempt to restore a glorious past (= the Golden Age in Tamil Nadu), a central ideological emplacement of the agrarian myth.

7.7 Aristocratic Versions of the Agrarian Myth: The Darwinian

Unsurprisingly, the landlord pastoral is now relatively uncommon. The most usual aristocratic version of the agrarian myth on film has been, and remains, the 'red-in-tooth-and-claw' variant, and the earliest and most notorious version of this genre is *The Birth of a Nation* (1915), directed by D.W. Griffiths.[61] Like *Gone With The Wind*, Griffiths' *The Birth of a Nation* not only depicts the aftermath of the American Civil War but contrasts this unfavourably with an idealized image of life on the antebellum Southern plantation, a bucolic arcadia where kindly landowners are surrounded by happy and loyal slaves. Northern abolitionists and blacks are represented as intruders into this tension-free and essentially benign context, and the former are blamed for the ensuing disruption and conflict. Unlike its pastoral counterpart, however, *The Birth of a Nation* portrays the fightback by the Southern planter class, and its culmination in the formation of the Ku Klux Klan, described by titles in the film as defending 'Aryan' purity and 'the organization that saved the South from the anarchy of Black rule'. Justification for the latter takes the form not merely of racist stereotypes (white females in landowning families pursued by rapacious blacks) but also – and more significantly – the Southern conservative fear that northern abolitionism would convert their hitherto 'naturally docile' unfree plantation workforce into an uncontrollable free black 'mob-in-the-streets'.[62]

The most enduring variant of the 'red-in-tooth-and-claw' aristocratic version of the agrarian myth, however, and certainly the most influential, is to be found in the vampire legend. Perhaps the most significant ideological role in the conceptual framing of a discourse about the interrelationship between traditional/folkloric identity/values and Nature were German Expressionist films, an imbrication which according to Kracauer anticipated the rise of fascism in two specific ways.[63] Hence the emphasis of films such as *The Cabinet of Doctor Caligari* (1919) on the non-real (= mythical/supernatural) diverted attention from socio-economic realities, while the 'imaginary tyrant' theme – whereby authoritarianism is represented as the only alternative to chaos – paved the way for the real tyrant in the form of Hitler. The problematic nature of this psychologistic reading notwithstanding, it is the case that the sub-text of these films in general – and one in particular – does indeed lend support to an explicitly 'red-in-tooth-and-claw' variant of the agrarian myth.

The example which illustrates this contention is the film *Nosferatu*, a classic of German Expressionist cinema directed by F.W. Murnau and released in 1922.[64] It could be argued that this influential film is not just a metaphor for the fears/interests of a traditional aristocratic landowning class menaced by an ascendant bourgeoisie, in its struggles against which it invokes many of the themes associated with the agrarian myth, but also demonstrates additionally how a particular character projects the interests of the landowning class into realm of 'popular culture'.[65] In short, it is a film about a conflict involving the bourgeoisie and a landlord class in which an embattled Nature itself intervenes on the side of the latter (its present custodians). Not the least important effect of this filmic representation of the landlord class is a relay in statement (soil = land = Nature = nation = identity) that is supportive of its claims to be an authentic bearer of an indigenous Germanic national identity, rooted like the peasantry in the soil itself and also in the myths/legends/traditions that spring from this.

7.8 Reel Images of the Land beyond the Forest

Widely perceived as the epitome of the Gothic horror genre, *Nosferatu* is ostensibly a film about vampirism, the supernatural, and death/corruption/decay.[66] However, the film is also centrally about something else: a landed aristocrat (Count Orlock/Nosferatu) from the distant past (the fifteenth century) who has never died, and consequently whose power continues to be exercised in the present.[67] That is, about the refusal on the part of a member of the landlord class to cede political and economic control over his/(its) rural domain. Most significantly, therefore, the film has a twofold political sub-text, each element of which possesses its origins in the Romantic reaction against the revolutionary changes at the end of the eighteenth century. On the one hand it entails a shift away from Enlightenment rationality to a concept of the irrational/individual self, and on the other it is a discourse about the struggle by a declining aristocracy, whose rule over the countryside is threatened by a rising industrial capitalism in the towns.[68]

Thematically, the film concerns the way in which the supernatural power of Count Orlock/Nosferatu is rooted in the countryside, and its discourse is structured by all the elements of the aristocratic 'red-in-tooth-and-claw' version of the agrarian myth.[69] Although subject to decay, his castle is nevertheless protected by the local rural population, by the Carpathian woods and by the beasts which inhabit this: that is, by Nature itself.[70] In order to retain his demonic power, moreover, Count Orlock/Nosferatu remains during the daytime in an earth-filled coffin, again symbolically reproducing his link with the land and Nature itself.[71] His rural domain is similarly depicted as the locus of a supernatural power that is the object of folkloric myth/legend, and thus traditional/innate. That a landlord such as Count Orlock should prey on the peasantry in the surrounding countryside is, it is inferred, both a-temporal and 'natural'.[72]

This particular aspect is reinforced by the manner in which the vampire sustains eternal life: to maintain himself, Count Orlock/Nosferatu draws the life-blood of those around him, in the process destroying them, a metaphor for the quotidian appropriation by a landowner of surplus labour from his estate workforce.[73] Since those bitten by a vampire themselves become one on death, its power is reproduced and thus symbolically perpetuated in reincarnated human form. Although Count Orlock/Nosferatu dies, therefore, his influence (= malign spirit) does not, living on in the victims he has in turn rendered undead.[74] Most significantly, the film also charts the extension of this power (embodied, literally, in the undead) from the countryside into the town, the domain of a nascent and threatening bourgeoisie, thereby reproducing another central ideological emplacement of the agrarian myth.[75]

In contrast to the aristocratic (and plebeian) pastoral version of the agrarian myth, where the countryside is depicted cinematically in terms of light/tranquillity, *Nosferatu* represents the explicitly Darwinian variant, the countryside as an arena of darkness, death, violence and foreboding, a place that is Nature 'red-in-tooth-and-claw' as its current owners – the landlord class – struggle to retain control over it.[76] Like the pastoral, however, the 'red-in-tooth-and-claw' variant depicts Nature/land as eternal and sacred, an ancient/'natural' (and oriental) form of existence predicated on folklore/myth/legend which accordingly resists historical attempts to change values/identity linked to this.[77] Whereas the plebeian version of the agrarian myth portrays the enduring nature of the peasantry, *Nosferatu* by contrast presses the same claim in relation to the landlord class.

7.9 Sex, Death and Emancipation

Recent accounts of the resurgence from the late 1950s onwards in the domain of popular culture in metropolitan capitalism of films about Dracula stress both a break with themes projected by Murnau's *Nosferatu* and a simultaneous recuperation of an earlier, more authentic discourse. Not only is socio-economic context no longer as important, but the focus has now shifted onto the element of sexuality which, it is inferred, corresponds to a politically subversive (not to say progressive) discourse linked to the wider issue of women's liberation.[78] Since the late nineteenth century literary version of the Dracula story is equated with a challenge to Victorian family values, which repress sexuality in general and that of women in particular, its popularity in the highly successful British films produced by the Hammer studios in the period from the late 1950s to the early 1970s has been attributed, among other things, to a politically progressive discourse about sexual emancipation devoid of class content.[79]

What is not pointed out in such over-optimistic analyses is that the theme of a sexually predatory aristocrat has other, less progressive, antecedents which are entirely consistent not just with the agrarian myth and class conflict but also with the way in which sexuality features in films about Dracula.[80] Hence the *droit de seigneur* included the specific historical practice in Europe of *ius primi noctis*, or the feudal right of a landlord to the first night with the bride of his tenant, a form of landlord power exercised over females in a peasant household that is also consonant with the symbolic depiction of predation by a nobleman against young females.[81] Much the same kind of power has until recently been exercised by landholders in areas of the so-called Third World, reported instances of which range from the landlord class in the United Provinces of India at the beginning of the twentieth century, to the eastern lowlands of Peru prior to the agrarian reform of the late 1960s, and to village headmen in the Indian state of Tamil Nadu during the 1980s.[82]

It is unsurprising that, like Murnau, Herzog has also directed a film about the Dracula legend, *Nosferatu the Vampyre* (1978), perceived by himself and others as the version closest to the 1922 film by Murnau.[83] Significantly, a number of important parallels exist between Herzog and Murnau: each of them grew up in a farming environment, and landscape is central to their films. In Herzog's version of the Dracula legend, as in Murnau's, the theme of 'Nature under attack' is combined with that of 'Nature on the attack'. Herzog's film not only allocates an important role to landscape, therefore, but – like Murnau – his version of the Count similarly evinces power derived from Nature itself; Herzog also attempts to reproduce filmically the visual impact of the character as played by Max Schrenk. There are, however, crucial differences between the content of the two versions: whereas for Murnau the emphasis is on the terror generated by Count Orlock as the source of his power, for Herzog by contrast the character is a tragic one that evokes pity, even sympathy.[84] In short, Count Orlock, who for Murnau is beyond redemption, is for Herzog redeemable.

Most significantly, the character of Jonathan Harker, the solicitor's agent and traditionally the bulwark of resistance to the Count, is in the Herzog version bitten by Dracula and becomes thereby the principal source for the propagation of the latter's influence. In other words, in this particular variant of the Dracula legend not only is it the representative of the urban middle class who is symbolically overwhelmed by and thus finally succumbs to the rural based mystical/folkloric power of the landlord class, but the latter is presented in a sympatic light, as deserving the 'understanding' of the audience and capable of redemption. Although unintentional, therefore, the Dracula legend as depicted by Herzog amounts to a recuperation of the agrarian myth as interpreted by landlordism. The same is true of another film on the same theme, produced in the same decade: *The Wicker Man.*

7.10 From Feudal Vampire to Capitalist Batman

Set in the Western Highlands during the Spring of 1973, the plot of *The Wicker Man* (1973), directed by Robin Hardy, is about how a policemen from the Scottish mainland, Sargeant Howie, is lured to Summerisle in response to an anonymous note reporting a missing girl. In the course of his investigation, the policeman discovers that the islanders, who subscribe to pre-Christian beliefs, are faced with economic ruin due to the failure of the previous harvest. Thinking that the islanders intend to sacrifice the missing girl so as to ensure a plentiful harvest, Howie rescues her, only to find that it is he who is to be the ritual victim. The film ends with his death, burned alive inside the eponymous wicker man.[85]

The two main characters are one another's 'other'. On the one hand, therefore, the policeman, Sargeant Howie, represents the power of the state and gives voice to the discourse of science/rationality. By contrast, Lord Summerisle is a landed aristocrat who gives voice to the ensemble of meanings which structure the anti-modern discourse of the agrarian myth. Not only does he embody the durability of ancient and seemingly immutable rural tradition, therefore, but he also symbolizes the pre-Christian/pre-Scientific (= irrational/mystical) belief in the power of Nature. In a crucial scene involving both protagonists, Lord Summerisle explains to Howie that a century ago the island was purchased by his ancestor, an agronomist who not only introduced modern farming methods based on new varieties of fruit but also reintroduced paganism ('gave them back old gods'). In his turn, the present Lord Summerisle was himself taught by his own father 'to love Nature and fear it, rely on it and appease it'.[86]

The conflict between these two protagonists, respresentatives of rationality/ science/the modern State and irrationality/mysticism/ancient tradition, is the sub-text of the film. Like Count Orlock in *Nosferatu*, Lord Summerisle refuses to cede political and economic control over his rural domain. Having flown to the island, Sargeant Howie is informed by the first inhabitants he encounters that it is private property, and that consequently he cannot remain there without the permission of the owner, Lord Summerisle. Indeed, every- where he goes, Howie's authority is challenged/questioned by the islanders, and the alternative source of authority – that of Lord Summerisle – is con- stantly invoked. The resolution to this conflict reinforces the agrarian myth. Unlike the Dracula films, in the majority of which the power of the landlord class, in the person of the vampire, is (momentarily) checked, if not actually destroyed, in *The Wicker Man* it survives; much rather it is the representative of the state (and by implication its power) who is destroyed.[87]

This in turn underlines two crucial differences between *Nosferatu* and *The Wicker Man*. First, unlike *Nosferatu*, which is dark and threatening, and where the terror emanating from landlordism is explicit, *The Wicker Man* by contrast is light and (seemingly) benign. This cinematic distinctiveness underlines a crucial aspect of the threat posed by Lord Summerisle: namely, landlord-as- deceiver, or landlord-as-trickster. And second, unlike Count Orlock in the Dracula legend, the ideologically anti-modern Lord Summerisle is clearly a modern capitalist landlord, producing apples for the export market.[88] The apparent contradiction between Lord Summerisle's economic role and his espousal of pre-capitalist beliefs is hinted at towards the end of the film.

Surrounded by the islanders, Howie begs for his freedom, telling them that the crop failure of the previous year was due not to unappeased gods of Nature but rather to the unadaptability of new fruit varieties to the island soil. Howie's final words before being imprisoned in the wicker man are to warn that, in the event of further harvest failures, the island workforce will turn on Lord Summerisle himself. Not only does the representative of the state attempt to counter the irrationalism of a mystical explanation with the rationality of a scientific one, therefore, but in doing so he also reveals the way in which the agrarian myth fuses with populism, and why: namely, the attempt by Lord Summerisle to deflect blame for an existing or potential crisis (crop failure) from economic causes (property relations, landlordism) to non-economic ones (the appeasement of ancient deities, in the process reaffirming the innateness of 'natural' identity based on an immutable Nature), the object being to secure the reproduction of the existing social order.[89]

Like landlords in many different historical contexts, the most recent mani-festations of the aristocratic 'red-in-tooth-and-claw' version of the cinematic agrarian myth suggest not only that landlords have become capitalists but also that their rural power base has now extended into the city. Films such as Tim Burton's *Batman* (1989) and *Batman Returns* (1992) represent the outcome of this process, or the fusion of the European Dracula legend with American *film noir*. Unlike other cinema 'superheroes' of the 1980s and 1990s, the characterization of Batman/Bruce Wayne in terms of 'good'/'bad' is deliberately ambiguous ('he is as dangerous for Gotham city as the Joker . . .'), thereby reproducing one of the main elements of the Dracula myth (hero/anti-hero). Not only is Batman/Bruce Wayne depicted/described as a 'winged vigilante' who attacks and kills petty criminals, therefore, but the parallels with Dracula/Nosferatu are explicit ('They say he can't be killed, that he drinks blood . . .').[90] A seemingly domesticated Count Orlock, still disguised as a bat but with his socio-economic power intact, can now exercise this same mythical/individual force/(terror) over the urban dystopia of Gotham city, but in a populist manner so as to ensure the reproduction of the existing social order in the town as well as in the countryside. Unlike the vampire of legend and earlier films such as *Nosferatu*, where the power of the urban bourgeois constitutes a threat, in *Batman* the hero/anti-hero has himself become part of that power.

7.11 Conclusion

As projected through the medium of popular film culture, the agrarian myth is about the desirability of redemption linked to the innateness of Nature and thus rural existence and traditional identities based on this. In the 'red-in-tooth-and-claw' variant of the agrarian myth, in both its plebeian and aristocratic forms, power not only emanates from the native soil, but is symbolically and constantly replenished by violence and bloodletting. Generally speaking, the powerful-landlordism variant tends to coincide with the 'red-in-tooth-and-claw' image of Nature, while the weak-landlordism version by contrast is compatible with the pastoral vision of Nature. In the former, landlordism exercises a reign of terror over a subordinate peasantry, whereas in the latter members of the landlord class are not presented as a threat to peasants, with whom consequently they coexist harmoniously.

What is important, therefore, is the fact that the ideological sub-text inform-ing the pastoral and 'red-in-tooth-and-claw' variants of the agrarian myth is in both cases the same. Each asserts the 'naturalness' of tradition and identity based on blood (= family/kinship/ethnicity/nationalism) and soil (= the rural), and simultaneously celebrates violence as an equally 'natural' defence of such attributes. Accordingly, in both the aristocratic and plebeian versions of the agrarian myth, the 'red-in-tooth-and-claw' variant is a defence of the ideological viability of the pastoral, and an attempt to restore to Nature the harmony and tranquillity of latter form, thereby making 'natural' once again the ahistorical rural identities of landlord and peasant.

The apparently distinct versions of the agrarian myth are thus more accurately interpreted as two points on the same continuum, in that landlords prefer (and indeed propagate) the pastoral version, since here their rule is not challenged, but will fight any attempts to change this, either by the peasantry or by non-rural elements in the urban sector. As a result of this conflict, either the pastoral image of Nature is transformed into its 'other', the 'red-in-tooth-and-claw' variant characterized by struggle, or the latter is converted into the former. In either case, peasants and the peasantry, or landlordism and landlords as a class, remain intact. In other words, the reaffirmation of that rural essentialism proclaimed by the agrarian myth.

The significance of the agrarian myth for film lies in the fact that much recent analysis of this medium has tended to eschew history and politics. Consequently, film has been seen either as a self-referential, hermetic language, or as devoid of fixed symbolic meaning. In contrast to such views, which dehistoricize and thus depoliticize the analysis of film content, it has been argued in this chapter that important elements both of the agrarian myth and of populist discourse continue to pervade film, in particular the sense of loss of identity as embodied in alienation from the city, (= the state, industry, corruption and social decay). This sense of loss is in turn coupled (explicitly or implicitly) with a nostalgia for the contrasting purity/values of the countryside, the locus of an authentic (and thus non-alienated) identity.

The difficulty this poses for popular culture is that such a project of innateness based on the antithesis between rural = good and urban = bad has been and remains an important ideological emplacement of the political right (see Chapters 1 and 5). Although the presence of a town/countryside divide is noted in passing by some film criticism, therefore, the political sub-text informing this dichotomy is rarely revealed, let alone interrogated. If a discourse which happens to be conservative is labelled as 'authentic' – regardless of whether or not it emanates from the grassroots – then what ends up being celebrated in the domain of 'popular culture' is precisely a conservative politics.

NOTES

1. It should be emphasized that the films produced by Powell and Pressburger themselves belonged to a much wider – though less 'popular' – cultural phenomenon:

namely, British Neo-Romanticism. The latter movement, which lasted from the mid-1930s until the mid-1950s, was characterized by a rejection of materialism and a corresponding aesthetic nostalgia for a vanishing landscape, its mythology and enduring (= 'natural') values, and consequently an accompanying sense of spiritual loss, sentiments embodied in the work of painters such as John Craxton, Leslie Hurry and Cecil Collins as well as better-known artists like John Minton, Graham Sutherland and John Piper. As has been noted by Mellor [1987: 9], the current recuperation by postmodernism of this earlier Neo-Romantic cultural framework is to a large degree premissed on a shared epistemology.

2. For the films of Powell and Pressburger, see Durgnat [1970], Christie [1978, 1985] and Aldred [1987]; for those produced by Ealing Studios, see Barr [1974, 1977] and Ellis [1975]. This 'Merrie England' imagery is particularly evident in Powell and Pressburger films such as A Canterbury Tale (1944), a nostalgic invocation of an ever-present/ever-powerful English pastoral that erases history in the name of myth and nostalgia for a rural 'golden age', and I Know Where I'm Going (1945), which projects a similar theme in the form of a heroine who rejects marriage to an industrialist (= modernity, manufacturing) in order to marry a landowner (= tradition, agriculture). Much the same is true of the films produced by Ealing Studios, which reproduce stereotypically populist images of 'community'. As noted by Barr [1977: 5]: 'Asked to invent a typical Ealing comedy plot, one might produce something like this. A big brewery tries to absorb a small competitor, a family firm which is celebrating its 150th anniversary. The offer is gallantly refused, whereupon the boss's son goes incognito from the big firm to infiltrate the small one and sabotage its fortunes. Gradually, he is charmed by the family brewery and by the daughter of the house, saves the company from ruin, and marries into it. Officials and workers unite at the wedding banquet to drink the couple's health in a specially created brew. To make it really Ealing, lay on the contrasts. The brewery names: Ironside against Greenleaf. Grim offices and black limousines against country lanes, ivy-covered cottages, horses, bicycles. Autocratic rule against the benevolent paternalism of a grey-haired old man who collects Toby Jugs. The beer itself: quantity against quality, machines against craftsmanship. The people and their manners: very harsh, very gentle. Small is beautiful.' 'This', Barr concludes, 'it will be guessed, is no invention. The film is called Cheer Boys Cheer, and Balcon produced it at Ealing in 1939'. That such arcadian views find an echo in the views of Conservatives about the nature of the postwar settlement is clear from the description of the latter by one such [Amery, 1944: 153] as '[a] beauty-loving Merrie England'.

3. In the film A Matter of Life and Death (1946), therefore, Powell and Pressburger draw a visual and politico-ideological contrast between an arcadian technicolour England and a monochrome heaven, the latter representing a vision of what for them was an unacceptable socialist utopia (on which see Christie [1985: 78]). On this point Durgnat [1970: 29, 30] comments: '[this film] is generally taken as an extravaganza, a vague, eccentric, enjoyable contraption advocating closer ties with the USA. But the politics of this "Halfway Heaven" are far more precise. They express perennial Tory criticisms of the Socialist Utopia – that is, the Welfare State. [. . .] This Heaven is a futurist Utopia. It's a planned society. It's machine-like . . . Heaven's values are those of the collectivity . . . Planned, bureaucratic, idealistic, totalitarian, colourless, theoretic – all these are the words Tories like to use of Socialism. Once again, we come to a city, and we opt out.' Similarly, in the

Ealing Studio film *Passport to Pimlico* (1949) a small-scale community (= urban village) declares its independence not just from the larger and thus bureaucratic British state but also and thereby from socialism, in the process reinventing an 'a-political' wartime unity and inaugurating free enterprise by eliminating rationing and controls [*Barr, 1977*: 94–107].

4. There are, of course, exceptions to this general rule. A recent one is the film *Land and Freedom* (1995), directed by Ken Loach, in which the complexities of agrarian reform in Spain during the Civil War are depicted in a dramatic fashion (a political debate between the protagonists) unconnected with the plebeian version of the agrarian myth (for the director's own views about this, see Fuller [1998: 102–4]).

5. As Raymond Williams [*Britton, 1991*: 106] reminds us: 'What was often not noticed on the left, and is perhaps not fully noticed even today, is that there are others besides radicals and democrats who are interested in being popular. What was supposed to be a monopoly in one selected sense of the people fighting for their rights and freedoms, turned out to be very different . . . Certainly radicals and democrats fought for the new [media] forms and the new freedoms, but so did commercial entrepreneurs [and] capitalists from that day to this. They saw their own versions of possibility in the new technologies, the new audiences which were being formed . . .'

6. Hence the importance attached by the Bolsheviks to the role of film in the construction of a new economic and political identity for the Russian peasant. For a description by Vertov of the impact of cinema on Russian peasants during the 1920s, see Michelson [1984: 51, 52, 60–2]. This political role became crucial during the collectivization of the 1930s, as evidence by films such as *Earth* (1930) directed by Dovzhenko, *Peasants* (1935) by Ermler, *Snatchers* (1935) by Medvedkin, and Eisenstein's *The General Line* (1928) and *Bezhin Meadow* (1937) [*Leyda, 1960*: 325–26; *Charrière et al., 1974*: 69ff., 89ff.; *Eisenstein, 1987*: 38–58]. An example of prematurely over-optimistic political judgement about the necessarily progressive political character of film is Kracauer [1995: 24], who thought initially, and mistakenly, that – where capitalism was concerned – cinema always 'exposes disintegration instead of masking it'.

7. Noting that '[n]o historical situation has ever found a more direct expression . . . than the crisis of capitalism . . . did in this montage technique', Hauser [1982: 625–6] cautioned that '. . . the identification of the phenomena juxtaposed sometimes becomes so dead in the process that dialectic threatens to degenerate into an empty series of metaphors. Moreover, we must not forget that the photographic technique of the film with its interest in detail and its preference for real props meets the materialism of the reflection of reality halfway. Yet it still remains questionable whether the whole technique of placing the props in the foreground is not itself the product of an already existing materialism rather than a process of conditioning such a materialism.'

8. On these points, see Eisenstein [1943], Pudovkin [1958], Arnheim [1933] Potamkin [*Jacobs, 1977*], and Kracauer [1960; 1995]. The centrality to film of time/space/plot reordering is outlined in the theory of editing/montage associated with the work of Eisenstein and Pudovkin.

9. In this connection, it is impossible to overlook the important political role of film music in the reproduction of ideological forms (the longing for, 'belonging' to, and celebration of nationalism/religion/Nature) that are themselves supportive of the

agrarian myth. Nowhere perhaps is this crucial function more evident than the way in which the music produced for the Hollywood cinema during the 1930s and 1940s was a pastiche of (and thus reproduced the nostalgia inherent in) its nineteenth century Romantic variant [*Flinn*, 1992]. Since the interpretation by the audience of the cinematic image is to an important degree structured by an accompanying melody the imperceptibility of which makes such ideological framing all the more effective, the resulting 'innocence'/'naturalness' of the music permits a powerful emotional conditioning of the visual experience in terms of its dramatic/spiritual/mythic/real/positive/negative meaning.

10. Hence the capacity to compose the 'reality' both of the problem-to-be-solved and of the solution itself, while at the same time denying/downplaying the very process of ideological construction, results in 'naturalizing' not just the resulting discourse but the political outcome.

11. This point was made by Kracauer [1995: 291] during the 1920s, when he highlighted the basic contradiction posed by commercial pressure on film-makers in capitalist contexts: the need to offer the cinema audience (of workers) hope by providing a critique of the existing society without simultaneously subverting capitalism itself. For this reason, he observes [*Kracauer*, 1995: 291–2], 'the films made for the lower classes are even more bourgeois than those aimed at the finer audiences . . . they smuggle in a respectable way of thinking [and] give the blackest settings a pink tinge, and smear reds liberally everywhere'.

12. This entails a capacity to propose as inevitable (= 'natural') a benign/malign outcome which in reality would not occur, as encapsulated both in positive thematic stereotypes (such as 'justice always prevails', 'the little man always wins', and 'good always conquers evil', etc.) and in equally improbable plot resolutions that are negative ('socialist revolutions always fail', 'the crowd is always irrational', etc.).

13. This may extend from the reinforcement of values/authority under threat (as in the case of *Nosferatu*; see below), and either challenging politically unfavourable interpretations or endorsing favourable ones of specific events, to the recuperation of events/issues/subjects regarded as no longer relevant.

14. In the case of 1930s Japan, for example, cinematic representations of the agrarian myth involved the defence of rural tradition and nationalism, as embodied in the peasant/soldier alliance (with its themes of the poverty and betrayal of them both). This discourse was projected in films such as *Earth* (1939), chronicling the struggle to survive by peasant farmers, *Man-Slashing, Horse-Piercing Sword* (1930), the theme of which is a soldier who first steals from and then unites with poor farmers in a common struggle against an oppressive government, and also *Humanity and Paper Balloons* (1937), in which a samurai warrior, rather than dying gloriously in battle, has to sell his sword to buy rice and then commits suicide in a dishonourable fashion. For these films, see Richie [1972: 43–4, 45, 51], who does not himself make these points. For similar themes of 'peasant-as-warrior-defending-the-nation', see Chapter 7.

15. On the one hand, therefore, an individual member of the working class succeeds in improving his/her own particular situation, but the structure itself remains intact. On the other hand, where structural change does occur, it is attributed not to mass agency but to individual endeavour. Either way, agency and change which follows from its exercise is attributed to the individual and not to the mass.

16. There are of course many examples of films the plot of which have been shifted

from wider political concerns to individual issues, a process that can occur at any one of three stages: the transition from book to film script (*Passage to India*), from the latter to the film itself (*Lawrence of Arabia, Reds*), and from the produced to the distributed version of the film (*Spartacus*). An example of the shift of emphasis in the course of a transition from book to film is E.M. Forster's *Passage to India* as filmed in 1984 by David Lean. As one commentator [*Couto*, 1986: 10] has noted, Lean 'does away with the political framework of the novel altogether and reduces it to a racial confrontation to illustrate cultural differences and to define codes that reiterate the white man's ethic'. An example of the same kind of transition effected between the production and distribution of a film is *Spartacus* (1960), directed by Stanley Kubrick and scripted by Dalton Trumbo, where the (ultimately unsuccessful) attempt by slaves to obtain their freedom from Rome is situated within the narrative about a developing relationship between two individual ex-slaves, Spartacus himself and Varinia. However, recently restored cuts indicate that originally the film was as much about political struggles within Rome itself, involving the democratic impulse of Gracchus and the attempt by Crassus to establish a patrician dictatorship, as about the slave rebellion against Rome or the love between Spartacus and Varinia. The same transition effected between script and filming is *Lawrence of Arabia* (1962), again directed by David Lean, the screeplay of which underwent substantial rewriting and consequently re-emphasis. The intial script was written by Michael Wilson, a blacklisted American communist living in exile, while the final version was produced by an English playwright, Robert Bolt. The difference between these two versions is outlined in Turner [1994: 73, 82]: 'Wilson's first draft [of the film script] was written very much as a political drama. Although Lawrence is never less than the principal character, Wilson's interest in the colonialism versus nationalism theme, with Lawrence caught in the middle, took precedence. Lawrence's sexuality was never one of Wilson's major concerns . . . [The substitute scriptwriter, Beverley] Cross remembers Wilson's script as "totally practicable and totally shootable. It was all political action and when it wasn't it was all politics. I think David [Lean] wanted to get away from the politics of Wilson's scripts." The screenplay that began to emerge [after Wilson's contract was terminated] was structurally identical to Wilson's. The meaning of it changed considerably. Whereas Wilson took a political view of Lawrence and the Arab Revolt, Bolt's approach was psychological.' Yet another and more recent example of a similar shift of focus is the film *Reds* (1981), directed by Warren Beatty, where the emphasis on the politics of the Russian Revolution and the struggles for American socialism, as portrayed in the initial script by Trevor Griffiths, was – as in the case of *Spartacus* – subsequently transformed into a love story about two of the protagonists, John Reed and Louise Bryant [*Poole and Wyver*, 1984: 122–39].

17. Illustrations supporting this claim about the political effects of an epistemological shift from society to individual are provided by Kracauer [1995: 291–304] in an essay about 'popular culture' and cinema ('Little Shopgirls go to the Movies') written during the 1920s, in which he identified eight themes which dominated film plots during that period. These were: 'Clear Road', 'Sex and Character', 'Nation in Arms', 'The World Travellers', 'The Golden Heart', 'The Modern Haroun al Raschid', 'Silent Tragedies' and 'Close to the Edge'. Common to most of the latter were the following discursive elements. Social conditions categorized as 'problems' (poverty and misery) are indeed displayed, but causes are individualized and solutions are confined within the framework of capitalism. Hence it

is an individual from the working class, and not the working class itself, which is redeemed, an outcome that is presented as a satisfactory (= 'natural') conclusion. Moreover, such redemption is presented as a reward for virtue, which in turn validates a central emplacement of bourgeois ideology: that wealth is the result of, and a just return for, hard work and thrift, and thus unconnected with property ownership/control and surplus-value extraction/accumulation. Supportive of this displacement is the discursive celebration of 'ordinaryness', or the theme that the-rich-are-really-people-just-like-everyone-else (for a similar point, see Arnheim [1933: 173–4]). Their problems are presented as being those of humanity at large (individuals who fall in love, have feelings, die, etc.), and wealth accordingly confers no special privilege nor is it deemed to be responsible for the misery which exists. Similarly, patriotic films glorify war as an end in itself, a socio-economically non-determined event that is projected in terms of an acceptable sacrifice made by the individual for his country. Unlike capital, which reaps material benefits from war, the films considered by Kracauer emphasize and naturalize the non-material elements (honour, heroism) conferred as 'rewards' for 'those below' who sacrifice themselves in battle.

18. The significance of the anti-hero as a focus of attraction/repulsion is that it is precisely through such figures that a cinema audience not normally receptive to this viewpoint can be persuaded to consider different ideological outcomes. Hence the value to populist discourse of what might be termed the 'redeeming features' of an otherwise unacceptable characterization. The political implications of this are obvious, and have been aptly encapsulated in an observation by Rotha [1949: 588] that 'Nazi propaganda did not seek to convince but to impress'. Accordingly, the initial object is not so much to convert to an opposed politico-ideological viewpoint as to challenge perceptions of the latter as wholly and unredeemably negative. In short, to relativize what has hitherto been presented and considered as absolutely 'other'.

19. No attempt will be made here to elaborate on the connection between populism and the Hollywood western, since it is already well documented (see, for example, Richards [1973: 270ff.], Wollen [1974: 94ff.], Stanfield [1996]).

20. Nowell-Smith [1976: 7] argues that most of Pasolini's films are structured by the following discursive oppositions:

Urban/bad	Rural/good
Present	Past
Repression	Freedom
Technology	Nature
Bourgeoisie	Peasantry/lumpenproletariat

The column on the left represents what Pasolini regards as undesirable, whereas that on the right is composed of the categories/attributes of which he approves. The similarity between these oppositions and the discourse-for/discourse-against of 'new' populism generally and Fanon, Marcuse and Foucault in particular (see previous chapters) is too obvious to require further comment.

21. Pasolini himself came from a a well-to-do peasant background [*Nowell-Smith*, 1976: 2]. 'If there is one constant, one invariant', notes Stack [1969: 7], 'it is Pasolini's uncritical attachment to the peasantry, an attachment which can be presented in the light of Marxism, but more consistently in the light of a backward-looking romanticism'. This is confirmed by Nowell-Smith [1976: 3], who observes

of Pasolini that not only was he ignorant of (and thus rejected) the political economy of Marx and Lenin, adopting instead the culturalism found in Gramsci, but 'the Communism that attracted him [Pasolini] was that of the peasantry and in particular the – predominantly Catholic – peasantry of Friuli'. For Pasolini's romanticization of the lumpenproletariat, in films such as *Accattone* (1961) and *Mama Roma* (1962), see Nowell-Smith [1976: 3–4].

22. On this point, see Francese [1994: 31].
23. This point is hinted at by Stack [1969: 9] when he observes in relation to the films *Oedipus Rex* (1967) and *Theorem* (1968) that Pasolini 'lays increasing stress on the need to restore a . . . mythological dimension to life, a sense of awe and reverence to the world: a sense which, he believes, the peasantry still sustain, though the bourgeoisie has done all in its power to destroy it. This emphasis on the spirituality of the peasantry, their semi-pagan consciousness of super-natural meanings and forces, is obviously difficult to reconcile with a Marxist political analysis. In fact, rather than politics, it is sex which Pasolini now seems to see as the main threat to the bourgeoisie . . . by associating sex with pagan mythology . . . and pagan mythology with the peasantry, Pasolini is able to reconcile the idea of sexual liberation with his attachment to the peasantry.' Much the same is true of the way in which sexuality is depicted in the film *The Wicker Man* (see below).
24. It should be emphasized that the 1960s do not constitute the point at which films in postwar Germany recommenced projecting the agrarian myth. Designed to influence returning wartime refugees, the *Heimatfilme* genre of the 1950s similarly constructed idealized images of landscape and engaged in anti-urban celebrations of rural homeland [*Kaes*, 1992: 14–15].
25. On the *arbeiterfilm*, see Collins and Porter [1981].
26. Kaes [1992: 165] defines 'heimat' in the following way: 'The high value placed on the simple life in the provinces "with their belief in law and order" dates back to the Heimat movement of the 1890s, which had arisen in reaction to rapid industrialization and the concomitant shift from rural to urban living. In the ideology of this antimodern, antiurban movement, Heimat was precisely that which was abandoned on the way into the cities; from then on the word "Heimat" began to connote "region", "province" and "country". Since the era of industrialization, German literature has weighted this term with emotional connotations almost to the breaking point: Heimat means the site of one's lost childhood, of family, of identity. It also stands for the possibility of secure human relations, unalienated, precapitalist labor, and the romantic harmony between the country dweller and nature. Heimat refers to everything that is not distant and foreign.'
27. On these points see Kaes [1992], who argues persuasively that themes (such as the recuperation of a 'popular' national identity) projected in the films of directors associated with the New German Cinema (Fassbinder, Reitz and Syberberg) prefigure the revisionist debates in Germany about the meaning/(normalization) of the Nazi era.
28. The link between on the one hand this process of normalization and on the other the celebration of a 'from below' film discourse associated with the depoliticized portrayal of 'popular culture' as 'natural' is delineated by Kaes [1992: 189]: 'Because the film for the most part identifies with the knowledge and consciousness of its protagonists, it often loses the distance necessary for a critical depiction of their behaviour. The characters – most of whom are basically opportunistic conformists – appear to us as they appear to themselves; the linear, chronological

narrative mode of *Heimat* restricts our perspective to that of the characters, so that we experience history through their eyes. The viewer is free to criticize the characters' point of view; but when a realistic narrative is so closely attuned to its characters, it is difficult to make the leap from identification to critical distance. Outsiders, who in realistic narratives are often the source of alternative critical perspectives, remain conspicuously absent in the episodes that deal with the Hitler years.' Despite the fact that nearly half the episodes are situated in the Nazi era, therefore, 'the annihilation of the Jews is almost completely excluded from the plot' [*Kaes*, 1992: 185, 187]. The political inference is clear: the rural population depicted in *Heimat* did not know about – and could thus not be held accountable for – the Holocaust.

29. Some 25 million people in Germany itself saw one episode of *Heimat* and all eleven were seen by nine million viewers [*Kaes*, 1992: 163]. According to one observer [*Kaes*, 1992: 164, 169, 170]: 'Reitz's radical regionalism, his peasant characters, his use of dialect, and his minute, often nostalgic descriptions of everyday life in the village have no equivalent in contemporary German literature or film. His film evokes associations of the "homeland" and "blood and soil" literature of the Nazi era – associations that must be regarded as dangerous . . . The film is filled with images of provincial life: quiet shots of landscapes, of people working, of objects and banal daily routines – long wordless passages in which the camera goes on a voyage of discovery or sequences in which people chat in an almost improvised way. Women sing at the spinning wheel, grouped in a painterly composition; the village smith stands at his anvil, pounding the wheel as sparks fly; [the central character] Maria kneads dough: the film lingers over such genre scenes . . . "heimat" in this film means first of all a place outside of history, removed from progress, caught in cyclical time, a place that seems subject only to nature and the seasons.'

30. For the ideological importance and influence of the 'mountain' film genre, as mediated in the work of Leni Riefenstahl and Luis Trenker, see Kracauer [1947: 110–12, 257–63]. The film *The Blue Light* (1932), directed by Riefenstahl, is described by Kracauer [1947: 259] in the following terms: 'Beautiful outdoor shots stress the indissoluble ties between primitive people and their natural surroundings . . . [c]lose-ups of genuine peasant faces thread through the whole of the film; these faces resemble landscapes molded by nature itself, and in rendering them, the camera achieves a fascinating study in facial folklore.' In other words, a film genre in which 'mountain', Nature, 'nation' and 'peasant' are symbolically interchangeable.The importance of this politico-ideological matrix is that in her other films, such as *Olympia* (1936) and *Triumph of the Will* (1934), the cult of the 'perfect body' is similarly presented by Riefenstahl as a synonym for 'perfect nature'. Accordingly, a powerful visual image of 'perfect Nature', already projected into the domain of 'popular culture' by means of her 'mountain' films, is here equated not just with 'nation' but also with a 'natural'/ever-present peasantry. Mountains not only symbolize 'perfect Nature', therefore, but also thereby permit the physical to merge with and thus become one with the spiritual (mountains-as-the-abode-of-the-Gods). The significance of this ideological fusion emerges most clearly and powerfully in the notorious opening scene of *Triumph of the Will*, where the plane on which Hitler is travelling to address the Nuremburg rally descends from the clouds, setting up a potent ideological relay-in-statement: the origin of this journey appears to be the mountains, the epitome of 'perfect Nature', which in turn

symbolically embody the eternal/ancient (= enduring) presence not only of God but also of the nation and through this 'the people'. This multiplicity of powerful symbolic identities is thereby projected onto the person of the Nazi leader himself in his descent from this sacred physical/mystical space (= God/Nature/nation/ people).

31. For the expansion in German cinema attendance see Wollenberg [1948: 38], and for 'blood and soil' cinematic themes see Petley [1979: 130–38].

32. For these points, see Hinz [1980: 110ff., 175–7]. The agrarian populist iconography structuring painting in Nazi Germany is clear from an 1941 essay by F.A. Kauffmann (cited in Hinz [1980: 77–78]) outlining its genres: '. . . our contemporary painting frequently portrays the faces and figures of *men who follow the old callings close to nature*: farmers, hunters, fishermen, shepherds, and woodcutters . . . Again and again we see. the farmer on his land. We see him plowing, sowing, reaping, and gathering his winter's wood. We see him against a background of earth and sky with the fruitful soil under his heavy shoes, a modest but proud ruler over his dutiful animals and his own well-tended fields . . . Where there is so much feeling for the soil in which we are rooted, the *pure landscape* is bound to be an object of artistic interest . . . These landscapes are *representations of the fatherland* . . . a piece of the Reich that demands our loyalty, . . . our all-nourishing mother that yields her best to us, certain of our undying loyalty' (original emphasis).

33. A common link between the agrarian myth and *film noir* is that both reproduce a prelapsarian gender stereotype. Since women are equated with Nature, females in the city symbolize a distortion of Nature/nature itself, as is borne out by the following oppositions:

Urban/bad	Rural/good
Film Noir	The Pastoral
Dangerous woman	Safe woman
Whore/temptress/seducer	Steadfast/Faithful
Impure/lover	Pure/mother/wife
Death	Life

That the agrarian myth remains a sub-text even in more recent – and highly acclaimed – examples of the *film noir* genre is evident from the admission by the Robert Towne, who wrote the script for *Chinatown* (1974) directed by Roman Polanski, that one object of his narrative was to highlight what he perceived as the despoilation of Nature in the Los Angeles region (see Thomson [1997: 83ff.]).

34. On this point, see Vernet [1993]. The extent to which the projection within the domain of 'popular culture' of petty bourgeois fears of domination by monopoly capital persisted in the post-war era, and its reproduction within the discourse of the political right, is evident for example from the way in which *film noir* was interpreted by the French. Accordingly, both the definition in France of *film noir* as a specific cinematic genre spanning the decade 1945–55 and its appeal to French audiences can be linked to the ideological anxieties of Poujadism, a conservative reaction on the part of the French petty-bourgeoisie threatened by monopoly capital. Thus the central character in *film noir*, the private detective, strives to save the (capitalist) system from itself: he embodies and reaffirms its essential moral virtues (self-sufficiency, innovativeness, tenacity, justice, and what Orwell referred to as 'decency') in the role of the lone individual taking on large-scale/

collective forces of corruption (the agents of the state, big business, powerful gangsters).

35. The trilogy, which consists of *The Godfather* (1972), *The Godfather Part II* (1974), and *The Godfather Part III* (1990), was rightly perceived as a prefiguring filmic representation of the kind of business ethics exhibited by capitalism during the Reagan and Thatcher era.

36. The romanticization by Coppola of mafia activity as an empowering grassroots challenge to landlordism reproduces the idealized stereotype associated with the seminal text by Hobsbawm [1969b]: namely, banditry as a systemically redistributive mechanism (= 'Robin Hood' activity) and thus as a form of revolutionary social protest. This view has been strongly criticized by others (for example, Blok [1972], Li Causi [1975]) who point out that the historical role of bandits/ brigands/mafiosi was much rather as enforcers of existing class relations and power structure in the countryside. The theme of gangster-as-enforcer-of-landlord-interests explicitly structures a more recent treatment modelled on Coppola's *The Godfather*, but set in the context of rural India: the Tamil film *Thevar Magan* (1992).

37. Hence the initial act of migration itself, by Vito Corleone from rural Sicily to urban America at the turn of the century, which is presented in the form of flash-backs in the second part, corresponds to a corrupting transition, with a consequent loss of innocence/purity. The same is true of the first part of the trilogy, in which the rural Sicilian idyll is an episode during which Michael Corleone finds temporary refuge and personal happiness, and a context where violence is depicted filmically in terms of an intrusion rather than – as in urban New York or Las Vegas – endemic. The subsequent return to America coincides with his transition to mafia boss, symbolizing both a loss of happiness on his part and also the corruption inherent in the exercise by him of absolute power in the urban underworld. That there should be a physical contrast in the film between the light/openness of the Sicilan episode and the dark/closed images of urban New York is clear from a comment by film's photographer [*Cowie*, 1997: 59] that 'I maintained that all the scenes in Sicily should be sunny, far off, mythical, a more romantic land . . . [s]o all the material shot there was grounded in this sunny landscape. [The Sicilian sequences were] softer, more romantic, in contrast to the harder newspaper look of the New York scenes.'

38. The physical shift is from the urban United States, which symbolizes the evil/impure, to a rural Sicily representing both legality and the goodness/purity of the agrarian myth. It is important to note, however, that in rural Sicily the Corleone family continue to enjoy wealth and power, the inference being that in this context they have now become part of the landlord class. Coppola himself is a substantial landowner, being the proprietor of a wine producing estate of some 1,500 acres in the Napa Valley of California.

39. Although that between the three 'city slickers' is important, the main relationship in the film is between Mitch and an aged but tough trail boss Curly (played by Jack Palance), who respresents all the vanishing values of the 'old west' (simplicity, honesty, bravery). Both are involved in the key scene, which concerns the birth of a calf, a 'natural' process assisted by Mitch, and symbolizing not just his own rebirth, as someone who now shares the 'natural' values hitherto embodied in Curly, but also that of Nature itself. This calf is rescued by the 'city slickers' twice: once from two of the accompanying cowhands, who threaten to kill it (and thus the

agrarian myth and Nature itself), and once from the flooded river. When Curly dies, Mitch resists the suggestion of the other 'city slickers' to abandon the live-stock and save themselves ('a cowboy shouldn't leave his herd'), and leads the cattle across a flooded river to the pastoral landscape beyond. The film ends not just with the 'city slickers' becoming men once again, but with them having done this as a result of having acquired from Curly the traditional values of the 'old west'. Urban redemption is effected, therefore, as a consequence of rediscovering and sticking to the values of Nature, of the 'old west', and of Curly. Unsurpris-ingly, Mitch takes the calf (= Nature) back home with him to his children in the city, symbolizing the importance of preserving these same values in order to trans-mit them to the next generation.

40. On this point, see among others, Pirie [1973: 36–7] and Biskind [1983: 123ff., 137ff.]. As Pirie [1973: 34] points out, the Quatermass BBC television series of the early 1950s [Kneale, 1959; 1960a; 1960b] and the subsequent films derived their power from the subversion of an internal and thus ordinary, quotidian existence by an external/extraordinary force, a process in which the human form is itself no longer 'natural'. Biskind [1983: 139] makes much the same point when he observes that '[f]ar worse than invasion, what these films anxiously imagined was the loss of community, the estrangement of . . . Us from Them'. Like other films in this genre, Invasion of the Body Snatchers [Biskind, 1983: 143, 144] 'is an activist film that dramatizes the need for eternal vigilance. Falling asleep is dangerous. When people doze off, become unaware, pods snatch their bodies . . . The film strives not to reassure but to alarm, not to tranquilize, but to mobilize, both the audience watching the film and the audience within the film . . . Both Invasion and Them! imagine attacks from exotic aliens, but the issue at stake in the two films is who's right, the individual or the group, and who commands authority, amateurs or experts, the people or the state . . . The fact that the hero succeeds in convincing his neighbors he's right is not only an expression of the radical right's populist optimism, but also a rehabilitation of common sense . . .'

41. In warfare, such a maneouvre (pretending-to-be-other-than-oneself) is considered to be the most heinous of military offences and, like treachery (also a form of pretending-to-be-other-than-oneself), is punishable by death.

42. On this point see Newman [1988: 51], who comments: 'Psycho is the first of many suggestions that the bypassed backwaters might nurture a homicidal hatred for the city slickers who have taken over from cowboys as emblems of Americana. Nobody stops at the Bates Motel since they built the new highway . . . Whenever the Beautiful people [= urban dwellers] are foolhardy enough to get off the free-ways, the festering old-timers have been leaving their rocking chairs and revving their chainsaws.'

43. Discourse about the 'revenge of Nature' has a long lineage in popular culture. Hence the ease with which inhabitants of an advanced capitalist society revert to a 'primitive'/'natural'/(savage) state informs non-horror films such as Buñuel's The Exterminating Angel (1962) and Peter Brook's Lord of the Flies (1963). The 'revenge of Nature'-as-horror-film possesses its most recent origin in Hitchcock's The Birds (1963), where the confrontation between Nature and humanity is set in California, the locus of American agribusiness. The same theme pervades a number of important films produced during the 1970s and after: for example, Willard (1970), Phase IV (1974), Jaws (1975), Piranha (1978), and Tremors (1990), in which Nature is represented symbolically by rats, ants, man-eating fish,

and giant carnivorous worms, and films such as Boorman's *Deliverance* (1972) and Walter Hill's *Southern Comfort* (1981), in which the 'revenge of Nature' theme is projected specifically in environmental terms. As the example of Val Guest's *The Day the Earth Caught Fire* (1961) indicates, the 'revenge of Nature'-as-ecological-disaster theme is by no means confined to the horror genre. In the 'revenge of Nature' film *Day of the Animals* (1977), humanity comes under simultaneous attack from both symbolic representatives of Nature: animals and the environment.

44. For Werner Herzog, see Sandford [1981: 48–62]. Contrasting the different approaches of Truffaut's *L'Enfant Sauvage* and Herzog's *The Enigma of Kaspar Hauser* to the same theme, Sandford [1981: 54] observes that while the former 'tackles the "wild boy" of Aveyron from the perspective of French rationalism, adopting the viewpoint of his educator, Herzog's [film] is steeped in German Romanticism, with its respect for the virtues of the "natural", the "wild", for the irreducible mysteries at the dark heart of life'.

45. Hence the focus of an early documentary film, *Fata Morgana* (1970), is on the damaging effect of humanity and economic development on the African environment (and *vice versa*), while that of a later one, *La Sufriere* (1976), is on physionomy of the abandoned/deserted townscape in Guadeloupe threatened by a potential (and in the event unrealized) volcanic eruption. Much the same is true of the non-documentary film, *The Enigma of Kaspar Hauser* (1974), where the main protagonist symbolizes the 'natural' state of humanity, a projection of Rousseauesque 'primitive goodness' who successfully confronts/questions but is eventually destroyed by (an urban/European) 'civilized' humanity.

46. According to Peary [1981: 2], *Aguirre* is 'an enormous cult favorite in such places as Mexico, Venezuela, Algiers, Paris, and America, where its distributor, New Yorker Films, reports that it is the one picture in its catalog that is never out of circulation'. For the historical inaccuracies and political evasions of the film, see Carnes [1995].

47. A central theme in *Gone With The Wind* is that 'land is . . . the only thing that lasts'. About the film version one commentator [*Umphlett*, 1983: 135] has observed: 'There is probably no more nostalgic subject in American social history than the idealized picture of this vanished world – the *antebellum* South, rife with magnolia-scented, plantation scenes of crinoline-attired belles; tall, straight-backed suitors; and their devoted black servants, field and house workers alike, laughing, singing, and apparently loving their routine existence, all this played out in fairy-tale innocence within and before a white-columned mansion of gleaming elegance'.

48. This film belongs to what is referred to as Ray's Zamindar trilogy: the other two are *Devi* (1959) and *Monihara* (1961).

49. The film effects a contrast between on the one hand an affectionate portrayal of the landlord character Biswambhar Roy, who owns an elephant and a white horse and displays a refined appreciation of traditional Bengali culture, and on the other the philistine businessman Mahim Ganguli, who owns only lorries and whose ostentatious cars are the epitome of modern vulgarity. The discourse of *The Music Room* is accordingly structured not just by a dichotomy between urban = undesirable and rural = desirable but also by the following oppositions.

Urban (= bad)	Rural (= good)
Mahim Ganguli	Biswambhar Roy
Bourgeois/businessman	Landlord
Car (technology)	Elephant (Nature)
Economic power	Cultural power

50. In both films the decline of the landlord class is represented by a process of symbolic destruction. By fire in *Gone With The Wind,* the burning of Atlanta signalling the demise of the antebellum plantation, and by water in *The Music Room,* in which the landlord's wife and son are drowned in a river during a storm. In both cases, therefore, Nature (fire, water) is to be found among the ranks of those ranged against a declining landlordism, a contrast with the 'red-in-tooth-and-claw' variant of the aristocratic version of the agrarian myth.

51. See Chapter 1 for the ideology of the Southern Agrarians. Many of these same themes surface in a subsequent example of the landlord pastoral, only this time with Mexican workers taking the place of black slaves: the film *Giant* (1956), directed by George Stevens. When oil is discovered on his smallholding, Jett Rink abandons his agrarian roots and becomes a rich businessman: his character, which embodies a series of negative traits (racism, alcoholism), symbolizes the perils of change (from rural to urban). By contrast, the character of Bick Benedict, the large Texan landholder within whose domain the smallholding was located, is imbued with positive traits: not only does he continue to uphold traditional rural values increasingly under threat from the oil millionaire, but he also defends 'his' Mexicans from racist exclusion and/or abuse.

52. On these and the following points, see Hay [1987: 138ff.]. The important ideological role of film for Italian fascism during the 1930s is clear from an instruction issued to directors (cited in de Grazia [1986: 249]) that 'We shall use the sunburnt faces of our peasants . . . Let us encourage productions that examine labour in the fields and workshops; let us make a film that is closer to us and to the time we live in; with the people and for the people we shall give life to a new fascist film'.

53. As Hay [1987: 132] points out, *strapaese* embodied a concept of 'ruralism' as opposed to 'urbanism' (*stracittà*), and essentially meant 'a desire to recuperate "agricultural values"', the proponents of which 'believed their vision to be a necessary antidote to a culture that had been "contaminated" by technological society, with its machines imported from abroad and an ideology "alien" to that of provincial communities'.

54. In Blasetti's film *Sole* (1929), the presence of potential conflict between two rival claims to land (the Pontine marshes outside Rome) is resolved, and rural harmony and 'community' restored, an outcome blessed by Nature in the form of the sun.

55. The plot of *Terra Madre* involves the return of an urbane/(urbanized) aristocrat to his country estate, which he intends to sell to a speculator. The pastoral metaphors deployed in this *strapaese* film all symbolize rural purity and urban decadence. En route to the estate, the aristocrat's car (= industry) becomes stuck in the mud (= halted by Nature). Like the film *Sole,* the potential conflict between rival claims to the land are solved by the marriage of the aristocrat to the daughter of the overseer on his estate, an act which symbolizes the rejection of finance capital (= speculator), the 'un-natural' city and modernity generally, and – in the form of the aristocratic repossession of land – the reaffirmation of 'natural' hierarchy and the celebration of Nature itself. The new/(old) landlord is thus a populist emblem

of class conciliation, in the double form of hypergamy and protection of the peasants against the speculator.

56. For Visconti's *The Leopard*, see Nowell-Smith [1967: 101ff.].

57. A similar criticism can be made of a subsequent film by the same director, *The Last Emperor* (1987), in which a sympathetic portrayal of Pu Yi, the last Emperor of China, depicts him as an essentially benign and powerless figure caught up in events not of his making and beyond his capacity to influence. Together with this film, *The Sheltering Sky* (1990) and *Little Buddha* (1993) have been described as Bertolucci's orientalist trilogy, which in the course of a television interview the director himself attributed to his dislike of 1980s Italy and a corresponding search on his part for the 'golden age'/'primitive' otherness in the Third World ('I was looking for a place of innocence, where the consumerism hadn't yet got hold', *Bernado Bertolucci: Scene by Scene*, BBC2, 18 Sept. 1999). Bertolucci replicates not only the endorsement of a pristine Eastern 'otherness' that informs the agrarian myth, therefore, but also the reason for holding such a view: like Pasolini and Marcuse, he adheres to the stereotype of metropolitan capitalist countries as corrupted-by-consumerism.

58. A similar case has been made by Balagopal [1988] with regard to N.T. Rama Rao in Andhra Pradesh. In India generally, the impact of the agrarian myth on popular culture has increased and not decreased as a consequence of the expansion of the electronic media. The impact of the cinema, and particularly television, has grown in India over recent times: by 1988 television coverage extended to include some 62 per cent of the population, and 11 million sets were watched by 90 million people [*Rudolph*, 1992]. In terms of its media presence, the agrarian myth has also disappeared, only to reappear once again. During the 1920s more than 70 per cent of Indian films had a mythological content, and rural existence was depicted in positive terms; after Independence, this mythological focus was replaced by social themes, in which the town was depicted in positive terms, as a source of enlightened values and liberation from the agrestic servitude of a backwards-looking and socially anachronistic village existence. On this point, see Das Gupta [1991: 34, 36, 45ff., 166]. From the 1970s onwards, however, this cinematic trend has been reversed: not only has the mythological film once again returned to prominence, but it has done this in a way that naturalizes (or makes real) the usually highly stylized presentation of Hindu mythology. Similarly, urban India is now recast politically as the locus not only of a uniformly hostile and corrupt state but also as a negative secular/alienated form of existence. The latter is in turn counterposed to a similarly recast and idealised concept of the village, the repository of traditional/religious values now depicted as positive and associated with the purity of an unchanging/ever-present (= authentic) indigenous culture threatened by a specifically urban, western/'foreign', greedy and anti-traditional secularism.

59. See Pandian [1992: 54–64].

60. See Pandian [1992: 44–7, 53].

61. Like Capra a populist, Griffiths came from a comfortable Southern rural background; his father was a slaveowning landholder who had fought for the Confederacy during the Civil War. On the subject of the connection between Griffiths' own background, his films and political beliefs a recent text has noted: '... the Populist attitudes that manifested themselves in so many of Griffiths' films certainly had their beginnings [in his farm upbringing] ... Some of the best, most strongly felt passages in his later movies ... were evocations of country people,

country life. He respected the values he learned there [and] mourned their passing
. . .' [*Schickel, 1984: 28–9, 30*].

62. For the anti-socialist views of Thomas Dixon, on whose 1905 book *The Clansman*
the film was based, and who warned that a free black worker would become an
urban 'mob-in-the-streets', see Schickel [1984: 79–80]. A subsequent novel by
Dixon, *Comrades*, published in 1909, was the source for the anti-socialist film
Bolshevism on Trial (1919), directed by Harley Knoles [*Brownlow, 1990, 443–5*].
Significantly, Griffith himself 'found in [*The Clansman*] dozens of points in
common with his family's mythology' [*Schickel 1984: 207*].

63. See Kracauer [1947].

64. Murnau himself came from Westphalia, described by Eisner [1969: 99] as 'a
region of vast pastures where enormous peasants breed heavy-boned plough-
horses'; not only did he retain a nostalgia for the countryside generally, but its
landscape pervaded his films to the degree that 'Nature participates in the action'.
Of all the film versions of the Dracula legend, Murnau's *Nosferatu* is widely
regarded as being the closest to its prefiguring nineteenth century literary sources:
the poetic dramas of Lord Byron (particularly *The Giaour*, published in 1813), and
the novel by Bram Stoker [1897/1993]. The latter contains a fairly precise set of
binary oppositions, which is supportive of the agrarian myth: on the one hand,
therefore, Dracula himself is synonymous with aristocratic power, landlordism,
ruralism, ancient tradition, pre-Christian beliefs, and Nature, while most of those
ranged against him (Professor Van Helsing, Dr Seward, Jonathan Harker) are
either scientists or middle class professionals who epitomize in turn a modern/
urban/scientific outlook combined with Christian beliefs. In short, the struggle is
one between a representative ensemble of Western, rational, forward-looking
Victorians, and an Eastern, backwards-looking, non-rational, Transylvanian
'other'. In terms of European culture generally and agrarian populism in particular,
however, Byron is perhaps the more important influence. A patrician exponent of
individual rebellion, a proponent of sexual 'transgression', and an advocate of
nationalism, Byron – like Count Dracula – is the epitome of the romantic anti-hero:
a noble, doom-laden 'fatal man' [*Praz, 1933: 76–81*], or the kind of Gothic villain
whose presence structures much of his work. Again like Dracula, he also belongs
to an ancient landowning aristocracy under threat throughout most of Europe from
an ascendant urban industrial bourgeoisie, and thus to a class mobilized for a pre-
emptive ideological offensive: as Brinton [1926: 149] observes, '[a]fter the
dissolution of the ideals of the old régime, he [Byron] could join in the search for
new ones . . .' Herein lies the populist element, or the capacity to exert 'from-
above' influence in an ostensibly non-class and politically progressive manner
(espousing nationalism, defending the rural oppressed against the urban oppressor,
or country versus town, and endorsing individual as distinct from collective
dissent/opposition) over the formulation of an emerging and – from the viewpoint
of a landowning class – a potentially threatening 'from-below' discourse.
According to the same source [*Brinton, 1926: 154*], Byron is a radical conservative, 'a true heir of the literary Jacobins in his faith in Nature, in his devotion to
liberty, in his sympathy for the oppressed, and in his hatred of the old régime . . .
But he was in many respects even more orthodox than he has been painted. He was
rather more conscious of his aristocratic position than it would seem, to a plebeian
mind, he should have been; and it is noticeable that, though he is as bitter against
kings as any Jacobin, he is not equally bitter against nobility.'

65. One reading [*Wasson*, 1966] of the vampire myth actually suggests that, in its literary form [*Stoker*, 1993], Dracula symbolizes the struggle between Central European fascism and Western democracy.

66. The text of the actual film itself is contained in Manvell [1973: 53–95], while a different version by the scriptwriter Henrik Galeen, on which the former was based, is contained in Eisner [1973: 227–72].

67. This element emerges clearly in the late nineteenth century novel where, in the words of the Count himself [*Stoker*, 1993: 19], 'here [in Transylvania] I am noble; I am *boyar*; the common people know me, and I am master . . . I have been so long master that I would be master still – or at least that none other should be master of me'.

68. For more on this point, see Chapter 1.

69. An important characteristic of the film *Nosferatu* is that Murnau's use of external locations enhance the credibility of the way in which the supernatural is portrayed by naturalizing it. That the agrarian myth is an important component of this particular film is hinted at by Pirie [1977: 41] when considering the significant role in its discourse of landscape. '[I]n one vital respect', he observes, '*Nosferatu* did point prophetically and courageously to the true destiny of the vampire picture. This was in its use of exteriors. If there is one magic ingredient of the vampire genre in literature or the cinema, one that sometimes even supercedes the vampire himself, it is the *landscape* he inhabits. . . . . [Bram Stoker] was a great Gothic writer, and he knew how to evoke a *feeling* from landscape . . . The vampire may be the active agent of terror, but the passive agent is the landscape he inhabits' (original emphasis). Eisner [1969: 151ff.] also notes the significance of landscape, but in regard to German Expressionist cinema. Neither Pirie nor Eisner, however, make the connection between landscape and class, and between the supernatural power of Count Orlock/Nosferatu and the fact that he is also a landowning aristocrat.

70. The extent to which Nature, animals, forests, peasants and the Count are all mutually interdependent and even symbolically interchangeable is evident from the novel, where Dracula is able to assume the form and command the obedience of animals and the natual elements (wind, mist, storm). Similarly, the local peasantry, who 'attach themselves as a rule to some great noble or *boyar*', protect the Count and – alongside the natural elements and animals – fight on his behalf against his opponents/pursuers [*Stoker* 1993: 36–8, 311–13].

71. This interpretation is supported by the description [*Eisner*, 1973: 239] of Count Orlock/Nosferatu as 'a creature . . . grown up on his native soil – from which alone he draws his powers'. The same point is made even more strongly in the novel by Stoker [1993: 199, 201, 229, 242, 248, 252], where those ranged against the Count repeatedly emphasize the need to deprive him of the source of his power: Dracula's 'earth-home', or his symbolic link with the Transylvanian land.

72. The nature of this power exercised by Dracula-as-landlord over the Transylvanian peasantry emerges clearly from an episode in the novel by Stoker [1993: 20], where the Count explains that the exact location of gold which belongs to him that is hidden in the ground of the surrounding countryside is revealed only on one night in the year. Since the latter is also the night on which 'evil spirits [who] are supposed to have unchecked sway' are present, Dracula's gold is in fact protected from the peasantry who might otherwise find it. The symbolism of this episode is not difficult to discern: gold is congealed surplus labour appropriated by the land-

lord, whose control over this is exercised by a combination of terror (= the legend of the vampire) and false consciousness (= superstitious beliefs) on the part of peasants who, because of a fear of vampirism, dare not reclaim that which is rightfully theirs.

73. The politico-ideological and mystical interrelationship between blood, earth and the Count is particularly marked in the novel by Stoker [1993: 20, 118, 194], where Dracula observes that 'there is hardly a foot of soil in all this region [= Transylvania] that has not been enriched by the blood of men . . .'. Not only does Count Dracula draw sustenance from each, but in so far as blood and soil lie at the root of a discourse about Nature and nationality, are both fundamental conditions of existence (blood = soil = Nature = life), and also nourish the representative of the landlord class, Dracula-as-landowner becomes thereby a potent embodiment of an unchanging/unchangeable national identity that has its origins in the countryside. Significantly, it is his attempt to take the blood from members of the bourgeoisie that leads in the end to the defeat of Dracula, thereby underlining the sub-text of the novel as being one about conflict between the landlord class and capitalists over the right to appropriate surplus-labour from the workforce.

74. Other texts view the outcome in more positive terms, as signalling the triumph of the 'white-collar character-types' [*Huaco*, 1965: 49]. The latter accordingly interprets the ending of *Nosferatu* as a victory for 'the heroic bourgeois housewife, Nina', who traps Count Orlock/Nosferatu until the rays of the sun destroy him. The over-optimism of this reading is evident from the fact that in the film she also dies; not merely is 'the heroic bourgeois housewife, Nina' killed by the vampire but as a consequence she will be converted into one of his kind. In his other films Murnau 'delighted in portraying the coarseness of the lower middle-classes, besotted with eating and drinking and reeling under the effects of the fresh outdoor air' [*Eisner*, 1969: 109], which suggests that – unlike Stoker – the director of *Nosferatu* did not himself endorse the notion of 'the heroic bourgeois'.

75. Both the threat to the urban and its possible effects are clear from the novel by Stoker [1993: 44–5; also 149] where, having encountered Dracula 'gorged with blood . . . like a filthy leech, exhausted with repletion', Jonathan Harker observes that '[t]his was the being I was helping to transfer to London, where, perhaps for centuries to come, he might, amongst its teeming millions, satiate his lust for blood, and create a new and ever-widening circle of semi-demons to batten on the helpless'. The element of threat/repulsion/horror is underlined by the way in which Count Orlock/Nosferatu is first seen/experienced by the cinema audience: not only is he looking directly at and simultaneously advancing towards the camera (and thus the urban audience), but he is also emerging from darkness (his castle in his rural domain, the realm of supernatural power exercised by him over and through the undead).

76. It is perhaps significant that the pastoral version of the agrarian myth structures *Sunrise* (1927), a subsequent film directed by Murnau in America (on which see Eisner [1973: 167–85]). The plot concerns the attempted seduction of a peasant farmer by a city vamp, who tempts him with wonderful images of urban nightlife. The farmer undertakes to kill his wife, sell his land and go with the vamp to the city. Reconciled with his wife, the farmer chases the city woman and the evil she represents from the countryside, a process of redemption accompanied/symbolized by the sun rising over the rustic idyll. There are clear differences between *Sunrise*, where the rural is depicted as a realm of light and tranquillity, and *Nosferatu*,

where by contrast it is presented as the domain of darkness and terror. The latter distinction notwithstanding, both *Nosferatu* and *Sunrise* not only reproduce the town/country opposition but also the aggressor/victim polarity: in each case, it is the countryside that is the object of a threat which emanates from the town (in the form of urban inhabitants/existence/values). With only a little exaggeration, therefore, it might be argued that *Nosferatu*, made in Germany, is Murnau in/(on) his Junker mode/(road), whereas *Sunrise*, made in the United States five years later, is Murnau in/(on) his peasant mode/(road).

77. Not only the peasant pastoral *Lost Horizon* (see previous chapter) but also the aristocratic 'red-in-tooth-and-claw' *Nosferatu* are orientalist, and both emphasize the 'naturalness', the power and the longevity of the agrarian myth. Like the inhabitants of Shangri-La, Dracula does not grow old. Although Transylvania is described in the book [*Stoker*, 1993: 3] as 'one of the wildest and least known portions of Europe', the character Jonathan Harker observes that when travelling towards it '[t]he impression I had was that we were leaving the West and entering the East . . .'. Accordingly, the journey undertaken by Dracula himself in the opposite direction, from Carpathia to England, licenses an orientalist discourse about the 'invasion' of the urban/industrial/rational/scientific West by a correspondingly rural/agrarian/irrational/mystical East.

78. For sexuality as the dominant theme in films about Dracula, see Pirie [1977: 88, 90, 98ff.]. The view about the unimportance of socio-economic context is held by Tudor [1974: 208]. To some degree, the latter is contradicted by Pirie [1973: 98], who draws attention to the continuity of these films with the original Gothic themes structuring this discourse.

79. Hence the view [*Pirie*, 1977: 26, 31] that 'Dracula's success as a character is no historical accident. The novel in which he appears is one of the most extraordinary works of popular fiction ever written, an astonishing culmination of the sado-erotic strains and stresses of the entire Victorian age. It is a book of immense unconscious power, weaving a spell of sex, blood and death around the reader which remains quite unaffected by time. On one level at least, the character of the Count can be construed as the great submerged force of Victorian libido breaking out to punish the repressive society which had imprisoned it; one of the more appalling things the Count perpetually does to the matronly women of his Victorian enemies (in the novel and in the best of films) is to make them sensual . . . It is not surprising that once [Bram Stoker] hit on a theme as visually arresting and sexually liberating as the demon aristocratic vampire, what he eventually wrote should have proved irresistible to film-makers of the 20th century.' On the question of class, Porter [1983: 207] claims that Hammer studios 'consistently shunned the problems of the contemporary world and set its horror films at the high point of Victorian capitalism . . . economic and class conflicts were effectively eliminated from the narrative'. This is a view which is disputed here, since the agrarian myth is centrally about class and class struggle.

80. Equally relevant in this regard is the discursive compatibility between the Dracula legend and the religious mythology/rituals of Roman Catholicism, an effect of which is to highlight the traditional support provided by a reactionary church for the landowning class, and thus to challenge the politically progressive nature of the vampire film genre. Ostensibly about the triumph of Christianity over Evil, the Dracula legend in fact mimics and reinforces the symbolic structure of religious belief and ritual. Hence the Roman Catholic priest, like Count Dracula, is clothed

in black, and both consume the blood of a sacrificial victim: one at night, the other during the daily celebration of Holy Communion. As in the case of the Count, the person of Christ not only takes different forms (Holy Ghost, God the Father) but is himself the subject of resurrection: each of them has plural identities, rises from the dead, and lives eternally.

81. The element of *droit de seigneur* is itself a common enough cinematic theme, extending from Eisenstein's unfinished film *Que Viva Mexico* (1931), *via* Schaffner's *The War Lord* (1965), to Gibson's *Braveheart* (1995).

82. Peasants and agricultural labourers on an agrarian co-operative in eastern Peru where this writer carried out fieldwork during the mid-1970s reported that during the pre-reform era the young unmarried women in their households were regularly harassed sexually by landowners for whom they worked. According to Briggs [1920: 43], at the start of the twentieth century in the Indian state of Uttar Pradesh *ius primae noctis* was a practice whereby a landlord obtained sexual favours from the wife of an untouchable in exchange for material 'favours' granted her spouse. In the case of Tamil Nadu, Pandian [1992: 59] observes that 'in certain villages [in the border area between Tiruchi and South Arcot districts] every woman had to spend her nuptial night with the village *Nattanmai* (headman)'. Equating sexual predation by landlords on female members in tenant households with emancipation/liberation is not so dissimilar from a central argument of the now discredited Freyre/Tannenbaum thesis [*Freyre*, 1956; *Tannenbaum*, 1947], which maintained that among the reasons why plantation slavery in Latin America was less onerous than its North American counterpart was an absence of racism, itself due to the prevalence of sexual relations between white male planters and black female slaves.

83. For an account of Herzog's version of *Nosferatu*, see Sandford [1981: 60–63].

84. On this point see Sandford [1981: 62], where he observes that, like Kaspar Hauser, Count Orlock/Dracula is a figure 'of pity [who] yearns for affection and understanding – and here he is very much in that Herzog tradition of characters, both real and ficticious, whom the world rejects because they are different'.

85. Although categorized as belonging to the horror genre (see, for example, Newman [1988]), *The Wicker Man* is in purely visual terms not a film that inspires terror; even the immolation of Howie is far less explicitly visceral than, for example, that of Grandier in *The Devils* (1971), directed by Ken Russell. The undeniable element of shock generated by *The Wicker Man* derives from four interconnected elements: the fact that the audience is encouraged to identify with the character of Howie and his concern for the 'missing' girl, the unexpectedness and ease of his deception, the finality and untroubled manner in which superstition overcomes rationality, and the closeness of the episode to the audience in terms of time and space.

86. As in other films projecting the discourse of the agrarian myth, *The Wicker Man* is based on a polarity between rural (= good) and urban (= bad) that also involves the following oppositions:

Urban/bad	Rural/good
Sgt Howie	Lord Summerisle
The State	The Community
Present	Past
Modernity	Tradition
Non-natural	Nature

The column on the right contains the positive components, as these appear to the islanders, while the negative ones are on the left. Significantly, the image of the Hare is a symbolically crucial motif recurring throughout the film. For example, the 'missing' girl is compared to a hare, and when Howie – suspecting that she has been murdered – exhumes her coffin, it contains only a hare. In folklore, the Hare is associated with a multiplicity of interlocking symbols, all of which are central to the concerns of *The Wicker Man*: the rebirth of Nature in springtime (= Easter, Mayday), the fertility of crops and women, the trickster, and sacrifice.

87. That Howie is identified as such by the islanders is clear from the three reasons given by them for immolating him: not only because he is a virgin and a fool (= Punch), therefore, but also because he 'comes as a representative of the Law'.

88. In the course of his search for the 'missing' girl, Howie encounters a boat anchored in the local harbour containing numerous empty boxes on which are stencilled the words 'Summerisle Apples', and which will be used to transport the harvested crop to external markets.

89. This is confirmed by the fact that anti-modern beliefs had not existed all along, but were reintroduced by Lord Summerisle's grandfather at the same time as agricultural production was modernized.

90. Like Count Orlock, moreover, Batman/Bruce Wayne lives in what is unmistakeably a Gothic castle.

Conclusion

Possessing its more immediate historical, epistemological and political roots in the conservative reaction to the rationalist discourse of the Enlightenment, the agrarian myth argues for the centrality of the rural/urban divide, and reaffirms the enduring cultural and economic importance of an innate 'peasant-ness' not just to rural but also to national identity and existence. This view informed European nationalism in the nineteenth century, the 'old' populisms and nationalisms which emerged during the 1890s, the 1920s and the 1930s in Europe, the United States, Latin America and Asia, and also the discourse of 'otherness'/'difference' shared by variants of the 'new' populism and the 'new' political right, both of which re-emerged in many of these same contexts from the 1960s onwards and consolidated in the 1990s.

Notwithstanding the variety in contextually-specific forms, such as *nohonshugi* in Japan, 'Merrie England' in the UK, Inca 'communism' in Peru, *heimat* in Germany, *strapaese* in Italy and *narodnichestvo* in Russia, what is striking about the discourse of the agrarian myth is its epistemological uniformity across time and space. In all these places and at all these periods, therefore, the structure and components of the agrarian myth are basically the same. Its discourse-for proclaims the desirability – if not the actual presence – of an arcadian existence close to and in accord with Nature, an idyllic/harmonious village community in which small-scale economic activity undertaken by peasant family farms generates the elements of rural tradition constitutive of national identity. Because they all foment the rural class formation/struggle that results in depeasantization, and thus not only erode cultural and national identity but may also lead to socialism, the discourse-against of the agrarian myth expresses opposition to the large-scale, to economic activity linked to technology/science and mechanization, to finance capital, industrialization and economic growth, and to the locus of these institutions/processes: the urban, the state, the banks, the working class (= 'the mob in the streets') and an equally threatening and 'alien' (= non-'natural'/'foreign') internationalism.

By itself, however, the agrarian myth cannot accomplish anything, and is soon consigned to the realm of academic study (= the esoteric, the folkloric), within which it circulates and from which it never escapes. Only when deployed as part of wider ideological struggle is it capable of exercising a political impact, and this is precisely the role of populism. The latter is such an effective mobilizing discourse from the viewpoint of a ruling class precisely because it acknowledges and proclaims a caring attitude about the effects of capitalism (and thus permits the expression of an ideological unity with the working class), but avoids solutions that would entail its systemic overthrow (and thus frustrates/displaces action/agency that could eliminate the material causes of these effects). Accordingly, the fusion of populism with the agrarian myth is perhaps the only way in which the political right can attempt to generate a mass following, which it does by invoking the legitimacy of 'popular culture' in seeking to obtain grassroots support for nationalist politics. As the examples of the United States and Russia during the late nineteenth century, and Europe, the United States, Latin America and Asia during the 1920s and 1930s all confirm, this populism does by mobilizing the support of the historical bearers of 'popular culture', the peasantry, in defence of the nation and thus against external 'foreign impositions' (= finance capital, socialism) deemed responsible both for the capitalist crisis and thus for its effects, economic de-peasantization and cultural de-essentialization.

Peasant de-essentialization is accordingly equated by populism not just with alienation but also with estrangement from a 'natural' identity celebrated/consecrated by 'popular culture' as the authentic essence of nationalism. The fact that, at different conjunctures and in different contexts, 'popular culture' linked to the agrarian myth either overlaps with or actually is the foundation myth (an homogeneous peasantry = the people = the nation) serves to reinforce the politico-ideological potency of this kind of mobilization. Hence the efficacy of a discourse which claims 'we (= peasants) made the land productive and thus the nation what it is today: without us and the work we did it would not now exist'. A populist grassroots mobilization based on the 'popular culture' of the agrarian myth thus becomes a defence not only of the peasantry but also – and more powerfully – of national identity.

Central to populism as a mobilizing ideology, therefore, is the kind of identity projected in this process: specifically the displacement of class consciousness/struggle by ethnic/national identity/antagonism. Given that rural movements, which have some middle/poor peasant membership and may in some circumstances even draw on the support of agricultural workers, nevertheless mobilize on the basis of rich peasant objectives, how such an economic and political contradiction is sustained *ideologically* must be related in turn to the form/content of the mobilizing discourse (= populism) which focusses on the presentation/projection of issues and identity in a non-class manner. And it is precisely this kind of deflecting role, which suggests the possibility of identities/interests not only unconnected with class but also that can be shared with landlords or rich peasants (we-*are*-all-the-same by virtue of being rural-not-urban, peasants-not-workers, nationals-not-'foreigners'), that populism discharges either for an emerging/aspiring agrarian bourgeoisie or an established one faced with an economic or political crisis.

Essentialist views about the peasantry which inform populist discourse can be mobilized both by rich peasants and also by landlords in defence of their own class interests. In the case of rich peasants, for example, this discourse takes the form of 'we-are-no-different-from-other-smallholders', while landlords similarly maintain that 'we-are-no-different-from-other-rural-subjects'. Both adhere to a view of a 'natural' peasant cultivator – the *sine qua non* of the agrarian myth – with whom each claims ideological affinity on the basis of a shared interest in landholding, the process of agricultural production, and its accompanying cultural traditions and practices. As its filmic/literary depictions confirm, the contrasting manifestations of the agrarian myth, the pastoral and the explicitly Darwinian, can apply equally to peasant economy and landlordism. In the pastoral each is depicted as harmonious, while in the Darwinian each is engaged in struggle.

Towards the latter half of the nineteenth century, and throughout the first half of the twentieth, populism was a mobilizing ideology that reflected the political and economic interests of the rural rich. In late nineteenth-century Russia, therefore, it projected the interests of the nobility and during the early twentieth that of the kulaks. In Eastern Europe at this conjuncture, agrarian populism reflected the interests of rich peasants and/or commerical farmers, while in the United States it was the ideology of farmers faced with foreign competition and Southerners lamenting the loss of plantation society and values. Agrarian populism was also the mobilizing discourse of the rich peasantry led by Gandhi in India, for whom the target was colonialism generally, and in particular foreign – but not domestic – landlordism. In Japan and Italy during the 1920s and 1930s, it reflected the interests of landlords faced with 'from below' struggles by tenants, whose antagonism was thereby refocused on to 'the urban' and/or 'the foreigner'.

With the demise of the landlord class as a result of the post-war land reform programmes, populism shifted to reflecting the political and economic interests of capitalist farmers and rich peasants in the rural Third World, who – like landlords during the pre-war era – were similarly faced with a potential/actual 'from below' challenge. It was the mobilizing ideology deployed by the Latin American rich peasantry engaged in cash-crop cultivation. In Peru during the late 1950s and early 1960s by capitalist tenants growing coffee in La Convención, and in the 1980s by better-off peasants growing coca in the Upper Huallaga Valley; and in Colombia during the 1970s, also by coffee-growing small agrarian capitalists. The same was true of India, where agrarian populism was similarly the mobilizing discourse invoked by rich peasant tribals in West Bengal during the late 1960s and early 1970s, and also by rural capitalists who led and/or participated in the new farmers' movements which emerged in Green Revolution areas during the late 1970s and early 1980s. The similarity between the mobilizing discourse of the latter and that of the Hindu political right (the BJP/VHP/RSS) at the same conjuncture serves to warn against attempts to classify populism as progressive.

Accordingly, a frequent mistake made by those occupying many different positions on the political spectrum is that populism constitutes a leftwards movement by the political right; namely, that the espousal of populism is an indicator that the right is becoming politically more progressive. It is argued here that the opposite is the case: it is not the right that has shifted leftwards but much rather the left that has shifted rightwards, in the process becoming less progressive politically. It is important to note in this regard that the mere presence in peasant and/or farmer movements of activists from the political left cannot of itself be taken as evidence for the advocacy of socialist policies. Much rather the contrary, since agrarian mobilizations such as ANUC in Colombia, FIR and Sendero Luminoso in Peru, Naxalism in West Bengal and the new farmers' movements in India generally all suggest that what happens in these circumstances is that, rather than advocating a specifically socialist programme, grassroots leftist organizations, such as Maoist/Trotskyist tendencies in Peru and Colombia or the CPI/CPI(M)/CPI(ML) in pre- and post-Independence India, simply lock onto existing policy/programmes. In other words, what is frequently accepted at face value as socialism is not actually socialist but much rather a variety of populism, its emanation from left-wing circles notwithstanding.

The sole exception, when it is permissible for socialists to unite with populists, is in (usually historical) contexts when the main political opponent is not capitalism but feudalism, and it is necessary to struggle for the displacement of the latter by the former, in the process realizing the national identity that is itself to be challenged and discarded along with capitalism. Under no circumstances is it possible for socialists to espouse populist programmes/policies in a context that is already capitalist, since this amounts to a defence of rather than an attack against the latter system. Yet – as the examples of the CPI, the CPI(M) and the CPI(ML) in India, and the FIR and Sendero in Peru all testify – this is precisely what has been done in many Third World contexts where socialists have discharged a major theoretical/organizational role in peasant and/or farmer movements.

That contemporary forms of agency generated by a combination of the agrarian myth and populism are not confined to the Third World is evident from two mobilizations which occurred in one particular metropolitan capitalist context during the late 1990s: the mass support received by the

Countryside Alliance in England, and the way in which the funeral of Diana Princess of Wales became the occasion for the celebration of her 'caring' role and the expression of 'popular' resentment against 'non-caring'/'traditional' British royalty. Significantly, this 'popular' outpouring of positive/negative sentiment was led by a member of the landowning aristocracy (her brother) and, supported by an heterogeneous ensemble of the bourgeoisie (New Labour 'modernizers', wealthy media celebrities, and elements of the non-tabloid press), constituted a manifestation directed not against the monarchy as such but rather against its current and proximate incumbents. Rather than a discourse-for which invokes republicanism, and with it a potential systemic challenge to capitalism itself, therefore, this populist mobilization confined itself to a discourse-against the target of which is only those perceived to be 'non-caring'/'traditional' components of the ruling class (= 'the establishment'), and not the ruling class as a whole. Not only does the capitalist system – the source of inequality, poverty and oppression – escape scrutiny, but in the process the institution of monarchy is itself rehabilitated.

Such attempts by conservatives and those on the political right to mobilize grassroots support on the basis of the agrarian myth have encountered their strongest opposition from Marxism, the theoretical and political 'other' of populism and neo-populism. The distinction between the latter and Marxism concerning the link between capitalist development, the peasantry, and a transition to socialism is reflected in the different epistemologies and outcomes of the agrarian question and the agrarian myth. For Marxism, accumulation entails not only the concentration of landownership and the development of the productive forces but also the process of class differentiation of smallholders into rural capitalists and workers. Differentiating the peasantry into rich, middle, and poor strata, Lenin argued that capitalist penetration of agriculture converted the former into a rural bourgeoisie and the latter into de facto rural labour, while middle peasants (or petty commodity producers) were 'depeasantized'. Not only is the historical subject of Marxism the proletariat formed by capitalism itself in the course of class struggle generated by large-scale urban industrial development, therefore, but the political objects and desired outcomes of this process are the revolutionary capture of the state and a transition to socialism.

Unlike Marxism, both populism and neo-populism deny that such a connection exists. For neo-populists, therefore, rural change is different not only in terms of content and outcome but also in that it is endogenous to the peasant family farm. Chayanovian theory denies that capitalist penetration of agriculture entails 'depeasantization', and argues instead that the economic reproduction of each individual peasant family farm is governed by the development cycle of the domestic group, and not by surplus appropriation.

Not only does such a process not entail class formation consequent on peasant differentiation, therefore, but it cannot generate systemic change, in the form of a transition either to capitalism or to socialism. This opposition between on the one hand small-scale 'people's' production and on the other large-scale capitalism or socialism is central to populism, which regards the state as the mechanism whereby the latter appropriates resources produced by the former. Peasants are forced to pay for industrialization, which populists maintain is an alien/urban/capitalist/socialist phenomenon the cost of which is the destruction of peasant family farming and the growth of a 'dangerous' proletariat. Rather than signalling the decline of Chayanovian theory, postwar capitalist expansion was accompanied by its return.

The period immediately following the Second World War was characterized not so much by the absence of the agrarian myth as by a diminution in its influence. Among the more important reasons for this were its pre-war complicity with the rise of fascism, and its incompatibility with the requirements of capital accumulation at that particular conjuncture. Essentialist concepts of the peasantry as self-sufficient smallholders hindered the expansion in the Third World both of consumer demand for commodities produced by capital, and also the formation of an industrial reserve army of labour. From the late 1960s onwards, however, as capitalism was faced with a resurgence in class conflict, this situation changed: across a wide range of debate and activity both populism and the agrarian myth began to re-emerge. This process informed not only the 'popular culture' of American, European and Indian film, therefore, but also rural grassroots movements in the Third World together with political discourse about these, and development theory itself, where the post-war decline in peasant economy has been accompanied by a conceptual re-essentialization of the peasantry: initially by neoclassical theory as an economic subject, and then by postmodernism as a cultural subject.

In terms of theory, this recuperation within the domain of 'popular culture' of peasant essentialism (= 'peasant-ness') was itself premissed – indeed, was ultimately dependent – on an additional process: the displacement of working class revolutionary agency, together with the accompanying possibilities of systemic transformation/emancipation. Inherited subsequently by the postmodern 'new' populism, this particular displacement stems from earlier anticolonial/anti-imperial discourse associated with the work of Fanon and Marcuse. Although too much of a Marxist to argue that emancipation from capitalism would be the task exclusively of the rural 'underprivileged' in the Third World, Marcuse did on occasion appear to create a space for just such a view, not least by his opposition between the non-revolutionary 'incorporated' working class of metropolitan capitalism and the pre-revolutionary 'unincorporated' social forces in the so-called Third World – of which the peasantry was an important component. Like exponents of the postmodern variants of the 'new' populism, therefore, Marcuse and Fanon imply that capitalism cannot be transcended; the conclusion of the former is that consequently no change must be attempted, while that of both the latter is to seek an alternative revolutionary subject. It is argued here that, in the end, both positions are not that dissimilar.

In contrast to the perception that in the Third World a connection between populism, the agrarian myth and nationalism ceased with decolonization, therefore, the collapse of actually-existing socialism in the 1990s has been accompanied by the reactivation of most/all of the elements (for example, ethnicity, religion) associated with populism and the agrarian myth. This is especially true in places where there has been – and is currently – an attempt to protect existing smallholding agriculture from global capitalist competition, or to re-create peasant family farming. The expansion of neo-liberal capitalism, which is incorporating large sections of the peasantry in Third World and ex-/actually-existing socialist countries into an international industrial reserve army of labour, is being accompanied by a worldwide resurgence of nationalism and a corresponding displacement of socialist ideas by 'new' populist ones. Among other things, this licenses the re-emergence of folkloric variants of reactionary nationalism linked to the agrarian myth.

A combined effect of the collapse of socialism and the resurgence of national/ethnic conflict has been the abandonment of Marxist solutions to problems of underdevelopment and their replacement with postmodern 'new' populist ones. The latter consist of analytical approaches based on new social movements theory, the Subaltern Studies project, ecofeminism, the impasse position, and the 'post-development' and 'post-colonial' framework, all of which claim that the 'voice-from-below' in the so-called Third World is determined not by class formation but by ethnic/peasant/tribal/gender identity. Similarly, 'new' populist agency is based not on class struggle culminating in revolutionary transformation, the political objectives of which are the capture of the state and a transition to socialism, but rather on 'everyday forms of resistance', an 'a-political'/'above-politics' process which eschews confrontation with the state and seeks only redemocratization.

An academic equivalent of New Age mysticism, postmodernism challenges the necessity of development and the existence of class, both of which are dismissed as universal/'foundational' Eurocentric metanarratives. What exponents of the 'new' populism fail to understand is that what they regard as positive in postmodern theory, the focus on non-class identity, is something that is by no means unique to postmodernism, whereas the negative element – the denial of the possibility of development – is actually an effect of its central epistemological tenet: undecidability. It is precisely as a result of this latter element that postmodernism cannot endorse a politics, since to do so would require a privileging of one specific viewpoint as correct, a 'judgemental' process the efficacy of which postmodernism denies.

In much contemporary social theory influenced by postmodernism this process of de-objectification/de-privileging of attempts to construct an existence beyond the self amounts at times to solipsism. One effect is to fragment reality, which is reduced to the epistemological status of an epiphenomenon of the 'self'. A de-objectified 'reality' that does not – indeed cannot – extend beyond the perception of the individual becomes thereby whatever any/every subject claims it to be. Not only is this 'reality' now reducible to the individual, but it is also deemed to be the basis of a subjectively-based process of self-empowerment, simply by virtue of 'being-mine/being-yours'. There is accordingly no longer an 'out there' to be perceived, only competing perceptions of an 'out there'. Instead of objectivity, therefore, there are now only contesting subjectivities, each of which advances rival claims to truth, and between which one is no longer able to judge.

One consequence of an 'out-there' objective 'reality' being non-existent is it cannot be changed, a position that is so convenient for owners of real estate. In addition to valorizing the view of the indigenous subject in relation to that of the colonizer, therefore, such de-objectification/depriviveging also confers political acceptability on landlords' or capitalists' view of existence, now deemed to be as 'valid' as that of a tenant or worker. Another is the reification of nationalism and ethnicity. The inference that culture, ethnicity and 'difference' were somehow 'discovered' by the postmodernist 'new' populism, and are therefore concepts about which Marxism and Marxists have remained silent, is of course untrue. Marxism and Marxists have long pronounced on these issues, but – unlike postmodernism and the 'new' populists – have insisted that without reference to the class position of those involved, it is impossible either to understand 'difference', to explain why culture takes the form it does, or why some forms of identity but not others surface at particular moments. To treat phenomena such as culture, ethnicity and 'difference' generally as innate, and thus as inexplicable in terms of relations beyond themselves, as postmodern 'new' populists seem intent on doing, is to indulge in the most fundamental form of idealism, a procedure that forbids analysis and allows only description.

For postmodernism, class is doubly unacceptable: not merely is it equated with an Eurocentric metanarrative, but it also categorizes the subject as victim. In much of the development theory influenced by postmodernism (= 'the subaltern', 'post-colonialism', 'everyday forms of resistance', 'eco-feminism', etc.) it is no longer possible to present the 'other' (= tribals, women, peasants, ethnic groups, etc.) as victim, since this is perceived as demeaning and/or disempowering. Accordingly, as 'victimhood' is equated by postmodern 'new' populist theory with passivity, and as self-empowerment on the part of the subject negates victimhood, the rejection of passivity through the de-victimization of the subject entails among other things the abandonment of class identity. Because of the latter, and a failure to distinguish between a progressive/modern anti-capitalism and a romantic anti- (or post-) modern form the roots of which are located in the agrarian myth, the response by many academics/intellectuals/activists to global capitalist expansion and/or crisis has been to endorse forms of grassroots agency which are supportive of conservative/nationalist ideology.

The importance of the 'new' populism, and one of the reasons for its political acceptability, is that its anti-capitalism is widely regarded as a socio-economically progressive project. The undeniable and enduring attraction of the 'new' populism, therefore, lies in the fact that it appears to endorse the voice-'from-below', and thus champions the oppressed in their opposition to capitalism. In part, this stems from an epistemological process of devictimiza-tion which entails a rejection of passivity: it is no longer acceptable to (re-) present the 'other' as victim, a conceptual approach extended to a wide variety of hitherto mute/disempowered sociological categories. Hence the laudable desire on the part of those anaysing the role of the peasantry to devictimize it, thus dispelling historically discredited notions of passivity by emphasizing the agency/empowerment of 'those below'.

This, it could be argued, lies behind at least some of widespread intellectual endorsement of postmodernism. Faced with setbacks, many of those who used to be on the left have opted to abandon what has now become an academically, ideologically and politically unfashionable struggle and adopt the discourse/politics of the 'new' populism. For exponents of the latter, it has been necessary to reinterpret all grassroots struggle as victorious and its political objectives as accomplished: what Marxism categorizes as forms of oppression, therefore, can now be (re-) presented/(reinvented) as a forms of rural grassroots empowerment and celebrated as such. The difficulty with this is that 'everyday forms of resistance' is not (as 'new' populists claim) merely a variant form of grassroots mobilization that is more effective than revolu-tionary activity, with which it has much in common. In many Third World contexts to which this kind of framework has been applied, it is clear that 'everyday forms of resistance' refers not so much to a radical and politically progressive 'from below' movement as to *counter*-revolutionary agency generated and headed by those whose private property rights have been threatened with expropriation by an incoming socialist regime that has succeeded in capturing the state.

In contrast to the view that their anti-capitalism is sufficient evidence of the politically progressive character of the peasant and/or new farmers' movements in Latin America and India, it is argued in this book that anti-capitalism can take two diametrically opposed forms: progressive and reactionary, and that many of the peasant and/or farmers' movements fall into the latter camp. Accordingly, such mobilizations have been located in the more distinctly undemocratic political tradition of conservative populism, with its emphasis on 'the felt' (= sentimental/emotional) which naturalizes both a mystical concept of Nature and the ethnic/national/gender identities that derive from this. That an overlap exists between the essentialist view of peasant/'popular' culture which structures much postmodern theory about development and the populist Thirdworldism of the European 'new' right is unsurprising, not least because each attributes underdevelopment in the Third World to an innate, socio-economically ineradicable and culturally empowering 'difference'/'otherness'.

As in the 1920s and 1930s, therefore, so 1980s and 1990s conservatism is not of itself incompatible with an endorsement of grassroots empowerment, much rather the contrary. It does, however, insist on a particular kind of grassroots empowerment (and thus discursively places limits on this process). If 'others' or 'those below' want in turn to invoke and exercise an analogous form of 'difference' – a specifically *cultural* one – then in the view of those on the political right this is not just fine but – since it adheres to the same principle – is actually to be encouraged, so long as it does not undermine or threaten the 'distinctiveness' of the existing ruling class, the culture of which is built on (and indeed symbolizes) its own *economic* power. Two points can be made in this connection. First, this is one of the reasons why historically the right has always objected (in terms of a culturally-eroding imposition of 'sameness') to the invocation by those on the left of univerals. And second, this is precisely the way in which the political right imbues its discourse with a spuriously 'democratic' veneer: by invoking the right to 'cultural difference' in this manner it not only protects the *economic* interests of the ruling class but does so in a way that is apparently innocent politically and even disinterestedly plebeian – the basis of the 'new' populism, in other words.

Precisely because it operates largely within the domain of 'the cultural', the discourse-for/discourse-against of both the 'new' populism and the 'new' right recognizes and simultaneously negates the threat that emanates from 'marginality' and 'alienation': by re-defining the latter as 'difference', each is banished as a problem. In cultural (but not economic) terms, therefore, the 'marginal' that is 'alienated' is recategorized merely as 'other': 'there is nothing *wrong* with being the way you are', this discourse proclaims, 'you are simply *different*'. This concept of 'difference'/'otherness' fuses with and is supportive of a 'new'-populist/'new'-right Thirdworldism: in contrast to the agrarian question of Marxism, which focuses on the way peasant *economy* changes, the agrarian myth of populism seeks to recuperate peasant essentialism by shifting the focus onto the way in which peasant *culture* (= the root of 'otherness'/'difference') remains the same.

Not only is this Thirdworldism compatible with the pluralistic endorsement of religious/ethnic/national heterogeneity on the part of the 'new' right and the 'new' populism but the discourse-for of both the latter has converted the element of a politically unacceptable (= economically disempowering) cultural subordination and economic exploitation associated with alienation into a neutral form of 'otherness'. The distinctiveness of the so-called Third World 'other' has, in short, been reconstructed as an empowering form of cultural 'difference'. Economic 'difference' as a form of 'otherness'/'not-us' is displaced by cultural 'difference' as the definition of identity, the consequence of which is that economic 'difference' is no longer perceived as alienating or exploitative but merely organizationally 'other'; not only does economic 'difference' no longer have to be explained or changed, but it is epistemologically reduced to and in effect becomes part of 'cultural' difference, henceforth to be celebrated as such. The 'new'-populist/'new'-right discourse is accordingly a relativistic analytical framework in which it is possible to assert that the rich and powerful are simply culturally 'different' from the poor and powerless, and the economic 'difference' of the latter is not merely part of their culture but much rather a form of empowerment. Both the fact of economic 'difference' and its cause are thereby banished from this discourse.

Bibliography

A Correspondent, 1987, 'Other Side of Punjab Crisis', *Economic and Political Weekly*, Vol.22, No.33.

Aass, S., 1980, 'The Relevance of Chayanov's Macro Theory to the Case of Java', in Hobsbawm, Kula, Mitra, Raj, and Sachs (eds.) [1980].

Abelson, E. (ed.), 1988, *A Mirror of England: An Anthology of the Writings of H.J. Massingham (1888–1952)*, Bideford: Green Books.

Adler, F., 1994, 'Left Vigilance in France', *Telos*, Nos.98–99.

Ahmad, A., 1992, *In Theory: Classes, Nations, Literatures*, London: Verso.

Ahmad, A., 1995, 'Postcolonialism: What's in a Name?', in de la Campa, Kaplan and Sprinker (eds.) [1995].

Akram-Lodhi, H., 1995, 'M.H. Khan, A.V. Chayanov and the Family Farms of the North-West Frontier (Pakistan)', *The Journal of Peasant Studies*, Vol.22, No.2.

Alavi, H. and J. Harriss (eds.), 1989, *Sociology of 'Developing Societies': South Asia*, London: Macmillan.

Alavi, H., 1973, 'Peasant Classes and Primordial Loyalties', *The Journal of Peasant Studies*, Vol.1, No.1.

Alavi, H., 1979, 'Peasants and Revolution', in Desai (ed.) [1979].

Alberti, G. and E. Mayer (eds.), 1974, *Reciprocidad e intercambio en los Andes peruanos*, Lima: Instituto de Estudios Peruanos.

Aldred, N., 1987, 'Powell and Pressburger's Film Fantasies of Britain', in Mellor (ed.) [1987].

Alexander, K.C., 1981, *Peasant Organizations in South India*, New Delhi: Indian Social Institute.

Alfaro, J. and T. Ore, n.d., *El desarrollo del capitalismo en La Convención y los nuevos movimientos políticos de campesinos con tierra 1963–1973*, Lima: Memoria de Bachiller, Universidad Católica del Peru.

All India Kisan Sabha, 1981, *New Peasant Upsurge – Reason and Remedies: Documents and Resolutions, AIKS Meeting November/December 1980*, New Delhi: AIKS.

Althusser, L., 1969, *For Marx*, London: Allen Lane.

Altieri, M. and S.Hecht (eds.), 1990, *Agroecology and Small Farm Development*, London: IT Publications.

Ambedkar, B.R., 1946, *What Congress and Gandhi have done to the Untouchables*, Bombay: Thacker & Co., Ltd.

Amery, L.S., 1944, *The Framework of the Future*, London: Oxford University Press.

Amin, S., 1984, 'Gandhi as Mahatma: Gorakhpur District, Eastern UP, 1921–22', in Guha (ed.) [1984].

Amiran, E. and J. Unsworth (eds.), 1993, *Essays in Postmodern Culture*, New York: Oxford University Press.

Amis, K., 1961, *Lucky Jim*, Harmondsworth: Penguin Books.

Amnesty International, 1983, *Political Killings by Governments*, London: Amnesty International Publications.

Anderson, W.K. and S.D. Damle, 1987, *The Brotherhood in Saffron: The Rashtriya Swayamsevak Sangh and Hindu Revivalism*, New Delhi: Vistaar Publications.

Aranda, A. and M. Escalante, 1978, *Lucha de clases en el movimiento sindical Cusqueño, 1927–1965*, Lima: G. Herrera, Editores.

Archetti, E.P. and S. Aass, 1978, 'Peasant Studies: An Overview', in Newby (ed.) [1978].

Arnheim, R., 1933, *Film*, London: Faber & Faber.

Assadi, M., 1994, ' "Khadi Curtain", "Weak Capitalism" and "Operation Ryot": Some Ambiguities in Farmers Discourse, Karnataka and Maharashtra 1980–93', *The Journal of Peasant Studies*, Vol.21, Nos.3/4.

Athreya, V., Djurfeldt, G. and S. Lindberg, 1990, *Broken Barriers: Production Relations and Agrarian Change in Tamil Nadu*, New Delhi: Sage Publications.

Atkinson, D., 1977, 'Russian Rationality', *Peasant Studies*, Vol.5, No.2.

Bagchi, A.K., 1993, ' "Rent-Seeking", New Political Economy and Negation of Politics', *Economic and Political Weekly*, Vol.28, No.34.

Bahro, R., 1982, *Socialism and Survival*, London: Heretic Books.

Bailey, R.B., 1958, *Sociology Faces Pessimism: A Study of European Sociological Thought Amidst a Fading Optimism*, The Hague: Martinus Nijhoff.

Balagopal, K., 1986, 'Agrarian Struggles', *Economic and Political Weekly*, Vol.21, No.32.

Balagopal, K., 1987a, 'An Ideology for the Provincial Propertied Class', *Economic and Political Weekly*, Vol.22, Nos.36/37.

Balagopal, K., 1987b, 'An Ideology for the Provincial Propertied Class', *Economic and Political Weekly*, Vol.22, No.50.

Balagopal, K., 1988, *Probings in the Political Economy of Agrarian Classes and Conflicts*, Hyderabad: Perspectives.

Banaji, J., 1976, 'Chayanov, Kautsky, Lenin: Considerations Towards a Synthesis', *Economic and Political Weekly*, Vol.11, No.40.

Banaji, J., 1980, 'The Comintern and Indian Nationalism', in Panikkar (ed.) [1980].

Banaji, J., 1990, 'Illusions About the Peasantry: Karl Kautsky and the Agrarian Question', *The Journal of Peasant Studies*, Vol.17, No.2.

Banaji, J., 1994, 'The Farmers' Movements: A Critique of Conservative Rural Coalitions' *The Journal of Peasant Studies*, Vol.21, Nos.3/4.

Bann, S. and K. Kumar (eds.), 1993, *Utopias and the Millenium*, London: Reaktion Books.

Bardhan, P., Datta-Chaudhuri, M. and T.N. Krishnan (eds.), 1993, *Development and Change: Essays in Honour of K.N. Raj*, Bombay: Oxford University Press.

Barker, M., 1979, 'Racism: The New Inheritors', *Radical Philosophy*, No.21.

Barker, M., 1981, *The New Racism: Conservatives and the Ideology of the Tribe*, London: Junction Books.

Barnett, A. and R. Scruton (eds.), 1998, *Town and Country*, London: Johathan Cape.

Barnouw, E. and S. Krishnaswamy, 1980, *Indian Film*, New Delhi: Oxford University Press.

Barr, C., 1974, ' "Projecting Britain and the British Character": Ealing Studios', *Screen*, Vol.15, No.2.

Barr, C., 1977, *Ealing Studios*, London: David & Charles.

Barry, N.P., 1986, *On Classical Liberalism and Libertarianism*, London: Macmillan.

Barthakur, S. and S. Goswami, 1990, 'The Assam Movement', in Sen (ed.) [1990].

Baskaran, S.T., 1981, *The Message Bearers: Nationalist Politics and the Entertainment Media in South India, 1880–1945*, Madras: Cre-A.

Basu, K. and A. Mishra, 1993, 'Sustainable Development and the Commons Problem: A Simple Approach', in Bardhan, Datta-Chaudhuri and Krishnan (eds.) [1993].

Basu, T. *et al.*, 1993, *Khaki Shorts and Saffron Flags: A Critique of the Hindu Right*, New Delhi: Orient Longman.

Bataille, G., 1985, *Visions of Excess: Selected Writings, 1927–1939*, Manchester: Manchester University Press.

Bataille, G., 1988, *The Accursed Share – Volume I*, New York: Zone Books.

Bataille, G., 1991, *The Accursed Share – Volumes II and III*, New York: Zone Books.

Bataille, G., 1992, *Theory of Religion*, New York: Zone Books.

Bataille, G., 1994, *The Absence of Myth*, London: Verso.

Bates, R.H., 1993, ' "Urban Bias": A Fresh Look', in Varshney [1993c].

Baudin, L., 1961/1928, *A Socialist Empire: The Incas of Peru*, Princeton, NJ: D. Van Nostrand.

Baudrillard, J., 1975, *The Mirror of Production*, St. Louis, MO: Telos Press.

Baudrillard, J., 1981, *For a Critique of the Political Economy of the Sign*, St Louis, MO: Telos Press.

Baudrillard, J., 1983, *In the Shadow of the Silent Majorities, or The End of the Social*, New York: Semiotext(e).

Bauer, P.T., 1971, *Dissent on Development: Studies and Debates in Development Economics*, London: Weidenfeld & Nicolson.

Bausinger, H., 1990, *Folk Culture in a World of Technology*, Bloomington, IN: Indiana University Press.

Baxter, C., 1971, *The Jana Sangh: A Biography of an Indian Political Party*, Bombay: Oxford University Press.

Beik, W., 1993, 'Debate: The Dilemma of Popular History', *Past and Present*, No.141.

Béjar, H., 1970, *Peru 1965: Notes on a Guerrilla Experience*, New York: Monthly Review Press.

Bell, D., 1962, 'The Debate on Alienation', in Labedz (ed.) [1962].

Bell, D., 1971, 'Post-Industrial Society: The Evolution of an Idea', *Survey*, Vol.17, No.2.

Bell, J.D., 1977, *Peasants in Power: Alexander Stamboliski and the Bulgarian Agrarian National Union, 1899–1923*, Princeton, NJ: Princeton University Press.

Belloc, H., 1924, *Economics for Helen*, London: The Knickerbocker Press.

Belloc, H., 1936, *An Essay on the Restoration of Property*, London: The Distributist League.

Belton, J., 1994, *American Cinema/American Culture*, New York: McGraw Hill.

Bendersky, J.W., 1983, *Carl Schmitt: Theorist for the Reich*, Princeton, NJ: Princeton University Press.

Bendix, R., 1960, *Max Weber: An Intellectual Portrait*, London: Heinemann.

Benvenuto, S., 1994, 'Beyond Left and Right', *Telos*, Nos.98–99.

Berger, P.L., 1979, 'In Praise of Particularity: The Concept of Mediating Structures', in *Facing Up to Modernity*, London: Penguin Books.

Berger, P.L., 1987, *The Capitalist Revolution*, Aldershot, Hants: Wildwood House.

Bergquist, C., 1993, 'Labor History and Its Challenges: Confessions of a Latin Americanist', *The American Historical Review*, Vol.98, No.3.

Berlin, I., 1978, *Russian Thinkers*, London: The Hogarth Press.

Berlin, I., 1990, *The Crooked Timber of Humanity*, London: John Murray.

Betz, H.-G., 1994, *Radical Right-wing Populism in Western Europe*, New York: St. Martin's Press.

Beverley, J. and J. Oviedo (eds.), 1993, *The Postmodernism Debate in Latin America*, Durham, NC: Duke University Press.

Bhabha, H., 1987, 'Remembering Fanon: "What does the black man want?"', *New Formations*, No.1.

Bhabha, H., 1991, 'Conference Presentation', in Mariani (ed.) [1991].

Bhattacharya, H., 1990, 'Communism, Nationalism and the Tribal Question in Tripura', *Economic and Political Weekly*, Vol.25, No.39.

Bhowmik, S., 1981, *Class Formation in the Plantation System*, New Delhi: People's Publishing House.

Bideleux, R., 1985, *Communism and Development*, London: Methuen.

Biehl, J., 1995, '"Ecology" and the Modernization of Fascism in the German Ultra-Right', in Staudenmaier and Biehl (eds.) [1995].

Billig, M., 1993, 'Nationalism and Richard Rorty: The Text as a Flag for *Pax Americana*', *New Left Review*, 202.

Biskind, P., 1983, *Seeing is Believing: How Hollywood Taught Us to Stop Worrying and Love the Fifties*, London: Pluto Press.

Blackburn, R. (ed.), 1972, *Ideology in Social Science*, London: Fontana.

Blanco, H., 1972, *Land or Death: The Peasant Struggle in Peru*, New York: Pathfinder Press.

Blinkhorn, M. (ed.), 1990, *Fascists and Conservatives: The Radical Right and the Establishment in Twentieth Century Europe*, London: Unwin Hyman.

Block, W. and L.H.J. Rockwell (eds.), 1988, *Man, Economy and Liberty: Essays in Honor of Murray Rothbard*, Auburn: Ludwig von Mises Institute.

Blok, A., 1972, 'The Peasant and the Brigand: Social Banditry Reconsidered', *Comparative Studies in Society and History*, Vol.14, No.4.

Bodemann, Y.M., 1986, 'The Green Party and the New Nationalism in the Federal Republic of Germany', in Miliband *et al.*, (eds.) [1986].

Booth, D., 1985, 'Marxism and Development Sociology: Interpreting the Impasse', *World Development*, Vol.13, No.7.

Booth, D., 1992, 'Social Development Research: An Agenda for the 1990s', *European Journal of Development Research*, Vol.4, No.1.

Booth, D., 1993, 'Development Research: From Impasse to a New Agenda', in Schuurman (ed.) [1993].

Booth, D. (ed.), 1994, *Rethinking Social Development*, Harlow: Longman Scientific & Technical.

Bosanquet, N., 1986, 'Hayek and Friedman', in Cohen *et al.* [1986].

Bose, P.K., 1985, *Classes and Class Relations among Tribals of Bengal*, Delhi: Ajanta Publications.

Bose, S. (ed.), 1990, *South Asia and World Capitalism*, Delhi: Oxford University Press.

Bosworth, R.J.B., 1993, *Explaining Auschwitz and Hiroshima: History Writing and the Second World War, 1945–1990*, London: Routledge.

Bourque, S.C., and K.B. Warren, 1989, 'Democracy Without Peace: The Cultural Politics of Terror in Peru', *Latin American Research Review*, Vol.24, No.1.

Boyd, R., Cohen, R. and P.Gutkind (eds.), 1989, *International Labour and the Third World: The Making of a New Working Class*, Aldershot: Avebury.

Boyte, H.C., Booth, H. and S. Max, 1986, *Citizen Action and the New Populism*, Philadelphia, PA: Temple University Press.

Boyte, H.C. and F. Riessman (eds.), 1986, *The New Populism: The Politics of Empowerment*, Philadelphia, PA: Temple University Press.

Bradby, B., 1982, ' "Resistance to Capitalism" in the Peruvian Andes', in Lehmann (ed.) [1982].

Bradford, G., 1989, *How Deep is Deep Ecology?*, Hadley, MA: Times Change Press.

Bradford, M.E., 1985, *Remembering Who We Are: Observations of a Southern Conservative*, Athens, GE: The University of Georgia Press.

Bramwell, A., 1985, *Blood and Soil: Richard Walther Darré and Hitler's 'Green Party'*, Bourne End: The Kensal Press.

Bramwell, A., 1989, *Ecology in the Twentieth Century*, New Haven, CT: Yale University Press.

Brass, P.R. and M. Franda (eds.), 1973, *Radical Politics in South Asia*, Cambridge, MA: MIT Press.

Brass, T., 1982, 'The Sabotage of Anthropology and the Anthropologist as Saboteur', *Journal of the Anthropological Society of Oxford*, Vol.XIII, No.2.

Brass, T., 1986, '*Cargos* and Conflict: The Fiesta System and Capitalist Development in Eastern Peru', *The Journal of Peasant Studies*, Vol.13, No.3.

Brass, T., 1995a, 'Old Conservatism in "New" Clothes', *The Journal of Peasant Studies*, Vol.22, No.3.

Brass, T., 1995b, 'A Reply to Utsa Patnaik: If the Cap Fits . . .', *International Review of Social History*, Vol.40, Part 1.

Brass, T., 1999, *Towards a Comparative Political Economy of Unfree Labour: Case Studies and Debates*, London and Portland, OR: Frank Cass.

Bree, K.M., 1991, *The Women of the Klan: Racism and Gender in the 1920s*, Berkeley, CA: University of California Press.

Briggs, G.W., 1920, *The Chamars*, Calcutta: Association Press.

Briggs, L.T. *et al.* (eds.), 1986, *Identidades andinas y lógicas del campesinado*, Lima: Mosca Azul Editores.

Brinton, C., 1926, *The Political Ideas of the English Romanticists*, Oxford: Clarendon Press.

Britton, A. (ed.), 1991, *Talking Films*, London: Fourth Estate.

Broome, J.H., 1963, *Rousseau: A Study of his Thought*, London: Edward Arnold.

Brosnan, J., 1978, *Future Tense: The Cinema of Science Fiction*, London: McDonald & Jane's.

Brown, J., 1972, *Gandhi's Rise to Power: Indian Politics 1915–22*, London: Cambridge University Press.

Brownlow, K., 1990, *Behind the Mask of Innocence*, London: Jonathan Cape.

Buck, J.L., 1930, *Chinese Farm Economy*, Chicago, IL: University of Chicago Press.

Bukatman, S., 1993, *Terminal Identity: The Virtual Subject in Post-Modern Science Fiction*, Durham, NC: Duke University Press.

Bukharin, N., 1927, *The Economic Theory of the Leisure Class*, New York: International Publishers.

Burdick, J., 1993, *Looking for God in Brazil*, Berkeley, CA: University of California Press.

Burger, J., 1987, *Report from the Frontier: The State of the World's Indigenous Peoples*, London: Zed Press.

Burke, P., 1981, 'The "Discovery" of Popular Culture', in Samuel (ed.) [1981].

Burns, E.M., 1963, *Ideas in Conflict*, London: Methuen.

Bush, R., Johnston, G. and D. Coates (eds.), 1987 *The World Order: Socialist Perspectives*, Oxford: Polity Press.

Bustamente, J.A. *et al.* (eds.), 1992, *US–Mexico Relations: Labor Market Inter-dependence*, Stanford, CA: Stanford University Press.

Buttel, F.H. and H. Newby (eds.), 1980, *The Rural Sociology of the Advanced Societies: Critical Perspectives*, London: Croom Helm.

Cahm, E. and V.C. Fisera (eds.), 1978, *Socialism and Nationalism*, Vol.1, Nottingham: Spokesman.

Callinicos, A., 1989, *Against Postmodernism*, Cambridge: Polity Press.

Calman, L.J., 1992, *Toward Empowerment: Women and Movement Politics in India*, Boulder, CO: Westview Press.

Cameron, I. and D. Pye (eds.), 1996, *The Western*, London: Studio Vista.

Campi, A., 1994, 'Gianfranco Miglio's Challenge', *Telos*, No.100.

Cancian, F., 1989, 'Economic Behaviour in Peasant Communities', in Plattner (ed.) [1989].

Canovan, M., 1981, *Populism*, London: Junction Books.

Cantril, H., 1982, *The Invasion from Mars: A Study in the Psychology of Panic*, Princeton, NJ: Princeton University Press.

Cardoza, A.L., 1982, *Agrarian Elites and Italian Fascism: The Province of Bologna, 1901–1926*, Princeton, NJ: Princeton University Press.

Carnes, M.C. (ed.), 1995, *Past Imperfect: History According to the Movies*, London: Cassell.

Castells, M., 1977, *The Urban Question*, London: Edward Arnold.

Castells, M., 1983, *The City and the Grassroots: A Cross-Cultural Theory of Urban Social Movements*, London: Edward Arnold.

Castles, S. and M.T. Miller, 1993, *The Age of Migration: International Population Movements in the Modern World*, London: Macmillan.

Castro Pozo, H., 1924, *Nuestra Comunidad Indígena*, Lima: Editorial 'El Lucero'.

Castro Pozo, H., 1936, *Del Ayllu al Cooperativismo Socialista*, Lima: Biblioteca de la Revista de Economia y Finanzas.

Caute, D., 1970, *Fanon*, London: Fontana.

Cavaliero, G., 1977, *The Rural Tradition in the English Novel 1900–1939*, London: Macmillan.

Centre National de la Recherche Scientifique (CNRS), 1967, *Les Problèmes Agraires des Amériques Latines*, Paris: Éditions du CNRS.

Chakrabarty, D., 1984, 'Trade Unions in an Hierarchical Culture: The Jute Workers of Calcutta, 1920–50', in Guha (ed.) [1984].

Chakrabarty, D., 1992, 'Marxism and Modern India', in Ryan (ed.) [1992].

Chakrabarty, D., 1995, 'Modernity and Ethnicity in India: A History for the Present', *Economic and Political Weekly*, Vol.30, No.52.

Chandra, N.K., 1983, 'Agricultural Workers in Burdewan', in Guha (ed.) [1983].

Chapkis, W. and C. Enloe (eds.), 1983, *Of Common Cloth: Women in the Global Textile Industry*, Washington: Transnational Institute.

Charlesworth, N., 1985, *Peasants and Imperial Rule: Agriculture and Agrarian Society in the Bombay Presidency, 1850–1935*, Cambridge: Cambridge University Press.

Charrière, J. *et al.*, 1974, *The Complete Films of Eisenstein*, London: Weidenfeld & Nicolson.

Chatterjee, P., 1983, 'More on Modes of Power and the Peasantry', in Guha (ed.) [1983].

Chatterjee, P., 1984, 'Gandhi and the Critique of Civil Society', in Guha (ed.) [1984].

Chatterjee, P., 1986, *Nationalist Thought and the Colonial World: A Derivative Discourse?*, Delhi: Oxford University Press.

Chatterjee, P., 1989, 'Caste and Subaltern Consciousness', in Guha (ed.) [1989].

Chattopadhyay, B., Sharma, S.C. and A.K. Ray, 1987, 'Rural/Urban Terms of Trade, Primary Accumulation and the Increasing Strength of the Indian Farm Lobby', in Chattopadhyay and Spitz (eds.) [1987].

Chattopadhyay, B. and P. Spitz (eds.), 1987, *Food Systems and Society in Eastern India*, Geneva: UNRISD.

Chavarría, J., 1979, *José Carlos Mariátegui and the Rise of Modern Peru, 1890–1930*, Albuquerque, NM: University of New Mexico Press.

Chayanov, A.V., 1966, *The Theory of Peasant Economy* (edited by Daniel Thorner, Basile Kerblay and R.E.F. Smith), Homewood, IL: The American Economic Association.

Chayanov, A.V., 1991, *The Theory of Peasant Cooperatives*, London: I.B. Tauris.

Cheles, L., Ferguson, R. and M. Vaughan (eds.), 1991, *Neo-Fascism in Europe*, London: Longman.

Chomsky, N., 1982, *Towards a New Cold War: Essays on the Current Crisis and How We Got There*, London: Sinclair Browne.

Chossudovsky, M., 1986, *Towards Capitalist Restoration? Chinese Socialism after Mao*, London: Macmillan.

Chossudovsky, M., 1988, 'World Unemployment and China's Labour Reserves', in Southall (ed.) [1988].

Christie, I., 1985, *Arrows of Desire: The Films of Michael Powell and Emeric Pressburger*, London: Waterstone.

Christie, I. (ed.), 1978, *Powell, Pressburger, and Others*, London: British Film Institute.

CIDA, 1966, *Tenencia de la tierra y desarrollo socio-económico del sector agrícola: Peru*, Washington, DC: Panamerican Union.

Clark, C., 1984, 'Development Economics: The Early Years', in Maier andSeers (eds.) [1984].

Clastres, P., 1977, *Society Against the State*, Oxford: Blackwell.

Clifford, J. and G. Marcus (eds.), 1986, *Writing Culture: The Poetics and Politics of Ethnography*, Berkeley, CA: University of California Press.

Cockett, R., 1995, *Thinking the Unthinkable: Think-Tanks and the Economic Counter-Revolution, 1931–1983*, London: Fontana.

Cohen, G. *et al.*, 1986, *The New Right: Image and Reality*, London: The Runnymede Trust.

Cohen, R., 1987, *The New Helots*, Aldershot: Gower Publishing.

Colburn, F.D., 1989, 'Introduction', in Colburn (ed.) [1989].

Colburn, F.D., 1994, *The Vogue of Revolution in Poor Countries*, Princeton, NJ: Princeton University Press.

Colburn, F.D. (ed.), 1989, *Everyday Forms of Peasant Resistance*, New York: M.E. Sharpe.

Collins, R. and V. Porter, 1981, *WDR and the Arbeiterfilm: Fassbinder, Ziewar and others*, London: BFI.

Conkin, P.K., 1988, *The Southern Agrarians*, Knoxville, TS: University of Tennessee Press.

Cooper, A., 1988, *Sharecropping and Sharecroppers' Struggles in Bengal 1930–1950*, Calcutta: K.P. Bagchi.

Cooper, F., 1994, 'Conflict and Connection: Rethinking Colonial African History', *The American Historical Review*, Vol.99, No.5.

Cooper, F., Mallon, F.E., Stern, S.J., Isaacman, A.F. and W. Roseberry (eds.), 1993, *Confronting Historical Paradigms: Peasants, Labor, and the Capitalist World System in Africa and Latin America*, Madison, WI: University of Wisconsin Press.

Copjec, J. (ed.), 1993, *Shades of Noir,* London: Verso.

Corbridge, S., 1990, 'Post-Marxism and Development Studies: Beyond the Impasse', *World Development*, Vol.18, No.5.

Corbridge, S., 1994, 'Post-Marxism and Post-Colonialism: The Needs and Rights of Distant Strangers', in Booth (ed.) [1994].

Couto, M., 1986, 'The Raj Films: A Study in Cultural Imperialism', *Splice*, No.2.

Cowie, P., 1997, *The Godfather Book*, London: Faber & Faber.

Cox, T.M., 1979, *Rural Sociology in the Soviet Union*, New York: Holmes & Meier.

Cox, T.M. and G. Littlejohn (eds.), 1984, *Kritsman and the Agrarian Marxists*, London: Frank Cass.

Craig, W.W., 1967, *From Hacienda to Community: An Analysis of Solidarity and Social Change in Peru*, Latin American Program Dissertation Series No.6, Cornell University.

Craig, W.W., 1969, 'Peru: The Peasant Movement of La Convención', in Landsberger (ed.) [1969]

Crump, J., 1993, *Hatta Shuzo and Pure Anarchism in Interwar Japan*, New York: St Martin's Press.

Cuadros, C., 1949, 'El arriendo y la reforma agraria en la provincia de La Convención', *Revista Universitaria*, 96.

Curran, J. and V. Porter, (eds.), 1983, *British Cinema History*, London: Weidenfeld & Nicolson.

Curtin, C., 1987, 'Chayanov and Peasants in the West of Ireland', in *Peasants*, Wageningen: Studium Generale.

Curtiss, J.S. (ed.), 1963, *Essays in Russian and Soviet History*, Leiden: E.J.Brill.

Cutler, A., 1975, 'The Concept of Ground-Rent and Capitalism in Agriculture', *Critique of Anthropology*, Nos.4–5.

Dahrendorf, R., 1959, *Class and Class Conflict in an Industrial Society*, London: Routledge & Kegan Paul.

Dange, S.A., 1969, *Driving Forces of History: Heroes and Masses*, New Delhi: People's Publishing House.

Darling, M.L., 1940, 'Presidential Address', *Proceedings of the First Conference held at Delhi, February 24th and 25th, 1940*, Bombay: The Indian Society of Agricultural Economics.

Das, A.N., 1983a, 'Agrarian Change from Above and Below: Bihar 1947–78', in Guha (ed.) [1983].

Das, A.N., 1983b, *Agrarian Unrest and Socio-economic Change in Bihar 1900–1980*, New Delhi: Manohar Publications.

Das, A.N., 1988, 'Farmer Power: A Symposium on the Growing Unrest in the Country-side', *Seminar*, No.352.

Das, A.N., Rojas, F. and P.Waterman, 1984, 'The Labour Movement and Labouring People in India', in Das, Nilkant and Dubey (eds.) [1984].

Das, A.N., Nilkant, V. and P.S. Dubey (eds.), 1984, *The Worker and the Working*

Class: A Labour Studies Anthology, New Delhi: Public Enterprises Centre for Continuing Education.

Das Gupta, C., 1991, *The Painted Face: Studies in India's Popular Cinema*, New Delhi: Roli Books.

Datta, P.K., 1991, 'VHP's Ram at Ayodhya: Reincarnation through Ideology and Organization', *Economic and Political Weekly*, Vol.26, No.44.

Datta, P.S., 1989, 'Emerging Differentiation in a Traditional Tribal Economy (The case of the Khasi-Jaintias of Meghalaya)', in Karna (ed.) [1989].

Davis, J.A. (ed.), 1979, *Gramsci and Italy's Passive Revolution*, London: Croom Helm.

Davis, K. and M.S. Bernstein (eds.), 1991, *Resources, Environment, and Population: Present Knowledge, Future Options*, New York: Oxford University Press.

de Benoist, A., 1994, 'Three Interviews with Alain de Benoist', *Telos*, Nos.98–99.

de Benoist, A., 1995, 'End of the Left-Right Dichotomy: The French Case', *Telos*, 102.

de Grazia, V. 1986, 'The Formation of Fascist Low Culture', in Donald and Hall (eds.) [1986].

de Janvry, A., 1980, 'Social Differentiation in Agriculture and the Ideology of Neopopulism', in Buttel and Newby (eds.) [1980].

de la Campa, R., Kaplan, E.A. and M. Sprinker (eds.), 1995, *Late Imperial Culture*, London: Verso.

Deák, I., 1965, 'Hungary', in Rogger and Weber (eds.) [1965].

Debray, R., 1967, *Revolution in the Revolution? Armed Struggle and Political Struggle in Latin America*, New York: Monthly Review Press.

Debray, R., 1973, *Prison Writings*, London: Allen Lane.

Debray, R., 1975, *Che's Guerrilla War*, London: Penguin Books.

Debray, R., 1979, *Teachers, Writers, Celebrities*, London: Verso.

Desai, A.R. (ed.), 1979, *Peasant Struggles in India*, Delhi: Oxford University Press.

Desai, A.R. (ed.), 1986, *Agrarian Struggles in India after Independence*, Delhi: Oxford University Press.

Desai, A.R., 1979, 'Unconventional Anthropology of "Traditional" Peasantry', in Desai (ed.) [1979].

Desai, M., Rudolph, S.H. and A. Rudra (eds.), 1984, *Agrarian Power and Agricultural Productivity in South Asia*, Delhi: Oxford University Press.

Deutscher, I., 1954, *The Prophet Armed*, London: Oxford University Press.

Deutscher, I., 1955, *Heretics and Renegades*, London: Hamish Hamilton.

Deva, A.N., 1946, *Socialism and the National Revolution*, Bombay: Padma Publications Ltd.

Dews, P., 1980, 'The "New Philosophers" and the End of Leftism', *Radical Philosophy*, 24.

Deyo, F.C., 1989, *Beneath the Miracle: Labor Subordination in the New Asian Industrialism*, Berkeley, CA: University of California Press.

Dhanagare, D.N., 1975, *Agrarian Movements and Gandhian Politics*, Agra: Institute of Social Sciences, Agra University.

Dhanagare, D.N., 1983, *Peasant Movements in India 1920–1950*, Delhi: Oxford University Press.

Dhanagare, D.N., 1988, 'An Apolitical Populism', *Seminar*, No.352.

Dhanagare, D.N., 1990, 'Shetkari Sanghatana: The Farmers' Movement in Maharashtra – Background and Ideology', *Social Action*, Vol.40, No.4.

Dhanagare, D.N., 1994, 'The Class Character and Politics of the Farmers' Movement in Maharashtra during the 1980s', *The Journal of Peasant Studies*, Vol.21, Nos.3/4.

Diamond, I., and G.F. Orenstein (eds.), 1990, *Reweaving the World: The Emergence of Ecofeminism*, San Francisco, CA: Sierra Club Books.

Diamond, L. *et al.* (eds.), 1989, *Democracy in Developing Countries: Latin America*, Boulder, CO: Lynne Rienner Publishers.

Diggins, J.P., 1994, *Up from Communism: Conservative Odysseys in American Intellectual Development*, New York: Colombia University Press.

Dobb, M., 1955, 'Full Employment and Capitalism [1950]', in *On Economic Theory and Socialism: Collected Papers*, London: Routledge & Kegan Paul.

Dolbeare, K.M. and J.K. Hubbell, 1996, *U.S.A. 2012: After the Middle-class Revolution*, Chatham, NJ: Chatham House Publishers.

Dolbeare, K.M. and P. Dolbeare, 1976, *American Ideologies*, Boston, MA: Houghton Mifflin.

Donald, J. and S. Hall (eds), 1986, *Politics and Ideology*, Milton Keynes: Open University Press.

Donnelly, I., 1960/1890, *Ceasar's Column: A Story of the Twentieth Century*, Cambridge, MA: The Belknap Press of Harvard University Press.

Dore, R.P., 1959, *Land Reform in Japan*, London: Oxford University Press.

Drage, G., 1904, *Russian Affairs*, London: John Murray.

Dreyfus, H.L. and H. Hall (eds.), 1992, *Heidegger: A Critical Reader*, Oxford: Blackwell.

Drucker, P., 1993, *Post-Capitalist Society*, London: Butterworth-Heinemann.

Dube, L., 1986, 'Seed and Earth: The Symbolism of Biological Reproduction and Sexual Relations of Production', in Dube, Leacock and Ardner (eds.) [1986].

Dube, L., Leacock, E. and S.Ardner (eds.), 1986, *Visibility and Power: Essays on Women in Society and Development*, Delhi: Oxford University Press.

Dupré, L., 1985, 'A Conservative Anarchist: Eric Voegelin 1901–1985', *Clio*, Vol.14, No.4.

Durando, D., 1993, 'The Rediscovery of Ethnic Identity', *Telos*, No.97.

Durgnat, R., 1970, *A Mirror for England*, London: Faber & Faber.

Durrenberger, E.P. (ed.), 1984, *Chayanov, Peasants, and Economic Anthropology*, London: Academic Press.

Durrenberger, P. and N.Tannenbaum, 1992, 'Household Economy, Political Economy, and Ideology: Peasants and the State in Southeast Asia', *American Anthropologist*, Vol.94, No.1.

Duyker, E., 1987, *Tribal Guerrillas: The Santals of West Bengal and the Naxalite Movement*, New Delhi: Oxford University Press.

Dwivedi, O.P., 1990, '*Satyagraha* for conservation: Awakening the spirit of Hinduism', in Engel and Engel (eds.) [1990].

Eagleton, T., 1983, *Literary Theory*, Oxford: Basil Blackwell.

Eatwell, R., 1992, 'The Nature of the Right, 2: The Right as a Variety of "Styles of Thought"', in Eatwell and O'Sullivan (eds.) [1992].

Eatwell, R., 1995, *Fascism: A History*, London: Chatto & Windus.

Eatwell, R. and N. O'Sullivan (eds.), 1992, *The Nature of the Right: American and European Politics and Political Thought Since 1789*, London: Pinter Publishers.

Ebert, R., 1995, *The Little Book of Hollywood Clichés*, London: Virgin Books.

Eckstein, S., 1989, 'Power and Popular Protest in Latin America', in Eckstein (ed.) [1989].

Eckstein, S. (ed.), 1989, *Power and Popular Protest: Latin American Social Movements*, Berkeley, CA: University of California Press.

Eder, K., 1993, *The New Politics of Class: Social Movements and Cultural Dynamics in Advanced Societies*, London: Sage Publications.

Edinburgh, Duke of, 1989, *Living Off the Land*, London: BBC Books.

Eidelberg, P.G., 1974, *The Great Rumanian Peasant Revolt of 1907*, Leiden: E.J. Brill.

Eisenstein, H., 1984, *Contemporary Feminist Thought*, London: Unwin Paperbacks.

Eisenstein, S., 1943, *The Film Sense*, London: Faber & Faber.

Eisenstein, S., 1987, *Nonindifferent Nature: Film and the Structure of Things*, Cambridge: Cambridge University Press.

Eisner, L.H., 1969, *The Haunted Screen*, London: Thames & Hudson.

Eisner, L.H., 1973, *Murnau*, London: Secker & Warburg.

Eliade, M., 1954, *The Myth of the Eternal Return*, New York: Pantheon Books.

Ellis, F., 1988, *Peasant Economics*, Cambridge: Cambridge University Press.

Ellis, J., 1975, 'Made in Ealing', *Screen*, Vol.16, No.1.

Engel, J.R. and J.G. Engel (eds.), 1990, *Ethics of Environment and Development*, London: Belhaven Press.

Engineer, A.A., 1992, 'Communal Conflict after 1950: A Perspective', *Economic and Political Weekly*, Vol.27, No.34.

Epstein, K., 1970, 'Three Types of Conservatism', in Richter (ed.) [1970].

Erdman, H.L., 1967, *The Swatantra Party and Indian Conservatism*, Cambridge: Cambridge University Press.

Eribon, D., 1992, *Michel Foucault*, London: Faber & Faber.

Escobar, A. and S.E. Alvarez (eds.), 1992, *The Making of Social Movements in Latin America*, Boulder, CO: Westview Press.

Espinoza, G. and C. Malpica, 1970, *El problema de la tierra*, Lima: Biblioteca Amauta.

Etzioni, A., 1990, *The Moral Dimension: Toward a New Economics*, New York: The Free Press.

Etzioni, A., 1993, *The Spirit of Community: Rights, Responsibilities and the Communitarian Agenda*, New York: Crown.

Evans, T., 1996, *Conservative Radicalism*, Oxford: Berghahn Press.

Evers, T., 1985, 'Identity: the Hidden Side of New Social Movements in Latin America', in Slater (ed.) [1985].

Fanon, F., 1963, *The Wretched of the Earth*, New York: Grove Press.

Fanon, F., 1967, *Toward the African Revolution*, New York: Monthly Review Press.

Fanon, F., 1968, *Black Skin, White Masks*, London: MacGibbon & Kee Ltd.

Farias, V., 1989, *Heidegger and Nazism*, Philadelphia, PA: Temple University Press.

Ferkiss, V.C., 1957, 'Populist Influences on American Fascism', *Western Political Quarterly*, Vol.10, No.2.

Ferkiss, V.C., 1961, 'Populism: Myth, Reality, Current Danger', *Western Political Quarterly*, Vol.14, No.3.

Ferkiss, V.C., 1993, *Nature, Technology, and Society: Cultural Roots of the Current Environmental Crisis*, London: Adamantine Press.

Ferraresi, F., 1987, 'Julius Evola: Tradition, Reaction, and the Radical Right', *Archives Européennes de Sociologie*, Vol.28, No.1.

Ferry, L. and A. Renaut, 1990, *Heidegger and Modernity*, Chicago, IL: University of Chicago Press.

Feuer, L., 1963, 'What Is Alienation? The Career of a Concept', in Stein and Vidich (eds.) [1963].

Fifteen Southerners, 1981, *Why the South Will Survive*, Athens, GE: The University of Georgia Press.

Figueroa, A., 1984, *Capitalist Development and Peasant Economy in Peru*, Cambridge: Cambridge University Press.

Filler, L., 1976, *Appointment at Armageddon: Muckraking and Progressivism in American Life*, Westport, CT: Greenwood Press.

Finley, M.I., 1975, *The Use and Abuse of History*, London: Chatto & Windus.

Fioravanti, E., 1974, *Latifundio y Sindicalismo Agrario en el Peru*, Lima: Instituto de Estudios Peruanos.

Fioravanti-Molinié, A., 1982, 'Multi-levelled Andean Society and Market Exchange: The Case of Yucay (Peru)', in Lehmann (ed.) [1982].

Fitzhugh, G., 1960, 'Sociology for the South [1854]', and 'Cannibals All! [1857]', in Wish (ed.) [1960].

Flinn, C., 1992, *Strains of Utopia: Gender, Nostalgia, and Hollywood Film Music*, Princeton, NJ: Princeton University Press.

Fontana, B., 1988, *Benjamin Constant: Political Writings*, Cambridge: Cambridge University Press.

Ford, G., 1992, *Fascist Europe: The Rise of Racism and Xenophobia*, London: Pluto Press.

Forster, E.M., 1947/1909, 'The Machine Stops', in *The Collected Stories of E.M. Forster*, London: Sidgwick & Jackson.

Fortunati, V., 1993, 'The Metamorphosis of the Apocalyptic Myth: From Utopia to Science Fiction', in Bann and Kumar (eds.) [1993].

Foster, G.M., 1962, *Traditional Cultures*, New York: Harper & Brothers.

Foster, G.M., 1965, 'Peasant Society and the Image of Limited Good', *American Anthropologist*, Vol.67, No.2.

Foucault, M., 1971, *Madness and Civilization: A History of Insanity in the Age of Reason*, London: Tavistock.

Foucault, M., 1975, 'Film and Popular Memory: An Interview with Michel Foucault', *Radical Philosophy*, No.11.

Foucault, M., 1977, *Discipline and Punish: The Birth of the Prison*, London: Allen Lane.

Foucault, M., 1978, *The History of Sexuality: Volume I*, London: Allen Lane.

Foucault, M., 1991, *Remarks on Marx*, New York: Semiotext(e).

Foucault, M. and M. Blanchot, 1990, *Foucault/Blanchot*, New York: Zone Books.

Foweraker, J. and A.L. Craig (eds.), 1990, *Popular Movements and Political Change in Mexico*, Boulder, CO: Lynne Rienner.

Fox, J. (ed.), 1990, *The Challenge of Rural Democratization*, London: Frank Cass.

Fox, R.G., 1990, 'Gandhian Socialism and Hindu Nationalism: Cultural Domination in the World System', in Bose (ed.) [1990].

Fox-Genovese, E., 1991, *Feminism Without Illusions: A Critique of Individualism*, Chapel Hill, NC: University of North Carolina Press.

Francese, J., 1994, 'Pasolini's "Roman Novels", the Italian Communist Party, and the Events of 1956', in Rumble, and Testa (eds.) [1994].

Franda, M., 1979, *Small is Politics: Organizational Alternatives in India's Rural Development*, New Delhi: Wiley Eastern.

Fraser, R., 1988, *1968: A Student Generation in Revolt*, London: Chatto & Windus.

Freyre, G., 1956, *Masters and Slaves*, New York: Alfred A. Knopf.

Frierson, C.A., 1993, *Peasant Icons: Representations of Rural People in Late 19th*

Century Russia, New York: Oxford University Press.

Fritzsche, P., 1990, *Rehearsals for Fascism: Populism and Political Mobilization in Weimar Germany*, New York: Oxford University Press.

Fröebel, F. *et al.*, 1980, *The New International Division of Labour*, Cambridge: Cambridge University Press.

Fuentes, M. and A.G. Frank, 1989, 'Ten Theses on Social Movements', *World Development*, Vol.17, No.2.

Fuller, G. (ed.), 1998, *Loach on Loach*, London: Faber & Faber.

Furth, C. (ed.), 1976, *The Limits of Change: Essays on Conservative Alternatives in Republican China*, Cambridge, MA: Harvard University Press.

Gadgil, D.R., 1945, *Regulation of Wages and Other Problems of Industrial Labour in India*, Poona: Gokhale Institute of Politics and Economics.

Gamble, A., 1988, *The Free Economy and the Strong State*, London: Macmillan.

Geertz, C., 1988, *Works and Lives: The Anthropologist as Author*, Stanford, CA: Stanford University Press.

Genovese, E.D., 1994, *The Southern Tradition: The Achievement and Limitations of an American Conservatism*, Cambridge, MA: Harvard University Press.

George, J., 1984, *Politicization of Agricultural Workers in Kerala – A Study of Kuttanad*, Calcutta: K.P. Bagchi.

Geras, N., 1998, *The Contract of Mutual Indifference*, London: Verso.

Ghose, S., 1971, *Socialism and Communism in India*, Bombay: Allied Publishers.

Gianotten, V. *et al.*, 1985, 'The Impact of *Sendero Luminoso* on Regional and National Politics in Peru', in Slater (ed.) [1985].

Gill, S.S., 1994, 'The Farmers' Movement and Agrarian Change in the Green Revolution Belt of Northwest India', *The Journal of Peasant Studies*, Vol.21, Nos.3/4.

Gingrich, N., 1995, *To Renew America*, New York: Harper-Collins.

Glendening, M.-H., 1994, 'Towards a Postmodern Conservatism', in Perryman (ed.) [1994].

Godechot, J., 1972, *The Counter-Revolution: Doctrine and Action, 1789–1804*, London: Routledge & Kegan Paul.

Gonzales, A. and G. Torre (eds.), 1985, *Las Parcelaciones de las Cooperativas Agrarias del Peru*, Chiclayo: Centro de Estudios Sociales "Solidaridad".

Goodwyn, L., 1976, *Democratic Promise: The Populist Moment in America*, New York: Oxford University Press.

Goodwyn, L., 1978, *The Populist Moment: A Short History of the Agrarian Revolt*, New York: Oxford University Press.

Goodwyn, L., 1986, 'Populism and Powerlessness', in Boyte and Riessman (eds.) [1986].

Goodwyn, L., 1991, 'Rethinking "Populism": Paradoxes of Historiography and Democracy', *Telos*, No.88.

Gortz, A., 1980, *Ecology as Politics*, Boston, MA: South End Press.

Gortz, A., 1982, *Farewell to the Working Class*, London: Pluto Press.

Goswami, M.C., 1983, 'Peasants and Neo-Peasants in Northeast India and their New Dimension', in Mencher (ed.) [1983].

Gott, R., 1970, *Guerrilla Movements in Latin America*, London: Nelson.

Gottfried, P., 1990a, 'Preface' to Sunic [1990].

Gottfried, P., 1990b, *Carl Schmitt*, London: The Claridge Press.

Gottfried, P., 1994, 'Miglio's Political Quest', *Telos*, No.100.

Gottfried, P. and T. Fleming, 1988, *The Conservative Movement*, Boston, MA: Twayne Publishers.

Gough, K., 1979, 'Indian Peasant Uprisings', in Desai (ed.) [1979].

Gough, K., 1989, *Rural Change in Southeast India 1950s to 1980s*, Delhi: Oxford University Press.

Government of India, 1991, *National Agricultural Policy: Views of Standing Advisory Committee on Agriculture (SAC)*, Jullundur: Government Printing Press.

Graham, B., 1990, *Hindu Nationalism and Indian Politics*, Cambridge: Cambridge University Press.

Gray, J., 1993, *Beyond the New Right: Markets, Government and the Common Environment*, London: Routledge.

Green, L.B., 1925, *The Planter's Book of Caste and Custom*, Colombo: The Times of Ceylon Co.

Greene, G., 1972, *Graham Greene on Film: Collected Film Criticism, 1935–39*, New York: Simon & Schuster.

Greenhough, P.R., 1982, *Prosperity and Misery in Modern Bengal: The Famine of 1943–44*, New York: Oxford University Press.

Gress, F., 1986, 'The New Right in France and the Federal Republic of Germany', in Cohen *et al.* [1986].

Griffiths, R., 1983, *Fellow Travellers of the Right: British Enthusiasts for Nazi Germany 1933–39*, Oxford: Oxford University Press.

Gross, D., 1986, 'Symposium on *Soviet Peasants*', *Telos*, No.68.

Guerin, D., 1974, *Fascism and Big Business*, New York: Pathfinder Press.

Guha, Ramachandra, 1989, 'Saboteurs in the Forest: Colonialism and Peasant Resistance in the Indian Himalaya', in Colburn (ed.) [1989].

Guha, Ranajit, 1982a, 'Preface', in Guha (ed.) [1982].

Guha, Ranajit, 1982b, 'On Some Aspects of the Historiography of Colonial India', in Guha (ed.) [1982].

Guha, Ranajit, 1983, *Elementary Aspects of Peasant Insurgency in Colonial India*, Delhi: Oxford University Press.

Guha, Ranajit, 1989, 'Dominance Without Hegemony and Its Historiography', in Guha (ed.) [1989].

Guha, Ranajit (ed.), 1982, *Subaltern Studies I*, Delhi: Oxford University Press.

Guha, Ranajit (ed.), 1983, *Subaltern Studies II*, Delhi: Oxford University Press.

Guha, Ranajit (ed.), 1984, *Subaltern Studies III*, Delhi: Oxford University Press.

Guha, Ranajit (ed.), 1985, *Subaltern Studies IV*, Delhi: Oxford University Press.

Guha, Ranajit (ed.), 1987, *Subaltern Studies V*, Delhi: Oxford University Press.

Guha, Ranajit (ed.), 1989, *Subaltern Studies VI*, Delhi: Oxford University Press.

Guillet, D., 1980, 'Reciprocal Labour and Peripheral Capitalism in the Central Andes', *Ethnology*, Vol.XIX, No.2.

Gunn, S., 1989, *Revolution of the Right: Europe's New Conservatives*, London: Pluto Press.

Gupta, A.K. (ed.), 1986, *Agrarian Structure and Peasant Revolt in India*, New Delhi: Criterion Publications.

Gupta, D., 1988, 'Country–Town Nexus and Agrarian Mobilization: Bharatiya Kisan Union as an Instance', *Economic and Political Weekly*, Vol.23, No.51.

Gupta, D., 1992, 'Peasant "Unionism" in Uttar Pradesh: Against the Rural Mentality Thesis', *Journal of Contemporary Asia*, Vol.22, No.2.

Guru, G., 1992, 'Shetkari Sanghtana and the Pursuit of "Laxmi Mukti"', *Economic and*

Political Weekly, Vol.27, No.28.

Habermas, J., 1987, *The Philosophical Discourse of Modernity*, Cambridge, MA: The MIT Press

Habermas, J., 1989, *The New Conservatism: Cultural Criticism and the Historians' Debate*, Cambridge: Polity Press.

Hackett, A.P. and J.H. Burke, 1977, *Eighty Years of Bestsellers, 1895–1975*, New York: R.R. Bowker.

Hall, S. and M. Jacques (eds.), 1989, *New Times: The Changing Face of Politics in the 1990s*, London: Lawrence & Wishart.

Hamacher, W., Hartz, N. and T. Keenan (eds.), 1989, *Responses: On Paul de Man's Wartime Journalism*, Lincoln, NE: University of Nebraska Press.

Hardgrave, R.L., 1973, 'The Kerala Communists: Contradictions of Power', in Brass and Franda (eds.) [1973].

Hardiman, D., 1981, *Peasant Nationalists of Gujarat: Kheda District 1917–34*, Delhi: Oxford University Press.

Hardiman, D., 1987, *The Coming of the Devi: Adivasi Assertion in Western India*, Delhi: Oxford University Press.

Hardin, G., 1960, *Nature and Man's Fate*, London: Jonathan Cape.

Hardin, G., 1977, *The Limits of Altruism: An Ecologist's View of Survival*, Bloomington, IN: Indiana University Press.

Hardin, G., 1993, *Living Within Limits: Ecology, Economics, and Population Taboos*, New York: Oxford University Press.

Hardin, G. and J. Baden (eds.), 1977, *Managing the Commons*, San Francisco, CA: W.H. Freeman.

Harris, M., 1966, 'The Cultural Ecology of India's Sacred Cattle', *Current Anthropology*, Vol.7, No.1.

Harris, M., 1974, *Cows, Pigs, Wars, and Witches: The Riddles of Culture*, New York: Random House.

Harris, M., 1992, 'Anthropology and the Theoretical and Paradigmatic Significance of the Collapse of Soviet and East European Communism', *American Anthropologist*, Vol.94, No.2.

Harrison, M., 1975, 'Chayanov and the Economics of the Russian Peasantry', *The Journal of Peasant Studies*, Vol.2, No.4.

Harrison, M., 1977, 'The Peasant Mode of Production in the Work of A.V. Chayanov', *The Journal of Peasant Studies*, Vol.4, No.4.

Harrison, T., 1995, *Of Passionate Intensity: Right-wing Populism and the Reform Party of Canada*, Toronto: University of Toronto Press.

Harriss, J., 1994, 'Between Economism and Post-Modernism: Reflections on Research on "Agrarian Change" in India', in Booth (ed.) [1994].

Harvey, D., 1989, *The Condition of Postmodernity*, Oxford: Blackwell.

Harvey, N., 1990, *The New Agrarian Movement in Mexico, 1979–90*, London: Institute of Latin American Studies.

Hasan, Z., 1989a, *Dominance and Mobilisation: Rural Politics in Western Uttar Pradesh, 1930–80*, New Delhi: Sage Publications.

Hasan, Z., 1989b, 'Self-Serving Guardians: Formation and Strategy of the Bharatiya Kisan Union', *Economic and Political Weekly*, Vol.24, No.48.

Hasan, Z., 1994, 'Shifting Ground: Hindutva Politics and the Farmers' Movement in Uttar Pradesh', *The Journal of Peasant Studies*, Vol.21 Nos.3/4

Hauser, A., 1982, *The Sociology of Art*, London: Routledge & Kegan Paul.

Havens, T., 1974, *Farm and Nation in Modern Japan: Agrarian Nationalism, 1870–1940*, Princeton, NJ: Princeton University Press.

Hawthorn, G., 1991, ' "Waiting for a Text?": Comparing Third World Politics', in J. Manor (ed.), *Rethinking Third World Politics*, London: Longman.

Hawthorn, G., 1993a, 'Liberalization and "Modern Liberty": Four Southern States', *World Development*, Vol.21, No.8.

Hawthorn, G., 1993b, 'Listen to the Women', *London Review of Books*, Vol.15, No.20.

Hay, J., 1987, *Popular Film Culture in Fascist Italy*, Bloomington, IN: Indiana University Press.

Haya de la Torre, V.R., 1936a, *¿A dónde va Indoamérica?,* Santiago de Chile: Biblioteca America.

Haya de la Torre, V.R., 1936b, *El Antimperialismo y el Apra*, Santiago de Chile: Ediciones Ercilla.

Hayek, F.A., 1967, 'The Principles of a Liberal Social Order', in *Studies in Philosophy, Politics and Economics*, London: Routledge & Kegan Paul.

Hayes, M., 1994, *The New Right in Britain*, London: Pluto Press.

Haynes, D. and G. Prakash (eds.), 1991, *Contesting Power: Resistance and Everyday Social Relations in South Asia*, Delhi: Oxford University Press.

Hecker, J.F., 1969, *Russian Sociology: A Contribution to the History of Sociological Thought and Theory*, New York: Augustus M. Kelley.

Heidegger, M., 1969, *Discourse on Thinking*, New York: Harper & Row.

Henderson, J. and M. Castells (eds.), 1987, *Global Restructuring and Territorial Development*, London: Sage.

Herzen, A., 1956, *From the Other Shore*, London: Weidenfeld & Nicolson.

Hewitt, W.E., 1998, 'From Defenders of the People to Defenders of the Faith: A 1984–1993 Retrospective of CEB Activity in São Paulo', *Latin American Perspectives*, Vol.25, No.1.

Hicks, J.D., 1931, *The Populist Revolt: A History of the Farmers' Alliance and the People's Party*, Minneapolis, MN: The University of Minnesota Press.

Hicks, J.D., 1963, *Republican Ascendancy, 1921–33*, New York: Harper & Row.

Hilton, J., 1933a, *Lost Horizon*, New York: Grosset & Dunlap.

Hilton, J., 1933b, *Knight Without Armour*, London: Ernest Benn.

Hilton, J., 1934, *Goodbye Mr Chips*, London: Hodder & Stoughton.

Hilton, J., 1938, 'A Chapter of Autobiography', in *To You, Mr. Chips*, London: Hodder & Stoughton.

Hindess, B. (ed.), 1977, *Sociological Theories of the Economy*, London: Macmillan.

Hinz, B., 1980, *Art in the Third Reich*, Oxford: Basil Blackwell.

Hirst, P., 1998, 'Can Rutland Learn from Jutland?', in Barnet and Scruton (eds.) [1998].

Hobart, M. (ed.), 1993, *An Anthropological Critique of Development*, London: Routledge.

Hobsbawm, E.J., 1967, 'Problèmes agraires à La Convención (Pérou)', in Centre National de la Recherche Scientifique (CNRS) [1967].

Hobsbawm, E.J., 1969a, 'A Case of Neo-Feudalism: La Convención, Peru', *Journal of Latin American Studies*, Vol.1, No.1.

Hobsbawm, E.J., 1969b, *Bandits*, London: Weidenfeld & Nicolson.

Hobsbawm, E.J., Kula, W., Mitra, Ashok, Raj, K.N. and Ignacy Sachs (eds.), 1980, *Peasants in History: Essays in Honour of Daniel Thorner*, Calcutta: Oxford University Press.

Hoeveler, J.D., 1991, *Watch on the Right: Conservative Intellectuals in the Reagan Era*, Madison, WI: University of Wisconsin Press.

Hofstadter, R., 1962, *The Age of Reform: From Bryan to FDR*, London: Jonathan Cape.

Hofstadter, R., 1969, 'North America', in Ionescu and Gellner (eds.) [1969].

Hofstadter, R., and S.M. Lipset (eds.), 1968, *Turner and the Sociology of the Frontier*, New York: Basic Books.

Hojman, D.E. (ed.), 1990, *Neo-liberal Agriculture in Rural Chile*, London: Macmillan.

Hojman, D.E. (ed.), 1993, *Change in the Chilean Countryside*, London: Macmillan.

Holbo, P.S., 1961, 'Wheat or What? Populism and American Fascism', *Western Political Quarterly*, Vol.14, No.3.

Hoogvelt, A., 1987, 'The New International Division of Labour', in Bush, Johnston and Coates (eds.) [1987].

Huaco, G.A., 1965, *The Sociology of Film Art*, New York: Basic books, Inc..

Hudson, W.H., 1887, *A Crystal Age*, London: T. Fisher Unwin.

Huizer, G., 1970a, 'Peasant Unrest in Latin America: its Origins, Forms of Expression, and Potential', doctoral thesis, University of Amsterdam.

Huizer, G., 1970b, 'Emiliano Zapata and the Peasant Guerrillas in the Mexican Revolution', in Stavenhagen (ed.) [1970].

Huizer, G., 1973, *Peasant Rebellion in Latin America*, Harmondsworth: Penguin Books.

Hunt, D., 1979, 'Chayanov's Model of Peasant Household Resource Allocation', *The Journal of Peasant Studies*, Vol.6, No.3.

Husain, A. and K. Tribe (eds.), 1984, *Paths of Development in Capitalist Agriculture*, London: Macmillan.

Iggers, G. (ed.), 1991, *Marxist Historiography in Transformation: East German Social History in the 1980s*, Oxford: Berg Publishers.

Ignatieff, M., 1998, 'Where Are They Now?' *Prospect/The London Observer*.

Ionescu, G., 1969, 'Eastern Europe', in Ionescu and Gellner (eds.) [1969].

Ionescu, G., and E. Gellner (eds.), 1969, *Populism*, London: Weidenfeld & Nicolson.

Isaacman, A.F., 1993, 'Peasants and Rural Social Protest in Africa', in Cooper, Mallon, Stern, Isaacman, and Roseberry (eds.) [1993].

Iyer, R. (ed.), 1960, *South Asian Affairs*, Illinois: Southern Illinois University Press.

Jackson, C., 1993, 'Women/Nature or Gender/History? A Critique of Ecofeminist "Development"', *The Journal of Peasant Studies*, Vol.20, No.3.

Jackson, G.D., 1974, 'Peasant Political Movements in Eastern Europe', in Landsberger (ed.) [1974].

Jacobeit, S., 1991, 'Clothing in Nazi Germany', in Iggers (ed.) [1991].

Jacobs, L. (ed.), 1977, *The Compound Cinema: The Film Writings of Harry Alan Potamkin*, New York: Teachers College, Columbia University Press.

Jasny, N., 1972, *Soviet Economists of the Twenties*, London: Cambridge University Press.

Jefferies, R., 1939/1885, *After London*, London: J.M. Dent.

Jenkins, T., 1977, 'The Death of Marx: A Media Event', *Journal of the Anthropological Society of Oxford*, Vol.VIII, No.3.

Jodha, N.S., 1990, 'Depletion of Common Property Resources in India: Micro-Level Evidence', in McNicoll and Cain (eds.) [1990].

Jones, A.K., 1990, 'Social Symbiosis: A Gaian Critique of Contemporary Social Theory', *The Ecologist*, Vol.20, No.3.

Jonsson, U., Köll, A.-M. and R. Pettersson, 1991, 'What is Wrong with a Peasant-based Development Strategy? Use and Misuse of Historical Experiences', in Mörner and Svensson (eds.) [1991].

Joseph, G.M. and D. Nugent (eds.), 1994, *Everyday Forms of State Formation*, Durham, NC: Duke University Press.

Joshi, Sharad, 1993, 'Farmers and Dunkel', unpublished manuscript, Pune.

Kaes, A., 1992, *From Hitler to Heimat: The Return of History as Film*, Cambridge, MA: Harvard University Press.

Kafka, F., 1973, *Shorter Works – Volume I*, London: Secker & Warburg.

Kalecki, M., 1976, *Essays on Developing Economies*, Hassocks: Harvester Press.

Kamenka, E. (ed.), 1982, *Community as a Social Ideal*, London: Edward Arnold.

Kannan, K.P., 1988, *Of Rural Proletarian Struggles: Mobilization and Organization of Rural Workers in South-West India*, Delhi: Oxford University Pess.

Kaplinsky, R., 1993, 'Export Processing Zones in the Dominican Republic: Transforming Manufactures into Commodities', *World Development*, Vol.21, No.11.

Karanikas, A., 1966, *Tillers of a Myth: Southern Agrarians as Social and Literary Critics*, Madison, WI: University of Wisconsin Press..

Karna, M.N. (ed.), 1989, *Peasant and Peasant Protests in India*, New Delhi: Intellectual Publishing House.

Kaser, M. (ed.), 1966, *Soviet Affairs*, London: Oxford University Press.

Katsiaficas, G., 1987, *The Imagination of the New Left: A Global Analysis of 1968*, Boston, MA: South End Press.

Kautsky, J.H., 1956, *Moscow and the Communist Party of India*, New York: MIT Press.

Kautsky, K., 1988, *The Agrarian Question* (2 vols.), London: Zwan Publications.

Kazin, M., 1995, *The Populist Persuasion: An American History*, New York: Basic Books.

Kerblay, B., 1966, 'The Russian Peasant', in Kaser [1966].

Kerblay, B., 1971, 'Chayanov and the Theory of Peasant Economies', in Shanin (ed.) [1971].

Kermode, F., 1991, *The Uses of Error*, Cambridge, MA: Harvard University Press.

Kirk, J.G. (ed.), 1968, *America Now*, New York: Antheneum.

Kirk, R., 1968, 'The African Example: American Ritualistic Liberalism in Action', in Kirk (ed.) [1968].

Kirk, R., 1978, *The Conservative Mind: From Burke to Eliot*, South Bend, IN: Gateway Editions Ltd.

Kitching, G., 1982, *Development and Underdevelopment in Historical Perspective*, London: Methuen.

Kneale, N., 1959, *The Quatermass Experiment*, London: Penguin Books.

Kneale, N., 1960a, *Quatermass II*, London: Penguin Books.

Kneale, N., 1960b, *Quatermass and the Pit*, London: Penguin Books.

Knowlton, J. and T. Cotes, 1993, *Forever in the Shadow of Hitler? Original Documents of the Historikerstreit*, Princeton, NJ: Humanities Press.

Kofi, T.A., 1978, 'Peasants and Economic Development: Populist Lessons for Africa', in Smith and Welch, Jr. (eds.) [1978].

Kohn, M., 1995, *The Race Gallery: The Return of Racial Science*, London: Jonathan Cape.

Koonz, C., 1987, *Mothers in the Fatherland: Women, the Family, and Nazi Politics*, New York: St. Martin's Press.

Korovkin, T., 1992, 'Peasants, Grapes and Corporations: The Growth of Contract Farming in a Chilean Community', *The Journal of Peasant Studies*, Vol.19, No.2.

Kosambi, D.D., 1956, *An Introduction to the Study of Indian History*, Bombay: Popular Book Depot.

Kracauer, S., 1947, *From Caligari to Hitler: A Psychological History of the German Film*, London: Dennis Dobson.

Kracauer, S., 1960, *Theory of Film*, New York: Oxford University Press.

Kracauer, S., 1995, *The Mass Ornament: Weimar Essays*, Cambridge, MA: Harvard University Press.

Kremnev, I. [ps. A.V. Chayanov], 1977/1920, 'The Journey of My Brother Alexei to the Land of Peasant Utopia', in Smith (ed.) [1977].

Kripa, A.P., 1992, 'Farmers' Movement in Karnataka', *Economic and Political Weekly*, Vol.27, No.23.

Krishnaji, N., 1986, 'Agrarian Relations and the Left Movement in Kerala', in Desai (ed.) [1986].

Krishnaji, N., 1995, 'Family Size and Wealth: Standing Chayanov on His Head in the Indian Context', *The Journal of Peasant Studies*, Vol.22, No.2.

Kucherov, A., 1963, 'Alexander Herzen's Parallel between the United States and Russia', in Curtiss (ed.) [1963].

Kühl, S., 1994, *The Nazi Connection: Eugenics, American Racism, and German National Socialism*, New York: Oxford University Press.

Kumar, K., 1987, *Utopia and Anti-Utopia in Modern Times*, Oxford: Basil Blackwell.

Kumar, K. (ed.), 1988, *Congress and Classes: Nationalism, Workers and Peasants*, New Delhi: Manohar.

Kumar, R.,1989, *India's Export Processing Zones*, Delhi: Oxford University Press.

Kumarappa, B., 1935, *Village Industries and Reconstruction*, Allahabad: All India Congress Committee.

Labedz, L. (ed.), 1962, *Revisionism: Essays on the History of Marxist Ideas*, London: George Allen & Unwin.

Laclau, E., 1977, *Politics and Ideology in Marxist Theory*, London: New Left Books.

Laclau, E., 1985, 'New Social Movements and the Plurality of the Social', in Slater (ed.) [1985].

Laclau, E., 1990, *New Reflections on the Revolution of Our Time*, London: Verso.

Laclau, E., 1993, 'Power and Representation', in Poster (ed.) [1993].

Laclau, E. and C.Mouffe, 1985, *Hegemony and Socialist Strategy*, London: Verso.

Landsberger, H.A. and C. Hewitt, 1970, 'Ten Sources of Weakness and Cleavage in Latin American Peasant Movements', in Stavenhagen (ed.) [1970].

Landsberger, H.A. (ed.), 1969 *Latin American Peasant Movements*, Ithaca, NY: Cornell University Press

Landsberger, H.A. (ed.), 1974, *Rural Protest: Peasant Movements and Social Change*, London: Macmillan.

Large, S.S., 1981, *Organized Workers and Socialist Politics in Interwar Japan*, Cambridge: Cambridge University Press.

Larsen, N., 1993, 'Postmodernism and Imperialism: Theory and Politics in Latin America', in Amiran and Unsworth (eds.) [1993].

Lasch, C., 1991, *The True and Only Heaven: Progress and Its Critics*, New York: W.W. Norton.

Lasch, C., 1995, *The Revolt of the Elites and the Betrayal of Democracy*, New York: W.W. Norton.

Latin American Subaltern Studies Group, 1993, 'Founding Statement', in Beverley and Oviedo (eds.) [1993].

Latouche, S., 1993, *In the Wake of the Affluent Society: An Exploration of Post-Development*, London: Zed Press.

Latouche, S., 1996, *The Westernization of the World*, Cambridge: Polity Press.

Lehman, D., 1991, *Signs of the Times: Deconstruction and the Fall of Paul de Man*, New York: Poseidon Press.

Lehmann, D., 1990, *Democracy and Development in Latin America*, Cambridge: Polity Press.

Lehmann, D. (ed.), 1982, *Ecology and Exchange in the Andes*, Cambridge: Cambridge University Press.

Lejeune, C.A., 1931, *Cinema*, London: Alexander Maclehose.

Lenin, V.I., 1960, 'What the "Friends of the People" Are and How They Fight the Social Democrats', *Collected Works*, Vol.1, Moscow: Foreign Languages Publishing House.

Lenin, V.I., 1962, 'The Agrarian Programme of Social Democracy in the First Russian Revolution, 1905–1907', *Collected Works*, Vol.13, Moscow: Foreign Languages Publishing House.

Lenin, V.I., 1963, 'The Agrarian Question in Russia Towards the Close of the Nineteenth Century', *Collected Works*, Vol.15, Moscow: Foreign Languages Publishing House.

Lenin, V.I., 1964, 'The Development of Capitalism in Russia', *Collected Works*, Vol.3, Moscow: Foreign Languages Publishing House.

Lenin, V.I., 1966, 'Preliminary Draft Theses on the Agrarian Question', *Collected Works*, Vol.31, Moscow: Progress Publishers.

Lenneberg, C., 1988, 'Sharad Joshi and the Farmers: The Middle Peasant Lives!', *Pacific Affairs*, Vol.61, No.3.

Levidow, L., 1991, 'Women Who Make the Chips', *Science as Culture*, 10.

Levitas, R. (ed.), 1986, *The Ideology of the New Right*, Cambridge: Polity Press.

Levitas, R., 1986, 'Ideology and the New Right', in Levitas (ed.) [1986].

Levy, E., 1991, *Small-Town America in Film: The Decline and Fall of Community*, New York: Continuum.

Lewis, N., 1953, *A Single Pilgrim*, London: Jonathan Cape.

Lewis, O., 1962, *The Children of Sánchez*, London: Martin Secker & Warburg.

Lewis, O., 1966, *La Vida: A Puerto Rican Family in the Culture of Poverty*, New York: Random House.

Lewis, O., 1967a, 'The Children of Sánchez, Pedro Martínez and La Vida', *Current Anthropology*, Vol.8, No.5.

Lewis, O., 1967b, 'Reply', *Current Anthropology*, Vol.8, No.5.

Leyda, J., 1960, *Kino: A History of the Russian and Soviet Film*, London: George Allen & Unwin.

Leys, C., 1996, 'Rational Choice or Hobson's Choice? The "New Political Economy" as Development Theory', *Studies in Political Economy*, No.49.

Li Causi, L., 1975, 'Anthropology and Ideology: The Case of "Patronage" in Mediterranean Societies', *Critique of Anthropology*, Nos.4–5.

Lieten, K., 1988, 'The Indian National Congress and the Control over Labour: The Need for a Passive Revolution', in Kumar (ed.) [1988].

Lindberg, S., 1990, 'Civil Society Against the State? Farmers' Agitation and New Social Movements in India', paper presented at the XII World Congress of Sociology, Madrid.

Lindberg, S., 1994, 'New Farmers' Movements in India as Structural Response and Collective Identity Formation: The Cases of Shetkari Sanghatana and the BKU', *The Journal of Peasant Studies*, Vol.21, Nos.3/4.

Lipietz, A., 1992, *Towards a New Economic Order: PostFordism, Ecology and Democracy*, Cambridge: Polity Press.

Lipset, S.M. and A. Solari (eds.), 1967, *Elites in Latin America*, New York: Oxford University Press.

Lipton, M., 1977, *Why Poor People Stay Poor: A Study of Urban Bias in World Development*, London: Temple Smith.

Lipton, M., 1993, 'Urban Bias: Of Consequences, Classes and Causality', in A. Varshney (ed.) [1993c].

Littlejohn, G., 1973a, 'The Peasantry and the Russian Revolution', *Economy & Society*, Vol.2., No.1.

Littlejohn, G., 1973b, 'The Russian Peasantry: A Reply to Teodor Shanin', *Economy & Society*, Vol.2, No.3.

Littlejohn, G., 1977, 'Peasant Economy and Society', in Hindess (ed.) [1977].

Littlejohn, G., 1987a, 'L.N. Kritsman: The Russian Peasantry 1920–1930', in *Peasants*, Wageningen: Studium Generale.

Littlejohn, G., 1987b, 'Chayanov's Theory of the Peasant Economy', in *Peasants*, Wageningen: Studium Generale.

Livingston, J., Moore, J. and F. Oldfather (eds.), 1976, *The Japan Reader: Volume One – Imperial Japan 1800–1945*, London: Penguin Books.

Lohia, R., 1963, *Marx, Gandhi and Socialism*, Hyderabad: Navahind Publications.

Long, N., 1977, *An Introduction to the Sociology of Rural Development*, London: Tavistock Publications.

Loomis, C.P. and J.A. Beegle, 1946, 'The Spread of German Nazism in Rural Areas', *American Sociological Review*, Vol.11, No.6.

Lora, R., 1971, *Conservative Minds in America*, Chicago, IL: Rand McNally.

Löwy, M., 1998 'Marxism and Romanticism in the Work of José Carlos Mariátegui', *Latin American Perspectives*, Vol.25, No.4.

Lukacs, G., 1971, *History and Class Consciousness*, London: Merlin Press.

Lukacs, G., 1980, *The Destruction of Reason*, London: The Merlin Press.

Lundahl, M. and T. Svensson (eds.), 1990, *Agrarian Society in History: Essays in Honour of Magnus Mörner*, London: Routledge.

Lüthi, D., 1993, 'Krishna and Catir Naccu: Feature Film as a Political Medium', *Visual Anthropology*, Vol.5, Nos.3–4.

Luxemburg, R., 1951, *The Accumulation of Capital*, New York: Monthly Review Press.

Lyotard, J.F. and J.-L. Thébaud, 1985, *Just Gaming*, Manchester: Manchester University Press.

Macciocchi, A.-M., 1979, 'Female Sexuality in Fascist Ideology', *Feminist Review*, No.1.

Macey, D., 1993, *The Lives of Michel Foucault*, New York: Pantheon Books.

MacIntyre, A., 1981, *After Virtue*, London: Duckworth.

Maclachlan, M.D. (ed.), 1987, *Household Economies and their Transformations*, New York: University Press of America.

Macpherson, C.B., 1972, 'Politics: Post-Liberal-Democracy?', in Blackburn (ed.) [1972].

Maier, C.S., 1988, *The Unmasterable Past: History, Holocaust, and German National Identity*, Cambridge, MA: Harvard University Press.

Maier, G.M. and D. Seers (eds.), 1984, *Pioneers in Development*, New Delhi: Oxford University Press.

Malia, M.E., 1955, 'Herzen and the Peasant Commune', in Simmons (ed.) [1955].

Malinowski, B. and J. de la Fuente, 1982, *Malinowski in Mexico: The Economics of a Mexican Market System*, London: Routledge & Kegan Paul.

Mallon, F., 1983, *The Defense of Community in Peru's Central Highlands*, Princeton, NJ: Princeton University Press.

Mallon, F., 1994, 'The Promise and Dilemma of Subaltern Studies: Perspectives from Latin American History', *The American Historical Review*, Vol.99, No.5.

Mannheim, K., 1953, *Essays on Sociology and Social Psychology*, London: Routledge & Kegan Paul Ltd.

Manor, J., 1992, 'BJP in South India: 1991 General Election', *Economic and Political Weekly*, Vol.27, Nos.24–25.

Manuel, F.E., 1972, *Freedom from History*, London: University of London Press.

Manuel, F.E. (ed.), 1967, *Utopias and Utopian Thought*, Boston, MA: Beacon Press.

Manuel, F.E. and F.P. Manuel, 1979, *Utopian Thought in the Western World*, Oxford: Basil Blackwell.

Manuel, P., 1993, *Cassette Culture: Popular Music and Technology in North India*, Chicago, IL: University of Chicago Press.

Manvell, R., 1973, *Masterworks of the German Cinema*, London: Lorrimer Publishing.

Marchand, P., 1989, *Marshall McLuhan: The Medium and the Messenger*, New York: Ticknor & Fields.

Marcus, J., 1995, *The National Front and French Politics*, London: Macmillan.

Marcuse, H., 1969, *An Essay on Liberation*, London: Allen Lane.

Marcuse, H., 1970, *Five Lectures*, London: Allen Lane.

Marcuse, H., 1976, *Revolution or Reform?* , Chicago, IL: New University Press.

Mariani, P. (ed.), 1991, *Critical Fictions: The Politics of Imaginative Writing*, Seattle: Bay Press.

Mariátegui, J.C., 1968/[1928], *Siete Ensayos de Interpretación de la Realidad Peruana*, Lima: Biblioteca Amauta.

Marin, L., 1993, 'The Frontiers of Utopia', in Bann and Kumar (eds.) [1993].

Martin, J.W. and C.E. Ostwalt (eds.), 1995, *Screening the Sacred: Religion, Myth, and Ideology in Popular American Film*, Boulder, CO: Westview Press.

Mattick, P., 1978, *Anti-Bolshevik Communism*, London: Merlin Press.

Mazumdar, S., 1995, 'Women on the March: Right-wing Mobilization in Contemporary India', *Feminist Review*, No.49.

McBride, J., 1992, *Frank Capra: The Catastrophe of Success*, London: Faber & Faber.

McClintock, C., 1984, 'Why Peasants Rebel: The Case of Peru's Sendero Luminoso', *World Politics*, Vol.27, No.1.

McClintock, C., 1989a, 'Peru's Sendero Luminoso Rebellion: Origins and Trajectory', in Eckstein (ed.) [1989].

McClintock, C., 1989b, 'Peru: Precarious Regimes, Authoritarian and Democratic', in Diamond *et al.* (eds.) [1989].

McCormick, J., 1992, *The Global Environmental Movement: Reclaiming Paradise*, London: Bellhaven Press.

McGilligan, P. (ed.), 1997, *Six Screenplays by Robert Riskin*, Berkeley, CA: University of California Press.

McLeod, W.H., 1991, *Popular Sikh Art*, Delhi: Oxford University Press.

McLuhan, M., 1949, 'The Psychopathology of Time & Life', *Neurotica*, 5.

McLuhan, M., 1951, *The Mechanical Bride: Folklore of Industrial Man*, New York: Vanguard Press.

McLuhan, M. and Q. Fiore, 1967, *The Medium is the Massage*, New York: Bantam Books.

McNicoll, G. and M.Cain (eds.), 1990, *Rural Development and Populations: Institutions and Policy*, New York: Oxford University Press.

Mehlman, J., 1983, *Legacies of Anti-Semitism in France*, Minneapolis, MI: University of Minnesota Press.

Mehta, U., 1992, 'Indian Agriculture Since Independence', in Shah (ed.) [1992].

Mellor, M., 1989, 'Turning Green: Whose Ecology?', *Science as Culture*, No.6.

Mellor, D. (ed.), 1987, *A Paradise Lost: The Neo-Romantic Imagination in Britain 1935–55*, London: Lund Humphries.

Melucci, A., 1989, *Nomads of the Present: Social Movements and Individual Needs in Contemporary Society*, London: Hutchinson Radius.

Mencher, J.P. (ed.), 1983, *Social Anthropology of Peasantry*, Bombay: Somaiya Publications

Merchant, C., 1992, *Radical Ecology: The Search for a Livable World*, London: Routledge.

Meyer, J.A., 1976, *The Cristero Rebellion: The Mexican People between Church and State 1926–1929*, Cambridge: Cambridge University Press.

Michelson, A. (ed.), 1984, *Kino-Eye: The Writings of Dziga Vertov*, London: Pluto Press.

Mies, M., 1986, *Patriarchy and Accumulation on a World Scale*, London: Zed Press.

Mies, M. and V. Shiva, 1993, *Ecofeminism*, London: Zed Press.

Mies, M., Bennholdt-Thomsen, V. and C. von Werlhof, 1988, *Women: The Last Colony*, New Delhi: Kali for Women.

Miglio, G., 1993, 'The Cultural Roots of the Federalist Revolution', *Telos*, No.97.

Miliband, R., 1985, 'The New Revisionism in Britain', *New Left Review*, No.150.

Miliband, R. *et al.*, (eds.), 1986, *Socialist Register 1985/86*, London: Merlin Press.

Miller, James, 1993, *The Passion of Michel Foucault*, New York: Simon & Schuster.

Miller, Jonathan, 1971, *McLuhan*, London: Fontana.

Miller, R., 1987, 'Some Reflections on Foreign Research and Peruvian History', in Miller (ed.) [1987].

Miller, R. (ed.), 1987, *Region and Class in Modern Peruvian History*, Liverpool: Institute of Latin American Studies.

Miroshevsky, V., 1942, 'El "populismo" en el Perú: papel de Mariátegui el la historia del pensamiento social latinoamericano', *Dialéctica*, Vol.1 (May–June).

Mishra, S.N., 1987, 'Private Property Formation among the Highland Tribal Communities of North-East India', *Social Science Probings*, Vol.4, No.4.

Mitra, A., 1977, *Terms of Trade and Class Relations*, London: Frank Cass.

Mitrany, D., 1951, *Marx Against the Peasant*, Chapel Hill, NC: University of North Carolina Press.

Mitter, S., 1986, *Common Fate, Common Bond: Women in the Global Economy*, London: Pluto Press.

Montague, A. (ed.), 1980, *Sociobiology Examined*, New York: Oxford University Press.

Montoya, R., 1986, 'Identidad étnica y luchas agrarias en los Andes Peruanos', in

Briggs *et al.*, (eds.) [1986].

Moore, B., 1967, *Social Origins of Dictatorship and Democracy: Lord and Peasant in the Making of the Modern World*, London: Allen Lane.

Moore, M., 1976, 'Horses, Households and Villages in Peasant Russia', *Peasant Studies*, Vol.5, No.2.

Morales, E., 1989, *Cocaine: White Gold Rush in Peru*, Tucson, AR: University of Arizona Press.

Morgan, R., 1992, *The Word of a Woman: Feminist Dispatches 1968–1992*, New York: W.W. Norton.

Mörner, M. and T. Svensson (eds.), 1991, *The Transformation of Rural Society in the Third World*, London: Routledge.

Morris, W., 1970/1885, *News from Nowhere*, London: Routledge.

Morton, A.L., 1952, *The English Utopia*, London: Lawrence & Wishart.

Morton, M.J., 1972, *The Terrors of Ideological Politics: Liberal Historians in a Conservative Mood*, Cleveland, OH: Press of Case Western Reserve University.

Mosley, O., 1936, *Fascism: 100 Questions Asked and Answered*, London: BUF Publications.

Mosse, G., 1966, *Nazi Culture: Intellectual, Cultural and Social Life in the Third Reich*, London: W.H. Allen.

Mosse, G.L., 1978, *Nazism: An Historical and Comparative Analysis*, Oxford: Basil Blackwell.

Mumford, L., 1934, *Technics and Civilization*, London: Routledge.

Munck, R., 1988, *The New International Labour Studies*, London: Zed Press.

Murray, C., 1990, *The Emerging British Underclass*, London: Institute of Economic Affairs.

Murray, C., 1994, *Underclass: The Crisis Deepens*, London: Institute of Economic Affairs.

Nadkarni, M.V., 1987, *Farmers' Movements in India*, New Delhi: Allied Publishers.

Namboodiripad, E.M.S., 1959, *The Mahatma and the Ism*, New Delhi: People's Publishing House.

Namboodiripad, E.M.S., 1966, *Economics and Politics of India's Socialist Pattern*, New Delhi: People's Publishing House.

Nash, G.T., 1976, *The Conservative Intellectual Movement in America*, New York: Basic Books.

National Labour Institute Report, 1986, 'Post-Independence Peasant Movements in Ryotwari Areas of Andhra Pradesh', in Desai (ed.) [1986].

Neira, H., 1968, *Los Andes: Tierra o Muerte*, Madrid: Editorial ZYX.

Neocleous, M., 1996, 'Friend or Enemy? Reading Schmitt Politically', *Radical Philosophy*, No.79.

Netting, R. McC., 1993, *Smallholders, Householders: Farm Families and the Ecology of Intensive, Sustainable Agriculture*, Stanford, CA: Stanford University Press.

Newby, H. (ed.), 1978, *International Perspectives in Rural Sociology*, Chichester: John Wiley.

Newman, K., 1988, *Nightmare Movies: A Critical History of the Horror Film, 1966–88*, London: Bloomsbury.

Nicholson, L. and S. Seidman (eds.), 1995, *Social Postmodernism*, Cambridge: Cambridge University Press.

Nisbet, R., 1966, *The Sociological Tradition*, London: Heinemann.

Nisbet, R., 1980, *History of the Idea of Progress*, London: Heinemann.

Nisbet, R., 1986, *Conservatism*, Milton Keynes: Open University Press.

Nolan, M., 1988, 'The *Historikerstreit* and Social History', *New German Critique*, No.44.

Nolte, E., 1966, *The Three Faces of Fascism*, New York: Holt, Reinhart & Winston.

Normano, J.F., 1949, *The Spirit of Russian Economics*, London: Dennis Dobson Ltd.

Norris, C., 1990, *What's Wrong with Postmodernism*, London: Harvester Wheatsheaf.

Norris, C., 1993, *The Truth about Postmodernism*, Oxford: Blackwell.

Nove, A., 1990, 'The Return of Chayanov', in Lundahl and Svensson (eds.) [1990].

Nowell-Smith, G., 1967, *Visconti*, London: British Film Institute.

Nowell-Smith, G., 1976, 'Pasolini's Originality', in Willemen (ed.) [1976].

Nozick, R., 1974, *Anarchy, State and Utopia*, Oxford: Basil Blackwell.

Nuñez, L., 1993, 'Women on the Streets: Vending and Public Space in Chile', *Economic and Political Weekly*, Vol.28, No.44.

O'Brien, C.C. and W.D. Vanech (eds.), 1969, *Power and Consciousness*, New York: New York University Press.

O'Hanlon, R., 1988, 'Recovering the Subject: *Subaltern Studies* and Histories of Resistance in Colonial South Asia', *Modern Asian Studies*, Vol.22, No.1.

Omvedt, G., 1986, 'Peasants and Women: Challenge of Chandwad', *Economic and Political Weekly*, Vol.21, No.48.

Omvedt, G., 1988, 'New Movements', *Seminar*, No.352.

Omvedt, G., 1989, 'Ecology and Social Movements', in Alavi and Harriss (eds.) [1989].

Omvedt, G., 1990a, 'The Farmers' Movement in Maharashtra', in Sen (ed.) [1990].

Omvedt, G., 1990b, *Violence Against Women: New Movements and New Theories in India*, New Delhi: Kali for Women.

Omvedt, G., 1990c, 'Ambedkar and Dalit Labor Radicalism: Maharashtra, 1936–1942', *South Asia Bulletin*, Vol.10, No.1.

Omvedt, G., 1991a, 'Theorists of the Peasantry Should at Least Have Their Feet on the Ground: A Response to Banaji', *The Journal of Peasant Studies*, Vol.19, No.1.

Omvedt, G., 1991b, 'Shetkari Sanghatana's New Direction', *Economic and Political Weekly*, Vol.26, No.40.

Omvedt, G., 1993a, 'Of Brahmins, Sacred and Socialist', *Economic and Political Weekly*, Vol.28, No.44.

Omvedt, G., 1993b, 'Farmers' Movement: Fighting for Liberalisation', *Economic and Political Weekly*, Vol.28, No.50.

Omvedt, G., 1994a, 'Peasants, Dalits and Women: Democracy and India's New Social Movements', *Journal of Contemporary Asia*, Vol.24, No.1.

Omvedt, G., 1994b, '"We Want the Return for Our Sweat": The New Peasant Movement in India and the Formation of a National Agricultural Policy', *The Journal of Peasant Studies*, Vol.21, Nos.3/4.

Omvedt, G. and C. Galla, 1987, 'Ideology for Provincial Propertied Class?', *Economic and Political Weekly*, Vol.22, No.45.

Omvedt, G. and B. Patankar, 1992, 'The Non-Brahman Movement and the Class-Caste Debate', in Shah (ed.) [1992].

Ong, A., 1987, *Spirits of Resistance and Capitalist Discipline: Factory Women in Malaysia*, Albany, NY: State University of New York Press.

Ortega y Gasset, J., 1950, *The Revolt of the Masses*, New York: Mentor Books.

Ortega y Gasset, J., 1961, *The Modern Theme*, New York: Harper Torchbook.

Orwell, G., 1949, *Nineteen Eighty-Four*, London: Secker & Warburg.

O'Sullivan, N., 1976, *Conservatism*, London: J.M. Dent.

O'Sullivan, N., 1992, 'The New Right: The Quest for a Civil Philosophy in Europe and America', in Eatwell and O'Sullivan (eds.) [1992].

Ostwalt, C.E., 1995, 'Hollywood and Armageddon: Apocalyptic Themes in Recent Cinematic Presentation', in Martin and Ostwalt (eds.) [1995].

Ott, H., 1993, *Martin Heidegger: A Political Life*, London: Harper Collins.

Palmer, B.D., 1990, *Descent into Discourse: The Reification of Language and the Writing of Social History*, Philadelphia, PA: Temple University Press.

Pandey, G., 1991, 'Hindus and Others: The Militant Hindu Construction', *Economic and Political Weekly*, Vol.26, No.52.

Pandian, M.S.S., 1992, *The Image Trap: M.G.Ramachandran in Film and Politics*, New Delhi: Sage.

Panikkar, K.N. (ed.), 1980, *National and Left Movements in India*, New Delhi: Vikas Publishing House.

Paredes, S., 1974, *Las clases sociales en el campo*, Lima: Ediciones Bandera Roja.

Parkinson, D. (ed.), 1993, *Mornings in the Dark: The Graham Greene Film Reader*, London: Carcanet.

Passmore, J., 1972, *The Perfectibility of Man*, London: Duckworth.

Passmore, J., 1978, *Science and Its Critics*, London: Duckworth.

Pathy, J., 1976, 'Political Economy of Kandhaland', *Man in India*, Vol.56, No.1.

Pathy, J., 1984, *Tribal Peasantry: Dynamics of Development*, New Delhi: Inter-India Publications.

Pathy, S., 1987, 'Class Formation in an Indian Tribe: The Saora', *Social Science Probings*, Vol.4, No.4.

Patnaik, U., 1979, 'Neopopulism and Marxism: The Chayanovian View of the Agrarian Question and Its Fundamental Fallacy', *The Journal of Peasant Studies*, Vol.6, No.4.

Patnaik, U., 1991, 'Food Availability and Famine: A Longer View', *The Journal of Peasant Studies*, Vol.19, No1.

Patnaik, U., 1995, 'On Capitalism and Agrestic Unfreedom', *International Review of Social History*, Vol.40, Part 1.

Pavier, B., 1981, *The Telengana Movement 1944–51*, New Delhi: Vikas Publishing House.

Pavloff, V.N., 1978, 'Revolutionary Populism in Imperial Russia and the National Question in the 1870s and 1880s', in Cahm and Fisera (eds.) [1978].

Peary, D., 1981, *Cult Movies*, London: Vermillion.

Pefanis, J., 1991, *Heterology and the Postmodern: Bataille, Baudrillard and Lyotard*, Durham, NC: Duke University Press.

Pennock, J.R. and J.W.Chapman (eds.), 1978, *Anarchism*, New York: New York University Press.

Perryman, M. (ed.), 1994, *Altered States: Postmodernism, Politics, Culture*, London: Lawrence & Wishart.

Petley, J., 1979, *Capital and Culture: German Cinema 1933–45*, London: British Film Institute.

Petras, J., 1990, 'Retreat of the Intellectuals', *Economic and Political Weekly*, Vol.25, No.38.

Petrovich, M.B., 1963, 'V.I. Semevskii (1848–1916): Russian Social Historian', in Curtiss (ed.) [1963].

Petrovich, M.B., 1968, 'The Peasant in Nineteenth Century Historiography', in

Vucinich (ed.) [1968].

Phillips, K.P., 1982, *Post-Conservative America: People, Politics and Ideology in a Time of Crisis*, New York: Random House.

Piccone, P., 1994, 'Confronting the French New Right', *Telos*, Nos.98–99.

Pieterse, J.N. (ed.), 1992, 'Emancipations, Modern and Postmodern', a special issue of *Development and Change*, Vol.23, No.3.

Pieterse, J.N., 1992, *White on Black: Images of Africa and Blacks in Western Popular Culture*, New Haven, CT: Yale University Press.

Pirie, D., 1973, *A Heritage of Horror: The English Gothic Cinema 1946–1972*, London: Gordon Fraser.

Pirie, D., 1977, *The Vampire Cinema*, London: Quarto Books.

Pirie, M., 1988, *Micropolitics: The Creation of Successful Policy*, Aldershot: Wildwood House.

Plattner, S. (ed.), 1989, *Economic Anthropology*, Stanford, CA: Stanford University Press.

Pois, R.A., 1986, *National Socialism and the Religion of Nature*, London: Croom Helm.

Poole, M. and J. Wyver, 1984, *Powerplays: Trevor Griffiths in Television*, London: British Film Institute.

Popkin, S.L., 1979, *The Rational Peasant*, Berkeley, CA: University of California Press.

Porter, R. and M. Teich (eds.), 1988, *Romanticism in National Context*, Cambridge: Cambridge University Press.

Porter, V., 1983, 'The Context of Creativity: Ealing Studios and Hammer Films', in Curran and Porter (eds.) [1983].

Portes, A. *et al.*, 1989, *The Informal Economy: Studies in Advanced and Less Developed Countries*, London: Johns Hopkins Press.

Poster, M. (ed.), 1993, *Politics, Theory, and Contemporary Culture*, New York: Columbia University Press.

Pouchepadass, J., 1980, 'Peasant Classes in Twentieth Century Agrarian Movements in India', in Hobsbawm *et al.* (eds.) [1980].

Prakash, G., 1994, 'Subaltern Studies as Postcolonial Criticism', *The American Historical Review*, Vol.99, No.5.

Prakash, G., 1995, 'Postcolonial Criticism and Indian Historiography', in Nicholson and Seidman (eds.) [1995].

Prakash, G., (ed.), 1992, *The World of the Rural Labourer in Colonial India*, Delhi: Oxford University Press.

Prasad, P.H., 1989, *Lopsided Growth: Political Economy of Indian Development*, Bombay: Oxford University Press.

Prasad, P.H., 1991, 'Rise of Kulak Power and Caste Struggle in North India', *Economic and Political Weekly*, Vol.26, No.33.

Praz, M., 1933, *The Romantic Agony*, Oxford: Clarendon Press.

Preston, P., 1990, 'Populism and Parasitism: The Falange and the Spanish Establishment 1939–75', in Blinkhorn (ed.) [1990].

Pudovkin, V.I., 1958, *Film Technique*, London: Vision Press.

Pumaruna, A. (ps. Ricardo Letts), 1968, *Peru: Revolución: Insurección: Guerrillas*, Lima: Ediciones Vanguardia Revolucionaria.

Puntambekar, S.V. and N.S. Varadachari, 1926, *Hand-spinning and Hand-weaving: An Essay*, Ahmedabad: The All-India Spinners' Association.

Quijano, A., 1965, 'El movimiento campesino del Peru y sus líderes', *América Latina*, No.4.

Quijano, A., 1967, 'Contemporary Peasant Movements', in Lipset and Solari (eds.) [1967].

Rabinow, P. (ed.), 1984, *The Foucault Reader*, London: Penguin Books.

Rahnema, M. and V. Bawtree (eds.), 1997, *The Post-Development Reader*, London: Zed Books.

Ranga, N.G., 1946, *The Colonial and Coloured Peoples: A Programme for Their Freedom and Progress*, Bombay: Hind Kitabs Publishers.

Ranga, N.G., 1968, *Fight for Freedom*, New Delhi: S. Chand.

Rao, C.R., 1972, *The Historic Telengana Struggle: Some Useful Lessons from its Rich Experience*, New Delhi: Communist Party of India.

Rao, C.R. and S. Faizee, 1989, *Babri Masjid Ram Janam Bhoomi Controversy – Dangerous Communal Situation*, New Delhi: CPI.

Rao, M.S.A. (ed.), 1986, *Studies in Migration*, New Delhi: Manohar.

Rawls, J., 1993, *Political Liberalism*, New York: Columbia University Press.

Ray, K. and S.K. Jha, 1987, 'Assessing Shetkari Sanghatana', *Economic and Political Weekly*, Vol.22, No.51.

Redclift, M., 1988, 'Agrarian Social Movements in Contemporary Mexico', *Bulletin of Latin American Research*, Vol.7, No.2.

Redfield, R., 1930, *Tepoztlan, A Mexican Village: A Study of Folk Life*, Chicago, IL: University of Chicago Press.

Redfield, R., 1941, *The Folk Culture of Yucatan*, Chicago, IL: University of Chicago Press.

Redfield, R., 1956, *Peasant Society and Culture*, Chicago, IL: University of Chicago Press.

Reed, T.V., 1992, *Fifteen Jugglers, Five Believers: Literary Politics and the Poetics of American Social Movements*, Berkeley, CA: University of California Press.

Reinaga, F., 1969, *La Revolución India*, La Paz: Ediciones PIB (Partido Indio de Bolivia).

Reinhardt, N., 1988, *Our Daily Bread: The Peasant Question and Family Farming in the Colombian Andes*, Berkeley: University of California Press.

Reissman, F., 1986, 'The New Populism and the Empowerment Ethos', in Boyte and Reissman (eds.) [1986].

Richards, J., 1970, 'Frank Capra and the cinema of populism', *Cinema*, No.5.

Richards, J., 1973, *Visions of Yesterday*, London: Routledge & Kegan Paul.

Richards, J. and D. Sheridan (eds.), 1987, *Mass-Observation at the Movies*, London: Routledge & Kegan Paul.

Richards, P., 1983, 'Ecological Change and the Politics of African Land Use', *African Studies Review*, Vol.26, No.2.

Richards, P., 1985, *Indigenous Agricultural Revolution*, London: Hutchinson.

Richards, P., 1986, *Coping with Hunger*, London: Allen & Unwin.

Richards, P., 1990, 'Indigenous Approaches to Rural Development: The Agrarian Populist Tradition in West Africa', in Altieri and Hecht (eds.) [1990].

Richie, D., 1972, *Japanese Cinema*, London: Secker & Warburg.

Richter, M. (ed.), 1970, *Essays in Theory and History*, Cambridge MA: Harvard University Press.

Ridge, M., 1962, *Ignatius Donnelly: The Portrait of a Politician*, Chicago, IL: University of Chicago Press.

Ridgeway, J., 1990, *Blood in the Face: The Ku Klux Klan, Ayran Nations, Nazi Skinheads, and the Rise of a New White Culture*, New York: Thunder's Mouth Press.

Riesman, D., 1953, *Thorstein Veblen: A Critical Interpretation*, New York: Charles Scribner's Sons.

Rodriguez, J., 1994, *Our Lady of Guadaloupe: Faith and Empowerment among Mexican-American Women*, Austin, TX: University of Texas Press.

Rogger, H. and E. Weber (eds.), 1965, *The European Right: An Historical Profile*, London: Weidenfeld & Nicolson.

Rohdie, S., 1970, 'A Structural Analysis of *Mr Deeds Goes to Town*', *Cinema*, No.5.

Röpke, W., 1948, *Civitas Humana: A Humane Order of Society*, London: William Hodge.

Röpke, W., 1950, *The Social Crisis of Our Time*, Glasgow: William Hodge.

Röpke, W., 1964, 'South Africa: An Attempt at a Positive Appraisal', *Schweizer Monatshefte*, 44th Year, No.2 (May).

Rorty, R., 1989, *Contingency, Irony, Solidarity*, Cambridge: Cambridge University Press.

Rose, M.A., 1991, *The Post-Modern and the Post-Industrial: A Critical Analysis*, Cambridge: Cambridge University Press.

Rotha, P., 1949, *The Film Till Now*, London: Vision Press.

Rothbard, M.N., 1970, 'Confessions of a Right-wing Liberal', in Silverman (ed.) [1970].

Rothbard, M.N., 1978, 'Society without a State', in Pennock and Chapman (eds.) [1978].

Rowbotham, S., 1999, 'Locked in the Ivory Tower', *The Times Higher*, 13 Nov.

Roy, A., 1993, 'Pressure to Curb People's Movements', *Economic and Political Weekly*, Vol.28, No.52.

Roy, K.C. and C.A. Tisdell, 1992, 'Gandhi's Concept of Development and Nehru's Centralized Planning', in Roy, Tisdell and Sen (eds.) [1992].

Roy, K.C., Tisdell, C.A. and R.K. Sen (eds.), 1992, *Economic Development and the Environment*, Calcutta: Oxford University Press.

Rudolph, L.I., 1992, 'The Media and Cultural Politics', *Economic and Political Weekly*, Vol.27, No.28.

Rudolph, L.I. and S.H. Rudolph, 1984, 'Determinants and Varieties of Agrarian Mobilization', in Desai, Rudolph and Rudra (eds.) [1984].

Rudolph, L.I. and S.H. Rudolph, 1987, *In Pursuit of Lakshmi: The Political Economy of the Indian State*, Chicago, IL: Chicago University Press.

Rumble, P. and B. Testa (eds.), 1994, *Pier Paolo Pasolini: Contemporary Perspectives*, Toronto: University of Toronto Press.

Rushing, J.H. and T.S. Frentz, 1995, *Projecting the Shadow: The Cyborg Hero in American Film*, Chicago, IL: University of Chicago Press.

Ryan, A. (ed.), 1992, *After the End of History*, London: Collins & Brown.

Ryan, A., 1986, 'Roger Scruton and Neoconservatism', in Cohen *et al.* [1986].

Sacchi, F., 1994, 'The Italian New Right', *Telos*, Nos.98–99.

Safa, H.I., 1995, *The Myth of the Male Breadwinner: Women and Industrialization in the Caribbean*, Boulder, CO: Westview Press.

Sahlins, M., 1972, *Stone Age Economics*, Chicago, IL: Aldine Atherton.

Sahlins, M., 1985, *Islands of History*, Chicago, IL: University of Chicago Press.

Said, E.W., 1978, *Orientalism*, London: Routledge & Kegan Paul.

Said, E.W., 1993, *Culture and Imperialism*, London: Chatto & Windus.

Said, E.W., 1994, *Representations of the Intellectual*, London; Random House.

Salutos, T. and J.D. Hicks, 1951, *Agricultural Discontent in the Middle West 1900–1939*, Madison, WI: University of Wisconsin Press.

Salutos, T., 1968, 'The Professors and the Populists', in Salutos (ed.) [1968].

Salutos, T. (ed.), 1968, *Populism: Reaction or Reform?*, New York: Holt, Rinehart & Winston.

Salvadori, M., 1979, *Karl Kautsky and the Socialist Revolution 1880–1938*, London: New Left Books.

Samuel, R., 1995, *Theatres of Memory*, London: Verso.

Samuel, R. (ed.), 1981, *People's History and Socialist Theory*, London: Routledge & Kegan Paul.

Sánchez, R., 1977, 'The Model of Verticality in the Andean Economy: A Critical Reconsideration', *Bulletin of the Society for Latin American Studies*, No.27.

Sánchez, R., 1982, 'The Andean Economic System and Capitalism', in Lehmann (ed.) [1982].

Sanderson, S.E. (ed.), 1985, *The Americas in the New International Division of Labor*, New York: Holmes & Meier.

Sandford, J., 1981, *The New German Cinema*, London: Eyre Methuen.

Sargent, L.T. (ed.), 1995, *Extremism in America*, New York: New York University Press.

Sarkar, S., 1997, *Writing Social History*, Calcutta: Oxford University Press.

Sarkar, T., 1991, 'The Woman as Communal Subject: Rashtrasevika Samiti and the Ram Janmabhoomi Movement', *Economic and Political Weekly*, Vol.26, No.35.

Sarkar, T. and U. Butalia (eds.), 1995, *Women and Right-wing Movements: Indian Experiences*, London: Zed Press.

Sarup, M., 1988, *Post-Structuralism and Postmodernism*, Hemel Hempstead: Harvester.

Sassen, S., 1988, *The Mobility of Labor and Capital: A Study in International Investment and Capital Flow*, Cambridge: Cambridge University Press.

Sathyamurthy, T.V., 1990, 'Indian Peasant Historiography: A Critical Perspective on Ranajit Guha's Work', *The Journal of Peasant Studies*, Vol.18, No.1,

Sawers, L. and W.K. Tabb (eds.), 1984, *Sunbelt/Snowbelt: Urban Development and Regional Restructuring*, New York: Oxford University Press.

Sawyer, R., 1986, *Slavery in the Twentieth Century*, London: Routledge & Kegan Paul.

Saxton, A., 1990, *The Rise and Fall of the White Republic: Class Politics and Mass Culture in Nineteenth Century America*, London: Verso.

Schickel, R., 1984, *D.W. Griffith and the Birth of Film*, London: Pavilion Books.

Schulman, M.D., Garrett, P.M. and B.A. Newman, 1989, 'Differentiation and Survival among North Carolina Tobacco Farmers: An Empirical Perspective on the Lenin-Chayanov Debate', *The Journal of Peasant Studies*, Vol.16, No.4.

Schuurman, F.J. (ed.), 1993, *Beyond the Impasse: New Directions in Development Theory*, London: Zed Press.

Scott, A.M., 1994, *Divisions and Solidarities: Gender, Class and Employment in Latin America*, London: Routledge.

Scott, J.C., 1976, *The Moral Economy of the Peasant: Rebellion and Subsistence in Southeast Asia*, New Haven, CT: Yale University Press.

Scott, J.C., 1985a, 'Socialism and Small Property – or – Two Cheers for the Petty Bourgeoisie', *Peasant Studies*, Vol.12, No.3.

Scott, J.C., 1985b, *Weapons of the Weak: Everyday Forms of Peasant Resistance*, New Haven, CT: Yale University Press.

Scott, J.C., 1989, 'Everyday Forms of Resistance', in Colburn (ed.) [1989].

Scott, J.C., 1990, *Domination and the Arts of Resistance*, New Haven, CT: Yale University Press.

Scott, J.C., 1995, 'State Simplifications: Nature, Space and People', paper presented at the Conference on 'Agrarian Questions', Wageningen, 22–24 May.

Scott, J.C. and B.J. Tria Kerkvliet (eds.), 1986, *Everyday Forms of Peasant Resistance in South-East Asia*, London: Frank Cass.

Seidel, G., 1986, 'Culture, Nation and "Race" in the British and French New Right', in Levitas (ed.) [1986].

Selbourne, D., 1985, 'A Political Morality Re-examined', in Selbourne (ed.) [1985].

Selbourne, D., 1987, *Left Behind: A Journey Through British Politics*, London: Jonathan Cape.

Selbourne, D. (ed.), 1985, *In Theory and in Practice: Essays on the Politics of Jayaprakash Narayan*, Delhi: Oxford University Press.

Sen, A., 1987, 'Subaltern Studies: Capital, Class, and Community', in Guha (ed.) [1987].

Sen, G. (ed.), 1992, *Indigenous Vision: Peoples of India Attitudes to the Environment*, New Delhi: Sage.

Sen, I., 1990, 'Introduction', in Sen (ed.) [1990].

Sen, I. (ed.), 1990, *A Space Within the Struggle: Women's Participation in People's Movements*, New Delhi: Kali for Women.

Sen, S., 1972, *Agrarian Struggle in Bengal 1946–47*, New Delhi: People's Publishing House.

Sen, S., 1982, *Peasant Movements in India: Mid-Nineteenth and Twentieth Centuries*, Calcutta: K.P. Bagchi.

Sengupta, N., 1982, 'Background of the Jarkhand Question', in Sengupta (ed.) [1982].

Sengupta, N., 1989, 'From Peasant to Tribe: Peasant Movements in Chotanagpur', in Karna (ed.) [1989].

Sengupta, N. (ed.), 1982, *Fourth World Dynamics: Jharkhand*, Delhi: Authors Guild Publications.

Shackleton, J.R. and G. Locksley (eds.), 1981, *Twelve Contemporary Economists*, London: Macmillan.

Shah, G., 1991, 'Tenth Lok Sabha Elections: BJP's Victory in Gujarat', *Economic and Political Weekly*, Vol.26, No.51.

Shah, G. (ed.), 1992, *Capitalist Development: Critical Essays*, London: Sangam Books.

Shanin, T., 1973, 'Gary Littlejohn's review of T. Shanin, *The Awkward Class*', *Economy & Society*, Vol.2, No.2.

Shanin, T., 1976, 'The "Invisible Hand" – A Comment', *Peasant Studies*, Vol.5, No.2.

Shanin, T., 1981, *The Awkward Class*, Oxford: The Clarendon Press.

Sheehan, T., 1980, 'Paris: Moses and Polytheism', in Montague (ed.) [1980].

Sheehan, T., 1981, 'Myth and Violence: The Fascism of Julius Evola and Alain de Benoist', *Social Research*, Vol.48, No.1.

Shanin, T. (ed.), 1971, *Peasants and Peasant Societies*, London: Penguin Books.

Sherman, A.L., 1992, *Preferential Option: A Christian and Neoliberal Strategy for Latin America's Poor*, Washington, DC: The Institute on Religion and Democracy.

Shils, E., 1981, *Tradition*, Chicago, IL: University of Chicago Press.

Shiva, V., 1988, *Staying Alive: Women, Ecology and Survival in India*, London: Zed Press.

Shiva, V., 1990, 'Development as a New Project of Western Patriarchy', in Diamond and Orenstein (eds.) [1990].

Shiva, V., 1991a, *The Violence of the Green Revolution: Third World Agriculture, Ecology and Politics*, London: Zed Books.

Shiva, V., 1991b, *Ecology and the Politics of Survival*, New Delhi: Sage Publications.

Shiva, V., 1992a, 'Women's Indigenous Knowledge and Biodiversity Conservation', in Sen (ed.) [1992].

Shiva, V., 1992b, 'Biodiversity, Biotechnology and Profits', in V.Shiva (ed.) [1992].

Shiva, V., 1993a, 'Farmers' Rights, Biodiversity and International Treaties', *Economic and Political Weekly*, Vol.28, No.14.

Shiva, V., 1993b, *Monoculture of the Mind: Biodiversity, Biotechnology and 'Scientific' Agriculture*, London: Zed Books.

Shiva, V., 1998, *Biopiracy: The Plunder of Nature and Knowledge*, Dartington: Green Books.

Shiva, V. (ed.), 1992, *Biodiversity: Social and Ecological Perspectives*, Dehradun: Natraj Publishers.

Silva, P., 1990, 'Agrarian Change Under the Chilean Military Government', *Latin American Research Review*, Vol.25, No.1.

Silverman, H.J. (ed.), 1970, *American Radical Thought: The Libertarian Tradition*, Lexington, MA: D.C. Heath .

Simmons, E.J. (ed.), 1955, *Continuity and Change in Russian and Soviet Thought*, Cambridge, MA: Harvard University Press.

Simon, D. (ed.), 1990, *Third World Regional Development: A Reappraisal*, London: Paul Chapman Publishing.

Singh, C., 1978, *India's Economic Policy: The Gandhian Blueprint*, New Delhi: Vikas Publishing House.

Singh, C., 1981, *Economic Nightmare of India: Its Cause and Cure*, New Delhi: National Publishing House.

Singh, K.S., 1985, *Tribal Society in India*, Delhi: Manohar Books.

Sinha, I., 1982, *Some Questions Concerning Marxism and the Peasantry*, New Delhi: Communist Party Publication.

Sinha, S., Greenberg, B. and S. Gururani, 1997, 'The "New Traditionalist" Discourse of Indian Environmentalism', *The Journal of Peasant Studies*, Vol.24, No.3.

Singelmann, P., 1981, *Structures of Domination and Peasant Movements in Latin America*, Columbia, MO: University of Missouri Press.

Sivanandan, A., 1990, *Communities of Resistance: Writings on Black Struggles for Socialism*, London: Verso.

Skar, H.O., 1982, *The Warm Valley People*, Oslo: Universitetsforlaget.

Sklair, L., 1990, 'Regional Consequences of Open-door Development Strategies: Export Zones in Mexico and China', in Simon (ed.) [1990].

Slater, D. (ed.), 1985, *New Social Movements and the State in Latin America*, Amsterdam: CEDLA.

Sluga, H., 1993, *Heidegger's Crisis: Philosophy and Politics in Nazi Germany*, Cambridge, MA: Harvard University Press.

Smith, A.K. and C.E. Welch, Jr. (eds.), 1978, *Peasants in Africa*, Waltham, MA: African Studies Association, Brandeis University.

Smith, R.E.F., 1977, 'Notes on the Sources of George Orwell's 1984', in Smith (ed.) [1977].

Smith, R.E.F. (ed.), 1977, *The Russian Peasant in 1920 and 1984*, London: Frank Cass.

Snowden, F.M, 1979, 'From Sharecropper to Proletarian: the Background to Fascism in Rural Tuscany, 1880–1920', in Davis (ed.) [1979].

Snowden, F.M., 1986, *Violence and the Great Estates in the South of Italy: Apulia 1900–1922*, Cambridge: Cambridge University Press.

Sohn-Rethel, A., 1978, *Economy and Class Structure of German Fascism*, London: CSE Books.

Sorel, G., 1916, *Reflections on Violence*, London: George Allen & Unwin.

Sorel, G., 1969, *The Illusion of Progress*, Berkeley, CA: University of California Press.

Soucy, R., 1995, *French Fascism: The Second Wave, 1933–1939*, New Haven, CT: Yale University Press.

Southall, R. (ed.), 1988, *Labour and Unions in Asia and Africa*, London: Macmillan Press.

Spretnak, C., 1986, 'Postmodern Populism: The Greening of Technocratic Society', in Boyte and Reissman (eds.) [1986].

Spretnak, C., 1990, 'Ecofeminism: Our Roots and Flowering', in Diamond and Orenstein (eds.) [1990].

Stack, O., 1969, *Pasolini on Pasolini*, London: BFI/Thames & Hudson.

Stanfield, P., 1996, 'Country Music and the 1939 Western: From Hillbillies to Cowboys', in Cameron and Pye (eds.) [1996].

Staudenmaier, P. and J. Biehl (eds.), 1995, *Ecofascism: Lessons from the German Experience*, Edinburgh: AK Press.

Stavenhagen, R., 1967, 'Review', *Current Anthropology*, Vol.8, No.5.

Stavenhagen, R. (ed.), 1970, *Agrarian Problems and Peasant Movements in Latin America*, New York: Anchor Doubleday.

Stein, M. and A.Vidich (eds.), 1963, *Sociology on Trial*, Englewood Cliffs, NJ: Prentice-Hall.

Stepan, A., 1978, *The State and Society: Peru in Comparative Perspective*, Princeton, NJ: Princeton University Press.

Stichter, S. and J.L. Parpart (eds.), 1990, *Women, Employment and the Family in the International Division of Labour*, London: Macmillan.

Stoker, B., 1897/1993, *Dracula*, Ware, Hertfordshire: Wordsworth Editions.

Stradling, R. and M. Hughes, 1993, *The English Musical Renaissance 1860–1940: Construction and Deconstruction*, London: Routledge.

Sundarayya, P., 1972, *Telengana People's Struggle and its Lessons*, Calcutta: Communist Party of India (Marxist).

Sunic, T., 1990, *Against Democracy and Equality: The European New Right*, New York: Peter Lang.

Taguieff, P.-A., 1990, 'The New Cultural Racism in France', *Telos*, No.83.

Taguieff, P.-A., 1994a, 'Discussion or Inquisition? The Case of Alain de Benoist', *Telos*, Nos.98–99.

Taguieff, P.-A., 1994b, 'Origins and Metamorphoses of the New Right', *Telos*, Nos.98–99.

Taguieff, P.-A., 1995, 'Political Science Confronts Populism', *Telos*, No.103.

Tannenbaum, F., 1947, *Slave and Citizen*, New York: Alfred A. Knopf.

Tarchi, M., 1995, 'In Search of Right and Left', *Telos*, 103.

Tarde, G., 1905, *Underground Man*, London: Duckworth.

Taussig, M., 1987, *Shamanism, Colonialism, and the Wild Man: A Study in Terror and Healing*, Chicago, IL: University of Chicago Press.

Tawney, R.H., 1932, *Land and Labour in China*, London: George Allen & Unwin.

Tawney, R.H., 1938, *Agrarian China*, Shanghai: Kelly and Walsh.

Taylor, C., 1992, 'Heidegger, Language and Ecology', in Dreyfus and Hall (eds.) [1992].

Taylor, L., 1983, *Maoism in the Andes: Sendero Luminoso and the Contemporary Guerrilla Movement in Peru*, Liverpool: Centre for Latin American Studies, Working Paper 2.

Taylor, L., 1987, 'Agrarian Unrest and Political Conflict in Puno, 1985–1987', *Bulletin of Latin American Research*, Vol.6, No.2.

Thompson, E.P., 1991, *Cultures in Common*, London: Merlin Press.

Thompson, P.B., 1992, *The Ethics of Aid and Trade*, Cambridge: Cambridge University Press.

Thomson, D., 1997, *Beneath Mulholland*, New York: Alfred A. Knopf.

Tidmarsh, K., 1960, 'The Soviet Reassessment of Mahatma Gandhi', in Iyer (ed.) [1960].

Timms, E. and D. Kelley (eds.), 1985, *Unreal City: Urban Experience in Modern European Literature and Art*, Manchester: Manchester University Press.

Timms, E., 1985, 'Expressionists and Georgians: Demonic City and Enchanted Village', in Timms and Kelley (eds.) [1985].

Tönnies, F., 1955, *Community and Association*, London: Routledge & Kegan Paul.

Totten, G.O, 1960, 'Labor and Agrarian Disputes in Japan following World War I', *Economic Development and Cultural Change*, Vol.IX, No.1, Part II.

Trotzky, L., 1918, *The Bolsheviki and World Peace*, New York: Boni & Liveright.

Trotsky, L., 1934, *The History of the Russian Revolution*, London: Victor Gollancz.

Trotsky, L., 1936, *The Third International After Lenin*, New York: Pioneer Publishers.

Trotsky, L., 1940, *The Living Thoughts of Karl Marx*, London: Cassell.

Trotsky, L., 1945, *The First Five Years of the Communist International*, New York: Pioneer Publishers.

Trotsky, L., 1962, *The Permanent Revolution and Results and Prospects*, London: New Park Publications.

Trotsky, L., 1969, 'The Three Conceptions of the Russian Revolution', *Writings 1938–39*, New York: Merit Publishers.

Trotsky, L., 1971, 'What is National Socialism?', in *The Struggle Against Fascism in Germany*, New York: Pathfinder Press.

Tudor, A., 1974, *Image and Influence: Studies in the Sociology of Film*, London: George Allen & Unwin.

Tupayachi, I., 1959, 'Un Ensayo de Econometría en La Convención', *Revista Universitaria*, 117.

Turner, A., 1994, *The Making of David Lean's Lawrence of Arabia*, Surrey: Dragon's World.

Twelve Southerners, 1951/[1930], *I'll Take My Stand: The South and the Agrarian Tradition*, New York: Peter Smith.

Ulmen, G., 1995, 'Reflections of a Partisan: Julien Freund (1921–1993)', *Telos*, No.102.

Umphlett, W.L., 1983, *Mythmakers of the American Dream: The Nostalgic Vision in Popular Culture*, Lewisburg: Bucknell University Press.

Utechin, S.V., 1964, *Russian Political Thought*, London: J.M. Dent.

van Onselen, C., 1977, 'South Africa's Lumpenproletariat Army: "Umkosi Wa Ntaba" – "The Regiment of the Hills", 1890–1920', *Collected Seminar Papers on the Societies of Southern Africa in the 19th and 20th Centuries*, London: Institute of Commonwealth Studies (University of London).

Vanaik, A., 1994, 'Situating the Threat of Hindu Nationalism – Problems with Fascist Paradigm', *Economic and Political Weekly*, Vol.29, N.28.

Vanaik, A., 1997, *The Furies of Indian Communalism: Religion, Modernity and Secularization*, London: Verso.

Vanaik, A., 1998, 'Marxist-Thompsonian History' *Economic and Political Weekly*, Vol. 33, No. 21.

Vann Woodward, C., 1938, *Tom Watson: Agrarian Rebel*, New York: Macmillan.

Vann Woodward, C., 1960, *The Burden of Southern History*, New York: Vintage Books.

Vann Woodward, C., 1989, *The Future of the Past*, New York: Oxford University Press.

Varshney, A., 1993a, 'Introduction: Urban Bias in Perspective', in Varshney [1993c].

Varshney, A., 1993b, 'Self-Limited Empowerment: Democracy, Economic Development and Rural India', in Varshney [1993c].

Varshney, A. (ed.), 1993c, *Beyond Urban Bias*, London: Frank Cass.

Venturi, F., 1960, *Roots of Revolution: A History of the Populist and Socialist Movements in Nineteenth Century Russia*, London: Weidenfeld & Nicolson.

Vernet, M., 1993, '*Film Noir* on the Edge of Doom', in Copjec (ed.) [1993].

Vidal, G., 1992, *Screening History*, London: Andre Deutsch.

Vidyarthi, L.P., 1970, *Socio-cultural Implications of Industrialisation in India: A Case Study of Tribal Bihar*, New Delhi: Research Programmes Committee, Planning Commission.

Vieux, S. and J. Petras, 1996, 'Selling Structural Adjustment: Intellectuals in Uniform', *Economic and Political Weekly*, Vol.31, No.4.

Villanueva, V., 1967, *Hugo Blanco y la rebelión campesina*, Lima: Libreria-Editorial Juan Mejía Baca.

Vinogradoff, E.D., 1975, 'The "Invisible Hand" and the Russian Peasant', *Peasant Studies*, Vol.4, No.3.

Vinogradoff, E.D., 1976, 'Reply', *Peasant Studies*, Vol.5, No.2.

Viski, K., 1932, *Hungarian Peasant Customs*, Budapest: Vajna.

Volosinov, V.N., 1973, *Marxism and the Philosophy of Language*, New York: Seminar Press.

Voltaire, 1947 [1758], *Candide, or Optimism*, Harmondsworth: Penguin Books.

Vucinich, W.S. (ed.), 1968, *The Peasant in Nineteenth Century Russia*, Stanford, CA: Stanford University Press.

Wakukawa, S., 1976, 'The Tenant Movement', in Livingston, Moore, and Oldfather (eds.) [1976].

Walicki, A., 1969, *The Controversy over Capitalism: Studies in the Social Philosophy of the Russian Populists*, Oxford: Clarendon Press.

Walicki, A., 1975, *The Slavophile Controversy: History of a Conservative Utopia in Nineteenth Century Russian Thought*, Oxford: Clarendon Press.

Walicki, A., 1980, *A History of Russian Thought from the Enlightenment to Marxism*, Oxford: Clarendon Press.

Ward, I., 1992, *Law Philosophy and National Socialism: Heidegger, Schmitt and Radbruch in Context*, Bern: Peter Lang.

Warriner, D., 1950, *Revolution in Eastern Europe*, London: Turnstile Press.

Wasson, R., 1966, 'The Politics of Dracula', *English Literature in Transition*, Vol.9, No.1.

Watts, M., 1992, 'Peasants and Flexible Accumulation in the Third World: Producing under Contract', *Economic and Political Weekly*, Vol.27, No.30.

Weber, E., 1964, *Varieties of Fascism*, New York: Van Nostrand Reinhold.

Weber, E., 1965, 'Romania', in Rogger and Weber (eds.) [1965].

Weber, E., 1966, 'The Men of the Archangel', *Journal of Contemporary History*, Vol.1, No.1.

Wegierski, M., 1994, 'The New Right in Europe', *Telos*, Nos.98–99.

Weiner, M., 1989, *The Indian Paradox: Essays in Indian Politics*, New Delhi: Sage Publications.

Welch, D., 1983, *Propaganda and the German Cinema 1933–45*, Oxford: Clarendon Press.

Wells, H.G., 1895, *The Time Machine*, London: Heinemann.

Wharton, C.R. (ed.), 1970, *Subsistence Agriculture and Economic Development*, London: Frank Cass.

Wiener, M.J., 1981, *English Culture and the Decline of the Industrial Spirit 1850–1980*, Cambridge: Cambridge University Press.

Wignaraja, P. (ed.), 1992, *New Social Movements in the South: Empowering the People*, London: Zed Books.

Wilde, L., 1985, *Sorel and the French Right*, Nottingham: Trent Polytechnic.

Wiles, P., 1969, 'A Syndrome, not a Doctrine', in Ionescu and Gellner (eds.) [1969].

Willan, B., 1984, *Sol Plaatje: South African Nationalist 1876–1932*, London: Heinemann.

Willemen, P. (ed.), 1976, *Pier Paolo Pasolini*, London: British Film Institute.

Williams, R., 1973, *The Country and the City*, London: Chatto & Windus.

Williams, R., 1985, 'The Metropolis and the emergence of Modernism', in Timms and Kelley (eds.) [1985].

Williamson, J., 1989, 'Even New Times change', *New Statesman*, 7 July.

Wish, H. (ed.), 1960, *Antebellum: The Writings of George Fitzhugh and Hinton Rowan Helper on Slavery*, New York: Capricorn Books.

Wolf, E.R., 1966, *Peasants*, Englewood Cliffs, NJ: Prentice-Hall.

Wolf, E.R., 1971, *Peasant Wars of the Twentieth Century*, London: Faber & Faber.

Wollen, P., 1974, *Signs and Meaning in the Cinema*, London: Secker & Warburg.

Wollenberg, H.H., 1948, *Fifty Years of German Film*, London: Falcon Press.

Wood, C., 1987, *The Moplah Rebellion and Its Genesis*, New Delhi: People's Publishing House.

Woodhouse, J., 1991, 'Tales From Another Country: Fictional Treatments of the Russian Peasantry, 1847–1861', *Rural History*, Vol.2, No.2.

World Bank, 1992, *World Development Report 1992: Development and the Environment*, New York: Oxford University Press.

Worsley, P., 1984, *The Three Worlds: Culture and World Development*, London: Weidenfeld & Nicolson.

Wortman, R., 1967, *The Crisis of Russian Populism*, Cambridge: Cambridge University Press.

Yadav, Y., 1993a, 'Political Change in North India: Interpreting Assembly Election Results', *Economic and Political Weekly*, Vol.28, No.51.

Yadav, Y., 1993b, 'Towards an Indian Agenda for the Indian Left', *Economic and Political Weekly*, Vol.28, No.41.

Yonghong, S., 1989, 'Export Processing Zones in China', *Economic and Political Weekly*, Vol.24, No.7.

Zamosc, L., 1986, *The Agrarian Question and the Peasant Movement in Colombia*, Cambridge: Cambridge University Press.

Zamosc, L., 1989, 'Peasant Struggles of the 1970s in Colombia', in Eckstein (ed.) [1989].

Zamosc, L., 1990, 'The Political Crisis and the Prospects for Rural Democracy in Colombia', in Fox (ed.) [1990].

Zamyatin, Y., 1977/1924, *We*, Harmondsworth: Penguin Books.

Author Index

A Correspondent, 139
Aass, S., 180
Abelson, E., 261
Adler, F., 222, 228
Ahmad, A., 153, 178, 213
Akram-Lodhi, H., 180
Alavi, H., 6, 144, 154, 156, 159, 162, 166, 181, 182, 184, 186
Alberti, G., 43, 94
Aldred, N., 293
Alexander, K.C., 125
Alfaro, J., 88, 90, 91, 92, 95
All India Kisan Sabha, 136
Althusser, L., 41
Alvarez, S.E., 171
Ambedkar, B.R., 51, 124
Amery, L.S., 293
Amin, S., 51
Amis, K., 178
Amnesty International, 124
Anderson, W.K., 136, 137, 138
Aranda, A., 88, 89, 90, 91
Archetti, E.P., 180
Arnheim, R., 294, 297
Assadi, M., 130, 131
Athreya, V., 127, 128
Atkinson, D., 43

Baden, J., 173, 177, 178
Bagchi, A.K., 172, 213
Bahro, R., 170
Bailey, R.B., 225
Balagopal, K., 125, 132, 135, 305
Banaji, J., 44, 126, 135, 139
Bann, S., 260
Barker, M., 228
Barnett, A., 231
Barr, C., 293, 294
Barry, N.P., 124
Barthakur, S., 138
Baskaran, S.T., 51
Basu, K., 178, 221
Basu, T., 136, 137, 138
Bataille, G., 143, 217, 218, 220

Bates, R.H., 131
Baudin, L., 55
Baudrillard, J., 184, 197, 220
Bausinger, H., 173
Bawtree, V., 171
Baxter, C., 132
Beegle, J.A., 58
Beik, W., 46
Béjar, H., 88, 89, 90
Bell, D., 41, 214
Bell, J.D., 58, 59
Belloc, H., 22, 46, 50
Bendersky, J.W., 221
Bendix, R., 41
Bennholdt-Thomsen, V., 135, 173
Benvenuto, S., 221
Berger, P.L., 225, 230
Bergquist, C., 176
Berlin, I., 43
Bernstein, M.S., 178
Betz, H.-G., 221
Bhabha, H., 213, 227
Bhattacharya, H., 125
Bhowmik, S., 126
Bideleux, R., 133
Biehl, J., 221, 231
Billig, M., 179
Biskind, P., 302
Blanchot, M., 218
Blanco, H., 88, 89, 90, 91, 92, 93, 94, 95
Blinkhorn, M., 39
Block, W., 124
Blok, A., 301
Bodemann, Y.M., 221, 231
Booth, D., 171, 173, 174, 181
Booth, H., 223, 230
Bosanquet, N., 221
Bose, P.K., 126
Bourque, S.C., 97
Boyd, R., 169
Boyte, H.C., 223, 230
Bradby, B., 43
Bradford, G., 178
Bradford, M.E., 50

Bramwell, A., 58, 178, 220
Brass, T., 48, 92, 93, 94, 95, 128, 171, 175, 186, 222, 229
Bree, K.M., 138
Briggs, G.W., 310
Brinton, C., 41, 306
Britton, A., 294
Broome, J.H., 41
Brosnan, J., 259
Brown, J., 51, 52
Brownlow, K., 306
Buck, J.L., 266
Bukharin, N., 180
Burdick, J., 174
Burger, J., 183
Burke, J.H., 257
Burke, P., 41
Burns, E.M., 190
Bustamente, J.A., 169
Butalia, U., 221

Callinicos, A., 170, 176, 182
Calman, L.J., 171
Campi, A., 221
Cancian, F., 180
Canovan, M., 43, 45, 46, 49, 172, 266
Cantril, H., 259
Cardoza, A.L., 39, 58
Carnes, M.C., 303
Castells, M., 147, 148, 169, 170, 171, 173, 174, 183, 185
Castles, S., 169
Castro Pozo, H., 53
Caute, D., 214
Cavaliero, G., 46
Chakrabarty, D., 171, 182, 212
Chandra, N.K., 182
Chapkis, W., 169
Charlesworth, N., 52
Charrière, J., 294
Chatterjee, P., 51, 182, 183
Chattopadhyay, B., 128, 131, 132
Chavarría, J., 54
Chayanov, A.V., 43, 180, 188, 226, 237ff., 256, 257, 264, 265, 266, 268, 269 (see also Kremnev, I.)
Cheles, L., 221
Chomsky, N., 170
Chossudovsky, M., 97, 169, 188
Christie, I., 293
CIDA, 89, 92
Clark, C., 127

Clastres, P., 184
Clifford, J., 172
Cockett, R., 221
Cohen, G., 221
Cohen, R., 169
Colburn, F.D., 181, 182, 185, 188
Collins, R., 298
Conkin, P.K., 50, 263
Cooper, A., 123
Cooper, F., 182, 223
Corbridge, S., 171, 174, 181
Couto, M., 296
Cowie, P., 301
Cox, T.M., 42, 43
Craig, A.L., 171
Craig, W.W., 88, 89, 90, 92, 95
Crump, J., 57
Cuadros, C.F., 89
Curtin, C., 180
Cutler, A., 180

Dahrendorf, R., 214
Damle, S.D., 136, 137, 138
Dange, S.A., 125
Darling, M.L., 181
Das Gupta, C., 305
Das, A.N., 51, 126, 128, 135, 182
Datta, P.K., 139
Datta, P.S., 126
Davis, K., 178
de Benoist, A., 198, 221
de Grazia, V., 304
de la Fuente, J., 179
Deák, I., 58, 60
Debray, R., 89, 176, 219
Desai, A.R., 123, 154, 181
Deutscher, I., 93, 257
Deva, A.N., 25, 52
Dews, P., 184
Deyo, F.C., 169
Dhanagare, D.N., 51, 52, 123, 127, 128, 131, 132, 135
Diggins, J.P., 221
Djurfeldt, G., 127, 128
Dobb, M., 169
Dolbeare, K.M., 41, 44, 45, 223, 228
Dolbeare, P., 44, 45
Donnelly, I., 237ff., 255, 256, 261, 262, 263, 264, 265, 266, 268, 269
Dore, R., 57
Drage, G., 47
Drucker, P., 214

Dube, L., 138
Dupré, L., 124
Durgnat, R., 293
Durrenberger, P., 43, 180
Duyker, E., 126, 127
Dwivedi, O.P., 137

Eagleton, T., 219
Eatwell, R., 176, 221, 225
Ebert, R., 271
Eckstein, S., 171, 182
Eder, K., 171
Edinburgh, Duke of, 177
Eidelberg, P.G., 39, 59
Eisenstein, H., 134
Eisenstein, S., 294
Eisner, L.H., 306, 307, 308
Eliade, M., 173
Ellis, F., 43
Ellis, J., 293
Engineer, A.A., 124
Enloe, C., 169
Epstein, K., 40, 226
Erdman, H.L., 53
Eribon, D., 214, 215, 223
Escalante, M., 88, 89, 90, 91
Escobar, A., 171
Espinosa, G., 91
Etzioni, A., 238, 254, 255
Evans, T., 224
Evers, T., 162, 164, 183, 184, 185, 187, 188

Faizee, S., 137
Fanon, F., 214, 215, 216, 224, 227, 229, 276, 297
Farias, V., 212
Ferguson, R., 221
Ferkiss, V.C., 39, 178, 220
Ferry, L., 212, 218
Feuer, L., 41
Fifteen Southerners, 50
Figueroa, A., 43
Filler, L., 49
Finley, M.I., 260
Fioravanti, E., 88, 89, 90, 91, 92, 95
Fioravanti-Molinié, A., 43
Fiore, Q., 219, 220
Fitzhugh, G., 50
Fleming, T., 221, 223, 228, 231
Flinn, C., 295
Fontana, B., 176
Ford, G., 221

Forster, E.M., 261, 262, 265, 296
Fortunati, V., 261
Foster, G.M., 135, 179
Foucault, M., 172, 173, 176, 183, 214, 218, 223, 229, 276, 297
Foweraker, J., 171
Fox, J., 171, 186, 187
Fox, R.G., 51
Fox-Genovese, E., 134
Francese, J., 298
Franda, M., 133
Frank, A.G., 171
Fraser, R., 223
Freyre, G., 310
Frierson, C.A., 47
Fritzsche, P., 58
Fröbel, F., 169
Fuentes, M., 171
Fuller, G., 294

Gadgil, D.R., 98
Galla, C., 132, 135
Gamble, A., 221
Garrett, P.M., 44
Geertz, C., 172
Gellner, E., 43
Genovese, E.D., 50
George, J., 125
Geras, N., 176
Ghose, S., 125
Gianotten, V., 84, 97, 183
Gill, S.S., 127, 131, 136
Gingrich, N., 221
Glendening, M.-H., 223
Godechot, J., 40
Gonzales, A., 187
Goodwyn, L., 45, 266
Gortz, A., 170
Goswami, M.C., 135
Goswami, S., 138
Gott, R., 88, 97
Gottfried, P., 221, 222, 223, 228, 231
Gough, K., 123, 124, 125
Government of India, 127, 128, 129, 130, 131, 132, 133
Graham, B., 132
Gramsci, A., 183
Gray, J., 198, 221
Green, L.B., 124
Greenberg, B., 172
Greene, G., 266
Greenhough, P.R., 123

Gress, F., 221, 224
Griffiths, R., 261
Guerin, D., 40
Guha, Ramachandra, 182
Guha, Ranajit, 147, 157, 159, 161, 164, 171,
   182, 183, 184, 185, 186, 187, 188, 227
Guillet, D., 94
Gunn, S., 221
Gupta, A.K., 123
Gupta, D., 127, 132
Guru, G., 132
Gururani, S., 172
Gutkind, P., 169

Habermas, J., 218, 221
Hackett, A.P., 257
Hall, S., 170
Hamacher, W., 212
Hardgrave, R.L., 126
Hardiman, D., 52
Hardin, G., 173, 177, 178, 179
Harris, M., 46, 170
Harrison, M., 43
Harrison, T., 45
Harriss, J., 181, 185
Hartz, N., 212
Harvey, D., 218
Harvey, N., 128
Hasan, Z., 127, 131, 132, 135, 136
Hauser, A., 294
Havens, T., 57
Hawthorn, G.P., 176
Hay, J., 304
Haya de la Torre, V.R., 53, 54, 55, 56, 57
Hayek, F.A., 198, 176
Hayes, M., 221
Haynes, D., 181
Heidegger, M., 220
Henderson, J., 169
Herzen, A., 9
Hewitt, C., 184
Hewitt, W.E., 174
Hicks, J.D., 49
Hilton, J., 237ff., 255, 258, 260, 261, 262,
   263, 264, 265, 266, 268, 269
Hinz, B., 300
Hirst, P., 170
Hobart, M., 176
Hobsbawm, E.J., 88, 89, 90, 301
Hoeveler, J.D., 221
Hofstadter, R., 45, 49, 123, 259
Hojman, D.E., 169

Holbo, P.S., 39
Hoogvelt, A., 169
Huaco, G.A., 308
Hubbell, J.K., 41, 223, 228
Hudson, W.H., 261
Hughes, M., 46
Huizer, G., 88, 89
Hunt, D., 180
Husain, A., 136

Ignatieff, M., 176
Ionescu, G., 39, 43, 58, 60
Isaacman, A.F., 223

Jackson, C., 134
Jackson, G.D., 45, 58, 59, 60, 61
Jacobeit, S., 58
Jacobs, L., 294
Jacques, M., 170
Jasny, N., 43, 48
Jefferies, R., 243, 261
Jenkins, T., 176
Jha, S.K., 135
Jodha, N.S., 178
Jones, A.K., 47
Jonsson, U., 180
Joseph, G.M., 181
Joshi, S., 129, 133

Kaes, A., 298, 299
Kafka, F., 237
Kalecki, M., 131
Kamenka, E., 254
Kannan, K.P., 125
Kaplinsky, R., 169
Karanikas, A., 224
Karna, M.N., 123
Katsiaficas, G., 223
Kautsky, J.H., 125
Kautsky, K., 42
Kazin, M., 44, 45, 223, 224, 228
Keenan, T., 212
Kerblay, B., 43
Kerkvliet, B.J., 181
Kermode, F., 212, 219
Kirk, R., 50, 177, 225, 227
Kitching, G., 43, 47, 180
Kneale, N., 302
Kofi, T.A., 180
Kohn, M., 228
Köll, A.-M., 180
Koonz, C., 138

Korovkin, T., 169
Kosambi, D.D., 135
Kracauer, S., 286, 294, 295, 296, 297, 299, 306
Kremnev, I., 238, 257, 265, 266, 267, 268, 269–70 (*see also* Chayanov, A.V.)
Kripa, A.P., 130, 132, 136
Krishnaji, N., 125, 180
Kucherov, A., 48
Kumar, K., 256, 260
Kumar, R., 169
Kumarappa, B., 51, 133, 137

Laclau, E., 162, 164, 170, 171, 183, 185, 187, 188
Landsberger, H.A., 184
Large, S.S., 57
Larsen, N., 217
Lasch, C., 45, 237, 238, 254, 255, 265
Latin American Subaltern Studies Group, 182
Latouche, S., 147, 171, 172, 205, 216, 217, 223, 224, 225
Lehman, D., 212, 218
Lehmann, D., 174
Lejeune, C.A., 271
Lenin, V.I., 42
Lenneberg, C., 127, 136
Levidow, L., 169
Levitas, R., 221, 224
Levy, E., 259
Lewis, N., 65
Lewis, O., 179
Leyda, J., 294
Leys, C., 213
Li Causi, L., 301
Lieten, K., 51
Lindberg, S., 127, 128, 131, 135
Lipietz, A., 170
Lipset, S.M., 49
Lipton, M., 131, 180
Littlejohn, G., 42, 44, 180
Locksley, G., 221
Lohia, R., 25, 52, 53
Long, N., 43
Loomis, C.P., 58
Lora, R., 50, 225
Löwy, M., 54
Lukacs, G., 47, 186, 220
Luxemburg, R., 168
Lyotard, J.-F., 158, 197, 231

Macciocchi, A.-M., 138

MacIntyre, A., 238, 254
Maclachlan, M.D., 180
Macpherson, C.B., 214
Malia, M.E., 42
Malinowski, B., 179
Mallon, F., 182, 223
Malpica, C., 91
Mannheim, K., 40
Manor, J., 136
Manuel, F.E., 260
Manuel, F.P., 260
Manvell, R., 307
Marchand, P., 212, 219, 220
Marcus, G., 172
Marcus, J., 222
Marcuse, H., 214, 215, 216, 223, 224, 229, 276, 297
Mariátegui, J.C., 53, 54, 55, 56
Marin, L., 270
Mattick, P., 41
Max, S., 223, 230
Mayer, E., 43, 94
Mazumdar, S., 221
McBride, J., 257, 258, 259, 260
McClintock, C., 82, 83, 84, 85, 97, 187
McCormick, J., 178
McGilligan, P., 257, 258
McLuhan, M., 219, 220
Mehlman, J., 212
Mehta, U., 128, 135
Mellor, D., 293
Mellor, M., 178
Melucci, A., 171
Merchant, C., 134, 178
Meyer, J.A., 56
Michelson, A., 294
Mies, M., 134, 135, 173, 205
Miliband, R., 170
Miller, James, 212, 214, 217, 229, 230
Miller, Jonathan, 219
Miller, M.T., 169
Miller, R., 185, 187
Miroshevsky, V., 54
Mishra, A., 178
Mishra, S.N., 126
Mitra, A., 131
Mitrany, D., 39, 43, 58
Mitter, S., 169
Montoya, R., 97
Moore, B., 123
Moore, M., 43
Morales, E., 97

Morgan, R., 135
Morris, W., 243, 261
Morton, A.L., 259
Morton, M.J., 45
Mosley, O., 224, 227, 231
Mosse, G., 58, 217
Mouffe, C., 164, 188
Mumford, L., 220
Munck, R., 169
Murray, C., 263

Nadkarni, M.V., 123, 127, 128, 129, 130, 132, 135, 136, 139
Namboodiripad, E.M.S., 125
Nash, G.T., 50, 125, 225
National Labour Institute Report, 127
Neira, H., 88, 89, 90, 91, 92
Neocleous, M., 221
Netting, R.McC., 187
Newman, B.A., 44
Newman, K., 302, 310
Nisbet, R., 173
Nolte, E., 40
Normano, J.F., 47, 48
Norris, C., 170, 212
Nove, A., 43
Nowell-Smith, G., 297, 298, 305
Nozick, R., 125
Nugent, D., 181
Nuñez, L., 216

O'Brien, C.C., 170
O'Hanlon, R., 157, 183
O'Sullivan, N., 40, 176, 221, 225
Omvedt, G., 41, 124, 125, 130, 131, 132, 133, 134, 135, 136, 137, 171, 205
Ong, A., 169
Ore, T., 88, 90, 91, 92, 95
Ortega y Gasset, J., 215, 228, 229, 230
Orwell, G., 257, 300
Ostwalt, C.E., 261
Ott, H., 39, 212

Palmer, B.D., 170
Pandey, G., 138
Pandian, M.S.S., 305, 310
Paredes, S., 96
Parkinson, D., 259
Parpart, J.L., 169
Passmore, J., 260, 265
Patankar, B., 124
Pathy, J., 126, 184

Pathy, S., 126
Patnaik, U., 44, 48, 123
Pavier, B., 123
Pavloff, V.N., 39
Peary, D., 303
Pefanis, J., 218
Petley, J., 300
Petras, J., 152, 176, 178, 213
Petrovitch, M.B., 48
Pettersson, R., 180
Phillips, K.P., 45, 221, 223
Piccone, P., 221, 222, 224, 228
Pieterse, J.N., 171, 176, 266
Pirie, D., 302, 307, 309
Pirie, M., 125
Pois, R.A., 58
Poole, M., 296
Popkin, S.L., 182
Porter, R., 40
Porter, V., 298, 309
Portes, A., 169
Pouchepadass, J., 51, 123, 124
Prakash, G., 171, 181, 182, 213, 214
Prasad, P.H., 124, 132
Praz, M., 306
Preston, P., 39
Pudovkin, V.I., 294
Pumaruna, A., 88
Puntambekar, S.V., 135

Quijano, A., 88, 90, 184

Rabinow, P., 214, 223
Rahnema, M., 171
Ranga, N.G., 25, 51, 53
Rao, C.R., 123, 137
Rao, M.S.A., 126
Rawls, J., 238, 254, 255
Ray, A.K., 128, 131, 132
Ray, K., 135
Redclift, M., 163, 182, 183, 184, 186, 187
Redfield, R., 179
Reed, T.V., 223
Reinaga, F., 216
Reinhardt, N., 96, 97
Reissman, F., 230
Renaut, A., 212, 218
Richards, J., 259, 297
Richards, P., 135, 180
Richie, D., 295
Ridge, M., 256
Ridgeway, J., 230

Riesman, D., 49
Rodriguez, J., 213
Rogger, H., 39
Rohdie, S., 259
Rojas, F., 126
Röpke, W., 187, 189–90, 225, 226, 229, 230, 232
Rorty, R., 153, 179, 238, 254, 255
Rose, M.A., 220
Roseberry, W., 223
Rotha, P., 297
Rothbard, M.N., 125, 224
Rothwell, L.H.J., 124
Rowbotham, S., 176
Roy, K.C., 132
Rudolph, L.I., 127, 128, 132, 135, 305
Rudolph, S.H., 127, 128, 132, 135
Ryan, A., 221

Sacchi, F., 221, 222, 223, 224, 225, 231
Safa, H.I., 169
Sahlins, M., 135, 171, 180, 184
Said, E.W., 170, 266
Salutos, T., 188
Salvadori, M., 136
Sánchez, R., 43, 94
Sanderson, S.E., 169
Sandford, J., 303, 310
Sargent, L.T., 229, 263
Sarkar, S., 227
Sarkar, T., 136, 137, 138, 221
Sarup, M., 182, 184
Sassen, S., 169
Sathyamurthy, T.V., 171
Sawers, L., 169
Sawyer, R., 175
Schickel, R., 306
Schulman, M.D., 44
Schuurman, F.J., 171
Scott, A.M., 216
Scott, J.C., 6, 82, 144, 147, 154, 155, 156, 158, 159, 162, 163, 164, 165, 166, 171, 172, 175, 180, 181, 182, 183, 184, 185, 186, 187, 188, 216, 217, 225
Scruton, R., 198, 231
Selbourne, D., 170
Sen, A., 183, 185
Sen, I., 135, 138
Sen, S., 51, 123
Sengupta, N., 183
Shackleton, J.R., 221
Shah, G., 136

Shanin, T., 43, 44, 81, 171, 180
Sharma, S.C., 128, 131, 132
Sheehan, T., 221
Sheridan, D., 259
Sherman, A.L., 216
Shils, E., 173
Shiva, V., 129, 130, 134, 135, 171, 205, 230, 265
Silva, P., 169
Singelmann, P., 90
Singh, C., 128, 132
Singh, K.S., 184
Sinha, I., 136
Sinha, S., 172
Sivanandan, A., 170
Skar, H.O., 94
Sklair, L., 169
Slater, D., 164, 171, 183, 184, 185, 187, 188
Sluga, H., 212
Smith, R.E.F., 257
Snowden, F.M., 58
Sohn-Rethel, A., 39
Sorel, G., 217
Soucy, R., 228
Southall, R., 169
Spretnak, C., 171, 172, 230
Stack, O., 297, 298
Stanfield, P., 297
Stavenhagen, R., 179
Stepan, A., 92
Stern, S.J., 223
Stichter, S., 169
Stoker, B., 306, 307, 308, 309
Stradling, R., 46
Sundarayya, P., 123
Sunic, T., 221, 224

Tabb, W.K., 169
Taguieff, P.-A., 202, 221, 222, 223, 224, 225, 231
Tannenbaum, F., 310
Tannenbaum, N., 180
Tarchi, M., 198, 221
Tarde, G., 244
Taussig, M., 97
Tawney, R.H., 266
Taylor, C., 220
Taylor, L., 92, 97
Teich, M., 40
Thébaud, J.-L., 231
Thompson, E.P., 147, 171, 227
Thompson, P.B., 178

Thomson, D., 300
Tidmarsh, K., 52, 125
Timms, E., 46
Tisdell, C.A., 132
Tönnies, F., 46, 47
Torre, G., 187
Totten, G.O., 57
Tribe, K., 136
Trotsky, L., 9, 42, 43, 49, 61, 65, 88, 93, 94, 95, 98, 143, 170, 189
Tudor, A., 309
Tupayachi, I., 89
Turner, A., 296
Twelve Southerners, 50

Ulmen, G., 221
Umphlett, W.L., 303
Utechin, S.V., 43, 47

van Onselen, C., 216
Vanaik, A., 212, 227
Vanech, W.D., 170
Vann Woodward, C., 50, 256, 262, 263
Varadachari, N.S., 135
Varshney, A., 111–12, 131
Vaughan, M., 221
Venturi, F., 43
Vernet, M., 300
Vidal, G., 271
Vidyarthi, L.P., 126
Vieux, S., 213
Villanueva, V., 88, 89, 91, 92
Vinogradoff, E.D., 43
Viski, K., 58
Volosinov, V.N., 157, 183
Voltaire, 1

von Werlhof, C., 135, 173
Wakukawa, S., 57
Walicki, A., 43, 46, 47, 48, 218
Ward, I., 221
Warren, K.B., 97
Warriner, D., 58
Wasson, R., 307
Waterman, P., 126
Watts, M., 169
Weber, E., 9, 39, 58, 59, 60, 61
Wegierski, M., 222, 223, 224, 225, 228, 230, 231
Weiner, M., 127
Wells, H.G., 244, 259, 261
Wharton, C.R., 177, 180
Wiener, M.J., 46
Wignaraja, P., 171
Wilde, L., 217
Wiles, P., 39
Willan, B., 175
Williams, R., 46
Wolf, E.R., 6, 82, 144, 154, 156, 159, 162, 163, 165, 166, 179, 180, 181, 183, 184, 186, 187
Wollen, P., 297
Wollenberg, H.H., 300
Wood, C., 123
Woodhouse, J., 47
World Bank, 134
Wortman, R., 47
Wyver, J., 296

Yadav, Y., 124, 136
Yonghong, S., 169

Zamosc, L., 81–2, 96, 97, 185, 186, 187
Zamyatin, Y., 257, 265

Subject Index

Film titles are followed by the year in which the film appeared.

A Canterbury Tale (1944) 293
A Matter of Life and Death (1946) 293
academy, the 5, 147, 151, 152–3, 166, 176,
178, 188, 222, 230, 312, 320
Accattone (1961) 298
agency
individual 102–3, 151, 154, 155, 167, 196,
239, 241, 274–5, 295, 306 (*see also*
resistance)
land invasions 4, 70, 81
mass 38, 70, 102–3, 154, 155, 167, 194–5,
215, 216, 247, 274–5, 295, 306, 313 (*see
also* revolution)
agrarian myth, variants of
aristocratic/landlord 7, 8, 23, 25, 197, 239,
255, 271, 280, 281–7, 291–2, 303–4,
309, 314
frontier spirit 3, 10, 49
golden age 3, 4, 7, 22, 27, 28, 38, 50, 135,
149, 155, 173, 203, 205, 230, 245, 250,
255, 285, 293, 305
heimat 3, 205, 276, 298–9, 312
Inca communism 4, 27–29, 34, 38, 44,
55–6, 84, 97, 214, 312
indigenismo 3, 10, 29, 54, 55, 216–7
Merrie England 3, 22, 38, 178, 196, 209,
261, 272, 293, 312
narodnichestvo 3, 10, 22–3, 49, 209, 312
nohonshugi 3, 10, 22, 25, 30–1, 34, 57, 196,
205, 209, 312
pastoral 7, 8, 25, 46, 149, 205, 208, 231,
240, 243, 244, 250, 254, 260, 267, 269,
271, 272, 275–9, 281–5, 291–2, 303–4,
309, 314 (*see also* utopia)
plebeian/peasant 7, 8, 239, 255, 271, 272,
275–81, 291–2, 309, 314
social darwinian 7, 8, 23, 47, 149, 177, 178,
208, 217, 218, 232, 243, 256, 260, 272,
280–1, 285–91, 292, 304, 309, 314
strapaese 3, 205, 276, 283, 304, 312
volksgemeinschaft 3, 25, 32, 57, 196, 205,
209, 277
agrarian question 1, 2, 17, 28, 36, 54, 96, 131,
316, 322 (*see also* class formation;
Lenin; Marxism)
agrarian reform 33, 38, 71–2, 78, 81, 82, 86,
92, 112, 125, 132, 154, 294, 314
Aguirre, Wrath of God (1972) 276, 281
Algeria 154
Alianza Popular Revolucionaria Americana
(APRA) 27–9, 54, 66, 68, 69, 70, 90, 94
(*see also* Haya de la Torre, Víctor Raúl)
alienation 1, 6, 13–14, 30, 36, 41, 57, 144,
187, 191, 192–4, 209, 211, 215, 225,
313, 321, 322
All India Anna Dravida Munnetra Kazhagam
(AIADMK) 284
All India Kisan Sabha 51, 52, 127, 136
allegados (*see* sub-tenants)
Amazonia 281
American Communist Party 49
American road 42 (*see also* agrarian question)
Amish 279
anarchism 52, 57, 124, 224
Ancient Rome 266, 296
Andhra Pradesh 100, 101, 102, 125, 127, 305
anti-Americanism 198, 199, 200, 206, 211,
224, 231, 277
anti-industrialism 2, 10, 23, 24, 25, 30, 33, 50,
59, 114, 119, 121, 125, 132, 133, 134,
137, 147, 172, 198, 201–2, 203, 206,
219, 220, 223, 224–5, 230, 241, 253,
257, 261, 266, 312
anti-intellectualism 24, 45, 170, 196, 241, 246,
255, 267
anti-semitism 2, 32, 33, 38, 58, 60, 228, 242,
246, 253, 260, 262, 263
anti-urbanism 2, 7, 9, 10, 20, 21, 22–3, 24, 26,
30, 32, 33, 35, 39, 46, 57, 59, 84, 85, 86,
99, 111, 114, 120, 121, 130, 137, 195,
198, 203, 220, 224, 226, 241, 253, 257,
261, 269–70, 312, 314
apartheid 150, 175, 189–90, 227
Arachnophobia (1990) 8, 275, 281
Argentina 49
arrendire (*see* tenants)

Asphalt Jungle, The (1950) 278
Assam 126, 135, 136, 138
Australia 49, 175, 178
Austria 221
ayllu (*see* kinship)
ayni (*see* exchange labour)

banditry 301
Bataille, George 217, 218
Batman 279, 291, 311
Batman (1989) 291
Batman Returns (1992) 291
Bezhin Meadow (1937) 294
Bharat versus India 111, 121, 130–1 (*see also* Joshi, Sharad; urban bias)
Bharatiya Janata Party (BJP) 4, 41, 54, 99, 117–20, 121, 122, 130, 136, 137, 139, 150, 227, 315
Bihar 26, 51, 101, 104, 124, 127, 169, 175
Birth of a Nation (1915) 282, 285
Black Narcissus (1947) 262
Blair, Tony 209, 232
Blanchot, Maurice 196, 212
Blanco, Hugo 3, 4, 39, 56, 66, 67, 70ff., 74ff., 77ff., 80, 81, 82, 84, 85, 86–7, 88–9, 90, 92, 93, 95, 96, 113, 114, 116, 181, 186
blood 35, 58, 208, 212, 218, 263, 308, 309
Bolivia 54, 216–7
Bolshevism 34, 36, 42, 49, 54, 213, 248, 253, 264, 265, 294
Bolshevism on Trial (1919) 306
Braveheart (1995) 310
Brazil 174–5
British Union of Fascists 224, 227
Bukharin, Nicolai 95
Bulgaria 33, 34, 38, 58, 59
Bulgarian Agrarian Union 33, 34, 59, 60
bureaucracy 9, 24, 30, 58, 85, 119, 121, 156, 185, 268, 278, 294
Byron, Lord 306

Cambridge University 223
Canada 49, 221
capital
   finance 2, 3, 7, 10, 24, 25, 30, 32, 33, 37, 38, 41, 49, 50, 53, 57, 126, 191, 209, 239, 240, 241, 242, 245, 246, 247, 248, 250, 251, 253, 255, 257, 260, 262–3, 264, 267, 277, 304, 312, 313 (*see also* moneylenders)

   foreign 3, 20, 21, 22, 23, 28, 29, 37, 49–50, 99, 120, 121, 126, 137, 148, 149, 191
   monopoly 24, 80, 103, 116, 300 (*see also* capital, foreign)
   relocation 145, 165
capitalism 1, 16, 19, 21, 36, 28, 40, 42, 72, 75, 79, 81, 82, 88, 119, 120, 133, 143, 145–6, 148, 150, 163–4, 165, 168, 172, 187, 203, 212, 215, 216, 218, 219, 224, 237, 248, 263–4, 269, 290, 291, 296–7, 301, 315, 316
Carpathia 287, 309
caste 26, 51, 101, 104, 111, 112, 119, 121, 124, 127, 132, 137, 159, 168, 179, 284–5
Castro Pozo, Hildebrando, 27
Chayanov, A.V. 6, 7, 17, 18, 19, 23, 43, 44, 54, 81, 111, 130, 134, 135, 144, 153–55, 158, 163, 165, 166, 180, 182, 184, 185, 187, 190, 226, 238, 239–40, 242, 245, 250, 251, 252, 253, 256, 257, 264, 265, 266, 268, 316–7 (*see also* neo-populism; peasant economy)
Chernyshevskii, N.G. 47
Chesterton, G.K. 22, 220
Chile 169, 185
China 95, 125, 145, 146, 154, 165, 169, 188, 240, 248, 258, 266
Chinatown (1974) 300
Chinese Communist Party 97, 258
Christian Slovak People's Party 33, 61
City Slickers (1991) 8, 275, 279
class
   collaboration 26, 49, 51, 57, 93, 125, 149, 255, 283, 305
   formation 2, 3, 9, 15, 18, 20, 36, 75, 81, 104ff., 144, 149, 156, 159, 160, 163, 166, 188, 209, 210, 213, 239, 247, 248 251–3, 254, 312, 317 (*see also* labourers, agricultural; rich, middle and poor peasants)
   struggle 2, 3, 4, 9, 13, 15–17, 30–1, 36, 42, 46, 50, 52, 57, 69ff., 76, 77, 78, 81, 86, 89, 94, 100ff., 102ff., 106ff., 111, 116, 118, 119, 120, 121, 124, 128, 144, 149, 151, 156, 157, 159, 166, 167, 170, 172, 180, 182, 186, 188, 194, 199, 207, 210, 213, 215, 226, 244, 247, 255, 284, 285, 286ff., 308, 309, 312, 316, 317
co-operatives 82
coca 83, 85, 86, 97, 187, 314
coffee 3, 67ff., 82, 85, 86, 89, 91, 97, 314

collectivization 2, 9, 17, 27, 34, 55, 71, 154, 165, 166, 188, 226, 294
Colombia 3, 39, 54, 66, 80–2, 85, 86, 96, 97, 112, 167, 168, 188, 314, 315
colonialism 3, 4, 14, 26, 28, 29, 36, 38, 51, 52, 53, 99, 100, 104, 114, 115, 120, 122, 125, 129, 135, 151, 153, 156, 157, 164, 178, 182, 184, 185, 187, 190, 192, 193, 194, 195, 201, 204, 209, 211, 213, 214, 215, 216, 249, 250, 296, 314, 317 (*see also* post-colonialism)
communalism 4, 98, 101, 102, 112, 117, 118, 119, 120, 121, 122, 124, 136, 137, 138, 139, 168 (*see also* consciousness, false)
Communist Party of India
    CPI 54, 102, 103, 104, 116, 121, 124, 125, 126, 136, 137, 168, 315
    CPI (M) 103, 121, 125, 168, 315
    CPI (ML) 103, 106–7, 121, 126–7, 168, 315
    (*see also* Maoism)
communitarianism 238–9, 253, 254
community, rural or village 2, 4, 7, 11, 15, 17, 23, 27, 28, 29, 30, 34, 36, 48, 53, 54, 55, 60, 74, 84, 86, 93, 94, 99, 106, 114, 121, 133, 137, 150, 206, 207, 220, 230, 237, 238ff., 253–4, 255, 257, 261, 274, 277, 293, 294, 312
compadrazgo (*see* kinship)
Congress Party 27, 51, 52, 103, 108, 110, 116, 124, 127, 136
Congress Socialist Party 51
consciousness
    class 2, 19, 20, 30, 37, 60, 65, 80, 103, 106, 122–3, 160, 161, 167, 168, 186, 202, 247, 264, 273
    false 5, 19, 20, 30–1, 37, 60, 85, 101, 102, 121, 122–3, 124, 161, 167, 168, 183–4, 208, 284–5, 290
conservatism 11–12, 13–14, 19, 20, 40, 43, 45, 46, 50, 85, 120, 132, 144, 149, 151, 152, 156, 162, 166, 173, 174–5, 176, 190, 191, 196, 210, 225, 226, 229, 230, 241, 242, 260, 265, 271, 292, 293, 300, 306, 312, 320
consumerism 137, 146, 147, 195, 200, 215, 225, 276, 305
Count Orlock (*see Nosferatu*; vampire legend)
Countryside Alliance 207–9, 210, 316
crisis, capitalist 2, 3, 7, 10, 20, 22, 24, 25, 32, 37, 38, 46, 123, 136, 138, 145, 146, 168,

169, 175, 215, 230, 241, 243, 246, 249, 252, 253, 255, 258, 259, 313, 314
Cristero movement 56
Croatia 34, 35, 59, 61
Croatian Peasant Party 33, 59, 61
Crosby, Bing 237
Cuba 91, 154
culture, popular 1, 2, 10, 46, 50, 12ff., 22, 31, 92, 123, 148, 149, 156, 157, 167, 172, 174, 183, 192, 193, 194, 197, 202, 210, 237ff., 254ff., 271ff., 292ff., 313, 317
    conservatism and 14, 19, 25, 35, 37, 124, 199–200, 201ff., 204, 206, 208, 213, 218, 226, 229, 230, 313, 321
    landlordism and 25, 286ff.
    nationalism and 12–14, 19, 25, 28, 30, 31ff., 35, 37, 102, 123, 124, 149, 168, 200, 204, 205, 207, 209, 212, 313
    populism and 3, 19, 21, 25, 35, 37, 38, 123, 148, 153, 199–200, 207, 208, 313, 317
Czechoslovakia 33, 34, 35, 58, 60, 61

Dange, S.A. 102
Darré, Richard Walther 32, 58
de Benoist, Alain 198, 200, 201, 202, 205, 221, 228, 231
de Man, Paul 196, 212
de-essentialization (*see* alienation; essentialism)
death 91, 101, 119, 120, 124, 173, 193, 201, 214, 218, 230, 237, 239, 240, 244, 247, 256–7, 267, 287, 289, 295, 302, 304, 308, 309, 311 (*see also* eternal present; golden age; time/timelessness)
debt bondage 76, 87, 95, 125, 175 (*see also* labour, unfree)
deculturation 2, 41, 56, 119, 138, 150, 191, 203, 225, 229, 231, 312, 313 (*see also* alienation; nationalism)
Deliverance (1972) 303
democracy, bourgeois 24, 28, 38, 41, 45, 72–3, 81, 99, 111, 115, 116, 127, 131, 137, 146, 153, 157, 161, 163, 164, 167, 174, 176, 179, 187–8, 199, 221, 260, 307, 318
demography 15, 18, 82, 177, 316 (*see also* Chayanov, A.V.; neo-populism)
depeasantization 1, 2, 10, 14, 17, 18, 24, 34, 36, 41, 48, 110, 116, 143, 145, 154, 162, 165–6, 209, 216, 230, 247, 249, 256, 257, 264, 312, 313, 316

Derrida, Jacques 218
Deva, A.N. 25, 26, 29, 51, 52, 192
development
   economic 5, 36, 114, 145–6, 156, 171, 172,
      180, 193, 199, 201, 203, 205, 206, 211,
      213, 225, 226, 230, 231–2, 254, 312
   studies 5, 152–3, 154, 174, 176, 177, 181,
      184, 223, 317 (*see also* post-
      development)
Devi (1959) 303
Diana, Princess 207, 208, 233, 316
difference 1, 6, 37, 115, 148, 150, 160, 171,
      174, 190, 191, 198, 200, 201ff., 206, 210,
      228, 312, 319, 321 (*see also*
      postmodernism)
differentiation, peasant 15, 17, 24, 36, 42, 43,
      53, 72, 74, 81, 86, 88, 96–7, 99, 103,
      104, 107, 113, 116, 126, 130, 154,
      250–1, 316–7 (*see also* depeasantization;
      labourers, agricultural; rich, middle and
      poor peasants)
directors, film
   Beatty, Warren 296
   Bertolucci, Bernardo 283, 284, 305
   Blasetti, Alessandro 283, 304
   Boorman, John 303
   Brook, Peter 302
   Buñuel, Luis 302
   Burton, Tim 291
   Capra, Frank 7, 237, 240–1, 242, 245, 248,
      249, 250, 252, 253, 258, 259–260, 305
   Coppola, Francis Ford 278, 301
   Dovzhenko, Alexander 294
   Eisenstein, Sergei 294, 310
   Ermler, Friedrich 294
   Fassbinder, Rainer Werner 276, 298
   Feyder, Jacques 264
   Fleming, Victor 282
   Gibson, Mel 310
   Griffiths, D.W. 285, 305–6
   Guest, Val 303
   Hardy, Robin 289
   Herzog, Werner 276, 281, 288, 303, 310
   Hill, Walter 303
   Hitchcock, Alfred 261, 302
   Huston, John 278
   Korda, Alexander 259, 261
   Kubrick, Stanley 296
   Lang, Fritz 244
   Lean, David 296
   Loach, Ken 294

Murnau, F.W. 286, 288–9, 306, 308, 309
Pasolini, Pier Paolo 275–6, 283, 297, 305
Polanski, Roman 300
Powell, Michael 262, 292–3
Pressburger, Emeric 262, 292–3
Pudovkin, V.I. 294
Ray, Satyajit 282, 303
Reitz, Edgar 276–7, 298
Riefenstahl, Leni 299
Russell, Ken 310
Schaffner, Franklin 310
Spielberg, Steven 281
Stevens, George 304
Truffaut, François 303
Underwood, Ron 279
Visconti, Luchino 283, 284, 305
Weir, Peter 279
Welles, Orson 259
disempowerment 159, 163–4, 191, 210–11,
      217, 319–20, 322 (*see also* empower-
      ment)
distributism 22, 46, 50
Donnelly, Ignatius 7, 238, 245, 249, 250, 251,
      252, 253, 255, 256
Dostoevsky, F.M. 47
Dracula 279, 280, 288ff., 291, 307, 309
droit de seigneur 288, 310
dual power 4, 56, 67, 70–1, 73–4, 75, 76–7,
      79, 84, 86–88, 91, 92, 93, 181–2 (*see
      also* Blanco, Hugo; Trotsky, L.D.)
Dunkel, Arthur 109, 110, 129, 139 (*see also*
      GATT)
dystopia 7, 237, 242ff., 246ff., 253–4, 255ff.,
      291 (*see also* utopia)

Earth (1930) 294
Earth (1939) 295
ecofeminism 4, 39, 41, 114ff., 117, 120, 122,
      123, 134, 136, 149, 170, 172, 190, 210,
      230, 318
ecology 6, 46, 47, 115, 119, 135, 137, 148,
      170, 172, 177, 197, 206, 220, 230–1
Ecuador 54
Egypt 49
Eichberg, Henning 198, 221, 231
empowerment 1, 6, 111, 112, 113, 118, 120,
      122, 131, 134, 138, 144, 148, 149, 150,
      151, 153, 171, 174, 175, 176, 178, 179,
      188, 191, 201, 205, 210, 213, 216, 222,
      225, 226, 230, 273, 319–20 (*see also*
      disempowerment)

endism 45, 169, 173, 176, 215, 245, 261
Engelgardt, A.N. 23
England 22, 46, 73, 146, 178, 206–9, 228–9,
    231, 232–3, 242, 243, 257, 260, 261,
    272, 292–3, 312
Enlightenment 5, 6, 11, 14, 23, 40, 115, 148,
    150, 156, 193–4, 201, 206, 211, 214,
    227, 286
environment 4, 99, 114, 118, 121, 132, 133,
    134, 147, 198, 199, 206, 207, 231, 281
essentialism 1, 4, 6, 11–12, 20, 21, 23, 30, 34,
    38, 57, 77, 79–80, 82, 84, 86, 87, 96,
    134, 135, 144, 147, 153, 163, 166, 175,
    187, 190, 195, 196, 198, 209, 210,
    213–4, 314, 317, 322 (see also depeasan-
    tization; peasant economy; Nature)
estate, rural 67, 70, 72, 74, 76, 86, 93, 164
estrangement, urbanization as 278, 279, 280–1
    (see also alienation)
eternal present 74, 201, 205, 225, 245, 272
ethnicity 2, 7, 11, 25, 28, 30, 31, 33, 34, 35,
    53, 54, 58, 59, 83, 97, 104, 106, 111,
    112, 115, 120, 122, 126, 138, 143, 145,
    147, 150, 153, 156, 157, 167, 168, 183,
    193, 202, 217, 228, 248, 251, 253–4,
    262, 268, 291, 304, 318, 319
Evola, Julius 198, 201, 205, 221, 223, 225, 231
exchange labour 43, 76, 93–4
Expressionism, German 286, 307
Exterminating Angel (1962) 302

family, the 2, 11, 14, 24, 30, 57, 58, 130, 150,
    154, 208, 249, 279, 288, 291
Fanon, Franz 6, 29, 39, 57, 144, 186, 190,
    191, 192, 193, 194, 195–6, 201, 204, 209,
    211–12, 214, 218, 223, 297, 317, 318
farm, peasant family (see peasant economy;
    neo-populism)
farmers' movements, new 4, 39, 41, 45, 52,
    88, 99, 107ff., 111ff., 117ff., 121–3, 127,
    128, 129, 130ff., 148, 149, 167, 170, 208,
    268, 315, 321
    Bharatiya Kisan Sangh (BKS) 107, 136
    Bharatiya Kisan Union (BKU) 107, 110,
        114, 127
    Karnataka State Farmers' Association
        (KRRS) 108, 110, 114, 130, 136
    Shetkari Sanghatana 41, 110, 113, 127,
        131, 133, 135, 136
    Tamil Nadu Agriculturalists' Association
        (TVS) 107–8

fascism 1, 3, 10, 20, 30–35, 38, 39, 40, 47,
    58–61, 121, 149, 151, 152, 153, 175,
    189, 191, 196, 202, 205, 212, 217, 218,
    220, 222, 227, 228, 231, 233, 263, 275,
    277, 283, 284, 286, 304, 307, 317 (see
    also right, new; post-fascism)
Fata Morgana (1970) 303
feudalism 16, 18, 27, 28, 29, 52, 54, 55, 67,
    72, 76, 84, 98, 103, 116, 158, 161, 173,
    218, 224, 288 (see also semi-feudalism)
fiesta system 93, 94
film
    audience 259, 295, 297, 299, 300, 308, 310
    capitalism and 294
    class struggle and 273–4, 275, 282, 288,
        296, 309
    politics and 25, 294, 295, 296
    populism and 25, 272–4, 293
Fitzcarraldo (1982) 276, 281
Foreign Correspondent (1940) 261
Foucault, Michel 39, 144, 156, 157, 183, 191,
    192, 193–4, 195, 196, 204–5, 206, 212,
    214, 215, 217, 223, 229–30, 297
France 40, 73, 212, 218, 221, 225, 228, 300
Freund, Julien 198, 221
Friedman, Milton 164, 198, 221

Gandhi, M.K. 25, 26, 38, 45–6, 51, 102, 111,
    113–14, 115, 119, 124, 125, 127, 130,
    132–3, 135, 137, 171, 179, 192, 219, 314
GATT 109, 110, 121, 122, 124, 129, 130, 139
gemeinschaft 22, 46–7
gender 4, 11, 58, 99, 111, 113, 114, 119, 120,
    121–22, 123, 131–2, 134, 135, 136, 138,
    145, 147, 156, 157, 159, 167, 169, 173,
    175, 183, 198, 205, 222, 230, 246, 266,
    278, 279, 285, 288–9, 299, 300, 304,
    308, 309, 310, 311, 318
genres, film
    arbeiterfilm 276, 298
    Ealing 271, 272, 293–4
    film noir 7, 275, 278, 291, 300
    gangster 275, 278–9, 301
    horror 7, 275, 280, 286ff., 289ff., 302–3,
        308, 310
    mountain 244, 261, 299–300
    mythological 118, 305
    red scare 278, 280
    science fiction 7, 242, 244, 275, 280
    westerns 275, 279, 297, 301–2
Germany 3, 10, 23, 31–2, 33, 35, 38, 39, 41,

46, 57, 58, 73, 175, 220, 221, 244, 252, 261, 276, 286ff., 298, 299–300, 309, 312
gesellschaft 22, 46–7
Giant (1956) 304
Gondo Seikyo 30, 57 (*see also nohonshugi*)
Gone With The Wind (1939) 8, 25, 50, 282–3, 285, 303, 304
goodness, primitive 14, 37, 41, 48, 184, 197, 204, 205, 230, 245, 249, 250, 303 (*see also* Rousseau, J.J.)
Gramsci, Antonio 156, 157, 183, 199, 224, 298
green revolution 106, 108, 115, 128, 139, 169, 177, 180, 315
Greene, Graham 250, 259
Gujarat 26, 51, 117, 136

hacienda (*see* estate, rural)
Haryana 128
Haya de la Torre, Víctor Raúl 27–9, 38, 44, 54, 55, 56, 75, 94, 192
Hayek, Friedrich 198, 212, 221
hegemony 162, 164, 182, 187, 188, 200 (*see also* Gramsci, Antonio)
Heidegger, Martin 39, 196–8, 212, 220
Heimat (1984) 275, 276
Herder, J.G. 12
Herzen, A.I. 47, 48
high/low 244–5, 249, 250, 253, 261, 301
Hilton, James 7, 238, 240–1, 242, 245, 250, 252, 253, 257, 258, 261
Hindus 99, 101–2, 104, 106, 114, 119, 120, 124, 126, 136, 137, 139
history-from-below 151, 175, 178, 192, 227, 277
Hitler, Adolf 58, 286, 299
Hollywood 261, 295
Hollywood Ten 260
Holocaust 299
Hong Kong 145
Hope, Bob 237, 254
Hungarian National Socialist Workers' Party 33, 34, 58
Hungary 32, 33, 38, 45, 58, 59, 60, 165

I Know Where I'm Going (1945) 293
impasse 148, 154, 170, 171, 173–4, 181, 188, 222, 318
Imperialism 6, 21, 27, 52, 54, 84, 85, 98, 103, 125, 137, 190, 192, 317 (*see also* colonialism)

Independent Smallholders' Party 32
India 1, 2, 3, 4, 10, 21, 25–7, 38, 47, 49, 51–2, 54, 88, 98ff., 123ff., 146, 147, 149, 154, 160, 164, 167, 168, 169, 170, 171, 180, 181, 186, 192, 208, 212, 219, 227, 282, 288, 296, 301, 303, 310, 315, 321
indigo 26
industrialization 9, 10, 12, 15, 17, 36, 46, 111, 114, 119, 132, 145, 201, 219, 240, 252, 253, 292, 298, 316
informal sector 170, 216
instinctivism 7, 191, 195–6, 207, 217, 231, 233 (*see also* Sorel, Georges)
international division of labour, new 145, 169
Invasion of the Body Snatchers (1956) 280, 302
Iran 229–30
Ireland 180
Iron Guard 33, 58, 61
It's a Wonderful Life (1946) 241, 260
Italian Communist Party (PCI) 213, 276
Italy 3, 10, 31, 35, 37, 38, 39, 40, 58, 220, 222, 223, 225, 227, 276, 283, 298, 304–5, 312, 314

Japan 3, 10, 30–1, 34, 35, 38, 39, 57, 109, 146, 295, 312, 314
Java 180
Jaws (1975) 302
Jews 32, 33, 38, 59, 60, 230, 299
Joshi, Sharad 39, 41, 52, 96, 109, 110, 111, 113, 114, 115, 119, 127, 128, 129, 130, 131, 132, 133, 135, 136, 137, 139, 170
Junkers 41 (*see also* landlords)

Karnataka 109, 117, 127, 128, 130, 136, 139
Kautsky, K. 17, 136
Kerala 104, 125
Khrushchev, Nikita 90
kinship 28, 29, 43, 75, 76, 93, 94–5, 105, 107, 150, 159, 162, 228, 274, 291
Knight Without Armour (1937) 264
Kondrat'ev, N.D. 23, 48
Korea 145
Krishak Lok Dal (peasants' party) 27
Kritsman, L.N. 42
Ku Klux Klan 41, 229, 285
kulaks (*see* rich peasants)

L'Enfant Sauvage (1970) 303
La Convención province 3, 56, 66, 67ff., 71ff.,

74ff., 77ff., 80, 81, 84, 85, 86, 88–95, 314
La Follette, Robert M. 49
La Sufriere (1976) 303
labour
  cooperative 28–9, 43, 94
  reserve army 5, 143, 145, 165, 169, 317, 318
  unfree 25, 50, 52, 55, 76, 125, 151, 161, 175, 178, 186, 229, 232
labour-rent 4, 67, 70, 72, 76, 78, 87, 89, 94, 95
labourers, agricultural 4, 15–16, 21, 30, 31, 36, 41, 52, 58, 60, 66, 69, 71, 76, 77, 79, 91, 94, 99, 100, 101, 103, 104, 105, 106, 107, 109, 112, 116, 120, 122, 125, 126, 128, 129, 131, 139, 148, 160, 164, 167, 168, 182, 207, 232, 247, 284–5, 310, 313
  (*see also* proletariat)
Land and Freedom (1995) 294
landlords 2, 3, 4, 8, 12, 16, 20, 23, 26, 27, 28, 29, 31, 37, 38, 41, 42, 47, 51–2, 54, 55, 56, 57, 58, 59, 66, 67, 68, 69, 70, 72, 73, 76, 77, 78, 80, 84, 86–88, 92, 94, 95, 100, 101, 103, 106, 108, 112, 116, 119, 122, 123, 124, 125, 159, 161, 163, 164, 181, 186, 187, 207, 208, 232, 242, 259–60, 272, 273, 274, 275, 281ff., 286ff., 291–2, 301, 306, 307, 308, 310, 313, 314, 316, 319
  good/bad 69, 71, 284–5, 291, 304, 306
  weak/powerful 282ff., 284ff., 288ff., 291, 303–4, 306, 307
landscape 7, 22, 46, 261, 272, 277, 288, 293, 298, 299, 300, 301, 302, 306, 307
Lawrence of Arabia (1962) 296
League of the Archangel Michael 33, 34
Lenin, V.I. 15, 17–18, 36, 42, 54, 75, 131, 154, 155, 156, 165, 166, 316
light/dark 7, 250, 261–2, 287, 290, 301, 308, 309
limited good 135, 179
Lipton, Michael 111, 113
Little Buddha (1993) 305
Lohia, Rammanohar 25, 29, 51, 192
London 207
Lord of the Flies (1963) 302
Lost Horizon (1937) 7, 238, 240–1, 242, 245, 246, 248, 249, 250, 252, 253, 254, 255, 257, 258, 259, 261, 262, 264, 267, 269, 309
Lost Horizon (1973) 257–8

lumpenproletariat 31, 61, 185, 186, 193, 195, 196, 212, 215, 216, 276, 297–8
Luxemburg, R. 17, 145, 146, 168

mafia (*see* banditry)
Maharashtra 109, 113, 117, 136
Major, John 271
Malaysia 53, 145
Mama Roma (1962) 298
Man-Slashing, Horse-Piercing Sword (1930) 295
Maoism 3, 4, 66, 67, 80, 83–5, 86, 93, 96, 97, 113, 121, 127, 186, 315
Marcuse, Herbert 6, 29, 39, 57, 144, 190, 191, 192, 193, 194, 195–6, 200, 204, 209, 212, 213, 214, 215, 218, 223, 297, 305, 317, 318
Mariátegui, José Carlos, 4, 27–9, 38, 44, 54, 55, 56, 75, 192, 214
Marxism 5, 10, 13, 14, 15–17, 19–20, 27, 34, 36, 41, 43, 45, 53, 55, 75, 80, 86, 103, 116, 131, 136, 147, 148, 149, 154, 156, 158, 159, 160, 161, 162, 166, 173, 174, 191, 194, 210, 214, 237, 243, 247, 255, 260, 283, 297, 316, 319
masculinity 134, 138, 149, 230, 279
massification 2, 9, 203, 229
McLuhan, Marshall 196–8, 212, 219–20
metanarratives, Eurocentric 5, 6, 148, 149, 152, 156, 159, 166, 182, 186, 188, 193, 197, 201, 211, 212, 318
Metropolis (1926) 244
Mexico 29, 56, 91, 128, 154, 179
mezzadria (*see* tenants)
middle peasant 15, 17, 33, 34, 36, 59, 69, 71, 76, 81, 83, 84, 88, 91, 94, 97, 105, 111, 116, 119, 125, 127, 132, 136, 154, 158, 159, 161, 162, 165, 167, 183, 313, 316
  thesis 6, 44, 82, 97, 154, 155, 156, 166, 183, 186
Miglio, Gianfranco 198, 221, 227
Mikhailovskii, N.K. 48
mink'a (*see* labour, cooperative)
Mises, Ludwig von 55, 212
mob-in-the-streets 12, 32, 51, 121, 135, 226, 238, 244, 247, 248, 256, 262, 263, 264, 285, 306, 312 (*see also* proletariat)
modern/anti-modern, discourse 11, 20, 22, 23, 32, 40, 45, 53, 115, 120, 143–4, 150, 171, 180, 184, 195, 197, 201, 206, 211,

217, 224, 230, 233, 247, 248, 252, 256, 261, 289
moneylending 59, 116, 126, 175, 246, 264, 284
Monihara (1961) 303
moral economy 6, 82, 83, 97, 144, 147, 149, 155, 156, 166, 182, 185, 186, 187
Moscow 240, 248, 251, 252, 257, 266–7
Mr Deeds Goes to Town (1936) 241
Mr Smith Goes to Washington (1939) 241
music 22, 294–5
Muslims 101–2, 104, 119, 120, 137, 138
Nanjundaswamy, M.D. 108, 109, 110, 113, 129
National Peasant Association (ANUC) 3, 39, 66, 80–2, 85–6, 96, 112, 167, 168, 315
nationalism 1, 3, 10, 11, 12–14, 20, 21, 22ff., 28, 30, 33, 34, 35–6, 38, 41, 53, 57, 58, 59, 60, 61, 97, 99, 102, 114, 115, 116, 117, 118, 121, 122–3, 124, 125, 129, 130, 136, 137, 138, 143, 144, 146, 147, 148, 149, 150, 152, 153, 168, 179, 190, 191, 193, 196, 202, 211, 215, 227, 228, 238, 239, 242, 252, 256, 265, 275, 276, 283, 284, 295, 296, 312, 318, 319 (*see also* Nature; Slavophiles)
Nature
   active/on-the-attack 7, 8, 147, 149, 173, 272, 280, 281, 286ff., 302
   female as 113, 114, 115, 120, 122, 123, 134, 138, 172, 300, 304, 311
   landlords as 37, 306, 307
   nation and 2, 32, 37, 53, 58, 98, 113, 119, 120, 122, 123, 130, 144, 179, 207, 231, 261, 277, 286, 291–2, 299–300, 308
   passive/under-attack 7, 8, 119, 120, 138, 150, 272, 281, 288
   peasants as 9, 12, 13, 26, 32, 35, 53, 58, 59, 98, 113, 122, 123, 158, 198, 210, 226, 243, 249, 264, 267, 299, 300, 307
Naxalites 4, 39, 96, 104–7, 112, 124, 126, 127, 167, 186, 315 (*see also* Maoism)
Nazis 39, 40, 58, 218, 261, 298–9, 300
Nehru, Jawaharlal 113–14, 132
neo-liberalism 120, 147, 150, 152, 164, 165, 169, 172, 176, 177, 188, 190, 212, 213, 225, 229, 254, 318
neo-populism 4, 10, 14, 17–19, 20, 43, 84, 116, 128, 158, 166, 316
Neo-Romanticism 293
NEP 48

New German Cinema 276, 281, 298
New York 239, 246, 247, 248, 251, 252, 263
NGOs 151, 174, 175
1900 (1976) 8, 282, 284
Nosferatu (1922) 8, 275, 282, 286–9, 290, 295, 306, 307, 308
Nosferatu the Vampyre (1978) 276, 288, 310
nostalgia 7, 20, 144, 197, 212, 218, 261, 292, 293, 295, 306 (*see also* golden age; post-modernism)

Oedipus Rex (1967) 298
Olympia (1936) 299
Orage, A.R. 22
organicism 11, 23, 134, 205, 222
orientalism 7, 51, 205, 210, 223, 227, 230, 238, 241, 245, 249–50, 253–4, 262, 266, 305, 309
otherness, cultural 7, 32, 46, 101, 105, 147, 150, 153, 178, 179, 183, 190, 193, 198, 200, 202, 203, 210, 221, 225, 227, 255, 269
   agrarian myth and 1, 32, 33, 38, 192, 189ff., 211ff., 245, 249, 254, 272
   populism and 1, 32, 33, 38, 112, 147, 150, 171–2, 189ff., 207, 224, 242, 252, 254, 269
Oxford University 269

paganism 47, 206, 222, 230, 231, 276, 290, 298
Pakistan 102, 138, 180
Passage to India (1984) 296
Passport to Pimlico (1949) 294
patriarchy 114–5, 134, 230 (*see also* gender)
peasant economy 2, 9, 11, 15, 17, 22, 27, 35, 43, 44, 48, 81, 82, 86, 94, 115, 133, 135, 143–4, 145–6, 158, 166, 169, 189, 203, 205–6, 225–6, 232, 248, 250, 251, 252, 254, 257, 261, 264, 267–8, 273, 274, 295, 314, 316, 318 (*see also* Chayanov, A.V.; neo-populism; middle peasant thesis)
peasant movements 1, 2, 3, 32, 51, 56, 58, 85, 123, 132, 149, 154, 166, 182, 183, 208, 321 (*see also* farmers' movements, new)
peasant-as-warrior 11, 30, 36, 239, 256, 295 (*see also* nationalism)
Peasants (1935) 294
peasants, discourse about 11–12, 47, 248, 275ff., 278ff., 280–1, 287, 291–2, 294, 297

People's Party 24, 256
permanent revolution 67, 72–3, 93
Peru 3, 10, 27–9, 38, 39, 54, 55, 56, 57, 66, 73ff., 76, 80, 82ff., 88, 91, 92, 93, 96, 112, 167, 168, 185, 187, 208, 281, 288, 310, 312, 314, 315
Peruvian Communist Party (PCP) 66, 68, 69, 70, 71, 90
Peruvian Socialist Party (PSP) 27–9
Phase IV (1974) 302
Piranha (1978) 302
planning 2, 9, 100, 226, 237, 240, 248, 265
plantations 49, 50, 101, 104, 124, 175, 178, 219, 285, 303, 310, 314
Poland 41, 181
poor peasants 4, 15, 16, 21, 29, 30, 33, 34, 37, 52, 58, 66, 69, 70, 71, 76, 78, 79, 81, 87–88, 91, 94, 95, 99, 100, 103, 105, 107, 109, 110, 111, 112, 119, 120, 122, 136, 154, 155, 159, 161, 164, 165, 167, 168, 182, 186, 187, 284, 313, 316
populism
    agrarian myth and 2, 4, 6, 10ff., 39ff., 65ff., 88ff., 98ff., 123ff., 143ff., 168ff., 237ff., 254ff., 271ff., 292ff., 312ff.
    anti-capitalism of 2, 3, 7, 10, 20, 23, 25, 26, 30, 36, 45, 53, 118, 119, 148, 149, 150, 164, 165, 168, 173, 185, 191, 197, 198, 199, 200, 204, 205, 213, 214, 219, 237, 242, 246, 247, 250, 253–4, 255, 269, 278, 289–90, 306, 313, 320, 321
    anti-socialism of 2, 3, 7, 10, 15ff., 20, 21, 23, 25, 30, 34, 36, 38, 44, 45, 50, 53, 58, 60, 98, 107, 117, 119, 146–8, 164, 168, 173–4, 197, 198, 204, 213, 214, 221, 231, 237, 238, 240, 242, 243, 246, 247–8, 250, 252, 253, 261, 264, 313
    as a-political 2, 4, 7, 10, 19, 37, 38, 39, 45, 108, 111, 118–9, 124, 148, 149, 150, 151, 172, 176, 197, 198, 207, 209, 217, 220, 221, 231, 271, 272, 292, 318
    as common sense 153, 199, 221, 222, 231, 241, 259, 302
    as mobilizing ideology 2, 4, 10, 15, 19ff., 33, 34, 37, 44, 56, 66, 75, 86, 88, 99, 108, 111, 112, 113, 123, 144, 151, 196, 206ff., 217, 239, 271, 313, 314
    as third way 2, 10, 189, 225
    new 1, 2, 5, 6, 15, 39, 54, 117, 123, 143ff., 146ff., 148ff., 150ff., 165–68, 171, 172, 190ff., 194ff., 199ff., 204ff., 206ff.,
        209–11, 212ff., 312ff. (*see also* moral economy; ecofeminism; post-colonialism; post-capitalism; post-Marxism; resistance; social movements, new; subaltern studies)
    old 1, 3, 15, 54, 144, 147, 148, 149, 166, 171, 188, 191, 194, 204, 209ff., 237, 272
post-capitalism 39, 190, 191, 210, 213–14
post-colonialism 6, 39, 130, 147, 182, 190, 191, 193, 201, 204, 210, 213, 318
post-development 5, 148, 149, 171, 172, 318
post-fascism 213, 222, 238 (*see also* fascism; right, new)
post-Marxism 5, 39, 148, 149, 174, 176, 190, 210, 213
postmodernism 1, 5, 6, 20, 39, 44, 97, 115, 117, 123, 143, 148, 149, 150, 151, 152, 153ff., 156, 166, 171, 172, 176, 179, 180, 184, 190, 191, 192, 193, 196–8, 201, 204, 210, 212, 213, 217, 218, 219, 220, 227, 293, 317, 318, 319, 320, 321
Poujadism 300
producer/consumer balance 18, 180 (*see also* Chayanov, A.V.; neo-populism)
Progressive Movement 24, 49
proletariat 7, 12, 13, 15, 19, 23, 26, 29, 36, 40, 41, 47–8, 57, 72, 76–7, 94, 110, 116, 121, 161, 172, 185, 191, 194, 195, 210, 211, 215, 219, 226, 239, 240, 242, 244, 245, 246, 247, 248, 252, 253, 255, 257, 263, 264–5, 268, 316 (*see also* labourers, agricultural)
Prussian road 42, 131 (*see also* agrarian question)
Psycho (1960) 302
Puerto Rico 179
Punjab 115, 136, 139

Quatermass II (1956) 280
Que Viva Mexico (1931) 310

racism 120, 149, 175, 202, 213, 224, 228, 238, 246, 247, 263, 285, 296, 304
Rama Rao, N.T. 305
Ramachandran, M.G. 8, 282, 284–5
Ranga, N.G. 25, 26, 29, 51, 52, 53, 192
Rashtriya Swayamsewak Sangh (RSS) 4, 41, 54, 99, 117ff., 121, 122, 136, 137, 138, 227, 315
red-in-tooth-and-claw (*see* agrarian myth, social darwinian)

redemption, spiritual 47, 58, 137, 204, 229, 244, 267, 278, 289

Reds (1981) 296

religion 2, 11, 12, 15, 23, 24, 26, 30, 35, 40, 47, 56, 69, 90, 101, 102, 104, 111, 112, 118, 119, 122, 124, 126, 134, 137, 138, 149, 150, 156, 174, 196, 201, 202, 206, 213, 214, 219, 222, 230, 242, 244, 245, 251, 254, 255, 261, 262, 268, 289, 298, 309–10, 318

remunerative prices 108–9, 116, 118, 127–8, 130, 136, 146

resistance (everyday forms of) 1, 5, 15, 17, 29, 39, 44, 65, 117, 122, 144, 147, 148, 149, 150, 151, 154, 155, 156, 158, 162, 163, 164, 165, 166, 167, 171, 175, 181, 183, 185, 188, 190, 191, 196, 205, 210, 216, 217, 229, 280, 318, 320

revolution 1, 2, 9, 11, 12, 15, 16, 17, 26, 32, 36, 40, 72, 77, 94, 103, 144, 147, 155, 161, 162, 164, 166, 188, 191, 210, 212, 248, 255, 262, 264, 265, 296, 316

Revolutionary Left Front (FIR) 3, 4, 66, 67, 69, 71, 72, 73, 76, 85–6, 90, 112, 167, 168, 186, 315 (*see also* Blanco, Hugo)

rich peasants 2, 3, 4, 6, 15, 16, 18, 20, 21, 22, 26, 35, 37, 43, 51, 58, 61, 65, 66, 67, 69, 70, 71, 75, 76, 78, 79, 80, 81, 83, 84, 85, 86–7, 91, 92, 93, 94, 95, 97, 99, 105, 106, 107, 108–9, 110, 111, 112, 113, 116, 122, 125, 126, 127, 132, 154, 155, 159, 160, 161, 162, 163, 165, 167, 182, 185, 186, 187, 188, 313, 314, 319

right, political 1, 4, 10, 19, 44, 49, 98, 117, 118, 119, 123, 124–5, 132, 138, 146, 153, 175, 190, 193, 196ff., 198, 200, 201ff., 209ff., 212, 232, 253, 265, 292, 313, 316, 321

new 1, 2, 5, 6, 41, 190, 191, 198ff., 204ff., 209–11, 220–1, 222, 223, 228, 238, 312, 321, 322

Road to Hong Kong (1962) 237

Romania 33, 34, 35, 38, 58, 59, 60, 61, 181

Romanticism 12, 40–1, 47, 205, 286, 295, 306

Röpke, Wilhelm 189–90, 225–6

Rosenberg, Alfred 32

Rousseau, J.J. 13–14, 37, 41, 158, 192, 204, 214, 230

rural identity
  as redemption 24, 241, 278, 279
  authenticity of 6, 9, 14, 23, 26, 27, 28, 33,

34, 36, 39, 47, 119, 167, 187, 196, 204, 209, 241, 249, 292, 313 (*see also* essentialism; nationalism)
  loss of 2, 7, 10, 11, 13, 22, 25, 30, 33, 36, 47, 84, 155, 158, 197, 210, 219, 242, 250, 292, 298 (*see also* alienation)

Russia 3, 15, 17, 18, 22ff., 25, 33, 34, 43, 48, 57, 73, 75, 125, 127, 145, 146, 154, 165, 181, 218–9, 221, 227, 240, 248, 250, 251, 252, 257, 264, 267, 269–70, 272, 294, 296, 312, 313, 314

Santals 106, 126

Santo Domingo 263

Schmitt, Carl 198, 221

Schrenk, Max 288

science/rationality 6, 10, 11, 22, 114, 115, 121, 134, 148, 191, 193, 196, 201, 214, 215, 217, 221, 230, 265, 289, 290, 306, 312

Scotland 289

scriptwriters, film
  Bolt, Robert 296
  Galeen, Henrik 307
  Griffiths, Trevor 296
  Riskin, Robert 257, 258
  Trumbo, Dalton 260, 296
  Wilson, Michael 296

secularism 53, 118, 119, 132, 137, 305

Semevskii, V.I. 23, 48

semi-feudalism 28, 80, 84, 105, 167

Sendero Luminoso 3, 39, 66, 80, 82–5, 86, 93, 112, 113, 167, 168, 186, 315

sexuality 134, 193, 198, 202, 204, 212, 214, 222, 276, 285, 288–9, 296, 298, 306, 309

Shangri-La 240, 244, 245, 248, 249, 250, 252, 254, 255, 258, 261, 262, 263, 266, 269, 309 (*see also* utopia)

Shiva, Vandana 39, 114–5, 129, 130, 133, 134, 135, 170, 171, 205, 265

Sicily 279, 301

Singapore 145

Singh, Charan 111, 113, 114, 119, 121, 122, 128, 130, 133

Slavophiles 23, 31, 41, 43, 46–7, 57, 59, 252, 269 (*see also* Russia)

small-scale, large-scale 2, 9, 15, 17–19, 20, 23, 35, 37, 147, 148, 154, 197, 198, 199, 203, 224, 228, 239, 241, 253, 275, 293, 300–01, 312, 317

Snatchers (1935) 294

social movements, new 5, 39, 41, 44, 82, 83,

97, 115, 117, 118, 135, 136, 144, 147, 148, 149, 154, 156ff., 159, 162, 163, 164, 165–6, 167, 170, 171, 173, 174, 183, 184, 188, 190, 197, 199, 205, 207, 210, 220, 228, 238, 318
socialism 2, 3, 9, 10, 11, 16, 17, 18, 28, 36, 38, 53, 56, 73, 75, 79, 97, 98, 99ff., 103, 104, 111, 113, 116, 121, 124, 137, 143, 145, 146, 149, 154, 155, 156, 157, 162, 165, 166, 167, 170, 182, 185, 188, 211, 240, 243, 248, 250, 253, 265, 272, 293–4, 296, 312
Sole (1929) 304
Sorel, Georges 7, 191, 196, 207, 217, 218, 233
South Africa 150, 175, 189–90, 216, 226, 227
Southern Agrarians 25, 50, 219, 224, 249, 283, 304
Southern Comfort (1981) 303
soviet 73–4
Soviet Union (*see* Russia)
Spain 28, 29, 39, 221, 294
Spartacus (1960) 296
Spencer, Earl 207, 208, 209, 232
Stalin, Joseph 95, 165, 257
state, the 2, 4, 9, 17, 24, 33, 37, 43, 50, 70, 71, 73–4, 75–6, 100, 108–9, 110, 111, 123, 128, 130, 131, 148, 159, 163, 164, 169, 172, 185, 187, 188, 198, 199, 206, 207, 212, 226, 240, 246, 251–2, 278, 289, 290, 292, 312, 316
Stoker, Bram 306, 308
strikes 4, 31, 41, 51, 69, 70, 91, 169
sub-tenants 67, 68, 69, 70, 72, 76, 77, 78, 86, 90, 91, 95, 95
Subaltern Studies 5, 39, 41, 44, 51, 52, 54, 117, 124, 144, 147, 149, 153, 154, 156–8, 159–60, 161, 162, 164, 166, 167, 170, 171, 182, 183, 186, 187, 190, 204, 205, 210, 227–8, 238, 318
sugarcane 26
Sunrise (1927) 308
Swatantra Party 27, 51

Tachibana Kozaburo 30 (*see also nohonshugi*)
Taiwan 145
Tamil Nadu 25, 125, 136, 284–5, 288, 301, 310
Tarchi, Marco 198, 221, 222
taxation 111–12, 121, 127, 131, 136
Tebhaga movement 100, 101, 103, 123 (*see also* tenants)

technology 15, 18, 114, 125, 132, 133, 154, 173, 237, 242, 248, 252
technophobia 114, 115, 125, 134, 195, 197–8, 199, 201, 206, 220, 221, 225, 226, 230, 241, 242, 247, 248–9, 259, 265, 266, 312
Telengana movement 100, 101
television 118, 198, 213, 233, 305
tenants 3, 12, 26, 31, 42, 57, 58, 66, 67, 68, 69, 70, 71, 76, 77, 78, 79, 80, 86, 90, 91, 92, 94, 95, 99, 100, 106, 125, 181, 207, 288, 314, 319
Terra Madre (1931) 283, 304
Thailand 145
The Birds (1963) 302
The Blue Light (1932) 299
The Cabinet of Doctor Caligari (1919) 286
The Day the Earth Caught Fire (1961) 303
The Devils (1971) 310
The Enigma of Kaspar Hauser (1974) 276, 303
The General Line (1928) 294
The Godfather trilogy (1972–90) 278–9, 301
The Last Emperor (1987) 305
The Leopard (1963) 8, 282, 284, 305
The Music Room (1958) 8, 282–3, 303–4
The Quatermass Experiment (1954) 280
The Sheltering Sky (1990) 305
The Terminator (1984) 143
The Thing (1951) 280
The War Lord (1965) 310
Them! (1954) 280, 302
Theorem (1968) 298
Thevar Magan (1992) 301
Things to Come (1936) 259, 261
Tibet 240, 250, 258
Tikait, M.S. 107, 109, 110, 113, 114, 129, 139 (*see also* BKU)
time/timelessness 135, 173, 201, 205, 220, 240, 242–3, 245, 253–4, 262, 287, 294, 299, 310 (*see also* eternal present)
Tolstoy, L.N. 47
town/country divide
    rural = good 2, 30, 35, 37, 51, 56, 57, 59, 84, 112, 121, 130, 207, 208, 215, 231, 232, 244, 273, 278, 279, 283, 291–2, 297, 303–4, 305, 306, 309, 310, 312
    urban = bad 2, 30, 35, 37, 56, 57, 59, 84, 112, 121, 130, 207, 215, 231, 232, 244, 273, 278, 279, 281, 283, 291–2, 297, 303–4, 305, 306, 309, 310, 312

trade
  free 109, 110, 118, 122, 127, 129, 130, 139,
    146, 166
  terms of 108, 111, 112, 128 (*see also* urban
    bias)
tradition, rural 2, 9, 11, 12ff., 20, 22, 23ff., 30,
    34, 35, 40, 43, 55, 60, 84, 85, 86, 94, 113,
    115, 120, 122, 124, 129–30, 133, 134,
    135, 145, 149, 155, 158, 162, 167, 172,
    173, 179, 185, 186, 191, 195, 201, 203,
    204, 205, 206, 207, 208, 212, 214–5, 232,
    242, 255, 259, 261, 274, 277, 278, 279,
    286, 287, 289, 291, 295, 304, 306, 312
Tremors (1990) 302
tribals 4, 27, 45, 53, 103, 104ff., 106ff., 111,
    115–16, 117, 125, 126, 135, 136, 147,
    148, 150, 157, 168, 179, 183, 197–8, 205,
    216, 220, 231, 315, 318
Tripura 104, 125
Triumph of the Will (1934) 299
Trotsky, L.D. 4, 15, 17, 36, 42, 54, 72, 73, 74,
    76, 77, 89, 93, 95
Trotskyism 3, 66, 67, 72–4, 77, 80, 81, 86–7,
    89, 96, 113, 154, 186, 315

Uganda 239, 249, 251, 252, 256, 269
underworld, urban 239, 244–5, 247, 301
    (*see also film noir*; gangster film; mob-in-
    the-streets)
unionization 31, 41, 68–9, 78–9, 86, 88, 89–89,
    102, 125, 169, 175
United States 1, 3, 10, 23ff., 28, 33, 41, 44–5,
    48, 49, 50, 109, 123, 146, 178, 188, 203,
    206, 213, 219, 221, 223, 224, 228, 229,
    231, 239, 241, 246, 247, 249, 250, 251,
    255, 256, 259, 263, 266, 273, 277, 278,
    279, 280, 281, 296, 301, 302, 303, 308–9,
    312, 313, 314
untouchables 103, 124
urban bias 53, 84, 108, 109, 111–12, 113, 114,
    116, 119, 120, 128, 130, 131, 133, 135
urbanization 237
utopia 7, 48, 217, 237, 242ff., 248ff., 253–4,
    255ff., 293 (*see also* dystopia)
Uttar Pradesh 109, 119, 127, 310

vampire legend 285ff., 290, 291, 306, 307–8
Veblen, Thorstein 24, 49
Venezuela 5
verticality 43–4
Vietnam 145, 154
violence 4, 101, 113, 115, 120, 122, 124, 138,
    149, 162, 173, 196, 216, 217, 218
Vishwa Hindu Parishad (VHP) 4, 41, 54, 99,
    117, 119, 120, 121, 122, 136, 137, 227,
    315

West Bengal 4, 39, 100, 101, 102, 104–7, 112,
    115, 121, 123, 124, 127, 167, 303–4,
    315
Westphalia 306
Wicker Man (1973) 8, 279, 282, 289–90, 310
Willard (1970) 302
Witness (1985) 8, 275, 279
Wordsworth, William 13–14, 37, 41, 204
World Bank 130, 134

Yugoslavia 150